Protocol Design for Local and Metropolitan Area Networks

Protocol Design for
Local and Metropolitan Area
Networks

Paweł Gburzyński

Department of Computing Science
University of Alberta

PRENTICE HALL, ENGLEWOOD CLIFFS, NEW JERSEY 07632

Library of Congress Cataloging-in-Publication Data

Gburzynski, Pawel.
   Protocol design for local and metropolitan area networks/ by
Pawel Gburzynski
      p. cm.
   Includes bibliological references and index.
   ISBN: 0-13-554270-7
   1. Computer network protocols. 2. Local area networks (Computer
networks) . 3. Metropolitan area networks (Computer networks) .
I. Title.
  TK5105.7.G39 1996
  004.8'8--dc20   95-11160
                               CIP

Acquisitions editor: **ALAN APT**
Editorial/production supervision
and interior design: **SHARYN VITRANO**
Copy editor: **ALICE CHEYER**
Cover designer: **WENDY ALLING JUDY**
Manufacturing buyer: **DONNA SULLIVAN**
Editorial assistant: **SHIRLEY McGUIRE**
Supplements editor: **BARBARA MURRAY**

 ©1996 by Prentice-Hall, Inc.
A Simon & Schuster Company
Englewood Cliffs, New Jersey 07632

Printed in the United States of America

10 9 8 7 6 5 4 3 2 1

ISBN 0-13-554270-7

Prentice-Hall International (UK) Limited, London
Prentice-Hall of Australia Pty. Limited, Sydney
Prentice-Hall Canada Inc., Toronto
Prentice-Hall Hispanoamericana, S.A., Mexico
Prentice-Hall of India Private Limited, New Delhi
Prentice-Hall of Japan, Inc., Tokyo
Simon & Schuster Asia Pte. Ltd., Singapore
Editora Prentice-Hall do Brasil, Ltda., Rio de Janeiro

To the memory of Lucyna Nałęcz,

my mother's mother

Contents

Preface

Medium access protocols for local and metropolitan area networks (LANs and MANs) constitute an interesting class of distributed algorithms. Yet these protocols are seldom treated as abstract algorithms and discussed outside the context of the specific hardware on which they run. Typically, a document describing the functionality of the lowest layers in a LAN or MAN is full of cryptic acronyms, numbers, and charts, which obscure the fundamental principle on which these layers are based, often to the point of rendering it incomprehensible. In consequence, many professionals dealing with computer communication, e.g., system or LAN administrators, have only a vague idea of what happens at the bottom of the local network. They often assume that this hidden part is not much relevant, as the exact format of CPU instructions is irrelevant to a user of a high-level language.

It doesn't take much effort to demonstrate that the above analogy is misleading. In contrast to the CPU architecture, whose high-level characteristics can be easily inferred from its low-level numerical parameters (e.g., the clock rate) and validated with a simple set of benchmarks, the user-end performance of a LAN usually depends on several convoluted factors, including the actual "algorithm" of the medium access scheme. There are few more deceptive performance measures than the raw transmission rate of a network. Thus, it generally makes no sense to say that one network is better than the other just because its transmitters are able to pump bits faster into the medium. Yet, in the absence of better measuring rods, the nominal transmission rate is commonly used as a simple numerical determinant of network performance. The confusion is made worse by the fact that networks are very difficult to benchmark, because there are no universally accepted performance criteria that could be used to assess the general quality of a network with no reference to its offered load. In other words, a network suitable for one class of applications (e.g., providing a centralized file service to a distributed collection of workstations) may prove completely inadequate for another traffic pattern (e.g., delivering voice and video signals to its customers).

Many dexterous researchers who design and investigate network protocols also prefer to draw a line between medium access schemes and higher layers. There exist several formal protocol specification systems useful for expressing logical properties of high-level protocols, but all these systems fail to capture the essential phenomena occurring at the medium access level. The reason is that medium access protocols are strongly dependent on time. Phenomena like race conditions, finite and specific signal propagation speed in a medium, limited accuracy of independent clocks, latency in recognizing status changes of the medium, all contribute to the programming environment for medium access algorithms. In contrast to higher-level protocols, one cannot usually simplify this environment by focusing on some of its "logically relevant" fragments and leaving out the pieces that "obscure the picture." A medium access protocol designed under simplifying assumptions with respect to the time-related phenomena (e.g., assuming a perfect synchronization of independent clocks or the same propagation distance between all pairs of stations) may turn out to be completely unrealistic (and thus worthless), or its implementation may exhibit drastically different properties than the abstract prototype. As they appear in the literature, medium access protocols are not often presented as formal programs whose semantics would be self-evident. They are usually described in plain language, with quite a bit of handwaving, and their intended semantics leave room for misinterpretation.

The objective of this book is to demonstrate that medium access protocols are amenable to formal presentation in a way that makes this presentation practically indistinguishable from a realistic implementation. The software package introduced in this book, called SMURPH,[2] is a combination of a programming language (based on C++) and a simulator for executing programs expressed in that language. The programming language of SMURPH is capable of expressing the relevant physical phenomena occurring at the medium access level; thus, it can be used to specify medium access protocols. The simulator part of SMURPH is hidden from the user, in the same way that a run-time system of a general-purpose high-level programming language is hidden from the programmer. Its role is to provide a realistic model of the hardware on which real medium access protocols are executed. This way, SMURPH can be used as a performance-evaluation tool—for modeling networks and their protocols at the medium access level.

Chapters 1–7 introduce SMURPH, explain its features, and illustrate them with simple examples. This part constitutes a complete user guide to the package and, supplemented by the appendixes, contains all the information needed to run the software. The remaining chapters (8–11) present SMURPH specifications of a number of medium access protocols for local and metropolitan area networks. These

---

[2]See section B.1 in appendix B for information on retrieving and installing the package.

specifications are fully executable: the reader is strongly encouraged to play with the programs that come with the package. As a by-product of the presentation, a powerful problem-oriented library of SMURPH modules is built, which can be reused in other protocols—to be designed/implemented by the reader.

In the presentation, I try to avoid unnecessary jargon and keep the number of acronyms at the minimum. I focus on the logical (algorithmic) aspects of the protocols and leave out all the redundant or irrelevant elements of their commercial specifications. For example, in most cases the actual packet format used by or proposed for a given protocol is not important unless it is explicitly related to the operation of the medium access scheme. All parameters of the implementations that can be free are actually free, and the reader may adjust their values at will in experiments. Three exceptions to this rule, Ethernet (section 8.1), DQDB (section 9.5), and FDDI (section 10.3), are all well-established industrial standards. But even in these cases, I merely provide the "right" default values of some parameters, which are in principle flexible, within the limits of the medium access policy.

Although the primary reason for modeling a protocol in SMURPH is to evaluate its performance, this book includes no performance graphs and avoids comparing different networks and protocols in this respect unless a comparison helps explain the merits of a discussed feature. A comprehensive performance study of the protocols presented in chapters 8–11 would be a voluminous document and, for the sheer sake of size, must be deemed to lie beyond the scope of this book. On the other hand, partial and necessarily incomplete results could meet with accusations of favoritism. Should the reader have any doubts regarding my unsupported statements about the behavior of some protocols, the programs that come with the package will provide a friendly vehicle for verifying these statements.

This book is primarily addressed to college and university students taking courses in telecommunication and to people involved in performance evaluation of communication networks and protocols. The material in this book has been used by the author to teach a graduate course on local and metropolitan area networks. Other people have taught undergraduate courses on telecommunication in which SMURPH played the role of a virtual testbed for implementing solutions discussed in class and devised by the students in their projects. Students seem to like the idea of having a user-friendly environment for building realistic models of networks and protocols, rather than learning about them from the blackboard and solving assignments whose relation to the course subject is only superficial. After a while, they even start to appreciate the merciless exactness with which SMURPH exposes flaws in their designs. Especially with medium access protocols, many such flaws are subtle and often pass unnoticed under human scrutiny; they also might not have shown up in a simplified (e.g., slotted) simulator in which some critical aspects of reality have not been accounted for.

The chain of events leading to this book was initiated in December 1984 by Jay Majithia, who introduced me to the fascinating area of telecommunication. In 1986, Piotr Rudnicki, my long-time friend and collaborator, helped me find the right way of turning my obscure collection of simulators into a decent programming environment for modeling CSMA/CD protocols. Later, between 1986 and 1988, this environment evolved into LANSF—a presentable and documented package for simulating medium access protocols for local area networks. The idea of reorganizing LANSF and converting it from plain C to C++ was suggested in 1991 by Jacek Maitan, then with Palo Alto Lockheed Lab, who offered a small, but very valuable, grant to support my efforts. Throughout the entire project, numerous people helped me directly or indirectly by suggesting various improvements to the package, criticizing its existing features, or simply expressing their opinions on SMURPH. I would like to mention my students: Marcel Berard (who programmed the first modular version of the collision protocols discussed in chapter 8) and Nyan Lo (whose complicated project in SMURPH revealed a few weak spots of the package). Włodek Dobosiewicz, my illustrious co-researcher and friend, was never short of novel protocol concepts. The medium access schemes that we devised and analyzed together provided an excellent testbed for SMURPH and, at the same time, demonstrated its usefulness and flexibility. I am deeply indebted to all the users of LANSF and SMURPH from around the globe who found time to share with me their successes and failures, especially to Bill Atwood, Brian Bertan, Carlos Escobar, Constantine Manikopoulos, and Mart Molle. If not for them, this book would not have been written.

1

Introduction

1.1 STRUCTURE OF COMMUNICATION NETWORKS

The notion of communication is so general that any dynamic system (i.e., exhibiting some behavior) can be thought of as a communication system. A dynamic system usually consists of a number of separable components that perform some specific functions. To call this collection of parts a system, we must see some relation among them: their functions must be intertwined teleologically—by the **purpose** of the system they comprise. We can always view this correlation as *communication* among the system's parts.

When designing or investigating complex physical systems, we usually split them into components and treat these components individually. There is no such thing as a system in itself, which could be described completely without making a reference to its environment, i.e., treating it as part of a larger system. Consider a windmill as an example. To describe its functionality in detail, e.g., to forecast its performance during the season, one has to know something about the weather pattern in the area, especially winds (their strength, direction, timing). The weather in the area surrounding the windmill depends on the weather in a wider area; ultimately, on the weather patterns around the globe. But we would not normally expect a skilled windmill constructor to be well trained in meteorology. Although the two systems, the windmill and the world's climate, are in fact parts of a larger system encompassing many other components, most people will agree that the workings of a windmill can be discussed and explained satisfactorily without referring to the patterns of solar activity.

The windmill analogy applies well to the subject of this book—digital com-

1

munication networks. A communication network is always an important (usually critical) part of a larger system consisting of computers, video and audio equipment, specialized peripheral devices, and ... human beings using all this machinery. Ultimately, it is impossible to describe the functionality of a network without taking into account the structure and diversity of its supersystem. But it is possible and reasonable to treat the network as a separate entity whose internal workings can be explained and understood without assuming any specific application. This is possible, provided that we agree to respect the limitations arising from this approach. Examples of such limitations are given later.

1.1.1   Network Components

By a communication network[1] we understand a configuration of *stations* interconnected via *channels*.

Sometimes, when people say *channel* they mean a possibly complex configuration of wires (or other media), which may be additionally equipped with some integrated control mechanism. We assume here that all channels are simple, i.e., a channel is just a broadcast-type medium without any interesting structure. A piece of twisted-pair wire, a coaxial cable, a fiber-optic cable, a radio channel are all examples of a simple channel. To avoid confusion, we call such channels *links*. A complex channel may be built of a number of links.

The place where a station is connected to a link is called a *port*. No restriction on possible interconnections is imposed. In particular, one station can be connected to the same channel in several places (via different ports). Clearly, a station can be connected to a number of different channels and many stations can be connected to the same channel. A sample network configuration is presented in figure 1.1.

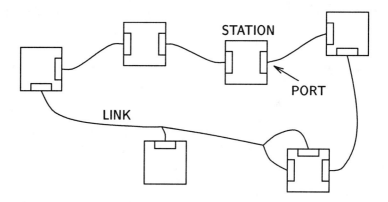

Figure 1.1   A sample network

---

[1]From now on, we skip the qualifier *communication* on the assumption that there are no other networks.

Stations are the network's processing units. They communicate by passing signals via links. These signals have some structure, namely, they consist of binary information—sequences of bits organized into chunks called *packets* or *frames*. The *communication protocol* executed by the network can be viewed as a distributed program whose parts are run by different stations. Thus, a station is a (specialized) computer executing a portion of the protocol program.

A link is characterized by two parameters: its length and its signal propagation speed. In fact, as several stations can be connected to one link in different places, we are interested in the length of the link segments between pairs of ports on the link. The signal propagation speed depends on the material of which the link is built. In all interesting cases, this speed is of the order of the speed of light but, of course, somewhat below this limit. Table 1.1 lists the signal propagation speed for a few typical link media.

Medium	Signal propagation speed
Sound in air	$0.000001c$
Twisted pair	$0.8c$
Coaxial cable	$0.8c$
Radio waves	$1c$
Optical fiber	$0.85c$

Table 1.1 Signal propagation speed for typical communication media as a fraction of c—the speed of light in vacuum

Another important attribute of a link is the transmission rate, usually expressed in bits per second (b/s). The transmission rate tells how fast information (packets) can be inserted (transmitted) into the link. This link attribute must be known to a station willing to use the link for transmission. Therefore, we prefer to associate it with ports rather than links. Normally, all ports on a given link have the same transmission rate (this is why it is reasonable to view the transmission rate as a link attribute), but exceptions from this rule cannot be precluded.

Medium	Transmission rate
Sound in air	100 Kb/s
Twisted pair	10 Mb/s
Coaxial cable	100 Mb/s
Radio waves	1 Gb/s
Optical fiber	1 Tb/s

Table 1.2 Maximum transmission rates for typical communication media

The theoretical maximum transmission rate of a link depends on the medium (see table 1.2);[2] however, the actual transmission rate used in the network is usually

---

[2]The numbers in table 1.2 give only a rough idea of the maximum achievable transmission rate. It is assumed that the medium is used in a network of a nontrivial (i.e., at least local area) size. Higher rates are possible over very short distances.

much lower than the theoretical maximum and is determined by the technology of the interface between links and stations. In our model, this interface is represented by ports.

1.1.2 OSI View on Protocol Structure

The network's behavior is governed by its communication protocol—a collection of rules that describe the actions to be taken by a station upon the occurrence of a specific event. Protocols are designed and implemented as distributed *event-driven* programs. An event-driven program is not supposed to read some data, perform some calculations, and finally produce some results. It operates in a perpetual cycle in which it responds to events triggered by its environment. One example of an event-driven program is an operating system.

It is not possible to write a book on protocols without mentioning the ubiquitous OSI view on the protocol structure. OSI stands for Open Systems Interconnection and comprises a set of recommendations[3] for identifying conceptual protocol layers necessary in every open communication network. The word *open* means here "general-purpose," i.e., a network capable of supporting typical, standard, common, distributed applications.

The OSI recommendation suggests a way of organizing network protocols and looking at various levels (layers) of their functionality. We will see shortly that it is not always possible to match the OSI layers accurately with the actual structure of a given protocol. Yet the functionality mentioned in the OSI model must always be present somewhere in the protocol structure. In our case, the familiarity with the OSI layer hierarchy will help us name and identify various elements of the protocol functionality, even though these elements will sometimes be misplaced with respect to the OSI model.

Complete networking interfaces implanted into existing computing systems are quite complicated and diverse. They consist of many different high-level protocols oriented for performing different types of networking "sessions" (e.g., file transfers, remote logins, electronic mail). These high-level functions are built on top of more primitive functions implementing their simpler but indispensable prerequisites: identifying hosts (stations) within name domains, establishing and maintaining connections, converting messages to packets, routing the packets to their proper destinations, accessing physical links, detecting errors and recovering from them, and so on. Owing to the very nature of networking, protocol programs running at different stations can be (and often are) designed and prepared by different teams of people, yet these programs must be able to "talk" to each other and obey the same protocol rules. It is obvious that to make wide networking possible, these rules must be clear; moreover, they must be organized according to the multiple levels of protocol functionality.

Organizing protocols into layers with well-defined functions and interfaces

---

[3]These recommendations were defined by the International Organization for Standardization (ISO).

serves a dual purpose. First, it makes protocols easier to describe and comprehend. Each layer can be presented, discussed, and understood independently of the
other layers. By replacing top layers, one can implement new high-level functions
taking advantage of the existing useful primitives implemented in the lower layers.
For example, an existing connection service can be used to implement file transfers
as well as remote logins. Second, lower layers can be replaced by their new versions,
better suited to the new technology, network configuration or topology, without
affecting the higher layers. For example, replacing a radio channel with a coaxial
cable may require reimplementation of the layer dealing with signal transmission
and error recovery, but this change should not affect the way of setting up a logical
connection between a pair of stations.

The terminology used to describe the OSI protocol hierarchy is best applied to
a standardized view on network geometry, even if the actual geometry is simpler and
more regular (which is often the case with local and metropolitan area networks).
This view is presented in figure 1.2. It has been inspired by the "official" structure
of ARPANET (which was one of the first wide-area networks) and provides us with
an adequate level of abstraction for discussing some interesting general networking
issues.

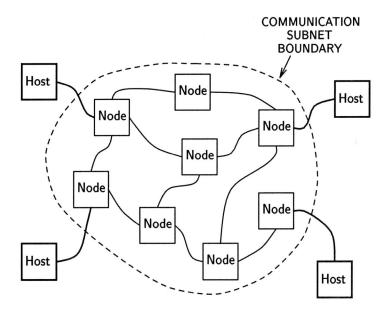

Figure 1.2 Standardized network structure

According to our view, a network consists of *hosts*, which are interconnected
via the *communication subnet*. Hosts are the primary communicating agents: any
useful *traffic* passing through the network is a result of some hosts being engaged

in a communication episode.[4] In real life, hosts are the primary computers connected to the network, which, besides contributing to the network load, perform operations not related directly to networking, e.g., running user programs, compilers and text editors. Hosts are identifiable at the highest possible level of the protocol hierarchy—by the human users. They are the only actual generators of the network's input and the ultimate end points for the traffic passed through the network.

The communication subnet consists of *internal nodes*[5] interconnected via *channels*. The nodes (we omit the adjective *internal* where it is not absolutely necessary) implement the functionality of the communication subnet by interfacing the hosts to the network and providing a means for passing messages among them.

The purpose of the communication subnet is to provide a transparent networking service to the hosts. A host should not be aware of the structure of the underlying communication subnet: all it directly perceives from the network is its interfacing node. Whenever it has a message addressed to some other host, it just passes the message (tagged with some information identifying the recipient) to the communication subnet (via its interfacing node). Then the communication subnet takes over and makes sure that the message reaches the target host.

According to the terminology introduced in section 1.1.1, both hosts and internal nodes are just *stations*, possibly with a diverse functionality. The channels may be complex, i.e., one channel may correspond to a number of links. In real life, especially in local area networking, the functionality of internal nodes is often absorbed by the hosts. Nonetheless, to retain an objective and "politically correct" view on the network and its protocol, we should always be able to logically isolate this functionality. For example, we should be able to make statements like "this piece of information never gets out of the communication subnet boundary," irrespective of the actual geometry of the network and the physical configuration of its stations.

Information passed through the communication subnet of a network is organized into transmission units called packets or frames. We make a distinction between *messages*, which are logical units of information processed by the hosts outside the communication subnet, and *transmission units*, which are physical blocks of information passed via channels among the stations. A message is characterized by the following attributes:

- Message sender, which is always one of the hosts
- Message receiver, which again is a host

---

[4]One would like to say *session*, but this word is used in the OSI terminology to describe something more specific.

[5]In the original terminology of ARPANET, internal nodes were called interface message processors (IMPs). This terminology is a bit outdated today and, trying to avoid unnecessary acronyms and obscure terms, we stick to the simpler name—*node*. For the same reason, we prefer the word *host* over the more fashionable technical term DTE (data terminal entry), denoting conceptually the same thing.

- Message contents, a sequence of bits with a definite length

One example of a message is a file to be transferred to another host. A character entered from the keyboard during a remote login session is also a message (assuming that all character strokes are immediately passed to the remote host).

Before it is transmitted, a message must be turned into one or more transmission units. Besides a fragment of the message contents, a transmission unit carries additional information, which is interpreted by the protocol layers processing the unit. Perceived by higher protocol layers (as portions of messages passed between pairs of hosts), these transmission units are called *packets*. Viewed from the bottom of the protocol hierarchy (as independent chunks of data subject to some physical processing within the communication subnet), the transmission units are called *frames*.

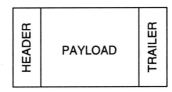

Figure 1.3   A typical packet layout

In this book we are concerned with lower protocol layers and, in most cases, we are not too interested in the specific message contents of a packet. Therefore, we need not differentiate between packets and frames, and we use *packet* to denote both types of entities.[6]

A packet usually consists of a *payload* part (see figure 1.3) enclosed between two contiguous chunks of control information. The interpretation of the packet structure depends on the protocol layer processing the packet. The packet header (transmitted first) usually identifies the packet's destination and sometimes it specifies the packet's type, length, and other attributes. The trailer (transmitted after the payload part) is mainly used for error detection and sometimes recovery. It may also contain a delimiter that allows the data-link layer (section 1.1.2.2) to detect the packet boundary.

The packet header is organized so that its portions relevant to lower protocol layers are located closer to the front. The structure of the trailer is usually much simpler, but it obeys a similar rule: the parts processed by lower layers are located closer to the end. The boundary between the header, the payload, and the trailer is shifted as the packet processing moves in the protocol hierarchy. On the way up, each layer strips the relevant portions of the header and trailer, uses the information in these portions to determine the packet's fate, and may decide to pass the leftover to the next upper layer. On the way down, each layer gets a packet from

---

[6]Although, in the light of the preceding remark, the term *frame* would seem better suited for our purpose.

its successor, adds the specific portions of the header and trailer, and passes the augmented packet down to the lower layer. Thus, the header and trailer perceived by a given layer can be viewed as fragments of the payload by a lower layer. Conversely, the payload perceived by one layer can be viewed as a complete packet by a higher layer. This interpretation stops when we get to the bottom of the protocol hierarchy. Then the packet becomes a complete frame and its individual bits are physically inserted into (or extracted from) the channel. On its way up, the packet ceases to exist when it crosses the boundary of the communication subnet; then it becomes part of a message transmitted or received by a host.

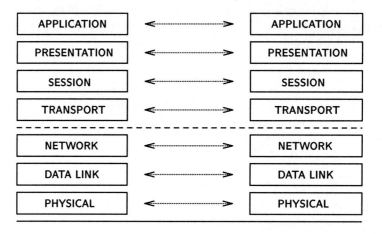

Figure 1.4 OSI protocol layer hierarchy

The standard seven-layer hierarchy of OSI (figure 1.4) specifies what kinds of operations are performed on packets or messages by a given layer. For each layer, there exists a collection of standards regarding the format of the interface with the neighboring layers and the semantics of the operations performed by the layer. Now we briefly discuss these operations in the general context of the OSI model. In section 1.1.3 we review some of them in the more specific context of local and metropolitan area networks.

1.1.2.1 Physical layer.   This layer is responsible for inserting raw information into a channel (on the sender's end) and receiving information from the channel (on the recipient's end). The responsibility of this layer can be stated succinctly as follows: "to make sure that a 0 or 1 bit inserted by the sender is received as the same bit by the recipient." Any special signals (not convertible into binary digits), e.g., markers used to determine packet boundaries, collisions (section 1.1.3), are also handled in this layer.

The input to the physical layer consists of a sequence of zeros and ones. The physical layer (almost always implemented entirely in hardware) converts this se-

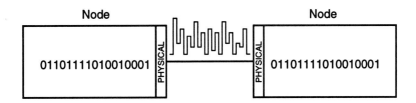

Figure 1.5   The operation of the physical layer

quence into signals (e.g., electric pulses, light modulation) suitable for the channel medium. The output from the physical layer is a sequence of zeros and ones into which the signals received from the channel are converted. This is illustrated in figure 1.5.

1.1.2.2   Data-link layer.   The data-link layer is responsible for error-free transmission of packets between pairs of directly connected nodes. Note that no routing problems occur in this layer: the identity of the receiver is known, and it must be one of the nodes connected to the sender via a direct channel. The operation of the data-link layer is illustrated in figure 1.6.

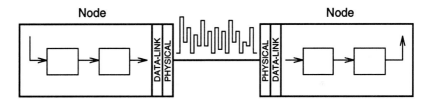

Figure 1.6   The operation of the data-link layer

Header interpretation in the data-link layer is usually simple. The entire packet is treated as a stream of bits to be submitted to the physical layer. Sometimes, the packet must be preceded by a special sequence of signals, which will be used by the receiver to synchronize its clock to the incoming packet. This sequence is called a *preamble* and, although it always occurs in the packet (frame) context, it rightfully belongs to the physical layer.

Error detection is usually performed by computing the CRC (cyclic redundancy check) checksum, which is a function of all the bits in the packet (note that the headers used by the upper layers are treated as payload by the data-link layer). The value of this function is stored in the trailer appended to the packet. Upon reception, the value of CRC is recomputed by the receiver's data-link layer and compared with the value stored in the trailer. If the two values do not match, it is assumed that the packet has been received incorrectly.

Several error recovery techniques can be used. By increasing the redundancy of CRC, it is possible to rebuild the correct structure of the packet, provided that the damage is not excessive. Acknowledgment packets are commonly used to notify the sender about the success/failure of its transmission. With this approach, the header prepended by the data-link layer must include a field for storing the packet's serial number. The range of this number depends on the *window size*—the number of packets that can be transmitted in a row before the first of them is acknowledged. In the simplest case, the window size is 1 and the packet serial number can be represented by a single bit (see section 1.2.4 for illustration).

The data-link layer is also responsible for detecting dormant neighbors (nodes) and reporting their status to the higher layer. This is accomplished by sensing timeouts, e.g., the lack of an acknowledgment after an excessively long period of time.

Another issue handled by the data-link layer is buffer space control. If packets arrive faster than they can be absorbed by higher layers, the node will eventually run out of buffer space. Thus, it must be able to ask its neighbor to slow down. Conversely, when a sufficient amount of buffer space becomes available, the neighbor should be notified that it may resume the normal speed.

1.1.2.3 Network layer. The network layer provides for error-free packet transmission among (not necessarily neighboring) nodes within the communication subnet. The most important issue resolved by this layer is routing, i.e., selecting the path within the graph of the communication subnet to be traveled by the packet on its way to the destination. The input to the network layer consists of packets addressed to some specific nodes. Based on the destination address and using some optimization criteria, the sending node determines to which of its neighbors the packet should be relayed and passes the packet to the data-link layer. Upon a packet reception, the data-link layer determines whether the packet is addressed to a host connected to the receiving node. If this is the case, the packet is forwarded to the host; otherwise, it is routed again—to another internal node. The operation of the network layer is illustrated in figure 1.7.

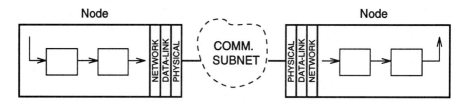

Figure 1.7 The operation of the network layer

The network layer must be able to detect inactive, faulty, or saturated nodes and modify its routing decisions accordingly. The status of the node's immediate neighbors is perceived via the feedback from the data-link layer. Information about more distant regions of the communication subnet is collected via special status packets exchanged by the nodes or by timing packets (and replies) sent (received) via different routes.

1.1.2.4   Transport layer.   Starting from the transport layer, the communication subnet becomes transparent and its structure is no longer visible. The transport layer organizes communication between hosts (see figure 1.8). Its responsibilities can be outlined as follows:

- Identifying hosts within the network name domain. Symbolic names of the hosts are turned into addresses recognizable by the nodes.
- Turning messages into packets (at the sender's end) and assembling messages from packets (at the receiver's end).
- Transforming the packet interface to the communication subnet into network services (e.g., datagrams, virtual circuits, broadcast messages).

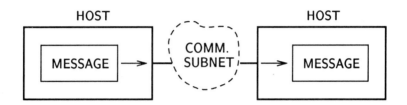

Figure 1.8 The operation of the transport layer

The network services offered by the transport layer are raw and should be viewed as a logical functionality rather than as a user interface. Datagrams are independent, individually addressable, typically short messages that can be received out of sequence, i.e., not necessarily in the order in which they were transmitted. This service is in principle unreliable: datagrams may be lost, and it is up to the user to ensure the consistency of communication.

A *virtual circuit* is a reliable logical channel connecting a pair of hosts. Such a channel must be explicitly established and closed (of course, these operations belong to the transport layer). Data sent along a virtual circuit are guaranteed to arrive at the other end in the same order in which they were transmitted.

1.1.2.5   Session layer.   This layer consists of the elementary networking tools offered by the operating system, e.g., via system calls (figure 1.9). Its role is to turn the raw functionality of the transport layer into a collection of usable programming primitives.

The boundary between the transport layer and the session layer separates the lower protocol layers (which are transparent to the user) from the upper layers (which offer some tangible functionality). One example of a service offered by the session layer is UNIX[7] *sockets* (visible as system calls). Generally, the session

---

[7]UNIX is a registered trademark of UNIX System Labs, Inc.

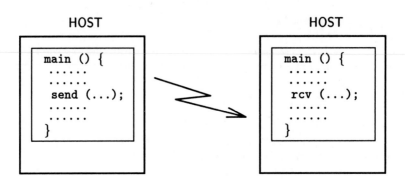

Figure 1.9 The operation of the session layer

layer should provide tools for communicating multiple processes running on different hosts. Note that these tools should be network-transparent, i.e., processes running on the same hosts should be able to communicate in the same way as remote processes. The concept of RPC (remote procedure call) also belongs to the session layer.

1.1.2.6 Presentation layer. The primary goal of the presentation layer is to eliminate differences between machines (their hardware and operating systems). This layer is responsible for presenting information transferred over the network in a uniform network-transparent way. In particular, issues like character conversion (e.g., ASCII to EBCDIC and vice versa), encryption/decryption, the resolution of big/little endian conflict, are all handled in the presentation layer. Another common operation performed in the presentation layer is *data compression.*

1.1.2.7 Application layer. This layer is intended to contain all networking applications and application-specific solutions related to networking. The application layer comprises useful programs and subroutines built on top of the session and presentation layers. For example, general file transfer protocols (FTP, TFTP), the Telnet protocol, UNIX commands: rlogin, rsh, rcp, the network file system (NFS) all belong to the application layer. Other utilities that fit into this layer are the electronic mail service and the Internet news facility.

1.1.3   Application of the OSI Model to LAN/MAN Protocols

Local and metropolitan area networks represent a pragmatic approach to the OSI recommendations, as far as the three bottom layers are concerned. From the viewpoint of implementing these layers, LANs and MANs are characterized by the following properties:

- Uniform and very specific type of media used to implement communication channels. The physical layer in a LAN or MAN can use its own standards for signal transmission.

- Relatively high reliability of channels. Error correction in the data-link layer may not be necessary (although error detection is still important). The responsibility for recovering from errors can be delegated to higher layers (transport, session).

- Short distances and low reaction time allow the protocols to use short time-outs. This is another argument for delegating error handling to higher layers.

- Regular topologies and conceptual uniformity of the network make routing problems simple or trivial. Consequently, the network and data-link layers may be difficult to tell apart.

Let us consider briefly two examples.

Ethernet, which is still one of the most popular local area networks, is based on the bus topology. The bus is a single, uniform, broadcast-type medium interconnecting all stations. The structure of the communication subnet is identical with the configuration of hosts (there is no concept of relaying packets). In consequence, the network layer is nonexistent: a packet transmitted to one station reaches all stations in due time.

Actually, the situation is slightly more complicated. The collision protocol of Ethernet (described in more detail in section 8.1) guarantees that a successfully transmitted packet reaches the most distant station in the network without damage. Some people would say that this is guaranteed by the data-link layer: packets are transmitted by the data-link layer and all stations can be viewed as neighbors directly connected via the same shared channel. Others may argue that the transmission rules could have been different if the packet were addressed to the closest neighbor of the transmitting station. By accounting for the possibility that the packet's recipient may be a long distance away from the transmitter, the transmission protocol assumes some responsibilities of the network layer. Moreover, the algorithm for rescheduling colliding transmissions (the *backoff algorithm*) implicitly assumes the existence of other stations (*nodes*) trying to transmit their packets at the same time. Thus, its purpose is to resolve congestion, which is clearly a responsibility of the network layer.

The concept of collision handling is an integral part of the Ethernet idea. Its presence is clearly visible in the physical layer (collisions are physical phenomena), in the data-link layer (the minimum packet length must guarantee that all collisions are detected while packets are being transmitted), and in the controversial network layer (congestion resolution by the backoff algorithm). Thus, collision handling in Ethernet cannot be assigned to one specific layer in the OSI hierarchy.

Another example that we would like to mention in the same context is FDDI (discussed in more detail in section 10.3). FDDI is a ring network aimed at *campus area applications* in which stations are arranged in a circular structure shown in figure 10.1. Packets travel in one direction only, either clockwise or counterclockwise. To be able to transmit a packet, a station must acquire the *token*—a special control packet permanently circulating in the ring. Again, one may ask several questions regarding the fitness of the OSI model to describe the operation of FDDI. Are the token-passing rules part of the data-link layer, or do they rather belong to the network layer? As in the case of Ethernet, we have to answer that these rules constitute an integral part of the FDDI concept. The physical layer makes it possible to identify the token as a special packet and remove it from the network in a simple and reliable way. The data-link layer makes sure that the station holding the token is allowed to transmit its packets for a prescribed amount of time; then it is expected to pass the token to its successor. Again, some people would argue that the counting of the token-holding time belongs to the network layer (the node is cognizant of the presence of other nodes waiting for the token). Everybody will probably agree that the lost token recovery procedure belongs to the network layer. But besides this somewhat unorthodox responsibility, the network layer in FDDI is as trivial as in Ethernet. Packets are not routed: each station has only one output port.

Yet another intriguing property of the FDDI protocol is its packet-stripping rules: the station holding the token disconnects the ring and removes from it all traffic arriving from upstream. Moreover, stations are expected to recognize their own packets, after they have made a full circle through the ring, and strip them partially. The precise placement of the packet-stripping rules within the OSI layer hierarchy may also pose some problems.

If we take a closer look at other local and metropolitan networking solutions discussed in this book (e.g., DQDB, Metaring, MNA), we see that they all suffer from a more or less serious incompatibility with the OSI model. Although the functionality postulated in the model is present in all these networks, the exact classification of this functionality in terms of OSI layers may be difficult and controversial. On the other hand, all protocols for LANs and MANs have something in common. Most of them are built in such a way that single channels are shared by multiple stations. This is clearly visible in Ethernet, where there is just one global link shared by all stations. But even in the case of FDDI, the ring can be viewed as a single logical channel consisting of a number of physical links connecting adjacent stations. A packet inserted into the ring travels the entire logical channel before it is partially stripped by the sender and eventually removed by a token-holding station.

A MAC-level (medium access control) protocol for a network in which a single channel can be shared by a number of transmitters can be completely described by a collection of rules for arbitrating channel access. Even in linked LANs, (e.g., Manhattan Street Networks—section 11.3), in which channels are not shared by multiple transmitters, the transmission rules resemble channel access rules. In the light of these observations, it is not surprising that a typical description of a LAN/MAN protocol (below the transport layer) looks like a list of conditions that must be fulfilled by a station in order to transmit a ready packet. Sometimes the station has no choice regarding the channel (link) on which the transmission takes place (Ethernet, FDDI, DQDB, Hubnet). Sometimes this choice is very limited and constrained by the transmission rules (Manhattan Street Network). Sometimes the station must take some action to manifest its willingness to transmit (DQDB). Regardless of the specific scenario, in all these cases we are talking about a *channel access algorithm*. Therefore, the portion of a LAN/MAN protocol below the transport layer is called the *medium access control* (MAC) *protocol.*

If we want to discuss LAN/MAN protocols as a separate category, we have to conclude that, besides the network topology, their MAC-level fragments are the only interesting subjects for discussion. Indeed, from the transport layer up, these protocols have really no features specific to local networking. These upper layers can (and should) be discussed generally without assuming any particular characteristics of the underlying communication subnet. After all, they were meant to make these characteristics irrelevant. Not surprisingly, when we look at the higher protocol layers, we see a good agreement with the OSI model, also in local and metropolitan networking.

1.2   AN OVERVIEW OF SMURPH

In chapters 2 through 7 we describe in detail the protocol-modeling system SMURPH, which is used later to implement several LAN/MAN protocols. In the remaining sections of the present chapter we give a brief overview of SMURPH, supported with a complete example of a protocol model. This overview should help the reader comprehend the material included in subsequent chapters.

1.2.1   The Goals of a Network Model

If modeling is useful at all, it is for two reasons: the model is cheaper and more flexible than the actual physical system. This applies to a wide range of systems, from space shuttles to bottle openers. Clearly, communication networks fit somewhere in between.

The designer of a brand-new protocol for a local area network seldom has complete a priori knowledge about its performance in the real world. Intuition gained with experience is certainly helpful in discovering new ideas, but it cannot replace exhaustive verification of these ideas in a confrontation with reality. Testing new concepts by building physical specimens may be expensive and in some cases just unthinkable. Therefore, modeling is an indispensable methodology in any serious development endeavor.

Even well-known and established networking solutions have at least a few installation parameters (e.g., the number of stations, their placement) that must be decided upon before a new network is physically configured or an existing network is reconfigured. If a reasonably accurate model exists for the network in question, it can be used to determine the best values of these parameters before the equipment is purchased and hardwired. Although this approach is seldom followed, especially when the configuration seems simple and relatively inexpensive, it never betrays its partisans. Many people would be quite surprised to learn how much they have been missing because of a poorly conceived network configuration.

Finally, models become extremely useful in education. One can hardly imagine a programming class in which students are not exposed to programming, or a driving school in which students are not given an opportunity to drive cars. But in some cases, hands-on training in the real environment is difficult or impossible. It may be too expensive or dangerous to expose the trainee to the real system, or the real system may not be flexible enough to give the trainee (and the instructor) sufficient feedback, e.g., with respect to the extreme or abnormal situations. In such cases (flying a large commercial aircraft is a good example), the training is carried out with the assistance of simulators. Note that even experienced pilots, who have mastered their aircraft, periodically exercise with simulators to develop reflexes needed to handle special situations that (fortunately) occur seldom in real life.

Not everybody would equate the relatively innocent activities of protocol design and network maintenance with designing and flying an aircraft. However, before purchasing your favorite networking equipment, you should ask the question, Has anybody flown this machinery under the conditions that I am going to fly it? Clearly, you would be more comfortable with your decision if the network designer were able to answer your question affirmatively.

As with many other physical systems, the performance of networks and protocols is usually investigated in two steps. First, a mathematical model of the network is built and a formal analysis of that model is carried out. Next, the results obtained by the mathematical modeling are verified by simulation. Unfortunately, exact and tractable mathematical models exist for very few networks and protocols—in most cases, one has to put up with simplifications. These simplifications make the model tractable, but at the same time they affect its accuracy: the model does not reflect the reality exactly and some details are lost.[8]

Cases when the impact of the simplifying assumptions on the accuracy of the model is investigated or at least discussed are rather rare. Most authors content themselves with "For the sake of simplicity, let us assume that...." The question of the accuracy of the model is thus left unanswered and one can only have some impression as to how well the model approximates reality. Note that if the impact of the simplifications were precisely known, there would be no need to introduce them (we would be able to build an exact model instead). Therefore, methodologically, simplifications are always unwanted and harmful because they introduce an essentially immeasurable amount of uncertainty into the research.

In the light of the above remarks, the role of simulation, as the second stage of the investigation, becomes very important: its purpose is to verify theoretical results obtained from simplified (and thus uncertain) models. However, as a self-contained method of arriving at conclusions, simulation is not much respected—at least, it is respected much less than (simplified) formal modeling. Among the reasons for that, the following two seem to prevail:

---

[8]A typical example of such a simplification is the assumption that all stations in a bus-type network are equally distant from one another.

- A formal model can be verified by another researcher much faster and with higher confidence than an obscure simulation program.
- A formal model usually gives a set of expressions describing the behavior of the investigated object. These expressions are (usually) more flexible and less complex than a simulation program. For example, to see how the value of a certain parameter affects the behavior of the investigated object, it is enough to evaluate the expressions produced by the model as functions of this parameter. A simulation program must be run a number of times to produce similar results.

In reality, the first reason is much more serious. It is very difficult to assign a scientific value to the output produced by someone else's program, especially when that output is a collection of obscure statistical data. Let us note, however, that should that lack of confidence disappear, simulation would turn out to be a pure investigation method of unquestionable quality. After all, we can accurately simulate any (realistic) network and any protocol, whereas only a few very simple networks and protocols have formal models that are both tractable and accurate at the same time.

The lack of the proper recognition of simulation in the performance analysis of networks results in an astounding phenomenon: many authors base their simulation programs on simplified models! The reasoning is as follows: The formal model is simplified, and the simulation model is intended to confirm (not verify?) the results obtained from the formal model, so let the simulation model be as close as possible to the formal model. In some other cases, the simplifications have a "long tradition" of being commonly accepted (so that it is "safe" to pretend that they are not simplifications). Most authors do not elaborate at all on the simulation models used to confirm their analytical results. It is not always clear whether these models are exact. Spectacular convergence of the analytical and experimental results raises serious doubts in many cases.

An extensive simulation study of Ethernet carried out by the author has demonstrated that simplified models are often misleading, especially when used to obtain quantitative conclusions. Even some innocent-looking simplifications may have a serious impact on the accuracy of quantitative or even qualitative results.

From the practical point of view, results obtained from experimental investigation of an exact simulation model are not less sound than theoretical results obtained with the help of a simplified analytical model. On the other hand, there is no excuse for using simplified simulation models, especially if an accurate model can be programmed with a reasonable effort. The problems of limited confidence about simulation results would easily be alleviated, or even eliminated, if every researcher used the same accurate model of the "real thing" being investigated. Then the question about the assumptions of the simulation model would be irrelevant, and the simulation results could easily be verified by independent researchers.

1.2.2   What Is SMURPH?

At the user's end, SMURPH is a programming language for expressing protocols
and network configurations in a natural and straightforward way. Unlike a regular
compiler, which translates input programs into forms that can be executed on a
given computer, SMURPH carries in itself its own "execution environment." Programs
in SMURPH are run on virtual hardware configured by the user. The acronym stands
for System for Modeling Unslotted Real-time Phenomena. This suggests that the
package was intended to model the flow of time in a class of physical systems. The
word *unslotted* means that the user has absolute freedom in specifying the flow of
time, as well as its granularity.

SMURPH can be viewed both as an implementation of a certain protocol specification language and a simulator oriented toward investigating medium access
control (MAC)-level protocols in communication networks. The simulation part is
almost completely invisible to the user. All simulation-related operations like creating and scheduling individual events and maintaining a consistent notion of time,
are covered by a high-level interface perceptible as a collection of abstract objects,
methods,[9] and functions. A protocol description in SMURPH looks like a program
that could be executed on hypothetical communication hardware. This program is
built from user extensions of some standard data types and interrupt-driven processes structured like *finite-state machines.* SMURPH emulates the communication
hardware on which the protocol is to be run and thus provides a realistic environment for its execution. We claim that this environment is realistic, because it
reflects all physical phenomena relevant from the viewpoint of communication, like
finite and specific propagation speed of signals, definite transmission rates, limited
accuracy of independent clocks, and faulty channels. It is conceivable to directly
translate SMURPH protocol code into actual protocol programs executable by real
network controllers.

SMURPH has been programmed in C++ and its protocol specification language
is an extension of C++. In this book, we assume that the reader is familiar with
C++ and with the concepts of object-oriented programming in general. This familiarity need not be very deep. In fact, it is possible to learn how to use SMURPH
without any prior experience in C++ (some of my students are living witnesses to
this statement), although such experience is certainly useful.

SMURPH is not a single interpreter for a variety of networks and protocols,
but it configures itself into a stand-alone modeling program for each particular
application. The users get at their disposal the full power of C++ augmented
by the power of a realistic, emulated environment for specifying, executing, and
monitoring communication protocols.

Although SMURPH does not purport to be a protocol verification system, it
offers some tools for protocol testing. These tools, the so-called *observers*, look
like programmable assertions describing sequences of protocol actions. In fact, they

---

[9]In the terminology of object-oriented programming, a *method* is a function belonging to a
specific object type. In C++, such functions are declared as class members.

provide an alternative (static) way of specifying the protocol; the run-time system of SMURPH checks whether the two specifications agree.

1.2.3 Structure of the Package

The structure of SMURPH is presented in figure 1.10. A protocol program in SMURPH is first preprocessed by smpp to become a C++ program. The code in C++ is then compiled and linked with the SMURPH run-time library. These operations are organized by mks (make smurph)—a generator script that accepts as arguments a collection of program files and options, and creates a stand-alone module, which is a simulator for the system described by the input program.

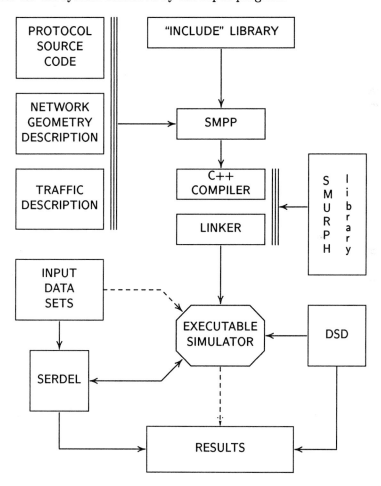

Figure 1.10 The structure of SMURPH

The linkable run-time library of SMURPH can be augmented by a source library of types—the "include" library. This library can be extended by the user; it typically contains descriptions of network topologies and traffic patterns. In chapters 8 through 11 we build our own library of types.

Protocol execution in SMURPH can be monitored, e.g., to investigate the protocol's performance. The package is equipped with an on-line display program (called DSD), which communicates with the simulator and displays on the terminal screen selected information in the form of a set of windows. This feature is useful for protocol debugging and peeking at the partial results of a potentially long simulation experiment. DSD and the simulator do not have to execute on the same machine.

A typical network performance study in SMURPH involves many independent experiments, e.g., to find a sufficient number of points of a performance curve. SMURPH is equipped with a simple tool called SERDEL (Supervisor for Executing Remote Distributed Experiments on a LAN), which helps organize such experiments on a local network of more or less homogeneous computers. SERDEL automatically starts new experiments as machines become available, migrates them from busy machines to idle ones, and checkpoints the experiments periodically to be able to recover from system crashes. With this approach a local network of reasonably fast workstations is turned into a parallel supercomputer. Owing to the independent character of individual experiments, the speedup from parallelism is perfectly linear.

1.2.4   Example: The Alternating-Bit Protocol

A good way to get the taste of SMURPH and understand its modus operandi is to analyze a number of examples. Many examples are to come in chapters 8 through 11, after we have become better acquainted with the protocol specification language of SMURPH. To initiate this acquaintance, we discuss in this section a SMURPH implementation of the well-known *alternating-bit protocol*, which illustrates a simple way of implementing a reliable packet delivery between a pair of directly connected nodes—in the data-link layer.

For the purpose of our illustration, we isolate a small fragment of the hypothetical communication subnet. This fragment, consisting of two neighboring nodes connected via two independent unidirectional links, is shown in figure 1.11. This simple network will constitute the backbone for our implementation of the alternating-bit protocol.

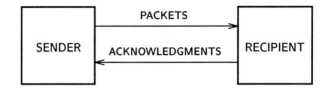

Figure 1.11   The network structure for the alternating-bit protocol

We assume that the two nodes (using the SMURPH terminology, we call them *stations*) communicate in one direction, i.e., one of them is the *sender* and the other is the *recipient* of the traffic. One of the two channels connecting the two stations is used for transfers from the sender to the recipient; the other is used by the recipient to send *acknowledgment packets* to the sender. Both channels are faulty, i.e., a packet inserted at one end of a channel may not arrive at the other end in good shape. In real life, it is usually reasonable to assume that the nature of a possible error introduced by a channel is restricted in the following way:

- Any damage to the packet contents is always detectable by the receiver. This means that a damaged packet will not be mistaken by the receiver for a valid packet whose contents are different from the transmitted original.
- The channel never inserts packets of its own. A packet arriving from the channel must have been inserted there (transmitted) by some station. Thus, the channel may be faulty, but it is not malicious.
- The channel does not reorder packets, i.e., packets inserted at one end of the channel arrive at the other end in the same order in which they were inserted, although possibly some of these packets are damaged.

The first postulate is usually secured by using checksums (CRC codes are a special class of checksums). Although checksums do not absolutely eliminate the possibility of an undetectable damage to a packet, they make this possibility so remote that for all practical purposes it can be ignored. Of course, one would expect that the higher protocol layers, and ultimately the application software, would "behave gracefully" even if a damaged packet somehow made it through the data-link layer. The protocol might get confused for a while, but it should not crash or go berserk.

The second postulate is even more natural. Although a "thermodynamic miracle" consisting of a formally valid packet appearing spontaneously in the channel cannot be excluded absolutely, its probability is comparable to the probability of the channel's hardware unexpectedly disintegrating into thin air.

The third postulate is warranted by the simplicity of our channels. The only way a packet is "processed" by a channel is by propagating the packet along the channel's medium.[10]

1.2.4.1 Protocol description.   The basic idea of the protocol is fairly simple. The sender transmits a packet and waits until it receives an acknowledgment from the recipient. If the acknowledgment does not arrive within some reasonable time interval, the sender keeps on retransmitting the packet until the acknowledgment eventually arrives. Simple as it sounds, this idea requires a bit of refinement before it can be turned into a working solution. First of all, the acknowledgment

---

[10]Some theoretical studies deal with abstract compound channels that may exhibit malicious behavior, e.g., insert an apparently valid packet. The alternating-bit protocol discussed here will not work with such channels, although there exist protocols capable of coping with problems of this kind.

itself is just a packet, and it also can be lost. This may result in the following scenario:

1. The sender sends a packet to the recipient. The packet arrives at the recipient undamaged and is received.

2. The recipient transmits an acknowledgment packet to the sender. The acknowledgment is damaged and lost.

3. The sender times out and retransmits the last packet. The packet arrives at the recipient undamaged and is received for the second time.

Thus, to interpret correctly the incoming packets, the recipient must take into account the possibility that the same packet will arrive more than once. All copies of the same packet, except the first undamaged copy, should be recognized as duplicates and ignored. A natural way to solve this problem is to tag packets with serial numbers. As the sender is going to keep on retransmitting the same packet until it concludes that at least one copy has successfully arrived at the destination, it can never happen that two retransmissions of the same packet are separated by another packet. Thus, the serial number can be represented by a single bit whose contents **alternate** with each new packet to be transmitted. Upon a packet arrival at the recipient, the meaning of this bit is either "previous packet" or "new packet," depending whether it agrees with or differs from the serial bit of the previously received packet.

It is not difficult to see that acknowledgment packets must also be tagged with serial numbers identifying the packets being acknowledged. Otherwise, the following scenario would be possible:

1. The sender transmits a packet p_1, which is successfully received by the recipient.

2. The recipient sends an acknowledgment, which arrives at the sender with no errors. The sender assumes (correctly) that p_1 has been received and transmits the next packet p_2.

3. Packet p_2 does not make it to the recipient. The recipient times out assuming that its acknowledgment did not make it to the sender and sends another acknowledgment for p_1.

4. The sender receives the acknowledgment and has no way to tell whether it is a duplicate acknowledgment for p_1 or a new acknowledgment for p_2.

This scenario demonstrates that detecting duplicate acknowledgments is as important as detecting duplicate packets. Thus, as with regular packets, acknowledgments must be tagged with serial numbers. Of course, a single **alternating** bit will do. It seems natural to make the contents of this bit match the serial number of the packet being acknowledged.

Now we can formulate the alternating-bit protocol in plain English. We start from the sender part.

Sender. The sender maintains a binary flag denoted `LastSent`. The role of this flag is to indicate the contents of the serial bit in the transmitted packet. Initially, `LastSent` contains zero.

1. When the station gets a packet to transmit, it inserts the contents of `LastSent` into the serial bit field of the packet header and transmits the packet. Having completed the packet transmission, the station sets up a timer and waits for the acknowledgment.
2. Upon the arrival of an acknowledgment packet, the station examines its serial bit field. If the contents of this field match the value of `LastSent` (the packet is acknowledged), `LastSent` is flipped and the station continues from 1. Otherwise, the acknowledgment packet is ignored and the station continues waiting.
3. If the timer goes off while the station is waiting for the acknowledgment, the last packet is retransmitted, the timer is reset, and the station continues waiting for the acknowledgment, as before.

Recipient. The recipient maintains a binary flag denoted `Expected`. This flag tells the contents of the serial bit in the next packet expected to arrive from the sender. Initially, `Expected` contains zero.

1. The station sets up a timer and starts waiting for a packet from the sender.
2. If the timer goes off, the station assumes that its previous acknowledgment packet has been lost. Thus, the station sends an acknowledgment packet with the serial bit field set to the reverse of `Expected` and then it continues at 1.
3. Upon a packet arrival from the sender, the station examines the packet's serial bit field. If the contents of this field match the value of `Expected`, the packet is received and an acknowledgment packet is sent with the serial bit field set to `Expected`. Then `Expected` is flipped and the station continues from 1.

1.2.4.2 Design considerations. Let us try now to turn the preceding informal description into a protocol program. Of course, we cannot assume at this moment that we want to encode this program in any specific language. We would rather postulate a possible structure of the protocol implementation; this will also give us some hints as to what kinds of constructs we should expect from a friendly language for protocol specification.

One rather obvious clue that we can get directly from the informal specification is the *event-driven* nature of the protocol program. The actions of this program are performed in response to certain events occurring outside the program (packet arrival, timer going off). We say that these events are triggered by the *protocol environment*. Clearly, the specification language should provide tools for the protocol program to perceive its environment. But what should be the level of this perception? For example, should we insist on accessing directly all the elements visible in the physical layer? That doesn't seem to make a lot of sense. In the majority of cases, the physical layer is implemented in hardware and the protocol designer cannot modify it at will. Moreover, from the viewpoint of the protocol logic, nothing exciting is happening at the physical level. Although the "physics" of turning bits into signals may be quite involved and based on fascinating phenomena, the actual implementation of this operation has little impact on the logical structure of the remaining protocol layers. The apparatus provided by the physical layer can be compared to computer hardware, especially the part of this hardware responsible for performing raw input/output operations. In SMURPH, the functionality of this layer is modeled by ports.

In the light of the preceding remarks, the lowest level at which we will perceive the protocol environment is the packet level. More specifically, we postulate that the following operations be built into the protocol environment:

- Start packet transmission. The operation accepts a packet buffer as an argument and starts transmitting the packet contents on the indicated port.
- Terminate packet transmission. We could assume that a packet transmission is terminated automatically when the entire packet has been transmitted. However, many MAC-level protocols require this operation to be controllable by the protocol program. For example, the Ethernet protocol may decide to abort the transmission prematurely, upon sensing a collision.
- Sense a packet arriving on the indicated port. This operation should be implemented as an *event* triggered by the packet arrival. The protocol program should be able to await the occurrence of this event.
- Sense the end of a packet arriving on the indicated port. With this operation (another *event*) the protocol can detect the packet boundary.

The protocol program is executed by stations. Thus, we have to assume that a station is a computer of sorts, equipped with a number of *processing units*. We do not want to postulate any specific architecture of these units. In real life, some elements of the protocol program above the physical layer can be (and usually are) implemented in hardware. In principle, however, starting from the data-link layer, the protocol is programmable, i.e., it can be expressed as a distributed algorithm reacting to events. We can imagine a scenario in which the protocol program written in a high-level language is compiled in such a way that its parts are transformed into hardware (e.g., VLSI).

In SMURPH, we assume that a station represents a computer capable of executing collections of processes. These processes are event-driven (they resemble interrupt-service routines from an operating system kernel), and they execute in parallel—as if each of them were assigned to a private processing unit. The generality of this approach implies a power of expression; its simplicity makes it realistic.

Revisiting the informal specification of the alternating-bit protocol, we can see that to make our model work we should add at least two more elements to the protocol environment. One such element is an alarm clock. To be flexible, we can assume that each protocol process has at its disposal a separate and independent timer, which can be set to an arbitrary time interval. When it goes off, the timer triggers an event, which can be perceived by the process that set it up.

Finally, we should take care of the input to the protocol that we want to model, i.e., the network must be supplied with packets to transmit. The protocol program must be able to learn whether a station has a ready packet awaiting transmission and, if so, to acquire the packet into the transmission buffer. From the viewpoint of the protocol, this part of the environment can be visible as a queue (or perhaps a collection of queues) storing messages awaiting transmission. It seems reasonable to make a distinction between *messages*, arriving to the network from outside, and *packets*, representing the transmission units. This way, the network model functions at the *transport layer*—as a vehicle for interconnecting hosts. If this view is inappropriate for a given model, we can always pretend that the messages are actually packets passed by the higher layer. Note that the interface to the message queue has again an event-driven character. Namely, if the queue is empty, the inquiring protocol process must be able to await an event triggered by a packet inserted into the queue.

We want the protocol part of our model to be logically indistinguishable from its hypothetical implementation viewed from a certain natural abstraction level. Note that all the postulates that we have formulated so far remain sensible if the word *model* is replaced with "possible implementation." However, the virtual nature of the model must manifest itself somewhere. Essentially, there are two parts to this manifestation. First, the way a network model is built is drastically different from the way a real network is put together. Second, a real network handles real traffic that originates at the applications, whereas a network model handles abstract, artificial traffic described explicitly by the experimenter. This traffic usually fits some *patterns* that are considered typical or interesting.

1.2.4.3 Stations and packet buffers. Now we are going to discuss a SMURPH implementation of the alternating-bit protocol. It seems natural to start from the data structures. Using the terminology of object-oriented programming, we call these structures *objects*. As we will see, many of our objects exhibit some kind of behavior. The dynamic nature of an object is manifested by a collection of functions defined within the object type. Such functions are called *methods*.

The geometry of the network backbone is described by a configuration of *stations*, *ports*, and *links*. Ports and links are objects whose types are built into SMURPH; the user seldom, if ever, defines private types to represent these objects. Of course, the actual object instances may differ in some attributes, e.g., links may be of various lengths, ports may be connected to various links at different places, and so on; however, the structure and functionality of all objects of a given type are the same. The nature of stations is somewhat different. The built-in station type is just a *chassis* for constructing actual station types. Let us look at the definition of the station type describing the sender from figure 1.11. Note that this definition does not actually create a single sender station but specifies the generic structure of such a station, which can be created in an arbitrary number of copies.

```
station SenderType {
  PacketType PacketBuffer;
  Port *IncomingPort, *OutgoingPort;
  Mailbox *AlertMailbox;
  int LastSent;
  void setup ();
};
```

A `SenderType` object consists of a packet buffer and two ports interfacing the station with the two links. It is easy to guess that `OutgoingPort` is used to transmit packets to the recipient, while the recipient's acknowledgments arrive via `IncomingPort`. The two ports are represented by pointers, which suggests that the actual objects are created somewhere explicitly. Indeed, the ports (and also the object pointed to by `AlertMailbox`) are built by the station's `setup` method announced in the definition of `SenderType`. We look at this method later.[11]

`AlertMailbox` points to an object called a *mailbox*, which will provide a communication tool for the processes run by the station. As we will see, the sender's part of the alternating-bit protocol will be implemented by two processes. These processes will be synchronized by exchanging simple notifications via `AlertMailbox`. The role of the integer attribute `LastSent` is clear from the informal protocol description in section 1.2.4.1.

The recipient station is very similar to the sender. The only difference is the lack of the packet buffer (which is replaced by the acknowledgment buffer) and the different name of the integer attribute (section 1.2.4.1).

```
station RecipientType {
  AckType AckBuffer;
  Port *IncomingPort, *OutgoingPort;
  Mailbox *AlertMailbox;
  int Expected;
  void setup ();
};
```

Packets transmitted by the sender arrive at the recipient on `IncomingPort`; the process uses the other port to send acknowledgments to the sender. Again, the recipient's protocol will be implemented as a pair of cooperating processes; these processes will communicate via `AlertMailbox`.

A station type defined with keyword `station` is derived from the built-in type `Station`. The built-in station type possesses a number of standard attributes that each station must have, but it lacks any ports or packet buffers. As one can hardly build a network from stations that cannot be connected anywhere, type `Station` is practically never used directly.

---

[11]The reader familiar with C++ would expect this end to be served by the object's *constructor*. Indeed, C++ constructors can also be used to initialize objects upon their creation. For reasons that will become clear later, it is more natural to initialize objects of SMURPH-specific types by their setup methods.

Types `Port` and `Mailbox` are built into SMURPH and, in contrast to type `Station`, it makes sense to use them directly. Types `PacketType` and `AckType` are derived from the standard type `Packet` in the following way:

```
packet PacketType {
  int SequenceBit;
};
packet AckType {
  int SequenceBit;
};
```

Not surprisingly, the two types are identical. Regular packets and acknowledgments are both tagged with sequence bits; the rest of the packet structure (represented by the implicitly prepended type `Packet`) is also common for the two defined types. Of course, the length of acknowledgments will most likely differ from the length of regular packets, but this detail will be reflected by the values of some standard packet attributes (defined in type `Packet`). So what is the reason for defining two separate packet types if their structure is identical? Note that we could make the two station types identical as well. The only real difference between these types is in naming two of their attributes.

One reason for keeping the packet and station types different is to enhance the clarity of the model. If this reason does not appeal to us, we should keep in mind that we are discussing here the implementation of an isolated fragment of a hypothetical larger protocol. For the purpose of this fragment, the simple structure of packets and acknowledgments is sufficient, but it may cease to be so if the alternating-bit protocol is embedded into a larger protocol structure.

Incidentally, one can claim that in a blown-up implementation of the protocol, the two station types actually **should** look identical. After all, the traffic between a pair of connected nodes is typically bidirectional. In such a case, it still might be better to retain the two separate station types and build a third type[12] combining their functionality.

1.2.4.4   The sender's protocol.   The program executed by the sender (a station of `SenderType`) consists of two processes. The simple idea is that each process takes care of one port. This idea can be recommended as a rule of thumb whenever the division of the protocol responsibilities among processes is not obvious. In our case, one of the processes, called the *transmitter*, will be responsible for transmitting packets to the recipient, whereas the other process, the *acknowledgment receiver*, will detect the recipient's acknowledgments and notify the transmitter about the relevant ones. The type declaration for the transmitter process is as follows:

```
process TransmitterType (SenderType) {
  Port *Channel;
```

---

[12]The multiple inheritance mechanism of C++ becomes handy here.

```
PacketType *Buffer;
Mailbox *Alert;
TIME Timeout;
void setup (TIME);
states {NextPacket, EndXmit, Acked, Retransmit};
perform;
};
```

This declaration is not complete—the setup method and the process code (announced by the keyword **perform**) will be specified later—but it lists all the attributes of the transmitter process. The first line identifies the process type and indicates the type of the station that will be running the process. The three pointers (**Channel**, **Buffer**, and **Alert**) are private handles to the station attributes referenced by the process. These pointers are set by the process's setup method.

Attribute **Timeout** of type **TIME** (which is a built-in SMURPH type) is also initialized by the setup method. It represents the acknowledgment waiting timeout (section 1.2.4.1). If a valid acknowledgment for the last transmitted packet is not received within this time, the packet is retransmitted.

The setup method takes one argument of type **TIME**, which gives the value to be assigned to **Timeout**. Its complete code is as follows:

```
void TransmitterType::setup (TIME tmout) {
    Channel = S->OutgoingPort;
    Buffer = &(S->PacketBuffer);
    Alert = S->AlertMailbox;
    Timeout = tmout;
};
```

S is an implicit standard attribute of the process, pointing to the station at which the process is running. Its type is "a pointer to the station type specified in parentheses with the **process** declaration."

The setup method assigns values to the process's attributes. The argument of **setup** must be specified at the moment when a process instance is created. We describe how this is done in section 1.2.4.6.

Note that the pointer attributes of the transmitter process are not absolutely needed: the process could reference the corresponding station attributes via the **S** pointer. In fact, one of the station attributes, **LastSent**, will be referenced by the transmitter this way. However, such references are generally more expensive (indirection overhead), textually longer, and less legible than direct references via process attributes. Keeping pointers to the relevant station attributes in local attributes of a process is a standard and recommended practice, perhaps except for simple variables that are modified by the process and shared with other processes (like **LastSent**).

The process's behavior is described in its *code specification*, which looks like a type-less and argument-less method. In the process type declaration, this method is announced with the **perform** keyword. We see later that this announcement is not redundant, as one can sensibly declare a code-less process type.

A process code method is structured and behaves like a finite-state machine. The states of this machine have names, which must be declared with the **states** specification. Let us look at the code method of our transmitter:

```
TransmitterType::perform {
  state NextPacket:
    if (Client->getPacket (Buffer)) {
      Buffer->SequenceBit = S->LastSent;
      Channel->transmit (Buffer, EndXmit);
    } else
      Client->wait (ARRIVAL, NextPacket);
  state EndXmit:
    Channel->stop ();
    Alert->wait (RECEIVE, Acked);
    Timer->wait (Timeout, Retransmit);
  state Retransmit:
    Channel->transmit (Buffer, EndXmit);
  state Acked:
    Buffer->release ();
    S->LastSent = 1 - S->LastEvent;
    proceed NextPacket;
};
```

The code method is divided into states. The sequence of statements at a given state is executed when the process "gets into" the state. Usually, some statements in this sequence describe conditions for entering other states. These conditions constitute the process's *transition function.*

Immediately after the process is created, it enters its first state labeled **NextPacket**. In this state, the process attempts to acquire a packet for transmission and store it in the station's packet buffer (pointed to by the process's attribute **Buffer**). **Client** is a pointer to the external dæmon supplying the network with traffic. Its **getPacket** method examines the message queue at the station running the process and either fills the indicated packet buffer with a new packet to transmit (returning *true*) or returns *false*. In the former case, the process sets the sequence bit of the new packet to the current value of **LastSent** and initiates its transmission by calling the **transmit** method of the station's output port (pointed to by **Channel**).

If the attempt to acquire a packet for transmission fails, the process executes the **wait** method of the **Client**. This way the transmitter declares that it wants to be resumed in state **NextPacket** when a message becomes queued at the station. By reaching the end of statements at its current state, the process suspends itself.

The **wait** method concept is common for many standard and user-defined dynamic objects. An object specifying a **wait** method is capable of generating events that can be perceived by processes. When a process executes the **wait** method of an object, we say that the process issues a *wait request* to the object.

The **transmit** method accepts two arguments. The first argument points to the packet buffer containing the packet to be transmitted. The second argument identifies the process's state to be assumed when the packet has been transmitted. Thus, the transmitter will be resumed in state **EndXmit** when the packet transmission is completed. Then, according to what we said in section 1.2.4.2, the process terminates the transmission explicitly, by calling the **stop** method of the output port. According to the protocol, the process will now wait for an acknowledgment from the recipient. This is accomplished by calling the **wait** method of the station's mailbox pointed to by the process's **Alert** attribute. Acknowledgments are intercepted by the other process running at the station (the acknowledgment receiver). Upon the arrival of a valid acknowledgment, the acknowledgment receiver will put a simple message (an alert) into the mailbox. Then the transmitter will be resumed in state **Acked** by the awaited **RECEIVE** event.

While expecting the acknowledgment alert, the transmitter process is also waiting for the timeout. The object pointed to by **Timer** is a general-purpose alarm clock that can be set to an arbitrary time interval indicated by the first argument of **wait**. When the timer goes off, the transmitter will be resumed in state **Retransmit**.

In state **EndXmit**, the transmitter awaits the occurrence of two events: the acknowledgment alert and the alarm clock going off. The earlier of the two events will be actually perceived by the process (the transmitter will be resumed in the corresponding state) and the second awaited condition will be then erased and forgotten.

If the alarm clock goes off before the acknowledgment is received, the process will end up in state **Retransmit**, where it simply restarts the packet transmission. In state **Acked**, into which the transmitter gets upon the reception of the acknowledgment, it *releases* the packet buffer, flips the **LastSent** bit, and moves directly to state **NextPacket**—to acquire a new packet for transmission. The operation of releasing the packet buffer (the **release** method) can be viewed as emptying the buffer and making it ready to accommodate a new packet.

The second process run by the sender station is even simpler. This time, we define it completely in one piece:

```
process AckReceiverType (SenderType) {
  Port *Channel;
  Mailbox *Alert;
  states {WaitAck, AckArrival};
  void setup () {
    Channel = S->IncomingPort;
    Alert = S->AlertMailbox;
  };
  perform {
    state WaitAck:
```

```
        Channel->wait (EMP, AckArrival);
      state AckArrival:
        if (((AckType*)ThePacket)->SequenceBit == S->LastSent)
          Alert->put ();
        skipto WaitAck;
    };
  };
```

The only part that requires a brief explanation is the code method. Upon creation, the process starts in state `WaitAck`, where it issues a wait request to the station's input port (`Channel` is set to point to `IncomingPort` by the setup method). The first argument of the `wait` method identifies the event awaited on the port. EMP stands for "end of my packet," which should read "the end of a valid packet addressed to the station running the process." Note that before the end of the acknowledgment packet is received, we cannot know whether the packet is valid. Upon the occurrence of this event, the process moves to state `AckArrival`.

`ThePacket` is a standard pointer of type `Packet*`, whose contents are set by port events triggered by packets; it points to the packet responsible for the event. In state `AckArrival`, the process examines the sequence bit of the arriving acknowledgment packet. If the contents of this bit are the same as the contents of `LastSent` (meaning the acknowledgment is for the current packet), an alert is put into the station's mailbox. This alert will be perceived by the transmitter, which will assume that the packet has been acknowledged. Having accomplished this simple task, the acknowledgment receiver moves back to state `WaitAck`—to await the arrival of another acknowledgment packet.

1.2.4.5   The recipient's protocol.   As does the sender, the recipient station runs two processes. One of them, the receiver, takes care of the incoming packets. The other process, the acknowledger, sends acknowledgments to the sender. Each of the two processes handles one of the two station's ports. The complete specification of the receiver is as follows:

```
process ReceiverType (RecipientType) {
  Port *Channel;
  Mailbox *Alert;
  TIME Timeout;
  states {WaitPacket, PacketArrival, ReAck};
  void setup (TIME tmout) {
    Channel = S->IncomingPort;
    Alert = S->AlertMailbox;
    Timeout = tmout;
  };
  perform {
    state WaitPacket:
      Channel->wait (EMP, PacketArrival);
```

```
        Timer->wait (Timeout, ReAck);
      state PacketArrival:
        if (((PacketType*)ThePacket)->SequenceBit == S->Expected) {
          Client->receive (ThePacket, Channel);
          S->Expected = 1 - S->Expected;
        }
        Alert->put ();
        skipto WaitPacket;
      state ReAck:
        Alert->put ();
        skipto WaitPacket;
    };
  };
```

The receiver uses a timeout to detect missing packets. The timeout value is the argument of the process's setup method and must be specified when the process is created. The first state of the receiver is WaitPacket, where the process waits for two events: the complete arrival of a valid packet addressed to the station (see section 1.2.4.4) and the timer going off. If the timer goes off first, the process gets to state ReAck, where it deposits an alert in the station's mailbox, notifying the acknowledger to resend the acknowledgment of the previous packet.

Upon a packet arrival, the receiver moves to state PacketArrival, where it examines the packet's sequence bit. If the contents of this bit are as Expected, the packet is "received" and Expected is flipped. Otherwise, the packet is ignored. In both cases, however, an alert is deposited in the mailbox to notify the acknowledger to send an acknowledgment packet. If the packet received is not the expected one, the acknowledgment (whose sequence bit is copied from Expected) will be for the previous packet.

The skipto operation used in the receiver is similar to the proceed operation from the previous processes. At this moment it is a bit too early to elaborate on the subtle difference between the two operations—we discuss it in section 4.5.1. To hint at this difference, let us just say that all port events persist until the modeled time is advanced. Therefore, moving directly (by proceed) from state PacketArrival to WaitPacket, the process would hit the same EMP event that previously forced it to state PacketArrival. Using skipto instead of proceed, the process makes sure that the modeled time is advanced—by the minimum possible amount, but enough for the EMP event to disappear from the port.

The operation of receiving a packet consists in calling the Client's receive method with the packet pointer passed as the first argument. The traffic dæmon supplies the network with traffic, and the same dæmon absorbs the traffic at its ultimate destination. The second argument of receive identifies the port on which the packet has arrived. Its role is discussed in sections 5.4.3 and 6.2.13.

The second part of the recipient's duties, i.e., sending acknowledgments to the sender, is performed by the following process:

```
process AcknowledgerType (RecipientType) {
  Port *Channel;
  AckType *Ack;
  Mailbox *Alert;
  states {WaitAlert, SendAck, EndXmit};
  void setup () {
    Channel = S->OutgoingPort;
    Ack = &(S->AckBuffer);
    Alert = S->AlertMailbox;
  };
  perform {
    state WaitAlert:
      Alert->wait (RECEIVE, SendAck);
    state SendAck:
      Ack->SequenceBit = 1 - S->Expected;
      Channel->transmit (Ack, EndXmit);
    state EndXmit:
      Channel->stop ();
      proceed WaitAlert;
  };
};
```

The process starts in state WaitAlert, where it awaits an alert from the receiver. When the alert arrives, the acknowledger moves to state SendAck. Here it sets the sequence bit of the acknowledgment packet to the reverse of Expected and transmits the acknowledgment packet, as discussed in section 1.2.4.4. Why is the serial bit of the acknowledgment set to the reverse of Expected? According to its name, Expected tells the "expected" contents of the serial bit for a new packet, whereas the acknowledgment is for the last packet that was successfully received.

1.2.4.6 The root process.   The object types discussed in the last three sections do not constitute yet an executable program in SMURPH. The following loose ends must be taken care of before the protocol can be executed:

- Input data parameterizing the experiment must be read in. These data typically specify the numerical parameters related to the network configuration (e.g., the lengths of channels) and traffic conditions (e.g., the mean message interarrival time).
- The network must be built, i.e., the stations and channels must be created and configured.
- Traffic conditions in the network must be described.
- The protocol processes must be created and started.
- If we want to see some results from running our protocol, we should make sure they are produced.

The task of coordinating these organizational activities is delegated to a special process that does not really belong to the protocol but nonetheless must be present in any complete SMURPH program. This process plays the role of function **main** in a C or C++ program. As every executable piece of code in SMURPH must belong to some process, the main function in a SMURPH program is actually a process. The type of this process must be named **Root** and its definition must be supplied by the user. The **Root** process will be automatically created in exactly one copy and started by SMURPH at the very beginning of the simulation. In the case of our alternating-bit protocol, type **Root** can be defined as follows:

```
process Root {
  void readData (), buildNetwork (), defineTraffic (),
    startProtocol (), printResults ();
  states {Start, Stop};
  perform;
};
```

The five methods of type **void** represent the five things that had to be taken care of, mentioned at the beginning of this section. Of course, the bodies of these methods must be provided by the user.

Note that no setup method is defined for **Root**. It would not be very useful in this case, although it could have been defined—as for any regular process.

To be executable, the **Root** process must specify a code method. The code method of our **Root** is as follows:

```
Root::perform {
  state Start:
    readData ();
    buildNetwork ();
    defineTraffic ();
    startProtocol ();
    Kernel->wait (DEATH, Stop);
  state Stop:
    printResults ();
};
```

As with any regular process, **Root** is started in its first state (**Start**). Then it reads the input data, configures the network, defines the traffic conditions, and creates the protocol processes. Having accomplished these steps, the process executes the **wait** method of Kernel—to await the end of the simulation experiment. The way we should look at it is that Kernel represents the simulator itself. The DEATH of the simulator means the end of the simulation run. Like everything important that happens during protocol execution, this event is perceptible by processes (the **Root** process in particular) via the **wait** method mechanism.

In state **Stop**, to which **Root** transits after Kernel's DEATH, the process prints out some results and disappears. How do we know that it disappears? Note that no wait requests are issued by `Root` in state `Stop`. A process that exhausts its list of statements at the current state without specifying any waking condition can never be resumed. Such a process effectively (and also literally) ceases to exist.

1.2.4.7   Protocol parameters.

Besides the four methods of `Root` (discussed later), three other code fragments are still missing: the setup methods for the two station types and the list of global variables used by the program. Note that no such variables were explicitly needed by the protocol (the items like `Client`, `ThePacket`, `Timer` do not really look like global variables), which is not surprising: by definition, the protocol program is local and its behavior can only be influenced by what happens at a given station. User-introduced global variables are needed, however, to organize the protocol into a stand-alone executable program. As we will see, the following "variables" are actually constants parameterizing the protocol and the experiment:

```
SenderType *Sender;
RecipientType *Recipient;
TIME TransmissionRate, SenderTimeout, RecipientTimeout, Distance;
Link *SenderToRecipient, *RecipientToSender;
double FaultRate, MessageLength, MeanMessageInterarrivalTime;
long MessageNumberLimit;
int AckLength;
```

`Sender` and `Recipient` will be set to point to the two stations of our network. `TransmissionRate` gives the channel's transmission rate. According to what we said in section 1.1.1, the transmission rate is associated with ports rather than channels. `SenderTimeout` and `RecipientTimeout` represent the two timeout intervals used by the transmitter and the receiver. `Distance` stands for the propagation length of the channels. We assume that both channels have the same length, which is expressed in time units, as the amount of time needed to propagate a signal across the channel. `SenderToRecipient` and `RecipientToSender` will point to the links representing the two channels. `FaultRate` gives the channel's error rate. Again we assume that the two channels are identical in this respect. The remaining variables are related to the traffic. `MessageLength` and `MeanMessageInterarrivalTime` parameterize the message arrival process. `MessageNumberLimit` specifies the number of messages to be passed through the network during the experiment. As soon as this number is reached, the `Kernel`'s DEATH event will be triggered and the simulation run will terminate. Finally, `AckLength` gives the length of the acknowledgment packet, which, of course, is specified in bits.

Some of these variables are initialized from the input data set. This is accomplished by the `readData` method of `Root` in the following simple way:

```
void Root::readData () {
  readIn (AckLength);
  readIn (TransmissionRate);
```

```
            readIn (FaultRate);
            readIn (Distance);
            readIn (SenderTimeout);
            readIn (RecipientTimeout);
            readIn (MessageLength);
            readIn (MeanMessageInterarrivalTime);
            readIn (MessageNumberLimit);
        };
```

1.2.4.8 Building the network. Before we discuss the next step performed by Root, which is the creation of the network backbone, we should look at the setup methods of the two stations:

```
        void SenderType::setup () {
          IncomingPort = create Port;
          OutgoingPort = create Port (TransmissionRate);
          AlertMailbox = create Mailbox (1);
          LastSent = 0;
        };
        void RecipientType::setup () {
          IncomingPort = create Port;
          OutgoingPort = create Port (TransmissionRate);
          AlertMailbox = create Mailbox (1);
          AckBuffer.fill (this, Sender, AckLength);
          Expected = 0;
        };
```

These two methods are very similar. Both stations create their ports and mailboxes and initialize the sequence bits. SMURPH objects are built using the **create** operation, described in section 2.4.7. The optional part in parentheses specifies the arguments of the setup method. The standard setup method of Port accepts the port's transmission rate as the argument. Note that the transmission rate is only specified for the output ports. Nothing is ever transmitted on the input ports, and their transmission rates are irrelevant.

The setup argument for a mailbox gives the mailbox's *capacity*: the number of elements that can be stored in the mailbox awaiting acceptance. In our case, the mailboxes are used to pass simple signals (alerts), which are stored and received one at a time.

The recipient's setup method initializes the acknowledgment buffer (note that the sender's packet buffer need not be initialized as it will be filled by the **getPacket** method of the Client—section 1.2.4.4). This is accomplished by the **fill** method of **Packet**. The first two arguments identify the sender and the receiver of the acknowledgment packet (stations), and the last argument gives the packet length.

The network backbone is built by the following method of the Root process:

```
void Root::buildNetwork () {
  Port *from, *to;
  Sender = create SenderType;
  Recipient = create RecipientType;
  SenderToRecipient = create Link (2);
  RecipientToSender = create Link (2);
  (from = Sender->OutgoingPort)->connect (SenderToRecipient);
  (to = Recipient->IncomingPort)->connect (SenderToRecipient);
  from->setDTo (to, Distance);
  (from = Recipient->OutgoingPort)->connect (RecipientToSender);
  (to = Sender->IncomingPort)->connect (RecipientToSender);
  from->setDTo (to, Distance);
  SenderToRecipient->setFaultRate (FaultRate);
  RecipientToSender->setFaultRate (FaultRate);
};
```

First, the two stations are created. Note that the stations' setup methods are automatically invoked, which results in their ports being built and set up. Next, the two links are created; the Link setup argument gives the number of ports that will be connected to the link. Then the ports are connected to their links and, for each link, the distance between the two ports is set (method setDTo).[13] Finally, for each link, the link fault (error) rate is set to FaultRate.

1.2.4.9 Defining traffic conditions.   Traffic conditions in the modeled network (the behavior of the Client dæmon) are described as a collection of *traffic patterns*. Only one traffic pattern is used in our program. Its type is declared in the following way:

```
traffic TrafficType (Message, PacketType) { };
```

The body of TrafficType is empty, which is not uncommon for a traffic pattern. The only reason we need to define our private traffic pattern, instead of relying on the standard type Traffic from which TrafficType descends, is that we have to indicate that the packets generated by the Client should be of type PacketType (which is nonstandard). This is accomplished by the part in parentheses. The two names appearing there specify the type of messages (the built-in type Message) and packets handled by the traffic pattern.

The traffic pattern type just declared is used in the following method of Root, which creates an instance of this type:

```
void Root::defineTraffic () {
  TrafficType *tp;
  tp = create TrafficType (MIT_exp + MLE_fix,
```

---

[13]The standard type Link represents broadcast channels; thus, from->setDTo(to,Distance) could be replaced with to->setDTo(from,Distance)—with the same effect.

```
        MeanMessageInterarrivalTime, MessageLength);
      tp->addSender (Sender);
      tp->addReceiver (Recipient);
      setLimit (MessageNumberLimit);
    };
```

In general, the list of setup arguments for a `Traffic` object can be long and tricky. A complete description of a traffic pattern consists of the arrival process (telling how and when messages arrive to the network) and the distribution of senders and receivers (which tells at which stations the arriving messages are queued for transmission and where they are destined). In our simple case, the three arguments describe a Poisson arrival process (exponentially distributed message interarrival time) with fixed-length messages. The mean message interarrival time and the fixed message length are given by the last two arguments; their values are read from the input data set. The trivial configuration of senders and receivers is described by the next two method calls. Finally, the call to `setLimit` defines the exit condition for the experiment: `Kernel`'s DEATH will occur as soon as `MessageNumberLimit` messages have been successfully received (see the `Client`'s method `receive` in section 1.2.4.5) at the recipient station.

1.2.4.10 Starting the protocol. The protocol program is started by creating all its processes. This part is done by the `Root`'s method `startProtocol`:

```
    void Root::startProtocol () {
      create (Sender) TransmitterType (SenderTimeout);
      create (Sender) AckReceiverType;
      create (Recipient) ReceiverType (RecipientTimeout);
      create (Recipient) AcknowledgerType;
    };
```

As all dynamically created SMURPH objects, the four processes constituting our implementation of the protocol are built with the `create` operation. Note that the syntax of this operation is somewhat different from its previous instances. The part in parentheses immediately following the keyword `create` identifies the station that is to own the created process. Setup arguments are specified for the transmitter and the receiver; these arguments give the timeout values used by the processes.

1.2.4.11 A sample data set. The data set for our program consists of a sequence of numbers to be read by `Root`'s method `readData` (section 1.2.4.7). For example, the following data set makes sense:

```
        Acknowledgment packet length    256
        Transmission rate               1
        Link fault rate                 0.0001
        Distance between stations       1000
        Sender timeout                  20000
```

```
Recipient timeout            40000
Message length               1024
Message interarrival time    16382
Message number limit         2000
```

While reading the input numbers, SMURPH ignores everything that cannot be interpreted as part of a number. Thus, the textual items are just comments.

The transmission rate of 1 means that the amount of time required to insert a single bit into an output port is equal to one time unit in our system. Therefore, time is measured in bits, which is natural for a homogeneous network—with the same transmission rate for all ports. Consequently, all time intervals, i.e., the channel length, the timeouts, and the message interarrival time, are specified in bits. Clearly, the acknowledgment packet length and message length are also in bits.

The link fault rate gives the damage probability for a single bit. A packet is considered damaged if at least one bit of the packet is damaged.

1.2.4.12 Producing results.   The last method of the Root process that still remains to be presented is printResults:

```
void Root::printResults () {
  Client->printPfm ();
  SenderToRecipient->printPfm ();
  RecipientToSender->printPfm ();
};
```

The printPfm method of the Client writes to the output file a standard collection of performance measures associated with the end-to-end traffic. By *end-to-end* we mean that these measures are taken at the two "ends" of the packet's trip through the network: at the sender and at the recipient. A similar method is defined for a link; it prints out the link-relative traffic statistics, e.g., the number of packets passed through the link.

There is a standard way of printing out (or displaying) information related to SMURPH objects, e.g., the Client, links, stations. The collection of the object's methods provided for this purpose is called the object's *exposure*. Thus, the printPfm method of the Client or a link is an element of its exposure.

At this moment, it is too early to discuss the complete output from our experiment. However, we can easily comprehend the link statistics, which tell us, among other things, how many packets have been damaged. The relevant fragments of the output file (produced on a PowerBook 140)[14] are as follows:

```
Time:           32102194       (Link 0) Performance measures:

Number of transfer attempts:              2250
```

---

[14]PowerBook is a registered trademark of Apple Computer, Inc.

```
        Number of transmitted packets:              2250
        Number of transmitted bits:              2304000
        Number of received packets:                 2000
        Number of received bits:                 2048000
        Number of transmitted messages:             2250
        Number of received messages:                2000
        Number of damaged packets:                   197
        Number of damaged bits:                   201728
        Throughput (by received bits):            0.0638
        Throughput (by trnsmtd bits):             0.0718
```

(Link 0) End of list

```
    Time:           32102194      (Link 1) Performance measures:

        Number of transfer attempts:                2230
        Number of transmitted packets:              2230
        Number of transmitted bits:               570880
        Number of received packets:                    0
        Number of received bits:                       0
        Number of transmitted messages:                0
        Number of received messages:                   0
        Number of damaged packets:                    62
        Number of damaged bits:                    15872
        Throughput (by received bits):                 0
        Throughput (by trnsmtd bits):             0.0178
```

(Link 1) End of list

The first link (number 0) is the one used for transmitting regular packets from the sender to the recipient. Link number 1 is the one used for sending acknowledgments in the opposite direction. Let us discuss link 0 first.

The number of transfer attempts (2250) is the same as the number of transmitted packets. This means that no packet transmissions were aborted: a started packet transmission was always continued to the last bit of the packet and eventually it was terminated by **stop** (section 1.2.4.4). Note that the fact that some packets have been damaged is not captured by these numbers. Obviously, the transmitter has no way of guessing that a packet being transmitted will be damaged on its way to the destination. The number of transmitted bits is just the product of the number of transmitted packets and the fixed packet (message) length (1024 bits).

The number of received packets is precisely 2000, which is not surprising if we recall the termination condition for our experiment. The number of transmitted/received messages is equal to the number of transmitted/received packets. In our case, there is a one-to-one correspondence between messages and packets, so these numbers must be equal. We explain later that it does not always have to be the case.

Note that the number of received packets plus the number of damaged packets does not add up to 2250, which is the number of transmitted packets. No reason to get alarmed here. It is perfectly legal for the sender to transmit two or more copies of the same packet, if an acknowledgment has been lost. This is what the serial bits are for—to detect packet duplicates and ignore them. Thus, the balance $2250 - 2000 - 197 = 53$ represents transmitted packet duplicates. One may still wonder why this number is less than the number of damaged acknowledgments. We leave the answer to this question as an easy exercise to the reader.

Note that acknowledgment packets are never "received." Indeed, the `Client`'s `receive` method is not called for acknowledgments, because they have nothing to do with the `Client`. Similarly, no messages are passed through the second link, as acknowledgments do not originate from messages.

The last two numbers in the link performance data tell the perceived throughput of the link. The first number gives the ratio of the number of bits `received` from the link to the total simulated time.[15] The second number accounts for all transmitted bits, i.e., the retransmitted packets contribute to the throughput. The "received" throughput of the second link is zero, as acknowledgments are never truly "received," i.e., they are never passed as arguments to the `receive` method of the `Client`.

BIBLIOGRAPHIC NOTES

Several books and papers describe the OSI reference model in much more detail than we have done in this chapter. A complete technical description of the OSI model can be found in *ISO* (1979). *Day and Zimmermann* (1983) give a brief introduction to the OSI model, including history, architecture, and terminology. *Bertsekas and Gallager* (1992) discuss the first three layers of the OSI hierarchy with a stress on theoretical aspects. *Miller and Ahamed* (1987) analyze technical issues related to the lower layers, including coding techniques and error detection and recovery. *Spragins, Hammond, and Pawlikowski* (1991) discuss all layers with stress on technical issues, including physical attributes of communication channels, coding and error detection techniques, standards and available networking equipment. More information on higher protocol layers can be found in *Henshall and Shaw* (1985). General discussion of coding techniques for error recovery is given in *Hideki* (1990). *Tanenbaum* (1988) discusses all protocol layers (including MAC-level protocols as a separate sublayer) and is highly recommended as a general, comprehensive handbook on networks and protocols. An overview of OSI-related communication standards, including a presentation of many commercially available networking products, is given by *Stallings* (1987a) (also see *Stallings* (1990)). In *Kochan and Wood* (1989) the reader will find a discussion of the networking tools available on UNIX systems and their placement in the OSI hierarchy.

---

[15]Note that the time is also expressed in bits; therefore, the throughput is *normalized*.

The development of ARPANET has played an important role in setting networking standards and terminology. This seminal network is referenced in all texts that mention the OSI protocol model. For a more detailed presentation, the reader may see *Davidson et al.* (1977), *McQuillan, Falk, and Richer* (1978), or *McQuillan* (1980).

Other protocol modeling and verification systems are discussed by *Budkowski and Dembinski* (1987), *Logrippo et al.* (1988), and *Holzmann* (1991). Although these systems are well suited for expressing high-level aspects of communication, the lack of a built-in notion of time makes them not so well equipped for expressing MAC-level protocols and carrying out performance evaluation studies. Nonetheless, *Holzmann* (1991) is a highly recommended, comprehensive reading, which nicely complements this book. The reader will find there a discussion of the reliability issues in the physical and data-link layers, a highly entertaining historical overview of telecommunication problems, and many valuable methodological hints related to protocol design and verification.

The predecessor of SMURPH, called LANSF, was described by *Gburzyński and Rudnicki* (1989a; 1991). Although LANSF was based on plain C and was much less convenient than SMURPH, it proved invaluable in our early research on protocols for bus-type networks. It was also used by other researchers, notably *Yang and Manikopoulos* (1992a; 1992b) and *Bertan* (1989).

The well-known alternating-bit protocol was formally defined by *Bartlett, Scantlebury, and Wilkinson* (1969) (see also *Lynch* (1968)).

A complete presentation of C++ can be found in *Stroustrup* (1991) and *Lippman* (1991).

PROBLEMS

1. The transmission rate of a ring network based on optical fiber channels is 100 Mb/s. How many meters of the fiber are filled with one bit? What is the propagation length of a 20 km ring?

2. Why is it explicitly postulated that the service provided by the network layer is error-free? Isn't the error-free nature of this service a direct consequence of the error-free data-link service?

3. Assume that the link fault rate is $1/k$, where k is the packet length. Does this mean that no packet ever gets through?

4. Modify the alternating-bit protocol in such a way that the two links can be assigned different fault rates. Draw a graph that shows the number of retransmissions (for regular packets) versus the fault rate of the acknowledging link. Interpret the results.

5. What is the minimum sensible timeout for the sender and the recipient in the alternating-bit protocol? What will happen if a shorter-than-sensible timeout is used? In the sample data set, the recipient timeout is longer than the sender timeout. What may be the reason for this difference?

6. Assume that you would like to test the correctness of the alternating-bit protocol in our implementation. Devise a collection of assertions that would convince you that the protocol operates correctly. Add your assertions to the protocol code and run it. Are they fulfilled?

7. Modify our network model to implement two-way reliable communication between a pair of symmetric nodes. You will have to be able to tell the difference between acknowledgment packets and regular packets. How can you do that without peeking into the forthcoming chapters?

8. In the sample output file presented in section 1.2.4.12, the "received" throughput is less than the "transmitted" throughput. Under what circumstances can the situation be reversed? Would you consider such a situation normal? Can it happen in the alternating-bit protocol?

9. Which of the following statements about the alternating-bit protocol are true?

   a. The number of received (regular) packets is never larger than the number of transmitted packets.
   b. Every lost acknowledgment results in a packet retransmission.
   c. The number of damaged packets is never less than the number of damaged acknowledgments.
   d. The "transmitted" throughput (for regular packets) can never be more than twice as high as the "received" throughput.

10. The message (and packet) length in the traffic pattern used in our experiment is fixed. Would the protocol operate correctly if this length were exponentially distributed?

2

SMURPH Types, Names, Operations

2.1 NAMING CONVENTIONS

SMURPH comprises a layer of macro definitions, type definitions, object declarations, and library functions imposed on C++. Thus, the protocol specification language accepted by the package consists of C++ augmented by some additional rules and constructs. We assume that the reader is familiar with C++ (perhaps superficially), and the elements of this language will not be discussed here unless they are essential for understanding the SMURPH features being presented.

The following rules have been used in introducing SMURPH-specific identifiers into the protocol specification language:

- The names of global variables and user-visible object attributes other than methods start with a capital letter and may contain both lower- and upper-case letters. If the name of a variable has been obtained by putting together a number of words, the first letter of each word is upper-case and all the other letters are lower-case. Examples of such names are `Time`, `Itu`, `TheStation`, `s->MQHead`. The last name stands for Message Queue Head.

- The names of functions and object methods start with a lower-case letter and may contain both upper- and lower-case letters. If the name of a function has been obtained by combining a number of words, each word except the first one starts with a capital letter and all other letters are lower-case. Examples: `setLimit(100)`, `pkt->frameSize()`.

- The names of operations (macros) that are intentionally new keywords added to the language start with lower-case letters and contain lower-case letters only. Examples: `traffic`, `station`, `proceed`. The names of macros that emulate functions or methods obey the same rules as the names of functions or methods. Similarly, the names of macros providing aliases for global variables obey the same rules as the names of variables. Examples: `idToStation(i)`, `ThePacket`, `Timer`.

- The names of symbolic constants (defined as macros) start with a sequence of capital letters optionally followed by "_" (underscore) and a sequence of lower-case letters (and possibly digits). Examples: `YES`, `MIT_exp`, `BIG_precision`, `PF_usr3`.

There exist some global variables, types, and functions that are not intended to be visible to the user. The names of such variables and types begin with "`zz_`" or "`ZZ_`." Most of the user-invisible methods are made private or protected within their objects.

2.2 EXTENSIONS OF STANDARD ARITHMETIC

Having been built on top of C++, SMURPH naturally inherits all the arithmetic machinery of this language. Most of the extensions to this machinery result from the need for a high-precision representation of the modeled discrete time.

2.2.1 Basic Integer Types

Although all C++ compilers offer the three standard integer types `int`, `short`, and `long` (including their `unsigned` versions), the actual range covered by these types may vary from machine to machine. Additionally, some compilers may introduce nonstandard integer types (e.g., type `long long`) intended to extend the available range of the built-in integer arithmetic. SMURPH is not very sensitive to the potential portability problems that may result from the idiosyncrasies of different machines/compilers with respect to the representation of the basic integer types. The only assumption made by the package is that a number of type `int` has at least 16 bits of precision, i.e., in the two's complement notation it covers the range from -32768 to 32767 inclusively. Besides, SMURPH expects that at least one of the built-in integer types (typically type `long`) offers at least 32 bits of precision. On machines with extended integer arithmetic (e.g., 64-bit `long` numbers), the package can take advantage of the extra range to implement `BIG` numbers (section 2.2.3) in an efficient way.

To make protocol programs indifferent to the peculiarities of the integer arithmetic across the various platforms on which the package has been (or will be) installed, SMURPH defines its private names for the most critical integer types. Depending on the availability and range of the actual built-in types, these private names are aliased to the pertinent standard type names, in a way that best matches the program's expectations as to the range covered by the numbers. Specifically, the package defines the following types:

Long

This type represents the shortest available built-in signed integer type with a guaranteed precision of 32 bits. Any integer number for which the 16-bit precision may be insufficient (but the 32-bit precision will do) should be declared as Long. In particular, all *Object* Ids (section 2.4.2) are numbers of type Long.

LONG

This alias is intended to represent the largest available built-in signed integer type. For example, if the given platform offers an efficient 64-bit long long arithmetic, type LONG can be aliased to long long. The primary purpose of type LONG is to provide the base type for implementing BIG numbers (see section 2.2.3).

IPointer

This is the smallest integer type capable of storing both an object of type Long and a pointer. A few functions of SMURPH use this type to represent the receiver of a message or packet (the relevant issues will be discussed in sections 5.2.1, 5.2.2, and 5.3.2).

Generally, the mapping of the above types to the actual built-in integer types is done automatically when the package is installed and the user need not be concerned with this mapping. It is simply recommended to use the SMURPH names listed here (according to the intended precision of the declared object) instead of the standard type name long, to which in most cases all three names are aliased anyway. To see an example of when it makes a difference, imagine a machine with 32-bit int numbers, 64-bit long numbers, and 64-bit pointers.[1] On such a machine, type Long will be aliased to int (SMURPH assumes that a 32-bit precision is all that is expected from type Long), and type LONG will be equivalenced with long (the maximum-precision integer type). The last type (IPointer) will be set to long (the smallest integer type accommodating a pointer as well as a Long integer number).

If the C++ compiler offers the type long long, the user has an option (see section B.1 in appendix B) to equivalence type LONG with long long rather than long. This decision affects the way of implementing type BIG, its consequences are discussed in section 2.2.3. To make sure that it makes sense, the user should compare the execution speed of the simulator with and without this option and then settle for the solution that gives the better performance.

From now on, we consequently avoid using type long explicitly. All simple integer numbers whose required range is potentially larger than that provided by the most conservative 16-bit type int will be declared as objects of type Long or LONG.

2.2.2   Time in SMURPH

As do all simulators, SMURPH provides tools for modeling the flow of time in a class of physical systems. Time in SMURPH is discrete, which means that integer numbers

---

[1]These parameters may describe a Digital Equipment Corporation Alpha processor.

are used to represent time instants and intervals. In the light of modern physics, the discrete nature of the modeled time is not really a limitation,[2] provided that the granularity of time sampling is not too coarse.

In SMURPH, the user is responsible for choosing the granularity of the modeled time. This granularity can be practically arbitrarily fine: it is determined by the physical interpretation of the time unit—the interval between two consecutive time instants. This interval is called the *indivisible time unit* and is denoted by ITU. The correspondence between the ITU and an interval of real time is not defined explicitly. All time-dependent quantities are assumed to be relative to the ITU, and it is up to the user to assign a meaning to it.

For example, in our alternating-bit protocol program (section 1.2.4), the ITU was implicitly defined as the amount of time needed to insert one bit into the network. This may be a natural choice for a homogeneous network in which all ports obey the same transmission rate. Otherwise, the ITU can be chosen in such a way as to represent the *greatest common divisor* of the "natural" time units occurring in the modeled system. The penalty for using a fine granularity of time is very low; thus, if you want to be on the safe side, you can make your ITU a few orders of magnitude smaller than the "natural" time unit for your system.[3] If you combine this approach with randomizing independent timers (section 4.5.2), you can be sure that you are not missing anything important because of an unrealistic "slotted" behavior of the model. We will see later how the careful modeling of time flow reveals hidden implementation problems in apparently simple protocols.

If two events modeled by SMURPH occur within the same ITU, there is in principle no way to order them with respect to their "actual" succession in time. In most cases the order in which such events are presented, i.e., trigger some operations in the protocol program, is nondeterministic. It is possible, however, to assign priorities to awaited events. This way, when multiple events occur at the same modeled time, they will be presented in the order of their priorities.

Although in many cases the ITU is a natural time unit from the viewpoint of the modeled system, is not necessarily natural from the viewpoint of the human observer. Therefore, besides the ITU, there exists another time unit—the so-called *experimenter time unit*, denoted by ETU—used to make the simulation data and results more legible to the human observer. The user declares the correspondence between the ITU and ETU by calling one of the following two functions:

```
void setEtu (double e);
void setItu (double i);
```

The argument of setEtu specifies how many ITUs are in one ETU; the argument of setItu indicates the number of ETUs in one ITU. The call

---

[2]In fact, real time is also discrete, namely, for two events separated in time by less than the so-called Planck interval (about 5.4×10^{-44}s) the concept of chronological ordering loses its meaning.

[3]In a homogeneous network, the author routinely uses 1/1000 of a bit insertion time.

```
setEtu (a);
```

is equivalent[4] to the call

```
setItu (1/a);
```

One of the two functions should be called only once, at the beginning of the network creation phase, before the first object of the network is built. Two global, read-only variables Itu and Etu of type double tell the relation between the ITU and the ETU. Itu contains the number of ETUs in one ITU and Etu, the reciprocal of Itu, contains the number of ITUs in one ETU.

If the ETU is not set explicitly (by setEtu or setItu), it is assumed to be equal to one ITU, i.e., by default, Itu = Etu = 1.0. Thus, in our implementation of the alternating-bit protocol in section 1.2.4, 1 ETU = 1 ITU = one bit insertion time.

2.2.3   Type BIG and Its Range

In many cases, the maximum range of built-in integer numbers available on a given machine is insufficient to represent long intervals of simulated time with a fine granularity. As a fine granularity of time is encouraged in SMURPH, the package is equipped with tools for performing arithmetic operations on potentially very big **non-negative** integer numbers. These tools are transparent to the user, i.e., objects representing time intervals look like yet another type of numeric entities with a standard collection of arithmetic operations and conversion rules.

Time instants and other potentially big non-negative integers should be declared as objects of type BIG or TIME. These two types are absolutely equivalent. Intentionally, TIME should be used in declarations of variables representing time instants or intervals, and BIG can be used to declare other big integers, not necessarily related to time.

When a simulator instance is created by mks (section B.2 in appendix B), the user may specify the minimum precision of type BIG with the -b parameter. The value of this parameter, which is always a single decimal digit, determines how type BIG is implemented. Any digit other than zero gives the requested precision of type BIG in multiples of 31 bits. For example, by specifying "-b 2" the user requests that a number of type BIG should cover at least the range from 0 to $2^{62}-1$. This happens to be the default range of BIG numbers.

The base type used to implement type BIG is LONG (section 2.2.1). If the requested precision of type BIG exceeds the precision of type LONG, several LONG numbers are put together to form a single BIG number. In such a case, type BIG is declared as a class whose data part consists of an array of LONG numbers. This class also defines a collection of methods that provide all standard arithmetic operations on BIG numbers as well as conversions between type BIG and other numerical types.

---

[4]Within the limitations of the floating-point arithmetic.

If type LONG happens to be represented on 32 bits (which is the most common case), the value of parameter -b (the precision digit) tells directly how many LONG numbers form a single BIG number. The most significant bit of each LONG component of this representation is left out for implementation reasons; the remaining 31 bits are significant and they contribute to the resultant precision of type BIG. For other sizes of type LONG, the interpretation of parameter -b is less straightforward. For example, suppose that the size of type LONG is 64 bits and the specified precision digit is 3. The requested size of type BIG is $3 \times 31 = 93$ bits. A single LONG number offers 63 bits of precision (regardless of the size of type LONG, the most significant bit is always left out); thus, type BIG will be declared as a class with the data part consisting of a two-element array of LONG numbers. The actual precision of type BIG will be 126, which is no less (but somewhat more) than 93. Note that precision digits 1 and 2 would both result in type BIG represented directly as LONG (in both cases the actual range covered by BIG numbers would be the same).

Some machines/compilers offer an extended long integer type declared as long long, whose size is equal to twice the size of the standard long type. If type long long is available, it may make sense to force type LONG to be equivalenced to long long rather than to long.[5] This possibility makes sense if the overhead of the extended long arithmetic provided by type long long is less than the overhead on simulating this arithmetic in SMURPH for type BIG consisting of two long objects. If it is not immediately clear which alternative will result in a better performance, the user should try them both and benchmark the execution time of a sample protocol program using a nontrivial precision of type BIG.

If the parameter -b (the precision digit) is 0, type BIG is emulated using type double floating-point numbers. In such a case, type BIG is declared as a class consisting of a single attribute of type double. All arithmetic operations (defined as methods of class BIG) assume that the integer part of the double number represents the actual BIG value. On most machines, this gives a precision that lies somewhere between 1 (31 bits) and 2 (62 bits) with most arithmetic operations performed directly on double numbers. If the resultant precision of type BIG is satisfactory, this solution may offer a visible performance improvement over precision 2, especially for the CPU architectures on which floating-point instructions can be executed in parallel with other operations.

As the value of parameter -b can only be a single decimal digit, mks imposes a limit on the precision of type BIG. In principle, this limit can be exceeded by modifying mks to accept two or even more precision digits. Note, however, that with the maximum currently available precision of 9 (which corresponds to 279 significant bits) one can simulate the life of the universe with the granularity of time corresponding to the Planck interval.

The protocol program has access to the symbolic constant BIG_precision, which tells how many numbers of type LONG constitute a single BIG number. If BIG_precision is −1 (the symbolic constant TYPE_double—section 2.2.5), it means

---

[5]We explain how this can be done in section B.1.

that type BIG is emulated using type double. The default precision of type BIG is 62 bits, which corresponds to the precision digit (parameter -b) of 2. Note that the value of BIG_precision for this default depends on the size of type LONG.

2.2.4 Arithmetic Operations and Conversions

The actual implementation of type BIG is completely transparent to the user. When the precision of BIG numbers is larger than the precision of type LONG (type BIG is a class rather than a simple type), the standard arithmetic operators +, -, *, /, %, ++, --, ==, !=, <, >, <=, >=, +=, -=, *=, /=, %= are automatically overloaded to operate on objects of type BIG. Combinations of BIG operands with types int, Long, LONG, and double are legal. If BIG is equivalent to LONG, the conversion rules for operations involving mixed operand types are defined by C++. Otherwise, if an operation involves a BIG operand mixed with a numeric operand of another type, the following rules are obeyed:

- If the type of the other operand is char, int, Long, or LONG, the operand is converted to BIG and the result type is BIG. One exception is the modulo (%) operator with the second operand being of one of the above types. In such a case, the second operand is converted to LONG and the result type is LONG.
- If the type of the other operand is float or double, the BIG operand is converted to double and the result type is double.
- An assignment to/from BIG from/to another numeric type is legal and involves the proper conversion. A float or double number assigned to BIG is truncated to its integer part.

Note. Overflow and error conditions for operations involving BIG operands are only checked if type BIG is implemented as a class consisting of several objects of type LONG.[6] The user can switch off this overflow checking by specifying the -m option of mks (see section B.2). Note that in principle it is illegal to assign a negative value to a BIG variable (even if not prohibited explicitly, it never makes sense). However, if type BIG is equivalent to LONG, such an operation passes unnoticed and the problem may show up later.

It is possible to check whether a BIG number can be safely converted to double. The function

```
int convertible (BIG a);
```

returns 1 if the BIG number a does not exceed the range of type double for the given machine, and 0 otherwise.

Explicit operations exist for converting a character string (an unsigned sequence of decimal digits) into a BIG number, and vice versa. In particular, the following function turns a BIG number into a sequence of characters:

---

[6]If the size of type LONG is 32 bits, this corresponds to the precision digit (the -b parameter of mks—section 2.2.1) between 2 and 9 inclusively.

```
char *btoa (BIG a, char *s = NULL, int nc = 15);
```

where a is the number to be converted to characters, s points to an optional character buffer to contain the result, and nc specifies the length of the resulting string. If s is absent (or NULL), an internal buffer is used. In any case, a pointer to the encoded string is returned as the function value.

If the number size exceeds the specified string capacity (15 is the default), the number is encoded in the format dd...ddEdd, where d stands for a decimal digit and the part starting with E forms a decimal exponent.

Note.   There is only one internal string buffer, which is overwritten with each call to btoa that specifies no explicit string buffer.

The following function converts a string of characters into a BIG number:

```
BIG atob (char *s);
```

The function processes the character string pointed to by s until it finds the first character that is not a decimal digit. Initial spaces and an optional plus sign are ignored.

2.2.5   Constants

One way to create a constant of type BIG is to convert a character string into a BIG object. If the constant is not too big (or should we rather say "not too BIG"), one can use a conversion from int or long, e.g., b = 22987 (we assume that b is of type BIG) or double. This works also in declarations; consequently, the following statements are legal:

```
BIG  b = 12;
TIME tc = 10e9;
const TIME cnst = 20000000000.5;
```

In the last case, the fractional part is ignored.

Three BIG constants BIG_0, BIG_1, and BIG_inf, are available directly. The first two represent 0 and 1 of type BIG, and the last one stands for an *infinite* or *undefined value* and is equal to the maximum BIG number representable with the given precision. This maximum value is reserved to express *infinity* (or an *undefined value*) and should not be used as a regular BIG number. For completeness, there exist constants TIME_0, TIME_1, and TIME_inf, which are exactly equivalent to the three BIG constants.

The following two predicates tell whether a BIG number is *defined* (or *finite*):

```
int def (BIG a);
```

returning 1 when a is defined (or definite), and 0 otherwise, and

```
int undef (BIG a);
```

which is a simple negation of **def**.

The following arithmetic-related symbolic constants are available to the protocol program:

TYPE_double   Equal to −1.   This is a type indicator (see constant BIG_precision in this list).

TYPE_long   Equal to 0. Another type indicator (see section 2.2.6 for a sample application).

TYPE_short   Equal to 1. An unused type indicator existing for completeness.

TYPE_BIG   Equal to 2. This is the BIG type indicator (section 2.2.6).

BIG_precision   Telling the precision of BIG numbers (section 2.2.3). For example, if BIG_precision equals TYPE_double, BIG numbers are emulated using double-precision floating-point arithmetic.

MAX_long   Equal to the maximum positive number representable with type long int. For the 32-bit two's complement arithmetic this number is 2147483647.

MIN_long   Equal to the minimum negative number representable with type long int. For the 32-bit two's complement arithmetic this number is −2147483648.

MAX_short   Equal to the maximum positive number representable with type short int. For the 16-bit two's complement arithmetic this number is 32767.

MIN_short   Equal to the minimum negative number representable with type short int. For the 16-bit two's complement arithmetic this number is −32768.

MAX_int   Equal to the maximum positive number representable with type int. In most cases, this number is equal to MAX_long or MAX_short.

MIN_int   Equal to the minimum negative number representable with type int. In most cases this number is equal to MIN_long or MIN_short.

There also exist constants MIN_Long, MAX_Long, MIN_LONG, and MAX_LONG, describing the range of types Long and LONG (section 2.2.1), according to the way these types have been aliased to the basic types.

2.2.6   Other Nonstandard Numeric Types

Some numbers, not necessarily representing time instants or intervals, can also be potentially big. One example of such a number is the counter of all information bits received at a station. On the other hand, using type BIG to represent all numbers that could potentially exceed the capacity of standard types int or long (Long, LONG) would be too costly in typical situations. Therefore, there exist three nonstandard flexible numeric types that can be used to express non-negative integer variables that typically fit into the `long int` range but which one would sometimes prefer to store as BIG numbers. Each of these types is in fact an alias (`typedef`) for either LONG or BIG, depending on the setting of some options of `mks` (section B.2). These three flexible types are as follows. By default, they are all equivalent to LONG.

DISTANCE   This type is used to represent propagation distances between ports (sections 3.2.1 and 3.3.2). A propagation distance is in fact a time interval; however, in most cases this interval is reasonably small and there is no need to use type BIG for its representation.

BITCOUNT   This type is used to declare variables counting individual information bits, e.g., transmitted or received, globally or at individual stations. Numerous such counters are used internally by SMURPH for calculating various performance measures.

RATE   This type is used to represent port transmission rates (section 3.3.1). The transmission rate of a port is a typically small time interval, which in most cases can be safely represented as a LONG integer value.

Five macros (symbolic constants) are associated with each of the three flexible types. For example, the following macros are related to type DISTANCE:

TYPE_DISTANCE   This is a symbolic constant that can have one of two values: TYPE_long (0) meaning that type DISTANCE is equivalent to LONG, or TYPE_BIG (2), which means that DISTANCE is equivalent to BIG.

MAX_DISTANCE   This macro is defined as BIG_inf if type DISTANCE is equivalent to BIG, or as MAX_LONG (equal to the maximum LONG number representable on the machine) otherwise.

DISTANCE_inf   The same as MAX_DISTANCE.

DISTANCE_0   This macro is defined as 0 if type DISTANCE is equivalent to LONG, or as BIG_0 otherwise.

DISTANCE_1   This macro is defined as 1 if type DISTANCE is equivalent to LONG, or as BIG_1 otherwise.

To obtain the corresponding macros for the other two types one should replace the world DISTANCE with BITCOUNT or RATE.

2.3 AUXILIARY OPERATIONS AND FUNCTIONS

In this section we list auxiliary functions provided by SMURPH. These functions can be viewed as an extension of the basic C++ run-time library.

2.3.1 Random Number Generators

All random number generators offered by SMURPH are based on the following function:

```
double rnd (int seed);
```

which returns a pseudo-random number of type `double` uniformly distributed in $[0, 1)$. By default, this function uses its private congruential algorithm for generating random numbers. The user can select the standard random number generator (the `drand48` family) by creating the simulator with the -8 option of `mks` (section B.2).

The argument of `rnd`, which must be `SEED_traffic` (0), `SEED_delay` (1), or `SEED_toss` (2), identifies one of three *seeds*. Each seed represents a separate pattern of pseudo-random numbers. The initial values of the seeds (which are of type `Long`) can be specified when the simulator is called (section B.3); otherwise, some default (always the same) values are assumed. This way simulation runs are replicable, which is important from the viewpoint of debugging.

Intentionally, each of the three seeds represents one category of objects to be randomized, in the following way:

SEED_traffic   Traffic-related randomized values (section 5.3), e.g., message interarrival intervals, message lengths, selection of the transmitter and the receiver.

SEED_delay   Values representing lengths of various (possibly randomized) delays not related to traffic generation. For example, the randomization of `Timer` delays for modeling inaccurate clocks (section 4.5.2) is based on this seed.

SEED_toss   Tossing (multisided) coins in situations when SMURPH must decide which of a number of equally probable possibilities to follow, e.g., selecting one of two or more waking events scheduled at the same ITU (section 4.4.1).

All random numbers needed by SMURPH internally are generated according to the preceding rules, but the user is not obliged to obey them. In most cases, the user need not use `rnd` directly.

When the simulator is restarted with the same value of a given seed, all randomized objects belonging to the category represented by this seed will be generated in exactly the same way as previously. In particular, two simulation runs with identical values of all three seeds will produce exactly the same results unless the declared CPU time limit is exceeded (section 4.9.3).

The following two functions generate exponentially distributed pseudo-random numbers:

```
TIME tRndPoisson (double mean);
LONG lRndPoisson (double mean);
```

When the precision of `TIME` is 1, the two functions are identical. The first function should be used for generating objects of type `TIME`, whereas the second one generates (`LONG`) integer values. The parameter specifies the mean value of the distribution. In both cases, the result is generated by transforming a uniformly distributed pseudo-random value obtained by a call to `rnd` with seed 0 (`SEED_traffic`).

The result is a double-precision floating-point number, which is rounded to an object of type TIME or LONG.

The following are four functions that generate uniformly distributed random numbers of type TIME and LONG:

```
TIME tRndUniform (TIME min, TIME max);
TIME tRndUniform (double min, double max);
LONG lRndUniform (LONG min, LONG max);
LONG lRndUniform (double min, double max);
```

In all cases, the result is between min and max inclusively. The functions call rnd with seed 0 (SEED_traffic).

Sometimes one would like to randomize a certain, apparently constant, parameter so that its actual value is taken with some *tolerance*. One example of such a situation is modeling the limited accuracy of a clock. The actual (measured) value of a time interval may vary from the postulated value within some (hopefully small) range. The following functions serve this end:

```
TIME tRndTolerance (TIME min, TIME max, int q);
TIME tRndTolerance (double min, double max, int q);
LONG lRndTolerance (LONG min, LONG max, int q);
LONG lRndTolerance (double min, double max, int q);
```

These functions generate random numbers according to the β distribution, which is believed to describe technical parameters that may vary within some tolerance. The functions call rnd with seed 1 (SEED_delay) and transform the uniform distribution into distribution $\beta(q, q)$, which is extended appropriately, so that the resultant random number is between min and max inclusively. Parameter q, which must be greater than 0, can be viewed as the "quality" of the distribution. For higher values of q the generated numbers have better chances to be closer to (min+max)/2. Reasonable values of q are between 1 and 10. The user should be aware that the higher the value of q, the more time is spent on generating a random number.

The following function simulates tossing a multisided coin:

```
Long toss (Long n);
```

It generates an integer number between 0 and n−1 inclusively. Each number from this range occurs with probability 1/n. The function calls rnd with seed 2 (SEED_toss).

There is an abbreviation for the most frequently used variant of toss. The function

```
int flip ();
```

returns 0 or 1, each value with probability 0.5. In fact, flip() is slightly more efficient than toss(1).

2.3.2   Input/Output

All standard functions and methods of C++ related to input/output are available from SMURPH. There are, however, some additional functions introduced by SMURPH that handle input from the *data file* and output to the *results file*. These two standard files are opened automatically by the program at the very beginning of execution. Their names are specified when the simulator is called (section B.3).

The data file represented by the global variable `Inf` of type `istream` is opened for reading and may contain some numeric data parameterizing the network topology and the protocols, e.g., the number of stations, the lengths of links, the minimum and maximum packet size, traffic distribution.

Note.   The data file is only accessible during the protocol *initialization phase*, i.e., while the `Root` process is in its first state (section 4.8). The file is closed before the protocol execution is started. Conceptually, the standard data file contains information needed to build the network and parameterize the protocol, but then the protocol is expected to live on its own—without any "hints" from the input file. Sometimes, additional input files are needed to supply run-time data, e.g., to feed trace-driven traffic generators. In section 5.5.3 we show how to handle such cases.

The results file, represented by the global variable `Ouf` of the standard C++ type `ostream`, is opened for writing and is intended to contain simulation results, e.g., performance data collected during simulation, control information produced by the protocol program. The most natural way to write some information to the results file is to *expose* some objects (section 7.3). In this section we discuss more elementary output operations offered by SMURPH.

The standard C++ operators `<<` and `>>` with a stream object as the first argument have been overloaded to handle `BIG` numbers. It is thus legal to write

$$\text{sp} >> \text{b};$$

or

$$\text{sp} << \text{b};$$

where `sp` is a pointer to a stream (it should be an `istream` in the first case and an `ostream` in the second) and `b` is an object of type `BIG` (or `TIME`). In the first case, a `BIG` number is read from the stream and stored in `b`. The expected syntax of the number in the input stream is the same as for `atob` (section 2.2.4), i.e., a sequence of decimal digits optionally preceded by a sequence of white spaces. It is also legal to put a plus sign immediately in front of the first digit. Note that there are no negative `BIG` numbers. The `<<` operation encodes and writes a `BIG` number to the stream. The number is encoded by a call to `btoa` (section 2.2.4) with the third argument (digit count) equal to 15. If the number has fewer than 15 digits, the initial spaces are stripped off.

The following functions read numbers from the data file:

```
void readIn (int&);
void readIn (Long&);
void readIn (LONG&);
void readIn (BIG&);
void readIn (float&);
void readIn (double&);
```

Each of these functions ignores in the *data* file everything that cannot be interpreted as the beginning of a number. A number expected by any of these input functions can be either integer (the first four functions) or real (the last two functions). An integer number begins with a digit or a sign (note that the minus sign is illegal for a BIG number) and continues for as long as the subsequent characters are digits. A sign not followed by a digit is not interpreted as the beginning of a number. A real number may additionally contain a decimal point followed by a sequence of digits (the fraction). The number of digits in the fraction may be zero, in which case the decimal point is not necessary. Decimal exponents are not allowed. A decimal point encountered in an expected integer number stops the interpretation of that number, i.e., the next number will be looked for starting from the first character following the decimal point.

The size of an integer number depends on the size of the object being read. In particular, the range of variables of type BIG (TIME) may be very big, depending on the declared precision of this type. Note that all values corresponding to time intervals must not be negative.

There are three simple features that help organize the data file in a more legible and concise way. If a number read by one of the preceding functions is immediately followed by a sign ("+," "−") and another number, then the two numbers are combined into one. For example, $120 + 90$ will be read as 210; similarly $1 − 0.5$ will be read as 0.5 if a real number is expected, or as 1 $(1 − 0)$ otherwise. The rule applies iteratively to the result and thus $1 + 2 + 3 + 4 − 5$ represents a single number (5). Another feature is the symbolic access to the last read number. Namely, the character "%" appearing as the first (or as the only) item of a sequence of numbers separated by signs stands for the last read value. For example, $15, \% − 4$ will be read as $15, 11$. If the type of the expected number is different from the type of the last read number, the value of "%" is undefined. One more feature provides an abbreviation for multiple consecutive occurrences of the same number. Namely, if a number m is immediately followed by a slash ("/"), followed in turn by an unsigned integer number n, the entire sequence is interpreted as n occurrences of number m. Again, all the expected numbers should be of the same type, otherwise the results are unpredictable. For example, the sequence 32.1/43 stands for 43 consecutive occurrences of 32.1.

The fact that only numeric data (together with a few other characters) are relevant and everything else is skipped makes it easy to include comments in the input data file. It is also possible to put a number in a comment. Namely, whenever an asterisk ("*") is encountered in the data file, the rest of the current line is ignored, even if it contains some numbers. One of the following functions can be used to write a data item to the results file:

```
void print (LONG n, char *h = NULL, int ns = 15, int hs = 0);
void print (double n, char *h = NULL, int ns = 15, int hs = 0);
void print (BIG n, char *h = NULL, int ns = 15, int hs = 0);
void print (char *n, int ns = 0);
void print (LONG n, int ns);
void print (double n, int ns);
void print (BIG n, int ns);
```

In all cases, the first argument identifies the data item to be written: it can be a number or a character string. In the three most general cases (the first three functions), the three additional arguments have the following meaning:

h   A textual title to precede the data item. No title will be printed if this argument is NULL.

ns   The number of character positions taken by the encoded data item. If the value of this argument is greater than the actual number of positions required, the encoded item will be right-justified with spaces inserted on the left.

hs   The number of character positions taken by the title. If this number is greater than the actual length of the title string, the title will be left-justified with the appropriate number of spaces added on the right. The total length of the encoded item, together with the title, is **ns+hs**.

The last three functions are abbreviations of the first three ones with the second argument equal to **NULL** and **hs** equal to 0, i.e., they print out items without titles.

Note. The last line of a complete SMURPH output file contains the string **@@@ End of output**. This string is used for special purposes, which are explained in appendix C, and it should never be written explicitly by the user program.

Note. SMURPH is equipped with its private version of the C++ i/o library and its private memory allocator/deallocator (**malloc**). Upon installation (section B.1) the user decides whether the SMURPH library is to be used in lieu of the standard one that comes with C++. The SMURPH versions of the library programs are more compact and better suited for their specific application than the standard versions. However, the i/o library that comes with the package contains only the essential functions and some standard i/o operations of C++ may not work. It is suggested that when the SMURPH version of the library is selected, the protocol programs restrict themselves to using the higher-level i/o interface described here and in section 7.3.

2.3.3   Operations on Flags

In a number of situations it is desirable to set, clear, or examine the contents of a single bit (flag) in a bit pattern. For example, a collection of binary flags is associated with every packet (section 5.2.2). SMURPH defines type FLAGS, which is equivalent to Long and, intentionally, is to be used for representing flag patterns. The following simple functions[7] provide elementary operations on binary flags:

```
FLAGS setFlag (FLAGS flags, int n);
FLAGS clearFlag (FLAGS flags, int n);
int flagSet (FLAGS flags, int n);
int flagCleared (FLAGS flags, int n);
```

The first two functions respectively set and clear the contents of the nth bit in flags. The updated pattern is stored in flags and also returned as the function value. Bits are numbered from 0 to 31; 0 is the number of the rightmost (least significant) bit.

The last two functions are predicates that tell the status of the nth bit in flags. Thus, flagSet returns 0 or 1, depending on whether the indicated bit is set or not, and flagCleared is the straightforward negation of flagSet.

2.3.4   Type Boolean

SMURPH defines type Boolean as char. This type is intended to represent simple binary flags that can have one of two values: 0 represented by the symbolic constant NO (standing for *false*) and 1 represented by the symbolic constant YES (which stands for *true*).

Boolean values are sometimes returned by functions and methods to manifest the OK/error status. By convention, value YES (1) stands for an error and NO (0) indicates that everything was OK. To avoid confusion, SMURPH defines two additional symbolic constants ERROR (1) and OK (0) representing the two Boolean values.

2.3.5   Error Handling

The run-time system of SMURPH handles errors via a standard exception-handling mechanism, which can also be accessed from the user protocol program. This simple mechanism offers the following three functions:

```
void excptn (char *string);
void assert (int cond, char* string);
void Assert (int cond, char* string);
```

The first function provides a standard way of terminating the simulation because of an error condition. The text passed as string is written to the standard

---

[7]These functions are implemented as macros.

output, standard error, and the simulation results file. When the simulation is aborted by **excptn**, SMURPH prints out a brief description of the context in which the error has occurred.

A call to **assert** or **Assert** is semantically equivalent to

$$\texttt{if (!cond) excptn (string);}$$

The difference between **assert** and **Assert** is that when the simulator is created with the **-a** option of **mks** (section B.2), all references to **assert** are physically removed from the program, whereas references to **Assert** are always active.

2.3.6   Identifying the Simulation Experiment

The following declarative operation, which can appear in any place where an **extern** declaration is legal, assigns a name to the protocol:

$$\texttt{identify } \textit{name};$$

The protocol identifier represented by *name* can be any piece of text that does not contain blanks. This text will be printed out in the first line of the results file, together with the current date and time (section 2.3.7).

If the protocol identifier contains blanks, it should be encapsulated in parentheses, e.g.,

$$\texttt{identify (Expressnet version B);}$$

or in quotation marks, e.g.,

$$\texttt{identify "A test version of Hubnet";}$$

A parenthesis within an identifier encapsulated in parentheses, or a quotation mark within a quoted string, can be escaped with a backslash.

2.3.7   Telling the Time and Date

The following function returns the number of seconds of CPU time used by the program from the beginning of the simulation run:

$$\texttt{double cpuTime ();}$$

Note. If the simulator has been restarted after a checkpoint (section B.4), **cpuTime** returns the accumulated execution time measured from the moment the program was originally called rather than the amount of time elapsed from the last restart.

The current date can be obtained by calling the following function:

$$\texttt{char *tDate ();}$$

which returns a pointer to the character string containing the date in the standard format **www mmm dd hh:mm:ss yyyy**, e.g.,

Fri May 19 10:30:13 MST 1995

Date/time in this format is included in the header of the results file, together with the experiment identifier (section 2.3.6).

2.4 SMURPH TYPES

By a SMURPH type we mean a compound, predefined, user-visible type declared as a class with some standard properties. We conveniently assume that BIG (and TIME), although usually declared as a class, is a simple type. In this section we are concerned with SMURPH types only—in the sense of this definition. The words *class* and *type* are used interchangeably to denote the same concept.

2.4.1 Type Hierarchy

Figure 2.1 presents the hierarchy of built-in basic SMURPH types. We assume that all of them are derived from a common ancestor called *class*, which reflects the fact that they are all compound types. Of course, no type named *class* exists in C++.

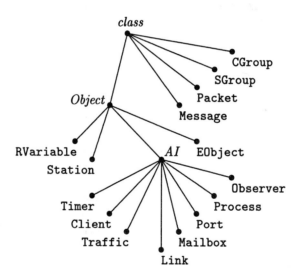

Figure 2.1 The hierarchy of user-visible compound types

All objects exhibiting dynamic behavior belong to type *Object*, which is an internal type, not visible directly to the user. This type declares a number of standard attributes and methods that each *Object* must have. Type EObject can be used to prefix user-defined subtypes of *Object*.

One property of an *Object* (or EObject) is that it can be *exposed*. By exposing an object we mean presenting some information related to the object in a standard way. This information can be *printed*, i.e., included in the output file produced by the simulator, or *displayed*, i.e., shown in a window on the terminal screen. These issues are discussed in detail in section 7.3.

Timer and Client stand for specific objects rather than types. Each of them occurs in exactly one copy. These objects represent some important elements of the protocol environment (section 4.1) and are static, in the sense that they exist throughout the entire execution of the simulator. The actual types of these objects are never used to derive new types; therefore, they are deemed uninteresting and are hidden from the user. Other *Object* types may be used to create new types; objects of these types may exist in multiple copies, and some of them may be dynamically created and destroyed during the simulation run.

All objects belonging to subtypes of *AI* (for activity interpreter) model some entities from the protocol environment. They are responsible for *triggering events* and thus modeling the flow of time. This is discussed in section 4.1.

2.4.2   Object Naming

Each *Object* has a number of attributes that identify it from the outside and a number of methods for accessing these attributes. The reason for so many identifiers mostly stems from the fact that the dynamic display program (DSD) responsible for exposing *Objects* on the screen (appendix A) must be able to identify individual *Objects* and recognize some of their general properties (section 7.3). Besides, *Object* identifiers are useful for locating the information related to particular objects in the results file.

The following seven identification attributes are associated with each *Object*:

- Class identifier
- Numerical Id attribute (*Object*'s serial number)
- Type name
- Standard name
- Nickname
- Base standard name
- Output (print) name

The *class identifier* of an *Object* is a number identifying the base SMURPH type to which the *Object* belongs. This attribute can be accessed by the parameter-less method getClass, e.g.,

```
int cl;
...
cl = obj->getClass ();
```

which returns the following values:

AIC_timer   if the object is the Timer AI

`AIC_client`	if the object is the `Client` AI
`AIC_link`	if the object is a `Link`
`AIC_port`	if the object is a `Port`
`AIC_traffic`	if the object is a `Traffic`
`AIC_mailbox`	if the object is a `Mailbox`
`AIC_process`	if the object is a `Process`
`AIC_observer`	if the object is an `Observer`
`AIC_rvariable`	if the object is an `RVariable`
`AIC_station`	if the object is a `Station`
`AIC_eobject`	if the object is an `EObject`

The *serial number* of an *Object*, also called its `Id`, tells apart different *Objects* belonging to the same *class*. This attribute is accessed by the method `getId`, e.g.,

```
int id;
...
id = obj->getId ();
```

With the exception of `Ports` and `Mailboxes`, all dynamically created *Objects* are assigned their `Ids` in the order of creation, in such a way that the first created *Object* in its *class* is numbered 0, the second is numbered 1, and so on. The numbering of `Ports` and `Mailboxes` is a bit more involved and is described in sections 3.3.1 and 4.7.3. The `Id` attribute of the `Timer` and the `Client` (which never occur in multiple copies) is equal to `NONE` (-1).

The *type name* of an *Object* is a pointer to a character string storing the textual name of the most restricted type (C++ `class`) to which the object belongs. This pointer is returned by the method `getTName`, e.g.,

```
char *tn;
...
tn = obj->getTName ();
```

The purpose of the *standard name* is to identify exactly one *Object*. The standard name is a character string consisting of the object's type name concatenated with the serial number, e.g., `MyProcess 245`. The two parts are separated by exactly one space. For a `Port` and a `Mailbox`, the standard name is built in a slightly trickier way. Namely, it contains as its part the standard name of the `Station` owning the object (sections 3.3.1, 4.7.3). For an object that always occurs in a single instance, the numeric part of the standard name is absent, i.e., the standard names of the `Timer` and the `Client` are just "Timer" and "Client," respectively. The pointer to the object's standard name is returned by the method `getSName`, e.g.,

```
char *sn;
...
sn = obj->getSName ();
```

The *nickname* is an optional character string, which can be assigned to the object by the user. This assignment is usually made when the object is created (section 2.4.7). The nickname pointer is returned by the method getNName, e.g.,

```
char *nn;
...
nn = obj->getNName ();
```

If no nickname has been assigned to the object, getNName returns the NULL pointer.

The *base standard name* is a character string built similarly to the standard name, except that the object's type name is replaced with the name of the base SMURPH type from which the object type has been derived. For example, assume that ms points to an *Object* of type MyStation, which has been derived (directly or indirectly) from Station. The (regular) standard name of this object is "MyStation *n*," whereas its base standard name is "Station *n*." The pointer to the base standard name is returned by the method getBName, e.g.,

```
char *bn;
...
bn = obj->getBName ();
```

Base standard names of objects that are direct instances of base types are the same as their (regular) standard names.

The *output name* of an *Object* is a character string, which is the same as the nickname, if the nickname is defined; otherwise, it is the same as the standard name. When an *Object* is exposed *on paper* (section 7.3), its output name is used as the default header of the exposure. The *Object*'s method getOName returns the pointer to the object's output name, e.g.,

```
char *on;
...
on = obj->getOName ();
```

Note. Character strings whose pointers are returned by getSName, getBName, and getOName are not constants. Thus, if a string returned by one of these functions is to be stored, it must be copied to a safe area. Strings pointed to by getTName and getNName are (intentionally) constants and do not change as long as the object in question is alive.

2.4.3   Type Derivation

Some of the types listed in figure 2.1 are templates to be used for creating problem-specific types defined by the user. For example, type Process can be viewed as a frame for defining types representing processes to be run at stations. One element of the process that must be provided by the user is a method describing the process *code*, i.e., its behavior. This element is specified in the user's part of the process type definition.

SMURPH provides a special way of deriving new types from the built-in ones. We have already seen how it is done in section 1.2.4. Now it is time to discuss this operation in detail. The simplest format of a SMURPH type declaration is as follows:

> *declarator typename* {
>
>   ...
>
>   *attributes and methods*
>
>   ...
>
> };

where *declarator* represents a keyword corresponding to a base SMURPH type (figure 2.1) and *typename* is the name of the newly defined type.

Example

> The declaration
>
> ```
> packet Token {
>     int status;
> };
> ```
>
> defines a new packet type called `Token`. This type is built as an extension of the standard type `Packet` and contains one user-defined attribute—the integer variable `status`.

The declarator keyword is obtained from the corresponding base SMURPH type by changing the first letter to lower-case. The base types that can be extended this way are `Message`, `Packet`, `Traffic`, `Station`, `Link`, `Mailbox`, `Process`, `Observer`, and `EObject`.

It is possible to define the new type as a descendant of an already defined type derived from the corresponding base type. In such a case, the name of the inherited type should appear after the new type name, preceded by a colon:

> *declarator typename* : *itypename* {
>
>   ...
>
>   *attributes and methods*
>
>   ...
>
> };

where *itypename* identifies the inherited type, which must have been declared previously with the same declarator. In fact, a declaration without *itypename* can be viewed as an abbreviation for an equivalent declaration in which *itypename* identifies the base type. In particular, the preceding declaration of type `Token` is equivalent to

```
packet Token : Packet {
    int status;
};
```

For the base types `Process`, `Mailbox`, and `Traffic`, a subtype declaration can optionally specify one or two *argument types* (sections 4.2, 4.7.2, 5.3.3). If present, these argument types are given in parentheses preceding the opening brace. Thus, the format of a subtype definition for these three base types is

> *declarator typename : itypename* (*argument types*) {
>
>   ...
>
>   *attributes and methods*
>
>   ...
>
> };

where the parts ": *itypename*" and "(*argument types*)" are independently optional.

Examples

The process type declaration

```
process Monitor (Node) {
    ...
};
```

defines the process type `Monitor` descending directly from the base type `Process`. The argument type should be a defined (or announced—section 2.4.5) station type; it tells the type of stations that will be running processes of type `Monitor`.

With the declaration

```
process SpecializedMonitor : Monitor (MyNode) {
    ...
};
```

one can build a subtype of `Monitor`. Processes of this type will be owned by stations of type `MyNode`.

The exact semantics of SMURPH type declarators will be described individually for each extensible base type. Every such operation is expanded into the definition of a class derived either from the corresponding base type or from the specified supertype. Some standard attributes (mostly invisible to the user) are automatically associated with this class. These attributes will be used by the run-time system of SMURPH.

The inherited supertype class is made `public` in the subclass. Following the opening brace of the type definition, the user can define attributes and methods of the new type. By default, all these attributes are `public`; the C++ keywords `private`, `protected`, and `public` can be used to specify access rights to the user-defined attributes.

2.4.4   Multiple Inheritance

Sometimes it may be convenient to define a SMURPH subtype as a direct descendant of more than one supertype. This may be especially convenient when creating libraries of types. The C++ concept of *multiple inheritance* has been naturally employed to offer this possibility. There are, however, a few problems that must be mentioned before the solution adopted in SMURPH can be explained. These problems stem from the following facts:

- It is meaningless to define types derived simultaneously from different base types. Thus, there should be a way of controlling whether a SMURPH type extension makes sense.

- An object of a type derived from multiple supertypes must have exactly one frame of its base type.

The first fact is obvious: what would it mean to have an object that is both a `Station` and a `Message` at the same time? The second fact is a consequence of the way in which objects derived from base SMURPH types are handled by the simulator. Internally, such an object is represented by various pointers and tags kept in its base type part. Having two or more copies of this part, besides wasting a substantial amount of space, would not agree well with the way objects are handled by the SMURPH run-time system.

In C++ it is possible to indicate that the frame corresponding to a given class occurs exactly once in the object frame, even if the class appears several times in the object's type derivation. This is achieved by declaring the class as `virtual` in the derivation sequence. Thus, one possible solution to be adopted in SMURPH would be to force each base type to occur as `virtual` in the derivation sequence of a user-defined type. This solution, however, would be quite costly. To make it work, one would always have to make the base types virtual, even if no multiple inheritance were used.[8] This would be too expensive, as the frame of a virtual subclass is referenced via a pointer, which substantially increases the cost of such a reference. Therefore, we came up with another simple solution. If the name of a newly defined SMURPH supertype is followed by `virtual`, e.g.,

```
station VirPart virtual {
    ...
};
```

it means that formally the type belongs to the corresponding base type, but the frame of the base type will not be attached to the type's frame.

The *itypename* part of a SMURPH subtype definition (section 2.4.3) may contain a list of type names separated by commas, e.g.,

---

[8]Note that the protocol program may be contained in several files, and the fact that no multiple inheritance is used in one file does not preclude it from being used in another one.

```
packet DToken : AToken, BToken, CToken {
    ...
};
```

This list represents the multiple inheritance sequence of the defined subtype. The following rules are enforced:

- The inheritance sequence may contain at most one nonvirtual type name (in the sense just described). If a nonvirtual type name is present, it must appear first in the sequence.
- If the name of the defined type is followed by `virtual` (this keyword must precede the colon), the inheritance sequence must not include a nonvirtual type.
- If the inheritance sequence contains virtual types only, but the keyword `virtual` does not follow the name of the defined type, the defined type **is not virtual**, i.e., the base type is implicitly added to the inheritance sequence (as the first element). Thus, only types explicitly declared as `virtual` are made `virtual`.

One disadvantage of this solution is that a virtual (in the SMURPH sense) type cannot reference attributes of the base type. This is not a big problem, as very few of these attributes may be of interest to the user. Virtual functions can be used to overcome this difficulty, should it become serious.

2.4.5   Announcing Types

A SMURPH subtype can be announced before being actually defined. This may be needed occasionally if the name of the type is required (e.g., as an *argument type*—section 2.4.3) before the full definition can take place. The following type declaration format is used for this purpose:

declarator typename;

where *declarator* has the same meaning as in section 2.4.3. The type name can be optionally followed by `virtual`, in which case the type is announced as virtual in the sense of section 2.4.4. Note that a full type definition must precede the use of this type in the inheritance sequence of another type.

2.4.6   Subtypes with Empty Local Attribute Lists

There are many cases when the local attribute list of a SMURPH subtype is empty, e.g.,

```
traffic MyTPattern (MyMType, MyPType) { };
```

This situation occurs most often for traffic patterns (subtypes of `Traffic`) and mailboxes (subtypes of `Mailbox`). In such a case, it is legal to skip the empty pair of braces, provided that the new type declaration cannot be confused with a type announcement (section 2.4.5). In particular, the definition of `MyTPattern` can be shortened to

`traffic MyTPattern (MyMType, MyPType);`

because, owing to the presence of the argument types, it does not look like a type announcement. On the other hand, in the declaration

`packet MyPType { };`

the empty pair of braces cannot be omitted, because otherwise the declaration would just announce the new packet type without actually defining it. Generally, an abbreviated type declaration (without braces) is treated as an actual type definition rather than as an announcement if at least one of the following conditions is true:

- The declaration contains argument types.
- The declaration explicitly specifies the supertype.

Thus, the declaration of `MyPType` can be written equivalently as

`packet MyPType : Packet;`

which, however, is hardly an abbreviation. On the other hand, the most common cases when the attribute list of a newly defined type is empty deal with subtypes of `Traffic` and `Mailbox`, and then argument types are usually present.

2.4.7   Object Creation and Destruction

If an object belonging to a base SMURPH type or its derived subtype is to be created explicitly, the following operation must be used for this purpose:

`obj = create typename ( setup args );`

where `typename` is the name of the object's type. The arguments in parentheses are passed to the object's setup method. If the object has no setup method or the list of arguments of this method is empty, the part in parentheses does not occur (the empty parentheses can be skipped as well). The operation returns a pointer to the newly created object.

The purpose of the setup method is to perform object initialization. If one is needed, it should be declared as

`void setup ( ...);`

within the object type definition. Argument-less C++ constructors can also be used in user-defined derived SMURPH types; however, there is no way to define and invoke upon an object creation a constructor with arguments. The role of such a constructor is played by `setup`. Nonextensible types (section 2.4.3) and types that need not be extended define appropriate standard/default setup methods. Their arguments and semantics will be discussed separately for each relevant basic type.

It is possible to assign a nickname (section 2.4.2) to the created object. The following version of `create` can be used for this purpose:

> `obj = create typename, nickname, ( ` *setup args* ` );`

where `nickname` is an expression that should evaluate to a character pointer. The string pointed to by this expression will be duplicated and used as the object's nickname. If the *setup args* part does not occur, the second comma together with the empty parentheses may be omitted.

The `typename` keyword (in both versions of `create`) can be optionally preceded by an expression enclosed in parentheses, i.e.,

> `obj = create (expr) typename ( ` *setup args* ` );`

or

> `obj = create (expr) typename, nickname, ( ` *setup args* ` );`

where `expr` must be either of type `int` or a pointer to an object belonging to a `Station` subtype. It identifies the station in the context of which the new object is to be created, and is relevant for some object types only (e.g., for processes). We have already seen an application of this syntax of `create` in section 1.2.4.10; more details are given in section 3.1.3.

Objects belonging to types `SGroup`, `CGroup`, `Station`, `Traffic`, `Link`, `Mailbox`, and `Port` can only be created and never explicitly destroyed. Methodologically, such objects represent some "hardware" elements that belong either to the network backbone or to the network environment, external from the viewpoint of the protocol. Objects that are elements of the protocol specification (processes, observers) or that are processed by the protocol (messages, packets, random variables, user-defined instances of types derived from `EObject`) can be created and then destroyed (deallocated). Object destruction is handled by the standard C++ operator `delete`. User-defined subtypes of *Object* must belong to type `EObject`, i.e., be actually subtypes of `EObject`. A declaration of such a subtype should start with the keyword `eobject` and obey the rules listed in sections 2.4.3 and 2.4.4. An `EObject` subtype may declare a setup method (or a number of such methods). Object instances of `EObject` subtypes should be generated by `create`, and they can be deallocated by `delete`.

Id attributes of `EObjects` reflect their order of creation starting from 0. This numbering is common for all subtypes of `EObject`.

Note. It is illegal to `create` an object of a virtual type (section 2.4.4).

BIBLIOGRAPHIC NOTES

Physical and philosophical considerations related to the nature of time can be found in several books aimed at a general audience, notably in *Coveney and High-*

field (1991), *Gribbin* (1988), and *Davies* (1992). In *Fritzsch* (1984), the reader will find an explanation of the concept of Planck time and an estimate of the age of the universe.

Concepts of event-driven, discrete time simulation are discussed by *Bratley, Fox, and Schrage* (1987), and many other authors, including *Law and Kelton* (1991), *Jeruchim, Balaban, and Shanmugan* (1992), *Ross* (1990), and *Fishman* (1990). All these books also cover to some extent random number generation. *Law and Kelton* (1991) and *Bratley, Fox, and Schrage* (1987) present the β distribution and show how to transform a uniform distribution into β (see also *Schmeiser and Babu* (1980)). *Niederreiter* (1992) gives a more involved course on random number generation and statistical methods of solving numerical problems. Congruential generators, their good properties and weak spots, are discussed by *Bratley, Fox, and Schrage* (1987), *Fishman* (1990), *Fishman and Moore* (1986), and *Marsaglia* (1968). Methods of converting uniform distributions into other distributions are discussed by *Ahrens and Dieter* (1972a; 1972b; 1980; 1982a; 1982b), *Ahrens and Kohrt* (1981), and *Devroye* (1981).

For an overview of commercially available software for simulating communication networks the reader may consult *Law and McComas* (1994). *Walch, Wolisz, and Wolf-Günther* (1994) give some interesting methodological suggestions regarding visualization techniques in network simulators.

C++ class derivation mechanism, including multiple inheritance, is discussed by *Lippman* (1991) and *Stroustrup* (1991) (see also *Stroustrup* (1989)).

PROBLEMS

1. What is the precision of TIME needed to model the behavior of Ethernet for two hours? Assume that the network transmission rate is 10 Mb/s and the time granularity is 0.001 of the bit insertion time. What will be the parameter of setEtu to set the ETU to 1 second?

2. Write a SMURPH program to determine empirically the density curve for the β distribution. Hint: You don't have to build a network for this experiment; all you need is a Root process. Investigate how this curve depends on the *quality* of the distribution.

3. Write a SMURPH program to determine by how much flip is faster than toss on your machine.

4. A SMURPH simulator is executed on a single sequential machine. The author claims that it can realistically model the time flow in a distributed system running many concurrent processes at the same time. How is it possible?

5. Write a SMURPH program to time the arithmetic operations on objects of type TIME. Determine how the execution time of these operations depends on the precision. You will see that multiplication and division are very expensive. Obviously, the author didn't bother to make these operations efficient. Why? Is precision 0 (TIME represented as double) useful on your machine?

6. Run the alternating-bit example with different precision of TIME, and draw a graph illustrating the execution time versus TIME precision. Why isn't this relation linear?

7. Modify the alternating-bit example to make it crash. Interpret the information displayed by SMURPH after the crash. How can you use this information to locate the problem.

8. The two station types in the alternating-bit protocol have a similar structure. Isolate the identical attributes of these types into a separate station type. Define the two station types used by the program as descendants of this type.

9. Add to the Root process in the alternating-bit program a code for printing out the name attributes of the stations, ports, mailboxes, links, and processes. Use the printing tools of SMURPH. What is the standard name of Kernel? Modify the relevant create operations to assign nicknames to the stations and processes.

10. Run the alternating-bit program for the following data set:

Acknowledgment packet length	256
Transmission rate	1
Link fault rate	0.000001
Distance between stations	1000
Sender timeout	20000
Recipient timeout	40000
Message length	32768
Message interarrival time	65536
Message number limit	66000

The results seem to be somewhat out of line (e.g., look at the number of transmitted bits in link 0). Why is it so? How can you remedy the problem without modifying the data set?

3

Building the Network

3.1 STATIONS

The geometry of the modeled network, although static from the viewpoint of the protocol program, is defined in SMURPH dynamically by explicit object creation and calls to some functions and methods. As perceived by the simulator, a network consists of *stations*, which are connected to *links* via *ports*. A station is a processing unit of the network. It can be viewed as hardware (a parallel computer) that runs a collection of *processes*. These processes implement a fragment of the protocol program run by the entire network.

A station is an object belonging to a type derived from `Station` (section 2.4.1). It is possible to create a station belonging directly to type `Station`, but such a station has no ports, so it cannot be connected to a link and consequently is not usable as a network component.

The standard type `Station` defines only two attributes visible to the user, which in most cases are not accessed directly. These attributes describe the queues of *messages* awaiting transmission at the station (section 5.3.7).

3.1.1 Defining Station Types

A new station type definition starts with the keyword `station` and obeys the rules introduced in sections 2.4.3 and 2.4.4. The setup method for a station type needs only to be defined if the type declares attributes that must be initialized when a station object of this type is created.

Examples

The declaration

```
station Hub {
    Port **Connections;
    int Status;
    void setup () { Status = IDLE; };
};
```

defines a new station type called Hub derived directly from Station, with two attributes: an array of pointers to ports and an integer variable. Upon the creation of a Hub object, the Status attribute will be set to IDLE. The array of port pointers is not initialized in the setup method, so presumably it will be created outside the object.

The Hub type just defined can be used to derive another station type, e.g.,

```
station SuperHub : Hub {
    TIME *TransferTimes;
    void setup (int hsize) {
        Hub::setup ();
        TransferTimes = new TIME [hsize];
    };
};
```

The SuperHub type inherits all attributes from Hub and declares one private attribute—an array of TIME values. The setup method of SuperHub has one argument specifying the size of TransferTimes. The setup method of the supertype must be called explicitly (unless the supertype initialization is not needed); hence the call to Hub's setup—to initialize the Status attribute.

Stations are the most natural candidates to be defined from virtual supertypes, according to the rules described in section 2.4.4. For example, the configuration of a station's ports is an element belonging to the network geometry definition, whereas the configuration of a station's buffers (section 5.2.3) belongs to the traffic specification. If we wanted to isolate the geometry component of a station, e.g., to put it into a library of network architectures, we would define a virtual station type defining the configuration of ports (and possibly other geometry-specific attributes). Similarly, another virtual station type describing traffic-related elements (e.g., the configuration of packet buffers) could be put into a library of traffic patterns. The only sensible way of combining such pieces into complete station types is to take advantage of the multiple inheritance apparatus of C++, in its SMURPH flavor discussed in section 2.4.4.

Example

Consider the following declaration:

```
station TwoBusInterface virtual {
  Port *Bus0Port, *Bus1Port;
  void setup (RATE tr) {
    Bus0Port = create Port (tr);
    Bus1Port = create Port (tr);
  };
};
```

which describes a station fragment. This fragment consists of two ports that are
created by the setup method (the details are explained in section 3.3.1). The two
ports may provide a station interface to a two-bus network without specifying any
other details of the station architecture. The next declaration,

```
station ThreeBuffers virtual {
  Packet Buf1, Buf2, Buf3;
};
```

can be viewed as a description of a Client interface (section 5.2.3) consisting of
three packet buffers. The two interfaces can be used together in a combined derived
definition, e.g.,

```
station MyStationType : TwoBusInterface, ThreeBuffers {
  RVariable *PacketDelay;
  void setup () {
    RATE MyTRate;
    PacketDelay = create RVariable;
    readIn (MyTRate);
    TwoBusInterface::setup (MyTRate);
  };
};
```

as independent building blocks for a new complete (nonvirtual) station type.

3.1.2   Creating Station Objects

Given a station type, a station object is generated by executing **create** (section 2.4.7). The serial number (the Id attribute—section 2.4.2) of a station object
reflects its creation order. The first-created station gets number 0, the second gets
number 1, and so on. The global read-only variable NStations of type int stores
the number of all stations created by the program.

The network geometry must be completely determined during the protocol
initialization phase, i.e., while the Root process is in its first state (section 4.8).
It is illegal to create new stations after the initialization is over. Once created, a
station can never be destroyed.

There exists one special station, which is created automatically at the very
beginning of program execution and, as do all stations, exists through the entire
simulation run. Formally, every SMURPH process must be owned by some station.
The purpose of this special station is to run the internal (*system*) processes of
SMURPH and also the user's Root process (section 4.8). This station is pointed

to by the global variable `System`, whose type (a subtype of `Station`) is hidden from the user. The `Id` attribute of the `System` station is `NONE` and its *type name* is `SYSTEM`. The structure of the `System` station is very simple. The station has no ports, no mailboxes, and no message queues. It cannot be configured into the network and it never appears as a member of the network configuration. We will see later (section 4.7.3) that it is possible to create a mailbox belonging to the `System` station. Such a mailbox can be used to synchronize user processes running outside the protocol, e.g., nonstandard traffic generators.

Sometimes it is convenient and natural to reference a station via its serial number (the `Id` attribute). For example, station numbers are used to identify senders and receivers of messages and packets (section 5.2). Quite often, during the network initialization phase, one would like to perform some operation(s) for all stations. In such a case, it is natural to use a loop, e.g.,

```
for (int i = 0; i < NStations; i++) ...
```

To make such operations possible, the following function[1] converts a station `Id` into a pointer to the station object:

```
Station *idToStation (int id);
```

The function checks whether the argument is a legal station number and if it is not, the execution is aborted. This checking is performed by invoking the following simple macro:

```
int isStationId (int id);
```

which expands into

```
((id) >= 0 && (id) < ::NStations)
```

This macro (available to the user program) is the recommended way of determining whether an integer number is a valid station `Id` (e.g., section 5.5.2).

Note. For symmetry, the following macro looks like a function that returns the `Id` attribute of a station (or any *Object*) whose pointer is specified as the argument:

```
int ident (Object *a);
```

This macro naturally expands into a call to `getId` (section 2.4.2).

3.1.3 Current Station

At any moment while the protocol program is running, and also during the network initialization phase, exactly one station must be "currently active." This station

---

[1]Implemented as a macro.

is pointed to by the global variable TheStation of type Station. This variable belongs to the so-called *process environment* (section 4.4.4). At the beginning of the initialization phase, TheStation points to the System station, then, as new user-defined stations are created, TheStation points to the last created station. Intentionally, TheStation is a read-only variable and should not be modified by the user. It is legitimate, however, to modify TheStation during the network initialization phase, to move explicitly to a different *current station*. This may be useful when creating an object that should belong to a specific station (e.g., a process or an RVariable). There exists a version of create with an argument specifying the station that should be assigned to TheStation before the actual object creation. The syntax of this operation is as follows (section 2.4.7):

$$\text{obj = create (expr) typename (} \textit{setup args} \text{);}$$

or

$$\text{obj = create (expr) typename, nickname, (} \textit{setup args} \text{);}$$

The effect is as if the create operation were preceded by one of the statements:

$$\text{TheStation = expr;}$$

or

$$\text{TheStation = idToStation (expr);}$$

depending on whether expr points to a Station object or produces an integer value. In the latter case, the integer value gives the Id attribute of the station in question. This way it is practically never required to assign anything to TheStation explicitly.

Note. The effect of specifying the new current station at create extends beyond the single create operation, i.e., TheStation is set to a new value before the object is created, but not reset to the previous value afterwards. For example, the sequence of commands

```
p1 = create (ns) Port;
mb = create (ns) Mailbox (4);
```

is equivalent to:

```
p1 = create (ns) Port;
mb = create Mailbox (4);
```

We will be often using sequences like the first one, to make the context of the create operations more visible. Sometimes such constructs may be misleading by suggesting a local character of the new context.

3.2   LINKS

Links are simple communication channels whose real-life counterparts can be implemented on the basis of some signal-passing media, e.g., a piece of wire, a coaxial cable, an optical fiber, a radio band. Links and stations are interfaced through ports. Ports can be viewed as some specific points (taps) on the links that the stations can use to send and receive information.

SMURPH links are objects belonging to type Link, which exists in four standard subtypes: BLink (equivalent to Link), ULink, PLink, and CLink. The purpose of a link is to model a simple communication channel. Two types of channel models, broadcast and unidirectional links, are built into SMURPH, each of the two types occurring in two marginally different flavors.

3.2.1   Propagation of Information in Links

A broadcast link is a uniform signal carrier (an information passing medium) with the property that information entered into any port connected to the link reaches all other ports of the link in due time. In a unidirectional link, information travels in one direction only: for any two ports p_1 and p_2 on such a link there is either a path from p_1 to p_2 or from p_2 to p_1, but never both. A typical physical implementation of a unidirectional link is a single, segmented fiber-optic channel.

Logically, the concept of a unidirectional link is somewhat redundant and may be confusing on the first reading. A real-life unidirectional fiber-optic channel is implemented as a chain of separate broadcast channels connected via active taps. Of course, it is possible in SMURPH to build unidirectional channels this way (in many cases this is actually the right way to do it). However, the built-in concept of a unidirectional link makes it easier to implement simple protocols exploring the idea of unidirectional channels and, what is more important, reduces the execution time of the model. The reader should view unidirectional links as a convenient shortcut, which may not be very realistic but which may prove quite handy if used with care.

Links are used to transmit information between stations. Section 6.1 explains what is meant by the somewhat evasive term *information*. For the purpose of this section, we can talk about passing "signals" (e.g., electric or photonic pulses) through the links. Unfortunately, the word *signals* is not a good choice as it is used to denote a simple "handshake" mechanism used for process synchronization (section 4.6.2). We seem to be running out of different words to name various kinds of "messages" passed between different agents, in different ways, and for different reasons. To separate the "things" passed through links from other types of "messages," we will call them "link activities," or simply "activities," if in the given context they cannot be confused with anything else. We see later that these terms correspond rather well with the general role played by the link model in the protocol environment.

Irrespective of the link type, the actual geometry of the link is described by the *link distance matrix*, which specifies the propagation distance between each pair of ports connected to the link. The propagation distance from port p_1 to port p_2 is equal to the (integer) number of ITUs required to propagate an activity from p_1 to p_2. If an activity, e.g., a packet transmission, is started on port p_1 at time t, that activity will appear on port p_2 at time $t + D_{p_1,p_2}$, where D is the link distance matrix. For a broadcast bidirectional link (types BLink and CLink), the propagation distance is independent of the direction, i.e., the propagation distance from p_1 to p_2 is the same as the propagation distance from p_2 to p_1. In other words, the distance matrix of a broadcast link is symmetric.[2]

For a unidirectional link (types ULink and PLink), the order in which particular ports were connected to the link (section 3.3.2) determines the propagation direction, i.e., if port p_1 was connected earlier than p_2,[3] then activities can propagate from p_1 to p_2, but not from p_2 to p_1. It means that an activity inserted into p_1 at time t will reach p_2 at time $t + D_{p_1,p_2}$ (as in a broadcast link), but no activity inserted into p_2 will ever arrive at p_1. Thus, the distance matrix of a unidirectional link is triangular.

If a unidirectional link has a strictly linear topology, i.e., for every three ports p_1, p_2, p_3 created in the listed order $D_{p_1,p_3} = D_{p_1,p_2} + D_{p_2,p_3}$, the link can be declared as PLink. This type can only be used to represent strictly linear, unidirectional links. Semantically, there is no difference between types PLink and ULink used to represent such a link; however, the PLink representation is usually much more efficient, especially when the link is very long compared to the duration of a typical activity inserted into it.

More information about the dynamics of links is given in section 6.2, where the concept of *collision* is discussed. For the purpose of this section, it is enough to say that there are two different methods of recognizing collisions in a bidirectional link. The existence of two types for representing a bidirectional link is a direct consequence of this fact. The two types BLink and CLink are semantically identical, except for the difference in interpreting collisions (section 6.2.10). Type BLink is equivalent to the simplest, generic link type Link. This is also the link type whose semantics best agree with the real-life semantics of regular, simple, uniform broadcast channels.

3.2.2   Creating Links

Link objects are seldom, if ever, referenced directly by the protocol program, with the exception of the network initialization phase when the links must be built and configured. It is technically possible to define a new link type with the operation

---

[2]In fact, distance matrices do not occur explicitly: they are distributed into *distance vectors* associated with ports rather than links.

[3]We assume that the two ports belong to the same link.

```
link newtypename : oldtypename {
   ...
};
```

but, in the present version of SMURPH, there is no way to create a link type that would be functionally different from all the existing, built-in link types. One potential use for the possibility of declaring a nonstandard link type is to augment the standard performance-measuring link methods by user-defined functions (section 7.1.3.2) or to declare a nonstandard link method for generating damaged packets (section 6.4).

If the *oldtypename* part is absent, the new link type is derived directly from Link. A link object is created by create—in a way similar to any other *Object* (section 2.4.7). The standard link setup method is declared with the following header (the same for all link types):

```
void setup (Long np, TIME at = TIME_0, int spf = ON);
```

Thus, at least one and at most three setup arguments are expected by the create operation for a link. The first (mandatory) argument, denoted by np, specifies the number of ports that will be connected to the link. The second argument (at) gives the so-called link *archival time* in ITUs. The archival time determines for how long descriptions of activities that have physically disappeared from the link are to be kept in the link database (section 6.1.1). The default value (0) means that any activity leaving the link is immediately forgotten. The last argument indicates whether standard performance measures are to be calculated for the link. With the default value (ON is a symbolic constant defined as 1), the standard performance measures will be collected; value OFF (0) turns them off.

Note. If the user declares private nonstandard performance-measuring methods for a link (section 7.1.3.2), they will be called even if the link has been created with spf = OFF.

A newly created link is raw in the sense that its geometry is not determined. Note that the setup arguments for a link say nothing about the link's distance matrix. The value of np specifies only the number of *slots* for ports that will be eventually connected to the link, but these ports are not created, nor is anything said about their geometric distribution. In fact, nothing is known at this moment about the geometry of the link: as we said in section 3.2.1, this geometry is determined by the list of distances between all pairs of ports.

The Id attributes of links (and also their standard names—section 2.4.2) reflect the order in which the links were created. The first created link gets number 0, the second—number 1, and so on. In many cases, when a link is to be referenced, it is possible to use either a pointer to the link object or the link number (its Id attribute). The function

```
Link *idToLink (int id);
```

converts a numeric link Id to the link pointer.[4] The global variable NLinks of type int contains the number of all links created so far. The simple standard macro

$$\text{int isLinkId (int id);}$$

returns YES, if the argument is a legitimate link Id, and NO otherwise.

3.2.3   Faulty Links

It is possible to declare that packets transmitted on a given link may be damaged with a certain probability. The following link method declares a fault rate for the link:

$$\text{void setFaultRate (double rate = 0.0, int ftype = FT\_LEVEL1);}$$

The first argument specifies the error rate per one bit. Its value must be between 0 and 1; usually it is much less than 1. The second argument gives the *processing type* for invalid packets. The details are given in section 6.4, after we have learned more about the way link activities trigger events on ports. For the purpose of this section, it is enough to say that a packet that has a damaged bit may not arrive at the destination.

By default, i.e., if setFaultRate is not called for a link, the link is assumed to be error-free, i.e., no packets are damaged by the link. Any new call to setFaultRate overrides the previous calls and redefines the faulty status of the link. In particular, by calling

$$\text{lnk->setFaultRate ();}$$

we declare the link pointed to by lnk as error-free.

Note.   To avoid unnecessary simulation overhead, the possibility of declaring links as faulty is switched off by default. To enable faulty links, the simulator must be created with the -z option of mks (section B.2).

3.3   PORTS

Ports are objects of the standard type Port, which is not extensible by the user. Therefore, there is no port operation that would define a Port subtype.

3.3.1   Creating Ports

There are two ways to create a port. One is to use the standard create operation (section 2.4.7).

The port setup method for this occasion is defined with the header

$$\text{void setup (RATE rate = RATE\_0);}$$

---

[4]This function is implemented as a macro.

where the optional argument specifies the port transmission rate (attribute `TRate`) as the number of ITUs required to insert a single bit into the port. Note that in SMURPH's perception, the transmission rate is the reciprocal of what we would normally call the transmission rate. The reason for this interpretation is the nature of the time unit (ITU), which is not (or at least should not be) larger than the (minimum) bit insertion time. In section 2.2.2 we postulated that all "natural" time units in the modeled system be multiples of the ITU. If this is the case, then the port transmission rates (which clearly fit into the category of natural time intervals) should also be expressible as natural numbers.

The `TRate` attribute of a port is only relevant if the port will ever be used for *transmission* (section 6.1) and determines the amount of time required to transmit a packet through the port. If nothing is ever transmitted on the port, i.e., the port is only used for reception or status sensing, the setup argument can be skipped, in which case the port's transmission rate is undefined (set to 0). Different ports belonging to the same link may have different transmission rates, although in most cases the nonzero rates of such ports are all the same and they reflect the global transmission rate of the link.

Ports are naturally associated with stations and links. From the viewpoint of the protocol program, the association of a port with a station is more important than its association with a link, as links are not directly perceived by the protocol. Therefore, a port can be declared statically within a station type and then created automatically when the station owning the port is created. The following declaration formats are legal:

```
Port portname;
Port portname = (rate);
Port portname = (rate, nickname);
Port portname = (nickname);
```

where *rate* should evaluate to an integer value of type `RATE` defined at the moment of creation and *nickname* should be a character string pointer. The first format declares a port with 0 (undefined) transmission rate and no nickname (section 2.4.2). With the second declaration format, a nonzero transmission rate can be assigned to a port that is to be used for transmission. With the third format, one can assign both a transmission rate and a nickname to the port (as if it were created by the second variant of `create` discussed in section 2.4.7). Finally, the last declaration format assigns a nickname to the port but leaves the rate unspecified, i.e., 0.

Regardless of which way a port has been created, from the very moment of creation it is associated with a specific station. If the port has been declared statically as a station attribute, the situation is clear: as soon as the station is created, the port comes into existence and is automatically assigned to the station. When a port is built by `create`, it is assigned to the *current station*, pointed to by the environment variable `TheStation` (section 3.1.3). The version of `create` with the station argument can be used; however, the most natural way to create ports is to do it from the station's setup method. The setup method will be called immediately after the station object has been created, and then `TheStation` will automatically point to the right station object. In particular, all ports in the alternating-bit protocol program in section 1.2.4 were created this way.

All ports belonging to one station are assigned numeric identifiers starting from 0 up to $n-1$, where n is the total number of ports owned by the station. This numbering of ports reflects the order of their creation and is used to construct the `Id` attributes of ports (section 2.4.2). Namely, the `Id` attribute of a port consists of two numbers: the `Id` attribute of the station owning the port and the station-relative port number determined by its creation order. Internally, these two numbers are combined into a single value. However, they appear separately in the port's standard name (section 2.4.2), which has the following format:

$$\text{Port } pid \text{ at } stname$$

where *pid* is the relative number of the port at its station and *stname* is the standard name of the station owning the port.

The `Station` method

```
Port *idToPort (int id);
```

converts the numeric station-relative port identifier into a pointer to the port object. An alternative way to do this conversion is to call a global function declared exactly as the preceding method, which assumes that the station owning the port is pointed to by `TheStation`, i.e., the port in question belongs to the current station.

3.3.2   Connecting Ports to Links

A port that has just been created, although it automatically belongs to some station, is not yet configured into the network. Two more steps are required to specify the port's place in the network geometry. The first consists in connecting the port to one of the links. Of course, the link to which the port is to be connected must have been created previously. One of the following two port methods can be used to connect a port to a link:

```
void connect (Link *l, int lrid = NONE);
void connect (int lk, int lrid = NONE);
```

In the first variant of `connect`, the first argument is a link pointer. The second variant allows the user to specify the link number (its `Id` attribute—section 3.2.2) instead of the link pointer.

A port connected to a link is assigned a link-relative numeric identifier, which in most cases is of no interest to the user. This identifier is a number between 0 and $n-1$, where n is the total number of ports connected to the link, and normally reflects the order in which the ports were `connected` to the link. For a unidirectional link (types `ULink` and `PLink`), the link-relative numbering of ports (which normally coincides with the connection order) determines the link direction. Namely, if A and B are two ports connected to the same unidirectional link, and the link-relative number of A is less than that of B, activities inserted into A will propagate to B, but not the other way around.

It is possible to assign an explicit link-relative number to a port by specifying this number as the second argument of `connect`. By default, this argument is `NONE` (-1), which means that the next unoccupied link-relative number is to be used. The user can force this number to be any number unused so far, but the resulting numbering of all ports that eventually get connected to the link must be consecutive and start from 0.

Example

Consider the following sequence of operations:

```
lk = create Link (NStations);
for (i = 0; i < NStations; i++)
  ((MyStation*) idToStation (i)) -> BusPort -> connect (lk);
```

The ports connected to the link `lk` are assigned the same link-relative numbers as the stations owning these ports. The same effect can be achieved in the following way:

```
lk = create Link (NStations);
for (i = 0; i < NStations; i++)
  ((MyStation*) idToStation (i)) -> BusPort -> connect (lk, i);
```

or by this somewhat less natural sequence:

```
lk = create Link (NStations);
for (i = NStations-1; i <= 0; i--)
  ((MyStation*) idToStation (i)) -> BusPort -> connect (lk, i);
```

With the last solution, the ports are created in the reverse order, but their link-relative positions are the same as in the previous two cases.

Link-relative port numbers should not be confused with station-relative port Ids. The former are only relevant at the network initialization phase, and once the link geometry has been determined, the user (and the protocol) can forget about them. If the link is bidirectional, the ordering of ports within the link can also be ignored. There exist methods of describing the link distance matrix that make no mention of the link-relative port numbers in such a case.

3.3.3   Setting Distance between Ports

One more operation required to complete the link description is the definition of the link distance matrix. This is done by assigning distances to all pairs of ports that have been connected to the link. One way to set a distance between a pair of ports is to call one of the following two global functions:

```
void setD (Port *p1, Port *p2, DISTANCE d);
void setD (Port p1, Port p2, DISTANCE d);
```

which both set the distance between the ports identified by the first two arguments.

The order in which the two ports occur in the argument list of setD is immaterial. For a bidirectional link (types Link/BLink and CLink), the distance from p1 to p2 must be the same as the distance from p2 to p1. For a unidirectional link (types ULink and PLink), only one of these distances is defined; this is determined by the link-relative numbers of the two ports—as described in section 3.3.2.

The following global distance setting functions[5] specify only one port each; the other port is assumed implicitly:

```
void setDFrom (Port *p, DISTANCE d);
void setDFrom (Port p, DISTANCE d);
void setDTo (Port *p, DISTANCE d);
void setDTo (Port p, DISTANCE d);
```

Each of the two variants of setDFrom sets the distance **from** port p to the port that was last used as the second argument of setD. For a bidirectional link, the direction is immaterial: the distance **between** the two ports is simply set to d. For a unidirectional link, it is checked whether the direction coincides with the link-relative ordering of the two ports (as explained in section 3.3.2) and if not, the program is aborted with a pertinent error message. Similarly, the two variants of setDTo set the distance **to** port p from the port that last occurred as the first argument of setD. The remaining rules are the same as for setDFrom.

These four functions also exist as methods of type Port. For such a method, the implicit port is the one determined by this, e.g.,

```
myPort->setDTo (otherPort, 12000);
```

sets the distance from myPort to otherPort according to the same rules as for the corresponding global function setDTo.

It is not illegal to define the same distance twice or more times, provided that all definitions specify the same value. For a strictly linear unidirectional link (type PLink—section 3.2.1), there is no need to define distances between all pairs of ports. As soon as enough distances have been provided to describe the entire link, SMURPH is able to fill the missing entries into the distance matrix on its own.

Examples

Let us revisit the link definition from the example at the end of section 3.3.2. The sequence of operations

```
for (i = 0; i < NStations-1; i++) {
    p1 = ((MyStation*) idToStation (i)) -> BusPort;
    for (j = i+1; j < NStations; j++) {
```

---

[5]All the global functions for setting the distance between a pair of ports also exist as Link methods. In any case, the two ports specified as explicit or implicit arguments to such a function must belong to the same link. For the corresponding Link method, the two ports must belong to the link owning the method.

```
    p2 = ((MyStation*) idToStation (i)) -> BusPort;
    setD (p1, p2, d);
  }
}
```

assigns the same distance d to every pair of ports connected to the link. Such a link can be viewed as a star with the center located d/2 ITUs from each port.

The code

```
for (i = 0; i < NStations-1; i++) {
  p1 = ((MyStation*) idToStation (i)) -> BusPort;
  for (j = i+1; j < NStations; j++) {
    p2 = ((MyStation*) idToStation (i)) -> BusPort;
    setD (p1, p2, d * (j-i));
  }
}
```

assigns a strictly linear geometry to the link (the distance between two neighboring ports is d). Note that the link-relative port numbers are never used. In fact, they are irrelevant in this case, as the link is bidirectional. Of course, we assume that the variables used in the example have been declared properly, i.e., i and j are both of type int, p1 and p2 are Port pointers, and the type of d is DISTANCE. The call to setD could be replaced by

```
p1 -> setDTo (p2, d * (j-i));
```

or

```
p1 -> setDFrom (p2, d * (j-i));
```

without affecting the code semantics.

If the link were of type PLink, the following simpler sequence would do the job:

```
for (i = 0; i < NStations-1; i++) {
  p1 = ((MyStation*) idToStation (i)) -> BusPort;
  p2 = ((MyStation*) idToStation (i+1)) -> BusPort;
  setD (p1, p2, d);
}
```

but the original double-loop code would still be fine (although somewhat redundant). Note that the sequence

```
p1 = ((MyStation*) idToStation (0)) -> BusPort;
for (i = 1; i < NStations; i++) {
  p2 = ((MyStation*) idToStation (i)) -> BusPort;
  setD (p1, p2, d * i);
}
```

would do the same job, as the distance information is sufficient to determine all the unspecified entries in the distance matrix. In the last code fragment, the call to setD could be replaced with

```
p1 -> setDTo (p2, d * i);
```

but

$$\texttt{p1 -> setDFrom (p2, d * i);}$$

would not work (it attempts to define an upstream distance).

It is possible to learn the distance between a pair of ports connected to the same link by calling the following port method:

$$\texttt{DISTANCE distTo (Port *p);}$$

which returns the distance from the current (`this`) port to the port pointed to by the argument. The method returns the undefined value (`DISTANCE_inf`—section 2.2.6) if the two ports are not connected to a link, belong to different links, or the distance between them has not been defined yet. The same undefined value is returned if the ports belong to the same link, but this link is unidirectional and `p` is located upstream with respect to the current port. A sure way to check whether two ports `p1` and `p2` are connected by a link segment at all is to evaluate the following condition:

```
p1->distTo (p2) != DISTANCE_inf || p2->distTo (p1) != DISTANCE_inf
```

Note that `distTo` is formally redundant. Distances between ports are set by the protocol program, so if this program needs to know these distances later, it can make sure to preserve them. The method is provided "just in case" (it turns out to be handy sometimes during the network creation phase), and it exists in one version only (there is no `distFrom` method).

While links of type `PLink` are checked against strictly linear shape, with the other link types it is possible to define links with unrealistic geometry. Note that while every realistic link geometry can be described by a distance matrix, there exist matrices (with non-negative entries) that do not describe realistic links.

Essentially, we can talk about two types of realistic links. A cable-based link is deemed realistic if it can be visualized as a tree consisting of linear cable segments. Note that the ports need not be located in the (proper) vertices of this tree. Another realistic link type is a radio-based link in which the distance between each pair of ports is the length of a straight line connecting these ports in 3-dimensional Euclidean space.[6]

The only restrictions verified by SMURPH are that the entries in the distance matrix are non-negative and that the matrix is symmetric (for a broadcast link), or triangular (for a unidirectional link). In particular, it is possible to define a link whose distance matrix does not even fulfill the *triangle inequality* (i.e., that for every three ports A, B, and C, $D_{A,C} \geq D_{A,B} + D_{B,C}$), which is a fundamental

---

[6]To be precise, we should admit occasional departures from the Euclidean character of this space resulting from the nonuniform atmospheric conditions along the signal's path and the existence of the so-called Kenelly-Heaviside zones. Most people would agree, however, that the first factor is generally negligible and the second irrelevant for the wave lengths typically used in data communication.

axiom of any sensible notion of distance.[7] From the viewpoint of SMURPH modeling, the realistic character of a link turns out not to be important. The model works consistently as long as all distances between pairs of ports are non-negative and, for a broadcast link, the same in both directions. The interpretation of direction in nonlinear unidirectional links is not always physically feasible, even if these links would make perfect sense as bidirectional channels. All realistic unidirectional links are expressible in the model, but not all expressible unidirectional links are realistic. Although not all SMURPH links have counterparts in the tangible world, they all seem to share a cozy room in the Platonic realm of conceivable beings.

BIBLIOGRAPHIC NOTES

Formal semantics of a broadcast communication channel are given by *Gburzyński and Rudnicki* (1989c). That paper describes formally the link mechanism of propagating activities and explains how these activities are turned into events perceived at ports. The notion of tree-realizable distance matrices is discussed by several authors. *Zaretski* (1965) gives necessary and sufficient conditions for an integer matrix to be representable as a tree and presents an algorithm for constructing the tree. Other algorithms are suggested by *Hakimi and Yau* (1964), *Boesch* (1968), *Patrinos and Hakimi* (1972), *Simões-Pereira and Zamfirescu* (1982), and *Culberson and Rudnicki* (1989), who propose the most efficient solution and demonstrate that its complexity achieves the lower bound.

More information about the physical aspects of communication channels used in networking can be found in *Spragins, Hammond, and Pawlikowski* (1991) and in *Freeman* (1989).

PROBLEMS

1. Run the variants of the alternating-bit protocol in section 1.2.4, with the link type replaced by CLink, ULink, and PLink. Do you observe any difference in the protocol behavior?

2. Redefine the geometry of links in the alternating-bit protocol by adding one extra port in the middle of each link. Create an additional station owning the two ports, and write two processes running at this station counting the packets passing by the extra ports. Verify that the numbers computed by the two processes agree with the link statistics produced by the simulator.

3. Assume that you have a bus network with an even number of stations. Each station has exactly one port connecting it to the bus. One half of the stations are located at one end of the bus and the other half are located at the other end. The distance between a pair of stations at one end of the bus is 10 ITUs (the stations form a star-shaped structure), and the distance between the centers of the stars is 10,000 ITUs. Program a function to build this network.

---

[7]Note that the fulfillment of the triangle inequality alone is not a sufficient condition for a link to be realistic.

4. Write a function accepting a `Link` pointer as an argument and checking whether the link is strictly linear.

5. Give an example of a distance matrix fulfilling the triangle inequality that does not represent a realistic, broadcast, cable-based link.

6. State formally a necessary and sufficient condition that must be satisfied by a distance matrix describing a realistic, broadcast, cable-based link.

7. Write a program to check whether a distance matrix is tree-representable. Consider incorporating your program into SMURPH, but remember: the tree-representability test must be optional. Some day somebody may find a good use for "unrealistic" links.

8. In a typical ring network, stations are connected into a circular structure in such a way that each station has two ports connecting it to two neighbors, each link has two ports, and there are exactly as many links as stations. Write a function that accepts two arguments, the number of stations N and the link length d, and builds a ring network in which all links are of the same length d.

9. A k-dimensional hypercube network consists of 2^k stations. Two stations are connected by a direct link, if and only if the binary representations of their addresses (numbers) differ on exactly one position. Write a function accepting two arguments, the dimension k and the link length d, and generating a hypercube network in which all links are of the same length d.

10. Write a function that generates a random network with N stations uniformly distributed within a planar, circular area with radius R. Assume that R is given in meters and the common transmission rate of the network is 1 Gb/s. The network is to be fully connected, i.e., there should be two unidirectional links between every pair of stations. The two links must be of the same length and, of course, they must go in the opposite directions. The length of a link should correspond to the geographic distance between the pair of connected stations. Choose your ITU small enough to express the link length with the accuracy of 0.0001 bit.

4

Processes

4.1 ACTIVITY INTERPRETERS: GENERAL CONCEPTS

A protocol program in SMURPH has the form of a collection of cooperating processes. Each process can be viewed as an *interrupt handler*: its processing cycle consists of being awakened by some event, responding to the event by performing some protocol-related activities, and going back to sleep to await the occurrence of another event.

The dæmons responsible for waking up processes are called *activity interpreters*. Formally, an activity interpreter, or AI,[1] is an object belonging to a type derived from *AI* (section 2.4.1). As any progress in protocol execution is a consequence of some events perceived by the protocol processes, we say that activity interpreters are responsible for advancing the modeled time.

Processes communicate with AIs in two ways. One way is to issue a *wait request* addressed to a specific AI. Such a request specifies a category of *events* to which the process would like to respond. The occurrence of an event from this category will *wake up* the process.

A process may also exhibit an *activity* that is perceived by an AI. Based on such activities, the AIs determine the timing of future events. Thus, the operation of an AI consists in transforming *activities* into *events*. This is what we mean by *interpreting activities*.

A typical example of an AI is a link, which is visible to processes as a collection of port AIs. A process, say P_1, may issue a wait request to a specific port, say p_1,

---

[1]This acronym has nothing to do with Artificial Intelligence.

e.g., to be awakened as soon as a packet arrives at p_1. Another process P_2 may start a packet transmission on port p_2 connected to the same link. This activity exhibited by P_2 will be transformed by the link into an event that will wake up process P_1 when, according to the propagation distance between p_1 and p_2, the packet arrives at p_1.

Different AIs use different means to learn about the relevant activities exhibited by processes. There is, however, a standard AI interface that a process can use to issue a wait request. This interface is provided by the following method:

```
void wait (etype event, int state, LONG order = 0);
```

where **event** identifies an event class (the type of this argument is AI-specific), and **state** identifies the process state (section 4.2) to be assumed when the awaited event occurs. The last argument (**order**) is optional and can be used to explicitly order the awaited events (section 4.4.1). When multiple events occur at the same modeled time (within the same ITU), this ordering determines the event that will actually be presented.

Note. The third parameter of **wait** can only be specified if the simulator was created with the -p option of **mks** (section B.2).

4.2 DEFINING PROCESS TYPES

A process is an object belonging to type **Process**. A process consists of private *data* and possibly shared *code* describing the process's behavior. To create a nontrivial process, i.e., a process that has nonempty code, one has to define a subtype of **Process**. Such a definition must obey the standard set of rules (sections 2.4.3, 2.4.4) and begin with the keyword **process**. Typically, it has the following layout:

```
process ptype : itypename ( ostype, fptype ) {
   ...
   local attributes and methods
   ...
   states { list of states };
   ...
   perform {
     the process code
   };
};
```

The two type arguments (*ostype* and *fptype*) are optional. If neither of them is specified, the parentheses can be omitted. If present, the two arguments identify respectively the type of the station owning the process and the type of the process's *parent*, i.e., the creating process.

Each process is always created by some existing process (this creating process is considered the parent of the process being created) and belongs to a specific station (which is called the process's owner). If both type arguments have been specified in the process type definition, the process type implicitly declares two standard attributes, denoted F (for father) and S (for station), that are pointers to the process's parent and owner. The implicit declaration of the two attributes is as follows:

$$ostype \quad *S;$$
$$fptype \quad *F;$$

i.e., the arguments *ostype* and *fptype* determine the type of the attributes F and S. If the argument types do not appear in the process type declaration header, the two attributes are not defined. This is legal as long as the process makes no reference to them. If only one type argument is specified within parentheses, it is interpreted as the owning station type. In such a case, the S pointer is defined while F is not. Although most processes do not "care about" their parents, they cannot get very far without referencing some attributes of their owners (e.g., see the processes from the alternating-bit example in section 1.2.4).

A setup method can be declared for a process type (section 2.4.7) to initialize the local attributes (the process's "data segment") upon process creation. The default setup method provided in type Process is empty and takes no arguments.

Note. A process B created from the setup method of another process A belongs to the creator of A rather than to A. To belong to A, B must be created from the A's code method.

The specification of the process code starting with the keyword perform[2] looks like the declaration of a (special) type-less argument-less method whose body is structured into a finite-state machine. The states of this machine must be announced with the states list within the process type definition and can be any C++ identifiers. These identifiers are interpreted as enumeration constants.

As for a regular method, the body of the code method can be defined outside the process type in the following way:

```
ptype::perform {
    ...
};
```

In such a case, the process type declaration must contain an announcement of the code method in the form

```
perform;
```

A process type declared as virtual (section 2.4.4) can neither specify nor announce a code method. Note that a virtual process type is by definition incomplete, and a code method can only be attributed to an executable (and thus complete) process.

---

[2]The resemblance to the well-known COBOL feature is accidental.

A process type T_2 derived from another process type T_1 naturally inherits all attributes and methods of T_1, including the setup method(s) and the code method. Of course, these methods can be redefined in T_2, in which case they subsume the corresponding methods of T_1. Although a subsumed setup method of T_1 can be referenced from T_2, there is no natural way to reference from T_2 the subsumed code method of the supertype. We will see later that it would not make much sense.

It is legal to have a complete (nonvirtual) process type that defines no code method of its own. A process of such a type can be run, provided that a code method is declared somewhere in a supertype. Note that this method may use virtual functions to communicate with the code-less subtype.

For complete examples of process type definitions, see the implementation of the alternating-bit protocol in section 1.2.4.

4.3   CREATING AND TERMINATING PROCESSES

As with any other *Object*, a process is created with the create operation (section 2.4.7). All activities of a protocol program are always performed from within some process; therefore, a (user-defined) process is always created by another process whose identity is well known at the moment of creation. This creating process becomes the *parent* of the created process and can be referenced via its F attribute (section 4.2). Similarly, each process belongs to a specific station. The identity of this station can be indicated explicitly by an argument of create (e.g., as for the processes from the alternating-bit protocol in section 1.2.4) or else the *current station* (section 3.1.3) becomes the process's owner.

Processes are assigned Id attributes in the order of their creation. As the first user process ever created is the Root process (section 4.8), the Id attribute of this process is always 0. Generally, Id attributes are not a convenient means of process identification. Unlike stations, links, and ports, processes can be destroyed dynamically; therefore, the allocation of Ids to the processes that are alive at any moment need not be consecutive. If a process P_1 is ever to be referenced by another process P_2 (we ignore the trivial reference by the parent when the process is created), a pointer to P_1 must be saved upon its creation and made available to P_2. Usually, such references only make sense among processes belonging to the same station. Thus, the most natural place to store a process pointer (if it needs to be stored at all) is at its owning station. In contrast to stations, links, and ports, there is no idToProcess method that would transform a process Id into a process pointer.

Whenever a process is run, its owner can be accessed via the process's S attribute (section 4.2) or via the global variable TheStation. The latter way of referencing the station owning the process is usually less convenient, as the type of TheStation is Station and, to be useful, it has to be cast to the proper subtype in most cases.

Note. It is not checked whether the types of the actual process's parent and its owning station agree with those specified with the process type definition (section 4.2). The pointers to the actual objects are simply cast to the specified types and assigned to F and S.

A process can terminate itself by calling the method

```
terminate ();
```

or by simply executing

```
terminate;
```

A process can also terminate another process by calling the function

```
terminate (Process *p);
```

or the method

```
p->terminate ();
```

where p points to the process being terminated.

A terminated process ceases to exist, its object is deallocated, and its description is erased from the system.

Note. If a process terminates itself (by calling "terminate();" or executing "terminate;"), any instructions following the termination statement are ignored.

Note. It is illegal to terminate a process (either by itself or from another process) if the process currently *owns* some dynamically allocable exposable objects (section A.7.1). Such objects must be deallocated before the process can be terminated. The Kernel process (section 4.8) is exempt from this rule, i.e., it is always legal to request Kernel termination (section 4.8), but this operation has a special meaning.

4.4   PROCESS OPERATION

A process is created, run, and eventually terminated. Even if a process does not terminate itself explicitly, it will be terminated by the simulator when the experiment is complete. A good understanding of the mechanism by which a process keeps itself alive is essential for understanding and predicting the behavior of SMURPH models.

4.4.1   Process Execution Cycle

Each process operates in a cycle consisting of the following steps:

1. The process is awakened by one of the awaited events.
2. The process responds to the event, i.e., it performs some operations specified by the protocol.
3. The process puts itself to sleep.

Before a process puts itself to sleep, it usually issues at least one wait request (section 4.1)—to specify the event(s) that will wake it up in the future. A process that goes to sleep without specifying a waking event effectively terminates itself. The result is as if the process issued `terminate` as its last statement (section 4.3).

To put itself to sleep, a process (its code method) can execute the statement

```
sleep;
```

or simply exit by exhausting the list of statements associated with the current state.

By issuing a wait request (using the `wait` method of an AI—section 4.1), a process identifies four elements describing its future waking condition:

- Activity interpreter responsible for triggering the waking event
- Event category
- Process state to be assumed upon the occurrence of the event
- Order of the awaited event

The first three items are mandatory. The last element can be left unspecified, in which case the default order of 0 is assumed. Note that the specified order can be negative, i.e., lower than the default.

If before suspending itself (going to sleep) a process issues more than one wait request, the multiple wait requests are interpreted as an **alternative** of waking conditions. This means that after the process becomes suspended, it will be waiting for a collection of event types, possibly coming from different AIs, and the occurrence of the **earliest** of those events will resume the process. When a process is awakened, its collection of awaited events is *cleared*, which means that in each operation cycle these events are specified from scratch.

It is possible that two or more events from the collection of the events awaited by a process occur at the same simulated time (within the same ITU). In such a case, the event with the lowest order is selected and this event actually restarts the process. If multiple events occurring at the same time have the same lowest order (e.g., the default order of 0), the waking event is chosen **nondeterministically** from among them.[3] In any case, whenever a process is awakened, this always results from exactly one event.

Note. Many protocols can be programmed without assuming any explicit ordering of events that can possibly occur within the same ITU. Therefore, for the sake of efficiency, the possibility of specifying the third argument of `wait` is switched on by a special option (`-p`) of `mks` (section B.2). Without this option, `wait` accepts only two arguments, and all events (except for the cases mentioned in sections 4.7.6 and 6.2.12) have the same (default) order.

The state identifier specified as the second argument of a wait request is an enumeration object viewed as an integer value. When the process is awakened

---

[3]Some exceptions are discussed in sections 4.7.6 and 6.2.12.

(always by one of the awaited events), the process code method is simply called (as a regular function) and the state identifier is presented in the global variable

```
int TheState;
```

which the process can reference to determine what has actually happened. The code method interprets the contents of **TheState** in a standard way, automatically directing control to the proper sequence of statements (state).

Because of the sequential nature of simulation in SMURPH, only one process can be active at a given moment of real time. However, the modeled time **does not flow** while a process is active, which means that from the viewpoint of the simulated time, multiple processes can be active simultaneously. It is important to realize that the only way to advance the simulated time is to put a process to sleep for a nonzero time interval. Although in many cases this time interval is determined implicitly by SMURPH and the actual sleeping is somewhat disguised, the basic idea is fairly simple: **the simulated time only flows when told to do so**.

Multiple processes whose waking events have been scheduled at the same ITU will be awakened in the order determined by the **order** attributes of those events. If several such processes are to be awakened by events with the same smallest order, the actual waking order is nondeterministic.

4.4.2   The Creation Event

A newly created process is automatically restarted within the ITU of its creation with the value of **TheState** equal to 0. Value 0 corresponds to the **first symbolic state** declared with the **states** command (section 4.2). The first waking event is assumed to have come from the process itself. In section 4.6 we explain that each process is also an activity interpreter capable of sending events to itself and to other processes.

The default order of the first waking event for a process is 0; therefore, multiple processes created within the same ITU will be awakened in an unpredictable order. The following **Process** method can be used to make this order predictable:

```
void setSP (LONG order);
```

The method can be called by the creator immediately after executing **create** (which returns a process pointer) or, preferably, from the created process's setup method. The argument of **setSP** specifies the order of the first waking event for the new process.

Note.   The simulator must be created with the -p option of **mks** in order for **setSP** to be usable.

4.4.3   The Process Code Method

A process code method is programmed in a way resembling a finite-state machine. An awakened process gets into a specific state and performs a sequence of operations associated with that state. By issuing wait requests, the process dynamically specifies the transition function that tells where to go from the current state upon the occurrence of certain interesting events. The layout of the process code method is as follows:

```
perform {
    state S0:
        ...
    state S1:
        ...
    state Sn-1:
        ...
};
```

Each **state** statement is followed by a symbol identifying one state. This symbol must be declared on the process's **states** list (section 4.2). The ellipses following a **state** statement represent instructions to be executed when the process wakes up in the given state. The interpretation of the contents of **TheState** is automatic: as soon as the process is awakened, control is switched to the proper **state** indicated by the value of **TheState**. When the list of instructions associated with the current state is exhausted, i.e., the code method attempts to fall through the **state** boundary, the process is automatically put to sleep.

The keyword **transient** can be used instead of **state** to allow the state to be entered directly from the preceding state. In other words, if the list of instructions of the state preceding a **transient** state is exhausted (and it does not end with **sleep**), the **transient** state will be entered and its instructions will be executed.

Example

The following is a sample process declaration:

```
process AlarmClock {
  TIME delay;
  setup (TIME intvl) {
    delay = intvl;
  };
  states {Start, GoOff};
  perform {
    state Start:
      Timer->wait (delay, GoOff);
    state GoOff:
      WakeUp->put ();
      proceed Start;
  };
};
```

This process can be viewed as an alarm clock that sends out a signal every **delay** time units. The exact semantics of the operations **Timer->wait**, **WakeUp->put**, and **proceed** are given in sections 4.5.1 and 4.7.5.

A process code method may declare local variables. If needed, all such declarations should occur after the opening keyword **perform** and before the first **state** statement.

Note.   Local variables declared in a code method do not survive state transitions, i.e., they cannot be used to pass information among different states. The only exception is entering a **transient** state directly by falling from the preceding state. Process attributes should be used for storing information that must be preserved across states.

Example

Consider the following code method:

```
perform {
  int PreviousState;
  state First:
    PreviousState = TheState;
    Timer->wait (delay1, Second);
  state Second:
    Timer->wait (delay2, PreviousState);
};
```

This method is not going to work. The contents of **PreviousState** are undefined in state **Second**, and an unpredictable value is used as the second argument of **wait**.

4.4.4   Process Environment

By the *process environment* we mean a collection of global variables readable by the active process that describe some elements of the process context or carry some information related to the waking event. Two such variables, **TheStation** (section 3.1.3) and **TheState** (section 4.4.1) have already been introduced formally. Two more variables in this category are

Time   Of type **TIME**. This variable tells the current simulated time measured in ITUs from the beginning of simulation.

TheProcess   Of type **Process**. This variable points to the object representing the currently active process. From the viewpoint of the process code method, the same object is pointed to by **this**.

Sometimes an event, besides just being triggered, carries some specific information. An example of such an event is a packet being heard on a port. The obvious information that should reach the awakened process along with this event is a pointer to the object representing the packet. There exist two general-purpose pointers that are used by AIs to pass information associated with events or related to some inquiries. They are declared as

```
void *Info01, *Info02;
```

These pointers are seldom, if ever, used directly. There exist numerous aliases (macros) that cast these pointers to the proper types corresponding to the potential types of data items that can be returned by events. For example, the following standard macrodefinition creates an alias that can be perceived as a packet pointer:

```
#define ThePacket ((Packet*)Info01)
```

We have already seen an application of this alias in the alternating-bit example (section 1.2.4). This and other aliases are discussed later at individual AIs.

4.5   THE TIMER AI

The Timer AI is the simplest and the most important of all activity interpreters. It is so simple that it does not deserve a separate chapter, yet it is important enough to be discussed first, together with the process concept. The inclusion of the Timer AI in this chapter is further motivated by the fact that Timer wait requests are implicitly used to implement two important process control operations.

Although it is formally a single object, Timer can be viewed as an unlimited number of alarm clocks that can be set and responded to individually by multiple protocol processes. This way the processes can explicitly measure and advance the simulated time.

4.5.1   Wait Requests

By issuing the wait request

```
Timer->wait (delay, where);
```

or

```
Timer->wait (delay, where, order);
```

where delay is an object of type TIME, the process declares that it wants to be awakened in state where, delay ITUs after the current moment.

Implicit wait requests to the Timer AI are issued by some compound statements. In particular, the operation

```
proceed newstate;
```

is used to branch directly (without awaiting any explicit event) to the state indicated by the argument. This is in fact a compound operation, which is equivalent (with a minor exception) to

```
Timer->wait (TIME_0, newstate, 0);
sleep;
```

With this solution, the branching is performed as an event that wakes up the requesting process at the target state within the current ITU.

Note that the default order of the wait request issued by proceed is 0. Thus, if other (e.g., explicit) wait requests possibly issued by the process can be fulfilled within the current ITU, they can take precedence over proceed and the operation may be ineffective. Moreover, other processes whose waking events have been scheduled for the current ITU can be run in the meantime. It is possible to assign an order to proceed by using one of the following two variants:

```
proceed newstate, order;
proceed (newstate, order);
```

where the second argument is an expression evaluating to a LONG integer number. This number will be used as the third argument of the implicit Timer wait request issued by the operation.

Another operation somewhat similar to proceed is

```
skipto newstate;
```

which is equivalent to

```
Timer->wait (TIME_1, newstate, 0);
sleep;
```

and performs a branch to state newstate with a 1-ITU delay. This operation is useful for skipping certain events that persist until time is advanced. We have already seen an example of such an event in section 1.2.4.5; we return to this topic in section 6.2.13.

As with proceed, it is possible to assign an order to the wait request issued by skipto. The following two variants of the operation are available:

```
skipto newstate, order;
skipto (newstate, order);
```

where the meaning of the second argument is exactly as for proceed. Section 6.1.2 gives other examples of implicit wait requests to the Timer.

Note. The two-argument variants of proceed and skipto are only available if the simulator has been created with the -p option of mks (section B.2).

Note. When a process is restarted by a Timer event, the two environment variables Info01 and Info02 are set to NULL, i.e., timer events carry no environment information. One exception is proceed. When a process wakes up at the target state of proceed, the environment variables contain their previous values—as they were at the moment when proceed was executed. In other words, proceed retains the environment of the previous state. On the other hand, skipto, which advances the modeled time, destroys the environment of the previous state.

4.5.2   Clock Tolerance

There exists only one global `Timer` AI, which would suggest that all stations in the network use the same notion of time and their clocks run in a perfectly synchronized fashion. Of course, in a realistic model of a physical system we often need to simulate the limited accuracy of local clocks, e.g., to model race conditions and other phenomena resulting from imperfect timing. Therefore, it is possible in SMURPH to specify *tolerance* for clocks. This means that the indication of an alarm clock may differ a bit from the actual time interval—within the specified margin.

Clocks at different stations may run with different tolerance. This idea boils down to randomizing slightly all delays specified as arguments of `Timer` wait requests issued by processes belonging to a given station. This randomization also affects implicit wait requests to the `Timer`, e.g., issued by `transmit` and `sendJam` (section 6.1.2). Of course, the zero interval used by `proceed` is never randomized (there is nothing to randomize); similarly, the 1-ITU delay of `skipto` is always accurate, even if the clock tolerance is extremely coarse.

Clock tolerances should be defined during the network initialization phase before creating stations (section 3.1). Each call to the function

```
void setTolerance (double deviation = 0.0, int quality = 2);
```

(re)defines the clock tolerance parameters, and the new definition affects all stations created thereafter until the tolerance parameters are overridden by a new definition, i.e., another call to `setTolerance`. Specifying `deviation` = 0 or `quality` = 0, or both, results in zero tolerance, i.e., absolutely accurate clocks. This is the default setting assumed before `setTolerance` is called for the first time.

With a nonzero clock tolerance in effect, the delay measured by the `Timer` may differ from the requested delay d_r by up to $\pm$`deviation` $\times d_r$ truncated to full ITUs. The actual deviation, which can be either positive or negative, is determined according to the distribution $\beta($`quality`, `quality`$)$ (section 2.3.1). Note that higher values of `quality` may result in increased execution time.

4.6   PROCESS AS AN AI

Figure 2.1 shows type `Process` as a descendant of *AI*, which suggests that a process can appear as an activity interpreter to another process. Indeed, processes can perceive themselves this way, which provides a simple mechanism for process communication and synchronization.

4.6.1   State Events

It is possible for a process, say P_1, to issue a wait request to another process, say P_2, to be awakened when P_2 enters a specific state. The first argument of `wait` specifying such a request is an integer enumeration value identifying a process state. One special value represented by the constant DEATH (-1) is used to denote the termination of the process to which the wait request is addressed.

Assume that a process P_1 issues a wait request to another process P_2, to be awakened when P_2 enters state S_w. In real time, P_1 will be awakened **after** P_2 is given control, which means that P_2 will complete its sequence of statements at S_w before P_1 is awakened. Note that the description of the awaited event is "process P_2 entering state S_w," so P_2 must actually "get into" the state to trigger the event. However, P_1 will be given control at the same virtual time (within the same ITU) as P_2. As we said earlier, the modeled time is not advanced while a process is executing its statements.

Typically, when a process creates another process, the two processes run in parallel, at least from the viewpoint of the simulated time. With the possibility of awaiting the termination of another process, one can implement a subroutine-like scenario in which a process creates another process and then waits for the termination of the child. For example, with the sequence

```
pr = create MyChild;
pr->wait (DEATH, Done);
sleep;
```

the current process spawns a child process and goes to sleep until the child is done. When that happens, the current process will resume its execution in state Done.

The first waking event for a process, triggered after the process's creation (section 4.4.2), is assumed to have been generated by the process itself. This forced event is called START, and it cannot be awaited explicitly.

It is legal for a process to wait for itself entering a specific state, although this possibility may seem somewhat exotic.

Example

Consider the following fragment of a code method:

```
  . . .
state First:
  TheProcess->wait (Second, Third);
  proceed Second;
state Second:
  sleep;
state Third:
  . . .
```

When the process wakes up in state Second, it apparently dies, as it does not issue any wait requests in this state (section 4.4.1). However, in its previous state, the process declares that it wants to get to state Third as soon as the very same process gets to state Second. According to what we said earlier, this wait request will actually be fulfilled when the process is done with the sequence of statements in state Second. Thus, after leaving this state, the process will wake up in state Third—within the current ITU. The effect is as if an implicit **proceed** operation to state Third were issued by the process at Second, before this state is actually entered. Note that **proceed** is just a special case of a wait request (section 4.5.1) and, if the process issues other wait requests that are fulfilled within the current ITU, the implicit **proceed** may be ineffective, i.e., the process may actually end up in another state. The **order** argument of the state wait request can be used to assign a higher priority to this transition.

The range of the wait request issued in state **First** is just one state ahead. According to what we said in section 4.4.1, all pending wait requests are cleared whenever a process is awakened.

In the sample code fragment presented here, the call to **wait** at state **First** does not have to be preceded by **TheProcess->**, as the wait request is addressed to the current process. It is recommended, however, to reference all *AI* methods with explicit remote access operators. Note that **this** used instead of **TheProcess** would have the same result.

User-defined state names are declared as enumeration-type attributes of the process type to which they refer. Therefore, when the state identifier of a process is referenced from another process, such a reference must be prefixed with the type of the process at which the state identifier has been declared. For example, the right way of referencing state **EndXmit** of the alternating-bit transmitter process, introduced in section 1.2.4.4, is **TransmitterType::EndXmit**.

4.6.2   Signal Passing

A process can also be viewed as a repository for *signals* (interrupts) that can be used as a simple means of process synchronization. More sophisticated interprocess communication tools, called *mailboxes*, are introduced in section 4.7.

4.6.2.1   Regular signals.   In the simplest case, a signal is deposited at a process by calling the following process method:

```
int signal (void *s = NULL);
```

where the argument can be a pointer to additional information—to be passed along with the signal. If the argument is absent, no signal-specific information is passed: it is assumed that the occurrence of the signal is the only event of interest. Formally, the signal is deposited at the process whose **signal** method is called. Thus, by executing

```
prcs->signal ();
```

the current process deposits a signal at the process pointed to by **prcs**, whereas each of the two calls

```
signal (ThePacket);
TheProcess->signal ();
```

deposits a signal at the current process.

A deposited signal can be perceived by its recipient via wait requests addressed to the process AI. A process can declare that it wants to await a signal occurrence by executing the following method:

```
prcs->wait (SIGNAL, where);
```

where **prcs** points to the process at which the awaited signal is expected to arrive and **where** identifies the state where the waiting process wants to be awakened upon the signal arrival. Note that the signal does not have to be deposited at the waiting process. For example, it can be deposited at the sender or even at a third party that is neither the sender nor the recipient of the signal.

If the signal is already pending at the moment when the wait request is issued, the waking event occurs within the current ITU. Otherwise, the event will be triggered as soon as a signal is deposited at the target process.

When a process is awakened because of a signal event, the signal is removed from the repository. Two environment variables are then set: **TheSender** (of type **Process***) pointing to the process that has sent (deposited) the signal, and **TheSignal** (of type **void***) returning the value of the argument given to **signal** by the sender. The two environment variables are aliases for **Info01** and **Info02**, respectively (section 4.4.4).

Only one signal can remain pending at a process at a time, i.e., multiple signals are not queued. The **signal** method returns an integer value that tells what has happened to the signal. The following values (represented by symbolic constants) can be returned:

ACCEPTED   The signal has been accepted, and there is a process already waiting for the signal. The signal has been put into the repository, and a waking event for the awaiting process has been scheduled. Note, however, that this event is not necessarily the one that will actually wake up the process (the process may have other waking events scheduled at the same ITU).

QUEUED   The signal has been accepted, but nobody is waiting for the signal at this moment. The signal has been put into the repository.

REJECTED   The repository is occupied by a pending signal, and the new signal has been rejected. The **signal** operation has no effect.

It is possible to check whether a signal remains pending at a process without trying to deposit another signal there. The following process method can be used for this purpose:

```
int isSignal ();
```

The method returns YES (1) if a signal is pending at the process, and NO (0) if the process's signal repository is empty. In the former case, the environment variables **TheSender** and **TheSignal** are set as for a signal received via a waking event. The signal is left in the repository and remains pending. The process method

```
int erase ();
```

behaves similarly to isSignal, except that the signal, if present, is removed from the repository.

The flexibility of selecting the signal repository makes it possible to create signal-based communication scenarios that are best suited for a particular application. For example, in a situation when a single process P_0 creates a number of child processes $P_1 \ldots P_k$ and wants to pass a signal to each of them, it is natural for P_0 to deposit each signal at the corresponding child. On the other hand, if each of the child processes $P_1 \ldots P_k$ is expected to produce a message for P_0, the most natural place for a child process to deposit such a signal is in its own repository. In the first case, the signal operation issued by P_0 will be addressed to a child and the child will issue a wait request to itself; in the second case, the child will execute its own signal method, and P_0 will issue a signal wait request to the child.

Example

> Assume that we want to implement a binary semaphore guarding a hypothetical critical section. The following simple process type may serve as a template for creating such semaphores:
>
> ```
> process Semaphore {
>   perform {
>     state Start:
>       signal ();
>       wait (DEATH, Start);
>   };
> };
> ```
>
> In its only state (entered upon startup), the process sends a signal to itself and then issues a wait request for its own termination. Thus, the process becomes permanently suspended. The role of the wait request is to keep the process alive; as we said in section 4.4.1, a process that exhausts its list of statements without specifying at least one wait request ceases to exist.
>
> The "full" status of the process's signal repository represents an open semaphore. We can now define the following two macrooperations implementing the classical operations P and V:
>
> ```
> #define P(sem,where) sem->wait (SIGNAL, where)
> #define V(sem)       sem->signal ()
> ```
>
> Note that the P operation takes two arguments. The first argument is the semaphore (a process pointer), and the second argument specifies the state where the calling process wants to get when the critical section has been successfully entered.

4.6.2.2 Priority signals.   Sometimes one would like to give a signal event a higher priority—to make sure that the signal is received immediately, even if some other waking events are scheduled at the same ITU. This is illustrated in the following example.

Example

Assume that the code method of some process P_1 includes the following fragment:

```
    ...
state Expecting:
  TheProcess->wait (SIGNAL, Signal);
  Timer->wait (Delay, Timeout);
state Signal:
    ...
state Timeout:
    ...
```

In state **Expecting** the process awaits two events: a signal to arrive at the process's own repository and a timeout. Assume that another process P_2, responsible for sending the signal awaited by P_1, executes the following code:

```
      ...
  state Sending:
    if (p1->signal () == ACCEPTED)
      proceed Accepted;
    else
      proceed Ignored;
  state Accepted:
      ...
  state Ignored:
      ...
```

Clearly, P_2 wants to find out whether the signal is actually received by P_1. Note, however, that according to the semantics of the **signal** operation described in section 4.6.2.1, P_1 cannot be absolutely sure that the signal will actually wake up process P_1, even though P_1 seems to be expecting the signal (**signal** returns ACCEPTED). The value returned by **signal** can be taken at its face value only if the process receiving the signal is not awaiting any other event that may be triggered at the same time (within the same ITU).

One obvious way to remedy this problem is to assign a very low order (section 4.4.1) to the wait request for the signal event. This solution works, but it requires cooperation from the signal recipient. It is also possible for the signal sender to indicate that the signal should be received immediately, irrespective of the order of the corresponding wait request. Such a communication mechanism can be interpreted as a "dangling branch" from one process to another and is called a *priority event*. Priority events can be triggered by some other operations, not only by signals sent in a special way. We see more of them in sections 4.7.6 and 5.4.2.

A process generating a priority event specifies in a deterministic way which process will be restarted next and in which state. This is why we can interpret a priority event as a branch to another process.

A signal priority event is triggered by calling the following method of **Process**:

```
int signalP (void *s = NULL);
```

where the meaning of **s** is the same as for the regular **signal** operation (section 4.6.2.1). Similarly to **signal**, **signalP** deposits a signal at the process. The following additional rules apply to **signalP**:

- At most one **signalP** operation can be issued by a process from the moment it wakes up until it goes to sleep. In fact, a somewhat stronger statement is true. Namely, at most one operation generating a priority event (including the **putP** operation, introduced in section 4.7.6) can be issued by a process after it wakes up and before it suspends itself. In other words, at most one priority event can remain pending at any moment.

- At the moment when **signalP** is executed, the signal repository must be empty, and there should be exactly one process waiting for the signal event on that repository. In other words, the exact deterministic continuation of the process generating the signal must be known at the moment when the **signalP** operation is issued.

The situation when nobody is waiting for a priority signal is not treated as a hard error. In such a case, **signalP** returns **REJECTED** and the operation has no effect. Note that the signal is not stored in the repository and **signalP** never returns **QUEUED**. If the signal is awaited at the moment when **signalP** is issued, the function returns **ACCEPTED**.

As soon as the process executing **signalP** is suspended, the waiting recipient of the signal is restarted. No other process is run in the meantime, even if some other events are scheduled to occur at the current ITU.

The recipient of a priority signal does not declare in any special way that it is awaiting a priority event: it just executes a regular signal wait request (section 4.6.2.1) with any (e.g., default) order. The fact that the transaction is to be processed as a priority event is indicated by **signalP**, and the order of the matching wait request is irrelevant. In sections 4.7.6 and 5.4.2 we give examples of situations where priority events are useful.

4.7   THE MAILBOX AI

The methods of process synchronization presented in section 4.6 take advantage of the fact that each process is an autonomous AI capable of triggering events that can be perceived by other processes. A more general way to communicate among processes, especially those running at the same station, is offered by the **Mailbox** AI.

4.7.1   General Concepts

The **Mailbox** AI provides a frame for defining mailbox types and creating objects of these types. As suggested by its name, a mailbox is a repository for messages that can be passed among processes. To differentiate these messages from the traffic messages handled by the `Client`, we may call them *notices*. A process can put a notice into a mailbox, remove the first notice from a mailbox, peek at the first notice in a mailbox, and suspend itself until a mailbox gets into a specific state.

Similar to processes and ports, mailboxes belong to stations. A mailbox belonging to a given station is intended to synchronize processes run by the station.

Depending on how a mailbox has been defined and created, its functionality may resemble a simple interrupt-passing mechanism or a virtual channel for transporting and queuing some objects. The capacity of a mailbox is limited and determined at the moment of its creation. Mailbox capacity can also be redefined dynamically, although this possibility is rather exotic. If the capacity of a mailbox is limited to zero or one, the mailbox behaves as a simple interrupt-passing device. If the limit is huge (e.g., `MAX_Long`—section 2.2.5), we get an essentially unlimited FIFO-type pipe. The type of elements stored in a mailbox can be specified along with the mailbox type declaration. If no such type is specified, the mailbox stores and passes simple *alerts* that carry no information other than their occurrence. Such a mailbox is called an *alert mailbox*. Otherwise, the mailbox can be used to store and retrieve objects of a simple type, e.g., pointers to compound objects. A mailbox of this type is called a *queue mailbox*. From now on, when we talk about a mailbox *element*, we mean either a queue item (for a queue mailbox) or an alert (for an alert mailbox).

At any moment, a mailbox (be it an alert mailbox or a queue mailbox) can be either empty or nonempty. A nonempty alert mailbox holds one or more pending alerts that await acceptance. As these alerts carry no information, they are all represented by a single counter. Whenever an alert is put into an alert mailbox, the mailbox element counter is incremented by one. Whenever an alert is retrieved from a nonempty alert mailbox, the counter is decremented by one. The *put* operation for such a mailbox has no arguments and the value returned by the *get* operation only tells whether the operation has been successful, i.e., the mailbox wasn't empty.

A nonempty queue mailbox can be viewed as a FIFO queue of the objects that have been put into the mailbox. The *put* operation for a queue mailbox identifies an element that is to be stored at the end of the mailbox queue. The *get* operation performed on a nonempty queue mailbox extracts the first element from the mailbox queue.

4.7.2   Defining Mailbox Types

The standard type `Mailbox` is usable directly. A mailbox of this type is a simple alert mailbox: a repository for alerts that, besides their occurrence, carry no information.

The mailbox capacity is determined when the mailbox is created (section 4.7.3), in a way that is independent of the type of elements stored in the mailbox.

A queue mailbox can only be created from a proper user-defined subtype of `Mailbox`. This subtype must specify the type of the elements to be stored in the mailbox queue.

A mailbox type declaration has the following format (section 2.4.3):

> **mailbox** *mtype* : *itypename* (*etype*) {
>
>   ...
>
>   *attributes and methods*
>
>   ...
>
> };

where *mtype* is the new mailbox type being defined. The optional argument in parentheses, if present, must identify a simple C++ type. This argument specifies the type of elements to be stored in the mailbox. Note that although the element type must be simple, i.e., it must be directly convertible into type (void*), compound objects can be stored via their pointers. In such a case, the type argument of the mailbox type declaration should be a pertinent pointer type. If the type argument is absent, the new mailbox type describes an alert mailbox.

Example

The following declaration describes a mailbox capable of storing integer values:

> **mailbox IntMType (int);**

Note the empty body of the declaration. As the type argument is present, the declaration will not be mistaken for a type announcement (section 2.4.6).

The attribute list of a mailbox type declaration is seldom nonempty: the basic purpose of a mailbox type extension is to specify the type of items to be stored in the mailbox. The user can monitor the standard operations on a queue mailbox by declaring within the mailbox class the following two virtual methods:

> **virtual void inItem** (*etype par*);
> **virtual void outItem** (*etype par*);

Each of the two methods has one argument whose type should coincide with the mailbox element type. The first method (**inItem**) will be invoked whenever a new item is inserted into the mailbox. The argument will then contain the value of the inserted item. Similarly, **outItem** will be called whenever an item (indicated by the argument) is removed from the mailbox. The two methods are independent, which means that it is legal to declare only one of them. For example, if only **inItem** is declared, no special (nonstandard) action will be performed upon an element removal. The methods have no effect for an alert mailbox.

Example

The mailbox type

```
mailbox (Process*) {
  void inItem (Process *p) {
    p->signal ();
  };
  void outItem (Process *p) {
    p->terminate ();
  };
};
```

describes a queue mailbox capable of storing process pointers. Whenever a process pointer is added to the mailbox, a signal is sent to the process. When a process pointer is removed from the mailbox, the process is terminated.

4.7.3   Creating Mailboxes

The ownership properties of mailboxes make them somewhat similar to ports (section 3.3.1) and packet buffers (section 5.2.3). A mailbox must belong to a specific station. The naming rules for mailboxes and ports are practically identical (section 3.3.1). The mailbox **Id** attribute combines the serial number of the station owning the mailbox and the serial number of the mailbox within the context of its station. The standard name of a mailbox (section 2.4.2) has the form

$$mtypename \ \text{\textbf{mid}} \ \textbf{at} \ stname$$

where *mtypename* is the type name of the mailbox (for the standard type it is **Mailbox**), *mid* is the station-relative mailbox number reflecting its creation order, and *stname* is the standard name of the station owning the mailbox.

The base standard name of a mailbox has the same format as the standard name, except that *mtypename* is always **Mailbox**.

The **Station** method

```
Mailbox *idToMailbox (int id);
```

can be used to convert the numeric station-relative mailbox identifier into a pointer to the mailbox object. An alternative way to do this conversion is to call a global function declared exactly as the preceding method, which assumes that the station in question is pointed to by **TheStation**.

One way to create a mailbox is to declare it statically within the station class, e.g.,

```
mailbox MyMType (ItemType) {
  ...
};
...
station MySType {
  ...
  MyMType Mbx = (1);
```

```
                            ...
                       };
```

The optional constructor argument for a mailbox should be a non-negative integer number that gives the mailbox capacity. The default capacity, assumed when no argument is specified, is 0. Although capacity-0 alert mailboxes are quite useful (section 4.7.4), it generally makes little sense to have a zero-capacity mailbox with a nontrivial element type.

Another way to create a mailbox is to do it dynamically, using the **create** operation (section 2.4.7). The standard setup method declared within the **Mailbox** type accepts one optional integer argument, which specifies the mailbox capacity. If no **create** argument is given, the capacity is assumed to be 0.

Although a mailbox must be created within the context of some station, for a dynamically created mailbox, this station can be **System**. The context of the **System** station is recommended for mailboxes that communicate among processes belonging to different (regular) stations.

Mailboxes are considered hardware components of their stations. Once created, a mailbox cannot be destroyed. As with ports, mailboxes cannot be created after the protocol has started, i.e., they must be all created during the network initialization phase, while the **Root** process is in its first state (section 4.8).

A mailbox type declaration can specify private setup methods. These methods are only accessible when the mailbox is created dynamically, with the **create** operation. As a private setup method subsumes the standard method that defines the mailbox capacity, it is possible to define this capacity explicitly (e.g., from a private setup method) by calling the **Mailbox** method **setLimit**. We present this method in section 4.7.5.

4.7.4   Mailbox Wait Requests

A process may suspend itself awaiting the nearest moment when a mailbox gets into a specific state. For example, assume that a process attempts to acquire an element from a mailbox and discovers that the mailbox is empty. The process may choose to put itself to sleep until some other process deposits an element into the mailbox. For example, by calling

```
                    mb->wait (NONEMPTY, GrabIt);
```

the process says that it wants to be awakened in state **GrabIt** at the nearest moment when the mailbox pointed to by mb becomes nonempty. If the mailbox happens to be nonempty at the moment when the request is issued, the event occurs immediately, i.e., within the current ITU.

Another event that can be awaited on a mailbox is **NEWITEM**. A process that executes

```
                    mb->wait (NEWITEM, GetIt);
```

will be restarted (in state GetIt) at the nearest moment when an element is put into the mailbox (section 4.7.5).

One should note the subtle difference between NONEMPTY and NEWITEM, which are in fact quite independent events. First of all, NEWITEM is only triggered when an element (or an alert) is actually added to the mailbox. Unlike NONEMPTY, it does not occur immediately if the mailbox already contains something. Moreover, no NONEMPTY event ever occurs on a capacity-0 mailbox. By definition, a capacity-0 mailbox is never NONEMPTY, and a wait request for this event addressed to a capacity-0 mailbox is illegal. On the other hand, a process can sensibly suspend itself on an (always empty) capacity-0 mailbox awaiting the NEWITEM event. The event will occur at the nearest moment when some other process executes the put operation (section 4.7.5) on the mailbox. Although nothing gets put into the mailbox (which is unable to hold even a single item), the NEWITEM event is triggered by an attempt to put something there. In fact, the following simple and important statement is true: "The only event that can be awaited on a capacity-0 mailbox is NEWITEM."

When a process is restarted by one of the two events just discussed, there is no guarantee that the mailbox is actually nonempty. This is obvious in the case of NEWITEM occurring on a capacity-0 mailbox but also possible for the NONEMPTY event. Namely, if multiple processes are waiting for NONEMPTY (or NEWITEM) on the same mailbox, they will be all restarted within the same ITU, as soon as something is put into the mailbox. Then one of the processes may clear the mailbox (remove the item that has just been put there) before the others are given a chance to look at it.

It is possible to issue a mailbox wait request that guarantees a delivery. A process calling

```
mb->wait (RECEIVE, GotIt);
```

will be awakened in state GotIt as soon as the mailbox becomes nonempty and the process is able to actually receive an element from the mailbox. As with NONEMPTY, the event occurs immediately if the mailbox is nonempty at the moment when the request is issued. Before the process code method is called, the first element[4] is removed from the mailbox.

Assume that two (or more) processes are waiting for RECEIVE on the same mailbox. When an element is put into the mailbox, only one of those processes will be restarted[5] and the element will be automatically removed from the mailbox. If some other processes are waiting for NONEMPTY or NEWITEM at the same time, all these processes will be restarted even though they may find the mailbox empty when they get to examine its contents.

If a RECEIVE event is triggered on a queue mailbox that defines the outItem method (section 4.7.2), the method is called with the removed item passed as the argument.

---

[4]For an alert mailbox, the ordering of elements (alerts) is irrelevant.

[5]According to the order attributes of the wait requests.

If the first argument of a mailbox wait request is a non-negative integer number, it represents the so-called *count event*, i.e., the number of elements that the mailbox must hold for the event to be triggered. A process issuing such a wait request will be awakened as soon as the number of elements stored in the mailbox reaches the specified value. In particular, if the specified element count is 0, the process will be restarted when the mailbox becomes empty. The symbolic constant EMPTY (defined as 0) can be used to identify this event. If the mailbox contains exactly the specified number of elements when the wait request is issued, the event occurs within the current ITU. Owing to the fact that multiple processes may be accessing a single mailbox at the same simulated time, the actual number of elements in the mailbox when the process is restarted may be different from the specified argument of wait.

When a process is awakened by a mailbox event, the environment variable TheMailbox (Info02) of type Mailbox, points to the mailbox on which the event has occurred. For a queue mailbox, and when it makes sense, the environment variable TheItem (Info01) of type void* contains the value of the item that has triggered the event. Note that for some events this value may not be up-to-date, i.e., the item indicated by TheItem may have been removed from the mailbox. For an alert mailbox, TheItem is always NULL.

For example, assume that a process is restarted by the NONEMPTY event on a queue mailbox. If the event is triggered immediately (the mailbox was nonempty when the wait request was issued), TheItem contains the value of the first item from the mailbox, as it was there when the nonempty status of the mailbox was perceived. If the NONEMPTY event is triggered by an item being put into the mailbox, the value of this item will be returned via TheItem.

The interpretation of TheItem for NONEMPTY, NEWITEM, and a count event is sensible under the assumption that only one process at a time is allowed to await events on the mailbox and remove elements from it.[6] The interpretation of TheItem for RECEIVE is always safe, even if the event is awaited by multiple processes at the same time. When a process is restarted by this event occurring on a queue mailbox, TheItem contains the value of the received item. Note that the item has been removed from the mailbox, so TheItem is the only handle to it.

4.7.5   Operations on Mailboxes

The following Mailbox method is used to insert an alert into an alert mailbox:

$$\text{int put ();}$$

For a queue mailbox, the method accepts one argument whose type coincides with the item type specified with the mailbox type declaration (section 4.7.2). The method returns one of the following three values (represented by symbolic constants):

---

[6]This seems to be a pretty common scenario.

ACCEPTED   The new element triggers an event that is currently awaited on the mailbox. The waking mailbox event has been scheduled at the current ITU. Note, however, that this event is not necessarily the one that will restart the waiting process. As for the **signal** operation discussed in section 4.6.2.1, it may happen that other events awaited by the process occur at the same ITU.

QUEUED   The new element has been accepted and stored in the mailbox, but it doesn't trigger any events immediately. This value is never returned for a capacity-0 mailbox.

REJECTED   The mailbox is full (it has reached its capacity), and there is no room to accept the new element.

If a **put** operation is issued for a queue mailbox that defines the **inItem** method (section 4.7.2), the method is called with the argument equal to the argument of **put**. This does not happen if the operation has been REJECTED.

One of the following two methods can be called to determine whether a mailbox is empty:

$$\text{int empty ();}$$
$$\text{int nonempty ();}$$

The first method returns YES (1) if the mailbox is empty, and NO (0) otherwise. The second method is a simple negation of the first.

The following method removes the first element from a mailbox:

$$\textit{etype}\ \textbf{get ();}$$

For an alert mailbox, *etype* is **int** and the method returns YES if the mailbox was nonempty (in which case one pending alert has been removed from the mailbox), and NO otherwise. For a queue mailbox, *etype* coincides with the mailbox item type. The method returns the value of the removed item if the mailbox was nonempty (in which case the first queued item has been removed from the mailbox), or 0 (NULL) otherwise. Note that 0 may be a legitimate value of an item; thus, in such a case, it is impossible to tell whether **get** succeeds or not. If 0 happens to be a legal item value, a call to **get** can be preceded by a call to **empty** (or **nonempty**)—to make sure that the mailbox status is perceived correctly.

If a successful **get** operation is executed for a queue mailbox that defines the **outItem** method (section 4.7.2), the method is called with the removed item passed as the argument.

It is possible to peek at the first item of a queue mailbox without removing the item. The method

$$\textit{etype}\ \textbf{first ();}$$

behaves like **get**, except that the first item, if present, is not removed from the mailbox. For compatibility, it is legal to call **first** for an alert mailbox. The method type is then **int**, and the returned value is exactly as for **nonempty**.

The methods put, get, and first set the environment variables TheMailbox and TheItem (section 4.7.4).   TheMailbox is set to point to the mailbox whose method has been invoked, and TheItem gives the value of the inserted/removed/looked-at item. For an alert mailbox, TheItem is always set to NULL.

One more useful operation on a mailbox is

$$\text{int erase ();}$$

which empties the mailbox. The method removes all elements stored in the mailbox, so that immediately after a call to **erase** the mailbox appears **empty**. The value returned by the method gives the number of removed elements. In particular, if **erase** returns 0, it means that the mailbox was empty when the method was called.

If **erase** is executed for a queue mailbox that defines the **outItem** method (section 4.7.2), the method is called individually for each removed item, with the removed item passed as the argument.

Operations on mailboxes may trigger events awaited by protocol processes. In particular, a put operation triggers NEWITEM and may trigger NONEMPTY, RECEIVE, and a count event. Operations get and erase may trigger count events (the latter triggers EMPTY).

Operations get, first, and nonempty performed on a capacity-0 mailbox always return 0. There is no way for such a mailbox to contain an element. The only way for a put operation on a capacity-0 mailbox to succeed is to match a wait request for NEWITEM that must be already pending when the put is issued. Note that even then there is no absolute certainty that the element will not be lost. Namely, the process to be awakened may be awaiting a number of other events (on different AIs) and some of them may be scheduled at the same ITU as the NEWITEM event. In such a case, the actual waking event will be chosen nondeterministically and it does not have to be the mailbox event. If the mailbox event must not be lost, the multiple events can be ordered (section 4.4.1) in such a way that the mailbox event is assigned the highest priority. Another way of coping with this problem is discussed in section 4.7.6.

Examples

Even if the NEWITEM event is the only event awaited by the process, synchronization based on capacity-0 mailboxes may be a bit tricky. Consider the process

```
process One (Node) {
  Mailbox *Mb;
  int Sem;
  void setup (int sem) { Sem = sem; Mb = &S->Mb; };
  states {Start, Stop};
  perform {
    state Start:
      if (Sem) {
        Mb->put ();
```

```
                  proceed Stop;
            } else
                  Mb->wait (NEWITEM, Stop);
        state Stop:
            terminate;
      };
   };
```

and assume that two copies of the process are started at the same station **s** in the following way:

```
                    create (s) One (0);
                    create (s) One (1);
```

At first sight, it seems that both copies should terminate (in state **Stop**) within the ITU of their creation. However, if **Mb** is a capacity-0 mailbox this need not be the case. Although the order of the **create** operations suggests that the process with **Sem** equal to 0 is created first, all we know is that the two processes will be started within the same (current) ITU. If the second copy (the one with **Sem** equal to 1) is actually run first, it will execute **put** before the second copy is given a chance to issue the **wait** request to the mailbox. Thus, the alert will be ignored and the second copy will be suspended forever (assuming that the alert will not arrive from some other process).

Of course, it is possible to force the right startup order for the two processes, e.g., by rewriting the setup method in the following way:

```
                 void setup (int sem) {
                   setSP (sem);
                   Sem = sem;
                   Mb = &S->Mb;
                 };
```

i.e., by assigning a lower order to the startup event for the first copy of the process (section 4.4.2). One may notice, however, that if we know the order in which things are going to happen, there is no need to synchronize them.

Another way to solve the problem is to replace the **put** statement with the following condition:

```
           if (Mb->put () == REJECTED) proceed Start;
```

This solution works, but it has the unpleasant taste of "indefinite postponement." It seems that the right way to make sure that both processes terminate is to create **Mb** as a capacity-1 mailbox and replace **NEWITEM** with **NONEMPTY** or, even better, **RECEIVE**. Note that with **NEWITEM** the solution still would not work. With **NONEMPTY**, the two processes would terminate properly, but the mailbox would end up containing a pending alert.

Now let us look at an example of a safe application of a capacity-0 mailbox. The two processes:

```
           process Server (MyStation) {
             Mailbox *Request, *Reply;
```

```
                        int Rc;
                        void setup () {
                          Rc = 0;
                          Request = &S->Request;
                          Reply = &S->Reply;
                        };
                        states {Start, Stop};
                        perform {
                          state Start:
                            Request->wait (RECEIVE, Stop);
                          state Stop:
                            Reply->put (Rc++);
                            proceed Start;
                        };
                      };
                      process Customer (MyStation) {
                        Mailbox *Request, *Reply;
                        void setup () {
                          Request = &S->Request;
                          Reply = &S->Reply;
                        };
                        states { ..., GetNumber, ...};
                        perform {
                          ...
                          state GetNumber:
                            Request->put ();
                            Reply->wait (NEWITEM, GetIt);
                          state GetIt:
                            Num = TheItem;
                          ...
                        };
                      };
```

communicate via two mailboxes, **Request** and **Reply**. Note that when the **Server** process issues the put operation for **Reply**, the other process is already waiting for NEWITEM on that mailbox (and is not waiting for anything else). Thus, **Reply** can be a capacity-0 mailbox. We assume that **Request** is a capacity-1 alert mailbox.

The method

$$\text{Long getCount ();}$$

returns the number of elements in the mailbox.

The capacity of a mailbox can be modified at any moment by calling the method

$$\text{setLimit (Long lim = 0);}$$

In particular, a call to this method can be put into a user-supplied setup method for a mailbox subtype (section 4.7.3). The argument of `setLimit` must not be negative. The new capacity cannot be less than the number of elements currently present in the mailbox.

4.7.6   The Priority Put Operation

As in the case of signal passing (section 4.6.2.2), it is possible to give a mailbox event a higher priority, to restart the process waiting for the event before anything else can happen. Besides the obvious solution of assigning the lowest order to the wait request for the mailbox event, it is possible to trigger a *priority event* on the mailbox. This approach assumes no cooperation on the recipient's part.

A priority event on a mailbox is triggered by a *priority put* operation implemented via the following `Mailbox` method:

$$\text{int putP ();}$$

For a queue mailbox, the method accepts one argument whose type coincides with the mailbox item type. The semantics of `putP` are similar to the semantics of regular `put`, in the sense that the operation is used to insert a new element into the mailbox. The following additional rules apply to `putP`:

- At most one operation triggering a priority event (`putP` or `signalP`— section 4.6.2.2) can be issued by a process from the moment it wakes up until it goes to sleep. This is equivalent to the requirement that at most one priority event can remain pending at any moment.

- At the moment when `putP` is executed, the mailbox must be empty and there must be exactly one process waiting on the mailbox for the inserted element. In other words, the exact deterministic fate of the new element must be known at the moment when the `putP` operation is issued.

The situation when no process is waiting on the mailbox on which a `putP` operation is executed is not treated as a fatal error. In such a case, the method returns REJECTED and has no other effect. Otherwise, the method returns ACCEPTED; note that QUEUED is never returned by `putP`.

As soon as the process that executes `putP` is suspended, the waiting recipient of the inserted element is restarted. No other process is run in the meantime, even if there are some other events scheduled to occur at the current ITU.

The recipient for a priority put operation does not declare in any special way that it awaits a priority put. It just executes a regular wait request[7] to the mailbox (for NEWITEM, NONEMPTY, or a count 1 event). The fact that the put operation is to be processed as a priority event is indicated by `putP`—at the sender's side.

---

[7]The order of this request is irrelevant.

Examples

Let us return to the second example from section 4.7.5 and assume that the `Customer` process communicates with two copies of the server in the following way:

```
state GetNumber:
  NRcv = 0;
  Request1->put ();
  Request2->put ();
  Reply1->wait (NEWITEM, GetIt);
  Reply2->wait (NEWITEM, GetIt);
state GetIt:
  Num = TheItem;
  if (!NRcv++) {
    Reply1->wait (NEWITEM, GetIt);
    Reply2->wait (NEWITEM, GetIt);
    sleep;
  }
```

The process wants to make sure that it receives both items; however, unless the servers use `putP` instead of `put`, one item can be lost. Namely, the following scenario is possible:

1. Server 1 executes `put` and the customer is scheduled to be restarted in the current ITU.

2. Before the customer is actually awakened, server 2 executes `put`. Thus, there are two events that want to restart the customer at the same time.

3. The customer is restarted, and it perceives only one of the two events. Thus, the second item is lost.

The problem can be eliminated by assigning a very low order to the wait requests issued by the customer. Another solution is to make the servers use `putP` instead of `put`. Then each put operation will be immediately responded to by the customer, irrespective of the order of its wait requests. Yet another solution is to create mailboxes `Reply1` and `Reply2` with capacity-1 and replace `NEWITEM` with `RECEIVE`.

Somebody might suggest rewriting the preceding code in the following, apparently equivalent, way:

```
state GetNumber:
  NRcv = 0;
  Request1->put ();
  Request2->put ();
transient Loop:
  Reply1->wait (NEWITEM, GetIt);
  Reply2->wait (NEWITEM, GetIt);
state GetIt:
  Num = TheItem;
  if (!NRcv++) proceed Loop;
```

One should be careful with such simplifications. Note that `proceed` (section 4.5.1) is actually a `Timer` wait request (for 0 ITUs). Thus, it is possible that when the second server issues putP, the customer is not ready to receive the item (although it will become ready within the current ITU).

SMURPH offers no immediate goto to another state. The operation

proceed newstate, MIN_long;

comes close to it, but it is still not guaranteed that no other wait request will use the same lowest-possible order. A safe goto operation can be simulated by a mailbox. For example, the following code does the job:

```
state GetNumber:
  NRcv = 0;
  Request1->put ();
  Request2->put ();
transient Loop:
  Reply1->wait (NEWITEM, GetIt);
  Reply2->wait (NEWITEM, GetIt);
state GetIt:
  Num = TheItem;
  GoTo->wait (NEWITEM, Loop);
  if (!NRcv++) { GoTo->putP (); sleep; }
```

GoTo can be an alert mailbox of any capacity, in particular 0. Note that the wait request to GoTo precedes the putP operations. Should it be the other way around, the putP operation would be REJECTED and ineffective.

4.8   ORGANIZATION OF THE PROTOCOL PROGRAM

From the user's perspective, all activities in SMURPH are processes. One system process is created by SMURPH immediately after the simulator is started and exists throughout the entire simulation run. This process is pointed to by the global variable Kernel of type Process and belongs to the System station (section 3.1.2). Before the simulation is started, Kernel creates one process of type Root, which must be defined by the user. This process is the root of the user process hierarchy, i.e., it is the direct or indirect parent of all user-defined processes. The Root process is created with the empty setup argument list; thus, if a setup method is defined within the Root type, it should take no arguments. The Root process is responsible for creating the network and starting the protocol processes (section 1.2.4.6). Then it should put itself to sleep awaiting the end of simulation, which is signaled as the termination of Kernel. The following structure of the Root process is recommended:

```
process Root {
  states {Start, Done};
  perform {
    state Start:
      read input data ...
```

```
                create the network ...
                define traffic patterns ...
                create protocol processes ...
                Kernel->wait (DEATH, Done);
              state Done:
                print output results
            };
          };
```

Of course, the particular initialization steps listed at state `Start` can be performed by separate functions or methods. The sequence of operations issued at the first state of the `Root` process is called the *network initialization phase*.

The termination of `Kernel` that manifests the end of the simulation run is illusory: in fact, `Kernel` never dies and, in particular, it can be referenced (e.g., exposed—section 7.3.5.10) in state `Done` after its apparent death. The user can define a number of termination conditions for the simulation run (section 4.9); it is also possible to terminate the simulation explicitly from a protocol process by executing

```
                Kernel->terminate ();
```

i.e., by requesting `Kernel` termination.

Note. Some elements of the network configuration and traffic generator (the `Client`) are actually built not sooner than just before the protocol is started, i.e., after the user's root process goes to sleep in its first state. Sometimes the user would like to perform some operations from the root (before giving control to the protocol) assuming that the network has been fully built at that moment. It is possible to force the complete network definition from the root process by calling the global function

```
                void buildNetwork ();
```

After it returns, any operations that add new elements to the network, e.g., create new stations, links, traffic patterns, are illegal.

4.9   TERMINATING SIMULATION

One way to terminate a simulation experiment is to do it explicitly from the protocol program, by terminating the `Kernel` process (section 4.8). Although simple, this way of stopping the simulator is seldom used. A protocol process is not normally expected to be able to abort the entire protocol; therefore, any termination conditions implanted into the protocol code look at least unnatural. If the termination condition is tricky and depends on some configuration patterns in the protocol state, it may be reasonable to define a special, independent process (or an observer—section 7.2.2) monitoring this condition and requesting `Kernel`'s termination upon its occurrence.

The simulator will terminate abnormally if it hits an error condition, gets aborted by the user, or runs out of events. The last situation occurs when all processes (including system processes) get into a state where no possible event can wake them up. This should not normally happen unless the standard Client is disabled (sections 5.5.1, B.3).

The simulation experiment will terminate automatically when any of the three limit values settable by the user has been reached. The following (global) functions can be used to specify these values:

```
setLimit (Long MaxNM, TIME MaxTime, double MaxCPUTime);
setLimit (Long MaxNM, TIME MaxTime);
setLimit (Long MaxNM);
```

If setLimit is not used, the simulation run will continue indefinitely, until it is terminated explicitly by the protocol program, killed by the user, hits an error, or runs out of events. Although typically setLimit is called from Root before the simulation is started (section 4.8), it can be called at any moment during the protocol execution. If the parameters of such a call specify limits that have been already met or exceeded, the experiment will terminate immediately.

4.9.1   Message Number Limit

The first argument of setLimit specifies the maximum number of messages that are to be entirely received at their destinations. The simulation experiment will be terminated as soon as the message number limit is reached. By receiving a message, we mean executing receive (sections 1.2.4.5, 5.4.3, 6.2.13) for its last packet.

When the -c SMURPH call option is used (section B.3), the message number limit is interpreted as the maximum number of messages to be generated by the Client and queued at senders. In this case, when the limit is reached, the Client is suspended and the simulation continues until all the messages that remain queued have been received at their destinations. This option (the so-called *flush mode*) is useful for modeling bursty traffic conditions: the simulation continues until the network has coped with all the pending traffic.

There exists a standard function

$$\text{void setFlush ();}$$

which, if called before the simulation is started, has the same effect as if the simulator has been invoked with the -c option.

Note.   If some messages are lost by the protocol, e.g., not all queued messages are ultimately delivered and received at their destinations, the termination condition in the flush mode will never be met. Note that a decent protocol should make sure that all queued messages are eventually delivered, even if some packets are lost on the way (section 1.1.2).

4.9.2   Simulated Time Limit

The second argument of `setLimit` declares the maximum interval of the simulated time in ITUs. The simulation stops as soon as the modeled time (the contents of variable `Time`) reaches the limit.

4.9.3   CPU Time Limit

The last argument of `setLimit` declares the limit on the CPU time used by the simulator. Owing to the fact that SMURPH checks against violation of this limit every few thousand simulation events, the CPU time limit may be slightly exceeded before the simulation run is eventually terminated.

If the specified value of any of these limits is 0, it actually stands for "no limit," i.e., any previous setting of this limit is canceled. If no value is given for a limit (the last two versions of `setLimit`), the previous setting of the limit is retained.

All three limits are viewed as an alternative of exit conditions, i.e., the simulation run stops as soon as **any** of the limits is met or exceeded. In particular, the process of emptying message queues in the flush mode, after the message number limit has been reached, can be stopped prematurely if one of the other two limits is reached in the meantime.

4.9.4   Exit Code

The protocol program, specifically the `Root` process (section 4.8), can learn the reason why the simulation run has been terminated. When the `DEATH` event for the `Kernel` process is triggered, the `int`-type environment variable `TheExitCode` (an alias for `Info01`) contains one of the following values:

`EXIT_msglimit`	The message number limit has been reached.
`EXIT_stimelimit`	The simulated time has reached the declared limit.
`EXIT_rtimelimit`	The CPU time limit has been reached.
`EXIT_noevents`	There are no more events to process, i.e., all the protocol processes and the `Client` have died.
`EXIT_user`	The simulation run has been terminated by the protocol program (by explicitly terminating the `Kernel` process).
`EXIT_abort`	The simulation run has been aborted by the user or because of an error condition.

The actual numerical values assigned to these symbolic constants are 0–5, in the order in which the constants are listed.

BIBLIOGRAPHIC NOTES

One may draw some parallels between the process view adopted in SMURPH and the concept of co-routines in SIMULA, e.g., see *Franta* (1977), *Dahl and Nygaard* (1967),

Dahl, Myhrhaug, and Nygaard (1970), *Birthwistle et al.* (1973), *Birthwistle* (1979). The basic idea of co-routines is to simulate parallelism in virtual time by controlled interleaving of the multiple execution threads in real time. The basic difference between the co-routine approach and SMURPH processes is that in SMURPH this interleaving is inherently stochastic and nondeterministic, whereas in SIMULA the nondeterminism must be simulated. A co-routine suspending itself must indicate explicitly its continuation, i.e., another co-routine that should take over. In SMURPH, this deterministic way of switching the process context is also possible, but it is definitely not the standard way.

Problems and methods of process communication and synchronization are discussed in numerous texts on operating systems, e.g., by *Brinch Hansen* (1973), *Deitel* (1990), *Silberschatz and Galvin* (1994), and *Tanenbaum* (1992).

PROBLEMS

1. Simplify the code of the alternating-bit protocol in section 1.2.4, avoiding the repetition of the same statements in different states.

2. Rewrite the alternating-bit protocol in section 1.2.4 in such a way that there is only one process running at each station, yet the modified implementation is functionally equivalent to the original.

3. Rewrite the alternating-bit protocol in section 1.2.4 using signals instead of mailboxes.

4. What wrong would happen if `skipto` in state `ReAck` in the receiver process in section 1.2.4.5 were replaced by `proceed`? Hint: The two events awaited in state `WaitPacket` can occur within the same ITU. Consider all possible events (regarding the receiver and acknowledger) that can be triggered within that ITU and their possible permutations. Which of those permutations must be eliminated? Can priority signals help?

5. A counting semaphore is a generalization of the binary semaphore that admits at most N processes at a time to the critical section. Implement a counting semaphore using mailboxes. Write a program to test your solution.

6. Does it make sense to have more than two states in the `Root` process? Can you suggest a possible application for such a scenario?

7. Rewrite the alternating-bit protocol in section 1.2.4, replacing the two links with mailboxes. Make sure that the propagation time is modeled accurately.

8. A co-routine in SIMULA uses the `resume` operation to transfer control to another co-routine specified as the argument of `resume`. The co-routine executing `resume` is suspended, and the resumed co-routine is restarted from the place of its last `resume`. Design macrooperations to implement a similar deterministic control transfer mechanism for SMURPH processes.

9. The two-process mutual exclusion problem, known from operating systems theory, is defined in the following way. Two independent processes P_1 and P_2 executing in

parallel communicate via shared memory. Atomic read/write operations are always consistent, even if the two processes reference the same location at the same time. For example, if P_1 wants to write quantity a into location m and, at the same time, P_2 wants to write b into the same location, then m will end up containing either a or b. The problem boils down to implementing two operations *lock* and *unlock* that would allow each of the two processes to execute a sequence of operations (a *critical section*) with *mutual exclusion*. If one process executes *lock*, then the other process should be blocked on its *lock* operation until the first process executes *unlock*. It must be absolutely guaranteed that only one process at a time can execute the sequence of statements in the critical section. The following algorithm was once proposed by *Hyman* (1966) as a solution to the two-process mutual exclusion problem (we assume that **first** and **second** are both initialized to zero):

```
P₁ {                                    P₂ {
    while (1) {                             while (1) {
        . . .                                  . . .
        first = 1                              second = 1
        while (turn != 0) {                    while (turn != 1) {
            while (second);                        while (first);
            turn = 0;                              turn = 1;
        }                                      }
        . . .                                  . . .
        critical section                       critical section
        first = 0;                             second = 0;
        . . .                                  . . .
    }                                      }
}                                       }
```

Unfortunately, this solution doesn't work, and it is possible for the two processes to get into the critical section at the same time. Write a SMURPH model of this two-process configuration to diagnose the problem with Hyman's solution.

10. Write a SMURPH model for the famous *Dining Philosophers* problem (*Dijkstra* (1971); see also *Deitel* (1990) or *Silberschatz and Galvin* (1994)). Design and implement a method for detecting deadlocks.

5

The Client

5.1 GENERAL CONCEPTS

The `Client` AI, which can be viewed as a union of all `Traffic` AIs, is a dæmon responsible for providing the network with traffic (at the sender's end) and absorbing the traffic (at the destination's end).

The absolutely indivisible unit of information transferred over the network is one bit; however, the traffic is quantized into two types of conceptually larger units: *messages* and *packets*. A message represents a single transaction arriving to the network from the outside. According to the OSI terminology introduced in section 1.1.2, messages correspond to the interface between the transport layer and the higher layers. From the viewpoint of the SMURPH protocol model, a message is characterized by the sender (i.e., the station at which the message is queued for transmission), the receiver (i.e., the station to which the message is to be sent), and the length (i.e., the number of bits).

The message arrival process is defined by the user as a collection of *traffic patterns*. Each traffic pattern is described by the distribution of potential senders and receivers and the distribution of the message interarrival time and length. A single simulation experiment may involve many different traffic patterns.

Each traffic pattern is managed by a separate activity interpreter called a `Traffic`. This AI is responsible for generating messages according to the distribution parameters specified by the user, queuing them at the sending stations, responding to *inquiries* about these messages, and triggering waking events related to the message arrival process. The `Client` AI is a union of all `Traffic` AIs. To illustrate what this means, assume that a protocol process P at a station S wants

126

to learn whether there is a message queued at S that has been generated according to traffic pattern T. To get this information, P will "ask" the specific `Traffic` AI whether a message generated by (sometimes we say "belonging to") this AI is queued at S. If P wants to learn whether there is **any** message awaiting transmission at S, it will address its inquiry to the `Client`. Similarly, P may decide to go to sleep awaiting the arrival of a message of some specific pattern, or it may await any message arrival at all. In the former case, the waking event will be triggered by the corresponding `Traffic` AI; in the latter case, it will be generated by the `Client`.

Each `Traffic` AI has its private message queue at every user-defined station. A `Client` message arriving to a station is queued at the end of the station's queue handled by the `Traffic` AI that has generated the message. Thus, the order of messages in the queues reflects their arrival order.

If the standard tools provided by SMURPH for defining the behavior of the `Traffic` AI turn out to be insufficient to describe a tricky traffic pattern, the user can program this behavior as a collection of processes. Numerous standard methods defined by type `Traffic` make this operation simple in most cases. The processes describing a nonstandard behavior of the `Client` can be run at the `System` station (section 3.1.2), so that they are well separated from the protocol processes.

Before a message can be transmitted over a communication channel (link), it must be turned into one or more *packets*. A packet represents a physical unit of information (a frame) that, besides information bits inherited from a message, usually carries some additional information required by the protocol (e.g., the header or trailer).

A typical execution cycle of a protocol process that takes care of transmitting packets at a station consists of the following steps (section 1.2.4.4):

1. The process checks if there is a message to be transmitted, and if so, acquires a packet from that message and proceeds to step 3.

2. If there is no message awaiting transmission, the process issues a wait request to the `Client` or some specific `Traffic` AI—to await a message arrival—and puts itself to sleep. When the waking event is triggered, the process wakes up at 1.

3. The process obeys the rules required by the protocol and transmits the packet.

4. When the transmission is complete, the process continues at 1.

The operation of acquiring a packet for transmission results in a portion of a message having been turned into a packet. The protocol may impose some rules as to the maximum (or minimum) packet length. It may thus happen that a single long message must be split into several packets, each packet transmitted individually to the destination.

SMURPH collects some standard performance measures, separately for each `Traffic` and globally for the `Client` (i.e., for all traffic patterns combined). The user is able to provide private performance-measuring methods that either augment or replace the standard ones.

5.2 MESSAGES AND PACKETS

SMURPH offers two standard base types **Message** and **Packet** that can be used to
define protocol-specific message and packet types. Note that these types are not
subtypes of *Object* (section 2.4.1). In many cases types **Message** and **Packet** need
not be extended by the user: they are usable directly.

5.2.1 Messages

Message types are defined according to the rules described in sections 2.4.3 and
2.4.4. The declaration of a message type starts with the keyword **message**.

Example

The declaration

```
message RMessage {
    int Route [N], RouteLength;
};
```

defines a message type called **RMessage**, which is derived directly from the base type
Message.

Messages are very seldom generated "by hand" in the protocol program, although, in principle, this is legal. In such an unlikely case, the message type may
declare a setup method and the regular **create** operation can be used to generate
an object of the message type. The default setup method defined in **Message** takes
no arguments and its body is empty.

Note. The version of **create** that assigns a nickname to the created object
cannot be used to generate a message. Nicknames can only be assigned to descendants of *Object* (section 2.4.2).

The standard type **Message** declares a number of **public** attributes that may
be of some interest to the user, especially if he or she is interested in programming
nonstandard traffic generators. Following are the user-visible attributes of **Message**:

```
Message      *next, *prev;
Long         Length;
IPointer     Receiver;
int          TP;
TIME         QTime;
```

Attributes **next** and **prev** are links used to store the message in a queue at the
sending station. They have been made publicly visible to facilitate programming of
nonstandard tools for putting messages into queues, extracting them, and turning
them into packets. Note that the names of these two attributes start with lower-
case letters, contrary to the naming rules detailed in section 2.1. This departure

should be viewed as an indication that **next** and **prev** have been made public "just in case" and that the likelihood of their being referenced explicitly by the user is minute.

Attribute **next** points to the next message in the queue and **prev** points to the previous message in the queue. For the last message in the queue, **next** contains **NULL**. The **prev** attribute of the first message in the queue points to a nonexistent dummy message whose **next** attribute coincides with the queue head pointer. We say more about this in section 5.3.7. This apparently obscure trick simplifies the operation of removing a message from the queue and makes it independent of the message location.

The **Length** attribute gives the message length in bits. The **Length** of a message generated by the standard **Client** is guaranteed to be a strictly positive multiple of 8. Thus, the standard traffic generator assumes that messages come in bytes or—according to the OSI terminology—in *octets*.

Attribute **Receiver** contains the **Id** (section 3.1.2) of the station to which the message is addressed. For a broadcast message (sections 5.3, 5.3.2) **Receiver** points to a data structure representing a *group* of stations.[1] One special value of the **Receiver** attribute is **NONE**, which means that the message is not explicitly addressed to any specific station. The actual destination of such a message can be decided upon by the protocol.

TP is the **Id** attribute of the traffic pattern (the **Traffic** AI) that has created the message (section 5.3). For messages generated in the standard way this attribute is set automatically. It is recommended to use negative TP values for messages that are generated explicitly (by **create**)—to avoid confusing them with messages created automatically by the **Client**.

QTime tells the time when the message was generated and queued at the sender. This attribute is used for calculating the *message delay* (section 7.1.2.1).

Besides these attributes, **Message** defines a few methods (e.g., the empty setup method). Another method of **Message** is

$$\text{virtual int frameSize ();}$$

which is automatically redefined in each subtype of **Message** and returns the size of the message data structure in bytes. It is mainly used for internal purposes. One more method defined in **Message** is discussed in section 5.4.1.4.

5.2.2 Packets

The declaration of a new packet type obeys the standard set of rules (sections 2.4.3, 2.4.4) and starts with the keyword **packet**.

Example

The following declaration defines a packet type that may correspond to the message type **RMessage** declared in section 5.2.1:

---

[1]This is why the type of **Receiver** is **IPointer** rather than **Long** (section 2.2.1).

```
packet RPacket {
  int Route [N], RouteLength;
  void setup (RMessage *m) {
    for (RouteLength = 0; RouteLength < m->RouteLength;
      RouteLength++)
        Route [RouteLength] = m->Route [RouteLength];
  };
};
```

The setup method copies the `Route` attribute of the message from which the packet is extracted into the corresponding packet attribute. This method is called automatically whenever a packet of type `RPacket` is acquired from a message (the type of this message is assumed to be `RMessage`).

Typically, packets are created automatically from messages by the `Client` when a protocol process requests a new packet for transmission. Sometimes it is desirable to create a nonstandard packet directly. In such a case the regular `create` operation can be used to explicitly generate an object of the packet type.

Note. As for messages, the nickname variant of `create` is not applicable to packets. Not being descendants of *Object*, packets cannot have nicknames.

A packet type may declare a setup method (or a collection of setup methods) to initialize its attributes upon the packet's creation. For standard packets, i.e., those generated automatically by the `Client`, one setup method has a special meaning (section 5.4.1.1). Namely, a user-defined packet type being a nontrivial extension of `Packet` (i.e., specifying some additional attributes) **must** declare the following setup method:

$$\texttt{void setup (mtype *m);}$$

where `mtype` is a message type, i.e., a subtype of `Message`. This method will be called automatically whenever a packet of the given type is acquired from a message—to set the nonstandard attributes of the packet. The argument m will then point to the message from which the packet is being extracted.

The public part of the `Packet` type specification contains the following attributes:

Long	ILength, TLength, Sender;
IPointer	Receiver;
int	TP;
TIME	QTime, TTime;
FLAGS	Flags;

Attributes Receiver, QTime, and TP are directly inherited from the message from which the packet was acquired. ILength contains the length of the *payload part* of the packet, i.e., the part that comes from the message and represents useful information. TLength is always greater than or equal to ILength and gives the *total length* of the packet, including the possible header and trailer required by the protocol. Both these lengths are in bits.

The `Sender` attribute contains the `Id` of the station sending the packet. No counterpart of this attribute is defined in type `Message`. A message is queued for transmission at a specific station, and only this station can be the sender of the message. Thus, the `Sender` attribute of a message is determined implicitly. On the other hand, a packet may be relayed through a number of intermediate stations on its way to the destination, and there is no implicit notion of the packet's original source.

`TTime` stands for *top time* and indicates the moment when the packet became ready for transmission (section 5.2.3). This time is used for measuring *packet delay*, which excludes the message queuing time (section 7.1.2.1).

Attribute `Flags` represents a collection of binary values describing various elements of the packet *status*. Five bits (27–31) are used by SMURPH; their meaning is discussed later. It is assumed that flags 0–9 will never be used by SMURPH; they are left for user applications. Ten symbolic constants `PF_usr0` ... `PF_usr9`, representing integer values from 0 to 9, provide access to these flags (section 2.3.3).

As with `Message`, the `Packet` type defines the virtual method `frameSize`, which returns the internal size of the packet data structure in bytes.

Nonstandard packets, i.e., packets created outside traffic patterns and the `Client`, should have their TP attributes negative or greater than the maximum valid traffic pattern Id (section 5.3.4). Two simple packet methods

```
int isStandard ();
int isNonstandard ();
```

tell a standard packet from a nonstandard one. A packet is assumed to be standard (`isStandard` returns 1 and `isNonstandard` returns 0) if it has been obtained from a message generated by one of the traffic patterns (i.e., if its TP attribute contains a valid traffic pattern Id). Otherwise, the packet is considered nonstandard and `isNonstandard` returns 1, while `isStandard` returns 0.

More methods of `Packet` are discussed later. One packet attribute that was not mentioned here is `Signature` of type `Long`. This attribute is only available if the simulator has been created with the `-g` (debugging) option of `mks` and is useful for monitoring individual packets, e.g., with observers. Its meaning is explained in sections 5.4.1.1 and 7.2.2.2.

5.2.3   Packet Buffers

Typically, when a protocol process decides to acquire a packet for transmission, it polls the `Client` (or one of the `Traffic` AIs), which, if there is a suitable message queued at the station, builds a packet and returns it to the process. The packet is returned into a *packet buffer* provided by the polling process (section 5.4.1.1).

Packet buffers are associated with stations. A packet buffer is just an object of a packet type (i.e., a subtype of `Packet`—section 5.2.2) declared statically within the station type.

Example

In the following declaration of a station type,

```
packet MyPType {
    ...
};
    ...
station MySType {
    ...
    MyPType Buffer;
    ...
};
```

`Buffer` is declared as a packet buffer capable of holding packets of type `MyPType`.

Packet buffers declared statically within a station class are called the station's *official buffers*. These official buffers are assigned internal identifiers, in the order of their declaration in the station type, and can be *exposed* (section 7.3.5.11) as part of the station structure. In principle it is legal, although not recommended, to use any packet structure, e.g., a packet created dynamically by the **create** operation, as a packet buffer. When a packet buffer is created this way, the setup argument list should be empty.

In real life, a station typically has a definite buffer pool, which belongs to the station's hardware. This pool is static and its size does not change as the protocol is running. Therefore, the recommended static configuration of packet buffers at a SMURPH station is not unrealistic. Note that it is possible to declare an array of packet buffers.

Note. It is illegal to declare a packet structure statically outside a station. Of course, this restriction does not apply to packet pointers, which can be declared anywhere.

A packet buffer can be either *empty* or *full*, which is determined by the contents of the PF_full flag (bit number 29) in the buffer's `Flags` attribute (section 5.2.2). This flag is irrelevant from the viewpoint of the packet contents: its meaning is restricted to the interpretation of the packet object as a buffer. Thus, the difference between a packet and a packet buffer boils down to the interpretation of a single bit in the packet's `Flag` attribute. This minor difference did not seem to warrant separating the two kinds of objects into different data types. On the contrary, in most cases it is very natural to treat packets and packet buffers as indistinguishable objects.

The following two simple `Packet` methods,

```
int isFull () {
    return (flagSet (Flags, PF_full));
```

```
};
int isEmpty () {
  return (flagCleared (Flags, PF_full));
};
```

can be used as predicates determining whether a packet buffer is full or empty without explicitly examining the PF_full flag. There exist other methods for examining other flags of packets; for all practical purposes, these methods completely disguise the packet flags concept under a more friendly interface.

In most cases, a packet buffer is filled by calling **getPacket** (e.g., section 1.2.4.4). In such a case, the buffer's PF_full flag is set automatically. The standard way to empty a packet buffer pointed to by buf is to call

```
buf->release ();
```

The purpose of **release** is to mark the buffer as empty (i.e., to clear the packet's PF_full flag) and to update certain performance measures (sections 5.4.3, 7.1.2.1). It should be called as soon as the contents of the buffer are no longer needed, e.g., after the packet has been completely transmitted, acknowledged, and so on, as required by the protocol.

There exist two Client's versions of **release**, which perform exactly the same action as the Packet's method. The preceding call is equivalent to

```
Client->release (buf);
```

or

```
Client->release (&buf);
```

The argument for the second version is a packet structure rather than a pointer.

Finally, two similar methods are available from traffic patterns. If TPat points to a traffic pattern, then each of the two calls

```
TPat->release (buf);
TPat->release (&buf);
```

is equivalent to buf->release(), with the exception that it checks whether the buffer being released holds a packet belonging to the traffic pattern pointed to by TPat.

A packet created directly by **create** has all its attributes undefined, except for Flags, which are cleared (set to all zeros), and TP, which is set to NONE. If a packet structure created this way is used as a packet buffer, its initial contents are irrelevant (note that the PF_full flag is initially cleared by **create**). It is possible to fill the contents of a packet explicitly, without having to acquire a packet from the Client. The following Packet method does the job:

```
void fill (Station *s, Station *r, Long tl, Long il = NONE,
  Long tp = NONE);
```

The first two arguments point to the stations to be used at the packet's sender and receiver, respectively. The third argument will be stored in the `TLength` attribute: it represents the total length of the packet. The next, optional, argument `il` gives the length of the packet's information part (payload). If it is unspecified (or equal to `NONE`), the information length (attribute `ILength`) is assumed to be the same as the total length. It is checked whether the information length, if specified, is not bigger than the total length. Finally, the last argument will be stored in the `TP` attribute of the packet. It cannot be equal to the `Id` of any defined traffic pattern: nonstandard packets are not allowed to pretend that they have been generated by the `Client`.

There exists an alternative version of `fill`, which accepts station `Ids` instead of pointers as the first two arguments. Either of the two station `Ids` (or both) can be `NONE`. If the receiver's `Id` is `NONE`, it means that the packet is not addressed explicitly to any station.

5.3   TRAFFIC PATTERNS

By a traffic pattern we understand here a single message arrival process described within the context of a single object belonging to type `Traffic`. The description of a standard message arrival process consists of two parts:

- The specification of senders and receivers, i.e., where the messages are to be queued for transmission and where they will be addressed
- The specification of the arrival timing and message length distribution, i.e., when the messages will be arriving to the network and how long they are going to be

To understand how the first part is handled, we need a few prerequisites that constitute the subject of the next two sections.

5.3.1   Station Groups

Sometimes a subset of stations in the network must be distinguished and identified as a single object. For example, to create a broadcast message, i.e., a message addressed to more than one recipient, one must be able to specify the set of all receivers as a single entity. A *station group* (an object of type `SGroup`) is just a set of station identifiers (`Id` attributes) representing a (not necessarily proper) subset of all stations in the network. An `SGroup` is created in the following way:

```
sg = create SGroup ( setup arguments );
```

where the setup arguments can be specified according to one of the following patterns:

```
()      (i.e., no setup arguments)
```

The communication group created this way contains all stations in the network.

$$(\text{int ns, int *sl})$$

If the first argument (ns) is greater than zero, it gives the length of the array passed as the second argument. This array contains the Ids of the stations to be included in the group. If the first argument is negative, its negation gives the length of sl, which is then assumed to contain the list of exceptions, i.e., the stations that are not to be included in the group. The group will consist of all stations in the network, except those listed in sl.

$$(\text{int ns, int n1, } \ldots)$$

The first argument specifies the number of the remaining arguments, which are explicit station Ids. The stations whose Ids are explicitly listed as arguments are included in the group.

$$(\text{int ns, Station *s1, } \ldots)$$

As above, but pointers to station objects are used instead of the Ids.

Note. Type SGroup does not descend from *Object*; therefore, objects of this types cannot be assigned nicknames.

The internal layout of type SGroup is not interesting to the user: there is no need to reference SGroup attributes directly.

In most cases, station groups are created as prerequisites for defining other objects, namely *communication groups* (section 5.3.2) and—via communication groups—traffic patterns (section 5.3.4). When a station group is used for this purpose, its pointer becomes an attribute of another data structure and the station group should not be altered or destroyed thereafter. It is illegal to execute delete on a station group pointer: once created, a station group cannot be destroyed.

Type SGroup defines the following two methods:

```
int occurs (Long sid);
int occurs (Station *sp);
```

which return YES (1) if the station indicated by the argument (either as an Id or as an object pointer) is a member of the group.

Stations within a station group are ordered. This ordering is relevant when the station group is used to define a communication group (section 5.3.2). If the station group has been defined by excluding exceptions or by using the empty setup argument list, the stations included in the group are ordered according to the increasing values of their Ids. In all other cases, the arrangement of the station within the group corresponds to the order in which the included stations have been specified.

Note. A station that has been specified twice counts as two separate elements. It makes no difference for determining whether a given station belongs to a station group but is significant when the group is used to define a communication group (section 5.3.2).

Example

The sequence of statements

```
int i, ex [EXSIZE];
SGroup *sgr1, *sgr2, *sgr3;
...
for (i = 0; i < NStations; i += 2) ex [i/2] = i;
sgr1 = create SGroup (-NStations/2, ex);
sgr2 = create SGroup (3, 2, 3, 3);
sgr3 = create SGroup;
```

creates three station groups: `sgr1` includes all odd-numbered stations, `sgr2` includes two stations with Ids 2 and 3 (note that station number 3 occurs twice within the group), and `sgr3` consists of all stations in the network.

5.3.2   Communication Groups

Communication groups (objects of type `CGroup`) are used (explicitly or implicitly) in definitions of refined traffic patterns. Intuitively, a communication group describes a set of senders and the associated set of receivers for a traffic pattern. Actually, the situation is (or at least can be) slightly more complicated, as the definition of a single traffic pattern may involve multiple communication groups. Whenever a new message arrives to the network, the `Client` must determine its *sender/receiver pair*, i.e., the values to be assigned to its attributes `Sender`[2] and `Receiver`. These values are determined based on the configuration of communication groups associated with the traffic pattern (`Traffic`) responsible for generating the message.

5.3.2.1   The structure and semantics of a communication group. A communication group consists of two station groups (section 5.3.1) and two sets of numeric weights associated with these groups. One group is called the *senders* group and contains stations that can be potentially used as senders of a message. Together with its associated set of weights, the senders group constitutes the *senders set* of the communication group. The other group is the *receivers* group and contains stations that can be used as receivers. The receivers group together with its associated set of weights is called the *receivers set* of the communication group.

A communication group can be either a *selection group*, in which the station group of receivers specifies individual stations, or a *broadcast group*, in which the receivers group is treated as a single object. In the former case, a message whose

---

[2]Note that the `Sender` attribute is implicit (section 5.2.2).

sender/receiver pair is determined from the group is addressed to one specific station selected from the receivers group. If the sender/receiver pair of a message has been produced from a broadcast group, the `Receiver` attribute of the message is set to point to the entire receivers group. In such a case, the message is addressed to all the stations in the receivers group at the same time. No weights are associated with the receivers of a broadcast communication group.

Assume that the definition of a traffic pattern T consists of a single communication group G (most traffic patterns are actually defined this way). Let G be a selection group and $S = \langle (s_1, w_1), \ldots, (s_k, w_k) \rangle$ be the set of senders of G. Similarly, by $R = \langle (r_1, v_1), \ldots, (r_p, v_p) \rangle$ we denote the set of receivers of G. The first element of each pair is a station number (`Id`), the other element is the associated weight. Assume that a message is to be generated according to T. The communication group G is used to determine the contents of the `Sender` and `Receiver` attributes of this message. The value to be assigned to the `Sender` attribute is chosen at random in such a way that the probability that a station $s_i : (s_i, w_i) \in S$ will be selected is equal to

$$P_S(s_i) = \frac{w_i}{\sum_{l=1}^{k} w_l}.$$

Thus, the weight of a station in the senders set specifies its relative frequency of being used as the sender of a message generated according to T.

Once the sender has been selected (let us assume that it is station s), the receiver of the message is chosen from the receivers set R in such a way that the probability of station r_i's being selected is equal to

$$P_R(r_i) = \frac{h_i}{\sum_{l=1}^{p} h_l},$$

where

$$h_i = \begin{cases} v_i & \text{if } r_i \neq s \\ 0 & \text{if } r_i = s \end{cases}.$$

In simple words, the receiver is determined at random in such a way that the chances that a particular station from the receiver set will be selected are proportional to its weight. However, the sender is excluded from the game, i.e., it is guaranteed that the message is addressed to another station. Note that the formula for P_R makes no sense when the sum in the denominator is zero. In such a case, SMURPH is not able to determine the receiver and the simulation is aborted with a pertinent error message.

Should G be a broadcast group, the problem of selecting the receiver would be trivial, namely, the entire receiver group would be used as a single object whose pointer would be stored in the `Receiver` attribute of the message (section 5.2.1).

5.3.2.2 Creating communication groups.

Section 5.3.6 explains that communication groups need not be (and seldom are) created directly. However, if the distribution of senders/receivers is particularly tricky, an explicitly created communication group (or a collection of communication groups) may improve the clarity of the traffic pattern definition. The following operation can be used to explicitly create a communication group:

$$cg = \texttt{create CGroup} \ (\ setup\ arguments\ );$$

Note. Like station groups, communication groups do not descend from *Object*; therefore, the nickname variant of `create` (section 2.4.7) is not applicable for a communication group.

The following configurations of setup arguments are acceptable:

```
(SGroup *s, float *sw, SGroup *r, float *rw)
(SGroup *s, float *sw, SGroup *r)
(SGroup *s, SGroup *r, float *rw)
(SGroup *s, SGroup *r)
```

The first, most general configuration specifies the senders group (`s`), the senders weights (the `float` array `sw`), the receivers group (`r`), and the receivers weights (array `rw`). The weights are assigned to individual members of the corresponding station groups according to their ordering within the groups (section 5.3.1). Note that if a station appears twice (or more times) within a group, it counts as two (or more) stations, and two (or more) entries are required for it in the weight array. The effect is as if the station occurred once with the weight equal to the sum of weights associated with all its occurrences.

With the remaining configurations of the setup arguments, one set (or both sets) of weights are not specified, and default weights are assumed for the unspecified set (or for both sets). In such a case, each station in the corresponding station group is assigned the same weight of $1/n$, where n is the number of stations in the group.

With the following two configurations of setup arguments, one can create a broadcast communication group:

```
(SGroup *s, float *sw, SGroup *r, int b)
(SGroup *s, SGroup *r, int b)
```

The value of the last argument can only be `GT_broadcast` (-1). Note that receivers weights are not specified for a broadcast communication group; there is no use for them, as all receivers are treated as a single set and the whole set is always selected as the single broadcast receiver. With the second configuration, default weights are assigned to the senders, as we have described.

Note. Like a station group (and for the same reason), a communication group can never be explicitly destroyed, i.e., it is illegal to execute `delete` on a communication group pointer.

Examples

The following sequence of operations creates a simple communication group in which all stations are legitimate senders and receivers, and their weights are equal:

```
SGroup *sg;
CGroup *cg;
...
sg = create SGroup;
cg = create CGroup (sg, sg);
```

The traffic generated from this communication group will be perfectly balanced among all stations.

Assume that we want to generate a skewed distribution of senders/receivers in which 20 percent of the stations are responsible for 80 percent of the traffic (this kind of skewedness is called the *Zipf distribution*). The following sequence of statements will do the job:

```
SGroup *sg;
CGroup *cg;
float W1, W2, Weights [MAXSTATIONS];
int i, nbiased;
...
nbiased = NStations * 0.8;
W1 = 0.2 / nbiased;
W2 = 0.8 / (NStations - nbiased);
for (i = 0; i < NStations; i++)
  Weights [i] = (i < nbiased) ?  W1 :  W2;
sg = create SGroup;
cg = create CGroup (sg, Weights, sg, Weights);
```

The probability of selecting a specific station whose Id is less than **nbiased** is equal to 0.2/nbiased. Thus, the probability of selecting any such station is 0.2.

Now assume that one half of all stations in the network are to be the senders of messages that are broadcast to the other half. For all senders, the likelihood of using a particular station is the same. The following is a sequence of statements creating a communication group for this occasion:

```
SGroup *sgs, *sgr;
CGroup *cg;
int i, Half [MAXSTATIONS/2];
...
for (i = 0; i < NStations/2; i++) Half [i] = i;
sgs = create SGroup (NStations/2, Half);
sgr = create SGroup (-NStations/2, Half);
cg = create CGroup (sgs, sgr, GT_broadcast);
```

Although with a single communication group it is possible to express bias in selecting the senders and receivers for a message, a correlation between classes of senders and receivers cannot be captured in this simple way. One needs multiple communication groups for specifying such subtle parameters of the senders/receivers distribution.

5.3.3   Traffic Type Declaration

A definition of a traffic pattern type obeys the rules described in sections 2.4.3 and 2.4.4, and has the following format:

> **traffic** *ttype* : *itypename* (*mtype, ptype*) {
>
>   ...
>
>   *attributes and methods*
>
>   ...
>
> };

where *mtype* and *ptype* are the names of the message type and the packet type (section 5.2.2) associated with the traffic pattern. All messages generated by the traffic pattern will belong to type *mtype*, and all packets acquired from this traffic pattern for transmission will be of type *ptype*. If these types are not specified, i.e., the parentheses together with their contents are absent, it is assumed that the standard types **Message** and **Packet** are to be used. If only one argument type occurs between parentheses, it determines the message type; the associated packet type is then assumed to be **Packet**.

The base traffic type **Traffic** can be used directly to create traffic patterns. Messages and packets generated by a traffic pattern of type **Traffic** belong to the basic types **Message** and **Packet**, respectively. A new traffic type definition is only required if at least one of the following two statements is true:

- The behavior of the standard traffic generator has to be changed by replacing or augmenting some of its methods.
- The types of messages or packets generated by the traffic pattern are proper subtypes of **Message** or **Packet**, respectively; i.e., at least one of these types is not basic.

The list of *attributes and methods* of a user-defined traffic type is seldom nonempty. Most often, the sole purpose of introducing a nonstandard traffic type is to bind a nonstandard message or packet type to a traffic pattern (e.g., section 1.2.4.9). The only legitimate items that may appear as attributes of a nonstandard traffic type are redeclarations of some virtual methods of **Traffic** and declarations of nonstandard variables used by these new methods. Essentially, there are two types of **Traffic** methods than can be overridden by user's declarations: the methods used in generating messages and transforming them into packets (section 5.5.2), and the methods used for calculating performance measures (section 7.1.2.3).

5.3.4   Creating Traffic Patterns

Traffic patterns should be built by the user's root process (section 4.8) after the network geometry has been defined. A single traffic pattern is created by the `create` operation, in the way described in section 2.4.7.

The standard setup methods built into `Traffic` accept the following configurations of arguments:

```
(CGroup **cgl, int ncg, int flags, ...)
(CGroup *cg, int flags, ...)
(int flags, ...)
```

The first configuration is the most general one. The first argument (`cgl`) points to an array of pointers to communication groups (section 5.3.2). This array is assumed to contain exactly `ncg` elements. The communication groups describe the distribution of senders and receivers for messages generated according to the created traffic pattern.

The second configuration specifies only one communication group and provides a shorthand for the situation when the array of communication groups contains exactly one element.

Finally, with the third configuration, the distribution of senders and receivers is not specified at the moment of creation (it can be specified later) and the definition of the traffic pattern is incomplete.

Argument `flags` is a collection of binary options that select the type of the message arrival process and indicate whether standard performance measures (section 7.1.2) should be calculated for the traffic pattern. The actual value passed as `flags` should consists of a sum (logical or arithmetic) of symbolic constants selected from the following list:

MIT_exp	The message interarrival time is exponentially distributed.
MIT_unf	The message interarrival time is uniformly distributed.
MIT_fix	The message interarrival time is fixed.
MLE_exp	The message length is exponentially distributed.
MLE_unf	The message length is uniformly distributed.
MLE_fix	The message length is fixed.
BIT_exp	The traffic pattern is *bursty*, and the burst interarrival time is exponentially distributed.
BIT_unf	The traffic pattern is bursty, and the burst interarrival time is uniformly distributed.
BIT_fix	The traffic pattern is bursty, and the burst interarrival time is fixed.
BSI_exp	Relevant only if BIT_exp, BIT_unf, or BIT_fix has been specified. The burst size is exponentially distributed.
BSI_unf	Relevant only if BIT_exp, BIT_unf, or BIT_fix has been specified. The burst size is uniformly distributed.

BSI_fix   Relevant only if BIT_exp, BIT_unf, or BIT_fix has been specified. The burst size is fixed.

SCL_on   This is the default setting. The standard Client processing for this traffic pattern is switched **on**, i.e., the traffic pattern will be used automatically by SMURPH to generate messages and queue them at the sending stations.

SCL_off   The standard client processing is switched **off**, i.e., the traffic pattern will not automatically generate messages. This option is useful when the traffic pattern is to be serviced by nonstandard pilot processes (section 5.5.3) supplied by the user.

SPF_on   Standard performance measures will be calculated for the traffic pattern (section 7.1.2). The user can still override or extend the standard methods that take care of this end. This is the default setting.

SPF_off   No standard performance measures will be computed for this traffic pattern.

It is illegal to specify more than one distribution type for a single distribution parameter, e.g., MIT_exp+MIT_unf. If no option is selected for a given distribution parameter, this parameter is not defined. For example, if none of BIT_exp, BIT_unf, or BIT_fix is specified, the traffic pattern is not bursty. It makes little sense to omit the specification of the message arrival time or message length distribution unless SCL_off is selected. SMURPH will complain about an incomplete definition of a traffic pattern for which the SCL_on flag is set, i.e., if the traffic pattern is to be controlled by the standard Client.

The number and interpretation of the remaining setup arguments depend on the contents of **flag**. All these arguments are expected to be **double** numbers. They describe the numeric parameters of the message arrival process in the following way and order:

- If MIT_exp or MIT_fix was selected, the next number specifies the mean message interarrival time in ETUs (section 2.2.2). For MIT_fix, this value gives the **exact** fixed message interarrival time. The **double** argument is then rounded to the nearest integer value. If MIT_unf was specified, the next two numbers determine the minimum and the maximum message interarrival time (also in ETUs). Note that these two numbers can be equal, which gives another way of specifying a fixed distribution of the message interarrival time.

- If MLE_exp or MLE_fix was included in the **flag** pattern, the next number specifies the mean message length in bits. If MLE_unf was selected, the next two numbers determine the minimum and the maximum message length (also in bits). The rules are the same as for the message interarrival time.

- If BIT_exp or BIT_fix was set, the next number specifies the mean burst interarrival time in ETUs (section 2.2.2). If BIT_unf was chosen, the next two numbers determine the minimum and the maximum burst interarrival time (also in ETUs). Again, the rules are the same as for the message interarrival time.

- If BSI_exp or BSI_fix was selected, the next number gives the mean burst size as the number of messages constituting the burst. If BSI_unf was chosen, the next two numbers determine the minimum and the maximum burst size, as for the message interarrival time.

According to the preceding description, the maximum number of the numeric distribution parameters is 8. Once again, we remind the reader that all of them must be double numbers, even those that determine the values of apparently integer quantities.

Note. As the number of arguments for the Traffic setup method is not known in advance, the header specification of this method is *incomplete*. This means that no automatic type conversion is performed for the numeric arguments. If the type of an actual argument is different from double, the results may be unpredictable.

Traffic patterns are *Objects*, which means that they are assigned name attributes, as described in section 2.4.2. The Id attributes of traffic patterns reflect their creation order. The first created traffic pattern is assigned Id 0, the second 1, and so on. The function

```
Traffic *idToTraffic (int id);
```

converts the traffic Id to the object pointer. The global variable NTraffics of type int contains the number of currently defined traffic patterns. As with stations and links, there exists a macro

```
int isTrafficId (int id);
```

that returns YES, if the argument is a legal traffic pattern Id, and NO otherwise.

5.3.5   The Standard Semantics of Traffic Patterns

A completely defined traffic pattern describes a self-contained message arrival process. For a nonbursty traffic, this process can be described as follows (we assume that when the simulation starts we are at step 1):

1. A time interval t_{mi} is generated at random, according to the message interarrival time distribution. The process sleeps for time t_{mi} and then moves to step 2.
2. A message is generated, its length is determined at random according to the message length distribution, its sender and receiver are selected using the list of communication groups associated with the traffic pattern. The message is queued at the sender, and the generation process continues at step 1.

With a bursty traffic pattern, it is assumed that messages arrive in groups called bursts. Each burst carries a specific number of messages that are to be generated according to similar rules as for a regular nonbursty traffic pattern. The process of burst arrival is described by the following sequence (again we assume that it starts at step 1):

1. An integer counter denoted by PMC (for pending message count) is initialized to 0.

2. A time interval t_{bi} is generated at random according to the burst interarrival time distribution. The process sleeps for time t_{bi} and then continues at step 3.

3. A random integer number s_b is generated according to the burst size distribution. This number determines the number of messages to be generated within the burst.

4. PMC is incremented by s_b. If the previous value of PMC was zero, a new process is started that is similar to the message generation process for a nonbursty traffic pattern and runs **in parallel** with the burst arrival process. Each time a new message is generated, the message arrival process decrements PMC by 1. When PMC goes to zero, the process terminates. Note that if the previous value of PMC (before adding s_b) was nonzero, the message arrival process is already active. Having completed this step, **without waiting for the termination of the message arrival process**, the burst arrival process continues at step 2.

Typically, the message interarrival time within a burst is much shorter than the burst interarrival time. In particular, it can be 0, in which case all messages of the burst arrive at once—within the same ITU. Note that when two bursts overlap, i.e., a new burst arrives before the previous one has been exhausted, the new burst adds to the previous burst.

The internal SMURPH processes implementing the preceding message generation algorithms are called *pilot processes* of the traffic patterns. In section 5.5.3 we list the code of the two standard pilot processes. We also show how to program nonstandard pilot processes describing user-defined message arrival patterns.

The procedure of determining the sender and the receiver of a newly arrived message, in the case when the traffic pattern is based on one communication group, was described in section 5.3.2.1. Now we discuss the case of multiple communication groups. Again let us assume that $S = \langle (s_1, w_1), \ldots, (s_k, w_k) \rangle$ and $R = \langle (r_1, v_1), \ldots, (r_p, v_p) \rangle$ are the sets of senders and receivers of a communication group $G = (S, R)$. If G is a broadcast group, we may assume that all v_i, $i = 1, \ldots, p$, are zeros (they are irrelevant in such a case). The value of

$$W = \sum_{i=1}^{k} w_i$$

is called the sender weight of group G. Assume that the definition of a traffic pattern T involves communication groups $G_1, \ldots, G_m$ with their sender weights

$W_1, \ldots, W_m$, respectively. Assume that a message generated according to T arrives to the network. The sender of this message is determined in such a way that the probability that a station $s_i^j : (s_i^j, w_i^j) \in S_j$ and $S_j \in G_j$ will be selected is equal to

$$P_S(s_i^j) = \frac{w_i^j}{\sum_{l=1}^m W_l}.$$

Thus, the weight of a station in the senders set specifies its relative frequency of being chosen as an actual sender with respect to all potential senders specified in all communication groups belonging to T. Note that the expression for P_S is meaningless if the sum of all W_l's is zero. Consequently, at least one sender weight in at least one selection group must be strictly positive.

Once the sender has been established, the receiver of the message is chosen from the receiver set R of the communication group that was used to determine the sender. If this communication group happens to be a broadcast group, the entire receivers group is used as the receiver. In consequence, the message will be addressed to all the stations listed in the receivers group, including the sender, if it occurs in R. For a nonbroadcast message, the receiver is selected from R, as described in section 5.3.2.1.

The senders set of a traffic pattern to be handled by the standard `Client` must not be empty: the `Client` must always be able to queue a generated message at a specific sender station. However, the receiver set can be empty, in which case the message will not be explicitly addressed to any specific station (its `Receiver` attribute will be `NONE`).

Examples

Despite the apparent complexity, the definition of a traffic pattern is quite simple in most cases. For example, to describe a uniform traffic pattern (in which all stations have equal chances to be used as senders or receivers) with a Poisson message arrival process and fixed-length messages, the following sequence of operations can be used:

```
traffic MyPattType (MyMsgType, MyPktType) {
};
MyPattType *tp;
SGroup *sg;
CGroup *cg;
double iart, lngth;
...
sg = create SGroup;
cg = create CGroup (sg, sg);
tp = create MyPattType (sg, MIT_exp+MLE_fix, iart, lngth);
```

`MyMsgType` and `MyPktType` are assumed to have been defined earlier; `iart` and `lngth` are variables of type `double` specifying the mean message interarrival time and the mean message length, respectively.

Now let us try something trickier. Assume that the population of stations is divided into half. The stations in the first half send messages to the other half and vice versa, but no station from a given half ever sends a message to another station in the same half. All stations are equally likely candidates for senders and, given a sender, the receiver is chosen from the other half in such a way that all eligible stations have the same chances. The traffic is bursty with a fixed burst size and exponential burst interarrival time. All messages within a burst arrive with an exponential interarrival interval, and the message length is uniformly distributed.

This traffic pattern cannot be defined with a single communication group, because of the correlation between senders and receivers. The following code will take care of this case:

```
Traffic *tp;
SGroup *fhalf, *shalf;
CGroup *cgs [2];
int i, fh [MAXSTATIONS];
double miart, minmsgl, maxmsgl, biart, bsize;
...
for (i = 0; i < NStations/2; i++) fh [i] = i;
fhalf = create SGroup (NStations/2, fh);
shalf = create SGroup (-NStations/2, fh);
cgs [0] = create CGroup (fhalf, shalf);
cgs [1] = create CGroup (shalf, fhalf);
tp = create Traffic (cgs, 2, BIT_exp+BSI_fix+MIT_exp+MLE_unf,
    miart, minmsgl, maxmsgl, biart, bsize);
```

We assume that messages and packets handled by the defined traffic pattern are of the standard types. This code only works as intended under the assumption that the number of stations NStations is even. Otherwise, the sender weights will be biased in favor of the stations in the "smaller half." The default sender weight assigned to each station in a given senders set is equal to $1/N$, where N is the number of stations in the set.

Note the order in which the numerical distribution parameters occur as the setup arguments for the Traffic create operation. According to what we said in section 5.3.4, the first number is interpreted as the mean message interarrival time. Then, as the message length distribution is uniform, the next two numbers are assumed to stand for the minimum and maximum message length in bits. The fourth number gives the mean burst interarrival time and the last number specifies the (fixed) burst size as the number of messages arriving to the network within one burst.

Let us consider one more example. This time, assume that a station number i is only allowed to send messages to station $i + 1 \bmod N$, where N is the number of all stations in the network. Thus, each sender has exactly one deterministic receiver. The message interarrival time and length are both exponentially distributed. The distribution parameters as well as the weights of particular senders are read from the input data file. This time we give a complete function creating our traffic pattern. We make this function a method of the Root process (section 4.8):

```
void Root::defineTraffic () {
  int i;
  SGroup *s, *r;
  CGroup **cg;
  float w [1];
  double mit, mle;
  readIn (mit); readIn (mle);
  cg = new CGroup* [NStations];
  for (i = 0; i < NStations; i++) {
    s = create SGroup (1, i);
    r = create SGroup (1, (i+1) % NStations);
    readIn (w [0]);
    cg [i] = create CGroup (s, w, r);
  }
  TPattern = create Traffic (cg, NStations, MIT_exp+MLE_exp,
    mit, mle);
}
```

Again, to avoid irrelevant complexity, we assume that the standard type `Traffic` is used as the type of our traffic pattern. We generate `NStations` communication groups, each group describing one sender/receiver pair.

Note that neither the station groups used to create the communication groups in these examples nor the communication groups themselves are ever deallocated. In accordance with what we said in sections 5.3.1 and 5.3.2.2, a station group used as a setup argument for a communication group becomes part of that communication group and must not be changed thereafter. No copy of the station group is made: the pointer to the station group becomes an attribute of the communication group. Similarly, a communication group specified as a setup argument for a traffic pattern becomes linked to that traffic pattern and should not be altered. SMURPH will signal an error if `delete` is attempted for a station or communication group.

5.3.6   Shortcuts

To define a simple traffic pattern, the user does not have to bother with communication groups. As a matter of fact, any traffic pattern that can be defined using explicit communication groups can be defined without them. Namely, by calling the following methods of `Traffic` the user can build the sets of senders and receivers dynamically, without putting them into groups first:

```
addSender (Station *s = ALL, double w = 1.0, int gr = 0);
addSender (Long sid, double w = 1.0, int gr = 0);
addReceiver (Station *s = ALL, double w = 1.0, int gr = 0);
addReceiver (Long sid, double w = 1.0, int gr = 0);
```

By calling `addSender` (or `addReceiver`) we add one sender (or receiver) to the traffic pattern, assign an optional weight to it, and (also optionally) assign it to a specific communication group. This approach can be viewed as an incremental way of building the communication groups implicitly. Its advantage over the technique described in the previous sections is that it is usually more concise and, for simple traffic patterns, the notions of station and communication groups need not come into play.

A call to `addSender` or `addReceiver` with the first argument equal to ALL[3] or without any arguments results in all stations being added to the group. The only legal value for `w` is then 1.0; the weights of all stations are the same and equal to 1/NStations.

Example

Let us consider again the first example from section 5.3.5, i.e., the uniform traffic pattern in which all stations have equal chances to be selected as senders and receivers. The message interarrival time is exponentially distributed, and the message length is fixed. With `addSender` and `addReceiver`, the same traffic pattern can be described in the following way:

```
traffic MyPattType (MyMsgType, MyPktType) {
};
MyPattType *tp;
double iart, lngth;
...
tp = create MyPattType (MIT_exp+MLE_fix, iart, lngth);
tp->addSender (ALL);
tp->addReceiver (ALL);
```

Note that before `addSender` and `addReceiever` are called, the traffic pattern, although formally created, is incompletely specified. If it were left in such a state, SMURPH would detect a problem while initializing the message generation process for this pattern.

It is legal to use `addSender` and `addReceiver` to supplement the description of a traffic pattern that was created with explicit communication groups. The two methods reference communication groups by numbers, and they assume that the explicit communication groups associated with the traffic pattern are numbered from 0 up, in the order of their occurrence on the list that was given as the first setup argument for the traffic pattern. Clearly, if there is only one communication group, its number is 0.

For `addReceiver`, if BROADCAST (-1) is put in place of `w`, the communication group is assumed to be a broadcast one. This must be consistent with the previous and future additions of receivers to the group.

Examples

Let us try to convert the remaining two examples from section 5.3.5 to their equiv-

---

[3]ALL is an alias for NULL.

alent forms devoid of explicit station and communication groups. The first of the two traffic patterns can be defined by the following code fragment:

```
Traffic *tp;
int i;
double miart, minmsgl, maxmsgl, biart, bsize;
...
tp = create Traffic (BIT_exp+BSI_fix+MIT_exp+MLE_unf,
  miart, minmsgl, maxmsgl, biart, bsize);
for (i = 0; i < NStations; i++) {
  if (i < NStations/2) {
    tp->addSender (i, 1.0, 0);
    tp->addReceiver (i, 1.0, 1);
  } else {
    tp->addSender (i, 1.0, 1);
    tp->addReceiver (i, 1.0, 0);
  }
}
```

Note that in contrast to its previous version, this code works correctly for an odd number of stations. The weight of each station in either senders set is 1.0, irrespective of how many stations fit into the set.

Here is the new version of the defineTraffic method from the last example in section 5.3.5:

```
void Root::defineTraffic () {
  int i;
  double mit, mle, w;
  readIn (mit); readIn (mle);
  TPattern = create Traffic (MIT_exp+MLE_exp, mit, mle);
  for (i = 0; i < NStations; i++) {
    readIn (w);
    TPattern->addSender (i, w, i);
    TPattern->addReceiver ((i+1) % NStations, 1.0, i);
  }
}
```

A traffic pattern defined with the help of station and communication groups can always be redefined (in an equivalent way) without these notions, using operations addSender and addReceiver. Moreover, as we can see from the examples, by avoiding the groups we get shorter and (arguably) more comprehensible definitions. A natural question to ask is, Do we really need the groups? They seem to be useful for at least one purpose: they make the semantics of traffic patterns easier to understand. Moreover, they still occur (although implicitly) in the specification of addSender and addReceiver. Without them, we would need quite a bit of handwaving to describe the exact meaning of the two operations.

5.3.7 Message Queues

Each station has two user-visible pointers that describe queues of messages awaiting transmission at the station. These pointers are declared within type `Station` in the following way:

Message **MQHead, **MQTail;

`MQHead` points to an array of pointers to messages, each pointer representing the head of the message queue associated with one traffic pattern. The `Id` attributes of traffic patterns (reflecting their creation order—section 5.3.4) index the message queues in the array pointed to by `MQHead`. Thus,

S->MQHead [i]

references the head of the message queue owned by station `S`, corresponding to the traffic pattern number `i`. Note that `S` is a standard process attribute identifying the station that owns the process (section 4.2).

Similarly, `MQTail` identifies an array of message pointers. Each entry in this array points to the last message in the corresponding message queue and can be used to append a message at the end of the queue in a fast way.

`MQHead` and `MQTail` are initialized to `NULL` when the station is created. The two pointer arrays are generated and assigned to `MQHead` and `MQTail` when the first message is queued at the station by `genMSG` (section 5.5.2). Thus, a station that never gets any messages to transmit has no message queues.

An empty message queue is characterized by both its pointers (i.e., `MQHead[i]` and `MQTail[i]`) being equal to `NULL`. The way messages are kept in queues is described in section 5.2.1. The `prev` pointer of the first message of an nonempty queue number i (associated with the ith traffic pattern) contains `&MQHead[i]`, i.e., it points to a fictitious message containing `MQHead[i]` as its **next** attribute.

It is possible to impose a limit on the length of message queues—individually at specific stations or globally for the entire network. This possibility may be useful for investigating the network behavior under extreme traffic conditions. By setting a limit on the number of queued messages, the user may avoid overflowing the memory area of the simulator. By calling the global function

void setQSLimit (Long lgth);

the user declares that the total number of messages queued at all stations together cannot exceed `lgth`. When `setQSLimit` is called as a `Traffic` method, it restricts the number of queued messages belonging to the given traffic pattern. It is also possible to call the function as a `Station` method, in which case it limits the combined length of message queues at the given station. The parameter can be skipped; it is then assumed to be `MAX_Long`, which effectively stands for "no limit."

Whenever a message is to be generated and queued at a station by `genMSG` (section 5.5.2), it is checked whether the queuing of the new message will not exceed one of three possible limits: the global limit on the total number of messages awaiting transmission, the limit associated with the traffic pattern to which the message belongs, or the limit associated with the station at which the message is to be queued. If any of the three limits is already reached, no message is generated and the action of genMSG is void.

Messages belonging to a traffic pattern that was created with the SPF_off indicator (section 5.3.4) are not counted against any of the three possible limits. For such a traffic pattern, genMSG always produces a message and queues it at the corresponding queue of the selected sender.

Note. By default, for reasons of efficiency, the size limit checking for message queues is disabled. The simulator must be created with the -q option of mks (section B.2) to enable this checking.

5.4   AI INTERFACE

Traffic patterns are activity interpreters, which means that they are perceived by the protocol program as event-triggering agents. A protocol process may issue a *wait request* to a specific traffic pattern, or to the Client representing the union of all traffic patterns, e.g., to await a message arrival at the station. It is also possible to *inquire* a specific traffic pattern, or the Client, e.g., for a packet to be transmitted. All these operations are implemented by a collection of methods defined within type Traffic. Most of these methods are also available from the Client.

5.4.1   Inquiries

A protocol process willing to acquire a packet for transmission can *inquire* for it in a number of ways. Such an inquiry can be addressed to

- A specific traffic pattern, if the process is explicitly interested in packets generated according to this pattern
- The Client, if the process does not want to specify the traffic pattern, i.e., any traffic pattern will do
- A message, if the process wants to explicitly indicate the message from which the packet is to be extracted

We refer to all these types of inquiries as *client inquiries*, although only a certain subset of them is implemented as a collection of methods actually belonging to the Client.

5.4.1.1   Acquiring packets from the Client.   The following method of the Client checks whether a message awaiting transmission is queued at the station and, if this happens to be the case, creates a packet out of this message:

```
int getPacket (Packet *p, Long min = 0, Long max = 0,
   Long frm = 0);
```

The first argument is a pointer to the packet buffer (section 5.2.3) where the acquired packet is to be stored. The remaining three arguments indicate the minimum packet length, the maximum packet length, and the length of the packet frame information (header and trailer), respectively. All these lengths are in bits.

The method examines all message queues at the current station. If the value returned by the method is NO, it means that all the queues are empty and no packet can be acquired. Otherwise, the earliest arrived message is chosen and a packet is created out of this message. This operation is performed by examining top messages in all queues at the current station. As messages are stored in queues in the order of their arrival, the top message in each queue is the earliest arrived message generated by the traffic pattern that handles that queue (section 5.3.7). If two or more message queues at the station have top messages with the same earliest arrival time, one of these messages is selected at random.

If max is greater than the message length, or equal to 0, which stands for "no limit," the entire message is turned into the packet. Otherwise, only max bits are extracted from the message and its remaining portion is left for further use. These bits will constitute the *payload* portion of the packet. If min is greater than the payload length obtained this way, additional bits are appended to the payload (we say that the packet is *inflated*)—up to the total size of min bits. The added bits count in the total length of the packet (e.g., they influence the packet's transmission time), but they are not considered to be information bits, e.g., they are ignored in calculating the *effective throughput* (sections 7.3.5.5, 7.3.5.10). Note that min can be greater than max, in which case the packet is always inflated.

Finally, frm bits are added to the packet length. This part is used to represent the length of various headers and trailers required by the protocol but not useful from the viewpoint of the packet information content.

The partitioning of the total packet size into the information part (payload) and the frame part (headers and trailers) is described by the values of two packet attributes: TLength and ILength (section 5.2.2). Let m point to the message from which the packet is extracted. The contents of TLength and ILength are determined according to the following algorithm:

```
ILength = (m->Length > max) ? max : m->Length;
TLength = ILength + frm;
if (ILength < min) TLength += min - ILength;
m->Length -= ILength;
```

Thus, TLength contains the total length of the packet, including headers, trailers, and the possible extra bits appended to the payload—to inflate it to the minimum size specified by the min argument of getPacket. ILength gives the length of the pure information content of the packet, i.e., the number of bits that have been extracted from the message.

The Flags attribute of a newly acquired packet is cleared, i.e., all flags are turned off except for the following:

- PF_full (flag number 29) is set unconditionally. Note that this is actually a

buffer flag (section 5.2.3) indicating whether the buffer contains a packet or
not.

- PF_last (flag number 30) is set if all bits of the message have been included
  in the packet. This flag indicates the **last** packet of its message.

- PF_broadcast (flag number 31) is set if the Receiver attribute of the packet
  (copied from the message) contains an SGroup pointer rather than a station
  Id (section 5.3.2).

The way the remaining attributes of the packet are filled is not difficult to
guess (it was partly described in section 5.2.2). The Sender attribute is set to
the Id attribute of the current station, i.e., the station running the process that
executes getPacket. TP and QTime are copied from the message. TTime is set to
the maximum of the old value of TTime (from the packet buffer) and QTime. (The
roles of QTime and TTime are explained in section 7.1.2.1.)

Before the message length is decremented, the packet's setup method is called
with the message pointer passed as the argument (section 5.2.2). The standard version of this method is empty. The user may (and should) define such a setup method
in subtypes of Packet—to set the nonstandard attributes. Note that generally the
setting of the nonstandard attributes of the packet may depend on the contents of
the message from which the packet has been acquired. In particular, this message
may belong to a proper subtype of Message and may carry nonstandard attributes
of its own.

If after subtracting the packet length, m->Length becomes equal to 0, the
message is discarded from the queue and deallocated as an object.

It is illegal to try to acquire a packet into a buffer that is not *empty* (section 5.2.3). After getPacket puts a packet into the buffer, the buffer status is
automatically changed to *full*.

If the simulator has been created with the -g (debugging) option of mks
(section B.2), each packet carries one additional attribute of type Long called
Signature. This attribute is set by getPacket in such a way that different packets
are assigned different signatures, in the order of their acquisition. The signature
of a packet acquired from the Client by getPacket is a non-negative number (the
first acquired packet gets signature zero) and the signature of a nonstandard packet,
e.g., filled explicitly by fill (section 5.2.3) is NONE (-1), unless the user modifies it
explicitly. Signatures are useful for tracing individual packets, e.g., with observers
(section 7.2.2.2) for an example.

Two environment variables (section 4.4.4) are set after a successful return
(with value YES) from getPacket. If the message from which the packet has been
acquired remains in the message queue (i.e., the packet's payload length is smaller
than the original message length), the environment variable TheMessage (Info01)
of type Message* points to that message. Otherwise, TheMessage contains NULL.
In either case, the environment variable TheTraffic (Info02) of type int returns
the Id of the traffic pattern to which the acquired packet belongs.

Following are the other variants of getPacket. All the rules just described, unless we explicitly say otherwise, apply to these other variants as well.

The following `Client`'s method works identically to the one already discussed:

```
int getPacket (Packet &p, Long min = 0, Long max = 0,
   Long frm = 0);
```

the only difference being that the packet buffer is passed by reference rather than pointer.

5.4.1.2 Qualified packet acquisition.

The standard way of selecting messages from queues (i.e., in the order of their arrival) may turn out to be inadequate to implement a tricky transmission protocol. For example, assume that we have a dual-bus network in which each bus is used for transfers in one direction only. A transmitter process running at a station connected to such a network may want to ask the `Client` for the earliest message going in a given direction. This direction can be determined based on the `Receiver` attribute of the message. In general, the predicate describing which message should be used to create a packet may be described by a compound and dynamic condition. The following method of the `Client` takes care of this end:

```
int getPacket (Packet *p, MTTYPE f, Long min = 0, Long max = 0,
   Long frm = 0);
```

where `f` is a pointer to a *qualifying function*, which should be declared as

```
int f (Message *m);
```

This function must be supplied by the user and programmed in such a way that it returns nonzero if the message pointed to by `m` satisfies the selection criteria, and zero otherwise.

The message from which the packet is to be extracted is determined as with the previous version of `getPacket`, but instead of the earliest arrived message the qualified version looks for the earliest arrived message that satisfies `f`. Again, if there are two or more earliest arrived messages satisfying `f` (i.e., all these messages have arrived at the same time), one of them is chosen at random.

Example

Assume that in a dual-bus network the stations are connected to the dual bus in the order of their Ids. Given a station with Id s, we say that a message queued at station s goes to the right if its `Receiver` attribute is greater than s; otherwise the message goes to the left. The following qualifying function can be used by a transmitter process servicing a port connected to the left-to-right bus:

```
int leftToRight (Message *m) {
  return (TheStation->Id < m->Receiver);
};
```

Now by calling:

```
getPacket (buf, leftToRight, min, max, frm);
```

the transmitter process will try to acquire a packet going to the right.

The concept of a qualifying function is powerful enough to implement all interesting message extraction schemes without resorting to shuffling the messages in their queues. Although technically possible, the latter approach does not seem very entertaining. If you think that tricky qualifying conditions may be difficult to program, note that nonstandard message attributes can assist the qualifying functions.

There exists a variant of qualified getPacket in which the buffer is passed by reference rather than by pointer.

5.4.1.3   Acquiring packets from traffic patterns.

The getPacket methods just described are defined within the Client, and they treat all traffic patterns globally. One possible way of restricting the range of a Client's getPacket to a single traffic pattern is to use one of the two qualified variants with the following qualifying function:

```
int f (Message *m) { return (m->TP == MyTPId); };
```

where MyTPId is the Id of the interesting traffic pattern. There is, however, a better (and more efficient) way to achieve the same result. Namely, all four of Client's versions of getPacket have their counterparts as methods of Traffic. Their configurations of arguments and behavior are identical to those of the corresponding Client's methods with the exception that the search for a message is restricted to the queue handled by the given traffic pattern. This means that an unqualified version of the method acquires the packet from the top message in the queue.

5.4.1.4   Acquiring packets from messages.

The two unqualified variants of getPacket also occur as methods of Message (with the same configurations of arguments). They are useful when the message from which a packet is to be extracted is known a priori. With the call

```
Msg->getPacket (buf, min, max, frm);
```

where Msg points to a message, the caller extracts a packet from Msg and stores it into buf. The algorithm determining the attributes of the new packet is the same as for the other versions of getPacket. Note that there is no need for a qualifying function in this case, as the message from which the packet is to be extracted is indicated explicitly.

Example

The Message variant of getPacket can be used to continue extracting packets from a long message. Consider the following two statements:

```
Client->getPacket (buf, min, max, frm);
Msg = TheMessage;
```

If `Msg` contains something different from NULL, it means that only a part of the message has been turned into the packet; the leftover remains queued and is pointed to by `Msg`. Next time around, we can use this message directly to acquire the next packet, for example:

```
if (Msg)
  Msg->getPacket (buf, min, max, frm);
else
  Client->getPacket (buf, min, max, frm);
Msg = TheMessage;
```

This approach may have some advantage over calling the `Client`'s version of the method repeatedly. If there are multiple traffic patterns (and multiple message queues), we have no guarantee that the subsequent calls to the `Client`'s version of `getPacket` will extract packets from the same message. This is because multiple messages in different queues may have the same earliest arrival time. This problem may be irrelevant, but if it is not, this code provides a simple solution.

There is no way for a `Message` variant of `getPacket` to fail. For compatibility with the other versions, the method always returns YES. If after the packet has been extracted, the message pointed to by `Msg` turns out to be empty (no bits left), its `prev` attribute is examined to determine whether the message belongs to a queue. If `prev` is NULL, it is assumed that the message does not belong to a queue and no further processing is undertaken. Otherwise, the empty message is dequeued and deallocated as an object. The user should make sure that the `prev` attribute of a message created in a nonstandard way (which should not be automatically dequeued by the `Message` version of `getPacket`) contains NULL.

5.4.1.5 Nondestructive inquiries.   Using one of the `getPacket` variants discussed in the previous sections, a process can acquire a packet for transmission or learn that no packet (of the required sort) is available. Sometimes one would like to learn whether a packet can be acquired without actually acquiring it. This is what we call a nondestructive inquiry about a packet. The following two methods of the `Client` are available for this purpose:

```
int isPacket ();
int isPacket (MTTYPE f);
```

The first version of `isPacket` returns YES if there is a message (of any traffic pattern) queued at the current station. Otherwise, the method returns NO. The second version returns YES if a message satisfying the qualifying function `f` (section 5.4.1.2) is queued at the station, and NO otherwise.

Two similar versions of `isPacket` are defined within `Traffic`, and they behave the same as the `Client`'s methods, except that they only look for packets belonging to the indicated traffic pattern.

If isPacket returns YES, the environment variable TheMessage (Info01) of type Message* points to the message located by the method,[4] and TheTraffic (Info02) of type int contains the Id of the traffic pattern to which the message belongs.

No isPacket method is defined for Message.

5.4.2   Wait Requests

When an attempt to acquire a packet for transmission fails (i.e., getPacket returns NO—section 5.4.1.1), the process issuing the inquiry may choose to suspend itself until a message arrives at the station. By issuing the wait request

Client->wait (ARRIVAL, TryAgain);

the process declares that it wants to be awakened when a message (of any traffic pattern) is queued at the station. Thus, the part of the process that takes care of acquiring packets for transmission may be as follows:

```
...
state TryNewPacket:
  if (!Client->getPacket (buf, min, max, frm)) {
    Client->wait (ARRIVAL, TryNewPacket);
    sleep;
  }
...
```

Of course, the order parameter (section 4.4.1) can be specified, as usual, to assign a priority to the Client wait request.

There are two ways of indicating that we are interested in messages belonging to a specific traffic pattern. One way is to put the Id of the traffic pattern in place of ARRIVAL in the preceding call to the Client's wait. The other, recommended solution is to use the Traffic's wait method instead, i.e., to call

TPat->wait (ARRIVAL, TryAgain);

where TPat is the pointer to the traffic pattern in question. Such a call indicates that the process wants to be restarted when a message belonging to the indicated traffic pattern arrives at the station.

The keyword ARRIVAL can be replaced with INTERCEPT, which turns the awaited arrival event into a *priority event* (section 4.6.2.2). The semantics of INTERCEPT are the same as ARRIVAL, except that INTERCEPT gets a higher priority (a lower order) than ARRIVAL, irrespective of the actual values of the order parameters specified with the requests.

Imagine that a process wants to intercept all messages arriving at the station, e.g., to preprocess them by setting some of their nonstandard attributes. At first sight, it would seem natural to program this process in the following way:

---

[4]Note that this is not necessarily the same message that will be located by a subsequent call to getPacket.

```
...
state WaitForMessage:
  Client->wait (ARRIVAL, NextMessage);
state NextMessage:
  ...
```
preprocess the message
```
  ...
```

However, this solution has one serious drawback. Assume that a message arrives at a station within the current ITU and two processes owned by the station are waiting for ARRIVAL. The waking events for both processes are scheduled to occur within the same current ITU, and there is no way to tell which process will *actually* run first (section 4.4.1). One way to make sure that the message preprocessor is run before any process that may use the message is to assign a low order to the wait request issued by the preprocessor and make sure that the other processes specify higher values. Another (safer) solution is to replace ARRIVAL in the wait request issued by the preprocessor with INTERCEPT. INTERCEPT is an event that, like the ARRIVAL event, is triggered when a message arrives and is queued at the station, but the process awaiting INTERCEPT will be given control before any other process waiting for ARRIVAL is awakened. Only one process at a station may be waiting for INTERCEPT at a time, unless each of the multiple INTERCEPT requests is addressed to a different traffic pattern and none of them is addressed to the Client.

The implementation of INTERCEPT is similar to the implementation of *priority signals* (section 4.6.2.2) and the *priority put* operation for mailboxes (section 4.7.6).

Whenever a process is awakened by a message arrival event (ARRIVAL or INTERCEPT), the environment variables TheMessage (of type Message*) and TheTraffic (of type int) (sections 4.4.4, 5.4.1.1) return a pointer to the new message and the Id of the message's traffic pattern, respectively.

5.4.3   Receiving Packets and Emptying Packet Buffers

The Client, understood as the union of all traffic patterns, provides a model of the network's user. This user originates all outgoing traffic at the sender's end, and absorbs all incoming traffic at the recipient's end. The Client wants to keep track of when packets/messages are (successfully) transmitted and when they reach their destinations. This information is primarily used for bookkeeping, i.e., calculating various performance statistics, discussed in detail in section 7.1.2.1. Some Client and Traffic methods provided for this purpose can also be used to program pilot processes for nonstandard traffic patterns.

As soon as a packet is formally received at the final destination, the protocol process handling this operation should execute the following method of the Client:

```
void receive (Packet *pkt, Port *prt);
```

where pkt points to the packet being received and prt is the pointer to the port on which the packet has arrived. The full list of variants of this method are given in section 6.2.13, and its semantics are discussed in section 7.1.2.1. For the purpose of this chapter, we can just view it as a manifestation of the fact that the packet has met its ultimate goal: it has reached the boundary of the network's world. We already saw an application of `receive` in the alternating-bit protocol in section 1.2.4.5.

Another important moment in the life of a packet is when the packet disappears from the view of its original sender. This happens when the sender (actually one of the protocol processes running at the sender) empties the packet buffer by calling

$$\texttt{Buf->release ();}$$

where `Buf` points to the packet buffer. Again, the exact semantics of this operation deal with performance measures, discussed in section 7.1.2.1. We can view `release` as an indication that the sender is done with the packet and it will not process this packet any further. One simple action performed by `release` is clearing the `PF_full` flag of the packet buffer (section 5.2.3). This operation marks the buffer as empty and makes it ready to accommodate a new packet.

The transmitter process of the alternating-bit protocol presented in section 1.2.4.4 `release`s the packet buffer after the packet has been acknowledged by the recipient. It is thus possible (and even typical) that the packet is `received` at the recipient's end before it is `released` by the original sender. Intermediate stations that relay packets originating somewhere else are not expected to `release` them.

Note.   Neither `receive` nor `release` should be executed for packets that do not belong to the `Client` (e.g., the acknowledgment packets in the alternating-bit protocol—section 1.2.4). Packets that have been created "by hand" have no underlying traffic patterns, and consequently they do not belong to the network's virtual user. Such packets are confined to the protocol's domain.

5.5   NONSTANDARD TRAFFIC PATTERNS

In this section we give more information about the internal workings of the `Client` and a few hints about programming nonstandard `Client` processes. The reader may want to skip this section on the first reading.

5.5.1   Suspending and Resuming Traffic Patterns

A traffic pattern is initially active unless the `SCL_off` option was selected upon its creation (section 5.3.4). An active traffic pattern is driven by the standard internal *pilot process* associated with the traffic pattern. The behavior of this process was described in section 5.3.5. Based on the setup parameters of the traffic pattern and its configuration of communication groups, the pilot process generates messages, fills their attributes, and queues them at their sending stations.

A traffic pattern can be activated and deactivated (suspended) dynamically by the protocol program. The following **Traffic** method deactivates an active traffic pattern:

`void suspend ();`

Calling **suspend** has no effect for a traffic pattern already being inactive. An active traffic pattern becomes inactive in the sense that its pilot process is suspended. From now on, the **Client** will not generate any messages described by the deactivated traffic pattern. This does not apply to user-defined pilot processes implementing nonstandard traffic patterns, i.e., the behavior of such processes is not directly affected by **suspend**. There exist tools that can be used by a nonstandard pilot process to perceive the suspended/resumed status of its traffic pattern and respond to the changes in this status.

The following **Traffic** method cancels the effect of **suspend** and resumes a suspended traffic pattern:

`void resume ();`

The operation has absolutely no effect on a traffic pattern that is already resumed when the method is called. Resuming a traffic pattern that was created with SCL_off does not start the standard pilot processes for the traffic pattern. If such a pattern is driven by nonstandard pilot processes supplied by the user, these processes are able to learn about the fact that the traffic pattern has been resumed. Calling **resume** for a suspended traffic pattern driven by the **Client** (SCL_on) has the effect of restarting the pilot process associated with the traffic pattern. The process is resumed at the exact place where it was previously suspended. In particular, if the traffic pattern is bursty (section 5.3.5), the pending message counter is not initialized to zero but left at its previous value.

The two operations are also available as methods of the **Client**. Calling the **Client** variant of a given method has the same effect as calling the method for all traffic patterns at the same time. Thus,

`Client->suspend ();`

deactivates all (active) traffic patterns and

`Client->resume ();`

activates all traffic patterns that are inactive.

It is possible to tell whether a given traffic pattern, or the **Client** perceived as a union of all traffic patterns, is suspended or active. The following two methods of **Traffic** return YES or NO, according to their names:

`int isSuspended ();`
`int isResumed ();`

The same methods exist as attributes of the `Client`. The `Client` is considered suspended if all traffic patterns are suspended, and resumed otherwise.

The most natural application of the suspend/resume feature of traffic patterns is in situations when the modeled network has to undergo a nontrivial[5] startup phase during which no traffic should be offered to the network. In such a case, all traffic patterns can be suspended by the `Root` process before the startup phase and resumed when the startup phase is over.

Note.   Normally, while a traffic pattern is deactivated, the modeled time that passes during that period affects its performance measures. For example, the effective throughput (sections 7.3.5.5, 7.3.5.10) calculated for a traffic pattern that has been suspended for excessive periods of time may be very low, even though the traffic might have been quite heavy during its activity periods. It is recommended to (re)initialize the standard performance measures for the traffic pattern (section 7.1.2.4) whenever its status changes from inactive to active. This suggestion also applies to the entire `Client`. (In most cases, all traffic patterns are deactivated and activated simultaneously.)

Although nonstandard pilot processes programmed by the user are not directly affected by `suspend` and `resume`, such processes are able to learn when their traffic patterns (or the entire `Client`) are suspended or resumed, and they can respond to these operations in a consistent way (section 5.5.3 for an illustration). Besides the two methods `isSuspended` and `isResumed` that can be used to poll a traffic pattern for its status, there exist two events that are triggered by the traffic pattern whenever this status changes:

SUSPEND   The event is triggered whenever the traffic pattern changes its status from resumed to suspended. If a wait request for SUSPEND is issued to a traffic pattern that is already suspended, the event occurs immediately, i.e., within the current ITU.

RESUME   The event is generated whenever the traffic pattern changes its status from suspended to resumed. If a wait request for RESUME is issued to a traffic pattern that is already resumed, the event occurs immediately.

A similar pair of events exists for the `Client`. The `Client` versions of SUSPEND and RESUME are triggered by the `Client` variants of `suspend` and `resume` operations. Such an operation must be *effective* to generate the corresponding event, i.e., the status of at least one traffic pattern must be actually affected by the operation.

5.5.2   Attributes and Methods of Traffic Patterns

In the course of their action, the pilot processes governing the behavior of traffic patterns call a number of methods declared within type `Traffic`. Most of these methods are virtual and user-accessible; consequently, they can be redefined in

---

[5]Meaning "taking some simulated time."

a user-declared subtype of `Traffic`. In this section we discuss briefly the public attributes and methods of traffic patterns that may be useful for implementing pilot processes.

The following attributes of `Traffic` store the options specified in the setup arguments when the traffic pattern was created:

```
char DstMIT, DstMLE, DstBIT, DstBSI, FlgSCL, FlgSUS, FlgSPF;
```

Each of the first four variables can have one of the following values:

UNDEFINED   If the distribution of the corresponding parameter (MIT—message interarrival time, MLE—message length, BIT—burst interarrival time, BSI—burst size) was not defined at the moment when the traffic pattern was created (section 5.3.4)

EXPONENTIAL   If the corresponding parameter is exponentially distributed

UNIFORM   If the corresponding parameter has uniform distribution

FIXED   If the corresponding parameter has a fixed value

The remaining three variables can take values `ON` or `OFF` (1 and 0, respectively). If `FlgSCL` is `OFF`, it means that the standard pilot process of the traffic pattern is permanently disabled. This will happen if the traffic pattern was created with `SCL_off`. The suspended/resumed status of the traffic pattern (which can change dynamically—section 5.5.1) is reflected by the value of `FlgSUS` (`ON` means "suspended" and `OFF` means "resumed").

If `FlgSPF` is `OFF` (`SPF_off` was selected when the traffic pattern was created), no standard performance measures are collected for the traffic pattern. The issues related to gathering performance statistics for traffic patterns are discussed in section 7.1.2.

Neither `DstMIT` nor `DstMLE` can be `UNDEFINED` unless the traffic pattern is permanently suspended, i.e., its behavior is never driven by a standard pilot process. It is possible for a nonstandard pilot process to ignore these distribution parameters, if it uses some other means to determine when messages arrive to the network and how long they are.

The following four pairs of attributes contain the numeric values of the distribution parameters describing the arrival process:

```
double ParMnMIT, ParMxMIT,
       ParMnMLE, ParMxMLE,
       ParMnBIT, ParMxBIT,
       ParMnBSI, ParMxBSI;
```

If the corresponding parameter (MIT—message interarrival time, MLE—message length, BIT—burst interarrival time, BSI—burst size) is exponentially distributed or fixed, the first attribute of a given pair contains the mean value of the distribution[6] and the value of the second attribute is irrelevant. If the parameter

_____
[6]For the fixed distribution, this is the exact value.

in question is uniformly distributed, the two attributes contain the minimum and maximum values. Otherwise, the parameter is undefined and the corresponding attributes have no meaning.

Note. The TIME values, i.e., `ParMnMIT`, `ParMxMIT`, `ParMnBIT`, `ParMxBIT` are kept in ITUs. Although the interarrival times were specified in ETUs when the traffic pattern was created (section 5.3.4), they are kept internally in ITUs—to avoid conversion overhead. Note, however, that their type is `double`, not TIME.

The following virtual methods of `Traffic` take part in the message generation process:

`virtual TIME genMIT ();`

This method is called to generate the time interval elapsing to the next message arrival. The standard version generates a random number according to the message interarrival time distribution.

`virtual Long genMLE ();`

This method is called to determine the message length. The standard version generates a random number according to the message length distribution. This number is guaranteed to be a strictly positive multiple of 8, i.e., it is rounded to the nearest multiple of 8 greater than zero.

`virtual TIME genBIT ();`

The method is called to determine the time interval elapsing to the next burst arrival. The standard version generates a random number according to the burst interarrival time distribution.

`virtual Long genBSI ();`

This method is called to generate the burst size (the number of messages within a burst). The standard version generates a random number according to the burst size distribution.

`virtual int genSND ();`

This method is called to determine the sender of a newly generated message. It returns the station `Id` of the sender, or `NONE` if no sender can be generated. The standard version determines the sender according to the configuration of communication groups associated with the traffic pattern, as discussed in section 5.3.5. Having generated the sender, the method sets the following two attributes of the traffic pattern:

```
Long    LastSender;
CGroup *LastCGroup;
```

LastSender is set to the station Id returned by the method. The pointer to the communication group used to generate the sender is stored in LastCGroup. These values are interpreted by the standard version of genRCV.

```
virtual IPointer genRCV ();
```

This method is called to generate the receiver for a newly generated message. It returns

- The station Id of the receiver, if the receiver is a single station
- A station group pointer, if the receiver is a station group (the broadcast case)
- NONE, if no receiver can be generated

In the second case, the value returned by genRCV must be cast to a station group pointer to be interpreted correctly. In most cases, however, this value is directly assigned to the Receiver attribute of a message. The type of this attribute is IPointer, which is compatible with Long (section 2.2.1); thus, the problem of interpreting the result of genRCV is seldom visible to the user.

Note. Given an integer number representing the Receiver attribute of a message/packet, SMURPH tells the difference between a station Id and a communication group pointer by examining the magnitude of this number. The operation isStationId (section 3.1.2) is used for this purpose. This simple approach is based on the assumption that a heap address can never be confused with a not too big, non-negative number between 0 and NStations − 1.

The standard version of genRCV assumes that LastSender and LastCGroup have been set by a preceding call to genSND. Thus, it only makes sense to call genRCV if genSND was executed a short while ago. The receiver is generated from the communication group pointed to by LastCGroup and is guaranteed to be different from LastSender (section 5.3.5).

```
virtual CGroup *genCGR (Long sid);
CGroup *genCGR (Station *s) {
  return (genCGR (s->Id));
};
```

The standard version of this method returns a pointer to the communication group containing the indicated station in the senders set. The station can be specified either via its Id or as a pointer to the station object. It may happen that the indicated station (assume that it is *s*) occurs in the senders sets of two or more communication groups. In such a case, one of these groups is chosen at random in such a way that the probability of a given group's being selected is equal to the ratio of the sender weight of *s* in this group to the sum of weights of *s* in all senders sets of all communication groups associated with the traffic pattern. The chosen communication group becomes the current group, i.e., its pointer is stored in

LastCGroup, and the Id attribute of the station specified by the argument is stored in LastSender.

One application of genCGR is in a situation when the sender is already known (e.g., it has been selected deterministically or in another nonstandard way), and a matching receiver must be generated (see section 9.4.3.2 for an example). By calling genCGR with the sender passed as the argument, we can prepare the ground for genRCV, so that the receiver will be generated according to the distribution of station weights.

If the specified station does not occur as a sender in any communication group associated with the traffic pattern (i.e., it cannot be a sender for this traffic pattern) genCGR returns NULL. This way the method can also be used to determine whether a station is a legitimate sender for a given traffic pattern.

```
virtual Message *genMSG (Long snd, IPointer rcv, Long lgth);
Message *genMSG (Long snd, SGroup *rcv, Long lgth);
Message *genMSG (Station *snd, Station *rcv, Long lgth);
Message *genMSG (Station *snd, SGroup *rcv, Long lgth);
```

This method is called to generate a new message and queue it at the sender. The sender station is indicated by the first argument, which can be either a station Id or a station object pointer. The second argument can identify a station (in the same way as the first argument) or a station group for a broadcast message. The last argument is the message length in bits.

The new message is queued at the indicated sender at the end of the queue corresponding to the given traffic pattern (section 5.3.7). A pointer to the message is also returned as the function value. If the action of genMSG is void because of the queue size limitations (section 5.3.7), the method returns NULL and generates no message.

Note.   Although declared as virtual, genMSG should not be redefined by the user.

Five more virtual methods of Traffic, intended to facilitate the collection of nonstandard performance measures, are discussed in section 7.1.2.3.

5.5.3   Programming Traffic Patterns

With the collection of methods presented in section 5.5.2, the task of describing the behavior of a traffic pattern is reasonably simple. Here we list the complete formal definitions of the standard pilot processes that were introduced informally in section 5.3.5. We start from the process driving a nonbursty traffic pattern.

```
process PilotNB {
  Traffic *TPat;
  void setup (Traffic *tp) { TPat = tp; };
  states {Wait, Generate};
```

```
perform {
  Long ml; int sn;
  state Wait:
    Timer->wait (TPat->genMIT (), Generate);
  state Generate:
    if (TPat->isSuspended ())
      TPat->wait (RESUME, Wait);
    else {
      sn = TPat->genSND ();
      ml = TPat->genMLE ();
      TPat->genMSG (sn, TPat->genRCV (), ml);
      proceed Wait;
    }
};
};
```

This process is logically equivalent to the standard pilot process actually run by SMURPH for a nonbursty traffic pattern. In reality, this process is somewhat disguised: for efficiency reasons there is just a single Client *service process* that emulates the behavior of all standard pilot processes for all active traffic patterns. However, functionally, there is no difference between the behavior of those emulated pilot processes and the behavior of PilotNB, except for handling abnormal conditions.[7] Note that the process detects when the traffic pattern becomes suspended (section 5.5.1) and refrains from generating traffic until the traffic pattern is resumed. The same way of responding to suspend/resume operations is recommended for user-programmed nonstandard pilot processes.

Now let us take care of the bursty traffic patterns. For this occasion, it is natural to prepare two pilot processes: one modeling burst arrival, the other responsible for generating individual messages. We start from the second process.

```
process PilotBM (Station, PilotBB) {
  Traffic *TPat;
  void setup (Traffic *tp) { TPat = tp; };
  states {Wait, Generate};
  perform {
    Long ml; int sn;
    state Wait:
      Timer->wait (TPat->genMIT (), Generate);
    state Generate:
      if (TPat->isSuspended ())
        TPat->wait (RESUME, Wait);
      else {
```

---

[7]For clarity, error-checking statements have been excluded from the presented version of the pilot process.

```
          sn = TPat->genSND ();
          ml = TPat->genMLE ();
          TPat->genMSG (sn, TPat->genRCV (), ml);
          if (--(F->PMC))
            proceed Wait;
          else
            terminate;
      }
   };
};
```

It should not be surprising that this process is very similar to its predecessor. The only difference is the presence of argument types and the added if statement at the end of the second state. Only the second argument type is relevant; it specifies the type of the process's parent—this will be the burst generation process. The message generator keeps on producing messages as long as the PMC counter of its parent process in nonzero. Each time a message is generated, PMC is decremented by 1. When the counter reaches zero, the process terminates itself.

The burst generator is defined as follows:

```
process PilotBB {
  Traffic *TPat;
  Long PMC;
  void setup (Traffic *tp) { TPat = tp; PMC = 0; };
  states {Wait, Generate};
  perform {
    Long oldPMC;
    state Wait:
      Timer->wait (TPat->genBIT (), Generate);
    state Generate:
      if (TPat->isSuspended ())
        TPat->wait (RESUME, Wait);
      else {
        oldPMC = PMC;
        PMC += TPat->genBSI ();
        if (!oldPMC && PMC) create PilotBM (TPat);
        proceed Wait;
      }
  };
};
```

Whenever a new burst is generated, the process adds its size (the number of messages to be generated within the burst) to PMC. If the previous value in PMC was zero and the new value is nonzero (it can never be negative), the message generator is created and it lives for as long as PMC remains greater than zero.

Note that to correctly interpret the suspended status of the traffic pattern, both processes, i.e., `PilotBM` and `PilotBB` have to sense this status. When the traffic pattern is suspended, `PilotBM` will be stopped in the middle of the current burst and `PilotBB` will refrain from generating more bursts until the traffic pattern is resumed.

If the built-in standard operation of traffic patterns is insufficient to express a tricky message arrival process, the user has three options:

- To substitute some of the virtual methods defined in type `Traffic` with their customized versions. For example, by replacing `genMIT` (section 5.5.2) the user may implant a private distribution of the message interarrival time into the standard pilot process.
- To leave the methods intact, but to provide a private pilot process. This way, the standard traffic generation procedures outlined in section 5.3.5 can be replaced with a user-defined algorithm.
- Combine the two approaches, i.e., program the traffic pattern from scratch.

Of course, the last solution is seldom, if ever, used. In most cases, the desired traffic generator is obtained with a few modifications to the standard procedure.

Example

Assume that we need a traffic pattern in which the message interarrival time has distribution β (section 2.3.1). This may correspond to a process in which the distribution is intentionally fixed but varies slightly because of the limited accuracy of the source. The other parameters of the message arrival process can be described using the standard means, e.g., the message length is fixed and the distribution of senders and receivers is even. All we have to do to define such a traffic pattern is to provide a nonstandard version of **genMIT**. Our definition may look as follows:

```
traffic MyPattern {
  int Quality;
  TIME genMIT () {
    return tRndTolerance (ParMnMIT, ParMxMIT, Quality);
  };
  void setup (double ml, double mnmit, double mxmit, int q) {
    Quality = q;
    Traffic::setup (MIT_unf+MLE_fix, mnmit, mxmit, ml);
    addSender (ALL);
    addReceiver (ALL);
  };
};
```

The standard pilot process for this traffic pattern is initialized as if the message interarrival time were uniformly distributed. The two standard attributes `ParMnMIT` and `ParMxMIT` are set by the standard setup method—as for a uniform interarrival time. They are later used by the customized version of **genMIT** to generate the actual interarrival time according to the β distribution.

Nonstandard pilot processes are mostly needed to implement correlated traffic patterns, e.g., in which received packets may trigger some events affecting the behavior of the traffic generator.

Example

Consider the alternating-bit protocol in section 1.2.4. The traffic generator used there operates independently of the rate at which the packets are absorbed by the network. We may try to modify it in such a way that no new messages are generated while the sender is waiting for an acknowledgment. Having generated a message, the pilot process will suspend itself until the message has been acknowledged. Then it will wake up, wait for a random amount of time determined by the interarrival time distribution, and generate another message.

To implement this simple modification, we have to supply our own version of the pilot process for the traffic pattern described by `TrafficType`. This process may look as follows:

```
process PilotAP (SenderType) {
  TrafficType *TP;
  Mailbox *Alert;
  void setup (TrafficType *tp) {
    TP = tp;
    Alert = S->AlertMailbox;
  };
  states {Wait, Generate};
  perform {
    Long ml; int sn;
    state Wait:
      Timer->wait (TP->genMIT (), Generate);
    state Generate:
      sn = TP->genSND ();
      ml = TP->genMLE ();
      TP->genMSG (sn, TP->genRCV (), ml);
      Alert->wait (NEWITEM, Wait);
  };
};
```

Note that the new pilot process is designed to run at the sender station. It accesses the station's mailbox, which is shared by the acknowledgment receiver and the transmitter. The event awaited by the pilot process on the mailbox is `NEWITEM`. Note that it does not interfere with the `RECEIVE` event awaited by the transmitter. When an alert is put into the mailbox by the acknowledgment receiver, both waiting processes will be restarted and the transmitter will remove the alert (section 4.7.4).

The only other modification required to put our pilot process to work is a slight adjustment of the `Root` method `defineTraffic`. Namely, `SCL_off` must be added to the traffic flags (to switch off the standard pilot process) and the statement

```
create (Sender) PilotAP (tp);
```

must be included, e.g., as the last statement of the method. Note that this statement must be executed after the traffic pattern has been created, as the traffic pattern pointer is the setup argument of the pilot process.

Sometimes the traffic pattern that we would like to model is *trace-driven*, i.e., it comes from measurements performed on a real physical configuration of communicating peers. In such a case, the arrival process is described by a sequence of empirical numbers specifying the arrival time, the sender/receiver pair and the message length. These numbers are typically stored in a file. Although SMURPH offers no explicit tools for implementing such traffic patterns, they are very easy to program.

Example

Assume that a file contains a list of quadruplets of the following form:

atime sender receiver length

describing an empirical (trace-driven) message arrival process. A SMURPH traffic pattern modeling this process can be defined in the following way:

```
traffic ETraffic {
  istream *IF;
  void setup (const char *fn) {
    IF = new istream (fn, "r");
    Traffic::setup (SCL_off);
  };
};
```

The setup method opens a file (an *input stream*, in the terminology of C++)[8] expected to contain a list of quadruplets describing the message arrival process. No attributes of the traffic pattern are defined, except for SCL_off, which permanently deactivates the standard pilot processes. This way, the Client will not attempt to use the traffic pattern to generate messages automatically. Note that this would not work, as the standard arrival parameters are left unspecified. The arrival algorithm will be described completely by the list of quadruplets read from a file. The name of this file will be specified when the traffic pattern is created.

A pilot process for our traffic pattern may look as follows:

```
process ETPilot {
  ETraffic *ETP;
  istream *IF;
  Long MLength, From, To;
  void setup (ETraffic *tp) { ETP = tp; IF = ETP->IF; };
  states {Wait, Generate};
```

---

[8]In this example, we assume that the package has been installed with its private i/o library (section B.1). Stream constructors and methods in other libraries may differ slightly from our tools, but these differences only affect the syntax of some operations.

```
perform {
  TIME t;
  state Wait:
    IF >> t;
    if (IF->eof ()) {
      delete IF;
      terminate;
    }
    IF >> From;
    IF >> To;
    IF >> MLength;
    assert (t >= Time, "Illegal arrival time");
    Timer->wait (t - Time, Generate);
  state Generate:
    ETP->genMSG (From, To, MLength);
    proceed Wait;
};
};
```

Upon creation, the process receives a pointer to the traffic pattern to be serviced. In its simple operation cycle, the process reads the quadruplets from the traffic pattern's input stream and interprets them until the end of file is reached. Then the pilot process closes the input stream and terminates itself.

It is not difficult to guess how the generation process is initialized. Assume that the list of quadruplets is in file **trafficdata**. The following sequence of statements, executed from the **Root** process, starts the traffic pattern:

```
ETraffic *EP;
...
EP = create ETraffic ("trafficdata");
create (System) ETPilot (EP);
```

Of course, it is possible to have multiple instances of **ETraffic** driven by different input files. Note, however, that the standard data file cannot be used for this purpose: it is closed immediately after the network initialization phase has been completed (section 2.3.2).

BIBLIOGRAPHIC NOTES

The role of the Poisson (exponential) distribution in modeling generic arrival processes is discussed in many textbooks on probability and statistics, e.g., *Feller* (1971), *Fisz* (1963), *Freund* (1992), and *S. Ross* (1989). The last book gives methods of simulating the Poisson distribution by the uniform distribution. Books on network performance analysis, e.g., *Schwartz* (1987) and *Stuck and Arthurs* (1985), and simulation, e.g., *Bratley, Fox, and Schrage* (1987), *Ross* (1990), and *Matloff* (1988), also cover this subject. In *Stuck and Arthurs* (1985), *Freeman* (1989), and *Spragins, Hammond, and Pawlikowski* (1991) the reader will find information about other distributions useful for modeling telecommunication systems. *Knuth* (1973) mentions the Zipf distribution and comments on its rule-of-thumb application for approximating many skewed distributions occurring in real life (see also *Zipf* (1949)).

The limitations of simple Poisson-based traffic models have been signaled by *Leland et al.* (1994) in the context of local area networking and *Paxson and Floyd* (1994) (in wide area networks). More realistic models of various traffic scenarios have been proposed recently by many authors, e.g., *Frost and Melamed* (1994), *Heyman and Lakshman* (1994), and *Stamoulis, Anagnostou, and Georgantas* (1994). Although the last paper addresses the issue of traffic models for ATM networks, the reader will find its contents relevant to networking in general.

PROBLEMS

1. Rewrite the definition of the traffic pattern in the alternating-bit protocol (section 1.2.4.9) using station and communication groups.

2. Write a qualifying function for the **Traffic** variant of **getPacket** selecting the last message from the queue.

3. Implement the modification to the alternating-bit protocol described in section 5.5.3. Determine the maximum throughput achieved by the modified protocol, and compare it with the maximum throughput achieved by the original version. Explain the results.

4. Write a SMURPH program implementing the sample traffic patterns discussed in section 5.3.5, and validate experimentally that the senders and receivers obey the intended distribution rules.

5. Write the full definitions of **genMIT**, **genMLE**, **genBIT**, **genBSI** implementing the standard functions of these methods, as described in section 5.5.2.

6. Among the virtual methods listed in section 5.5.2, **genMSG** is the trickiest one and the user should not try to replace it. Describe the actions performed by **genMSG**. Which of them require some knowledge about the interior of SMURPH to implement?

7. Instead of creating a complicated collection of communication groups, it is possible to provide substitutes for the standard methods **genSND** and **genRCV**. Write such methods for the sample traffic patterns discussed in section 5.3.5 and redefine these traffic patterns without using explicit or implicit communication groups.

8. Assume that a hypothetical transmitter process wants to acquire packets for transmission only if the length of the message queue is greater than l, where l is a parameter that can be specified by the process. Implement tools that could be used by the transmitter to acquire packets and await the interesting message arrival events.

9. Define the traffic type and program the pilot processes for a two-level bursty traffic pattern in which bursts arrive in bursts. Can you generalize your solution to k burst levels, where k is a parameter?

10. Design and implement a message preprocessor (section 5.4.2) that effectively changes the order in which messages are queued at the station to LIFO (i.e., turns the message queues into stacks).

6

The Port AI

6.1 ACTIVITIES

Links are not directly visible to protocol processes. The only place where they are explicitly referenced is in the network creation program executed by `Root` during the initialization phase (section 3.2). The interface between links and protocol processes is provided by ports. In this chapter, we give the functional characteristics of ports as perceived by protocol processes. Of course, it is impossible to talk about these characteristics without referring to links as the actual objects in which "things happen." Therefore, it may be helpful to visualize multiple ports connected to the same link as different fragments of the same activity interpreter—the Link AI. We say "something is inserted into the link" or "something is received from the link" when actually, as viewed by the process, the corresponding operations are performed on a port. It should be clear that when we say "the link" while talking about a port, we mean the link to which the port in question is attached.

There are three reasons why a process may wish to reference a port:

- To insert into the port (and thus into the underlying link) an *activity*, e.g., a packet
- To *inquire* the port about its current or past status, e.g., to check whether an activity is heard on the port
- To issue a *wait request* to the port, e.g., to await an activity to arrive at the port in the future

Two types of activities can be inserted into ports, namely *packet activities* and *jamming signals*. A packet activity carries a packet that represents some structured

174

portion of information exchanged between stations. A packet possesses a number of standard attributes (sections 5.2.2, 5.4.1.1) identifying, among other things, its original sender and the intended recipient. Packets model the transmission units exchanged between nodes in the data-link layer (section 1.1.2.2). Usually, the information passed in packets has been acquired from the Client and comes from the *user traffic* offered to the network. The operation of inserting a packet activity into a port is called a *packet transmission*.

Jamming signals (or jams for short) are special activities that are clearly distinguishable from packets. Their role is to model any special signals possibly required by the MAC-level protocol, e.g., packet preambles in FDDI (section 10.3.4.2) or collision jams in Ethernet (section 8.1.1.3). Although in principle such signals can be implemented by special (nonstandard) packets, the existence of jamming signals simplifies protocol programming in many cases. The name *jamming signals* is the legacy of an early version of our package, in which the primary purpose of the jamming signals was to represent the so-called collision jams used to enforce *collision consensus* in bus protocols based on collision detection.[1] Since then SMURPH has been used to model many other protocols, including collision-free protocols, which have no use for collision jams but often employ other special activities that can be conveniently modeled as jamming signals.

6.1.1 Processing of Activities in Links

Any activity inserted into a link must be explicitly started and explicitly terminated. When an activity is started, an internal object representing the activity is built and added to the link. The actual structure of this object is irrelevant from the user's point of view. Activities are entirely invisible and their contents are protected; thus, the protocol program cannot access activities (or their attributes) directly. However, we will mention some of those attributes and describe their role. This will help us explain how activities are processed and transformed into port events.

One attribute of an activity is its type: it sets apart packet activities from jamming signals. The *starting time* attribute tells the time (in ITUs) when the activity was started on its source port. Another attribute, the *finished time*, indicates the time when the activity was terminated. The difference between the *finished time* and the *starting time* is called the *duration* of the activity. One more activity attribute identifies its source port, i.e., the port on which the activity was inserted into the link.

If an activity represents a packet transmission, the packet structure is embedded into the activity structure and becomes its attribute. For simplicity, we usually make no distinction between an activity carrying a packet and the packet itself except where necessary to avoid confusion. This simplification is warranted by the fact that the only attribute of a packet activity directly perceptible by the protocol program is the packet carried by this activity. One should, however, keep

---

[1] These issues are discussed in more detail in section 8.1.1.3.

in mind that when we say "packet" meaning "a packet-carrying activity," we are talking about something more than just the packet.

The *finished time* attribute of an activity that has been started but not yet terminated is undefined, and so is the activity's duration. These elements become defined when the activity is terminated.

The rules describing how activities propagate along links were discussed in section 5.4.1.1. Assume that p_1 and p_2 are two ports connected to the same link. If the link is a regular broadcast link, the distance from p_1 to p_2 is the same as the distance from p_2 to p_1. For a unidirectional link, exactly one of the two distances is finite and the other is assumed to be infinite. If the distance from p_1 to p_2 is infinite, it means that no activity inserted into p_1 will ever reach p_2. For uniformity, we may think of the distance between a pair of ports belonging to different links as being always infinite.

If an activity is started on p_1 at time t_s, the beginning of this activity will arrive at p_2 at $t_s + D_{p_1,p_2}$, where D_{p_1,p_2} is the distance between $p1$ and $p2$ (an element of the link distance matrix—section 3.2.1). Similarly, if the activity is terminated at t_f, its end will be recognized at p_2 at $t_f + D_{p_1,p_2}$. Thus, given an activity and the link distance matrix, one can predict when the activity will be heard on any port connected to the same link as the activity's originating port.[2]

Two sets of activities are associated with each link. One set contains the *alive activities*, i.e., activities that at the given moment are "physically" present in the link. The other set is called the link *archive* and contains activities that have disappeared from the link. If an activity that was started on port p is terminated at time t, it will be removed from the alive set at time $t + d_{max}$, where d_{max} is the maximum distance from p to another port connected to the same link. Then the activity will be put into the link archive, where it will be kept for the amount of time determined by the link's *archival period*. The archival period is defined upon the link creation (section 3.2.2). If the length of this period is zero, no link archive is maintained and all activities that "physically" leave the link are immediately discarded and forgotten. The link archive can be viewed as a database describing the history of the link during some time window terminating at the current moment.

6.1.2   Starting and Terminating Activities

The two types of activities are terminated in the same way, but they are started differently. To start a packet transmission, one has to specify the packet buffer, whereas a jamming signal is just started and, besides its presence, carries no other information.

6.1.2.1   Packet transmissions.
The following port method can be used to start a packet transmission on the port (insert a packet activity into the port):

---

[2]One can also predict when the activity will be heard on a port connected to another link— never.

$$\text{void startTransfer (Packet *buf);}$$

where `buf` points to the buffer containing the packet to be transmitted (section 5.2.3). The method builds a data structure representing the new link activity, makes a duplicate of the packet pointed to by `buf`, and inserts this duplicate into the activity data structure. Then the activity is added to the pool of alive link activities. The starting time attribute of the activity is set to the current time (the contents of the global variable `Time`—section 4.4.4). The finished time is undefined and will remain so until the transmission has been terminated.

The pointer to the packet duplicate that has become part of the new activity inserted into the link is returned via the environment variable `ThePacket` (`Info01`) of type `Packet*`. This pointer can be used to reference the packet's instance that will be actually propagated along the link. The contents of the original packet (pointed to by `buf`) can be modified, e.g., erased, while the packet is being transmitted, without affecting the transmitted copy.

Another environment variable, `TheTraffic` (`Info02`) of type `int`, returns the TP attribute of the transmitted packet, i.e., the `Id` attribute of the traffic pattern to which the packet belongs.

A started packet transmission can be terminated in two ways. The port method

$$\text{int stop ();}$$

completes the transmission of the packet inserted by a previous call to `startTransfer`. A packet transmission terminated this way ends *normally*, which means that the packet trailer is formally appended to the packet and the packet's structure is complete. Another way to terminate a packet transmission is to call the port method

$$\text{int abort ();}$$

With `abort` the packet transmission is aborted, i.e., the packet is interrupted in the middle and presumed incomplete.

Formally, the amount of time needed to transmit a packet on a given port is equal to the product of the total packet length and the port transmission rate (section 3.3.1). Thus, a sample process code for transmitting a packet may look as follows:

```
...
state Transmit:
  MyPort->startTransfer (buffer);
  Timer->wait (buffer->TLength*MyPort->TRate, Done);
state Done:
  MyPort->stop ();
  ...
```

or at least it might look so if attribute `TRate` were not `private` within `Port`.

Note that there is no automatically enforced relation between a packet's length and its transmission time. The transmission is terminated explicitly by the protocol when the transmitting process concludes that the packet has been transmitted entirely (or that the transfer has to be aborted). Thus, the time spent on transmitting a packet need not have much to do with the contents of the packet's `TLength` attribute. This time is determined by the interval between the moments when the transmission of the packet was stopped and started. In particular, if a process starts transmitting a packet and then forgets to terminate it (by `stop` or `abort`), the packet will be transmitted forever.

In the majority of cases, the user would like to transmit the packet for the amount of time determined by the packet length multiplied by the port transmission rate, possibly aborting the transmission earlier if a special condition occurs. The port method

```
void transmit (Packet *buf, int done);
```

starts transmitting the packet pointed to by `buf` and automatically sets up the `Timer` to wake up the process in state `done` when the transmission is complete. The transmission still has to be terminated explicitly. Thus, the preceding code fragment is equivalent to

```
        ...
        state Transmit:
          MyPort->transmit (buffer, Done);
        state Done:
          MyPort->stop ();
        ...
```

Sometimes it is useful to know how much time it would take to transmit a packet on a given port without actually transmitting the packet. For example, imagine that a transmitting process has to delay its transmission by the amount of time required by some other process to transmit its packet without interference. Given a number of bits, the amount of time needed to transmit them on a given port can be obtained by directly multiplying this number by the port transmission rate. This operation is performed by the following port method:

```
TIME bitsToTime (int n = 1);
```

which converts a number of bits specified in the argument to the number of ITUs required to transmit these bits on the port. This conversion is performed by multiplying the integer argument by the port's transmission rate. Note that when the method returns zero (for a nonzero argument), it means that the transmission rate of the port is zero and the port cannot be used for transmission.

The transmission rate of a port can be changed dynamically by calling the following `Port` method:

```
RATE setTRate (RATE r);
```

where r is the new rate. The method returns the previous transmission rate of the port. As we said in section 3.3.1, different ports connected to the same link can have different transmission rates. The possibility of changing port transmission rates dynamically may be useful in modeling variable-rate channels, e.g., virtual channels with dynamically allocable bandwidth. It is also possible to change with one operation the transmission rates of all ports connected to a given link. This is accomplished by calling the following method associated with type Link:

```
void setTRate (RATE r);
```

Note that the Link variant of setTRate returns no value. It resets the transmission rates of all ports connected to the link, including the ports whose transmission rates were zero, to the value specified in the argument.

There is no getTRate method that would return the current transmission rate of a port.[3] Note, however, that the current rate of the port pointed to by p can be obtained by calling p->bitsToTime(), which returns the number of ITUs needed to insert a single bit into the port.

6.1.2.2 Jamming signals.   The port method

```
void startJam ();
```

starts emitting a jamming signal on the port. As with packet transmissions, jams must be explicitly terminated by stop or abort; in this case, both methods have identical semantics.

It is possible to start emitting a jamming signal and at the same time set the Timer for a specific amount of time. A call to the port method

```
void sendJam (TIME d, int done);
```

is equivalent to the sequence

```
MyPort->startJam ();
Timer->wait (d, done);
```

Both stop and abort return an integer value that tells the type of the terminated activity. This value can be either TRANSFER or JAM. It is illegal to attempt to interrupt a nonexistent activity, i.e., to execute stop or abort on an idle port.

If the terminated activity was a packet transmission, two environment variables ThePacket and TheTraffic are set—as for startTransfer or transmit. The first one points to the packet whose transmission is being terminated, the second tells the Id of the traffic pattern to which the packet belongs.

---

[3]Besides, attribute TRate cannot be referenced directly, because it is declared as **private** within Port.

Note. It is illegal to insert more than one activity at a time into a single port, i.e., if an activity is being inserted into a port, it must be terminated before another activity can be started on the same port. Note, however, that it is perfectly legitimate to have two ports connected to the same link and separated by the distance of zero ITUs. Such ports can be viewed as multiple instances of the same port. In fact, their locations on the link are indistinguishable. This way two or more activities can be inserted simultaneously into the same point on a link.

6.2   WAIT REQUESTS

The first argument of a wait request addressed to a port is a symbolic constant that identifies the event type. Later in this section we give the complete list of event types for the **Port AI** and, for each event type, explain the circumstances under which events of this type occur. By *circumstances* we mean configurations of activities in the link to which the port is connected.

To put this discussion on a formal ground, suppose that a wait request has been issued to a port p connected to a link l and that the set $A = \langle a_1, \ldots, a_n \rangle$ describes the configuration of activities in l as perceived by p. Each a_i from A has the following structure:

$$a_i = (k_i, s_i, f_i),$$

where k_i is the activity type, s_i is the starting time of a_i relative to p, and f_i is the finished time of a_i (also relative to p). Thus, s_i is equal to $\overline{s_i} + D_{p_i,p}$, where $D_{p_i,p}$ is the distance from the port on which the activity was inserted to p, and $\overline{s_i}$ is the actual starting time of the activity on port p_i. A similar transformation is performed on the *finished time* attribute. We assume that infinity augmented by anything non-negative remains infinity.

The activity type can be *transfer* (representing a packet transmission in progress or a packet transmission terminated by **stop**—section 6.1.2.1), *aborted* (indicating a packet transmission terminated by **abort**), or *jam* (which stands for a jamming signal).

By making the time attributes of the activities in A relative to p, we can ignore their originating ports. Moreover, we postulate that if s_i turns out to be infinite (i.e., the activity is not ever going to be heard on p), the activity does not appear in A. Thus, A contains only those activities that are actually perceived by p.[4] Note that f_i can be temporarily infinite but s_i is always finite.

At the moment when a process issues a port wait request, the current configuration of activities in the link (the set A) is examined and the occurrence time for the specified event is calculated based on this configuration. If later, while the wait request remains pending, something changes in the set of link activities that may result in a new prediction for the occurrence time of the awaited event, the

---

[4]A similar preprocessing of the link activities is performed by the simulator when it determines the timing of port events.

new configuration of link activities is reexamined and the event may be rescheduled accordingly. For example, assume that a process has issued a wait request to port p for the nearest beginning of a packet activity, but no such activity is currently present in the link. Clearly, the predicted time of occurrence for the awaited event is infinity. If a while later (or even within the same ITU, but *after* the wait request was issued), some process starts a packet transmission on a port connected to the same link as p, the event will be rescheduled to a definite time.[5]

The semantics of particular events that can be awaited on ports will be given in two parts: informally and formally. The informal part should be intuitively clear. It is quite possible that the reader (and also the author) could live happily without the formal part. The role of the formal part is to avoid any misunderstanding, however remote its possibility might be. In the formal description, we assume a static configuration of link activities (the set A) and give a condition that this configuration must satisfy in order for the awaited event to occur at time t. In the light of what we said in the preceding paragraph, such a description should read "the event occurs at the earliest moment t, not preceding the current time, when the configuration of activities in the link fulfills the specified condition."

For the purpose of this section, we assume that links are error-free, i.e., all activities inserted into a link reach all ports connected to the link[6] with no errors. Faulty links are discussed in section 6.4, and we explain there how the semantics of port events are affected by link errors.

The capital letter T stands for the current time, i.e., the contents of the system variable Time at the moment when the wait request is issued.

6.2.1   SILENCE

This event occurs at the beginning of the nearest silence period perceived by the port. The condition of its occurrence at time t is as follows:

$$\forall_{a_i \in A}(s_i > t \lor f_i \le t).$$

This condition describes all time instances when the port does not sense any activity. If no activity is heard on the port when the request is issued, the event occurs immediately, i.e., within the current ITU.

Note that the last ITU of an activity, i.e., the moment when the activity was finished does not count in the activity's duration time. This ITU may be the first ITU of a silence period, provided that no other activity is heard on the port at that time.

---

[5]Assuming the link is bidirectional or the port on which the packet is transmitted is located upstream of p.

[6]For a unidirectional link, we mean all ports located downstream from the port of insertion.

6.2.2 ACTIVITY

The event occurs at the beginning of the nearest activity heard on the port. The activity must be preceded by a silence period to trigger the event, i.e., two or more activities that overlap (from the viewpoint of the sensing port) are treated as a single continuous activity. If an activity is heard on the port when the request is issued, the event occurs within the current ITU.

Formally, the event is described by the following alternative of two conditions:

$$t = T \wedge \exists_{a_i \in A}(s_i \leq t \wedge f_i > t)$$

or

$$\exists_{a_i \in A}(s_i = t \wedge \forall_{a_j \in A, a_j \neq a_i}(s_j \geq t \vee f_j < t)).$$

The first condition describes the situation when an activity is heard at the port at the moment the wait request is issued. The second condition says that the event occurs at the moment when the beginning of an activity is heard at the port, provided that

- If any other activity is heard at the same time, that activity is just starting.
- No other activity terminates at this time.

Note that if an activity terminates at the moment when another activity starts (takes over), the two activities are treated as a continuous activity period (i.e., the event is not triggered at this moment, unless the wait request is just being issued).

6.2.3 BOT

The event (Beginning Of Transmission) occurs as soon as the port perceives the nearest beginning of a packet activity. The event occurs even if the packet activity overlaps with other activities, so it is up to the protocol process to recognize and interpret such situations. The simple formal condition for the occurrence of this event is as follows:

$$\exists_{a_i \in A}(k_i \neq jam \wedge s_i = t).$$

Note that a packet transmission terminated by abort (section 6.1.2.1) also triggers the BOT event.

6.2.4 EOT

The event (End Of Transmission) occurs when the nearest end of a packet terminated by stop (section 6.1.2.1) is heard at the port. Aborted transfer attempts, i.e., packets terminated by abort, do not trigger this event. As with BOT, an EOT event is recognized, even if some other activities are heard on the port when the event occurs. Formally, the event is described by the following condition:

$$\exists_{a_i \in A}(k_i = transfer \wedge f_i = t).$$

Although the end of an aborted packet transmission does not trigger EOT, it may trigger other events, e.g., SILENCE.

6.2.5   BMP

The event (Beginning of My Packet) occurs when the port perceives the beginning of a packet for which the current station (the one whose process issues the wait request) is the receiver (or one of the receivers, for a broadcast packet). This event is triggered even if other activities are heard on the port at the same time; thus, it is up to the protocol to detect and interpret such situations.

The formal condition describing this event is similar to the condition for the BOT event, except that the `Receiver` attribute of the packet carried by a_i must either be equal to `TheStation->Id` or point to a station group (section 5.3.1) containing the current station as a member.

6.2.6   EMP

The event (End of My Packet) occurs when the port perceives the end of a packet for which the current station is the receiver (or one of the receivers, for a broadcast packet). The event is only triggered if the packet was terminated by `stop`, but other activities heard on the port at the same time have no impact on the perception of the event.

The formal condition describing this event is similar to the condition for EOT, except that the `Receiver` attribute of the packet carried by a_i must either be equal to `TheStation->Id` or point to a station group (section 5.3.1) containing the current station as a member.

6.2.7   BOJ

The event (Beginning Of a Jamming signal) occurs when the port hears the nearest beginning of a jamming signal preceded by anything not being a jamming signal. If a number of jams overlap (according to the port's perception), only the first of those jams triggers the BOJ event, i.e., overlapping jams are heard as one continuous jamming signal. If a jam is being heard on the port when the request is issued, the event occurs immediately, i.e., within the current ITU.

As for ACTIVITY, the formal condition for this event consists of two alternative conditions:

$$t = T \wedge \exists_{a_i \in A}(k_i = jam \wedge s_i \leq t \wedge f_i > t)$$

or

$$\exists_{a_i \in A}(k_i = jam \wedge s_i = t \wedge \forall_{a_j \in A,(a_j \neq a_i \wedge k_j = jam)}(s_j \geq t \vee f_j < t)).$$

These conditions bear a close resemblance to the conditions for the ACTIVITY event, except that they ignore packet activities.

6.2.8   EOJ

The event (End Of a Jamming signal) occurs when the port hears the nearest end of a jamming signal (followed by anything not being a jamming signal). Two (or more) overlapping jams are heard as one, so the end of the last of such jamming signals will trigger the event. If no jam is heard when the request is issued, the event **does not** occur.

The formal condition for this event is as follows:

$$\exists_{a_i \in A}(k_i = jam \wedge f_i = t \wedge \forall_{a_j \in A, (a_j \neq a_i \wedge k_j = jam)}(s_j > t \vee f_j \leq t)).$$

This condition says that there exists a jam terminating at t, no jam continues past t, and no new jam is started at t. If a jamming signal starts exactly at the moment when another jamming signal terminates, the sensing port perceives the two activities as a single continuous jam.

6.2.9 ANYEVENT

This event occurs whenever the port begins to sense a new activity or stops sensing some activity. Overlapping activities are separated, e.g., two overlapping activities generate four separate events, unless some of those events occur within the same ITU. Although formally two activities starting (terminating) at the same time still generate two separate events, these events occur simultaneously, and they cannot be automatically told apart by the awakened process.

Formally, the condition for ANYEVENT is given by the following formula:

$$\exists_{a_i \in A}(s_i = t \vee f_i = t).$$

Note that the end of an aborted packet transmission triggers ANYEVENT, although it does not trigger EOT.

6.2.10 COLLISION

The event occurs when the earliest collision is sensed on the port. If a collision is present on the port when the request is issued, the event occurs immediately.

For any link type other than CLink (section 3.2.1) the formal condition for collision is described by the following alternative of conditions:

$$t = T \wedge \exists_{a_i \in A}(k_i = jam \wedge s_i \leq t \wedge f_i > t)$$

or

$$t = T \wedge \exists_{a_i, a_j \in A, a_i \neq a_j}(s_i \leq t \wedge f_i > t \wedge s_j \leq t \wedge f_j \leq t)$$

or

$$\exists_{a_i \in A}(s_i = t \wedge (k_i = jam \vee \exists_{a_j \in A, a_j \neq a_i}(s_j \leq t \wedge f_j > t)))$$

$$\wedge$$

$$\nexists_{a_i \in A}(a_i = jam \wedge s_i < t \wedge f_i \geq t)$$

$$\wedge$$

$$\nexists_{a_i, a_j \in A, a_i \neq a_j}(s_i < t \wedge s_j < t \wedge f_i \geq t \wedge f_j \geq t).$$

This somewhat complicated condition can be explained in simple words. By a collision, we mean a situation when the port perceives at least one jamming signal or two or more overlapping packet transmissions. This is stated by the first two components of the formula. They describe the situation of a collision being present at the port when the wait request is issued. The remaining parts of the formula capture the case of an awaited collision. They say that a collision occurs at time t when the port starts perceiving a jamming signal or at least two simultaneous packet transmissions (part 3), provided that no earlier collision is perceived at t (then the collision would have started before t). The latter condition is described by the last two parts. Part 4 says that no jamming signal that started before t is still heard or just being terminated. Part 5 says that no overlapping activities that started to overlap before t are still overlapping or just cease to overlap. In short words, an awaited collision (i.e., a collision that is not present at the moment when the wait request is issued) occurs at the nearest moment when the port starts perceiving a jamming signal or at least two overlapping packet transmissions. The collision ends as soon as the port gets into a state where it senses at most one packet transmission and no jamming signal.

The role of jamming signals in detecting collisions reflects their original purpose. As we said in section 6.1, jamming signals were originally intended to enforce collision consensus in bus protocols based on the concept of collision detection (e.g., Ethernet). In such protocols, a station sensing a collision is expected to emit a jamming signal—to make sure that the collision is clearly perceived by all interested parties.[7] Consequently, the presence of a jamming signal on the port, even unaccompanied by any other activity, is interpreted as a collision.

The collision semantics just described are shared by the link types BLink (Link), ULink, and PLink (section 3.2.1). Note that with these semantics, two (short) packets transmitted simultaneously from the opposite ends of a link can pass through each other and arrive at their destinations undamaged. All natural links, e.g., radio channels, cables, fiber-optics, behave in this manner.

In a link belonging to type CLink (section 3.2), collisions propagate, in the sense that when two packets meet in any place of the link, the interference spreads (as a kind of activity of its own) and is perceived in due time by all ports connected to the link. The jamming signals retain their meaning, i.e., a jamming signal heard on a port unconditionally triggers a collision. Note that CLink represents bidirectional links. For a unidirectional link, the concept of propagating collisions makes no sense. A formal description of the collision semantics in a CLink is complicated and cannot be given without making a reference to the link geometry. As CLinks are not used very often (they are a relic from an old version of SMURPH), we will not bother to present these semantics here. The reader who finds the CLink type useful will be able to use it by following the intuitive description in this paragraph.

---

[7]In section 8.1.1.3, we return to these issues in a more specific context.

6.2.11   Environment Variables

When a process is awakened by a port event, with the exception of ANYEVENT, the environment variable ThePort (Info02) of type Port* contains a pointer to the port on which the waking event has occurred. The contents of this variable may be useful if the process awaits events on multiple ports at the same time. According to our rule of thumb mentioned at the beginning of section 1.2.4.4, this should not happen very often.

If the waking event is caused by a packet perceived by the port (i.e., BOT, EOT, BMP, EMP, and ANYEVENT), the environment variable ThePacket (Info01) of type Packet* returns a pointer to the object representing the packet. This also applies to the ACTIVITY event caused by a packet activity. The object pointed to by ThePacket is a copy of the packet buffer given to startTransfer or transmit (section 6.1.2.1) when the transmission of the packet was initiated.

Note.   The object pointed to by ThePacket is deallocated when its carrying activity is removed from the link archive (section 6.1.1). Therefore, if the protocol program wants to save the packet for whatever reason, it cannot just save the pointer returned via ThePacket; it should rather make a copy of the packet object and save the copy instead.

With ANYEVENT, if two (or more) events occur at the same time (within the same ITU) only one of them (chosen at random) will be actually presented. The restarted process is able to learn about all events that occur at the current moment by calling the port method events (section 6.3.1).

When a process awaiting ANYEVENT is awakened, the environment variable TheEvent (Info02) of type int contains a value identifying the event type. The possible values returned in TheEvent are represented by the following symbolic constants:

TRANSFER	Beginning of a packet activity
ENDTRANSFER	End of a complete packet activity, terminated by stop
ABTTRANSFER	End of an aborted packet activity, terminated by abort
JAM	Beginning of a jamming signal
ENDJAM	End of a jamming signal

If the event type is TRANSFER, ENDTRANSFER, or ABTTRANSFER, ThePacket points to the corresponding packet object; otherwise, ThePacket is undefined.

6.2.12   Event Priorities

Sometimes it is necessary to assign different priorities to different events that can occur simultaneously on the same port.

Example

Consider the following fragment of a process code:

```
            ...
      state SomeState:
        MyPort->wait (BOT, NewPacket);
      state NewPacket:
        MyPort->wait (EMP, MyPacket);
        MyPort->wait (EOT, OtherPacket);
        MyPort->wait (SILENCE, Garbage);
            ...
```

Most likely, the intended interpretation of the wait requests issued in state NewPacket is as follows: "Upon detection of the end of a packet addressed to this station we want to get to state MyPacket; otherwise, if we get the end of a packet addressed to some other station, we want to continue at OtherPacket; finally, if the packet does not terminate properly (it has been aborted), we want to resume in state Garbage." The problem is that the three awaited events may occur (and usually occur) at the same time. Therefore, special measures must be taken to enforce a specific order in which the events are to be presented.

If the simulator has been created with the -p option of mks (section B.2), it is possible to use the third argument of the wait request to order the awaited events:

```
          ...
    state SomeState:
      MyPort->wait (BOT, NewPacket);
    state NewPacket:
      MyPort->wait (EMP, MyPacket, 0);
      MyPort->wait (EOT, OtherPacket, 1);
      MyPort->wait (SILENCE, Garbage, 2);
          ...
```

If the three-argument wait requests are not available (i.e., the simulator was not built with -p), some events occurring on the same port are ordered implicitly. This does not happen if the simulator has been created with -p: then it is assumed that the user wants to exercise full control over ordering events.

This implicit ordering of certain port events was inspired by the rather typical character of the preceding example. Our reasoning was as follows. Many protocols can be programmed without assigning order attributes to multiple events awaited simultaneously. On the other hand, the problem of processing the multiple events caused by the same packet in a certain (natural) order is common enough to warrant special attention. Therefore, if explicit event ordering is unavailable, we should make sure that this natural order is still enforced automatically. This way, protocols that want to receive the port events in order do not have to execute in the three-argument wait environment just for this sole reason.

Suppose that the simulator was created without -p, i.e., explicit event ordering is unavailable. Imagine that a packet arrives at a port, and there is a single process awaiting three different events that may be caused by the same packet arrival, namely: BMP, BOT, and ACTIVITY. The BMP event has the highest priority, i.e., it is the one that will be triggered if the packet happens to be addressed to the station running the process. On the other hand, ACTIVITY is the lowest-priority event and is only triggered when none of the two higher-priority events occurs. This rule only applies to events caused by the same packet. Events caused by multiple packets arriving at the same port at the same time can be randomly interleaved, although the subset of those events caused by any one packet is still ordered, as just explained.

The problem of multiple packets arriving all at the same time does not seem to be very serious. Most realistic protocols will treat such situations in a special way. Typically they will recognize a collision and ignore everything until the port gets into a "decent" state. Thus, the issue of correctly interpreting the events that correspond to a successful reception of a packet is then irrelevant.

Similarly, the events EMP, EOT, and SILENCE are assigned priorities such that EMP is the highest-priority event, whereas SILENCE has the lowest priority. Again, these priorities only apply to events caused by a single packet whose trailer is passing by the port. In particular, in the preceding example, the order in which the three events will be presented to the awaiting process agrees with the intended interpretation. Note that this will not be the case if the simulator has been created with -p and the default event ordering is assumed. The implicit ordering of port events is then switched off, and all not explicitly ordered port events occurring at the same time are equally likely candidates for waking up the process.

6.2.13   Receiving Packets

By sensing BMP and EMP events a process can recognize packets that are addressed to the current station. A packet triggering one of these events must be either a nonbroadcast packet whose Receiver attribute contains the Id of the current station or a broadcast packet with Receiver pointing to a station group including the current station.

Another way to determine whether a given packet is addressed to the current station is to call the packet's method:

int isMy ();

which returns nonzero if and only if the current station is the packet's receiver (or one of the receivers in the broadcast case).

Typically, the receiving process waits until it detects the end of the packet (event EMP) before assuming that the packet has been received completely. Then the process can access the packet via the environment variable ThePacket (section 6.2.11) and examine its contents. The most often performed operation after the complete reception of a standard packet (section 5.2.2) is

Client->receive (ThePacket, ThePort);

The sole purpose of this operation is to update performance measures associated with the traffic pattern to which the packet belongs and with the link from which the packet has been received. The semantics of `receive` are discussed in sections 7.1.2 and 7.1.3.1. From the viewpoint of this section it is enough to say that `receive` should always be executed for a standard packet (for which performance measures are to be collected) as soon as, according to the protocol's perception, the packet has been completely and successfully received at its final destination.

The following variants of `receive` are declared within `Client`:

```
void receive (Packet *pk, Port *pr);
void receive (Packet *pk, Link *lk = NULL);
void receive (Packet &pk, Port &pr);
void receive (Packet &pk, Link &lk);
```

The second version accepts a link pointer rather than a port pointer, and the last two versions are equivalent to the first two, except that instead of pointers they take objects as arguments. If the second argument is not specified, it is assumed to be `NULL`, which means that the link performance measures will not be affected by the packet's reception.

Exactly the same collection of `receive` methods are declared within type `Traffic`. The `Traffic` methods operate exactly like the corresponding `Client` methods, except that they additionally check whether the received packet belongs to the given traffic pattern. Thus, they can be viewed as simple assertions.

All versions of `receive` check whether the station whose process is executing the operation is authorized to receive the packet, i.e., if the packet is addressed to the station. A packet whose `Receiver` attribute is `NONE` (i.e., the packet is not explicitly addressed to any specific station) can be received by any station.

Examples

The following is a sample code method of a process responsible for receiving packets:

```
perform {
  state WaitForPacket:
    RcvPort->wait (EMP, NewPacket);
  state NewPacket:
    Client->receive (ThePacket, ThePort);
    skipto WaitForPacket;
};
```

Instead of `ThePort`, `RcvPort` could be used as the second argument of `receive`—with the same results. After returning from `receive`, the process uses `skipto` (section 4.5.1) to resume waiting for a new packet. Note that if `proceed` were used instead of `skipto`, the process would loop infinitely. Namely, the process would get to `WaitForPacket` without advancing the simulated time, and the previous `EMP` event would still be present on the port; it would restart the process immediately—within the same ITU and for the same packet.

Now let us modify our receiver to recognize and properly handle collisions. Note that packet boundary events like `BMP` and `EMP` are triggered even if the packet has been involved in a collision,[8] so it is up to the protocol to detect colliding packets. The following modified code method detects and ignores packets destroyed by collisions:

```
perform {
  state WaitForPacket:
    RcvPort->wait (BMP, MyPacket);
  state MyPacket:
    RcvPort->wait (COLLISION, Ignore);
    skipto Receive;
  state Receive:
    RcvPort->wait (EMP, GotIt);
    RcvPort->wait (COLLISION, WaitForPacket);
  state GotIt;
    Client->receive (ThePacket, ThePort);
    proceed WaitForPacket;
  state Ignore:
    skipto WaitForPacket;
};
```

The code is significantly more complicated than its previous version. We assume that it is legal for the beginning of a packet to touch the end of the previous packet; thus, we have to handle carefully all the simultaneous events that may occur at packet boundaries. The process has to monitor the packet reception from the moment the packet triggers the BMP event until its end (EMP) arrives at the port. A collision detected during that time causes the packet to be ignored. Note that the following simplified version of the code method would not work:

```
perform {
  state WaitForPacket:
    RcvPort->wait (BMP, MyPacket);
  state MyPacket:
    RcvPort->wait (COLLISION, WaitForPacket);
    RcvPort->wait (EMP, GotIt);
  state GotIt;
    Client->receive (ThePacket, ThePort);
    proceed WaitForPacket;
};
```

because a collision occurring at the very beginning of a packet reception would result in an infinite loop. The skipto statement in the correct version is needed to advance the time, so that upon detecting a collision in state Receive, the process can safely move to state WaitForPacket without having to worry that the last BMP event still remains pending. Note that the last statement in state GotIt is proceed rather than skipto. With skipto the process could miss the next BMP event, if it happened to coincide with EMP for the last received packet.

Often packets are not allowed to touch their neighbors. For example, Ethernet enforces *packet spacing* rules that guarantee a short period of silence between packets.

---

[8]Note that a collision may occur in the middle of a packet, not necessarily at the boundary.

Assuming that (valid) packets are always spaced, we can simplify our collision-aware receiver in the following way:

```
perform {
  state WaitForPacket:
    RcvPort->wait (BMP, MyPacket);
  state Receive:
    RcvPort->wait (COLLISION, Ignore);
    RcvPort->wait (EMP, GotIt);
  state GotIt;
    Client->receive (ThePacket, ThePort);
    proceed WaitForPacket;
  state Ignore:
    skipto WaitForPacket;
};
```

Now there is no danger in skipping one ITU behind the end of the currently received packet. We know that the next valid packet will start a while after the end of the previous one.

Note. A port event does not go away when the process awaiting it is awakened. The event remains pending until the modeled time is advanced by a sufficient amount, so that the event condition (section 6.2) disappears from the port. For the packet *boundary* events, i.e., BOT, BMP, EOT, EMP, this amount is just one ITU.

The Receiver attribute of a packet can be interpreted in two ways: as the Id of a single station or as a station group pointer (section 5.2.1). The latter interpretation takes effect for a broadcast packet. To tell whether a packet is a broadcast one, the receiver can examine its flag number 31 (PF_broadcast—section 5.4.1.1), which is set for broadcast packets. The two packet methods

```
int isBroadcast ();
int isNonbroadcast ();
```

determine the broadcast status of the packet without using this flag explicitly.

Another flag (number 30 or PF_last) is used to tell the last packet of a message. It is possible (section 5.4.1.1) that a single message is split into a number of packets that are transmitted and received independently. If the PF_last flag of a received packet is set, it means that the packet is the last (or the only) packet acquired from its message. This flag is used internally by SMURPH in calculating message delay (section 7.1.2.1). Two packet methods

```
int isLast ();
int isNonlast ();
```

check whether the packet is the last packet of a message without referencing the PF_last flag directly.

Examples

The following is an example of a process that receives packets from a port and passes them to another process for further processing:

```
process Rcvr (Node) {
  Port *RP;
  PMailbox *PM;
  void setup () { RP = S->RP; pm = S->PM; };
  states {Wait, Receive};
  perform {
    Packet *p;
    state Wait:
      RP->wait (EMP, Receive);
    state NewPacket:
      p = create Packet;
      *p = *ThePacket;
      PM->put (p);
      Client->receive (ThePacket, RP);
      skipto Wait;
  };
};
```

We assume that the two processes communicate via a queue mailbox belonging to their owning station. Note that a copy of the received packet is made and inserted into the mailbox. The original structure pointed to by ThePacket should not be used, unless we are absolutely sure that the packet will be processed within the current ITU. This structure will be deallocated when the packet's carrying activity is removed from the link archive.[9] The mailbox type PMailbox can be declared in the following way:

```
mailbox PMailbox (Packet*) { };
```

Now let us look at another example illustrating a relatively common problem with interpreting the contents of environment variables. Here is the code method of a hypothetical receiver:

```
perform {
  state WaitBMP:
    MyPort->wait (BMP, MyPacket);
  state MyPacket:
    Timer->wait (HdrTime, GotHeader);
    MyPort->wait (COLLISION, AbortReception);
  state GotHeader:
    if (ThePacket->TP == REQUEST)
      RqMbx->put (ThePacket->Sender);
    else
      RpMbx->put (ThePacket->Sender);
    proceed WaitBMP;
```

---

[9]Or just from the link, if the archive is not used.

```
        state AbortReception:
           skipto WaitBMP;
};
```

The process waits for the beginning of a packet addressed to its owning station. Upon detection of such a packet, the process moves to state MyPacket, where it simulates the reception of the packet header. Apparently, the process tries to make the action performed in state GotHeader dependent on some attribute of the packet (represented by the traffic type). Realistically, this attribute can become known to the process only after at least some portion of the packet header has been received. We assume that HdrTime gives the amount of time needed to receive this critical portion of the packet. While waiting for the reception of this portion, the process monitors the port for a collision. As soon as a collision is detected, the process aborts the reception and awaits another packet arrival event.

Unfortunately, the code at state GotHeader is not going to work. ThePacket is only defined after the process wakes up in consequence of a packet-related event. Most likely, the simulator will crash by referencing the TP attribute of a nonexistent packet; certainly, it will not do what we would like it to do.

The problem can be eliminated by preserving the contents of ThePacket in state MyPacket after receiving the BMP event. The pointer returned by the environment variable can be saved in a process attribute, and later, in state GotHeader, the process can reference that attribute instead of ThePacket, which points nowhere. Note that a local variable of the code method (declared after perform) is not going to work, as the values of such variables are destroyed by state transitions (section 4.4.3).

As illustrated by these examples, the values of the environment variables must be interpreted with care, not only after port events. If the information returned by an environment variable should be retained across subsequent state transitions, this information must be stored in a safe place, e.g., in a process attribute or a mailbox. Additionally, one has to remember about the temporary nature of the object pointed to by ThePacket. Even if the packet pointer returned by ThePacket is stored, the packet may disappear after a while. If we know a reasonable estimate of the length of the period for which a received packet may be needed, we can use a nonzero link archival time to guarantee the survival of the packet-carrying activity for that period. It seems that copying the packet is generally a better solution. First, the packet deallocation is then entirely controlled by the protocol process. Second, this solution closely resembles the way of handling the issue in a real network.

6.3 PORT INQUIRIES

By issuing a port wait request, a process declares that it would like to learn when something happens on the port in the future. Although it is possible that the awaited event occurs immediately (i.e., within the current ITU), the general character of a wait request makes such a scenario a special case of a future occurrence.

It is possible to ask a port about its present status, i.e., to determine the configuration of activities currently perceived by the port, or about its past status—within the time interval determined by the link's *archival time* (sections 3.2.2, 6.1.1).

Note that technically it is possible to examine the present status of a port via wait requests.

Example

The following fragment of a process code method determines whether the port pointed to by P is currently perceiving a period of silence:

```
state Check:
    P->wait (SILENCE, Silence, MIN_long);
    proceed Activity;
```

Note the very low order assigned to the wait request for SILENCE. The process makes sure that if no activity is perceived on P within the current ITU, the transition to Silence will take precedence over the transition to Activity (scheduled at the current ITU, but with the default order of 0).

With a bit of imagination, one could use this technique to implement all the interesting types of inquiries about the present status of a port. To facilitate such inquiries, type Port offers a collection of methods for performing them in a straightforward way, without issuing wait requests and forcing superfluous state transitions.

6.3.1   Inquiries about the Present

The port method

```
int busy ();
```

returns YES (1) if the port is currently perceiving any activity (a packet transmission, a jamming signal, or a number of overlapping activities), and NO (0) otherwise. There also exists a complementary method,

```
int idle ();
```

which is a simple negation of busy.

In the case when a number of activities are heard at the port at the same time, it is possible to determine their types by calling one of the following port methods:

```
int activities (int &t, int &j);
int activities (int &t);
int activities ();
```

With the first method, the two reference arguments return the number of packet transmissions (t) and the number of jamming signals (j) sensed by the port at the current moment. The method's value tells the total number of all activities perceived by the port, i.e., the sum of t and j. The second method does not explicitly return the number of jams; however, the method's value still gives the total number of all activities. The last method has no arguments and merely returns the total number of all activities perceived by the port.

In the case when exactly one packet transmission is sensed by the port and no other activity is heard at the same time, each of these methods sets the environment variable ThePacket (section 6.2.11) to point to the packet object. ThePort is always set to point to the port to which the inquiry was addressed.

Example

> There is no explicit inquiry about a collision perceived by the port within the current ITU, but such an inquiry can be modeled by the following function:

```
int collision (Port *p) {
  int t, j;
  p->activities (t, j);
  return j || (t > 1);
};
```

> Note that the Boolean formula at the return statement is essentially equivalent to the first two components of the COLLISION condition given in section 6.2.10.

When a process is awakened by ANYEVENT (section 6.2.9), it may happen that two or more simultaneous events have triggered the waking event. It is possible to learn how many events of a given type occur on the port at the current moment by calling the Port method

$$\text{int events (int etype);}$$

where the argument identifies the event type in the following way:

BOT   Beginnings of packets

EOT   Ends of packets (only the packets terminated by stop—section 6.1.2—are counted)

BOJ   Beginnings of jamming signals

EOJ   Ends of jamming signals

The method returns the number of events of the type indicated by the argument that are currently perceived by the port.

By calling activities a process can learn the number of packets that are simultaneously heard on a given port. Sometimes the process may wish to have a look at all these packets. The following port method can be used in such situations:

$$\text{Packet   *anotherPacket ()}$$

The method can be called after receiving one of the events BOT, EOT, BMP, or EMP, or after calling events with the second argument equal to BOT or EOT, or after calling activities.

When the method is called after the process has been restarted by one of the four packet events, its subsequent calls return pointers to all packets that trigger the event at the same time. These pointers are returned via the function value and also in `ThePacket`. If the `NULL` pointer is returned, it means that there are no more packets, i.e., all of them have been examined. If there are n packets that cause a given event simultaneously, n calls to `anotherPacket` are required to examine them all.

When called after `events`, the method behaves exactly as if the process were awakened by `BOT` or `EOT`, depending on the argument of `events`. After a call to `activities`, the method returns (in its subsequent calls) pointers to all packets currently heard on the port.

Note.   A call to `anotherPacket` in a context that does not fit into any of the circumstances just mentioned is treated as an error.

Examples

The following code method receives all packets arriving via the port pointed to by `P`, even if multiple packets arrive at the same time:

```
perform {
  state Wait:
    P->wait (EMP, Receive);
  state Receive:
    while (anotherPacket ())
      Client->receive (ThePacket, P);
    skipto Wait;
};
```

The only way to enter state `Receive` is after an `EMP` event; thus, it makes sense to call `anotherPacket` in that state.

The following process code method monitors all activities passing by port `P` and counts the number of jamming signals and packets longer than 1024 bits:

```
perform {
  int t, j;
  state Wait:
    P->wait (ANYEVENT, Monitor);
  state Monitor:
    NJams += P->events (BOJ);
    if (P->events (BOT))
      while (anotherPacket ())
        if (ThePacket->TLength > 1024) NPackets++;
    skipto Wait;
};
```

Note that `anotherPacket` is called after `events(BOT)`; thus, it will sweep through all packets whose beginnings are just being perceived by `P`. A modification of this method,

```
perform {
  int t, j;
  state Wait:
    P->wait (ANYEVENT, Monitor);
  state Monitor:
    if (P->events (BOJ) + P->events (BOT)) {
      NJams += P->events (BOJ);
      while (anotherPacket ())
        if (ThePacket->TLength > 1024) NPackets++;
    }
    skipto Wait;
};
```

will not work, as it makes no sense to call `anotherPacket` after `events(BOJ)`. The earlier call to `events(BOT)` does not help; what counts is the type of the most recent port inquiry.

One may object that the inquiries performed by `activities`, `events`, and `anotherPacket` are unrealistic. Perhaps they are, but it is not unconceivable that a signal-coding technique would make it possible, for example, to tell the number of packets involved in a collision. The "unrealistic" inquiries are provided for free by the SMURPH link model. Sometimes they can be useful for making convenient shortcuts that simplify the protocol model without affecting its realistic nature. Someone might want to use them for modeling complex channels that realistically admit some types of inquiries deemed unrealistic for regular, ether-type links.

6.3.2 Inquiries about the Past

In a real network it is impossible to ask a port about its past status. In SMURPH this possibility has been provided to simplify the code of some protocols. Of course, it is always possible to reprogram a protocol in such a way that no port inquiries about the past are made: processes can maintain their private databases of interesting past events. In this sense, port inquiries about the past are not unrealistic. They can be viewed as shortcuts that do not really increase the expressing power of the system. They just make the expression more concise in some cases.

Following are the port methods that perform port inquiries about the past. All these methods return values of type `TIME` and take no arguments.

lastBOA   The method returns the time when the last beginning of (any) activity (the end of the last silence period) was heard on the port. `TIME_0` is returned if no activity has been heard on the port within the link archival period. The method can also be called as `lastEOS` (for the last end of a silence period).

lastEOA   The method returns the time of the beginning of the current silence period on the port (the end of the last activity). The undefined value (`TIME_inf`) is returned if an activity is currently sensed on the port.

If no activity has been observed on the port within the archival period, TIME_0 is returned. The two port methods busy and idle (section 6.3.1) are actually macros that expand as undef(lastEOA()) and def(lastEOA()), respectively. The lastEOA method can also be called as lastBOS (for the last beginning of silence).

lastBOT   The method returns the time when the last beginning of packet was perceived by the port. TIME_0 is returned if no beginning of packet has been heard within the link archival period. The event is recognized even if the packet interferes with another activity or activities (i.e., another packet or a jamming signal).

lastEOT   The method returns the time when the last end of a complete packet activity (i.e., terminated by stop—section 6.1.2) was sensed by the port. If no end of packet has been heard on the port within the archival time period, TIME_0 is returned. As with lastBOT, the end of a packet will be recognized even if it overlaps with some other activities, provided that the packet was terminated by stop.

lastBOJ   The method returns the time when the last beginning of a jamming signal was heard on the port. Multiple overlapping jams are perceived as one; in such a case, only the beginning of the earliest jam is recognized. TIME_0 is returned if no jamming signal has been perceived by the port within the archival time period.

lastEOJ   The method returns the time when the last end of a jamming signal was sensed by the port. TIME_inf is returned if a jamming signal is currently perceived. If no jam has been heard on the port within the archival period, the method returns TIME_0. As with lastBOJ, multiple overlapping jams are treated as a single continuous jamming signal, and only the end of the last of those signals is recognized.

lastCOL   The method returns the time of the beginning of the last collision sensed by the port. By the beginning of a collision we mean the first moment when the collision was perceived by the port (section 6.2.10). TIME_0 is returned if no collision has been sensed on the port within the archival period.

It is possible to give formal conditions describing the values returned by these methods, based on the configuration of activities in the link and the link archive. These conditions are easy to derive from the conditions describing port events (section 6.2) and are left as an exercise to the reader.

If an inquiry is fulfilled by a packet activity, a pointer to this packet is returned via ThePacket, as for a port event. For compatibility, all inquiries set ThePort to point to the port to which the inquiry was addressed.

The history of past activities in a link is kept in the link archive (sections 3.2.2, 6.1.1) for the amount of time specified upon the link's creation. The link archival time says for how many ITUs a link activity is to be kept in the archive after its end formally disappears from the link. If no past inquiries are ever issued to a link (i.e., to a port connected to the link), the link's archival time should be set to 0. Otherwise, the archival time should be big enough to make sure that the protocol works correctly (i.e., all inquiries about the past are answered according to the protocol specification), but not too big—to avoid overloading the simulator with a huge number of archived activities.

Note that even if the link archival time is 0, i.e., link archive is not maintained at all, some operations looking like inquiries about the past may make perfect sense. For example, the methods busy and idle (section 6.3.1) implement special cases of such inquiries, and they work correctly regardless of the length of the link archival period. Generally, an inquiry about the past cannot be answered by examining the link archive alone. Note that for a long link, something that happened a while ago on one port may still belong to the realm of future events for another port. Thus, for a port located far from the link boundary, the link itself can be viewed as an archive.

Example

The following code method belonging to a transmitter process makes sure that packets inserted into the link are separated by silence periods not shorter than some minimum value represented by SilLength:

```
perform {
  TIME t;
  state Wait:
    if (!Client->getPacket (buf, min, max, frm))
      Client->wait (ARRIVAL, WaitClient);
    else if ((t = Time - lastEOA ()) < SilLength)
      Timer->wait (SilLength - t, Transmit);
    else
      proceed Transmit;
  state Transmit:
    Bus->transmit (buf, Done);
  state Done:
    Bus->stop ();
    buf->release ();
    proceed WaitClient;
};
```

We assume that no other activities can interfere with the packets transmitted by our process; thus, lastEOA in state Wait always returns a definite value. Of course, with this assumption, the code method could be rewritten without using lastEOA, in the following simpler way:

```
perform {
  state Wait:
    if (!Client->getPacket (buf, min, max, frm))
      Client->wait (ARRIVAL, WaitClient);
```

```
           else
             Bus->transmit (buf, Done);
         state Done:
           Bus->stop ();
           buf->release ();
           Timer->wait (SilLength, Wait);
     };
```

However, the simple solution would not work if more processes were allowed to transmit into the same link, whereas the previous solution could be easily modified to handle such situations.

No ready methods are provided for past inquiries about the beginning/end of a packet addressed to the current station. Such inquiries can be easily implemented by the user. They did not seem very useful, and they have been intentionally omitted. Indeed, there must be something wrong with a receiver process that did not grab its packet on time and now wants to excavate it from the link archive.

6.3.3   Some Problems Resulting from Time Discretization

In section 2.2.2 we argued that the discrete nature of the modeled time is not really a simplification insofar as modeling physical systems is concerned. We stand by this statement here. However, we would like to signal some potential problems that may show up if the granularity of time is too coarse or if its discrete nature is not understood properly by the programmer.

All these problems result from the fact that a port status perceived at time t (within the ITU number t) may, under some circumstances, change within the same ITU **after** it has been perceived.

Example

Consider the following simple process code method:

```
         perform {
           state Wait:
             P->wait (BOT, NewPacket);
           state NewPacket:
             while (anotherPacket ()) PCount++;
             skipto Wait;
         };
```

Apparently, the task of the process running this method is to intercept all BOT events on port P and count the number of packets passing by the port. The process takes two precautions:

- Count all packets arriving at the port simultaneously.
- Advance the time after each BOT event, so that when the process gets back to state Wait, the old BOT event is gone.

Clearly, all beginnings of packet activities arriving within the same ITU are handled by anotherPacket loop in state NewPacket. Then the time is advanced by one ITU and the process starts awaiting another BOT event. Can we safely claim that the process counts all packets passing by port P?

This example can be viewed as a representative of many similar situations fitting into the following general scenario:

- A process monitoring a given port wants to make sure that it intercepts all the relevant events.
- Because events do not disappear from the port until time is advanced, the process must advance the time before issuing a wait request for the next interesting event.
- It is possible that several events monitored by the process occur at the same time (within the same ITU).

Can the process organize its activities in such a way that no events are lost?

Of course, but sometimes the problem is trickier than it seems at first sight. Assume that the port P referenced by the preceding code method is also accessed by another process using it to transmit packets into the link. The following sequence of events is now possible:

1. A packet arrives at P. This packet has been inserted on another port, possibly quite distant from P.
2. The monitoring process wakes up in state NewPacket and registers the new packet.
3. The monitoring process puts itself to sleep for one ITU (the skipto operation).
4. The transmitter process wakes up within the current ITU and starts a packet transmission on P. Of course, this transmission reaches P immediately, i.e., within the current ITU.
5. The monitoring process gets to state Wait one ITU later and misses the last packet.

The problem has occurred because of the nondeterminism in restarting multiple processes whose waking events have been scheduled at the same ITU. Note that if the monitoring process were restarted after the transmitter, it would not miss the packet. Another element contributing to the problem is the fact that no time elapses between the moment when a packet is inserted into P and the moment when the same packet arrives at P. The distance from a given port to itself is always zero.

One way out is to assign a very low order (e.g., MIN_LONG—section 2.2.5) to the port wait request in the monitoring process. This way we would try to make sure that the process will wake up at the last possible moment within the ITU of the event occurrence. This approach will work in our example, but sometimes, because of the correlation between processes, even the lowest possible order does not guarantee that no other process will be run later within the same ITU. For example, imagine that a process P_1 awaits a signal that can be sent by another process P_2. Irrespective of how the wait requests of the two processes are ordered, P_1 will follow P_2, although they may both be run within the same ITU (if only P_2 delivers the signal awaited by P_1).

Therefore, the user should heed the following recommendations:

- Avoid using the same port for different purposes if you suspect that a race condition of the discussed type may occur. There is little penalty for adding extra ports to the links and absolutely no simulation overhead caused by these extra ports.

- Avoid introducing two or more ports separated by zero ITUs. From the viewpoint of the race problem discussed here, such ports are indistinguishable from a single port. Note that in real life it is impossible to perform two operations in precisely the same place and at precisely the same time. If something like this happens in your protocol and causes a problem, it most likely means that your time granularity is not fine enough. Then you should consider selecting a smaller ITU.

The two recommendations should be followed in all dubious or tricky cases; however, departures from them are permitted (and even welcome) as long as it is obvious that nothing wrong can happen. For example, the same port can be used for transmitting and receiving packets (which is most naturally done by two different processes), if the receiver process consistently ignores the packets transmitted by its station or if no packets can ever overlap.

6.4 FAULTY LINKS

A link can be declared as faulty, which means that a packet inserted into such a link may be damaged and may not make it to the destination in good shape, even if it does not interfere (collide) with other activities. In section 3.2.3 we showed how to specify an error rate for a link. Now we describe the adjustments to the link semantics needed to handle the faulty links.

6.4.1 Interpreting Damaged Packets

The faulty status of a link is described by two parameters of the `setFaultRate` method introduced in section 3.2.3. This method is declared with the following header:

```
void setFaultRate (double rate = 0.0, int ftype = FT_LEVEL1);
```

where `rate` gives the probability of damaging a single bit of a packet inserted into the link, and `ftype` specifies the *processing type* for damaged packets. Clearly, the value of `rate` must be between 0 and 1 and is usually much closer to 0 than to 1.

By default, i.e., before `setFaultRate` is called, the link is error-free and packets inserted into it are never damaged. A faulty link can be reverted to its error-free status by calling `setFaultRate` with the second argument equal to `NONE` (the value of the first argument is then irrelevant), with the first argument equal to 0 (the value of the second argument is then irrelevant), or both. In particular, an argument-less call to `setFaultRate` has this effect.

It is legal to change the fault characteristics of a link on the fly, i.e., while the protocol is running. This means that the link may suddenly become error-prone and later calm down, or vice versa. Of course, this operation can be controlled by a process, which makes it easy to model any interesting pattern of the link's malevolence.

The valid/invalid status of a packet is determined upon its transmission (by `transmit`—section 6.1.2.1) and stored in the packet's `Flags` attribute (section 5.2.2). Two flags are used for this purpose, and the packet can be damaged in two ways:

- The packet's header is unrecognizable and the packet's destination cannot be formally determined. This status is indicated by two flags `PF_hdamaged` (flag 28) and `PF_damaged` (flag 27), set simultaneously.
- The packet's header is correct, but the packet is otherwise damaged (e.g., its trailer checksum is invalid). This status is indicated by flag number 27 (`PF_damaged`) set and the other flag (`PF_hdamaged`) cleared.

Note that a packet that is *header-damaged* is also *damaged*, but not necessarily the other way around.

The damage status of a packet can always be determined directly by calling any of the following packet methods:

```
int isDamaged ();
int isValid ();
int isHDamaged ();
int isHValid ();
```

Each of these methods returns either `YES` or `NO`—in a natural way. Note that `isHDamaged` implies `isDamaged`; similarly, `isValid` implies `isHValid`.

Depending on the value of the second argument of `setFaultRate` (`ftype`), the damaged status of a packet can be interpreted automatically by suppressing certain events that are triggered by valid packets. Besides `NONE` (which makes the link error-free), the following three values of `ftype` are legal:

FT_LEVEL0   No automatic processing of damaged packets is in effect. Damaged packets trigger the same events and respond to the same inquiries as valid packets. The only way to tell a damaged packet from a valid one is to examine the packet's `Flags` attribute, e.g., with one of the methods just mentioned.

FT_LEVEL1   A header-damaged packet does not trigger the BMP event. A damaged packet does not trigger the EMP event (section 6.2.6). This also applies to anotherPacket (section 6.3.1) called after BMP (EMP), which ignores header-damaged (damaged) packets. The packet method isMy (section 6.2.13) returns NO for a header-damaged packet (but works as usual if the packet is damaged without being header-damaged).

FT_LEVEL2   The interpretation of damaged packets is as for FT_LEVEL1, but additionally events BOT and EOT are affected. Thus, a header-damaged packet does not trigger the BOT event, and a damaged packet does not trigger the EOT event. This also applies to anotherPacket and to the link inquiries about past BOT/EOT events (section 6.3.2).

Regardless of the processing type for damaged packets, events SILENCE, ACTIVITY, COLLISION, BOJ, EOJ, and ANYEVENT (section 6.2) are not affected by the damage status of a packet. Besides, jamming signals are never damaged.

Note that in the alternating-bit protocol in section 1.2.4, the default fault processing level (FT_LEVEL1) is assumed for both links. Thus, a damaged packet will not trigger the EMP event awaited by the receiver process (section 1.2.4.5). Similarly, a damaged acknowledgment will not trigger the EMP event awaited by the acknowledgment receiver (section 1.2.4.4). As the length of the packet (and acknowledgment) header is formally zero (getPacket is called with a single argument), no packet is ever header-damaged.

6.4.2 Damaging Packets

As we said in section 6.4.1, whether a packet is ever to be damaged is determined at the moment when the packet is inserted into the link. This operation is performed by calling the following link method:

```
virtual void packetDamage (Packet *p);
```

Note that packetDamage is declared as virtual; therefore, it can be overridden by the user in a Link subtype declaration.

The method is called automatically for each packet given as the argument to transmit (section 6.1.2.1). First, based on the length of the packet header, packetDamage determines the probability that the packet will be header-damaged. Let h denote the header length in bits.[10] The header is damaged with probability $1 - (1 - \text{rate})^h$. A uniformly distributed random number between 0 and 1 is generated, and if its value is less than the damage probability, the packet is marked as both header-damaged and damaged (the flags PF_hdamaged and PF_damaged are both set). Otherwise, the probability of the packet's being damaged (without being header-damaged) is determined based on the packet's ILength attribute and another random number is generated—in the same way as before. If this number turns

---

[10]This length is equal to p->TLength−p->ILength (section 5.4.1.1).

out to be less than the damage probability for the packet's payload, the packet is marked as damaged (PF_damaged is set, but PF_hdamaged is cleared). If the packet is not to be damaged at all, both damage flags are cleared.

Examples

Suppose that we would like to have a unidirectional link in which the packet damage probability is independent of the packet length but different for the header and payload. We may want to declare the following link type:

```
link MyULink : ULink {
  double PHdr, PPay;
  virtual void packetDamage (Packet *p) {
    if (rnd (SEED_toss) < PHdr) {
      setFlag (p->Flags, PF_hdamaged);
      setFlag (p->Flags, PF_damaged);
    } else if (rnd (SEED_toss) < PPay) {
      clearFlag (p->Flags, PF_hdamaged);
      setFlag (p->Flags, PF_damaged);
    } else {
      clearFlag (p->Flags, PF_hdamaged);
      clearFlag (p->Flags, PF_damaged);
    }
  };
  void setup (int np, double ph, double pp) {
    PHdr = ph; PPay = pp;
    ULink::setup (np);
  };
};
```

It is a good habit to explicitly clear the damage flags in a user-defined version of packetDamage if the packet is not to be damaged. Although these flags are automatically cleared by getPacket when a packet buffer is filled, they are carried over when packets are copied, relayed, and so on.

Now imagine that we want to have a link generating bursty faults, e.g., resulting from an external interfering source. The behavior of such a link can be modeled by a dedicated process, which may be defined as follows:

```
process LinkFaults {
  Link *LK;
  double MBIT, MBL, R;
  void setup (Link *lk, double *mbit, double *mbl, double *r) {
    LK = lk; MBIT = mbit; MBL = mbl; R = r;
  };
  states {WaitBurst, GenBurst, StopBurst};
  perform {
    state WaitBurst:
      Timer->wait (tRndPoisson (mbit), GenBurst);
    state GenBurst:
```

```
            lk->setFaultRate (R, FT_LEVEL2);
            Timer->wait (tRndPoisson (mbl), StopBurst);
        state StopBurst:
            lk->setFaultRate ();
            proceed WaitBurst;
    };
};
```

We assume that the mean burst interarrival time and mean burst duration are both exponentially distributed with the mean values specified upon process creation. Besides these mean values, the process setup method takes two more arguments: the pointer to the faulty link (the link can be of any link type) and the fault rate to be assumed during a burst.

Note. The possibility of declaring links as faulty is switched off by default— to avoid simulation overhead. To enable faulty links, the simulator must be created with the -z option of mks (section B.2).

BIBLIOGRAPHIC NOTES

Physical properties of various types of communication channels are discussed by *Freeman* (1989), *Bartee* (1985; 1986), and *Spragins, Hammond, and Pawlikowski* (1991). *Gburzyński and Rudnicki* (1989c) give a formal description of a simple communication channel and elaborate on the semantics of the port events listed in section 6.2. The reader will also find there a formal specification of collisions in a CLink. The concept of *collision consensus* in Ethernet is explained in the technical document *Ethernet* (1980) and also by *Metcalfe and Boggs* (1976). *Kamal* (1987) proposed a variant of Ethernet in which stations recognize how many parties have been involved in a collision. That paper supports our remarks at the end of section 6.3.1.

PROBLEMS

1. What would happen if the skipto statements from the two examples in section 6.3.1 were replaced by proceed?

2. Based on the formal conditions for port events given in section 6.2, give similar conditions for the port inquiries discussed in section 6.3.

3. Modify the alternating-bit protocol in section 1.2.4 in such a way that all packets (including acknowledgments) are furnished with headers. Calculate the expected ratio of damaged and header-damaged packets, and verify your calculations experimentally.

4. Define a process that will monitor a port, and count the number of packets undisturbed by jamming signals passing by the port. Overlapping packets must be counted separately.

5. Define a process implementing a correlated pattern of link failures. The probability of damaging a single bit should increase with the number of packet bits passed through the link within a given time window.

6. Define a single receiver process that will receive packets from two ports simultaneously. Make sure that the process receives correctly packets arriving at the same time (on different ports), ignores packets destroyed by collisions, and does not get into an infinite loop on the same pending port event. How would you generalize your solution for more than two ports? Why is it recommended that one receiver process should only handle one port?

7. Define a process that monitors a port and calculates the number of aborted packets passing by the port. Assume that packets can overlap in an arbitrarily malicious way. Hint: The end of an aborted packet activity triggers ANYEVENT, but not EOT. Note that when such an event occurs on the port, the packet causing the event is no longer there.

8. Design and implement a collection of processes that would serve as a two-way gate between two bidirectional broadcast links. The two links are represented by two ports passed to the processes upon their creation. The gate is expected to relay activities between the two ports in the following way:

   - An undisturbed (i.e., not colliding) packet activity is to be relayed as a packet activity (carrying the same packet).
   - A collision is to be relayed as a jamming signal.
   - Silence is to be relayed as silence.

9. Design and implement a variant of the alternating-bit protocol in which the two stations communicate via a single broadcast channel. Thus, besides the possibility of being damaged because of the faulty nature of the channel, a packet can be destroyed by colliding with another packet going in the opposite direction. Make sure that collisions are detected properly and the colliding packets are not received. How should a transmitting process handle a collision of its packet? Should it retransmit the packet immediately?

10. Generalize your solution from the previous question to multiple senders and recipients (occurring in pairs) sharing the same broadcast channel. Assume that the channel is star-shaped, i.e., the distance between a pair of ports is the same for all pairs. How does the channel utilization (in terms of useful bits passed through the channel) depend on the number of sender-recipient pairs? Does it depend on the length (or should we rather say diameter) of the channel?

7

Seeing Things Happen

7.1 MEASURING PERFORMANCE

The objective of a real network is to offer bandwidth to its users. The purpose of a network model is to demonstrate some facts about the behavior of its physical counterpart. These facts can be related to the performance of the investigated network. Then we are talking about some numbers or functions that give us an impression as to the suitability of the network for a class of applications. For example, the average amount of time elapsing after a message is queued at a station until it is delivered to its destination, measured at a given load, is a number that tells us something about the quality of service one can expect from the network. These facts can also be logical statements asserting some properties of the network that are not necessarily of a numerical nature. For example, the statement "packets arrive at the destination in the same order in which they have been sent" is part of the logical characteristics of the network.

In this section we deal with measuring performance, i.e., producing some numbers or functions that reflect certain observed quantitative parameters of the modeled network. These measured quantities are usually of a statistical character, which means that they are extracts from a reasonably large population of cases or samples. Some performance measures are calculated automatically by SMURPH. The user can easily collect additional statistical data, which augment or replace the standard measurements. Calculation of statistical performance measures (the standard ones as well as those defined by the user) is facilitated by the concept of a *random variable* represented by a special data type.

208

7.1.1   Type RVariable

An object of type `RVariable` is a data structure used for incremental calculation of some empirical distribution parameters of a random variable, whose values are discretely sampled. The actual collection of attributes of an `RVariable` is not very interesting. In fact, this type has been implemented in a somewhat tricky way—to make the operations efficient—and some of its functional attributes do not occur explicitly. A collection of standard methods cover all these attributes and it is neither necessary nor reasonable to try to reference them directly. Type `RVariable` is not extensible by the user.

As objects of type `RVariable` represent empirical random variables, we will be calling these objects simply *random variables* unless it would lead to confusion. Type `RVariable` takes care of the following parameters of a random variable:

- The number of samples (the number of times the random variable was probed). This attribute is referred to as the *counter* of the random variable.
- The minimum and the maximum values encountered so far.
- The mean value, the variance, and higher-order central moments. The number of central moments to be calculated is definable by the user.

A random variable can be viewed as a representation of the history of a measured quantity in a number of its observed values. At any moment, the attributes of the random variable reflect the statistical distribution parameters of the measured quantity, according to its values observed so far. A typical operation on a random variable consists in adding a new sample (value) to the random variable's history. We will simply say that the new value is added to the random variable. Whenever this happens, the parameters of the random variable are updated to include the new value. In particular, if the new value happens to be greater than the maximum value observed so far, the maximum value is adjusted accordingly, i.e., set to the new value.

Type `RVariable` declares a number of publicly visible methods for performing typical operations on random variables and for presenting their attributes in a legible form. The latter methods are based on the concept of *exposing* (discussed in section 7.3.5.4), which is common for all *Objects*.

7.1.1.1   Creating and destroying random variables.   Random variables are *Objects* (section 2.4.1): they must be created before they are used, and they may be released (`deleted`) when they are no longer needed. A random variable is created in the standard way (section 2.4.7), e.g.,

```
rv = create RVariable (ct, nm);
```

where `rv` is an `RVariable` pointer and both setup arguments are integer numbers. The first argument (`ct`) specifies the type of the sample counter. The value of this argument can be either `TYPE_long`, in which case the counter will be stored as a

LONG integer, or TYPE_BIG, in which case the counter will be an object of type BIG (TIME).

The second argument (nm) gives the number of central moments to be calculated for the random variable. This number must be between 0 and 32, inclusively. No moments are calculated if nm is 0. Note that the mean value and variance are moments number 1 and 2, respectively.

The setup method of RVariable is declared with the following header:

```
void setup (int ct = TYPE_long, int nm = 2);
```

Thus, if no setup arguments are specified at create, the random variable has a LONG sample counter and keeps track of two central moments, i.e., the mean value and variation.

The need for BIG counters stems from the fact that the number of accumulated samples can sometimes be larger than the capacity of type LONG. As we shall see, it is possible to add to a random variable an arbitrary number of samples in one step (all with the same value).

Being *Objects*, random variables are assigned Id attributes, which reflect their order of creation. Ids of random variables are not useful for internal identification. Random variables can be created and destroyed dynamically, and the allocation of Ids to the random variables alive at any given moment need not be consecutive. Unlike stations, links, and ports, random variables' Ids cannot be easily converted to object pointers. There is no operation that would transform the Id attribute of an RVariable into the pointer to the RVariable's structure. The only way to reference a random variable is via its pointer returned by create. Therefore, this pointer should never be ignored. A random variable can be assigned a nickname (section 2.4.2) upon its creation. The nickname version of create (section 2.4.7) should be used for this purpose. A random variable that is no longer needed can (and should) be erased by the standard C++ operation delete.

Example

The following sequence of operations creates three random variables:

```
rv1 = create RVariable;
rv2 = create RVariable, form ("RVar%1d", i), (TYPE_BIG, 4);
rv3 = create RVariable (TYPE_long, 0);
```

The first random variable is created with default setup arguments; thus, its counter type is LONG and the number of moments is 2 (the mean value and variance). The second random variable is assigned a nickname. Its counter is BIG and the random variable will handle four moments. Finally, the third random variable has no moments: only the minimum and maximum values will be computed.

Random variables do not naturally belong to other objects, e.g., the way processes belong to stations. Nonetheless, there exists a general object ownership hierarchy for all *Objects*, including random variables. This hierarchy is irrelevant from the point of view of the protocol program, and its sole purpose is to facilitate object identification for the dynamic display program DSD, presented in appendix A.

7.1.1.2 Operations on random variables.

When a new random variable is created, the value of its sample counter is initialized to zero. Whenever a new sample, or a number of samples, is to be added to the history of a random variable, the following RVariable method should be called:

$$\text{void update (double val, } ctype \text{ cnt = 1);}$$

where *ctype* is either LONG or BIG, depending on the type of the random variable's sample counter. The function increments the sample counter by cnt and updates the parameters of the random variable according to cnt occurrences of value val.

Example

> Consider the following sequence of operations:
>
> ```
> r = create RVariable (TYPE_long, 3);
> r->update (2.0, 1);
> r->update (5.0, 2L);
> ```
>
> The first call to update adds to the variable's history one sample with value 2, the second call adds two more samples with the same value of 5. Thus, after the execution of the three statements, s represents a random variable with three values: 2, 5, 5, and the distribution parameters of this random variable are
>
> | | |
> |---|---|
> | *minimum value* | 2.0 |
> | *maximum value* | 5.0 |
> | *mean value* | 4.0 |
> | *variance* | 2.0 |
> | *third central moment* | −2.0 |

Owing to the fact that the attributes of an RVariable do not represent directly the distribution parameters, a special operation is required to bring these parameters into tangible existence. This operation is implemented by the following method of RVariable:

$$\text{void calculate (double \&min, double \&max, double *m, } ctype \text{ \&c);}$$

All arguments of calculate are return arguments. The type of c (denoted by *ctype*) must be the same as the counter type of the random variable, i.e., either LONG or BIG. The four return arguments are filled (in this order) with the minimum value, the maximum value, the moments, and the sample counter. Argument m should point to a double array with no fewer elements than the number of moments declared when the random variable was created. The first element of the array (the element number 0) will contain the mean value, the second—the variance, the third—the third central moment, and so on.

Two random variables can be combined into one in such a way that the combined parameters describe a single sampling experiment in which all samples belonging to both source variables have been merged into one set of samples. The function

```
void combineRV (RVariable *a, RVariable *b, RVariable *c);
```

combines the random variables **a** and **b** into a new random variable **c**. The target random variable must exist, i.e., it must have been created previously.

If the two random variables being combined have different numbers of moments, the number of moments of the resulting RVariable is the minimum of the two numbers. If the counter types of the source random variables are different, the resulting counter type is BIG.

In practice, the need to combine two or more random variables or to extract the parameters of a random variable arises rather seldom. Note that these parameters can be printed out or displayed in a very natural and simple way—by *exposing* the random variable (section 7.3.5.4). Internally, SMURPH combines random variables used by individual traffic patterns (Traffic objects) to produce the global traffic statistics for the Client (section 7.3.5.5).

Note. combineRV is a global function, not a method of RVariable.

It is possible to erase the contents of a random variable, i.e., initialize its sample counter to zero and reset all its parameters. This is done by the following method of RVariable:

```
void erase ();
```

Each random variable is automatically erased when it is created.

Examples

Imagine that we would like to add some measurements to the alternating-bit protocol in section 1.2.4. The most natural thing to measure (and usually the most interesting element of network performance) is the average message delay, i.e., the average amount of time elapsing after a message arrives at the sender until it is received at the recipient. But such measurements are taken by SMURPH for free, so let us think about something more extravagant. For example, assume that we are interested in the average number of retransmissions for a regular packet. It may be an interesting exercise to draw a graph illustrating how this number depends on the channel error rate.

We should start by creating a random variable for this purpose. Somewhere among the declarations of global variables we may want to insert the statement

```
RVariable *NRetr;
```

and in the Root process, e.g., in method startProtocol, we will create the random variable in the following way:

```
NRetr = create RVariable;
```

Note that we are only interested in the average number of retransmissions, so we could get away with a single moment. If our random variable is created as shown, we get additionally the variance (and, of course, the standard deviation, which is just a square root of the variance). Had we been a bit more frugal, we would have written

`NRetr = create RVariable (TYPE_long, 1);`

In either case, the counter type can be LONG. What we want to count is the number of transmitted packets, and this number certainly fits into a LONG integer.

Now let us recall the structure of the transmitter process. We will need a counter that is set to zero at the moment when a new packet is acquired from the Client (state NextPacket). Then, whenever the packet is retransmitted (state Retransmit) we will increment this counter by 1. Fortunately, the first transmission is done in state NextPacket, immediately after the packet has been put into the buffer, so it will not be counted. (We only count retransmissions!) Finally, in state Acked the process is done with the packet. In this state we should add a new sample to the random variable. Thus, assuming that the retransmission counter has been declared as an attribute of TransmitterType, e.g.,

`int RCntr;`

we can rewrite the transmitter's code method as follows:

```
TransmitterType::perform {
  state NextPacket:
    if (Client->getPacket (Buffer)) {
      RCntr = 0; /* --- */
      Buffer->SequenceBit = S->LastSent;
      Channel->transmit (Buffer, EndXmit);
    } else
      Client->wait (ARRIVAL, NextPacket);
  state EndXmit:
    Channel->stop ();
    Alert->wait (RECEIVE, Acked);
    Timer->wait (Timeout, Retransmit);
  state Retransmit:
    RCntr++; /* --- */
    Channel->transmit (Buffer, EndXmit);
  state Acked:
    Buffer->release ();
    NRetr->update (RCntr); /* --- */
    S->LastSent = 1 - S->LastEvent;
    proceed NextPacket;
};
```

Three statements have been added to the original version of the code method—they are marked with the comment /* --- */. As the second argument of update is absent, the default value 1 is assumed. With this statement, we add to the history of the random variable one case of a packet's having been transmitted successfully after RCntr retransmissions.

One last thing we should do to complete our exercise is to print out the calculated mean value. The simplest way to do it is to add the statement

`NRetr->printCnt ();`

to the `printResults` method of the `Root` process. The collection of exposure methods for `RVariable` (discussed in detail in section 7.3.5.4) includes `printCnt` as the standard method to print out the *contents* of the random variable, i.e., the values of its parameters.

Now let us try something a bit trickier. Suppose that we would like to monitor the size of the message queue[1] at the sender. For example, we might be interested in the mean queue size and its variance in time. To calculate these parameters, we intercept all events that change the size of the message queue. Whenever the queue size changes, we record the time of the change and the new queue size. At the same time, we update a random variable representing the history of changes. Assume that at time t_1 the queue size became s_1 and later, at time t_2, it changes to s_2. Upon detecting this change, we add to the random variable $t_2 - t_1$ samples with the same value s_1. The meaning of this update is simple: for $t_2 - t_1$ ITUs the queue size has been s_1.

To implement this operation, we will need an additional process *intercepting* all message arrival events. Whenever a new message is queued at the sender, the process will increment the queue size counter (an attribute of the sender station). This counter will be decremented whenever a packet (message) is released. In both cases, the random variable will be updated accordingly.

The idea of a process intercepting message arrivals at a station was discussed in section 5.4.2. Our version of this process can be defined as follows:

```
process InterceptorType (SenderType) {
  states {Waiting, Intercepting};
  perform {
    state Intercepting:
      QSRvar->update (S->QSize, Time - S->LUTime);
      S->QSize++;
      S->LUTime = Time;
    transient Waiting:
      Client->wait (INTERCEPT, Intercepting);
  };
};
```

Note the simple trick that we play here. Would anything be wrong with the following code method?

```
perform {
  state Waiting:
    Client->wait (INTERCEPT, Intercepting);
  state Intercepting:
```

---

[1]In our implementation of the protocol, one message is always transformed into a single packet. Thus, in section 1.2.4 we talked about a packet queue rather than a message queue. Now, having learned how to tell messages from packets, we can be more formal.

```
                    QSRVar->update (S->QSize, Time - S->LUTime);
                    S->QSize++;
                    S->LUTime = Time;
                    proceed Waiting;
            };
```

Well, not necessarily. But just to be on the safe side, with the first version we keep in mind that two or more messages may arrive at the sender within the same ITU. With proceed, such an arrival event could be lost while the interceptor was waiting on the Timer to get back to state Waiting.

Two additional attributes are declared within SenderType:

```
                    TIME LUTime;
                    int QSize;
```

They should be both initialized to zero in the station's setup method. LUTime stands for the last update time and tells the time when the last change in the queue size was recorded. QSize gives the current size of the message queue. Clearly, at time 0 the queue is empty.

Having released the packet buffer, the transmitter should update the random variable and decrement the perceived queue size by executing the following three statements:

```
                    QSRVar->update (S->QSize, Time - S->LUTime);
                    S->QSize--;
                    S->LUTime = Time;
```

This time the random variable must be created by

```
                    QSRVar = create RVariable (TYPE_BIG);
```

as its sample counter counts time instants. Again, we only care about two central moments.

In section 7.1.2.3 we explain how our nonstandard measurements can be implemented in a simpler and "politically better" way.

7.1.2   Client Performance Measures

A number of performance measures are automatically calculated for each traffic pattern, unless the user decides to switch them off by selecting SPF_off when the traffic pattern is created (section 5.3.4). These measures consist of several random variables (objects of type RVariable) and counters, whose contents are updated automatically under certain circumstances.

7.1.2.1   Random variables.

Type Traffic declares six pointers to random variables. These random variables are created together with the traffic pattern, provided that the standard performance measures are not switched off. The RVariable pointers of Traffic are publicly available, in case the user would like to examine their contents in an unconventional way. In no circumstances should these contents be directly modified by the user program. A list of the performance measures represented by the random variables of `Traffic` follows. For each measure, we give in parentheses the name of the `Traffic` attribute (an `RVariable` pointer) pointing to the corresponding `RVariable`.

Absolute Message Delay (RVAMD). The absolute delay of a message m is the amount of time in ETUs (section 2.2.2) elapsing from the moment m was queued at the sender (this moment is indicated by the contents of the `Message` attribute `QTime`—section 5.2.1) to the moment when the last packet of m has been received at its destination. A packet is assumed to have been received when `receive` (section 6.2.13) is executed for the packet. Each reception of a complete message (operation `receive` executed for its last packet) belonging to the given traffic pattern generates one sample, which is added to the history of the random variable pointed to by `RVAMD`.

The `QTime` attribute of a message is set by `genMSG` (section 5.5.2) to the current time (variable `Time`) at the moment when the message is generated and queued at the sending station.

Absolute Packet Delay (RVAPD). The absolute delay of a packet p is determined as the amount of time in ETUs (section 2.2.2) elapsing after the packet became ready for transmission (the message queuing time is excluded) until p is `received` at its destination. The time when a packet becomes ready for transmission is calculated as the maximum of the following two values:

- The time when the buffer into which the packet has been acquired was last `released` (section 5.2.3)
- The time when the message from which the packet has been acquired was queued at the sending station (this time is given by the `Message` attribute `QTime`)

Note that it is illegal to acquire a packet into a full (nonreleased) buffer (section 5.4.1.1), and the above prescription for determining the ready time of a packet is well defined. The `TTime` attribute of an empty packet buffer (section 5.2.2) is used to store the time when the buffer was last `released`.

At first sight, it might seem natural to assume that the packet delay should be counted from the moment the packet is put into the buffer. However, the actual operation of acquiring the packet into one of the station's buffers can be postponed by the protocol to the very moment of starting the packet transmission. Thus, the numeric value of the packet delay would be dependent on the programming style of the protocol implementor.

Example

Consider the following simple transmitter code:

```
perform {
    state WaitClient:
```

```
        if (Client->getPacket (Buffer))
          proceed WaitTransmit;
        else
          Client->wait (ARRIVAL, WaitClient);
      state WaitTransmit:
        TheProcess->wait (SIGNAL, Transmit);
      state Transmit:
        MyPort->transmit (Buffer, Done);
      state Done:
        MyPort->stop ();
        Buffer->release ();
        proceed WaitClient;
  };
```

The process acquires a packet for transmission and then awaits permission to transmit, which arrives as a signal sent by some other process. One may think about rewriting the code method in the following way:

```
  perform {
    state WaitTransmit:
      TheProcess->wait (SIGNAL, WaitClient);
    state WaitClient:
      if (Client->getPacket (Buffer))
        proceed Transmit;
      else
        Client->wait (ARRIVAL, WaitClient);
    state Transmit:
      MyPort->transmit (Buffer, Done);
    state Done:
      MyPort->stop ();
      Buffer->release ();
      proceed WaitTransmit;
  };
```

The two versions of the transmitter code method may be perfectly equivalent from the operational point of view; however, they fill the packet buffer at different moments within the transmission cycle. The second version acquires the packet immediately before transmission. If the packet delay were counted from the moment of packet acquisition, it would be equal to the sum of the propagation delay and the packet transmission time (packet length), and consequently it would not be very useful as a performance measure. We would prefer to include the waiting time for the permission signal in the packet delay. Apparently, something interesting is going on during that time interval, e.g., the station negotiates its access rights to the channel, and the length of this period may be of interest to the user.[2]

The way the packet delay is measured makes sure that the two versions of the transmitter code method will produce exactly the same samples of this measure. When a packet is put into the buffer, its delay time is assumed to have started at

---

[2]This internal measure, called the packet access time, is discussed later in this section.

the moment when the buffer was emptied unless, of course, the packet was not ready at that moment. Then the time when the message was queued is used (note that the buffer was available at that moment and, in principle, it could have been used to accommodate the packet immediately upon the message arrival). Note that the two methods release the packet buffer at the same moments. The only sensible time to do it is immediately after the transmitter is done with the packet.

Intuitively, as soon as a packet buffer is emptied (by **release**) the buffer becomes ready to accommodate the next packet. In this sense, the next packet becomes automatically ready for transmission, provided that the packet is pending, i.e., its message is queued at the station.

Each reception (by **receive**) of a complete packet belonging to the given traffic pattern generates one sample to be included in the random variable pointed to by RVAPD.

Weighted Message Delay (RVWMD). The weighted message delay (also called the message bit delay) is the delay in ETUs (section 2.2.2) of a single information bit measured from the time the message containing that bit was queued at the sender to the moment when the packet containing that bit has been completely received at the destination. Whenever a packet p belonging to the given traffic pattern is received, p->ILength samples are added to the random variable pointed to by RVWMD, all with the same value equal to the difference between the current time (**Time**) and the time when the message containing the packet was queued at the sender. This difference, like all other delays, is expressed in ETUs.

Weighted message delay accounts for the possibility that a single message can be split into a number of packets and that different packets representing some portions of the original message may reach the destination at different moments. With the absolute message delay (RVAMD), the entire message is treated as a single transmission unit, whereas with the weighted message delay the delay suffered by the message is spread among all its packets—in proportion to their size.

Example

Imagine that a message transmitted from station s_1 to station s_2 was queued at time $t_0 = 4,224,000$ ITUs. The message is split into two packets p_1 and p_2, their payloads being of length 1024 and 768 bits respectively. Assume that p_1 arrives at s_2 at time $t_1 = 8,779,000$ ITUs and p_2 arrives at s_2 at time $t_2 = 11,897,000$ ITUs. Additionally, assume for simplicity that 1 ITU is equal to 1 ETU. The absolute delay of the message is just a single number (the message produces just one sample for RVAMD) equal to $t_2 - t_0 = 7,673,000$ ETUs.

With weighted message delay, the situation is a bit more complicated. The arrival of the first packet adds to the random variable 1024 samples, all with the same value of $t_1 - t_0 = 4,555,000$ ETUs. With the second packet, 768 new samples are added with the value of $t_2 - t_0 = 7,673,000$ ETUs. Assuming that these are the only packets received so far, the average weighted message delay accumulated in the random variable will be

$$\frac{1024 \times 4{,}555{,}000 + 768 \times 7{,}673{,}000}{1024 + 768} = 5{,}991{,}591 \text{ ETUs}$$

Note that this number is less than the absolute delay of the entire message, as some portion of the message arrived earlier than its last packet.

If a message is transmitted as a single packet, its absolute message delay is equal to the weighted delay of all its bits. Therefore, to observe a difference between the two measures, one has to deal with messages that are split into multiple packets.

Message Access Time (RVMAT).   The access time of a message m is the amount of time in ETUs elapsing from the moment the message was queued at the sender to the moment when the last packet of the message is `released` by the sender. Each operation of releasing the last packet of a message generates one data sample for the random variable pointed to by RVMAT.

Message access time can be viewed as the absolute message delay reduced by the distance to the destination and is useful in situations when we want to compare networks with different diameters.

Packet Access Time (RVPAT).   The access time of a packet p is the amount of time in ETUs elapsing from the moment the packet becomes ready for transmission (see *absolute packet delay*) to the moment when the packet is `released` by the sender. Each operation of releasing a packet generates one data sample for the random variable pointed to by RVPAT.

Packet access time can be viewed as the absolute packet delay reduced by the distance to the destination. Packet access time reduced by the packet transmission time (packet length expressed in ETUs) gives the actual amount of time spent by the transmission protocol on negotiating access to the network for the (successful) packet transmission.

Message Length Statistics (RVMLS).   Whenever a message belonging to the given traffic pattern is queued at a sender, one data sample containing the message length is generated and added to the random variable pointed to by RVMLS. Thus, this random variable collects statistics related to the length of messages generated according to the given traffic pattern.

The message length statistics are not very useful for a standard traffic pattern (they are easily predictable), but they can be used for nonstandard patterns, e.g., to verify their operation.

All standard random variables of traffic patterns are created with the number of central moments equal to two (section 7.1.1.1). Thus, only the mean value and variance (standard deviation) are calculated. If these statistics (plus the minimum and the maximum value) are insufficient, the user may collect other statistics using additional, private random variables.

The counter type for a standard random variable of a traffic pattern is LONG, except for RVWMD, whose counter type is BITCOUNT (section 2.2.6). Note that all standard random variables except RVWMD count packets or messages, whereas RVWMD samples individual bits and may occasionally require a larger counter capacity. Consequently, RVWMD is created with the following statement:

```
RVWMD = create RVariable (TYPE_BITCOUNT, 2);
```

Note that TYPE_BITCOUNT can be either TYPE_long or TYPE_BIG, depending on the setting of the -i option of mks (section B.2). By default TYPE_BITCOUNT is TYPE_long and bits are counted using type LONG, in the same way as messages and packets.

The contents of the standard random variables associated with a traffic pattern are automatically *exposed* (i.e., printed or displayed) when the traffic pattern is exposed in a certain way. One can also expose the Client, in which case the corresponding random variables of all traffic patterns will be combined (using combineRV—section 7.1.1.2) and the results exposed. These issues are discussed in detail in section 7.3.5.6. We saw an example of a Client exposure in section 1.2.4.12, where we showed how to produce output results from the alternating-bit protocol.

Note. If the number of messages received is large or the messages are long, the bit counter of the random variable used to calculate the weighted message delay may run out of range. This will result in a nonsensical (typically negative) value of the counter and incorrect values of the distribution parameters produced by the Traffic or Client exposure (sections 7.3.5.5, 7.3.5.6). In such a case, the simulator should be recreated with the -i option of mks (section B.2).

Note. If the standard performance measures have been switched off upon the creation of a traffic pattern (section 5.3.4), the standard random variables are not created and their pointers contain NULL.

7.1.2.2 Counters.   Besides the random variables, type Traffic defines the following user-accessible counters:

```
Long NQMessages, NTMessages, NRMessages, NTPackets, NRPackets;
BITCOUNT NQBits, NTBits, NRBits;
```

All these counters are initialized to zero when the traffic pattern is created. If the standard performance measures are effective for the traffic pattern, the counters are updated in the following way:

- Whenever a message is generated and queued at the sender (by the standard method genMSG—section 5.5.2), NQMessages (the number of queued messages) is incremented by 1 and NQBits (the number of queued bits) is incremented by the message size in bits.

- Whenever a packet is released (by `release`—section 5.4.3), `NTPackets` (the number of transmitted packets) is incremented by 1. At the same time `NTBits` (the number of transmitted bits) is incremented by the length of the packet's payload (attribute `ILength`) and `NQBits` is decremented by the same number. If the packet is the last packet of a message, `NTMessages` (the number of transmitted messages) is incremented by 1 and `NQMessages` is decremented by 1.

- Whenever a packet is `received`, `NRPackets` (the number of received packets) is incremented by 1 and `NRBits` (the number of received bits) is incremented by the length of the packet's payload. If the packet is the last packet of its message, `NRMessages` (the number of received messages) is incremented by 1.

Note that `NQBits`, `NTBits`, and `NRBits` are of type `BITCOUNT`, which is either `LONG` or `BIG`, depending on how the simulator was created (section B.2). If the performance statistics produced by the `Traffic` or `Client` exposure (sections 7.3.5.5, 7.3.5.6) include nonsensical (typically negative) counters, the simulator must be recreated with the `-i` option of `mks`.

Besides the publicly available collection of `Traffic` counters, there exist similar counters used by the `Client` to calculate messages, packets, and bits globally. These counters are used for internal purposes and are not directly visible to the protocol program. In principle, we could get away without even mentioning the internal counters of the `Client`. Normally, each of them contains the sum of the corresponding counters from all traffic patterns. For example, there is a global counter keeping the total number of messages received so far, irrespective of their traffic patterns. This counter is used to detect the simulation exit condition based on the message number limit (section 4.9.1). Its value is usually equal to the sum of all `NRMessages` counters over all traffic patterns. The situation becomes a bit more complicated if the standard performance measures for selected traffic pattern are reset (section 7.1.2.4) on an individual basis. Then the global counters may get "out of sync" with the `Traffic` counters. This issue is given some attention in section 7.1.2.4.

Another global counter of the `Client` is used for calculating the global throughput of the network. This throughput (which appears as an item of the `Client`'s exposure—section 7.3.5.5) is equal to the ratio of all the useful (payload) bits received at their destinations to the simulated time expressed in ETUs. Although this entity does not occur explicitly as a `Client` or `Traffic` attribute, it can be easily computed, e.g.,

```
BITCOUNT nb;
int i;
for (nb = 0, i = 0; i < NTraffics; i++)
  nb += idToTraffic (i) -> NRBits;
throughput = ((double) nb / (double) Time) * Etu;
```

Of course, the algorithm only works under the assumption that `Time` is greater than zero. The actual way the throughput is calculated is a bit simpler because of the existence of a global counter of all received bits. Clearly, the user can calculate the throughput for any single traffic pattern as

```
throughput = ((double) (tp->NRBits) / (double) Time) * Etu;
```

Normally, except for the situations discussed in section 7.1.2.4, the global throughput (calculated by SMURPH using the global counter) is equal to the sum of individual throughputs for all traffic patterns.[3]

7.1.2.3 Collecting nonstandard traffic statistics.

As mentioned in section 5.5.2, type `Traffic` declares a number of virtual methods that can be redefined by the user to modify the standard behavior of the traffic pattern. We introduce here five more such methods, which are useful for collecting nonstandard performance statistics. Actually, we should not say that these methods are useful for anything, because their default bodies are empty. It is their existence that is useful: the sole purpose of those methods is to be redefined in user subtypes of `Traffic`.

In the following list, *mtype* and *ptype* stand for the message and packet types associated with the traffic pattern.

```
void pfmMQU (mtype *m);
```

The method is called whenever a message is generated (by the standard method `genMSG`) and queued at the sender. The argument contains a pointer to the newly generated message.

```
void pfmPTR (ptype *p);
```

The method is called whenever a packet is **released** (section 5.4.3). The argument points to that packet.

```
void pfmPRC (ptype *p);
```

The method is called whenever a packet is **received** (section 5.4.3). The argument points to the received packet.

```
void pfmMTR (ptype *p);
```

The method is called whenever the last packet of a message is **released**. This operation can be viewed as releasing the entire message. The argument points to the packet being released.

```
void pfmMRC (ptype *p);
```

The method is called whenever the last packet of a message is **received**. This operation can be viewed as the reception of the entire message. The argument points to the packet being received.

---

[3]If we ignore the subtleties of the floating-point arithmetic.

Example

Let us revisit the second example from section 7.1.1.2. Instead of modifying the transmitter's code method, we could redefine some virtual methods of the traffic pattern leaving the transmitter code intact. This approach makes better sense, especially since we already have a nonstandard traffic type.

We augment the traffic type declaration in the following way:

```
traffic TrafficType (Message, PacketType) {
   RVariable *QSRvar;
   int LUTime, QSize;
   void setup (int flags, double mmit, double ml) {
      QSRvar = create RVariable (TYPE_BIG, 2);
      LUTime = TIME_0;
      QSize = 0;
      Traffic::setup (flags, mmit, ml);
   };
   void pfmMQU (Message *m) {
      QSRvar->update (QSize, LUTime);
      QSize++;
      LUTime = Time;
   };
   void pfmMTR (PacketType *p) {
      QSRVar->update (QSize, Time - LUTime);
      QSize--;
      LUTime = Time;
   };
};
```

These are practically all the modifications needed to perform our measurements. This time they have been put together into the traffic pattern, where they rightfully belong. The protocol code need not be aware of the fact that these measurements are being taken.

We have eliminated the interceptor process that was needed in the previous solution to intercept all message arrivals at the sender. This end is now taken care of by **pfmMQU**.

One simple element needed to complete our solution is the code for printing out the contents of the random variable pointed to by **QSRvar**. We can do it in a simple way, by executing the **printCnt** method of the random variable. We can also opt for a more formal and general way of handling this issue, and define a nonstandard *exposure* for our traffic type. In section 7.3 we explain how this can be done.

The preceding virtual methods are called even if the standard performance measures for the given traffic pattern are switched off. Note that the user redefinitions of these methods can determine the status of the standard performance measures by examining the **FlgSPF** attribute of the traffic pattern (section 5.5.2).

7.1.2.4   Resetting performance measures.   At any moment, the standard performance statistics of a traffic pattern (discussed in the previous sections) can be *reset*, which corresponds to starting the collection of these statistics from scratch. This is done by calling the following `Traffic` method:

`void resetSPF ();`

The method does nothing for a traffic pattern created with `SPF_off` (section 5.3.4), i.e., if no standard performance statistics are collected for the traffic pattern. Otherwise, it erases (section 7.1.1.2) the contents of the traffic pattern's standard random variables and resets its counters (section 7.1.2.2) in the following way:

```
NTMessages = NTMessages - NRMessages;
NRMessages = 0;
NTPackets = NTPackets - NRPackets;
NRPackets = 0;
NTBits = NTBits - NRBits;
NRBits = 0;
```

The new values of the counters (note that `NQMessages` and `NQBits` are not changed) are obtained from the previous values by assuming that the number of received messages (packets, bits) is now zero. In order to maintain consistency, the counters reflecting the number of transmitted items are not zeroed, but decremented by the corresponding counts of received items. This way, after they have been reset, these counters give the number of items "in transit." By the same token, the number of queued items is left intact.

Whenever `resetSPF` is executed for a traffic pattern, the traffic pattern's attribute `SMTime` of type `TIME` is set to the current time (the contents of variable `Time`). `SMTime` is initialized to `TIME_0` upon the creation of the traffic pattern. At any moment, it gives the time when the standard statistics of the traffic pattern were last reset. This is another way of saying that `SMTime` tells since when the standard performance statistics have been collected.

The `SMTime` attribute is user-accessible, and it can be used to properly calculate the throughput for the traffic pattern. The throughput formula we gave in section 7.1.2.2 only works under the assumption that the `NRBits` counter has never been reset, i.e., the received bits have been accumulating since time 0. The following formula is better, as it accounts for the possibility that the performance measures (and the counters) may have been reinitialized:

```
throughput = ((double)(tp->NRBits) / (double)(Time - tp->SMTime))
   * Etu;
```

Resetting the performance measures of a selected traffic pattern affects the `Client`'s performance measures but not the `Client`'s global counters (section 7.1.2.2). The `Client` does not have its own random variables; thus, it "globalizes" the performance measures by combining the random variables of all traffic patterns. The global performance statistics produced by the `Client`'s exposure (section 7.3.5.5) are always compilations of the statistics for individual traffic patterns. On the other hand, the `Client` uses its own (user-invisible) global counters for the transmitted and received messages, packets, and bits. These counters are not affected by calling `resetSPF` for a traffic pattern. In particular, the global throughput produced by the `Client`'s exposure (sections 7.1.2.2, 7.3.5.5) will account for all bits received since time 0.

It is possible to reset the standard performance statistics globally for the entire `Client` by executing the `resetSPF` method of the `Client`. This version of the method calls `resetSPF` for every traffic pattern and also resets the internal global counters of the `Client`. These counters are reset in a similar way as the local user-accessible counters of an individual traffic pattern.

The global effective throughput calculated by the `Client` (section 7.3.5.5) is produced by relating the total number of received bits to the time during which these bits have been received. This time is calculated by subtracting from `Time` the contents of an internal variable (of type `TIME`) that gives the time of the last `resetSPF` operation performed for the `Client`.

If the simulation termination condition is based on the total number of messages received (section 4.9.1), this condition will be affected by the `Client` variant of `resetSPF`. Namely, `resetSPF` zeros the global counter of received messages so that it will be accumulating toward the limit from scratch. In particular, if `Client`'s `resetSPF` is executed many times, e.g., in a loop, the termination condition may never be met, although the actual number of messages received during the simulation run may be bigger than the specified limit. The semantics of the `-c` SMURPH call option (sections 4.9.1, B.3) are also affected by the global variant of `resetSPF`. Namely, the total number of generated messages is reduced by the number of messages that were received at the moment when the method was invoked. According to what we said earlier, calling `resetSPF` for a traffic pattern has no impact on the global counters of the `Client` and consequently does not affect the termination conditions.

In most cases, if the standard performance measures are ever reset, it is done globally for the `Client` and only once during the simulation experiment. The main purpose of this operation is to make sure that all measurements start after the network has reached a steady-state behavior, i.e., it is past a possible warm-up phase during which the measured values may be uncertain.

Every `resetSPF` operation executed on a traffic pattern triggers an event that can be perceived by a user-defined process. This way the user may define a customized response to the operation, e.g., resetting nonstandard random variables or private counters. The event, labeled RESET, occurs on the traffic pattern even if the traffic pattern was created with SPF_off. A global `resetSPF` operation performed on the `Client` forces the RESET event for all traffic patterns and also for the `Client`.

7.1.3   Link Performance Measures

As with traffic patterns, certain standard performance statistics are collected for
links. Unlike the `Traffic` measures, the link statistics are not random variables:
they are just simple counters (similar to those associated with traffic patterns—
section 7.1.2.2) that keep track of how many bits, packets, and messages have passed
through the link. The user may switch off collecting these measures at the moment
when the link is created (section 3.2.2).

Type `Link` declares a number of virtual methods whose purpose is similar to
the role of the virtual methods of type `Traffic` discussed in section 7.1.2.3. These
methods are called automatically whenever a potentially interesting change occurs
in the status of a packet propagated along the link.

The following public link attribute tells whether the standard performance
measures are being collected for the link:

char FlgSPF;

This flag can take two values: `ON` (1) if the standard performance measures are
to be calculated for the link, or `OFF` (0) if the standard measurements are switched
off. The value of `FlgSPF` is determined by the contents of the `spf` argument passed
to the link's `setup` when the link is created (section 3.2.2). Unlike traffic patterns,
links are not equipped with methods for suspending and resuming the collection of
performance measures on the fly.

7.1.3.1   Counters.   Type `Link` declares the following publicly available
counters:

```
BITCOUNT NTBits, NRBits, NDBits;
Long NTJams, NTAttempts;
Long NTPackets, NRPackets, NDPackets, NHDPackets;
Long NTMessages, NRMessages;
```

All these counters are initialized to zero when the link is created. Then, if the
standard performance measures are effective for the link, the counters are updated
according to the following rules:

- Whenever a jamming signal is inserted into a port connected to the link,
  `NTJams` is incremented by 1. This happens when **startJam** or **sendJam** (section 6.1.2.2) is executed on one of the link's ports.
- Whenever a packet transmission is started on a port connected to the link,
  `NTAttempts` is incremented by 1. This happens when **startTransfer** or
  transmit (section 6.1.2.1) is executed on one of the link's ports.
- Whenever a packet transmission on a port connected to the link is terminated
  by **stop** (section 6.1.2.1), `NTPackets` is incremented by 1 and `NTBits` is incremented by the packet's payload length (attribute `ILength`). If the packet
  is the last packet of its message (i.e., its `PF_last` flag is set—section 5.4.1.1),
  `NTMessages` is incremented by 1.

- Whenever a packet is received from the link (by `receive`—section 6.2.13), `NRPackets` is incremented by 1 and `NRBits` is incremented by the packet's payload length. If the packet is the last packet of its message, `NRMessages` is incremented by 1.
- Whenever a damaged packet (section 6.4) is inserted into the link, `NDPackets` is incremented by 1 and the packet's payload length (attribute `ILength`) is added to `NDBits`. If the packet happens to be header-damaged, `NHDPackets` is also incremented by 1. Note that a header-damaged packet is also damaged; consequently, `NHDPackets` cannot be bigger than `NDPackets`.

Note that it is possible to call `receive` (section 6.2.13) without the second argument that normally identifies the link from which the packet is received. In such a case, the counters `NRPackets`, `NRBits`, and `NRMessages` will not be affected by the packet reception.

Note. The counters related to damaged packets, i.e., `NDPackets`, `NHDpackets`, and `NDBits`, are only available if the simulator has been created with the `-z` option of `mks` (section B.2).

7.1.3.2   Virtual methods.   Type `Link` declares a number of virtual methods, which are initially empty and can be redefined in a user extension of a standard link type. These methods are called automatically whenever a relevant change occurs in the status of a packet being propagated along the link. They look similar to the analogous `Traffic` methods discussed in section 7.1.2.3. Each method accepts one argument of type `Packet*`. Note that packets of different types may be transmitted along the same link; thus, the argument may have to be cast to the proper packet subtype pointer before being referenced.

A list of the virtual methods of `Link` follows:

```
void pfmPTR (Packet *p);
```

The method is called when a packet transmission on a port belonging to the link is terminated by `stop` (section 6.1.2.1). The argument points to the packet whose carrying activity is being terminated.

```
void pfmPAB (Packet *p);
```

The method is called when a packet transmission on a port belonging to the link is terminated by `abort` (section 6.1.2.1). The argument points to the packet whose carrying activity is being aborted.

```
void pfmPRC (Packet *p);
```

The method is called when a packet is received from the link by `receive` (section 6.2.13) with the second argument identifying the link. The argument points to the received packet.

```
void pfmMTR (Packet *p);
```

The method is called when a packet transmission on a port belonging to
the link is terminated by stop and the packet turns out to be the last packet of
its message. The argument points to the packet whose carrying activity is being
terminated.

```
void pfmMRC (Packet *p);
```

The method is called when the last packet of its message is received (by
receive) from the link. This only happens if the second argument of receive
identifies the link. The argument points to the received packet.

```
void pfmPDM (Packet *p);
```

The method is called when a damaged packet is inserted into the link. The user
can examine the packet flags (section 6.4) to determine the nature of the damage,
i.e., whether the packet is header-damaged or just damaged. The argument points
to the damaged packet.

It is possible to print out or display the standard performance measures related
to a link in a natural way—by exposing the link (section 7.3.5.8).

Example

Type Link offers no standard random variables for measuring distribution parameters related to the packets passing through the link. However, one can easily implement such statistics, should they prove useful. For example, assume that we want to
measure the length distribution of damaged packets in our alternating-bit protocol
(section 1.2.4). One possible place to perform such measurements is at the recipient
station in the receiver process (section 1.2.4.5). Note however, that in the present
version of the alternating-bit protocol damaged packets are never received. With
the default processing level for damaged packets (section 6.4.1) a damaged packet
does not trigger the EMP event awaited by the receiver process. Thus, we would
have to change the processing level to FT_LEVEL0 by specifying this constant as the
second argument of setFaultRate in section 1.2.4.8. Then we would have to modify
the receiver process to treat damaged packets in a special way, i.e., by sampling
their lengths without receiving them. If we wanted to take similar measurements for
the acknowledging channel, we would have to modify the acknowledgment receiver
process as well.

With the virtual methods of Link, we can implement our measurements in a way
that is transparent from the point of view of both the protocol processes and the
processing level for damaged packets. Namely, we can define a simple extension of
type Link,

```
link MLink {
  RVariable *DPS;
  void setup (int nports) {
    DPS = create RVariable;
```

```
                    Link::setup (nports);
        };
        virtual void pfmPDM (Packet *p) {
          DPS->update (p->ILength);
        };
    };
```

and use it instead of Link to build the channel(s) for which the distribution of damaged packets is to be measured. The contents of the random variable pointed to by DPS can be printed by printResults (section 1.2.4.12), e.g., as shown in section 7.1.1.2.

Note. The methods related to damaged packets are only available if the simulator has been created with the -z option of mks (section B.2).

7.2 TOOLS FOR PROTOCOL TESTING AND DEBUGGING

SMURPH provides the user with a few simple monitoring tools that can greatly help in the process of debugging and validating a protocol program, especially in those numerous cases when formal correctness proofs are infeasible.

The incorrectness of a protocol can manifest itself in one of the following two ways:

- Under certain circumstances, the protocol crashes and ceases to operate.
- The protocol seems to work, but it does not exhibit certain properties expected by the designer or implementor.

Generally, problems of the first type are rather easy to detect by extensive testing, unless the "certain circumstances" occur too seldom to be caught. Our experience indicates that the likelihood of finding a crashing error decreases much more than linearly with the running time of the protocol prototype. However, the specific nature of protocol programs, especially medium access control (MAC) protocols, makes them susceptible to errors of the second type, which may be more difficult to diagnose.

7.2.1 Protocol Tracing

One simple way to detect run-time errors is to assert simple Boolean properties. SMURPH offers some tools for this purpose (section 2.3.5). Once an error has been found, the detection of its origin may still pose a tricky problem. Often, one has to trace the protocol behavior for some time prior to the occurrence of the error to identify the circumstances leading to the trouble.

The natural event-driven structure of protocols programmed in SMURPH makes their local debugging relatively easy and straightforward. The author's experience indicates that the best way to find a bug in a protocol is to trace its actions while printing out the configurations of link activities (sections 7.3.5.7, 7.3.5.8) and the contents of user-defined variables.

There exists a global variable, `TracingTime` of type `TIME`, which can be set by the `-t` option of the simulator (section B.3). This variable can be used to determine whether the protocol tracing should be switched on or off. Intentionally, when `TracingTime` contains an undefined value (`TIME_inf`), the tracing is switched off. Otherwise, the variable shows the starting moment of the simulated time when the tracing should commence. Another variable, `TracedStation` (also settable by `-t`) optionally specifies the `Id` of the station to which the tracing should be restricted. By default, `TracedStation` contains `NONE`, indicating that the tracing is global. The standard macro

```
#define Debugging (def (TracingTime) && Time >= TracingTime && \
  (TracedStation == NONE || TracedStation == TheStation->getId ()))
```

returns `YES` if, according to the rules just outlined, the current event is to be monitored.

If the simulator has been created with the `-g` (debug) flag (section B.2), the global variables `TracingTime` and `TracedStation` are interpreted by SMURPH and the `-t` call option can be used to turn on the standard tracing. The standard tracing starts when the simulated time reaches the value in `TracingTime`. When the tracing is on, SMURPH writes to the results file (section 2.3.2) one line of text for each process-waking event to be triggered (note that if `TracedStation` is not `NONE`, the event must wake up a process owned by the indicated station). This line is printed **before** the restarted process is given control, and it includes the following items:

- Current simulated time
- Type name and `Id` of the AI (activity interpreter) generating the event
- Event identifier (in the AI-specific format—section 7.3.5.1)
- Station `Id`
- Type name and `Id` attribute of the process to be awakened (if a nickname is defined for the process, the nickname is printed instead—section 2.4.2)
- Identifier of the state to be assumed by the process

Example

Following is an initial fragment of the trace information for the alternating-bit protocol in section 1.2.4.

Time	AI/Idn	Event	Station	Process/Idn	State
0	ReceiverTyp/004	START	1	ReceiverTy/004	WaitPacket
0	Acknowledge/005	START	1	Acknowledg/005	WaitAlert
0	AckReceiver/003	START	0	AckReceive/003	WaitAck
0	Transmitter/002	START	0	Transmitte/002	NextPacket
628	Client	ARRIVAL	0	Transmitte/002	NextPacket

1652	Timer	wakeup	0	Transmitte/002	EndXmit
2652	Port/000	EMP	1	ReceiverTy/004	PacketArri
2652	Mailbox/000	RECEIVE	1	Acknowledg/005	SendAck
2653	Timer	wakeup	1	ReceiverTy/004	WaitPacket
2908	Timer	wakeup	1	Acknowledg/005	EndXmit
2908	Timer	wakeup	1	Acknowledg/005	WaitAlert
3908	Port/000	EMP	0	AckReceive/003	AckArrival
3908	Mailbox/000	RECEIVE	0	Transmitte/002	Acked
3908	Timer	wakeup	0	Transmitte/002	NextPacket
3909	Timer	wakeup	0	AckReceive/003	WaitAck
12155	Client	ARRIVAL	0	Transmitte/002	NextPacket
13179	Timer	wakeup	0	Transmitte/002	EndXmit
14179	Port/000	EMP	1	ReceiverTy/004	PacketArri
14179	Mailbox/000	RECEIVE	1	Acknowledg/005	SendAck
14180	Timer	wakeup	1	ReceiverTy/004	WaitPacket

The Id attribute for the AI triggering the waking event and for the process being awakened is limited to three decimal digits. Note that the activity interpreters that occur in single instances, e.g., the Client and Timer, have no Ids. If the actual Id is greater than 999, the value modulo 1000 is printed. Similarly, textual fields are limited (to 11 or 10 characters) and longer names are truncated.

Event identifiers appearing in column 3 are AI-specific. Typically, the event name coincides with the name of the symbolic constant identifying the event for the corresponding wait request. For the Timer AI, the event is always wakeup; it is clear that the event consists in the alarm clock going off at exactly the current moment (indicated by the first column). We say more about event identifiers in section 7.3.5.1.

Note that the first four events occurring at time 0 are the startup events for the protocol processes. According to what we said in section 4.6.1, these events formally arrive from the processes themselves. Note that the order in which the processes are started is different from the order in which they were created (section 1.2.4.10).

When the -t call option of the simulator is used together with -f (indicating the so-called *full tracing*—section B.3), SMURPH follows each line of the trace information with the dump of all links accessible via ports from the current station. This dump is obtained by requesting the mode-2 link exposure (section 7.3.5.8).

Example

Following is a short fragment of a full-trace output for the alternating-bit protocol. This fragment describes one waking event for the receiver process at station 1 (the recipient) caused by the Timer.

```
        Time      AI/Idn     Event Station   Process/Idn      State
        1082337    Timer     wakeup        1 ReceiverTy/004 WaitPacket
Activities in Link 0:
T       STime        FTime   St Port Rcvr   TP    Length  Signature
T       1080312     1081336   0   1   1     0     1024          67
(Link 0) End of list
```

```
Activities in Link 1:
T        STime              FTime     St Port Rcvr   TP    Length Signature
T        1082336            undefined  1   1    0    -1    256        -1
(Link 1) End of list
```

The format of the link exposure used to dump link activities for the purpose of tracing is discussed in section 7.3.5.8. The letter T points to a packet transmission, rather than to a jamming signal. STime and FTime give the activity's starting and finished time, respectively (section 6.1.1). Note that the packet activity in Link 1 (the acknowledging link) has not been terminated yet and its finished time is undefined. The remaining numbers specify (in this order):

- Id of the station whose process inserted the activity
- Station-relative Id of the port on which the activity was inserted (section 3.3.1)
- Receiver attribute of the packet, if the activity is a packet transmission
- TP attribute of the packet, i.e., the Id attribute of the traffic pattern to which the packet belongs
- Total packet length (attribute TLength)
- Packet's signature, i.e., a unique number assigned to the packet by getPacket (section 5.4.1.1)

The last three items are only present for a packet-carrying activity; they do not appear for a jamming signal. Note that the signature attribute of a packet is only present if the simulator has been created with the -g option of mks (section B.2). But to be able to get a protocol trace list one must have created the simulator with -g; thus, packet signatures always appear in a full-trace output.

Irrespective of the setting of the -t option (and irrespective of whether the simulator has been created with -g), it is always possible to write to the output file a line of trace information, possibly listing the snapshot contents of some protocol variables at the given moment. The function

$$\text{void trace (char *, ...);}$$

accepts a format string as the first argument. This format string is used to interpret the remaining arguments,[4] which are encoded and written to the output file. The printout is automatically terminated by a new line, so the format string need not end with the newline character. The printed values of the arguments are preceded by the current simulated time.

In appendix A we present DSD (a dynamic simulation display program), which provides a user end to the concept of screen exposing (section 7.3). As DSD is a separate (and in principle exchangeable) program, its description does not really belong to the SMURPH manual. However, we should at least remark in this section that the standard version of DSD is also very useful for debugging. When an error occurs, e.g., because of a failing assert or Assert (section 2.3.5), the simulator

---

[4]In the same way as in printf or form.

prints out, among other things, the simulated time of the failure. The user may call the simulator again under control of DSD, requesting to halt the program a while before the error occurrence. Then, it is possible to execute the protocol in the *step mode*, examining individual events and their environment. This procedure is described in detail in appendix A.

7.2.2   Observers

Regular static assertions (section 2.3.5) are Boolean statements expressing statically some dynamic properties of the program in which they appear. By employing assertions, the user reduces the complexity of the (dynamic) program whose behavior he or she is trying to understand, or express in an easily comprehensible way, to a collection of simple static formulas. Along these lines, one can draw an analogy between static assertions and observers. As assertions are typically used to transform the dynamic semantics of a sequential program into a set of static formulas, observers reduce the semantics of a parallel program to the semantics of a sequential program. An observer can be viewed as a dynamic assertion—a statement about a configuration of state transitions in a collection of protocol processes.

Examples

Consider the following statement about the behavior of the alternating-bit protocol in section 1.2.4: *If two consecutive entries of the transmitter process to state* EndXmit *are not separated by state* Retransmit, *then they must be separated by state* AckArrival *of the acknowledgment receiver process.* This statement is an example of a property expressible (and verifiable) by an observer.

In fact, statements verbalized by SMURPH observers can be more tricky than just raw assertions about state transitions. Observers have access to the protocol's data structures and environment variables; thus, the following statement about the alternating-bit protocol is also quite easy to assert in an observer: *If a packet is acquired for transmission with the sequence bit equal to ε (in state* NextPacket *of the transmitter), then no other packet is acquired for transmission until a packet with sequence bit equal to ε is received (in state* Receiving *of the receiver).* Note that this statement can be viewed as the "no-loss" property of the protocol.

All interesting properties of protocols are expressible as formal statements about the configurations of state transitions, possibly involving some local or global variables affected by the protocol.

7.2.2.1   Observer structure.   Observers are tools for expressing global assertions that may involve combined actions of many processes, possibly running at different stations. An observer is a dynamic object that resembles a regular protocol process. Unlike regular processes, observers never respond directly to the events caused by the protocol environment, nor do they generate events that may be perceived by the protocol. Instead, they are driven by state transitions of protocol processes. An observer may specify that it is to be awakened whenever a waking condition of a protocol process fulfills certain criteria. Thus, observers are able to monitor the behavior of the protocol viewed as a collection of finite-state machines.

An observer is an object belonging to an observer type. An observer type is defined in the following way:

```
observer otype : itypename {
    ...
    local attributes and methods
    ...
    states { list of states };
    ...
    perform {
        the observer code
    };
};
```

where *otype* is the name of the declared observer type and *itypename* identifies an already known observer type (or types), as described in section 2.4.3. As with a process code method, the observer code method can be just announced in the observer type definition and fully specified later, according to the following pattern:

```
observer otype : itypename {
    ...
    local attributes and methods
    ...
    states { list of states };
    ...
    perform;
};...
otype::perform {
    the observer code
};
```

The preceding layouts closely resemble a process type declaration (section 4.2). One difference is that the structure of observers is flat, i.e., an observer does not belong to any specific station, has no formal parent process (or parent observer) and no children. Observer types are extensible and can be derived from other user-defined observer types.

An observer type may declare a setup method (or a collection of setup methods—section 2.4.7), to initialize local attributes when an observer instance is created. The default observer setup method is empty and takes no arguments.

Observers are created by **create** in the regular way. Typically, all observers are created by the **Root** process, before the protocol execution is started. It is possible for an observer to create another observer (e.g., to verify some dynamic property that only arises in special and intermittent conditions). An observer can terminate itself, in which case it simply ceases to exist.

There is no formal reason against creating an observer from a regular protocol process, although, for methodological reasons, it is recommended to keep observers well separated from the protocol. If possible, the protocol should not be aware that it is being monitored.

The observer's code method has the same layout as a process code method:

```
perform {
    state OS₀:
        ...
    state OS₁:
        ...
    state OS_{p-1}:
        ...
};
```

where $OS_0, \ldots, OS_{p-1}$ are state identifiers listed with the **states** statement within the observer type declaration. Thus, like a regular process, an observer is a finite-state machine.

7.2.2.2 Observer operation.

Like a regular process, a newly created observer is started automatically in its first state, i.e., the first state occurring on the **states** list (section 7.2.2.1). From then on, the observer will sustain its operation by specifying waking conditions that will advance it to subsequent states. Like a regular process, an awakened observer performs some operations, specifies its new waking conditions, and goes to sleep. The waking conditions for an observer are described by executing just two types of statements:

```
inspect (s, p, n, ps, os);
timeout (t, os);
```

For both types of operations, the last argument is an observer state identifier, which should be one of the enumeration symbols occurring on the **states** list of the observer type declaration. It specifies the target state of the observer to be assumed when a certain condition is met. In the case of **inspect**, this condition involves a regular protocol process being restarted. For **timeout**, the condition is very simple: the observer will be resumed in the state indicated by **os** after the time interval specified by the first argument.

The first four arguments of **inspect** describe a class of scenarios when a regular protocol process is restarted. Their meanings are as follows:

s   Identifies the station to which the process belongs. It can be either a station object pointer or a station **Id** (an integer number).

p   Process type identifier. It should be a process type name declared with the **process** keyword (section 4.2).

n   Pointer to the character string containing the process nickname (section 2.4.2).

ps Process state identifier. It should be one of the symbols occurring on the **states** list of the process type declaration. Note that the process type is identified by **p**.

To understand the semantics of **inspect**, let us assume for simplicity that an observer has issued exactly one inspect request and put itself to sleep. The inspect request is interpreted as a declaration that the observer wants to remain suspended until the simulator awakes a regular process in a scenario matching the parameters of the **inspect**. Then, immediately after the restarted regular process **completes its action**, the observer will be awakened and the global variable **TheObserverState** will contain the value passed to **inspect** through **os**. As for a regular process (section 4.4.1), this value is interpreted automatically by the observer's code method, to select the proper observer state. This way, the observer is restarted in the state indicated by the last argument of the **inspect** operation, whose remaining arguments match the current waking scenario for a regular protocol process.

Any of the first four arguments of **inspect** can be ANY, which is a *wildcard* symbol meaning that the actual value of the corresponding attribute in the process awakening scenario is irrelevant.

Example

With the request

                inspect (TheStation, TransmitterType, "P1", Done, TDone);

the issuing observer declares that it wants to be resumed in state **TDone** when a process nicknamed "P1" whose type is **TransmitterType** running at the current station is awakened in state **Done**.

In most cases, some parameters of **inspect** are left unspecified. For example, with the request

                inspect (ANY, TransmitterType, ANY, ANY, WakeMeUp);

the observer will be restarted after any process of type **TransmitterType** is awakened in any state.

Note that the process type may be insufficient to identify exactly one process (a single station may be running multiple processes of the same type). It happens quite seldom, but if a problem of this kind arises, different processes of the same type running at the same station can be assigned different nicknames—to make them distinguishable by observers (section 2.4.7). Nicknames (as long as they differ across different processes of the same type run at the same station) can be used to identify processes uniquely. Of course, it is possible to identify a subclass of processes within a given type (or even across different types) by assigning the same nickname to multiple processes.

The process state identifier can only be specified if the process type identifier has been indicated as well (i.e., it is not ANY). A state is always defined within the scope of a specific process type; specifying a state without a process type makes no sense.

Example

The following inspect request is illegal:

```
inspect (0, ANY, "PierNick", NextPacket, GotIt);
```

Although the nickname may pretty well identify exactly one process running at station number 0, the state specification NextPacket cannot be accepted without a process type specification. Note that if we know that NextPacket is our state of interest, we must also know which process type the state belongs to. Thus, we may as well use this process type instead of ANY. Even if two or more different process types use the same names for some of their states, one should never assume that these de facto completely different states have anything in common.

There exist abbreviated versions of inspect accepting one, two, three and four arguments. In all these versions, the last argument specifies the observer's target state (corresponding to os in the full five-argument version), and all the missing arguments are assumed to be ANY. The interpretation of which arguments are present reflects their importance and relevance in practical situations. Thus, the single-argument version of inspect says that the observer is to be restarted after any event awaking any protocol process at any station. In the two-argument version, the first argument identifies the station to which the awakened process is expected to belong (s). The three-argument version accepts the station identifier as the first argument and the process type identifier (p) as the second argument. For the four-argument version, the first two arguments are the same as in the two-argument case, and the third argument identifies the process state (ps). Note that the nickname argument is deemed the least important one: to specify a nickname, one has to provide a full suite of arguments, even if some of them are ANY.

Example

The three inspect requests

```
inspect (ANY, Receiver, ORcv);
inspect (Stat, Monitor, Error, OErr);
inspect (TheStation, OAny);
```

are equivalent to

```
inspect (ANY, Receiver, ANY, ANY, ORcv);
inspect (Stat, Monitor, ANY, Error, OErr);
inspect (TheStation, ANY, ANY, ANY, OAny);
```

respectively.

When an observer is created (by **create**), it is initially started in the first state occurring on its **states** list, as a regular process would be. However, unlike a process, a newly created observer is started in its first state immediately—at the very moment when the **create** operation is issued. Note that the first waking event for a process may be separated from the process creation by other activities occurring within the same ITU (section 4.3).

The analogy between observers and regular processes extends onto inspect requests, which are in some sense similar to wait requests. In particular, an observer can issue a number of inspect requests before it puts itself to sleep. Like a regular process, an observer puts itself to sleep by exhausting the list of commands in its current state or by executing **sleep**.

In contrast to multiple wait requests issued by the same process, the order in which multiple inspect requests are issued is significant. Whenever a regular process completes its current action and suspends itself, SMURPH attempts to match the attributes of the process's waking scenario with the arguments of the pending inspect requests. For each alive observer, these inspect requests are examined in the order in which they were issued. The first inspect request that matches the waking scenario is chosen, and the observer is awakened in the state determined by the value of the **os** argument specified with that inspect. Multiple observers whose inspect requests match the same process waking scenario are restarted in the reverse order of their creation, i.e., the observer that was created last will be restarted first.

Example

Assume that an observer has issued the following sequence of inspect requests:

```
inspect (ThePacket->Receiver, receiver, ANY, Rcv, State1);
inspect (TheStation, ANY, ANY, ANY, State2);
inspect (ANY, ANY, ANY, ANY, State3);
```

The observer will wake up in **State1** if the next process restarted by SMURPH

- Is of type **receiver**, and
- Belongs to the station determined by the **Receiver** attribute of **ThePacket**, and
- Wakes up in state **Rcv**

Otherwise, if the next restarted process belongs to the current station, the observer will be awakened in **State2**. Finally, if the attributes of the process wake-up scenario do not match the arguments of the first two **inspects**, the observer will be awakened in **State3**. Note that the argument list of the last inspect matches all process waking scenarios.

These three inspect requests can be rewritten using the equivalent abbreviated versions of **inspect**:

```
inspect (ThePacket->Receiver, receiver, Rcv, State1);
inspect (TheStation, State2);
inspect (State3);
```

If multiple protocol processes are scheduled to be restarted at the same modeled time (within the same ITU), the actual order in which they are awakened is generally nondeterministic (section 4.4.1). With observers, the situation is much simpler. The algorithm for restarting observers can be described by the following informal program, executed every time a protocol process completes its sequence of actions:

```
for (o = ObserverList; o != NULL; o = o->next)
  for (p = o->InspectList; p != NULL; p = p->next)
    if (p->matching (TheStation, TheProcess, TheState)) {
      TheObserverState = p->State;
      run (o);
      break;
    }
```

As in most cases different observers are mutually independent, the actual order in which multiple observers are restarted by the same process awakening scenario is seldom relevant. Nonetheless, this order is deterministic. There exists a global list of observers that stores them in the reverse order of their creation. Multiple observers restarted by the same process awakening scenario are restarted according to their ordering on this list, i.e., the most recently created observers are restarted first.

An active observer has natural access to the environment variables of the regular process that has been awakened. Note that the observer is not activated until the process puts itself to sleep. Thus, the environment variables reflect the fact that the process has executed its sequence of statements at the monitored state.

Being in one state, an observer can branch directly to another state by executing

```
proceed nstate;
```

where `nstate` identifies the new observer state to be assumed. The semantics of this operation are different from that of `proceed` for a regular process (section 4.5.1). Namely, the observer variant of `proceed` branches to the indicated state immediately, the observer retaining full control during this operation. Note that no `skipto` operation is available for observers. Observers do not suffer from the problem of persisting waking conditions: a single observer cannot be restarted more than once by the same process awakening event.

Example

Consider the following fragment of an observer code method:

```
state Waiting:
  inspect (TheStation, Transmitter, Ready, CheckItOut);
state CheckItOut:
  assert (ThePacket->TP == NONE, "Illegal packet type");
  proceed Waiting;
```

Irrespective of what event has caused the **Transmitter** process to wake up in state **Ready**, there is no danger that by executing **proceed** the observer will get into an infinite loop. Unlike some events perceived by processes (e.g., section 6.2.13), the waking condition for an observer always disappears when the observer has been restarted.

Whenever an observer is restarted, its entire inspect list is cleared, so that new waiting conditions must be specified from scratch. This also applies to the **timeout** operation, which is used by observers to implement alarm clocks.

By executing **timeout(t,os)** the observer sets up an alarm clock, which wakes it up unconditionally **t** ITUs after the current moment if no process matching one of the pending inspect requests is restarted in the meantime. Observer timeouts are needed to implement assertions of the following kind: *There exists a moment in a definite future when the protocol executes a given sequence of actions.* The alarm clocks of observers are always accurate, i.e., the **timeout** interval is always precisely equal to the specified number of ITUs and is not subject to randomization (section 4.5.2).

An arbitrary number of observers can be defined and active at any moment. Different observers are completely independent in the sense that the behavior of a given observer is not directly affected by the presence or absence of other observers. Of course, an observer may affect the execution of other observers (or even protocol processes) by modifying some data structures shared with other observers (or processes). Although in some cases a cooperation of multiple observers may prove useful, it seldom makes sense to influence the protocol behavior from an observer. One natural exception is using observers to implement complicated termination conditions for a simulation experiment.

Example

The following observer terminates the simulation run as soon as the **Transmitter** process at station 0 has executed a prescribed number of state transitions:

```
observer Terminator {
  int NTransitions;
  void setup (int nt) { NTransitions = nt; };
  states {Sleeping, Counting};
  perform {
    state Sleeping:
      inspect (0, Transmitter, Counting);
    state Counting:
      if (--NTransitions <= 0) Kernel->terminate ();
      proceed Sleeping;
  };
};
```

An observer can terminate itself in exactly the same way as a regular process, i.e., by executing `terminate` (section 4.3) or by going to sleep without specifying at least one `inspect` or `timeout` request.

   Note.   When the simulator is built with the `-v` option of `mks` (section B.2) all observers are deactivated: all `create` operations for observers are void. This option is useful for switching off all observers (and reducing the simulation time) without having to modify the protocol program.

Examples

   Assume that we would like to augment our implementation of the alternating-bit protocol in section 1.2.4 by an observer verifying that no packets are ever lost, i.e., all packets acquired from the `Client` eventually reach the recipient station and are received there. We will express this property in the following somewhat weaker form: *If the transmitter process acquires a packet for transmission and the sequence bit of this packet is ε ($\varepsilon \in \{0,1\}$), then no other packet is acquired for transmission until a packet whose sequence bit is ε is received at the recipient's side.* The following observer verifies this property:

```
observer LostPackets {
  int SequenceBit;
  states {WaitNPkt, CheckNPkt, WaitRcv, CheckRcv, LostPkt};
  perform {
    state WaitNPkt:
      inspect (Sender, TransmitterType, NextPacket, CheckNPkt);
    state CheckNPkt:
      if (Sender->PacketBuffer.isFull ()) {
        SequenceBit = Sender->PacketBuffer.SequenceBit;
        proceed WaitRcv;
      } else
        proceed WaitNPkt;
    state WaitRcv:
      inspect (Recipient, ReceiverType, Receiving, CheckRcv);
      inspect (Sender, TransmitterType, NextPacket, LostPkt);
    state CheckRcv:
      if (((PacketType*)ThePacket)->SequenceBit == SequenceBit)
        proceed WaitNPkt;
      else
        proceed WaitRcv;
    state LostPkt:
      excptn ("Lost packet");
  };
};
```

Upon creation, the observer issues an inspect request to await the nearest moment when the transmitter process enters state `NextPacket`. Th observer's state `WaitNPkt` is the starting point of a cycle in which the observer monitors the fate of every packet acquired by the transmitter from the `Client`. Whenever the transmitter acquires a new packet, the observer moves to state `CheckNPkt`, where it first checks whether the packet buffer is nonempty and then, if this happens to be the case, saves the contents of the packet's sequence bit in the local variable SequenceBit. Note that the observer will be run **after** the transmitter has completed its sequence of operations in state NextPacket; thus, if a packet has been acquired in this state, the observer will be able to have a look at it.

In state WaitRcv, the observer executes two inspect operations: one to await the receiver's state Receiving; the other to detect another attempt of the transmitter to acquire a packet from the Client. The first inspect request describes the valid continuation of the protocol: a packet acquired for transmission must be eventually received at the recipient's side. If the transmitter attempts to acquire another packet for transmission before the previous one has been received, the observer gets to state LostPkt, where it aborts the experiment with a pertinent error message (section 2.3.5). In state CheckRcv, where the observer gets after the receiver process has completed the actions in state Receiving, it checks whether the sequence bit of the received packet matches the saved sequence bit of the packet last acquired for transmission. If this is the case, the observer has completed its cycle. Then it moves to state WaitNPkt to await another packet acquisition by the transmitter. Otherwise, the observer continues waiting in state WaitRcv.

Having asserted that no packets are ever lost by the alternating-bit protocol, we may want to verify whether no packet is ever received more than once, i.e., there are no duplicates. Formally, we will assert the following statement: *Every two packets consecutively received at the recipient station have different sequence bits.* Supported by the "no loss" property (and a bit of handwaving, which we conveniently leave as an exercise to the reader), this statement is equivalent to the claim that no packet is ever received more than once. The following simple observer will take care of this end:

```
observer DuplicatePackets {
  int SequenceBit;
  void setup () { SequenceBit = 1; };
  states {WaitRcv, CheckRcv};
  perform {
    int sb;
    state WaitRcv:
      inspect (Recipient, ReceiverType, Receiving, CheckRcv);
    state CheckRcv:
      sb = ((PacketType*)ThePacket)->SequenceBit;
      if (sb == SequenceBit)
        excptn ("Duplicate packet");
      SequenceBit = sb;
      proceed WaitRcv;
  };
};
```

The observer monitors the behavior of one process—the receiver. It just makes sure that two consecutively received packets have different sequence bits.

Taking advantage of packet signatures (sections 5.2.2, 5.4.1.1), we can make our observers a bit more powerful. In fact, signatures make it actually possible to assert the "no loss" property in a direct and complete manner. The simple modification of the preceding LostPackets observer consists in replacing the name SequenceBit with Signature in all its occurrences. Note, however, that to make this solution work, we have to create the simulator with the -g (debugging) option of mks (sections 5.4.1.1, B.2). The original version of the observer works regardless of the configuration of mks options, except for the -v option, which deactivates all observers.

7.3   EXPOSING OBJECTS

By *exposing* an object we mean making some information associated with the object directly visible to the user. This may involve either printing out this information to the results file (section 2.3.2) or displaying it on-line on the terminal screen. In the former case, the exposing is done exclusively by the simulator; in the latter case, the exposing is performed by a separate display program communicating with the simulator via IPC tools.[5]

7.3.1   General Concepts

Each *Object* type (section 2.4.1) carrying some dynamic information that may be of interest to the user can be made *exposable*. An exposable type defines a special method that describes how the information related to the objects of this type should be printed out or how it should be displayed on the terminal screen. By printing out information related to an object we understand including this information in the simulation output file; at the end of the simulation run this file will contain the results. By displaying information on the terminal screen we understand sending this information to DSD—a special display program (appendix A) that organizes it into a collection of windows presented on-line on the terminal. In the later case, the information is displayed dynamically, in the sense that it is updated periodically and in any moment it reflects a snapshot situation in the middle of the simulation run. Exposing by printing out, in the sense of the above definition, will be called exposing on paper, whereas dynamic exposing (displaying) will be called exposing on screen. The property of an exposure that says whether the information is printed or displayed will be called the *exposure form*.

The way an object is exposed is described by the **exposure** declaration associated with the object type. This declaration (resembling a method declaration) specifies the code to be executed when the object is exposed.

An object can be exposed in a number of ways, irrespective of the form (i.e., regardless of whether the exposure is on paper or on screen). Each such a way is called an *exposure mode* and is identified by a (typically small) non-negative integer number. Different exposure modes can be viewed as different kinds or fragments of information associated with the object.

---

[5]IPC stands for interprocess communication. In the Macintosh version of the package, the display program is integrated with the simulator (appendix D).

Moreover, some exposure modes may be optionally *station-relative*. In such a case, besides the mode, the user may specify a station to which the information printed (or displayed) is to be related. If no such station is specified, the global variant of the exposure mode is used.

For most of the standard *Object* types, the display modes coincide with the printing modes, so that for a given mode the same information is sent to paper and to the screen. However, each mode for any of the two exposure forms is defined separately. For example, consider the standard exposure of the `Client`, which defines the following four paper modes:

0. Information about all processes that have pending wait requests to the `Client`. If a station-relative variant of this mode is chosen, the information is restricted to the processes belonging to the given station.

1. Global performance measures taken over all traffic patterns combined. This mode cannot be made station-relative.

2. Message queues at all stations (global variant), or at one specified station (for the station-relative variant of this mode).

3. Traffic pattern definitions. No station-relative variant of this mode exists.

The first three modes are also applicable for exposing the `Client` on screen (and they send the same information to the display program), but the last paper mode is not available for the screen exposure.

In general, the format of the paper exposure need not be similar to the format of the corresponding screen exposure. The number of modes defined for the paper exposure need not be equal to the number of the screen exposure modes.

7.3.2 Making Objects Exposable

In principle, objects of any *Object* type (section 2.4.1) can be *exposed*, provided that they have been made *exposable*. All standard *Object* types are made exposable automatically. The user may declare a nonstandard subtype of *Object* as exposable and describe how objects of this type are to be exposed. It is also possible to declare a nonstandard exposure for an extension of an exposable standard type. This nonstandard exposure can either completely replace the standard exposure or merely supplement it.

The remainder of this section and section 7.3.3 may seem irrelevant to the user who is not interested in creating nonstandard exposable types. Certainly, these parts can freely be skipped on the first reading. However, besides instructing on how to expose objects of nonstandard types, this section also explains the mechanism of exposing objects of the standard types. This information may be helpful in understanding the operation of the display program described in appendix A.

7.3.2.1 The layout of an exposure method. All user-created subtypes of *Object* must belong to type `EObject` (sections 2.4.1, 2.4.7). To make such a subtype exposable, the user has to declare an *exposure* for it. The exposure declaration should appear as part of the type definition. It resembles the declaration of a regular method and has the following general format:

```
exposure {
  onpaper {
    exmode mp₀:
      . . .
    exmode mp₁:
      . . .
    . . .
    exmode mpₖ:
      . . .
  };
  onscreen {
    exmode ms₀:
      . . .
    exmode ms₁:
      . . .
    . . .
    exmode msₙ:
      . . .
  };
};
```

As with a regular method, it is possible to merely announce the exposure within the definition of an *Object* type and specify it later. An *Object* type is announced as exposable by putting the keyword `exposure;` into the list of its publicly visible attributes.

Example

The following declaration (section 2.4.1) defines a nonstandard exposable type:

```
eobject MyStat {
  LONG NSamples;
  RVariable *v1, *v2;
  void setup () {
    v1 = create RVariable;
    v2 = create RVariable;
    NSamples = 0;
  };
  exposure;
};
```

The exposure definition, like the specification of a regular method announced in a class declaration, must appear below the type definition in one of the program's files, e.g.,

```
MyStat::exposure {
  onpaper {
    exmode 0: v1->printOut (0);
    exmode 1: v2->printOut (0);
    exmode 2: print (NSamples, "Number of samples: ");
  }
  onscreen {
    exmode 0: v1->displayOut (0);
    exmode 1: v2->displayOut (0);
    exmode 2: display (NSamples);
  }
};
```

The meaning of the particular statements from the exposure code is explained later in this section. As is explained in section 7.3.4.1, the printOut method, defined for each *Object* type, offers a standard way of requesting a paper exposure of an exposable object. Similarly, displayOut is the standard method for requesting the object's screen exposure. In both cases, the argument identifies the exposure mode. Thus, the exposure method of a compound object may naturally invoke the exposure methods of its exposable attributes.

An exposure specification consists of two parts: the paper part and the screen part. Either of the two parts can be omitted; in such a case, the corresponding exposure form is undefined and the type cannot be exposed that way.

Each fragment starting with exmode m: and ending at the next exmode or at the closing brace of its form part contains code to be executed when the exposure with mode m is requested for the given form.

The exposure method has immediate access to the attributes of the exposed object: it has the same rights as a regular method declared within the exposed type. Additionally, the following two variables are accessible from the exposure code (they can be viewed as implicit arguments passed to the exposure method):

```
Long SId;
char *Hdr;
```

If SId is not NONE (-1), it indicates that the exposure is to be station-relative (section 7.3.1) and gives the Id of the station to which the exposed information is to be tailored. It is up to the exposure code to interpret this value, or ignore it (e.g., if it makes no sense to relate the exposed information to a specific station).

Variable Hdr is only relevant for a paper exposure. It points to a character string representing the header to be printed along with the exposed information. If Hdr contains NULL, it means that no specific header is requested. Again, the exposure code must perform an explicit action to print out the header; in particular, it may ignore the contents of Hdr, print a default header if Hdr contains NULL, and so on. The contents of Hdr for a screen exposure are irrelevant and they should not be interpreted there.

Any types, variables, and objects needed locally by the exposure code can be declared immediately after the opening **exposure** statement.

7.3.2.2   Superposing exposures.   If no exposure is defined for a subtype of an exposable type, the supertype exposure is inherited by the subtype. On the other hand, a subtype exposure, if declared, overrides the supertype exposure. Instead of completely eliminating the standard exposure from the view, the user may wish to just augment the supertype (standard) exposure by the new definition. In such a case, the supertype exposure method should contain a reference to the supertype exposure in the form

```
supertypename::expose;
```

Such a reference is equivalent to invoking the supertype exposure in the same context as the subtype exposure. The most natural place where the supertype exposure can be referenced is at the very beginning of the subtype exposure code, as in the following example:

```
exposure {
  int MyAttr;
  SuperType::expose;
  onpaper {
    ...
  };
  onscreen {
    ...
  };
};
```

If the supertype exposure does not contain the mode for which the subtype exposure has been called, the reference to the supertype exposure has no effect. Thus, the subtype exposure can just add new modes that are not serviced by the supertype exposure.

Example

As explained in section 7.3.5.11, the standard exposure of type **Station** offers five modes numbered from 0 to 4. Assume that we would like to program a private exposure for the station type **SenderType** from the alternating-bit protocol (section 1.2.4.3). We just want to add one more exposure mode, to print/display the status of the station's mailbox and the contents of the **LastSent** attribute.

As exposure methods do not belong to the protocol, it is generally preferable to specify them outside the exposed types. Thus, we will just announce **SenderType** as exposable by putting the keyword **exposure** in the attribute list of this type, e.g.,

```
station SenderType {
  PacketType PacketBuffer;
```

```
                    Port *IncomingPort, *OutgoingPort;
                    Mailbox *AlertMailbox;
                    int LastSent;
                    void setup ();
                    exposure;
                };
```

and define the exposure method later:

```
            SenderType::exposure {
              Station::expose;
              onpaper {
                exmode 5:
                  if (Hdr == NULL) Hdr = "SenderType exposure:";
                  print (Hdr); print ("\n\n");
                  AlertMailbox->printOut (2);
                  print (LastSent, "Last sent sequence bit: ");
              }
              onscreen {
                exmode 5:
                  AlertMailbox->displayOut (2);
                  display (LastSent);
              }
            };
```

Conveniently, type Mailbox defines a collection of standard exposures. One of these exposures (mode 2—section 7.3.5.3) produces information about the mailbox contents. The semantics of display are discussed in section 7.3.3.2.

By requesting the Station exposure, we make sure that the standard exposure modes for type Station are also available for type SenderType. Whenever an object of type SenderType is exposed, the Station's exposure method is called first. Assume that the mode of the requested exposure is between 0 and 4. Then the proper code fragment from the standard Station exposure will be selected and executed. As no mode in this range is defined in the local exposure method for SenderType, no action will be taken by this method. Conversely, if the requested mode is 5, the standard exposure method for type Station will not find a suitable code fragment and its action will be void. Then the SenderType exposure will take over.

Note. An exposure mode must be a non-negative number not greater than 4095. There is no other limitation. In particular, the exposure modes of a given (exposable) type need not occupy a consecutive range.

Note that a mode specified in a subtype exposure may be the same as a legal mode for a supertype exposure. If the supertype exposure is referenced from the subtype exposure, both code fragments will be executed, which will result in a combination of both exposures.

The supertype exposure can be referenced from any place of a subtype exposure, not only at the very beginning. It can even be referenced from a specific code fragment associated with one mode. Only the portion of the supertype exposure associated with the given mode will then be selected.

7.3.3   Programming Screen Exposures

The paper part of the exposure body is simple: it should contain statements that directly output the requested information to the results file. The `print` function—in its several versions discussed in section 2.3.2—is recommended for this purpose. Sometimes, the exposure method of a compound object whose attributes are themselves exposable invokes the exposure methods of the attributes. We have already seen how this can be done. The `printOut` method available for any *Object* type serves this end. We say more about this method in section 7.3.4.1.

7.3.3.1   The mechanism of screen exposures.

The issues related to programming the screen part of an exposure are somewhat more involved, although in most cases this part is shorter and simpler than the paper part. The main difference between the two exposure forms is that while the paper exposure can be interpreted as a regular function that is called explicitly by the user program to write some information to the output file, the screen exposure is called automatically by SMURPH—usually a number of times—asynchronously from the viewpoint of the protocol program. SMURPH invokes the screen parts of exposure methods to periodically update the contents of the windows displayed on the terminal screen. One simplification with respect to the paper case is that the exposure code need not be concerned with formatting the output: it just sends out raw data items, which are interpreted and organized by the display program (appendix A).

The part of the screen exposing process directly perceived by a protocol program in SMURPH is necessarily incomplete. The display program (which is in principle exchangeable and independent of the simulator) deals with all organizational aspects of exposing. Thus, this program determines the collection of exposures currently present on the screen (this collection is negotiated with the user), the screen layout, how often the screen contents are to be updated, and so on. The display program communicates with the simulator (using a special protocol described in a separate document)[6] and receives from it all information needed to maintain the dynamic contents of the screen. From the user point of view, the interaction between the simulator and the display program is not much relevant. Each window kept in existence by the display program is described by three parameters: the object to be exposed, the exposure mode of the object, and the station to which the exposure is to be related.[7] A complete description of a screen exposure for an *Object* type consists of two parts. The first part, visible by the protocol program, is the definition of the exposure method for the type in question. The second part, required by the display program, is a collection of window layouts (called

---

[6]This document comes with the source code of the package (section B.1).

[7]A special value of the third attribute identifies a global exposure, i.e., not related to any specific station.

templates—section A.6). The display program needs a separate window layout for each combination of an *Object* type and a display mode. Additionally, if a given mode occurs in station-relative and global variants, separate layouts should be provided for the two variants. Fortunately, building window templates is quite simple (and usually more entertaining than programming exposure methods). Of course, a suitable set of templates is provided for all the standard screen exposures. As this part is not really the simulator's business, we drop further discussion of it until section A.6. The reader who has managed to get to the present paragraph on the first reading should be assured that one can go a long way with SMURPH without having to program a single screen exposure.

Whenever the display program decides to refresh the contents of a specific window, it sends a message to the simulator. The simulator responds by invoking the corresponding exposure method (its screen part) with the proper mode. The SId parameter (section 7.3.2.1) is set to indicate whether the exposure is station-relative and, if so for which station. By executing its statements, the exposure method sends various items to the display program. These items are sent (and arrive at the display program) in a specific order, and this order is the only element of the window specification realized by the exposure method. The role of a window template is to instruct the display program where to put the images of subsequent items arriving from the simulator.

7.3.3.2 Displaying simple values.

Two types of items are sent by an exposure method to the display program: simple items (e.g., numbers, character strings), and *regions* representing modest (but compound) graphical objects (typically curves). A simple item is sent by calling one of the following functions available from a screen exposure method:

```
void display (LONG ii);
void display (double dd);
void display (BIG bb);
void display (char *tt);
```

Each of the four functions sends one data item to the display program. For the first three functions, the data item is a numeric value (an integer, a double, or a BIG number). The data item sent by the last method is a character string terminated by a null byte.

A simple data item passed to the display program by one of these functions is converted by that program into a character string and displayed within the exposure window, according to the template.

Example

The following sequence of statements can be used to display all seven name attributes of any *Object* (section 2.4.2):

```
display (getClass ());
display (getId ());
```

```
display (getTName ());
display (getSName ());
display (getNName ());
display (getBName ());
display (getOName ());
```

This sequence can be put at **exmode** of the screen part of an exposure method associated with any *Object* type. Like a regular method, the exposure method belongs to its object; thus, the name methods referenced by the exposure are automatically qualified to the object.

7.3.3.3   Regions.   A *region* is an aggregate of graphic information in the form of a collection of curves to be displayed within a rectangular area of a window. A region is handled by the display program as a single, albeit compound, item. It may be just a part of an exposure consisting of other items (simple items or regions), or it may be the only item of the exposure.

The part of the region display procedure visible by the exposure method consists of a sequence of statements that send to the display program a collection of planar points (x, y coordinates). These points can be clustered into a number of *segments*, each segment representing a separate line. The display program is responsible for presenting the segments in a rectangular area of the exposure window described in the window template (section A.6.7).

As regions are compound items, more than one operation is needed to generate a region. In particular, a region must be explicitly started and terminated. The functions

```
void startRegion (double xs, double xt, double ys, double yt);
void startRegion ();
```

are used to start a region, i.e., to indicate that subsequent display operations will generate the region contents.

The first function starts the so-called *scaled region*. The arguments have the following meaning:

xs   Starting value for the x coordinate, i.e., the x coordinate of the left side of the region's rectangle

xt   Terminating value for the x coordinate, i.e., the x coordinate of the right side of the region's rectangle

ys   Starting value for the y coordinate, i.e., the y coordinate of the bottom side of the region's rectangle

yt   Terminating value for the y coordinate, i.e., the y coordinate of the top side of the region's rectangle

The argument-less version of the function starts an *unscaled region*, i.e., a region whose scaling will be determined by the display program (section A.6.7).

A region is terminated by calling

$$\texttt{endRegion ();}$$

which informs the display program that nothing more will be put into the region.

Display statements executed between `startRegion` and `endRegion` send to the display program a number of segments.[8] One way to display a segment is to start it explicitly, then send the individual points of the segment, and finally terminate the segment by an explicit operation. The following function is used to start a segment:

$$\texttt{startSegment (Long att = NONE);}$$

where the argument, if specified, is a bit pattern defining segment attributes. The interpretation of the attributes is left to the discretion of the display program with the following recommendation for two standard fields (we assume that bits are numbered from the "little end," i.e., from the least significant position):

bits 0–1 The display style. Value 0 means that the segment will be displayed as a loose collection of points; value 1 indicates points connected with lines; value 2 specifies histograms, i.e., vertical stripes extending from the points down to the bottom of the region rectangle.

bits 2–5 The thickness of lines and points.

The version of DSD intended for nongraphic ASCII terminals ignores the thickness field. Points or lines are displayed using a designated character defined in the window template. The Macintosh version of the display program interprets both fields (section D.4). Future (more sophisticated) versions of DSD may interpret other fields, e.g., identifying the color of the segment. If the attribute argument is not specified (or if its value is `NONE`), default segment attributes are used. The default display style is 0.

A segment is terminated by calling

$$\texttt{endSegment ();}$$

The contents of a segment are described by calling the following function:

$$\texttt{void displayPoint (double x, double y);}$$

which gives the coordinates of one point of the segment. If the segment points are to be connected,[9] a line will be drawn between each pair of points consecutively defined by `displayPoint`. The first and the last points are not connected unless they are the only points of the segment.

Note. It is illegal to call `displayPoint` outside a segment, i.e., the function can only be called after `startSegment` and before `endSegment`. Similarly, `endSegment` is only allowed after `startSegment`, and `startSegment` can only be

---

[8]In most cases, there is just a single segment.

[9]This applies to the Macintosh version of the display program.

called between `startRegion` and `endRegion`. A call to `endRegion` must be preceded by a call to `startRegion`.

It is possible to display an entire segment with a single function call, but all the point coordinates must be prepared in advance in two arrays. One of the following two functions can be used to do the job:

```
void displaySegment (Long att, int np, double *x, double *y);
void displaySegment (int np, double *x, double *y);
```

The first argument of the first function specifies the segment attributes; default attributes are used with the second function. The two `double` arrays are expected to contain x and y coordinates of the segment points. The common size of these arrays (the number of points in the segment) is given by `np`.

Example

Suppose that we would like to define a nonstandard screen exposure for a station type to display the lengths of the message queues at the station. The number of message queues is equal to the number of traffic patterns. For each traffic pattern, we are interested in the number of messages belonging to this traffic pattern queued at the station.

The display will consist of a region presenting these lengths graphically, followed by the list of their numerical values. We start by defining a subtype of `Station`, e.g.,

```
station MStation {
  exposure;
};
```

The new station type introduces no new attributes except for the exposure method. By using `MStation` instead of `Station` to create new station types, we make sure that their exposures include the new option. As we remember from the example in section 7.3.2.2, type `Station` offers five standard exposure modes and it seems reasonable to retain them for `MStation`. Thus, we will assign mode 5 to the new exposure. The new mode will only be available in the screen form. The full definition of our exposure method is as follows:

```
MStation::exposure {
  int i, j, max, ml [20];
  Message *m;
  Station::expose;
  onscreen {
    exmode 5:
      for (i = 0, max = 0; i < NTraffics; i++) {
        ml [i] = 0;
        for (j = 0, m = MQHead [i]; m; m = m->next, ml [i] ++);
        if (ml [i] > max) max = ml [i];
      }
      startRegion (0.0, (double) (NTraffics-1), 0.0, (double) max);
      startSegment (022);
```

```
            for (i = 0; i < NTraffics; i++)
              displayPoint ((double) i, (double) ml [i]);
            endSegment ();
            endRegion ();
            for (i = 0; i < NTraffics; i++) display (ml [i]);
      }
    };
```

The segment attribute argument passed to **startSegment** indicates histograms, i.e., each point will be displayed as a strip starting at the bottom of the region rectangle.

In appendix A the reader will find information on the further steps needed to make a window, corresponding to a screen exposure mode on the simulator's side, appear on the terminal screen. One of these steps involves the preparation of a window template that assigns the various items produced by the exposure method to specific locations in the actual window.

7.3.3.4 Opening and closing screen exposures.

Let us recall the exposure method from the last example. One problem with it is the static size of the array used to store message queue lengths for individual traffic patterns. The method will not work if the number of traffic patterns is larger than 20. Of course, we could get rid of the array by recalculating the queue lengths immediately before executing **displayPoint**, but this would involve some unnecessary duplication of labor.We could also increase the array size to a much safer value, but this solution would not look very nice either. One may think about allocating the array dynamically at the beginning of the exposure code and deallocating it at the end. This would not look bad, but some people would consider it too expensive. Note that a screen exposure method may be invoked many times during a relatively short interval—to refresh the screen contents dynamically. Finally, we could make the array a station attribute (it could be allocated dynamically by the station's setup method), but then the station itself would have to care about its exposure, which could be rightfully perceived as a poor separation of concerns.

It would be helpful if the exposure method could learn when it is called for the first and last time in its display cycle. By a display cycle, we mean the time while the exposure's window is present on the screen and its contents are updated periodically. The first time around, when the exposure's window is opened, the exposure method would allocate the dynamic data structures needed to sustain its operation cycle. Then, when the window is closed and the method gets invoked for the last time, it would deallocate the objects allocated upon its first call. To make this idea work, we need a place where an exposure method could store its data structures that are to remain alive across its different invocations. Of course, one can always use attributes of the exposed object for this purpose, but, as we have said, this approach may not be methodologically correct.

The following three global variables available from an exposure method make it possible to implement this idea:

```
    int DisplayOpening, DisplayClosing;
    void *TheWFrame;
```

If `DisplayOpening` is YES, it means that the exposure mode has been invoked for the first time in its display cycle. Otherwise, `DisplayOpening` is NO. If upon recognizing the first invocation, the exposure code decides to allocate a dynamic data structure, the pointer to this structure should be stored in `TheWFrame` (the window frame). In subsequent invocations of the exposure method for the same display mode `TheWFrame` will contain the same pointer. It is important that the contents of `TheWFrame` are local to the display mode, not just to the exposure method. This way, different display modes are absolutely independent with respect to what dynamically allocable data structures they may want to use.

If `TheWFrame` is not NULL then when the window corresponding to the given exposure mode is closed, the exposure method is called for the last time with `DisplayClosing` set to YES. No display information should be sent in this case: the method should use its last invocation exclusively to deallocate the structure pointed to by `TheWFrame`. Note that the closing call is only made when `TheWFrame` is not NULL; exposures that do not store anything into `TheWFrame` are assumed to require no special closing action.

Example

Let us now rewrite the example from section 7.3.3.3 in such a way that the burdensome array is allocated dynamically:

```
#define ml ((int*) TheWFrame)
MStation::exposure {
  int i, j, max;
  Message *m;
  Station::expose;
  onscreen {
    exmode 5:
      if (DisplayOpening)
        TheWFrame = (void*) new int [NTraffics];
      else if (DisplayClosing) {
        delete (int*) TheWFrame;
        return;
      }
      for (i = 0, max = 0; i < NTraffics; i++) {
        ml [i] = 0;
        for (j = 0, m = MQHead [i]; m; m = m->next, ml [i] ++);
        if (ml [i] > max) max = ml [i];
      }
      startRegion (0.0, (double) (NTraffics-1), 0.0, (double) max);
      startSegment (022);
      for (i = 0; i < NTraffics; i++)
        displayPoint ((double) i, (double) ml [i]);
```

```
                    endSegment ();
                    endRegion ();
                    for (i = 0; i < NTraffics; i++) display (ml [i]);
        }
    };
    #undef ml
```

Note that when the exposure method determines that `DisplayClosing` is nonzero, it returns without executing the exposing code. The display program does not expect to receive anything from the exposure method in that case.

The simple features described in this section are not applicable to paper exposures. A paper exposure is always completed in one call—there is no notion of a display cycle during which the exposure method may be called a number of times to produce updated versions of the same sustained window. Thus, a paper exposure completes its job within a single invocation, and if it needs to allocate any objects to perform its task, it can handle them as any regular method would.

7.3.4   Interface with Exposures

Paper exposures resemble regular methods, or rather collections of methods (for different exposure modes) disguised as single methods. Communication with paper exposures is very simple. Exposing on paper is done explicitly by the protocol program (typically from the Root process—section 1.2.4.12), and the commands performing these operations look like regular method calls. With screen exposures the situation is somewhat trickier. Screen exposing is usually done outside the protocol program, asynchronously with its operation.

7.3.4.1   Invoking exposures.   Note that exposure methods have no explicit names, and consequently they cannot be invoked directly. Each *Object* type can define at most one exposure method; however, this method may define a practically arbitrary number of exposure modes. Additionally, a given mode may occur in a global or station-relative variant.

The following three methods automatically defined for each exposable *Object* type can be used to expose objects of this type:

```
    void printOut (int m, char *Hdr = NULL, Long SId = NONE);
    void printOut (int m, Long SId);
    void displayOut (int m, Long SId = NONE);
```

The first two methods expose the object on paper and they are commonly used by the protocol program to request a paper exposure. The third method exposes the object on screen, and it is almost never called explicitly.[10]

---

[10] As explained in section 7.3.5, `printOut` is also seldom called directly. Standard exposable types declare "alias methods" for paper exposures with different modes, which relieve the user of having to memorize the mode numbers.

The second method behaves identically with the first one with `Hdr` equal `NULL`. For all three methods, the first argument indicates the exposure mode. Depending on whether the exposure is on paper (the first two methods) or on screen (the last method), the appropriate code fragment from the object's exposure definition, determined by the form and mode (`m`), is selected and executed. For the first method, the contents of the second and third arguments are made available to the exposure method via variables `Hdr` and `SId` (section 7.3.2.1). With the second method, `Hdr` is set to `NULL`.

Usually, the protocol program does not request screen exposures directly, i.e., it does not call `displayOut`. The only exception is when the screen exposure code for a compound type T requests exposures of subobjects (attributes), which define their own exposure methods (sections 7.3.2.1, 7.3.2.2). In such a case, the exposure code for T may call `displayOut` for a subobject: this will have the effect of sending the subobject's display information to the display program—as a portion of T's exposure.

The interpretation of the display mode (argument `m`) is automatic: the value passed in `m` is used internally to select the proper `exmode` fragment of the exposure method. The remaining arguments, i.e., `SId` and `Hdr` (the latter is applicable to paper exposures only) are interpreted by the exposure method (sections 7.3.2.1, 7.3.2.2). In particular, if the given mode cannot be made station-relative, it may ignore the `SId` argument.

7.3.4.2   Communication with the display program.

The screen exposure of an object can be requested implicitly, practically at any moment, without the protocol program being aware of it. SMURPH cooperates with the display program using a special protocol, and generally this communication is transparent to the user. The exposure methods (their screen parts) send to the display program the data items to be displayed using the tools described in section 7.3.3. There exist a few additional functions and variables that make the display program partially visible to the protocol program—to the extent of providing some potentially useful features.

If the global integer variable `DisplayActive` contains `YES`, it means that the display program is currently active and *connected* to the simulator (section A.1). At any moment during such a connection (we call it a display session), the display program defines a number of windows, whose contents are to be refreshed periodically. A single window corresponds to one display mode of a single object. SMURPH maintains some internal description of the set of windows currently requested by the display program. From the simulator's point of view, such a window is a triplet: an object pointer, a display mode (an integer number), and (optionally) a station `Id`, if the window is related to a station. The simulator is not concerned with the window layout: it just sends to the display program the raw data generated by the object's screen exposure.

During a display session, SMURPH periodically calls the exposure methods corresponding to the active windows. By executing commands presented in section 7.3.3, the exposure methods send to the display program the data items to be displayed. Based on the window templates associated with the active windows, the display program interprets the data items and assigns them to the proper locations on the screen. The exposure methods are called every given number of events. The number of events separating two consecutive display updates (the so-called *display interval*) is kept in the global integer variable `DisplayInterval`. Both `DisplayActive` and `DisplayInterval` are read-only variables that should not be changed by the protocol program.

A protocol program may request connection to the display program explicitly, e.g., upon detecting a situation that may be of interest to the user. This is done by calling the following function:

<code>int requestDisplay (char *msg = NULL);</code>

which halts the simulation until a connection with the display program is established (section A.4). The function returns `OK` when the connection has been established and `ERROR`, if the connection was already established when the function was called (section 2.3.4). Note that `requestDisplay` does not time out: it waits indefinitely until the display program connects to the simulator.[11] The optional argument is a character string representing a textual message to be sent to the display program immediately after establishing a connection. The interpretation of the message is left to the discretion of the display program.[12]

The protocol program may send a textual message to the display program at any moment during the connection by calling the function

<code>char *displayNote (char *msg);</code>

where `msg` is a pointer to the message. The function returns an optional response of the display program (a character string pointer), or `NULL` when there is no specific response.[13] Value `NULL` is also returned if the simulator is not connected to the display program when the function is called.

Upon reception of a message from the simulator, the display program gets into the blocked state, i.e., it holds the simulator until an explicit action is taken by the user (sections A.8.1, D.5.4).

While the simulator is connected to the display program, the protocol program may request that the screen contents be updated before the end of the current display interval. By calling the function

<code>void refreshDisplay ();</code>

the protocol program explicitly sends the exposure information for the currently defined configuration of windows to the display program.

---

[11] In the Macintosh version of the package, the simulator is integrated with the display program and, in a sense, remains permanently connected to it. Thus, `requestDisplay` always returns `ERROR` in that version. As a side effect, it immediately forces an update for the screen contents, irrespective of how many events remain to the scheduled update (section D.5.6).

[12] The present versions of the program ignore this message.

[13] The present versions of the display program send no responses to the simulator.

7.3.5   Standard Exposures

Starting from section 7.3.5.2, we list and briefly discuss the standard exposures defined for the built-in *Object* types of SMURPH. There are some conventions that are obeyed (with minor exceptions) by all the standard exposures.

Unless explicitly stated, it is assumed by default that the number of screen exposure modes is the same as the number of paper exposure modes, and that the corresponding modes of both forms produce (i.e., print or send to the display program) exactly the same items of information. Thus, we do not discuss screen exposures except for the few special cases when their information contents differ from the information contents of the corresponding paper exposures. Each exposure is described by the list of items sent by the exposure to the output file or to the display program.

To save space (and also to encourage the reader to perform a few simple experiments with SMURPH) we do not present the actual layouts of the exposures in the output file or on the terminal screen. The user can easily write a simple program to produce the exposure in question and compare it with our description. Note that the layouts of the screen exposures depend on the display program and, formally, the simulator does not care about them. As we said in section 7.3.3.1, the only element of this layout shared by the two parties is the order in which individual items are sent by the simulator and received (presented) by the display program. Therefore, it makes sense to restrict our discussion of exposures to the specification of this order.

Each standard paper exposure is equipped with a default header (argument Hdr—sections 7.3.2.1, 7.3.4.1), which is printed at the beginning of the exposure, if no special header is provided by the user. Note that by specifying a null header (""), the user may eliminate the header completely. The standard header contains the *output name* of the exposed object (section 2.4.2). In most cases, the simulated time when the exposure was produced is also included in the header. Most standard exposures end with the line of text that looks like this:

$$(\textit{outputname}) \texttt{ End of list}$$

where *outputname* is the output name of the exposed object.

Example

Following is the standard paper exposure (mode 0) of the sender station from the alternating-bit protocol in section 1.2.4:

```
Time:       22013588      (SenderType 0) Sleeping processes:
                Process          AI/Idn      Event        State          Time
   AckReceiverType 3        Port/000          EMP  AckArrival      22014588*
   TransmitterType 2        Timer          wakeup  Retransmit      22032332*
                         Mailbox/000     RECEIVE        Acked      undefined
   (SenderType 0) End of list
```

The exposure has been produced by the following call:

```
Sender->printOut (0);
```

As we explain in section 7.3.5.11, mode 0 station exposure produces the list of pending wait requests issued by the processes owned by the station. Even left unexplained, the shown output is quite easy to interpret.

All standard exposable types define methods that provide abbreviations for requesting paper exposures without having to specify explicit numeric modes. With the mnemonic names of these methods, the user does not have to memorize the mode numbers. Wherever possible, these names obey simple and intuitive rules. For example, calling

```
rv->printCnt ();
```

where rv points to a random variable, we expose the contents of the random variable, i.e., print the values of its distribution parameters (section 7.1.1). This is equivalent to calling

```
rv->printOut (0);
```

The same method name (printCnt) can be used to request a paper exposure of other objects whose **contents** may be interesting to the user, specifically mailboxes, traffic patterns, and also the Client. The contents exposure of a traffic pattern produces the length of message queues of this traffic pattern at all stations. In this case, it corresponds to mode 2. Similarly, the method

```
ai->printRqs ();
```

where ai points to an activity interpreter (e.g., a port, a traffic pattern, the Client, the Timer, a process), prints out the list of pending wait requests addressed to the AI. This list has a similar form as the one from the last example.

In general, the type specification of a method that provides a mnemonic way of requesting paper exposures may have one of the following forms:

```
printxxx (char *hdr = NULL, Long sid = NONE);
printxxx (char *hdr = NULL);
```

where xxx stands for three or four letters identifying the information contents of the exposure. With the first version, by specifying a station Id as the second argument, it is possible to make the exposure station-relative (sections 7.3.1, 7.3.2.1); no station-relative exposure is available for the second version. For both versions, the optional first argument may specify a nonstandard header. For example, printCnt for a traffic pattern or the Client accepts a station Id. Thus, the call

```
Client->printCnt (NULL, 0);
```

produces the contents of all message queues at station number 0. The exposure will begin with a standard header.

While describing the information contents of an exposure, we ignore headers and other fixed text fragments. The user should have no problem identifying these parts in the output file. Fixed text fragments are never sent to the display program for a screen exposure. The specific dynamic data items appearing in exposures are discussed **in the order in which they are produced**, which, unless stated otherwise, is the same for both exposure forms.

Quite often, the output size of a list-type exposure may vary, depending on the number of elements in the list. For example, the number of pending wait requests associated with a given AI usually varies with time. All such exposures organize the output information into a sequence of rows, all rows obeying the same layout rules. Thus, in such cases, we describe the layout of a single row, understanding that the actual number of rows may be arbitrary.

7.3.5.1 Event identifiers.

Many standard exposures produce information about (pending) wait requests and various events. By default, only the wait requests issued by protocol processes and the events perceptible by these processes are listed. There are some internal processes of SMURPH that issue wait requests and respond to some special events that are rather exotic from the user's point of view. To include information about these internal requests and events in the exposed data, the simulator should be called with the -s option (section B.3). This also concerns the event information generated when the simulated protocol is being *traced* (section 7.2.1).

In the output produced by standard exposures, events are represented by symbolic identifiers. In the following sections, we list, separately for each AI type, the identifiers of the events generated by the AI.

Timer. A Timer event (section 4.5.1) is triggered when the delay specified in a pending Timer wait request elapses. If BIG_precision is 1, the event identifier is the numeric value of the delay in ITUs. Otherwise, the character string "wakeup" is used to represent all Timer events.

Mailbox. Mailbox events (section 4.7.4) are generated when items are stored in mailboxes or removed from mailboxes. The event identifier can be one of the character strings "NEWITEM," "NONEMPTY," "RECEIVE," or a number identifying a count event (section 4.7.4).

Port. The identifier of a port event (section 6.2) is a character string containing the symbolic name of the event (section 6.2). Thus, a port event identifier can be one of the following strings: "SILENCE," "ACTIVITY," "BOT," "EOT," "BMP," "EMP," "BOJ," "EOJ," "COLLISION," "ANYEVENT."

Client. For the Client, the event identifier can be one of the following character strings: "ARRIVAL," "INTERCEPT" (section 5.4.2), "SUSPEND," "RESUME" (section 5.5.1), "RESET" (section 7.1.2.4), or "arr_Trf*xxx*." The sequence *xxx* in the last string stands for the Id of the traffic pattern whose message arrival is awaited. This case corresponds to a Client wait request with the first argument identifying a traffic pattern (section 5.4.2).

Traffic. The event identifier for a Traffic AI is one of the following four strings: "ARRIVAL," "INTERCEPT" (section 5.4.2), "SUSPEND," "RESUME" (section 5.5.1), "RESET" (section 7.1.2.4).

Process. The event identifier for the process AI is one of the following character strings: "START," "DEATH," or a state name. The first string represents the virtual event used to start the process: a process that appears to be waiting for it is a new process that has just been created—within the current ITU. The DEATH event is triggered by the process termination. Like START, it occurs only once in the lifetime of a process. The state name represents an event that will be generated by the process AI when the process gets into the named state (section 4.6.1).

System Events. Link AIs do not generate directly any events that can be awaited by protocol processes. There exists a system process called LinkService, which takes care of removing obsolete activities from links and their archives. The following two system events are generated by link AIs and perceived by the LinkService process:

LNK_PURGE   Occurring when an activity should be removed from the link and possibly added to the archive

ARC_PURGE   Occurring when an activity should be removed from the link archive and destroyed

The following two internal events are generated by the Client AI and sensed by the system process called ClientService, which emulates the behavior of the standard pilot processes (section 5.5.3).

ARR_MSG   Occurring when a new message is to be generated and queued at a station

ARR_BST   Occurring when a new burst is to be generated

One more system process responding to an internal event is ObserverService. This process is responsible for restarting an observer after its timeout delay has elapsed. The timeout event is triggered by a nonexistent AI called Observer and its identifier is "TIMEOUT."

7.3.5.2   Timer exposure

Mode 0: Full Request List

Calling: printRqs (char *hdr = NULL, Long sid = NONE);

The exposure produces the full (long) list of processes waiting for the Timer. The list consists of rows with the following entries (produced in this order):

1. Simulated time in ITUs when the `Timer` event will occur.
2. Single-character flag that describes the status of the `Timer` request: "*" means that according to the current state of the simulation, the `Timer` event will actually restart the process, blank means that another waking event will occur earlier than the `Timer` event, and "?" says that the `Timer` event **may** restart the process, but another event has been scheduled at the same ITU and has the same order as the `Timer` event.
3. Id of the station owning the process, or "**Sys**" for a system process. This data item is not included in the station-relative variant of the exposure.
4. Process type name.
5. Process Id.
6. Identifier of the process's state associated with the `Timer` request, i.e., the state where the process will be restarted by the `Timer` event, should this event actually restart the process.
7. Type name of the activity interpreter that, according to the current state of the simulation, will restart the process.
8. Id of the activity interpreter, or blanks if the AI has no Id (`Client`, `Timer`).
9. Identifier of the event that will wake the process up.
10. Identifier of the state where, according to the current configuration of activities and events, the process will be restarted.

The station-relative version of the exposure restricts the list to the processes belonging to the indicated station.

Exactly the same items are sent to the display program with the screen version of the exposure.

Note. For all AIs, the standard mode 0 exposure produces similar information organized according to the preceding layout. When the time of the event occurrence (item 1) is not known at the moment of exposure (this cannot happen for a `Timer` wait request), the string "`undefined`" is produced in its place.

Mode 1: Abbreviated Request List

Calling: `printARqs (char *hdr = NULL, Long sid = NONE);`

The exposure produces the abbreviated list of processes waiting for `Timer` events. Each row of the list consists of the following entries (in this order):

1. Simulated time in ITUs when the `Timer` event will occur.
2. Character flag describing the status of the `Timer` request (as for mode 0).
3. Id of the station owning the process. This data item is not included in the station-relative variant of the exposure.
4. Process type name.
5. Process Id.

6. Identifier of the process's state associated with the **Timer** request.

Only user processes are included in the abbreviated list, even if the simulator was called with **-s** (section B.3). The station-relative version of the exposure restricts the list to the processes belonging to the indicated station.

Exactly the same items are sent to the display program with the screen version of the exposure.

7.3.5.3 Mailbox exposure

Mode 0: Full Request List

Calling: `printRqs (char *hdr = NULL, Long sid = NONE);`

The exposure produces the full list of processes awaiting events on the **Mailbox**. The description is the same as for the mode 0 **Timer** exposure, with the word "Timer" replaced by "Mailbox."

Mode 1: Abbreviated Request List

Calling: `printARqs (char *hdr = NULL, Long sid = NONE);`

The exposure produces the abbreviated list of processes awaiting events on the **Mailbox**. The description is the same as for the mode 1 **Timer** exposure, with the word "Timer" replaced by "Mailbox."

Mode 2: Mailbox Contents

Calling: `printCnt (char *hdr = NULL);`

The exposure produces information about the mailbox contents. The following four items are printed (in a single line):

1. Header argument, or the mailbox output name (section 2.4.2) if the header argument is not specified.

2. Number of elements currently stored in the mailbox.

3. Mailbox capacity (note that in principle mailbox capacities may change dynamically—section 4.7.5).

4. Number of pending wait requests issued to the mailbox.

The line containing the values of these items is preceded by a caption line identifying the items.

The screen version of the exposure sends to the display program the last three items, i.e., the mailbox name is not sent. Of course, the caption line is also absent.

Mode 3: Short Mailbox Contents

Calling: `printSCnt (char *hdr = NULL);`

The paper version of the exposure produces the same output as the mode 2 exposure, except that no caption line is printed. Thus, the output can be used as part of a longer output, e.g., listing the contents of several mailboxes. No screen version of this exposure is provided. Note that the screen version of the mode 2 exposure is already devoid of the caption line.

7.3.5.4 RVariable exposure

Mode 0: Full Contents

   Calling: `printCnt (char *hdr = NULL);`

The exposure outputs the contents of the random variable (section 7.1.1). The following data items are produced:

1. Number of samples.
2. Minimum value.
3. Maximum value.
4. Mean value (i.e., the first central moment).
5. Variance (i.e., the second central moment).
6. Standard deviation (i.e., the square root of the second central moment).
7. Relative confidence margin for the confidence level $1 - \alpha = 0.95$. This value is equal to half the length of the confidence interval at $\alpha = 0.05$ divided by the absolute value of the calculated mean.
8. Relative confidence margin for $\alpha = 0.01$.

   If the random variable was created with more than two moments (section 7.1.1.1), the list is continued with their subsequent values. If the number of moments is 1, items 5–8 do not appear; if it is 0, item 4 is skipped as well.

   Note. The confidence intervals are calculated based on the number of samples and the measured value of the mean. No attempt is made to account for the correlation among different samples, which may be quite strong in many cases. Therefore, the confidence intervals produced by the exposure should be treated with limited confidence.

   The screen version of the exposure contains the same numeric items as the paper exposure without item 8, i.e., only one confidence interval (at $\alpha = 0.05$) is displayed. This list of numeric items is preceded by a region (section 7.3.3.3) that displays graphically the history of 24 last exposed mean values of the random variable. The region consists of a single segment including up to 24 points. It is scaled by $(0, 23)$ in the x axis and (min, max) in the y axis, where min and max are the current minimum and maximum values of the random variable.

Mode 1: Abbreviated Contents

   Calling: `printACnt (char *hdr = NULL);`

The exposure outputs the abbreviated contents of the random variable. The following data items are produced:

1. Number of samples.
2. Minimum value.
3. Maximum value.
4. Mean value (i.e., the first central moment). This item is not included if the random variable does not have at least one moment.

The values are preceded by a caption line identifying individual items.

The screen version of the exposure contains the same numeric items as the mode 0 paper exposure, i.e., the mode 0 screen exposure without the region.

Mode 2: Short Contents

Calling: `printSCnt (char *hdr = NULL);`

The exposure produces the short contents of the random variable. The items produced are identical to those for mode 1. The only difference is that no caption line precedes the items, which makes it possible to expose multiple random variables in the form of a list. This can be done by exposing the first random variable in the list with mode 1 and the remaining ones with mode 2.

The screen version of the exposure contains the same numeric items as the paper exposure followed additionally by the standard deviation. If the random variable has less than two standard moments, the missing values are replaced by dashes (---).

7.3.5.5   Client exposure

Mode 0: Request List

Calling: `printRqs (char *hdr = NULL, Long sid = NONE);`

This exposure produces the list of processes waiting for `Client` and `Traffic` events. The description is the same as for the `Timer` exposure with mode 0, with the word "Timer" replaced by "Client" or "Traffic."

Mode 1: Performance Measures

Calling: `printPfm (char *hdr = NULL);`

This exposure lists the standard performance measures for all traffic patterns viewed globally, as if they constituted a single traffic pattern. The exposure is produced by combining (section 7.1.1.2) the standard random variables belonging to individual traffic patterns (section 7.1.2.1) into a collection of global random variables reflecting the performance measures of the whole `Client` and then exposing them with mode 0 (`printCnt`—section 7.3.5.4) in the following order:

1. RVAMD—absolute message delay
2. RVAPD—absolute packet delay
3. RVWMD—weighted message delay

4. RVMAT—message access time
5. RVPAT—packet access time
6. RVMLS—message length statistics

The data produced by this list of exposures are followed by the `Client` statistics containing the following items:

1. Number of all messages ever generated and queued at their senders.
2. Number of messages currently queued awaiting transmission.
3. Number of all messages completely received (section 6.2.13).
4. Number of all transmitted packets (terminated by `stop`—section 6.1.2.1).
5. Number of all received packets.
6. Number of all message bits queued at stations awaiting transmission. This is the combined length of all messages currently queued (item 2).
7. Number of all message bits successfully transmitted so far. This is the combined payload length of all transmitted packets (item 4).
8. Number of all message bits successfully received so far. This is the combined payload length of all received packets (item 5).
9. Global throughput of the network calculated as the ratio of the number of received bits (item 8) to the simulated time in ETUs.

The screen version of the exposure does not include the last nine items. The six random variables representing the global performance measures are exposed with mode 1 (section 7.3.5.4).

Mode 2: Message Queues

Calling: `printCnt (char *hdr = NULL, Long sid = NONE);`

This exposure produces information about message queues at all stations, or at one indicated station for the station-relative variant. The global variant prints one line of text for each station. This line consists of the following three items:

1. Station Id
2. Number of messages queued at the station
3. Number of message bits queued at the station, i.e., the combined length of all messages queued at the station

The station-relative variant of the exposure produces one row for each message queued at the indicated station. This row contains the following data:

1. Time in ITUs when the message was queued
2. Id of the traffic pattern to which the message belongs
3. Message length in bits
4. Id of the station to which the message is addressed, or the text "bcast" for a broadcast message

The global variant of the screen form produces a single item—a region that displays graphically the number of messages queued at every station. The region consists of a single segment containing NStations points (section 3.1.2) scaled by $(0, \text{NStations}-1)$ on the x axis and $(0, L_{max})$ on the y axis, where L_{max} is the maximum length of a message queue at a station. The y coordinate of a point is equal to the number of messages queued at the station (all traffic patterns combined) whose Id is determined by the x coordinate.

Mode 3: Traffic Definition/Client Statistics

Calling: `printDef (char *hdr = NULL);`

The paper form of this exposure prints out information describing the definition of all traffic patterns. This information is self-explanatory. The exposure assumes the standard interpretation of the `Traffic` attributes describing the distribution parameters of the message arrival process, as if all traffic patterns were driven by the standard pilot processes (section 5.5.3).

The screen variant of mode 3 displays the client statistics containing the same items as the client statistics printed by the mode 2 exposure. The order of these items is also the same except that the throughput is moved from the last position to the first.

7.3.5.6   Traffic exposure.   The exposure modes, their mnemonic abbreviations, and contents are identical to those of the `Client` with the following modifications:

- With mode 0, the list of processes is limited to the protocol processes awaiting events from the given traffic pattern.
- The performance measures produced by mode 1 refer to the given traffic pattern. The client statistics printed by mode 1 and displayed by mode 3 refer to the given traffic pattern, and they do not contain the throughput item.
- The output produced by the station-relative variant of mode 2 does not contain the traffic pattern Id: this output, as well as the output generated by the global variant, is restricted to the given traffic pattern.
- The information printed by the mode 3 exposure describes the definition of the given traffic pattern.

7.3.5.7   Port exposure

Mode 0: Request List

Calling: `printRqs (char *hdr = NULL);`

The exposure produces the list of processes waiting for events on the port. The description is the same as for the `Timer` exposure with mode 0, with the word "Timer" replaced by "Port." Note that no station-relative exposures are defined for ports: a port always belongs to some station, and all its exposures are implicitly station-relative.

Mode 1: List of Activities

Calling: `printAct (char *hdr = NULL);`

This exposure produces the list of all activities currently present in the link to which the port is connected, and in the link's archive. There exists an alias for the argument-less variant of the method: calling `printAct()` has the same effect as invoking `dump()`, the latter method to be used for debugging. The list is sorted in the nondecreasing order of the time when the beginning of the activity was, is, or will be heard at the port. Each activity takes one row consisting of the following items:

1. Single-letter activity type designator: "T"—a transfer (or an aborted transfer attempt), "J"—a jamming signal, "C"—a collision.
2. Starting time of the activity in ITUs, as perceived by the port.
3. Finished time of the activity in ITUs, as perceived by the port. If this time is not known at present (i.e., the activity is still being inserted into the link), the string "undefined" appears in this place.
4. Id of the station that generated the activity.
5. Station-relative number of the port (section 3.3.1) into which the activity was inserted.
6. Id of the receiver station or "bcst" for a broadcast packet.
7. Traffic pattern Id.
8. Packet signature (section 5.4.1.1).

Items 6–8 are meaningful for packets only. If the activity is not a packet transmission, a string of dashes ("---") appears in place of each of the three items. In the paper form of this exposure, item 8 (the packet signature) is only included if the simulator has been created with the -g option of mks (section B.2). Otherwise, packets carry no signatures. In the screen form, however, item 8 is always displayed,[14] but unless the simulator has been created with -g, the item is filled with dashes ("---").

If according to the port's perception, the current configuration of activities results in a future or present collision, a nonexistent activity representing the collision is included in the activity list. Only the first two attributes of this activity (i.e., the activity type designator and the starting time) are meaningful; the remaining items are printed as dashes ("---").

Exactly the same items of information are displayed with the screen form of the exposure.

---

[14]A display template (section A.6) is independent of the simulator, so its layout cannot be influenced by the options of mks.

Mode 2: Predicted Events

Calling: `printEvs (char *hdr = NULL);`

The exposure gives the timing of future or present events on the port (section 6.2). The description of each event takes one row consisting of the following items:

1. Event identifier (e.g., "ACTIVITY," "BOT," "COLLISION")
2. Time when the event will occur, or "---" if no such event is predictable at the current moment
3. Type of the activity triggering the event ("T" for a packet transmission, "J" for a jamming signal)
4. Id of the station that started the triggering activity
5. Station-relative number of the port on which the activity was started
6. Id of the receiving station if the triggering activity is a packet transmission ("---" is printed otherwise)
7. Traffic pattern Id of the triggering activity if the activity is a packet transmission ("---" is printed otherwise)
8. Total length of the packet in bits if the triggering activity is a packet transmission ("---" is printed otherwise)
9. Packet signature (see the comment regarding item 8 for the mode 1 Port exposure)

The list produced by this exposure contains exactly ten rows, one row for each of the ten event types discussed in section 6.2. If, based on the current configuration of link activities, no event of the given type can be anticipated, all entries in the corresponding row, except for the first one, contain "---."

The information displayed by the screen form of the exposure contains the same data as the paper form. Note that although the first item of each row is in fact static, this item is sent to the display program as a regular dynamic item.

7.3.5.8   Link exposure

Mode 0: Request List

Calling: `printRqs (char *hdr = NULL, Long sid = NONE);`

The exposure produces the list of processes waiting for events on ports connected to the link. The description is the same as for the Timer exposure with mode 0, with the word "Timer" replaced by "a port connected to the link." If the -s run-time option is selected (section B.3), the system processes waiting for internal events generated directly by the link AI (section 7.3.5.1) are included in the list.

The station-relative version of the exposure restricts the output to the processes belonging to the indicated station.

Mode 1: Performance Measures

Calling: `printPfm (char *hdr = NULL);`

The exposure outputs statistical data describing the amount of information passed through the link. The following items are produced (in this order):

1. Total number of jamming signals ever inserted into the link.
2. Total number of packet transmissions ever attempted (i.e., started—section 6.1.2.1) in the link.
3. Total number of packet transmissions terminated by `stop`.
4. Total number of information bits (packet's attribute `ILength`—section 5.2.2) transmitted via the link. A bit becomes transmitted if the transmission of the packet containing the bit is terminated by `stop`.
5. Total number of packets received on the link. A packet becomes received when `receive` (section 6.2.13) is executed for the packet. Note that the second argument of that `receive` must identify the link or one of its ports (sections 6.2.13, 7.1.3.1).
6. Total number of information bits received from the link.
7. Total number of messages transmitted via the link. A message becomes transmitted when the transmission of its last packet is terminated by `stop`.
8. Total number of messages received from the link. A message becomes received when `receive` is executed for its last packet. Note that the second argument of that `receive` must identify the link or one of its ports.
9. Number of damaged packets inserted into the link (section 7.1.3.1).
10. Number of header-damaged packets inserted into the link.
11. Number of damaged bits inserted into the link.
12. Received throughput of the link determined as the ratio of the total number of bits received on the link (item 6) to the simulated time expressed in ETUs.
13. Transmitted throughput of the link determined as the ratio of the total number of bits transmitted on the link (item 4) to the simulated time expressed in ETUs.

The screen version of the exposure displays the same items. The two throughput measures are displayed first and followed by the remaining items, according to the listed order.

Items 9, 10, and 11 do not appear in the link exposure if the simulator was not created with the -z option of `mks` (section B.2).[15]

---

[15]Note that if the simulator was not built with **-z**, the number of items sent by the screen version of the exposure to the display program is less than otherwise. As window templates are indifferent to the options of `mks`, the display program has no way of telling that some items from the exposure list should be selectively skipped. Thus, the only way out is to keep optional items at the end of the exposure list. If they do not arrive from the simulator, they will not be displayed, but their absence will not mess up the interpretation of any items that would have followed them,

Mode 2: Activities

Calling: `printAct (char *hdr = NULL, Long sid = NONE);`

This exposure produces the list of activities currently present in the link and the link's archive. The description of each activity takes one row that looks exactly like a row produced by the `Port` exposure with mode 1, with the following differences:

- Type "C" virtual activities are omitted, as collisions occur on ports, not in links.
- The starting and ending times reflect the actual starting and ending times of the activity at the port responsible for its insertion.
- In the station-relative version of the exposure, the `Id` of the station inserting the activity is not printed. Only the activities inserted by the indicated station are printed in this mode. Note that no station-relative version exists for the `Port` exposure.

The screen form of the exposure displays exactly the same items of information as the paper form.

7.3.5.9   Process exposure

Mode 0: Request List

Calling: `printRqs (char *hdr = NULL, Long sid = NONE);`

The exposure produces the list of processes waiting for events to be triggered by the `Process` AI (section 4.6). The description is the same as for the `Timer` exposure with mode 0, with the word "Timer" replaced by "Process."

The station-relative version of the exposure restricts the list to the processes belonging to the indicated station. As in the majority of cases a process waiting for an event from a process AI belongs to the same station as the AI, there seems to be little need for the station-relative version.

The screen form of the exposure displays exactly the same items of information as the paper form.

Mode 1: Wait Requests of This Process

Calling: `printWait (char *hdr = NULL);`

The exposure outputs the list of pending wait requests issued by the process. Each wait request is described by one row containing the following items (in this order):

1. Type name of the activity interpreter to which the request has been issued
2. `Id` of the activity interpreter or blanks, if the AI has no `Id` (e.g., `Timer`)

---

had the optional items been expected in the middle of the exposure. This is the primary reason for rearranging the screen version of the link exposure in such a way that its optional items are displayed last.

3. Identifier of the awaited event (section 7.3.5.1)

4. Identifier of the process state to be assumed when the event occurs

5. Time in ITUs when the event will be triggered, or the text "undefined" if the time is unknown at present

The screen form of the exposure displays the same items in exactly the same order.

7.3.5.10   Kernel exposure.   The `Kernel` process (section 4.8) defines a separate collection of exposure modes. These modes present information of a general nature.

Mode 0: Full Global Request List

Calling: `printRqs (char *hdr = NULL, Long sid = NONE);`

This exposure prints out the full list of processes waiting for some events. Each wait request is represented by one row containing the following data (in this order):

1. Id of the station owning the waiting process, or "Sys" for a system process. This item is not printed by the station-relative version of the exposure.

2. Process type name.

3. Process Id.

4. Simulated time in ITUs when the event will occur, or the text "undefined" if this time is unknown at present.

5. Single-character flag that describes the status of the wait request: "*" means that according to the current state of the simulation, the awaited event will actually restart the process, blank means that another waking event will occur earlier than the awaited event, and "?" says that the awaited event **may** restart the process, but another event awaited by the process is scheduled at the same ITU with the same order.

6. Type name of the activity interpreter expected to trigger the awaited event.

7. Id of the activity interpreter, or blanks if the AI has no Id (`Client`, `Timer`).

8. Event identifier (section 7.3.5.1).

9. State where the process will be restarted by the awaited event, should this event actually restart the process.

The station-relative version of this exposure lists only the wait requests issued by the processes belonging to the indicated station.

For multiple wait requests issued by the same process, the first three items are printed only once—at the first request of the process—and blanks are produced instead in the subsequent rows representing requests of the same process.

The screen form of the exposure displays the same items in exactly the same order.

Mode 1: Abbreviated Global Request List

Calling: `printARqs (char *hdr = NULL, Long sid = NONE);`

This abbreviated variant of the mode 0 exposure produces a single row of data per each sleeping process. This row has the same layout as for the mode 0 exposure. It describes the wait request that, according to the current state of the simulation, will restart the process.

The same items are produced by the screen form of the exposure.

Mode 2: Simulation Status

Calling: `printSts (char *hdr = NULL);`

The exposure prints out global information about the status of the simulation run. The following data items are produced (in this order):

1. UNIX process id of the simulator[16]
2. CPU execution time in seconds
3. Simulated time in ITUs
4. Total number of events processed by the simulator so far
5. Size of the simulator's event queue, i.e., the number of sleeping processes, including the system processes
6. Total number of messages ever generated and queued at the senders by the standard `Client`
7. Total number of messages entirely `received` (section 6.2.13)
8. Total number of queued bits, i.e., the combined length of all messages queued at the current moment
9. Amount of memory (in bytes) used for dynamically allocable data structures[17]
10. Global throughput determined as the total number of bits `received` so far divided by the simulation time in ETUs
11. Output name (section 2.4.2) of the last active station, i.e., the station whose process was last awakened
12. Output name of the last awakened process
13. Output name of the AI that woke the process up
14. Waking event identifier
15. State at which the process was restarted

Only items 1–10 are displayed by the screen form of the exposure—in the same order.

---

[16]In the Macintosh version of the package, this item does not occur.

[17]This value is updated when the nonstandard memory allocator is used (sections 2.3.2, B.1); otherwise it is displayed as zero. In the Macintosh version of the package, this item tells the number of bytes still available for allocation.

Mode 3: Last Event

No paper form.

This mode exists in the screen form only. It displays the information about the last awakened process, i.e., the last five items from the paper form of mode 3, in the same order as in the paper form.

7.3.5.11   Station exposure

Mode 0: Process List

Calling: `printPrc (char *hdr = NULL);`

This exposure prints out the list of processes belonging to the station and waiting for some events. Each wait request is represented by one row containing the following data (in this order):

1. Process output name (section 2.4.2).
2. Type name of the activity interpreter expected to trigger the awaited event.
3. Id of the activity interpreter, or blanks if the AI has no Id (`Client`, `Timer`).
4. Event identifier (section 7.3.5.1).
5. State where the process will be restarted by the awaited event, should this event actually restart the process.
6. Simulated time in ITUs when the event will occur, or the text "`undefined`" if this time is unknown at present.
7. Single-character flag that describes the status of the wait request: "`*`" means that according to the current state of the simulation, the awaited event will actually restart the process, blank means that another waking event will occur earlier than the awaited event, and "?" says that the awaited event **may** restart the process, but another event awaited by the process has been scheduled at the same ITU with the same order.

For multiple wait requests issued by the same process, the first item is printed only once—at the first request of the process—and replaced with blanks in the subsequent rows representing requests of the same process.

The screen form of the exposure displays the same items in exactly the same order.

Mode 1: Packet Buffer Contents

Calling: `printBuf (char *hdr = NULL);`

This exposure prints out the contents of the packet buffers at the station. One row of information is printed for each buffer, in the order in which the buffers have been declared (section 5.2.3). The following data items are included:

1. Buffer number (from 0 to $n-1$), where n is the total number of packet buffers owned by the station.

2. **QTime** attribute of the packet currently stored in the buffer (section 5.2.2), i.e., the time when the message from which the packet has been acquired was queued at the station.

3. Time when the packet became ready for transmission (attribute **TTime**— section 7.1.2.1).

4. **Id** of the packet's receiver or the string "**bcst**" for a broadcast packet.

5. **Id** of the traffic pattern to which the packet belongs.

6. Information length of the packet (attribute **ILength**—section 5.2.2).

7. Total length of the packet (attribute **TLength**).

8. Two standard flags of the packet: **PF_broadcast** and **PF_last** (section 5.4.1.1).[18] This item is a piece of text consisting of up to two possibly combined letters: B (for a broadcast packet) and L (for the last packet of a message). Blanks are printed if neither of the two flags is set.

9. Packet signature (see the comment regarding item 8 for the mode 1 **Port** exposure).

Items 2–9 are only printed if the packet buffer is nonempty; otherwise, the string "**empty**" is written in place of item 2 and dashes ("---") replace the remaining items.

The screen form of the exposure has exactly the same contents as the paper form.

Mode 2: Mailbox Contents

Calling: **printMail (char *hdr = NULL);**

The exposure prints information about the contents of all mailboxes owned by the station. One row of data is produced for each mailbox with the following items (in this order):

1. Station-relative serial number of the mailbox reflecting its creation order, or the mailbox nickname (section 2.4.2) if one is defined for the mailbox

2. Number of elements currently stored in the mailbox

3. Mailbox capacity

4. Number of pending wait requests issued to the mailbox

The screen form of the exposure produces exactly the same items.

Mode 3: Link Activities

Calling: **printAct (char *hdr = NULL);**

The exposure prints out information about port (link) activities started by the station. All links are examined, and all activities that were originated by the station

---

[18]The third flag (**PF_full**) associated with the packet buffer is not printed. When this flag is 0, the buffer is empty and no packet information is printed at all.

and are still present in the link or the link archive are exposed. One row of data per activity is produced with the following contents:

1. Station-relative number of the port (section 3.3.1) on which the activity was started
2. Id of the link to which the port is connected
3. Starting time of the activity
4. Finished time of the activity or the text "**undefined**" if the activity has not been finished yet
5. Activity type: "T" for a transfer, "J" for a jam
6. Id of the receiver (or "**bcst**" for a broadcast packet) if the activity carries a packet
7. Id of the traffic pattern to which the packet belongs
8. Total length of the packet in bits
9. Packet signature (see the comment regarding item 8 for the mode 1 **Port** exposure)

Items 6–9 are only printed if the activity carries a packet; otherwise, these items are replaced with dashes ("**---**").

Exactly the same data items are displayed by the screen form of the exposure.

Mode 4: Port Status

Calling: `printPort (char *hdr = NULL);`

The exposure produces information about the current status of the station's ports. One row of ten items is printed for each port. The first item is the port identifier. It can be either the station-relative serial number reflecting the port creation order, or the port's nickname if one is defined for the port (section 2.4.2). Each of the remaining items corresponds to one type of an event that can be present or absent on the port. If the item is "*******," the event is present (i.e., the port is currently perceiving the event). Otherwise, the item is "**...**" and the event is absent. The nine events are (in this order): ACTIVITY, BOT, EOT, BMP, EMP, BOJ, EOJ, COLLISION, ANYEVENT (section 6.2). They are identified by a caption line preceding the first row of items.

The screen form of the exposure displays the same information, except that "*******" is reduced to "*****" and "**...**" to "**.**" respectively. No caption line is sent to the display program.

7.3.5.12   System exposure.   The System station has its own two exposure modes that are used to print out information about the network topology/geometry. These modes have no screen forms.

Mode 0: Full Network Description

Calling: `printTop (char *hdr = NULL);`

Full information about the network configuration is printed out in a self-explanatory format.

Mode 1: Abbreviated Network Description

Calling: `printATop (char *hdr = NULL);`

Abbreviated information about the network configuration is printed. Again the output is self-explanatory.

Note.   The contents of mailboxes owned by the `System` station (section 4.7.3) can be printed/displayed using the mode 2 `Station` exposure.

7.3.5.13   Observer exposure

Mode 0: Information about All Observers

Calling: `printAll (char *hdr = NULL);`

The exposure produces information about all observers.[19] This information includes the list of pending inspect requests and timeouts (section 7.2.2.2). A single row of items describes one such request (or a timeout). For an inspect request, these items are as follows:

1. Output name of the observer
2. Id of the station specified in the inspect request or "ANY" (section 7.2.2.2)
3. Process type name from the inspect request or "ANY"
4. Process nickname or "ANY"
5. Process state or "ANY"
6. Observer state to be assumed should the inspect request become fulfilled

A pending `timeout` is printed in the form "Timeout at *time*," where the text "Timeout at" is printed as item 2 and the time (in ITUs) as item 3. The remaining items are blank.

For multiple entries corresponding to one observer, the observer's name (item 1) is printed only once (at the first entry), and it is blank in the subsequent entries belonging to the same observer.

Exactly the same items are displayed by the screen form of the exposure.

---

[19]We admit that this is not very elegant: to find out about all observers one has to expose any one of them.

Mode 1: Inspect List

Calling: `printIns (char *hdr = NULL);`

The exposure produces the same information as with mode 0, but restricted to the one observer whose exposure has been invoked. The layout of the list produced by this exposure is exactly as for mode 0 with the exception that the first item (the observer's output name) is absent.

The same information is produced by the screen form of the exposure.

BIBLIOGRAPHIC NOTES

The concept of a discrete random variable and its distribution parameters (moments, standard deviation) is introduced in any (sufficiently elementary) text on probability, in particular by *Feller* (1971), *Fisz* (1963), and *Mendehall and Scheaffer* (1973). Methodology of determining distribution parameters of random variables by discrete sampling during simulation (steady-state detection, confidence intervals) is discussed in many books on simulation, e.g., by *Bratley, Fox, and Schrage* (1987). Estimation of confidence intervals is one of the most important issues in simulation. For a deeper insight into these problems, the reader may refer to *MacDougall* (1987), *Fishman* (1990), *Kobayashi* (1978), *Welch* (1983), *Crane and Lemoine* (1977), *Iglehart* (1978), *Kleijnen* (1974-75), *Law* (1983) (this paper contains an excellent summary of techniques for the recognition of steady-state behavior), *Law and Kelton* (1982; 1984), *Starr* (1966), and *Chow and Robbins* (1965).

The idea of the observer as an independent agent monitoring the protocol behavior and verifying its compliance with specification was first published by *Ayache, Azéma, and Diaz* (1979). Examples of observers and their application to validating MAC-level protocols were given by *Groz* (1986), *Molva, Diaz, and Ayache* (1987), and *Berard, Gburzyński, and Rudnicki* (1991).

PROBLEMS

1. Devise an algorithm for calculating the nth moment of a random variable in an incremental way, i.e., assuming that new samples arrive dynamically and the previous samples are not stored. This way SMURPH computes distribution parameters for its random variables.

2. Write a SMURPH program to determine empirically the second, third, and fourth moments of the exponential distribution. Compare your results with analytically obtained values.

3. How would you determine that the behavior of the alternating-bit protocol (section 1.2.4) has reached a steady state? Implement an observer that starts at the beginning of the simulation run, monitors the network to detect the moment when its behavior becomes steady, then resets the `Client`'s performance measures and terminates itself.

4. The average packet delay (section 7.1.2.1) excludes the message queuing time at the sender. Define a nonstandard traffic type that will keep track of the *queued packet delay*, which, as for the message delay, will include the message queuing time at the sending station.

5. In the collision version of the alternating-bit protocol (see exercise 9 at the end of chapter 6) there is only one channel connecting the two stations. Implement a way of collecting statistics for this channel that will interpret regular packets and acknowledgments separately. Define a paper exposure method to print out your statistics.

6. The length of the confidence interval for an empirically determined mean value decreases with the square root of the number of samples. Explain why the length of the confidence interval calculated by SMURPH for weighted message delay (section 7.1.2.1) should generally be taken with a grain of salt.

7. As we said in section 7.2.2.2, observers can be used to implement complicated termination conditions for simulation experiments. Define an observer for the alternating-bit protocol in section 1.2.4 that will stop the simulation after a given number of packet retransmissions have taken place.

8. Add the two observers discussed at the end of section 7.2.2.2 to the alternating-bit protocol. Modify the acknowledgment receiver process by removing the `if` statement in state `AckArrival`, but leaving `Alert->put();` as an unconditional statement. Run the modified protocol until a problem is detected by one of the observers, and try to diagnose the problem using the tracing mechanism of SMURPH (section 7.2.1).

9. Sometimes a protocol gets into a *live-lock* scenario in which the protocol is apparently performing some nontrivial operations, but no progress is observed. What would you consider progress in the case of the alternating-bit protocol? Define an observer to detect the lack of such progress.

10. Define a nonstandard link type that will measure the distribution of the ratio of damaged packets to all packets inserted into the link. Provide an exposure method for this link type. Use your link type in the alternating-bit protocol. Read the relevant portions of appendix A, and figure out how to make sure that the screen part of your exposure will be interpreted properly by the display program.

8

Collision Protocols

8.1 ETHERNET

In this chapter we present a number of collision protocols and discuss their implementation in SMURPH. Although collision protocols are no longer considered an attractive research topic (it is commonly believed that all paths of their evolution have been explored and found blind), Ethernet—the simplest and best known representative of this family—continues to be the most popular local area network. This gives us a good reason to start our presentation from Ethernet. Even if we accept that collision protocols do not have a very bright future (which is by no means certain for the author), we should honor the simplicity and flexibility of Ethernet, and use it as inspiration in our pursuit of new solutions.

A technical description of a protocol is usually full of secret acronyms and buzzwords that make it difficult, if ever possible, to understand how the protocol really works. In our discussion, we will try to avoid unnecessary noise and obey the golden principle of Occam, which says that notions and concepts that are not necessary to explain a given phenomenon should not appear in the explanation. This rule will guide us through all the remaining chapters of this book.

All collision protocols constituting the subject of this chapter operate on bus networks based on uniform, broadcast-type media shared by all stations. If a station decides to insert an activity (e.g., a packet) into the channel, all the other stations will sense this activity in due time—depending on the distance between the sender and the sensing station.

Although in some protocols based on unidirectional segmented channels (e.g., Expressnet—section 9.2) the collision concept is also present, we generally do not

call them collision protocols. In such protocols, collisions play a secondary role
(and they are usually less destructive than in Ethernet), whereas in a true collision
protocol, collisions are the driving force of the medium access scheme. Protocols
of the latter kind are called CSMA/CD protocols, where CSMA/CD stands for
Carrier-Sense Multiple Access with Collision Detection. The meaning of the six
keywords in this acronym will become clear shortly.

8.1.1   The Ethernet Protocol

The backbone of Ethernet consists of a number of stations, say N, connected to a
single, uniform, broadcast-type channel called the bus. In the commercial network[1]
this channel is a tree-shaped link built of connected segments of coaxial cable,[2]
which offers a signal propagation speed of the order of $0.8c$, where c is the speed of
light in vacuum. Each station has a single port to the channel, which can be used
passively (i.e., to sense the channel status or receive a packet) or actively (i.e., to
transmit a packet).

8.1.1.1   Transmission rules.   The most interesting part of the Ethernet protocol (practically the only interesting part) is the set of transmission rules:

E1   (*Carrier Sense*) A station willing to transmit a packet listens to the bus
       (via its port). If the bus is perceived idle, the station is allowed to transmit,
       provided that the bus has been idle for the amount of time corresponding
       to the length of the so-called *interpacket space*.

E2   (*Multiple Access*) A station willing to transmit may find its port busy (there
       are multiple stations accessing the shared channel at the same time). In
       such a case, the station waits until the bus becomes idle. Then the station
       waits for the amount of time corresponding to the length of the interpacket
       space and starts transmitting the packet. Note that while waiting for the
       interpacket space, the station **does not monitor the port**. It starts trans-
       mitting unconditionally as soon as the interpacket space has been obeyed.

E3   (*Collision Detection*) While transmitting, the station monitors the bus for
       an interfering activity (a collision). As soon as a collision is detected, the
       station aborts the transmission, sends a short jamming signal and resched-
       ules the transmission after a randomized delay. The retransmission is carried
       out according to the same rules as the original transmission.

The reception part of the protocol is simple. Every station hears all the packets
passing through the bus and receives those whose receiver fields in the headers match
the station's address.

---

[1]Some people use the term *Ethernets* to denote a general class of networks based on the
concept of CSMA/CD. Although we do not follow this terminology, we will try to avoid misunderstanding by referring to the actual Ethernet as the *commercial network* or *commercial Ethernet*.

[2]Early versions of Ethernet used twisted pair.

8.1.1.2   Responsibilities of the medium access control (MAC) protocol.

If a packet has been transmitted entirely without a collision, the station assumes that the transmission has been successful. To be precise, we should say that the MAC-level protocol assumes that the transmission has been successful. There may be reasons, unknown to the transmitting station, why the packet may not make it to the destination; for example, the destination may be dead or broken. Such problems are to be detected and diagnosed by higher protocol layers (e.g., the transport layer—section 1.1.2.4).

Let us now ask what kind of guarantee one could reasonably expect from a decent MAC-level protocol for a bus network. In a bus network, the MAC-level protocol replaces the data-link layer and the network layer of the OSI model (section 1.1.2). The role of the communication subnet is played by the ubiquitous broadcast channel extending to all the hosts. It thus seems sensible to assume that the virtual network layer emulated by the medium access protocol has done its job if the transmitted packet is able to reach the most remote regions of the bus without damage. As no intermediate nodes take part in the packet's tour through the network, the network layer has no obligation to detect dead stations; this is for the transport layer, which deals with the end-to-end traffic.

In Ethernet a packet that has been transmitted without a collision is guaranteed to reach the virtual boundary of the communication subnet. This guarantee should read: "If nothing catastrophic happens to the network (e.g., disconnected cable, electromagnetic interference), the packet will reach the location of its destination without damage." As we will see, this simple postulate is the underlying principle of most MAC-level protocols, not only collision protocols for bus networks.

To stand up to its guarantee, the medium access protocol of Ethernet must know that a packet that has been transmitted without a collision will not collide later, on its way to the destination. This requirement (which is common for all CSMA/CD protocols) imposes a relation between the network diameter and the minimum length of a packet. Consider two stations s_1 and s_2 located at the opposite ends of the bus, as shown in figure 8.1. Let the distance between s_1 and s_2 be $d(s_1, s_2)$. Assume that, having sensed the bus idle, station s_1 starts transmitting a packet at time t. Shortly before the packet transmitted by s_1 reaches station s_2 (which happens at $t + d(s_1, s_2)$), s_2 decides to transmit a packet of its own. This transmission immediately collides with s_1's packet and the collision is recognized by s_2 at once. However, it will take another $d(s_1, s_2)$ time units for station s_1 to learn about the collision. This will happen when the beginning of the packet transmitted by s_2 reaches s_1, at time $t + 2d(s_1, s_2)$. Thus, s_1 recognizes the collision $2d(s_1, s_2)$ time units after it started transmitting the packet. Consequently, if all collisions are to be recognized while the packets involved are still being transmitted, the shortest packet must not be shorter than $2L$, where L is the maximum distance between a pair of stations.[3] In reality, because of the fact that collisions are not recognized

---

[3]In section 8.1.1.4 (table 8.1) we give the numerical parameters of the commercial network, including the minimum and maximum packet size.

instantaneously, the minimum safe packet length should be somewhat larger than $2L$.

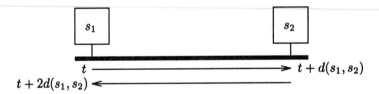

Figure 8.1 The worst-case collision scenario

More precisely, we should say that the transmission of the shortest packet in Ethernet must take at least $2L$ time units. However, we should be getting used by now to expressing time in bits (section 1.2.4.11). This makes sense for homogeneous networks (like Ethernet) in which all stations obey the same transmission rate. The transmission rate of Ethernet is 10 Mb/s, which means that one bit is equal to 10^{-7} seconds. Bits can also be used to measure distance between locations on the bus. Assuming that the signal propagation speed in Ethernet is $0.8c$ (about 240,000 km/s), the distance traveled by a signal within one-bit time is about 24 meters.

The role of packet spacing is twofold. First, boundaries between packets are clearly visible, which makes the work of the two bottom layers a bit easier. Second, packet spacing improves the protocol fairness. Note that, having sensed the bus busy, a station willing to transmit a packet waits until the bus becomes idle and then obeys the packet space, i.e., delays the transmission by a certain amount of time. During that time, the station does not monitor the bus for another activity and does not yield to transmission attempts of other stations.[4] Thus, if multiple stations start transmitting after detecting the same silence period in the bus, these stations will collide, rather than one station preempting the others. After the collision, they will resolve the contention in a randomized fashion, without any of the stations involved in the collision being privileged.

8.1.1.3 Collision processing. Having sensed a collision, a transmitting station aborts the transfer and emits a short *jamming signal*. The purpose of this activity is to make sure that all the other stations involved in the collision also recognize that a collision has occurred. The jamming signal prolongs the collision to a definite minimum duration independent of the sensitivity of the participating stations. To understand why this is needed, consider a collision scenario involving two stations s_1 and s_2. Assume that s_1 is slightly more sensitive than s_2, i.e., s_1 has a shorter collision recognition latency than the other station. By the *collision recognition latency* we understand the amount of time elapsing from the moment

---

[4]Note that with this approach successfully transmitted packets are still well separated by interpacket space intervals.

an interfering activity arrives at the station to the moment the station actually recognizes a collision.

The collision scenario is as follows. Station s_2 starts transmitting a packet at time t; this packet arrives at s_1 at time $t + d(s_1, s_2)$. Having sensed the bus idle, s_1 starts its own transmission at time $t+d(s_1, s_2)$—just an infinitesimal time before the packet being transmitted by s_2 arrives at s_1. Station s_1 recognizes the collision and aborts its transfer attempt at time $t + d(s_1, s_2) + l(s_1)$, where $l(s_1)$ is the collision recognition latency of station s_1. Thus, the interfering activity traveling toward s_2 is of length $l(s_1)$. But the collision recognition latency of station s_2 is larger than $l(s_1)$; thus, s_2 may not recognize the collision.

One can conceive of similar scenarios, involving more than two stations, in which the station with the longest collision recognition latency is not able to recognize that a collision has occurred. One may claim that it is very unlikely for s_1 to start its transmission precisely at the moment when it is reached by the packet transmitted by s_2. But this scenario need not be uncommon under reasonably heavy traffic conditions. Consider a strictly linear bus topology (as in figure 8.1), and assume that three stations s_1, s_2, and s_3 are connected to the bus in the order of their indexes, e.g., from left to right. Suppose that station s_3 has been transmitting for at least $2L$. When s_1 and s_2 become ready to transmit, they both sense the bus busy and are forced to wait for silence (i.e., the end of s_3's transmission). Assume that s_3 terminates its transmission at time t. Station s_2 is first to detect silence in the bus, which happens at time $t + d(s_2, s_3)$. Then it waits for the interpacket space, and at time $t+d(s_2, s_3)+p$ (where p is the length of the interpacket space), s_2 starts transmitting. Station s_1 senses the bus idle at time $t + d(s_1, s_3)$, obeys the interpacket space, and starts transmitting at time $t+d(s_1, s_3)+p$, i.e., at the moment when the packet transmitted by s_2 arrives at s_1.[5] This scenario is illustrated in figure 8.2, which shows the space/time *propagation diagram* for the activities of the three stations. Propagation diagrams are very useful for visualizing in a static way dynamic configurations of activities in linear buses. The unidimensional "space" of a linear bus is represented by the horizontal axis with the marked points representing the locations of the relevant stations. The vertical axis symbolizes the time. Activities emitted by stations are denoted by vertical bars. Shaded areas correspond to the space/time regions where activities are being heard. For example, in figure 8.2, at time $t + d(s_1, s_3) +p$, station s_1 starts perceiving the transmission of station s_2 and will continue perceiving this transmission until its end (not shown in the diagram) arrives at the station.

The jamming signals, whose rationale has been demonstrated, need not have any special structure. It might be reasonable to postulate that they consist of *noise* clearly distinguishable from a packet transmission. However, the jamming signal is usually just a continuation of the packet being transmitted. A transmitting station sensing a collision simply delays the abortion of its transmission for a short while— to make sure that the interfering activity perceived by the other transmitting station

---

[5]Note that if the bus is strictly linear, $d(s_1, s_3) = d(s_1, s_2) + d(s_2, s_3)$.

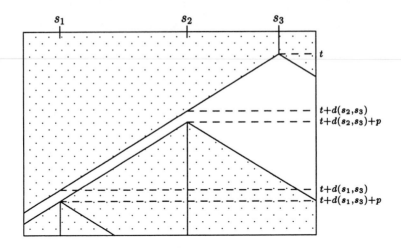

Figure 8.2 The propagation diagram of a two-station collision scenario following the transmission of a third station

(or stations) is not too short.

Another important element of the collision-processing mechanism is the *backoff algorithm*, i.e., the method of rescheduling transmissions after a collision. Clearly, the retransmission delay should be randomized; otherwise, the retransmitting stations would almost certainly get involved in another collision. In the commercial network the backoff delay is generated according to the following formula:

$$b = U(0, 2^{nc} - 1) \times 2L,$$

where nc is the number of collisions suffered by the packet so far (including the current collision), $U(a, b)$ stands for a uniformly distributed integer random number between a and b inclusively, and L is the network diameter, i.e., the maximum distance between a pair of stations.

Each station maintains a collision counter for the packet currently being processed. When a new packet is acquired for transmission, the collision counter is cleared. Then, whenever the packet suffers a collision, the collision counter is incremented by 1. This way, according to the formula, the average backoff delay grows as an exponential function of the number of collisions suffered by the packet. The actual waiting time is allotted in $2L$ increments. Note that two retransmissions scheduled $2L$ or more time units apart from each other are guaranteed not to collide, which need not be true for a smaller separation interval. Thus, the value $2L$ is sometimes called the *collision window* or, somewhat less fortunately, the *slot*. We will call it the *round-trip propagation delay*, which reflects the fact that $2L$ corresponds to the amount of time needed to travel twice the maximum distance in the network.

In the commercial network, the backoff function is *truncated* at the tenth collision, which means that once nc has reached 10, it does not grow any more. When the actual number of collisions reaches 15, this event is reported to the higher protocol layers as an abnormal condition.

8.1.1.4   Technical parameters of commercial Ethernet.   In the preceding sections we explained the operation of the MAC-level protocol of Ethernet without assuming any specific implementation parameters. Actually, in section 8.1.1.2 we mentioned the transmission rate of 10 Mb/s, but this number is known to virtually everybody who has ever heard about Ethernet. The signal propagation speed in the Ethernet bus (section 8.1.1) is a parameter of the coaxial cable and does not really belong to the Ethernet specification. The transmission rate of 10Mb/s, as well as the other parameters discussed later, is arbitrary: there is nothing in the conceptual design of Ethernet that precludes other transmission rates. In fact, the first experimental Ethernet network operated at 3 Mb/s.

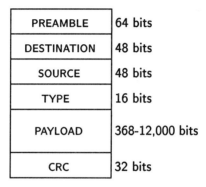

Figure 8.3 Packet format in Ethernet

Figure 8.3 depicts the packet format in the commercial network. The lengths of the different components of the header are specified in bits, although usually they are given in octets (bytes). Each field, including the payload field, takes an integer number of octets.

The frame starts with a 64-bit preamble consisting of alternating zeros and ones.[6] The role of the preamble is to tune the receiver's clock to the incoming packet. The problem is not the absolute clock rate, whose accuracy is well preserved across different stations. The tolerance of clocks used by Ethernet stations is no worse than 0.01 percent. With the preamble, the receiver has ample time to determine very precisely where the packet actually begins, i.e., when to start the clock to make sure that its ticks properly strobe the packet bits. The preamble belongs to the physical layer and some people do not consider it as part of the packet header. We count the preamble in the header: no packet is ever transmitted without it.

---

[6]The preamble starts with a 1 and ends with a 1. The last 1 is repeated twice and indicates the end of the preamble.

The preamble is followed by two 48-bit address fields with the destination address preceding the source address. A special value of the destination address field (all 1's) represents a broadcast packet, i.e., a packet that should be received by all stations in the network. The type field is unused by the MAC layer; it is reserved for the higher layers, e.g., to describe the packet type, whatever it means. As we are not concerned with the operation of the higher layers, we ignore this field (but count it in the header length).

The payload portion of the packet must be at least 46 octets long because of the constraints on the minimum packet length imposed by the collision detection mechanism (section 8.1.1.3). The maximum payload length of 1500 octets determines the size of a packet buffer at a station. Two such buffers are needed: one for transmission, the other for reception. The packet is closed by a 32-bit *frame check sequence*, which is the value of a CRC polynomial calculated from all the bits of the packet, including the header but excluding the preamble.

Three more numbers are needed to fully specify the protocol. The length of the interpacket space is 9.6 microseconds, which translates into 96 bits. The length of a jamming signal is between 32 and 48 bits, at the discretion of the colliding station. The round-trip propagation delay assumed by the backoff function (the value of $2L$) is 512 bits. Note that this value is hardwired into the backoff function—it is not determined based on the actual propagation diameter of the network.

Parameter	Value
Transmission rate	10 Mb/s
Round trip propagation delay	512 bits
Minimum packet payload length	368 bits
Minimum packet payload length	12,000 bits
Minimum total packet length	576 bits
Maximum total packet length	12,208 bits
Header length (including preamble)	176 bits
Trailer length	32 bits
Header length + trailer length	208 bits
Inter-packet space	96 bits
Jamming signal length	32–48 bits

Table 8.1 Numerical parameters of commercial Ethernet

Table 8.1 lists all the numerical parameters of the commercial network, including the packetization parameters. The minimum total packet length (including the preamble) is 576 bits, which, in accord with the collision detection requirements, is somewhat more than the maximum theoretical round-trip propagation delay of the network.

8.1.2 Ethernet Implementation in SMURPH

In this section we present a complete SMURPH program modeling the behavior of Ethernet, as described in the preceding sections. As Ethernet is a homogeneous network, it is convenient and natural to assume that time is measured in bits.

Thus, both ITU and ETU will correspond to the amount of time needed to insert a single bit into the network. With this assumption, the header of our program may look as follows:

```
identify Ethernet1;

#define MinPL       368    // Minimum payload length in bits
#define MaxPL     12000    // Maximum payload length in bits
#define FrameL      208    // Combined length of header and trailer

#define PSpace       96    // Interpacket space length in bits
#define JamL         32    // Length of the jamming signal in bits
#define TwoL        512    // Maximum round-trip delay in bits

#define TRate         1    // Transmission rate: 1 ITU per bit
```

The first three constants are packetization parameters of Ethernet. Note that we can pass them directly as arguments to getPacket (section 5.4.1.1) to make sure that the acquired packet fulfills the protocol's requirements. The last constant (TRate) will be used as the transmission rate of ports (section 3.3.1). We agreed that one bit insertion time should be equal to one ITU.

8.1.2.1 Station and process types.

Viewed from the MAC level, Ethernet is based on stations of the same type executing the same protocol. This protocol is described by two processes: the transmitter and the receiver. We define the types of all these objects as follows:

```
station EtherStation {
  Port *Bus;              // Port to the bus
  Packet Buffer;          // The packet to be transmitted
  void setup () { Bus = create Port (TRate); };
};

process Transmitter (EtherStation) {
  int CCounter;           // Collision counter
  Port *Bus;              // A copy of the bus port
  Packet *Buffer;         // Packet buffer pointer
  TIME backoff ();        // The standard backoff function
  void setup () {
    Bus = S->Bus;
    Buffer = &(S->Buffer);
  };
  states {NPacket, Retry, Xmit, XDone, XAbort, JDone};
  perform;
};
```

```
process Receiver (EtherStation) {
  Port *Bus;              // A copy of the bus port
  void setup () { Bus = S->Bus; };
  states {WPacket, Rcvd};
  perform;
};
```

For the time being, we ignore the Root process, which glues the program together, and the description of the network geometry and traffic pattern. We focus on the protocol specification, which should (and can) be done without assuming any specific network configuration and traffic conditions.

The station structure in our Ethernet model is quite simple. It consists of one packet buffer (storing packets of the standard type Packet) and one port to the bus. The setup method of EtherStation creates the port and sets its transmission rate to one ITU per bit.

Each of the two processes defines its private pointers to the relevant station attributes; these pointers are set by the processes' setup methods. We follow this approach in other examples. Although station attributes can be referenced from a process owned by the station via the S attribute of the process (section 4.2), accessing them via private copies is more convenient and makes the process code method shorter and easier to read. Of course, if the process wants to modify a station attribute, it must reference it directly (via the S pointer). Fortunately, the two processes run by EtherStation do not modify the attributes of their station. Both processes need access to the bus port; additionally, the transmitter will reference the station's packet buffer.[7]

The transmitter defines one integer attribute called CCounter, which will count collisions suffered by a packet awaiting a successful transmission. This attribute will be used in calculation of the backoff function, which is implemented as a transmitter's method.

8.1.2.2 Protocol operation.

Let us start by listing the code of the receiver process, which is almost trivial. The same (or a very similar) receiver code is used by many other protocols presented in this book. As we said in section 8.1.1.1, the reception part of the Ethernet protocol is very simple, at least insofar as the medium access level is concerned. Every station is expected to monitor the bus for packets addressed to it and receive these packets, provided that they arrive with no errors. This is accomplished by the following code method of Receiver:

```
Receiver::perform {
  state WPacket:
```

---

[7]In a real network the station is equipped with two buffers: one for a packet to be transmitted, the other for a received packet. In our model received packets are not assumed to be passed to higher protocol layers (we do not model these layers), and consequently the receiver's buffer is not needed.

```
        Bus->wait (EMP, Rcvd);
    state Rcvd:
    Client->receive (ThePacket, ThePort);
    skipto (WPacket);
};
```

There is little to explain. The process detects all EMP (End of My Packet) events on the bus port triggered whenever the end of a complete packet addressed to the station owning the process arrives at the port (section 6.2.6). For each EMP event, the packet causing it is received (sections 5.4.3, 6.2.13). Note that having received a packet, the process uses skipto (section 6.2.13) to get back to state WPacket, to make sure that the end of the received packet has disappeared from the port.

Before we discuss the code of the transmitter process, let us look at its backoff method used to generate the retransmission delay after a collision.

```
TIME Transmitter::backoff () {
    return TwoL * toss (1 << (CCounter > 10 ? 10 : CCounter));
};
```

The integer function toss (section 2.3.1) generates a uniformly distributed integer random number between 0 and $n - 1$, where n is the argument passed to the function. In the preceding method, the argument of toss is produced by shifting 1 CCounter positions to the left (or by ten positions if CCounter is greater than 10). This generates the proper power of 2 needed by the backoff formula introduced in section 8.1.1.3.[8]

The complete code method of the Ethernet transmitter is as follows:

```
Transmitter:: perform {
    TIME  LSTime, IPeriod;
    state NPacket:
      CCounter = 0;
      if (Client->getPacket (Buffer, MinPL, MaxPL, FrameL))
        proceed Retry;
      else
        Client->wait (ARRIVAL, NPacket);
    state Retry:
      if (undef (LSTime = Bus->lastEOA ()))
        Bus->wait (SILENCE, Retry);
      else {
        if ((IPeriod = Time - LSTime) >= PSpace)
          proceed (Xmit);
        else
```

---

[8]Incidentally, this approach to generating the retransmission delay closely resembles the way it is done in the commercial implementation of the protocol.

```
                    Timer->wait ((TIME) PSpace - IPeriod, Xmit);
            }
        state Xmit:
          Bus->transmit (Buffer, XDone);
          Bus->wait (COLLISION, XAbort);
        state XDone:
          Bus->stop ();
          Buffer->release ();
          proceed (NPacket);
        state XAbort:
          Bus->abort ();
          CCounter++;
          Bus->sendJam (JamL, JDone);
        state JDone:
          Bus->stop ();
          Timer->wait (backoff (), Retry);
    };
```

The process starts in state NPacket, where it clears CCounter and attempts to acquire a packet for transmission. With the arguments passed to getPacket (section 5.4.1.1), the payload of the acquired packet will be no shorter than MinPL (dummy bits will be appended to the payload if the message is shorter than MinPL) and no longer than MaxPL. FrameL bits will be added to the payload portion to represent the frame information, i.e., the header and trailer. Note that the value of FrameL (section 8.1.2) includes the preamble length. If no packet can be acquired (i.e., no message is queued at the station), the process issues a wait request to the Client—to be awakened by the nearest message arrival event—and goes to sleep. Upon message arrival, the transmitter will wake up again in state NPacket, where it will reexecute getPacket, this time successfully. Consequently, the transmitter will transit to state Retry. As CCounter has been cleared in state NPacket, the collision counter will start running from zero—for the newly acquired packet.

The first statement executed in state Retry assigns to LSTime the time when the last end of activity (the beginning of the current silence period) was heard at the bus port. According to section 6.3.2, when this value is undefined (function undef), it means that the port is currently perceiving an activity (i.e., the bus is sensed busy). In such a case, the process issues a wait request to the port awaiting the end of this activity, i.e., the beginning of a silence period. When this event occurs, the process will find itself back in state Retry, but this time the port will be sensed idle. If the port is idle (LSTime is defined), the transmitter checks whether the packet space has been obeyed. This happens to be the case if $Time - LSTime$ is not less than PSpace. Then the transmitter proceeds to state Xmit, where it starts the packet transmission. Otherwise, before moving to Xmit, the process waits for the residual amount of time required by the spacing rules, i.e., for the difference between the required spacing interval and the duration of the currently perceived silence period. Note that during this waiting the bus port is not monitored. Thus, even if an activity appears on the port in the meantime, the transmission will commence forcing a collision (sections 8.1.1.1, 8.1.1.2).

In state Xmit, the transmitter starts the packet transmission (section 6.1.2.1) and issues two wait requests. One of these requests is generated implicitly by transmit. The process will get to state XDone upon the completion of the transfer; this will only happen if the other event awaited by the transmitter (COLLISION) does not occur earlier. Let us follow the first alternative, i.e., assume that the packet has been transmitted without a collision. Then the process wakes up in state XDone, where it stops the transfer and releases (empties) the packet buffer (sections 5.2.3, 5.4.3). This completes the processing of the packet at the transmitter's end: the process moves to state NPacket to try to acquire another packet for transmission.

If a collision is detected while a packet is being transmitted (section 6.2.10), the process is restarted in state XAbort, where it aborts the transfer (section 6.1.2.1), increments the collision counter (used by the backoff function), and emits a jamming signal for JamL ITUs (section 6.1.2.2). After that time, the transmitter gets to state JDone, where the jamming signal is terminated. Then the process waits for the amount of time determined by the backoff function and moves to state Retry, to continue its attempts to transmit the packet successfully.

Note that it is not absolutely critical that the Ethernet jamming signals be actually represented by SMURPH jams. Upon sensing a collision, the transmitter could just continue the packet transmission for the amount of time corresponding to the required length of the jamming signal, with the same effect. As an easy exercise, the reader may try to modify the transmitter code along these lines.

In exactly one place (state Retry), the transmitter performs a port inquiry about the past (operation lastEOA). As we said in section 6.3.2, inquiries about the past are shortcuts, which are formally impossible in a real network without a special agent (i.e., process) keeping track of the activities within a sliding time window. Clearly, it is not impossible to implement such processes in SMURPH. The primary role of inquiries about the past is to make the protocol model more efficient and easier to comprehend; they do not increase the expressing power of our system.

8.1.2.3 The root process.

To make our implementation executable, we should create a virtual environment in which the protocol can run. This is done by the root process. We present here a complete root process that can be used as a driver for the protocol processes listed in section 8.1.2.2. In section 8.1.2.4, we show how to structure the protocol program, i.e., isolate its fragments so that they can be reused as building blocks in other protocol programs.

The type definition for the root process has the following layout:

```
process Root {
  void buildNetwork (int, TIME);
  void initTraffic ();
  states {Start, Stop};
```

```
  perform;
};
```

Besides the code method, the process defines two other methods:
buildNetwork, responsible for creating the stations and the bus, and connecting
these components into a network; and **initTraffic**, describing the traffic conditions. The first of the two methods is defined as follows:

```
void Root::buildNetwork (int ns, TIME bl) {
    int i, j;
    Link *lk;
    EtherStation *s;
    DISTANCE d;
    d = bl / (ns - 1);
    for (i = 0; i < ns; i++) create EtherStation;
    lk = create Link (ns, PSpace+10);
    for (i = 0; i < ns; i++) {
        s = (EtherStation*) idToStation (i);
        s->Bus->connect (lk);
        for (j = 0; j < i; j++)
            ((EtherStation*) idToStation (j))->Bus->
                setDTo (s->Bus, d * (i - j));
    }
};
```

The two arguments **ns** and **bl** specify the number of stations and the bus
length, respectively. It is assumed that the bus has a strictly linear topology and
the stations are equally spaced along it. The bus length is divided by the number of
stations minus 1 to produce the length d of a bus segment separating two neighboring
stations. Note that if **bl** is not divisible by **ns** $- 1$, the actual length of the bus will
be shorter than **bl** (it is always equal to the biggest multiple of **ns** $- 1$ not larger
than **bl**).

The method starts with building the stations. Then it creates a broadcast link
with slots for **ns** ports and with the archival time of **PSpace+10** ITUs (section 3.2.2).
Note that to respond correctly to the transmitter's inquiry issued in state **Retry**
(section 8.1.2.2), the link must remember what has happened on each port within the
last **PSpace** ITUs. Any activity that disappeared from the link earlier is irrelevant:
if no activity has passed through the link since then, packet spacing is necessarily
obeyed by all stations. It is reasonable to make the link archival period slightly
longer than the maximum depth of an inquiry addressed to the link's port. Obeying
this informal rule costs practically nothing and protects against possible problems
arising from the limited accuracy of stations' clocks. The safety margin added to
the archival time should be no less than $t_a \times dev$, where t_a is the nominal requested
archival time and *dev* is the maximum clock tolerance (**deviation**—section 4.5.2)
over all stations. In our case, the clock tolerance in the same for all stations and
equal to 0.0001; thus, the margin of 10 added to **PSpace** is much more than needed.

Having created the bus, buildNetwork enters a loop in which it traverses all stations from 0 to ns, connects their ports to the bus, and updates the bus's distance matrix. Note that when station number i is being connected to the bus, all stations numbered 0 through i − 1 have been connected already. The inner loop goes through all these stations and sets the distance between them and station i (sections 3.1.2, 3.3.3). For a station number j (j < i), this distance is equal to (i − j) × d (assuming a strictly linear bus topology with equally spaced stations). After the last station (number ns − 1) has been connected, the link's distance matrix is completely defined.

To keep things simple at the beginning, we assume that the traffic pattern in our network is uniform with all stations equally contributing to the network load. These conditions are set up by the following method:

```
void Root::initTraffic () {
  Traffic *tp;
  double mit, mle;
  readIn (mit);
  readIn (mle);
  tp = create Traffic (MIT_exp+MLE_exp, mit, mle);
  tp->addSender (ALL);
  tp->addReceiver (ALL);
};
```

The method reads two double numbers from the input data file and creates a traffic pattern for which these numbers specify the mean message interarrival time and mean message length. The distribution of these two parameters is exponential. All stations are legitimate senders and receivers of messages, with equal weights.

Let us now look at the code of the root process:

```
Root::perform {
  int n;
  Long NMessages;
  TIME BusLength;
  state Start:
    setEtu (1);
    setTolerance (0.0001);
    readIn (n);
    readIn (BusLength);
    buildNetwork (n, BusLength);
    initTraffic ();
    for (n = 0; n < NStations; n++) {
      create (n) Transmitter;
      create (n) Receiver;
    }
    readIn (NMessages);
```

```
          setLimit (NMessages);
          Kernel->wait (DEATH, Stop);
     state Stop:
          System->printTop ("Network topology");
          Client->printDef ("Traffic parameters");
          Client->printPfm ();
   };
```

The layout of this code method is typical. Most root processes have just two states: one assumed when the process is started and the other where the process wakes up to complete the simulation experiment. In the first state, the root process builds the network, describes the traffic conditions, and starts the protocol. Then it typically issues a wait request for Kernel's DEATH (section 4.8), to learn when the simulation exit conditions (section 4.9) have been met.

This is exactly what is performed by our present instance of the root process. Specifically, the process performs the following actions in state Start:

1. The relationship between the ITU and ETU is established (section 2.2.2). As a matter of fact, this operation is redundant: by default, 1 ETU = 1 ITU.

2. The clock tolerance (deviation) is set (section 4.5.2) to the maximum value acceptable in the commercial network.

3. The number of stations and the bus length in bits are read from the data file and passed as arguments to buildNetwork.

4. Traffic conditions in the network are defined (by calling initTraffic).

5. The protocol processes are started (two processes per station). Recall that the first argument of create (in parentheses) identifies the station owning the created process (section 2.4.7).

6. A number is read from the data file and used as the limit for the number of messages to be received at their destinations (section 4.9). This number provides the termination condition.

7. The process issues a wait request for Kernel's DEATH. This event will be triggered as soon as the declared number of messages have been received. Then the root process will run for the second (and last) time, in state Stop.

In its second state, the process writes some information to the output file. The printTop method of the System station exposes the network configuration (section 7.3.5.12) and writes to the output file its description. Similarly, the Client's exposure by printDef (section 7.3.5.5) produces the parameters of the traffic pattern. These two exposures echo to the output file the input specification of the network geometry and traffic conditions in a processed form. The second exposure of the Client (method printPfm) prints some simulation results: the standard collection of performance measures associated with the traffic pattern (section 7.3.5.5). When the list of statements in state Stop is exhausted, the program terminates.

The complete code of Ethernet, in the version discussed here, can be found in directory Examples/ETHER/Ethernet1 of the SMURPH package. The reader will also find there a sample data set for the simulator. This data set consists of five numbers, which are read by the root process (note that two numbers are read by initTraffic, which is not immediately clear from the Root's code method).

8.1.2.4 Structuring the protocol program.

The different pieces of code presented in the previous sections can be combined into a single file and compiled by mks (section B.2) to create a simulator instance. Putting all code into one file is seldom a good idea, regardless of the program's nature. Usually, it is much better to isolate some functionally related fragments into separate files, which can be treated as autonomous or semi-autonomous modules. These modules can be reused in other programs. For example, all the protocols presented in this chapter operate on bus networks with the same topology. It is natural to separate the network geometry description from the protocol: the former can be put into a library, from which it can be incorporated into many different protocol programs. Whenever we feel like playing with a different variant of the bus topology (e.g., nonlinear or with an uneven distribution of stations), we should make sure that the code for building a network according to the new prescription can be turned into a standard geometry module with the same interface as the other geometry modules already residing in the library. The same can be done with traffic specifications and with many common features of apparently different protocols. With the right modularization methodology, we will be creating a powerful problem-oriented library rather than a loose collection of independent protocol programs. This way, with the growing size of our library, new protocol programs will be easier to design and code. By keeping in mind that different modules should be autonomous, we will be forced to obey clear and simple interfacing rules. This will make our programs easier to comprehend and debug.

Directory Examples/ETHER/Ethernet2 contains a reimplementation of the Ethernet program, organized into the following modules:

- The protocol specification (files protocol.c, ether.h, and types.h).
- The root process. This process has been put into a separate file (root.c), as it is a driver that formally does not belong to the protocol.
- The network geometry description (files lbus.h and lbus.c). These two files describe a bus configuration with a number of stations equally spaced along the bus.
- The traffic specification (files utraffic.h and utraffic.c), describing a uniform traffic pattern with exponentially distributed message length and inter-arrival time.

Files types.h, protocol.c, and root.c are closely related, and their contents depend on each other. These contents can be viewed as the protocol-specific portion of the program. File ether.h defines the numerical parameters of commercial Ethernet (table 8.1). These parameters are in principle flexible,[9] and it seems natural

---

[9]They are fixed in the commercial network, but in our virtual world we are free to play with

to separate them from the protocol. The remaining files are protocol-independent and can be exchanged to define other bus topologies and other traffic patterns.

Let us look at `types.h` and focus on the changes with respect to the previous implementation:

```
#include "ether.h"
#include "lbus.h"
#include "utraffic.h"
station EtherStation : BusInterface, ClientInterface {
  void setup () {
    BusInterface::configure ();
    ClientInterface::configure ();
  };
};
process Transmitter (EtherStation) {
  int CCounter;        // Collision counter
  Port *Bus;           // A copy of the bus port
  Packet *Buffer;      // Packet buffer pointer
  TIME backoff ();     // The standard backoff function
  void setup () {
    Bus = S->Bus;
    Buffer = &(S->Buffer);
  };
  states {NPacket, Retry, Xmit, XDone, XAbort, JDone};
  perform;
};
process Receiver (EtherStation) {
  Port *Bus;              // A copy of the bus port
  void setup () { Bus = S->Bus; };
  states {WPacket, Rcvd};
  perform;
};
```

The types of the two processes are declared in exactly the same way as before. The station type is now composed of two virtual types (section 2.4.4): `BusInterface` and `ClientInterface`. The first of the two types defines the fragment of the station interfacing it to the bus, the other describes the station's interface to the `Client`. We assume that each of the virtual types declares a method called `configure`. This method is called from the `setup` method of `EtherStation` to initialize the corresponding fragment of the station structure.

Let us discuss the bus interface first. File `lbus.h` contains the following declarations:

---

noncommercial Ethernets.

```
station BusInterface virtual {
  Port *Bus;
  void configure ();
};
void initBus (RATE, DISTANCE, int, TIME);
```

The global function `initBus` will be called by `Root` to supply the parameters of the network configuration. These parameters have the following meaning (in the order of their occurrence in the function header):

- Transmission rate of all ports (in ITUs per bit—section 3.3.1)
- Bus length in ITUs
- Number of stations in the network
- Archival time of the link representing the bus

Although we have assumed that the transmission rate of ports in our Ethernet model is 1, we should not insist on implanting this assumption into a reusable library module. Therefore, the transmission rate is now a parameter of `initBus`.

The way the network is configured should be independent of the protocol and consequently independent of the actual layout of the station type. Thus, the module cannot assume any name or contents of the final station type and can only rely on the bus interface fragment (type `BusInterface`), which rightfully belongs to the geometry module. The other part of this module (file `lbus.c`) is as follows:

```
#include "lbus.h"
static Link *TheBus;
static RATE TR;
static DISTANCE D;
static int NP, NC;
static BusInterface **Connected;
void initBus (RATE r, DISTANCE l, int np, TIME ar) {
  TheBus = create Link (np, ar);
  TR = r;
  D = l / (np-1);  // The distance between neighbors
  NP = np;         // The number of stations to connect
  NC = 0;          // The number of stations connected so far
  Connected = new BusInterface* [NP];
};
void BusInterface::configure () {
  int i;
  Bus = create Port (TR);
  Bus->connect (TheBus);
  for (i = 0; i < NC; i++)
    Bus->setDTo (Connected[i]->Bus, D * (NC - i));
  if (NC == NP-1)
```

```
   delete Connected;
else
   Connected [NC++] = this;
};
```

Note that initBus does not actually build the network. The function merely creates the bus link, computes the distance between a pair of neighboring stations, and sets some global variables. It is assumed that stations are created elsewhere, but initBus must be called before the first station is created. Generally, the network configuration program, if it is to be set aside as an independent module, cannot be made responsible for creating stations whose complete structure is unknown to it. Therefore, the network is built step-by-step whenever a new station comes into existence. This is done by the configure method of BusInterface, which should be called by the station's setup method when the station is created by Root.

Whenever configure is called, the method creates the bus port (with the required transmission rate) and connects it to the bus. Then, for all stations that have been created so far, configure sets up the distance between their ports and the port of the newly created station. Finally, a pointer to the station is stored in array Connected, which has been allocated for this purpose by initBus. This only happens if the station is not the last station to be created. Otherwise, configure assumes that there will be no more processing, and the array is deallocated.

The need for a temporary array to store station pointers stems from the fact that configure does not know the actual station type and consequently does not know how to *cast* type Station to BusInterface. In particular, the following operation: (BusInterface*)idToStation(i) would not produce the intended result, as BusInterface contributes to the final station type via multiple inheritance. However, at the moment when configure is called (and only at that moment), the pointer to the BusInterface fragment of the station object is known and contained in this. By storing this pointer, the method is able to keep track of the relevant fragments of all stations that have been created, without knowing the complete layout of the station structure.

Example

The preceding approach to building network configurations is quite flexible. For example, suppose that you want to model a hybrid of two networks, e.g., Ethernet and Token Ring connected via a bridge. Thus, you will have stations of three types, e.g.,

```
station EtherStation : BusInterface, ClientInterface {
  void setup () {
    BusInterface::configure ();
    ClientInterface::configure ();
  };
};
station RingStation : RingInterface, ClientInterface {
```

```
              void setup () {
                RingInterface::configure ();
                ClientInterface::configure ();
              };
            };
            station Bridge : BusInterface, RingInterface {
              void setup () {
                BusInterface::configure ();
                RingInterface::configure ();
              };
            };
```

Assume that `RingInterface` is implemented according to rules similar to those used for `BusInterface`. Now, when the stations are created by `Root` (in an arbitrary order), they will be automatically and correctly interfaced with their subnetworks.

To turn the traffic specification into an independent module, we follow essentially the same approach as in the case of the geometry description. We list the contents of file `utraffic.h` specifying the part of the module visible to the protocol program:

```
            station ClientInterface virtual {
              Packet Buffer;
              Boolean ready (Long, Long, Long);
              void configure ();
            };
            void initTraffic ();
```

The role of `initBus` from the geometry module is played by function `initTraffic`, which is responsible for creating the traffic pattern. The function takes no arguments: the traffic parameters will be read from the data file. The station's method `ready` provides a new tool for packet acquisition.

To see how the module operates, let us look at its other file (`utraffic.c`), which has the following contents:

```
#include "utraffic.h"
static Traffic *UTP;
void initTraffic () {
  double mit, mle;
  readIn (mit);
  readIn (mle);
  UTP = create Traffic (MIT_exp+MLE_exp, mit, mle);
};
void ClientInterface::configure () {
  UTP->addSender (TheStation);
  UTP->addReceiver (TheStation);
```

```
};
Boolean ClientInterface::ready (Long mn, Long mx, Long fm) {
  return Buffer.isFull () || UTP->getPacket (&Buffer, mn, mx, fm);
};
```

The only item in this file that calls for some explanation is the **ready** method. The method returns YES when the station has a packet (belonging to the traffic pattern handled by the module) ready for transmission. If the station's packet buffer is nonempty, the method returns YES immediately; otherwise, it attempts to acquire a new packet and store it in the buffer. The three arguments passed to the method specify the packetization parameters for **getPacket**.

One may question the need for a special packet acquisition method that does very little beyond just calling **getPacket**. With a bit of imagination, we can see, however, that it helps the traffic module to separate concerns. This may not be very beneficial in the case of our simple uniform traffic pattern but becomes quite advantageous in more involved cases. Note that, in general, packet acquisition may be tricky; for example, it may differ from station to station, it may involve multiple traffic patterns examined in some order, it may reference objects that should be hidden from the protocol and contained entirely in the traffic module. Therefore, it is reasonable to postulate that the acquisition method is a station attribute and it comes as part of the traffic module interface.

Stations are configured with the traffic pattern dynamically, as they are created. Each station equipped with **ClientInterface** is added to the senders and receivers set of the traffic pattern (section 5.3.6) with the same weight of 1.

File **protocol.c** contains the code of the two protocol processes listed in section 8.1.2.2 with one little modification: the call to **getPacket** executed in state **NPacket** of the transmitter, i.e., the statement

```
    if (Client->getPacket (Buffer, MinPL, MaxPL, FrameL))
        proceed Retry;
```

is replaced with a call to **ready**:

```
        if (S->ready (MinPL, MaxPL, FrameL))
            proceed Retry;
```

The last interesting element of the modular implementation of Ethernet is the file **root.c**, containing the new definition of **Root**. The contents of this file are as follows:

```
        #include "types.h"
        process Root {
          states {Start, Stop};
          perform {
            int n;
            Long NMessages;
```

```
                    TIME BusLength;
                    state Start:
                      setEtu (1);
                      setTolerance (CTolerance);
                      readIn (n);
                      readIn (BusLength);
                      initBus (TRate, BusLength, n, PSpace + 10);
                      initTraffic ();
                      while (n--) create EtherStation;
                      for (n = 0; n < NStations; n++) {
                        create (n) Transmitter;
                        create (n) Receiver;
                      }
                      readIn (NMessages);
                      setLimit (NMessages);
                      Kernel->wait (DEATH, Stop);
                    state Stop:
                      System->printTop ("Network topology");
                      Client->printDef ("Traffic parameters");
                      Client->printPfm ();
                  };
                };
```

The clock tolerance is now represented by a symbolic constant CTolerance, defined in ether.h, along with the transmission rate (constant TRate defined as 1) and the other constants listed at the beginning of section 8.1.2.

In the other protocol programs presented in this book, we follow the same modularization rules as the ones just illustrated. Typically, we have three protocol-specific files: types.h, protocol.c, and root.c. Sometimes there will be additional files containing elements that are closely related to the protocol (and that cannot be reused in other programs) but that neither belong to the protocol (in which case they would have been put into protocol.c) nor are part of the initialization procedure (in which case they would have been put into root.c). Observers are examples of such elements.

All potentially reusable modules are stored in the include library (section B.1) kept in directory Examples/IncludeLibrary of the SMURPH package. From there they will be #included by the protocol-specific files. Usually, the ".h" portions of the library modules will be included by types.h, and the ".c" portions will be included by root.c.[10] To make sure that a library file is included at most once in a given source file, we encapsulate it into an #ifndef–#endif pair, according to the following scheme:

---

[10]Note that the ".c" files of the library modules cannot be precompiled and stored in binary form. Their binary versions generally depend on the configuration of mks parameters (section B.2) specified when the executable simulator is created.

```
#ifndef symbol
#define symbol
    ...
#endif
```

where *symbol* uniquely identifies the file name.[11]

Directory `Examples/ETHER/Ethernet3` contains yet another implementation of Ethernet in which the reusable modules have been removed from the protocol directory and put into the include library. Files `ether.h`, `lbus.h`, `lbus.c`, `utraffic.h`, and `utraffic.c` can be found in `Examples/IncludeLibrary`. Note that `utraffic.c` is now included by `root.c`. Otherwise, `mks` would not know that the file must be compiled together with the protocol-specific files.

Additionally, we have extracted from the Ethernet program the declaration of `EtherStation` and the complete specification of the receiver process. These fragments have been stored in files `etherstation.h` and `etherreceiver.h`, in `IncludeLibrary`. They are reused in other collision protocols for bus networks discussed in this chapter.

8.2   TREE COLLISION RESOLUTION

The simplicity and statistical nature of Ethernet have been found irritating by many people (including the author), who have spent considerable effort trying to come up with a better idea. One problem with Ethernet is its unpredictability: given a packet to be transmitted, there is no bound on the amount of time needed to transmit this packet successfully. As collisions in Ethernet are resolved statistically, a packet may collide an unpredictable number of times before it is eventually transmitted. This number cannot be limited a priori; thus, formally, packet delivery is not absolutely guaranteed.

It is not impossible that two packets in Ethernet will collide for a substantial amount of time, for example, one hour. Although the probability of this event is much smaller than the probability of the network's being damaged by an earthquake during that time, many people would claim that the nondeterminism of packet delivery is a serious drawback of Ethernet. In real-time applications, where packets are expected to arrive at predictable intervals, the random character of transmission rescheduling in Ethernet may actually show up, especially if the network consists of many heavily loaded stations. The reader is encouraged to carry out experiments to determine the distribution of packet access time in Ethernet under varying traffic conditions. These experiments will demonstrate that most packets suffer low access delays, even if the traffic is very heavy. On the other hand, quite a few packets will be less fortunate; some of them will be delayed for a very long time.

There have been several attempts to invent a CSMA/CD protocol that would

---

[11]Some macropreprocessors for C++ compilers feature the `#pragma once` specification, which can be used to indicate that a given file is to be included at most once. Unfortunately, this feature is not common enough to be relied upon.

impose an upper limit on the number of collisions suffered by a packet and that would make the packet access time bounded, regardless of the traffic conditions. The authors of these solutions did not want to give up the most advantageous and unbeatable property of Ethernet: zero access time in the absence of contention. Their objective was to devise a protocol that under light load would offer a mean access delay comparable to Ethernet's, but would also impose an upper bound on this delay. The Tree Collision Resolution protocol proposed by Capetanakis in 1979 is one attempt to meet this objective.

8.2.1   The Protocol

The role of any MAC-level protocol for a bus network is to determine the order in which competing stations should carry out their transfers to make them successful. In Ethernet the contending transmitters play a stochastic tournament to come up with a successful ordering of their transfers. A collision can be viewed as a game in the tournament: a station that reschedules its transmission "correctly" wins and transmits successfully, otherwise it loses and has to play again. To make this tournament more challenging, the stations are blindfolded, i.e., they do not see the moves of the other contenders. The only message a colliding station gets is that its transmission was scheduled incorrectly in the last game.

The basic idea of the Tree Collision Resolution protocol (TCR) is to make collisions useful. The protocol assumes that collisions are recognized by all stations in the network, not only by the participants, and used as synchronizing events that help the backlogged stations transmit their packets in a deterministic way. A collision in TCR carries some implicit information. This information allows the contending stations to split themselves into subsets in such a way that stations from different subsets will not collide further until they have transmitted their packets. The tournament nature of the protocol becomes clearly visible in TCR, because now the stations are not blindfolded (at least not completely). After a collision, the station learns whether it wins or loses. A station that wins is allowed to retransmit immediately. A station that loses must wait until all winners are done with their packets. A winner may collide again and become a loser in the new game; however, after a bounded number of games (collisions), there will be only one winner, which will transmit successfully. The remaining stations will continue the tournament, becoming subsequent winners and losers, until they are all done.

Each game (collision) divides the set of stations into two parts: the winners and the losers. Although the winners may still collide with other winners and the losers may still collide with other losers, the losers will not further collide with the winners. As each collision essentially halves the population of stations that are eligible to compete in the next game, the number of collisions suffered by a packet is limited.

At any moment, the network is perceived by stations as being in one of two different modes of operation. In the *uncontrolled mode*, TCR behaves like commercial Ethernet, i.e., a station may start transmission at any time provided that the bus is idle and the packet spacing rules have been obeyed. After a collision is sensed,[12] all stations switch to the *tournament mode*. The collision initiating the tournament counts as the first game, i.e., there are winners and losers from this collision.

To better understand the operation of the protocol, it is convenient to imagine that the network operates in a slotted manner. The slots (special signals that mark slot boundaries) are inserted into the bus by a dedicated station. Each slot may contain

- A valid packet transmission
- Silence
- A collision, i.e., an interference of two or more simultaneous transfer attempts

Slots are big enough to provide a means of global synchronization. In particular, the fate of any activity started within a slot can be determined and learned by all stations within the same slot. Thus, the length of a slot must be at least equal to the round-trip propagation delay of the bus ($2L$).

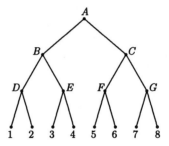

Figure 8.4   The tree structure for a network of eight stations

Let us imagine that all stations in the network are logically organized into a binary tree, as presented in figure 8.4. For simplicity, we may assume that the number of stations is a power of 2, although this is not important, because the binary tree need not be complete. This organization is absolutely unrelated to the distribution of stations along the bus: it is purely logical and may be based on certain globally known attributes of stations, e.g., their addresses or identifiers assigned by the network administrator. In the uncontrolled mode of operation, all stations are permitted to access the bus spontaneously. Thus, a station having a packet ready to transmit is allowed to do it immediately, i.e., at the nearest beginning of a slot. If the station transmits successfully, nothing special happens; as long as there are no collisions, the network remains in the uncontrolled mode.

Suppose that a collision occurs. This means that two or more stations have transmitted in the same slot. Let the slot in which the collision has been detected

---

[12]Note that a collision is detected by all stations, not only those that participate in the collision.

be numbered 0. All stations in the network recognize the collision and are able to tell that the tournament has started. The stations that were not trying to transmit in slot 0 are now deferred until the tournament is over and the network returns to the uncontrolled mode. This means that a station that gets a packet to transmit while the tournament is in progress must postpone its transfer attempt until the tournament is finished. The purpose of the tournament is to resolve the contention among the stations that were ready before the tournament started.

During the next slot (slot number 1) only the stations falling under node B of the virtual tree are allowed to play, i.e., attempt to transmit their packets. The stations located under C must wait until they learn that all contending stations from the left subtree have transmitted their packets successfully. Thus, the first collision divides the set of contenders into two groups: the stations belonging to the left subtree win, and the stations falling into the right subtree are proclaimed losers. All the winners are allowed to transmit in the next slot, i.e., slot number 1. The losers must wait until they know that all the winners have transmitted their packets. The same idea applies recursively to all subsequent collisions, with the set of potential contenders halved each time. For example, if more than one station transmits in slot 1, there will be another collision. Then the stations falling under node D will win and will be allowed to transmit in slot 2, whereas the stations located under E will have to wait until the winners are done.

It may happen that at a certain stage of the tournament the set of winners is empty. In such a case, the next slot will be silent, and the losers will learn that they are allowed to get back to the tournament. The operation of the protocol depends on the stations' ability to monitor activities in the slots and correctly interpret the status of the game.

Example

> Assume that stations 2, 3, 4, and 7 (see figure 8.4) all attempt to transmit in slot 0. After the collision, stations 4 and 7 are deferred, and stations 2 and 3 retransmit their packets in slot 1. Stations 2 and 3 collide again in slot 1, and they are both proclaimed losers. Note that at this moment they cannot possibly know that the set of winners is empty. They learn about this fact having perceived the silent slot number 2. Then they rejoin the tournament and collide once more in slot 3. This time station 2 wins and transmits successfully in slot 4. Station 3 detects the successful transmission of station 2 and concludes that it is the only remaining contender in subtree B. Note that station 3 does not have to detect an empty slot to find out that there are no more winners. The transmission in slot 4 was successful, and that transmission could only be performed by station 2—the only other legitimate contender at this level of the tournament. Thus, the transmission of station 3 in slot 5 completes the processing of subtree B.
>
> Note that to know that all stations falling under B are done, stations 4 and 7 have to monitor the activities in the bus carefully. After their first collision, the two stations expect one of the following three events:
>
> - An empty slot, indicating that the set of winners is empty, after which the

stations are allowed to retransmit their packets immediately

- A collision, informing the stations that there was more than one winner
- A successful transmission, indicating that one of the winners is gone

In the second case, it is no longer enough for stations 4 and 7 to detect a single empty slot to get back to the tournament. The two stations learn that there are at least two winners, and now they expect two successful transmissions before they are allowed to return to the game.

8.2.2   The Implementation

The only interesting element of the SMURPH implementation of TCR is the transmitter process. The other parts of this implementation, including the station structure and the receiver process, are borrowed directly from the Ethernet implementation discussed in section 8.1.2. Before we present the TCR transmitter, we discuss briefly a few implementation issues.

8.2.2.1   Keeping track of the tournament.

As long as the network remains in the uncontrolled mode, its behavior is practically identical to the behavior of Ethernet (section 8.1.1). The tournament starts with the first collision sensed in the uncontrolled mode. Let us focus on the issues related to maintaining the consistent notion of the tournament across different stations.

It is quite easy to determine the winner/loser status of a colliding station. A transmitter participating in the tournament maintains a counter (called Ply), which tells the number of collisions suffered by the packet since the beginning of the tournament. The value of this counter tells the level of the virtual tree of stations at which the last game was played. For example, the following method (which we associate with the transmitter process) returns YES if the station has lost in its last game:

```
Boolean Transmitter::loser () {
   return (S->getId () >> Ply) & 01;
};
```

The method assumes that the first collision that starts the tournament sets Ply to zero. From then on, Ply will be incremented by 1 with each collision in which the transmitter actively participates. The organization of the virtual tree of stations implied by loser is different from that presented in figure 8.4. According to the method, the station's position (left/right) in level-i subtree can be determined by looking at the ith bit of its address, assuming that the least significant bit of the address is numbered 0. For eight stations, their order at the leaves of the virtual tree is $0, 4, 2, 6, 1, 5, 3, 7$.[13] Note that the number of stations need not be a power of

---

[13] We would get the same order as in figure 8.4 if the address bits were processed from the most significant end. This would make the loser method a little bit trickier, because it would have to know the location of the most significant bit in the station address field.

2.

Of course, in a real network, the tree hierarchy can be determined in a more complicated way, possibly using a lookup table explicitly assigning leaf locations to stations. It should be noted that stations located closer to the left end of the leaf list are slightly privileged over the other stations. This privilege consists in a faster access to the medium, although the average number of collisions required to get this access is the same for all stations.

The problem of deciding when a loser is allowed to get back to the tournament seems a bit trickier at first sight. Another (related) question is when to proclaim that the tournament is over, i.e., when a station is allowed to resume the uncontrolled mode of operation.

Assume that at some point in the tournament station s transmits and collides. Let the slot of this collision be labeled 0. If s wins in this collision, there is no problem: the station is allowed to retransmit in slot 1. But suppose that s loses and has to wait until all the winners are gone. The station does not know the number of winners. Clearly, s is not allowed to transmit in the next slot; it has to monitor what happens in that slot and base its waiting time on the outcome of this observation. The following outcomes are possible:

- Slot number 1 is silent. The station concludes that the set of winners is empty and that it is allowed to transmit in slot 2.

- The slot contains a successful packet transmission. The station knows that there was only one winner (otherwise, the multiple winners would have collided). Thus, s is allowed to transmit in slot 2.

- The slot contains a collision. The station learns that there are multiple winners and it has to monitor the next two slots (2 and 3) to get a better picture of the situation.

In the third case, s learns that there are at least two winners. If slot 2 is silent, the station must still wait (it means that all the winners have lost their first game, but they remain winners with respect to s). If slot 2 brings a successful packet transmission, s must wait for yet another slot (3), because it knows that at least one more winner is still in the game. Note, however, that two successful transfers in slots 2 and 3 will indicate that all the winners are done with their packets. Indeed, had there been more than two winners, some of them would have collided in slot 2, slot 3, or both. A collision occurring in slot 2 or slot 3 is treated by s recursively, in the same manner as the collision in slot 1. This means that the station should add one slot to its waiting time. These observations suggest the following simple solution to the loser's dilemma.

A loser awaiting its time to get back to the tournament maintains a simple counter called `DelayCount`. This counter tells the number of slots that must pass before the loser is allowed to play again. When the station becomes a loser, the counter is set to 1, meaning that the station is not allowed to transmit in the next slot but it may be able to transmit one slot later if the scenario is favorable. Whenever the station senses a collision, `DelayCount` is incremented by 1. Whenever the station perceives a successful transmission or an empty slot, 1 is subtracted from the counter. When DelayCount descends to zero, the station gets back to the tournament and is allowed to transmit its packet in the next slot.

A similar counter that simulates the behavior of a "permanent loser" is used to tell when the tournament is over. This counter, called DeferCount, is set to 2 after the starting collision of the tournament and updated like DelayCount, assuming that the station remains a loser throughout the entire tournament. When DeferCount reaches zero (which means that all participating stations have transmitted their packets), the tournament is over.

The last problem to be solved is the elimination of the explicit slots. With a careful interpretation of the activities in the bus, it is possible for the stations to play the tournament in an unslotted environment. As long as there are no collisions, the network operates exactly like Ethernet. A station sensing a collision waits until it knows for sure that all the other stations have learned about the collision and all activities related to the collision (aborted packet remnants, jamming signals) have disappeared from the bus. This waiting time (which should be of order $2L$)[14] corresponds to skipping the remainder of the collision slot and advancing to the next slot boundary. Then, if the station turns out to be a winner, it is allowed to retransmit its packet. Otherwise, the station monitors the bus for another $2L$ time units, to determine the status of the next slot. There are three possibilities:

- No activity is sensed during the $2L$ period. Then the station assumes that the slot is empty.
- A transmission is sensed, which is eventually terminated by a valid packet trailer. This means that one of the winners has transmitted successfully in the slot.
- An activity is sensed that develops into a collision. This indicates the presence of multiple winners, which play another game.

This way, although no explicit slots are used, the slot concept is retained in a virtual sense, to the extent that makes it possible for the stations to play the tournament consistently. Note that the length of a virtual slot may vary. A slot filled with a successfully transmitted packet ends at the packet boundary, whose location depends on the packet length.

8.2.2.2 TCR transmitter. The correct recognition of slot boundaries and consistent interpretation of events in slots are critical prerequisites for an accurate implementation of TCR. If this implementation is to be realistic, it must account for the limited accuracy of independent clocks at different stations. Despite the clock discrepancies, the stations must properly "guess" the boundaries of the virtual slots, such that the perception of the tournament by different stations is the same. Like most protocol models discussed in this book, our model of TCR will be run with nonzero clock tolerance. To make sure that we do not miss anything important,

---

[14]With a safety margin added to compensate for the limited accuracy of independent clocks.

we will use a much finer time granularity than in the Ethernet model. This way we will account for situations in which clock discrepancies trigger race conditions occurring within a fraction of one bit insertion time. The time granularity will be a parameter of the model and will be read from the data file.

The contents of the file types.h from the SMURPH implementation of TCR are as follows. The reader will find this implementation in directory Examples/TCR1.

```
#include "ether.h"
#include "lbus.h"
#include "utraffic.h"
#include "etherstation.h"
#include "etherreceiver.h"
extern RATE TRate;
extern TIME SlotLength, GuardDelay, TPSpace, TJamL;
process Transmitter (EtherStation) {
  Port *Bus;
  Packet *Buffer;
  Boolean TournamentInProgress, Transmitting, Competing;
  int Ply, DelayCount, DeferCount;
  Boolean loser ();
  void setup () {
    Bus = S->Bus;
    Buffer = &(S->Buffer);
    TournamentInProgress = Transmitting = Competing = NO;
  };
  states {NPacket, Transmit, Busy, XDone, SenseEOT,
    SenseCollision, EndJam, NewSlot, EndSlot};
  perform;
};
```

The implementation of TCR involves quite a bit of recycling. The items inherited from Ethernet (which can be found in Examples/IncludeLibrary) were discussed in section 8.1.2. The time granularity (TRate) is now a global variable, which will be initialized by Root (read from the data file). TPSpace and TJamL are TIME versions of PSpace and JamL from the file ether.h. The numerical parameters of TCR, including packetization, packet spacing, and jamming signals, are the same as for Ethernet. Now, as TRate need not be equal to 1 and time is not measured directly in bits, the parameters expressing time intervals must be converted from bits to ITUs. This conversion will be performed by Root before the protocol is started.

SlotLength determines the length of a virtual slot (section 8.2.2.1) in the case when the slot is silent or contains a collision. This parameter, which is read from the data file, should be equal to $2L$ augmented by a small safety margin dependent on the clock tolerance. The size of this margin is related to GuardDelay, which represents a short compensating delay used by the transmitter to cover the uncertainty in the position of a slot boundary.

Besides the usual pointers providing local access to the relevant station attributes, the transmitter declares three Boolean flags, three counters, and one Boolean method. The role of the counters and the `loser` method was described in section 8.2.2.1. The three Boolean flags describe the station's perception of the tournament status and the station's role in the tournament. `TournamentInProgres` indicates whether a tournament is being played. This flag is set to YES at the first collision in the uncontrolled mode and reset to NO when the tournament is over (when `DeferCount` descends to zero). If `Transmitting` is YES, it means that the station is currently transmitting a packet. The value of this flag is used to determine whether the station actively participates in a collision. The last flag (`Competing`) tells whether the station takes part in the tournament or is deferred until the tournament is over. To participate in a tournament, a station must have had a packet ready when the tournament was started. This is another way of saying that the station was involved in the first collision of the tournament. All three flags are set to NO by the transmitter's setup method (note that this initialization agrees with their announced semantics). The integer counters are only relevant when a tournament is in progress; they will be initialized upon the first collision.

Following is the code method of the transmitter:

```
Transmitter::perform {
  state NPacket:
    if (S->ready (MinPL, MaxPL, FrameL))
      proceed Transmit;
    else {
      Client->wait (ARRIVAL, NPacket);
      Bus->wait (ACTIVITY, Busy);
    }
  state Transmit:
    Transmitting = YES;
    Competing = YES;
    Bus->transmit (Buffer, XDone);
    Bus->wait (COLLISION, SenseCollision);
  state Busy:
    Bus->wait (EOT, SenseEOT);
    Bus->wait (COLLISION, SenseCollision);
  state XDone:
    Bus->stop ();
    Transmitting = NO;
    Competing = NO;
    Buffer->release ();
    proceed SenseEOT;
  state SenseCollision:
    if (!TournamentInProgress) {
```

```
      Ply = DelayCount = 0;
      DeferCount = 1;
      TournamentInProgress = YES;
    }
    if (Competing) {
      if (Transmitting) {
        if (loser ()) DelayCount = 1;
        Ply++;
      } else
        DelayCount++;
    }
    DeferCount++;
    if (Transmitting) {
      Bus->abort ();
      Transmitting = NO;
      Bus->sendJam (TJamL, EndJam);
    } else
      Timer->wait (TJamL + SlotLength, NewSlot);
  state EndJam:
    Bus->stop ();
    Timer->wait (SlotLength, NewSlot);
  state NewSlot:
    if (Competing && DelayCount == 0)
      Timer->wait (GuardDelay, Transmit);
    else {
      Timer->wait (SlotLength, EndSlot);
      Bus->wait (ACTIVITY, Busy);
    }
  state EndSlot:
    if (--DeferCount == 0) {
      TournamentInProgress = NO;
      Timer->wait (GuardDelay, NPacket);
    } else {
      if (Competing) DelayCount--;
      proceed NewSlot;
    }
  state SenseEOT:
    if (TournamentInProgress)
      Timer->wait (TPSpace, EndSlot);
    else
      Timer->wait (TPSpace, NPacket);
};
```

We first discuss the process's operation in the uncontrolled mode. In this mode, the transmitter transits through states NPacket, Transmit, XDone, SenseEOT, and possibly Busy. As long as there are no collisions, the process mimics the behavior of Ethernet; its slightly different organization results from the need to accommodate the tournament.

In state NPacket, the transmitter checks whether there is a packet awaiting transmission at the station. The method ready, introduced in section 8.1.2.4 and defined in the traffic module, is used for this purpose. If the message queue is empty, the process awaits a message arrival event; upon its occurrence, the transmitter will move back to state NPacket and reexecute ready. Together with the Client's wait request, the transmitter issues a wait request to the bus port. Note that even if the station has no packet to transmit, it is expected to monitor activities in the bus, to maintain a consistent perception of the network's operation mode. The *carrier-sense* part of the protocol is thus implemented differently from the Ethernet model. The transmitter is constantly aware of the bus status (even when the station is passive) and need not refer to the link archive to obey the packet spacing rules. Consequently, as no inquiries about the past are issued to the bus, the link archival time can be declared as zero (section 3.2.2).

Assume that while waiting for a message arrival, the process is restarted by the bus ACTIVITY event—in state Busy. This activity can either develop into a successful transmission (in which case the process will find itself in state SenseEOT) or into a collision (forcing the transmitter to state SenseCollision). In the latter scenario, the network (as perceived by the station) enters the tournament mode. In state SenseEOT, the process sleeps for the packet space interval (note that TournamentInProgress is NO) and moves back to NPacket. This operation is semantically equivalent to the operation of the Ethernet transmitter (section 8.1.2.2) under similar circumstances.

Now suppose that ready at state NPacket returns YES. The process moves to state Transmit, where it initiates the packet transmission and (as in Ethernet) issues a wait request to the bus port to await a possible collision. At the same time, the process sets Transmitting and Competing to YES. The meaning of the first flag is obvious; the second indicates the process's participation in a possible tournament that will be triggered if the transmission collides. If the transmission is successful, the process wakes up in state XDone, where it terminates the transfer, resets the two flags to NO, releases the packet buffer, and moves to SenseEOT.

Let us now turn our attention to the tournament. The transmitter gets to state SenseCollision whenever it senses a collision in the bus. This collision may or may not involve a packet transmission initiated by the process (Transmitting == YES). The first condition checked in state SenseCollision is whether a tournament is currently in progress. If TournamentInProgress is NO, it means that the collision starts a new tournament; then Ply and DelayCount are initialized to 0, DeferCount is set to 1 (section 8.2.2.1), and TournamentInProgress is set to YES, to indicate the change in the network operation mode.

Suppose that the station participates in the tournament, i.e., its Competing flag is YES.[15] It is then determined whether the station has been playing the current game, i.e., has been involved in the current collision (Transmitting == YES as well). If this happens to be the case, the winner/loser status of the station is determined by a call to loser (section 8.2.2.1). If the station wins, its DelayCount remains intact—equal to 0. (This is equivalent to letting the station retransmit in the next virtual slot.) Otherwise, DelayCount is set to 1, to delay the retransmission by one slot.[16] In either case, Ply is incremented by 1 to indicate that the station has played one more game. If the station has not been involved in the collision (but it participates in the tournament), it means that the station is one of the losers from a previous game. In this case, DelayCount is incremented by 1, in accordance with the tournament rules outlined in section 8.2.2.1.

Irrespective of whether the station participates in the tournament, DeferCount is always incremented by 1 upon a collision. This counter simulates the behavior of a permanent loser, which participates in the tournament but loses every game, including the first one.

If the station is taking part in the collision (Transmitting == YES), the process aborts the transmission and emits a jamming signal. Then it terminates the jamming signal in state EndJam, delays for SlotLength time units, and moves to state NewSlot. If the station is passive, the transmitter just delays its further operation by the amount of time equal to SlotLength+TJamL ITUs and moves to NewSlot directly. In both cases, the process ends up in state NewSlot SlotLength + TJamL time units after it perceived the collision. Note that SlotLength is selected in such a way that when the station gets to state NewSlot all activities related to the collision have had ample time to disappear from the bus. At this moment, according to the name of the state, the transmitter marks the beginning of a new virtual slot.

There are two possibilities at NewSlot: The station is allowed to retransmit its packet (if it participates in the tournament and its DelayCount is zero), or it has to skip the slot monitoring its contents. In the first case, the station moves to state Transmit but delays this transition by GuardDelay time units. Let us forget about this delay until we get to the next section. To explain its rationale, we have to examine first all the possible paths leading from state NewSlot. One such path goes through state Transmit, with which we are already familiar. If the transmission develops into a collision, we will get back to state CollisionSensed. The transmitter will repeat the sequence of actions, and eventually it will get back to NewSlot. If the transfer is successful, the process will find itself in state SenseEOT, from which it will transit to EndSlot (note that now TournamentInProgress == YES). The end of a virtual slot containing a valid packet transmission (the transition from SenseEOT to EndSlot) is assumed TPSpace time units after the end of this transmission is actually perceived by the process. As the eligible stations are allowed to transmit at the beginning of a virtual slot, this way we make sure that they automatically

---

[15]Note that Competing is equivalent to Transmitting in the first collision of the tournament.

[16]The retransmission may be delayed further, depending on what happens within the next slot.

obey the packet spacing rules.

After a successful transmission, in state XDone, the process clears its Competing flag. This way the station leaves the tournament, if one is in progress, and is deferred until all the remaining stations involved in the tournament are done with their packets. During one tournament, any one participating station is allowed to transmit exactly once.

State EndSlot can be entered either from SenseEOT (as described), or from NewSlot if the slot turns out to be silent. Note that from the viewpoint of the tournament status, the two scenarios are equivalent. In both cases, DeferCount of any station sensing the end of the virtual slot must be decremented by 1. If the counter becomes zero after this operation, the tournament is proclaimed to be over (section 8.2.2.1) and the station resumes the normal mode of operation (delaying the transition to state NPacket by GuardDelay time units). Otherwise, if the station remains involved in the tournament, its DelayCount is decremented by 1. Then the transmitter moves to state NewSlot, where it decides to retransmit or wait, depending on the value of DelayCount.

8.2.2.3 Accounting for clock errors.

To understand the role of GuardDelay, assume that it is zero and consider the following scenario. Two stations s_1 and s_2 perceive a collision at times t_1 and t_2, respectively. The absolute difference between t_1 and t_2 can be as big as $d(s_1, s_2)$ (the distance between the two stations).[17] Assume that $t_2 = t_1 + d(s_1, s_2)$. The two stations mark the beginning of the next virtual slot at times

$$t_1^s = t_1 + \text{TJamL} + \text{SlotLength}$$

and

$$t_2^s = t_2 + \text{TJamL} + \text{SlotLength}.$$

Then they both wait for SlotLength time units to determine the contents of the new slot. Assume that this slot turns out to be empty. Formally, s_1 should learn about this fact at time

$$t_1^e = t_1^s + \text{SlotLength},$$

and the other station should conclude the same at time

$$t_2^e = t_2^s + \text{SlotLength}.$$

Let $D = \text{TJamL} + 2\text{SlotLength}$. Substituting $t_2 = t_1 + d(s_1, s_2)$, we get

$$t_1^e = t_1 + D$$

and

$$t_2^e = t_1 + d(s_1, s_2) + D.$$

---

[17]For example, assuming the linear bus topology and the collision occurring outside the segment between s_1 and s_2.

In reality, as clocks are allowed to be slightly inaccurate, the actual moments when the two stations mark the end of the slot are

$$\overline{t_1^e} = t_1 + D(1 + \delta_1)$$

and

$$\overline{t_2^e} = t_1 + d(s_1, s_2) + D(1 + \delta_2),$$

where δ_1 and δ_2 represent clock deviations at s_1 and s_2. Suppose that s_1 becomes eligible to transmit in the new slot and s_2 must still delay its retransmission for another slot. The transmission of s_1 will arrive at s_2 at time

$$t_1^a = \overline{t_1^e} + d(s_1, s_2),$$

which can be rewritten as

$$t_1^a = t_1 + d(s_1, s_2) + D(1 + \delta_1).$$

Now, if it happens that $\delta_1 < \delta_2$ (i.e., the clock at s_1 runs slightly faster than its counterpart at s_2), we have $t_1^a < t_2^e$. This means that the transmission of s_1 will be heard at the other station before s_2 marks the end of the previous slot. Consequently, s_2 will assume incorrectly that the previous slot was nonempty.

A similar problem occurs when a station concludes that the tournament is over and decides to transmit its packet in the uncontrolled mode. If the station does it a little bit too soon, immediately upon marking the end of the last virtual slot, it may confuse other (slower) stations that are still monitoring the last slot.

This problem can be eliminated by delaying a retransmission at a slot boundary by a small safety margin. This way, the transmitter makes sure that when the packet arrives at another station, that station will have marked the end of the previous slot and switched to a new one, even if its clock lags a little behind the clock of the transmitting station. To calculate the minimum safe length of `GuardDelay`, we have to know two values: the clock tolerance (i.e., the bound on the clock deviation at a station) and the maximum possible waiting time in the tournament mode without perceiving any activity in the bus. Assume that the stations are ordered according to their occurrence on the list of leaves in the tournament tree (figure 8.4). The worst-case delay scenario happens when the tournament involves two neighbors from this list. These stations will collide $\lceil \log_2(N) \rceil$ times, where N is the number of stations, before they finally transmit their packets successfully. Each time the two stations collide, `DeferCount` at all stations will be incremented by 1. Thus, finally, when the second of the two stations completes its packet transmission, every station in the network will have to wait for $\lceil \log_2(N) \rceil - 1$ empty virtual slots before switching to the uncontrolled mode. This operation must be done consistently with respect to the last slot of the tournament. If worse comes to worst, the two competing stations may go down immediately after their last collision,[18] in

---

[18] A realistic implementation of the protocol should include a recovery procedure that would allow a dormant station to resume its operation in a consistent way. In the case of TCR, *consistent* means conforming to the tournament rules. We do not consider these issues here, leaving them as an exercise to the reader.

which case neither of them will transmit. Therefore, the longest waiting time is[19]

$$D_{max} = (\lceil \log_2(N) \rceil + 2) \times \texttt{SlotLength} + \texttt{TJamL}.$$

`GuardDelay` must be greater than the maximum difference in clock indications accumulated while D_{max} is being measured:

$$\texttt{GuardDelay} > 2 \times \texttt{deviation} \times D_{max},$$

where `deviation` is the maximum relative discrepancy of a clock (section 4.5.2).

Note that `SlotDelay` must also include a safety margin compensating for the limited accuracy of measuring the $2L$ interval.[20] Having waited for `SlotLength` time units after the occurrence of a bus event, the station must know for sure that the event has propagated to all the other stations in the network and back to the sensing station. Thus,

$$\texttt{SlotDelay} > 2L(1 + \texttt{deviation}).$$

To be absolutely sure that nothing goes wrong, both `SlotLength` and `GuardDelay` should be augmented by the maximum difference in the latency with which stations recognize activities in the bus. This additional interval is fixed: it does not depend on the length of the waiting period.

For example, consider a network with 128 stations and the round-trip propagation delay of 512 bits. Assume that the maximum clock deviation is 0.01 percent (as in commercial Ethernet). What is the minimum safe value of `SlotLength` and `GuardDelay`?

We have `SlotDelay` $> 512 \times 1.0001 = 512.0512$. It seems reasonable to round this value up to an integer number of bits, or (to be absolutely safe) to the nearest multiple of 8. This way, we get `SlotDelay` $= 520$ bits. Note that this value is much larger than the absolute minimum; one can safely bet that it also covers the discrepancy in the latency of different stations.[21] The maximum idle waiting time in our network is $D_{max} = 9 \times 520 + 32$ (32 represents the length of a jamming signal), which yields 4712 bits. Thus, we have `GuardDelay` $> 2 \times 0.0001 \times 4712 = 0.9424$. Certainly, we will not advocate frugality in this case: setting `GuardDelay` to four or even eight bits will solve all our problems.

These estimates demonstrate that the problems of accounting for the limited accuracy of independent clocks are not very serious. Even with crude clocks, the safety intervals are very short, and their impact on the network performance is negligible. Note, however, that without these intervals the protocol would not operate correctly.

---

[19]Note that three more slots have to be added to the previous value of D: two empty slots in which the two disappearing stations should have transmitted, and one slot to clean up after the collision.

[20]Most likely, in a realistic commercial implementation of TCR, the value of `SlotDelay` would be hardwired into the protocol and overestimated—to guarantee the correct operation of the protocol in the longest feasible network.

[21]One can realistically expect this latency to be of the order of a single bit insertion time. After all, the stations are expected to recognize individual bits arriving at their ports.

8.2.2.4   TCR observers.   As a corollary from the previous section, we can say that the correctness of our implementation of TCR is by no means obvious. As a matter of fact, the first implementation of this protocol prepared by the author was incorrect, although it seemed to work: all packets were delivered and the maximum throughput achieved by the network looked reasonable. The disagreement of the protocol with its specification became apparent when the following simple observer was added to the program:

```
observer CObserver {
  int *CCount, MaxCollisions;
  void setup (int max) {
    CCount = new int [NStations];
    for (int i = 0; i < NStations; i++) CCount [i] = 0;
    MaxCollisions = max;
  };
  states {Monitoring, EndTransfer, Collision};
  perform {
    state Monitoring:
      inspect (ANY, Transmitter, XDone, EndTransfer);
      inspect (ANY, Transmitter, EndJam, Collision);
    state EndTransfer:
      CCount [TheStation->getId ()] = 0;
      proceed Monitoring;
    state Collision:
      if (++(CCount [TheStation->getId ()]) > MaxCollisions)
        excptn ("Too many collisions");
      proceed Monitoring;
  };
};
```

This observer monitors the number of collisions suffered by a packet and makes sure that this number is not greater than a maximum value specified when the observer was created. In a correct implementation of TCR, this number must be bounded by the maximum depth of the tournament game, i.e, $\lceil \log_2(N) \rceil$, where N is the number of stations. As we are going to reuse the observer in other collision protocols presented in this chapter, the maximum number of collisions is a setup parameter (it will be different for different protocols).

Let us have a closer look at the observer's behavior. The setup method creates an integer array (CCount) indexed by station Ids. The ith entry of this array stores the number of collisions suffered by the packet currently being processed by the transmitter of station i. Initially, all entries in CCount contain zeros.

In its first state, the observer awaits the Transmitter process at ANY station entering one of two states: EndTransfer or EndJam. In state EndTransfer the transmitter completes a successful packet transmission; in the other state, it terminates the jamming signal emitted in response to a collision. Whenever a packet is successfully transmitted, the observer resets the collision counter for the transmitting station to zero. Upon a collision, this counter is incremented by 1 and, at the same time, the observer checks whether the number of collisions remains within the declared bound.

One can think about a more comprehensive observer that monitors individual steps of the tournament and verifies that the tournament is played correctly. The implementation of a complicated protocol may (and perhaps should) involve two persons (or two teams)—one party implementing the protocol and the other developing a detailed observer (or a collection of observers). Both parties should base their work on the same protocol specification. They should negotiate together the general guidelines regarding the data structures and names of essential process states—to make sure that the observers can be naturally interfaced with the protocol processes.

To illustrate how this procedure can be carried out, let us develop an observer for TCR that asserts the formal correctness of tournaments. This observer will keep track of all stations competing for access to the bus and check whether they obey the tournament rules. The type declaration of our observer may look as follows:

```
#define Left  NO
#define Right YES
observer TCRObserver {
  int CurrentLevel;
  Boolean *Tree, **Players, TournamentInProgress;
  TIME CollisionCleared;
  void newPlayer (), removePlayer (),
    validateTransmissionRights (),
      descend (), advance ();
  states {SlotStarted, EmptySlot, CleanBOT, Success,
    StartCollision, ClearCollision, CollisionBOT, Descend};
  void setup ();
  perform;
};
```

The pointers Tree and Players (initialized by the setup method) are hooks to simple data structures used to describe the current stage of the tournament. The tournament mode of the network is indicated by the contents of TournamentInProgress. If this flag is YES, CurrentLevel tells the level at which the tournament is played. Level 0 corresponds to the root of the tournament tree.

The current status of the tournament is represented by two data structures. One of them, a Boolean array pointed to by Tree, describes the current path of the tournament in the virtual tree of stations. The array is indexed by the tournament level. Value NO (aliased as Left) at position i means that at level i the tournament has stepped into the left subtree. Similarly, if Tree[i] is YES (Right), the tournament is in its right subtree at level i. The other data structure, pointed to by Players, is a two-dimensional Boolean array indexed by tournament levels and stations. Value YES at position $< i, j >$ indicates that station j is playing in the tournament and it made a move (i.e., attempted to transmit its packet) at level i.

The methods declared within the observer type are used to mark some important events occurring during the protocol operation or to assert certain statements that must hold if the tournament is played according to the rules. Before we discuss them, let us see how the observer is initialized by its setup method:

```
void TCRObserver::setup () {
  int i, j, ml;
  for (ml = 1, i = 1; i < NStations; i += i, ml++);
  Tree = new Boolean [ml];
  Players = new Boolean* [ml];
  for (i = 0; i < ml; i++) {
    Players [i] = new Boolean [NStations];
    for (j = 0; j < NStations; j++)
      Players [i][j] = NO;
  }
  CurrentLevel = 0;
  TournamentInProgress = NO;
};
```

The first **for** loop calculates (in ml) the ceiling of the binary logarithm of NStations, which determines the maximum number of levels in a tournament. The value of ml is then used as the size of Tree, and also as the size of Players along one of its two dimensions. The second loop creates the rows of Players, the size of each row being equal to the number of stations. The inner loop clears the array. Tree need not be cleared: it will be set explicitly as the tournament progresses through its levels.

Whenever a station starts a packet transmission, newPlayer is called to register the station in the tournament. Note that even when the network (as perceived by the observer) operates in the uncontrolled mode, a station that starts a packet transmission must be considered a potential player. This potentiality will turn into a fact if the transmission develops into a collision. The simple code of newPlayer is as follows:

```
void TCRObserver::newPlayer () {
  Players [CurrentLevel][TheStation->getId ()] = YES;
};
```

A successful packet transmission recognized by the observer results in the removal from the pool of competitors of the station terminating the transfer. This is accomplished by calling the following method:

```
void TCRObserver::removePlayer () {
  Long lv, sid;
```

```
        sid = TheStation->getId ();
        for (lv = CurrentLevel; lv >= 0; lv--)
          if (Players [lv][sid])
            Players [lv][sid] = NO;
          else
            excptn ("Unknown player leaves the tournament");
};
```

The method examines all the open tournament levels, including the current level, and removes the station from every level. A station completing a packet transmission must have been registered on all active levels of the tournament. Even if the transmission is done in the uncontrolled mode, the transmitting station must have been registered at level zero (which is always open). As a by-product of its bookkeeping activities, removePlayer verifies that the station has been registered.

The tournament level (CurrentLevel) is incremented with every collision. This happens at the end of collision processing, when the observer knows that no more stations will get involved in the same collision. Then the observer calls its descend method:

```
void TCRObserver::descend () {
  Tree [CurrentLevel++] = Left;
  TournamentInProgress = YES;
};
```

The first collision perceived by the observer while the network is in the uncontrolled mode advances the tournament level to 1. After the first collision of a tournament, Players[0] describes the full population of players.

When the tournament descends one level (after a collision), Tree of the previous level is set to Left, to show that the stations in the left subtree of the new level get their turn first. This should read as an indication that at the previous level the tournament has progressed into the left subtree. Upon detection of an empty slot or a successful transmission in the tournament mode, the observer calls advance to move to the right subtree:

```
void TCRObserver::advance () {
  if (Tree [CurrentLevel - 1] == Left)
    Tree [CurrentLevel - 1] = Right;
  else {
    CurrentLevel--;
    for (int sid = 0; sid < NStations; sid++)
      if (Players [CurrentLevel][sid])
        excptn ("Some players have not transmitted");
    if (CurrentLevel)
      advance ();
    else
      TournamentInProgress = NO;
```

```
        }
    };
```

If the tournament is in the left subtree, it advances to the right subtree. Otherwise, the tournament already is in the right subtree, which means that its current level has been explored. In such a case, the tournament must advance to the right subtree of the closest level up which is still in its left subtree. This is accomplished by decrementing CurrentLevel and calling advance recursively. Of course, if CurrentLevel reaches zero during this operation, no further advance is possible. This marks the end of the tournament, and the observer assumes the uncontrolled mode of operation.

Whenever the tournament level is decremented (meaning that both subtrees of the previous level have been explored), the method checks whether all the stations registered at the previous level have been checked out (i.e., they have transmitted their packets successfully). This way, the observer makes sure that the tournament does not leave out any player. This property of the tournament is asserted for every single game.

At every transmission attempt, irrespective of its fate, the observer invokes the following method:

```
void TCRObserver::validateTransmissionRights () {
    Long lv, sid;
    if (TournamentInProgress) {
        sid = TheStation->getId ();
        for (lv = 0; lv < CurrentLevel; lv++)
            if (((sid >> lv) & 01) != Tree [lv])
                excptn ("Illegal transmission");
    }
};
```

The method checks whether the station initiating the transfer is authorized to do so in the context of the current tournament stage. In the uncontrolled mode, any station is allowed to start a packet transmission at any moment; thus, if TournamentInProgress is NO, the method does nothing. Otherwise, the method examines the tournament path and verifies that it leads to a subtree including the transmitting station as a leaf. This is the only place in the observer where the actual structure of the station tree (i.e., the ordering of its leaves) becomes relevant. Of course, this ordering must be the same as the one assumed by the transmitter (method loser—section 8.2.2.1).

The last item to be discussed in this section is the observer's code method, which puts the above pieces together:

```
TCRObserver::perform  {
    state SlotStarted:
        inspect (ANY, Transmitter, Transmit, CleanBOT);
        if (TournamentInProgress)
```

```
              timeout (SlotLength, EmptySlot);
      state EmptySlot:
        advance ();
        proceed SlotStarted;
      state CleanBOT:
        validateTransmissionRights ();
        newPlayer ();
        inspect (ANY, Transmitter, Transmit, CleanBOT);
        inspect (ANY, Transmitter, XDone, Success);
        inspect (ANY, Transmitter, SenseCollision, StartCollision);
      state Success:
        removePlayer ();
        if (TournamentInProgress) advance ();
        proceed SlotStarted;
      state StartCollision:
        CollisionCleared = Time + TJamL + SlotLength;
        proceed ClearCollision;
      state ClearCollision:
        timeout (CollisionCleared - Time, Descend);
        inspect (ANY, Transmitter, Transmit, CollisionBOT);
      state CollisionBOT:
        validateTransmissionRights ();
        newPlayer ();
        proceed ClearCollision;
      state Descend:
        descend ();
        proceed SlotStarted;
  };
```

The first state of the observer (SlotStarted) is the basic waiting state in the uncontrolled mode. This state is also assumed in the tournament mode to mark the beginning of a new virtual slot. The observer awaits a transmission attempt (transmitter's state Transmit—section 8.2.2.2). Also, if a tournament is being played (TournamentInProgress is YES), the observer awaits the end of a silent virtual slot. In the tournament mode, the silent (empty) slots must be detected as they advance the tournament. Method advance called in state EmptySlot takes care of this end.

Having detected a transfer attempt, the observer gets to state CleanBOT, where it validates the station's transmission rights and registers the station at the current level of the tournament. Then the observer issues three inspect requests:

- To learn about transmission attempts of other stations (transmitter's state Transmit). This is needed to make sure that all transmitting stations are validated and registered.
- To learn about the possible successful completion of the original transfer at-

tempt. When this happens, the observer will resume in state `Success`, where it will remove the station from the pool of contenders and advance the tournament (if one is being played).

- To detect a collision.

In the last case, the observer ends up in state `StartCollision`. Now the observer must wait until the collision is cleared, i.e., all the stations involved in it have manifested their presence. This happens `TJamL` + `SlotLength` time units after the collision was sensed (section 8.2.2.2). To mark this moment properly without missing any players, the observer calculates the time when the collision will be cleared (`CollisionCleared`) and proceeds to state `ClearCollision`, where it issues a timeout request for the residual interval `CollisionCleared` − `Time`. While waiting for this timeout, the observer inspects all new transfer attempts. Each such attempt is validated and registered in state `CollisionBOT`; then the observer moves back to state `ClearCollision` to await the moment when the collision has been processed completely.

When this finally happens, the observer will get to state `Descend`. It will then increment the tournament level (by calling `descend`) and move to `SlotStarted` to determine the outcome of the first game at the new level.

The complete definition of the observer described in this section can be found in files `tcrobserver.h` and `tcrobserver.c`, in directory `Examples/IncludeLibrary`. This observer will be reused in our second implementation of TCR (section 8.3.2.1).

8.2.2.5 The root process.   A complete program implementing TCR in the version presented in the preceding sections can be found in `Examples/ETHER/TCR1`. For the record, we present in this section the root process of this program:

```
process Root {
  states {Start, Stop};
  perform {
    int NNodes, i, lv;
    Long NMessages;
    TIME BusLength;
    state Start:
      readIn (TRate);
      setEtu (TRate);
      setTolerance (CTolerance);
      readIn (NNodes);
      readIn (BusLength);
      readIn (SlotLength);
      readIn (GuardDelay);
      BusLength *= TRate;
      SlotLength *= TRate;
      GuardDelay *= TRate;
```

```
      TPSpace = (TIME) PSpace * TRate;
      TJamL = (TIME) JamL * TRate;
      initBus (TRate, BusLength, NNodes);
      initTraffic ();
      for (i = 0; i < NNodes; i++) create EtherStation;
      for (i = 0; i < NStations; i++) {
        create (i) Transmitter;
        create (i) Receiver;
      }
      create TCRObserver ();
      for (lv = 1, i = 1; i < NStations; i += i, lv++);
      create CObserver (lv);
      readIn (NMessages);
      setLimit (NMessages);
      Kernel->wait (DEATH, Stop);
    state Stop:
      System->printTop ("Network topology");
      Client->printDef ("Traffic parameters");
      Client->printPfm ();
  };
};
```

The time granularity, represented by TRate, is now a parameter read from
the input file. One ETU is still equal to one bit insertion time, but this time
now consists of TRate ITUs. The clock tolerance is the same as in commercial
Ethernet; constant CTolerance is defined in file ether.h (section 8.1.2.4) included
from types.h (section 8.2.2.2).

All time intervals parameterizing the protocol, i.e., BusLength, SlotLength,
GuardLength, the length of the packet space interval and jamming signal duration,
are assumed to be given in bits. They are converted to ITUs (multiplied by TRate)
so that they can be used directly as arguments of Timer wait requests. The last two
parameters are borrowed from Ethernet. Note that PSpace and JamL are symbolic
constants defined in file ether.h (in Examples/IncludeLibrary).

The root process creates both observers described in section 8.2.2.4. The
setup argument for CObserver is the maximum number of collisions that can be
suffered by a single packet before a successful transmission. This number, equal to
the ceiling of the binary logarithm of NStations, is calculated in a loop.

File sample_data in the program's directory contains a sample data set. The
reader may want to verify that SlotLength and GuardDelay specified in that set
satisfy the requirements stated in section 8.2.2.3.

8.3 CSMA/CD-DP

The Tree Collision Resolution protocol achieves two objectives: it incurs absolutely no access overhead when the network is idle, and under heavy load the packet access time is still bounded. The limitations of TCR become visible under moderate traffic conditions. The reader is encouraged to experiment with the protocol, to determine the shape of its performance curve (mean packet access time versus throughput) and compare it with the performance curve of Ethernet. The curve for TCR starts very low (the access delay is zero[22] under very light load); however, in the medium range of traffic conditions, TCR tends to incur substantially higher access delays than Ethernet. This phenomenon results from the deterministic rules of the tournament in TCR. Assume that there are only two stations competing for medium access. Depending on their location in the tournament tree, the two stations may collide a number of times before one of them wins and the other loses. While the stations are waiting for nonexistent winners, the network remains idle and its bandwidth is wasted.

Another, already mentioned, problem with TCR is the slight bias in service received by different stations. Given a node in the tournament tree and two stations s_1 belonging to the left subtree rooted at the node and s_2 belonging to the right subtree, s_1 is favored over s_2.

One possible way of alleviating the first problem is to reduce the number of games. Consider the tree in figure 8.4, and assume that a tournament is started by a collision in slot 0. Normally, slot 1 is reserved for the stations in subtree B. If none of them is willing to play, the stations from subtree C will transmit in slot 2. A version of TCR is possible in which the tournament begins at a level deeper than zero. For example, slot 0 can be followed by four slots corresponding to nodes D, E, F, and G. If slot 1 turns out to be idle, the stations located under E will be allowed to transmit in slot 2. Similarly, if slots 1 and 2 are both idle, the stations in subtree F will be given their turn in slot 3. Finally, slot 4 is reserved for node G and can be used by a station located under this node, provided that all three preceding slots are empty. The number of contenders at level i of the tournament (counting the root as level 0) is $c_i = 2^{log_2 N - i}$. If the traffic intensity is known and the traffic is uniform, it can be shown that the best level to start the tournament is the one at which c_i/N is equal to the normalized traffic intensity (expressed in arrival bits per bit of time). Unfortunately, real traffic patterns are seldom uniform and their intensity is seldom static over sufficiently long periods.

The second problem can be eliminated completely in a relatively simple way. Namely, after the end of a tournament is recognized by all stations, the stations may switch their locations in the tournament tree, e.g., in a rotary manner.

---

[22]Note that with the standard way of measuring the packet access time, the time spent on transmitting the packet is included in the access time. Somewhat informally, we will say that a protocol incurs zero access delay if the packet access time (measured in the standard way— section 7.1.2.1) is equal to the time needed to transmit the packet.

8.3.1   The Protocol

CSMA/CD-DP (DP stands for Dynamic Priorities) can be viewed as a cousin of
TCR designed along the preceding suggestions. As with TCR, in the absence of
collisions the protocol mimics the behavior of Ethernet. Upon sensing a collision, the
stations enter a controlled mode of operation that resembles a trivialized tournament
in TCR. There is only one collision in this tournament. Following this collision, the
network remains in the controlled mode for as long as there are stations willing to
transmit their packets. Unlike TCR, this protocol allows new stations to join the
tournament, provided that they obey its simple rules.

Tournaments in CSMA/CD-DP start at the very bottom of the tournament
tree. This means that following the first (and only) collision of a tournament, every
station gets its private slot in which it can transmit successfully. Thus, there is little
sense in talking about a tournament tree or a tournament.[23] It is simply assumed
that all stations in the network are tagged with consecutive integer numbers starting
from zero. These numbers are called stations' *priorities*. The first slot following a
collision is reserved for the station with priority 0, the second for the station with
priority 1, and so on.

Following the end of a successful packet transmission (which is recognized by
all stations in the network), the stations switch their priorities cyclically, in the
following way:

$$\text{Priority = (Priority - 1) \% NStations;}$$

This way, no stations are permanently privileged and the protocol is fair.
Upon initialization, different stations are assigned different priorities from zero to
NStations − 1. After all stations have updated their priorities, these priorities
remain different; consequently, different stations are always assigned to different
slots.

CSMA/CD-DP is intended for unslotted networks, and the slots are virtual.
Upon sensing a successful packet transmission in the controlled mode, all stations
wait until the transfer is over. Then they switch their priorities and resume counting
slots, in the same way as after a collision. If the protocol operates correctly, no
collisions are possible in the controlled mode, as the slot size guarantees that no
two transmissions are scheduled less than $2L$ apart.

The controlled mode is exited when NStations consecutive slots have been
sensed idle. Note that this will happen after a successful transmission, unless the
stations involved in the collision that forced the network to the controlled mode
have gone dead before using their slots.

In the controlled mode, a station can join the tournament and transmit in its
slot, provided that it is ready to do so at the beginning of the slot. Thus, if there
is a continuous supply of packets, the network may remain in the controlled mode
for an undetermined amount of time.

---

[23]The term *tournament* emphasizes the close relation between TCR and CSMA/CD-DP.

Example

Assume that the network consists of eight stations and the allocation of priorities to these stations is described by the following table:

Station	0	1	2	3	4	5	6	7
Priority	3	5	0	2	7	1	4	6

Suppose that stations 1 and 5 collide. Following the collision, station 5 will transmit first (in slot 1). Then all stations will update their priorities, which will result in the following configuration:

Station	0	1	2	3	4	5	6	7
Priority	2	4	7	1	6	0	3	5

If no other stations have become ready in the meantime, station 1 will transmit in the fifth slot (i.e., slot number 4) following the end of the packet transmitted by station 5.

Note that if station 2 becomes ready before it marks the beginning of slot 0 following the collision of stations 1 and 5, it will transmit and preempt station 5. Then station 5 will receive priority 0 and will transmit in the first slot following the transmission of station 2.

The end of the successful transmission of station 1 is followed by eight virtual slots that give all stations, including station 1, an opportunity to transmit a packet in the controlled mode. If no station becomes ready before it marks the beginning of its slot, all these slots will be empty and the network will leave the controlled mode.

8.3.2   The Implementation

From the previous sections, it should be clear that CSMA/CD-DP and TCR have quite a bit in common. As we will shortly see, the two protocols have more in common than one might think. With the right organization of the transmitter, the difference between TCR and CSMA/CD-DP can be contained in a few simple lines of code.

8.3.2.1   TCR revisited.   Let us return to TCR and try to recode its transmitter, keeping in mind that this transmitter will be reused in CSMA/CD-DP and possibly in some other protocols based on the idea of collision-triggered tournaments. Such a tournament is characterized by a specific behavior assumed by a station upon sensing certain events in the bus. The relevant elements of this behavior are as follows:

- The station must be able to tell whether the network is in the tournament mode.

- The station must be able to tell when it is allowed to play, i.e., to transmit a packet in the tournament mode.

- The station may want to perform some protocol-dependent actions upon sensing a collision, an empty slot, or a successful packet transmission.

In the present version of the TCR transmitter (section 8.2.2.2), these elements are implanted into the transmitter and, not surprisingly, are TCR-specific. To separate them from the transmitter, we encapsulate these operations into methods and make these methods virtual. This way, specific transmitters for tournament-based protocols can be built by extending a common generic transmitter type. This generic transmitter type can be defined as follows:

```
process CTransmitter (EtherStation) {
  Port *Bus;
  Packet *Buffer;
  Boolean TournamentInProgress, Transmitting, Competing;
  void setup () {
    Bus = S->Bus;
    Buffer = &(S->Buffer);
    TournamentInProgress = Transmitting = Competing = NO;
  };
  virtual void onCollision () {};
  virtual void onEndSlot () {};
  virtual void onEOT () {};
  virtual Boolean participating () { return YES; };
  states {NPacket, Transmit, Busy, XDone, SenseEOT,
    SenseCollision, EndJam, NewSlot, EndSlot};
  perform;
};
```

The role of the three Boolean flags was described in section 8.2.2.2. These flags make sense for any tournament-based protocol, irrespective of the tournament rules. The protocol-specific actions taken on collisions, empty slots, and successful packet transmissions are represented by the three void virtual methods. The fourth method, returning a Boolean value, tells whether the station is allowed to transmit. Note that not all four virtual methods must be redefined in a subtype of CTransmitter. For example, if the transmitter is not expected to do anything specific after sensing an empty slot, it need not define its private version of onEndSlot. The default version of participating returns unconditionally YES, assuming optimistically (in the spirit of CSMA/CD) that in the absence of more specific rules a station should be allowed to transmit whenever possible.

The virtual methods can be composed into the code of the generic transmitter as follows:

```
CTransmitter:: perform {
  state NPacket:
    if (S->ready (MinPL, MaxPL, FrameL))
      proceed Transmit;
    else {
      Client->wait (ARRIVAL, NPacket);
```

```
      Bus->wait (ACTIVITY, Busy);
    }
  state Transmit:
    Transmitting = YES;
    Competing = YES;
    Bus->transmit (Buffer, XDone);
    Bus->wait (COLLISION, SenseCollision);
  state Busy:
    Bus->wait (EOT, SenseEOT);
    Bus->wait (COLLISION, SenseCollision);
  state XDone:
    Bus->stop ();
    Transmitting = NO;
    Competing = NO;
    Buffer->release ();
    proceed SenseEOT;
  state SenseCollision:
    onCollision ();
    if (Transmitting) {
      Bus->abort ();
      Transmitting = NO;
      Bus->sendJam (TJamL, EndJam);
    } else
      Timer->wait (TJamL + SlotLength, NewSlot);
  state EndJam:
    Bus->stop ();
    Timer->wait (SlotLength, NewSlot);
  state NewSlot:
    if (participating ())
      Timer->wait (GuardDelay, Transmit);
    else {
      Timer->wait (SlotLength, EndSlot);
      Bus->wait (ACTIVITY, Busy);
    }
  state EndSlot:
    onEndSlot ();
    if (TournamentInProgress)
      proceed NewSlot;
    else
      Timer->wait (GuardDelay, NPacket);
  state SenseEOT:
    onEOT ();
    if (TournamentInProgress)
      Timer->wait (TPSpace, NewSlot);
```

```
        else
            Timer->wait (TPSpace, NPacket);
};
```

This code was obtained by a direct and simple transformation of the transmitter code from section 8.2.2.2. In particular, the state names have been retained,
and most of the code at the states has been left intact. The portions corresponding to the specific nature of the tournament in TCR have been removed (states
SenseCollision, NewSlot, EndSlot, and SenseEOT). These fragments are now implemented in the corresponding virtual methods. One more difference that deserves
a few words is in the first Timer wait request issued in state SenseEOT. In the TCR
version, the process branches to state EndSlot, to decrement DeferCount and possibly DelayCount. In TCR, essentially the same action is performed after sensing
an empty slot and a slot filled with a complete packet. In the generic transmitter,
these actions should be separated: they need not be always the same.

The TCR transmitter can be redefined almost mechanically as a subtype of
CTransmitter, in the following way:

```
process Transmitter : CTransmitter (EtherStation) {
    int Ply, DelayCount, DeferCount;
    Boolean loser ();
    void onCollision () {
        if (!TournamentInProgress) {
            Ply = DelayCount = 0;
            DeferCount = 1;
            TournamentInProgress = YES;
        }
        if (Competing) {
            if (DelayCount == 0) {
                if (loser ()) DelayCount = 1;
                Ply++;
            } else
                DelayCount++;
        }
        DeferCount++;
    };
    void onEndSlot () {
        if (--DeferCount == 0)
            TournamentInProgress = NO;
        else if (Competing)
            DelayCount--;
    };
    void onEOT () { onEndSlot (); };
    Boolean participating () {
        return Competing && DelayCount == 0;
```

```
      };
    };
```

The `loser` method is the same as in section 8.2.2.1. Note that the `Transmitter` type defines no code method and consequently no states. The process inherits the code method of `CTransmitter`, with the virtual methods replaced by their protocol-specific redefinitions.

Directory `ETHER/TCR2` in `Examples` contains the new implementation of TCR based on the generic tournament transmitter. The generic transmitter has been put into `IncludeLibrary` (files `ctransmitter.h` and `ctransmitter.c`).

8.3.2.2 The transmitter for CSMA/CD-DP. The transmitter for CSMA/CD-DP can be implemented quite easily as an instance of the generic transmitter:

```
process Transmitter : CTransmitter (EtherStation) {
  Long Priority, DelayCount, DeferCount;
  void onCollision () {
    assert (!TournamentInProgress, "Collision in controlled mode");
    TournamentInProgress = YES;
    DelayCount = Priority;
    DeferCount = NStations;
  };
  void onEndSlot () {
    if (--DeferCount == 0)
      TournamentInProgress = NO;
    else
      DelayCount--;
  };
  void onEOT () {
    if (--Priority < 0) Priority = NStations - 1;
    DelayCount = Priority;
    DeferCount = NStations;
  };
  Boolean participating () {
    return DelayCount == 0 && S->ready (MinPL, MaxPL, FrameL);
  };
  void setup () {
    CTransmitter::setup ();
    Priority = S->getId ();
  };
};
```

This time the process needs a private version of the setup method, to initialize the station's dynamic priority (variable `Priority`). Upon sensing a collision, the process enters the controlled (tournament) mode and initializes `DelayCount` and `DeferCount`. The role of these counters is similar to the role of their counterparts in TCR. `DelayCount` gives the number of slots by which the station should delay its transfer attempt, and `DeferCount` tells the number of consecutive empty slots that must be perceived by the station before it may resume the uncontrolled mode. According to the protocol described in section 8.3.1, `DelayCount` is determined by the station's dynamic priority and `DeferCount` should be initialized to the number of stations in the network. While in the controlled mode, the station is allowed to transmit if `DelayCount` equals zero (of course, the station must also have a packet awaiting transmission). This condition is described by method `participating`.

Having sensed the end of an empty slot, the transmitter decrements `DeferCount`. If the counter has reached zero, the controlled mode is exited; otherwise, `DelayCount` is reduced by 1. At the end of a successful packet transmission, the process changes the station's priority (according to the formula given in section 8.3.1) and resets the counters, in the same way as after a collision.

CSMA/CD-DP is significantly simpler than TCR, perhaps to the point of making sophisticated observers unnecessary. Clearly, we can reuse in CSMA/CD-DP the simpler of the TCR observers (`CObserver`) discussed in section 8.2.2.4. The maximum number of collisions suffered by a packet in CSMA/CD-DP is one; thus, the setup argument for `CObserver` should be 1. The transmitter's private version of `onCollision` asserts that the collision occurs in the uncontrolled mode. No collisions are possible in the controlled mode, provided that the implementation is correct.

8.3.2.3   Accounting for clock errors.

The analysis of the impact of clock accuracy on protocol correctness is essentially the same as for TCR (section 8.2.2.3). In the case of CSMA/CD-DP, the worst-case waiting time for an activity in the bus is given by the following formula:

$$D_{max} = (N + 1) \times \texttt{SlotLength} + \texttt{TJamL},$$

which grows linearly with respect to the number of stations. For TCR, D_{max} is a logarithmic function of N; thus, TCR poses less stringent requirements on clocks than CSMA/CD-DP.

The preceding formula corresponds to the situation when two (or more) stations collide and then all contenders immediately go down. If no other station becomes ready to transmit before it marks the beginning of its virtual slot, the alive stations must wait until the collision is cleared (`SlotLength` + `TJamL`), and then for N empty slots, before they are allowed to leave the controlled mode (which operation must be done consistently).

The requirements for `SlotLength` are the same as in the case of TCR. To get an idea how the increased value of D_{max} affects `GuardDelay`, let us calculate the safe value of `GuardDelay` for the network with 128 stations and $2L = 512$ considered in section 8.2.2.3. Assuming `SlotDelay` = 520 bits, we get $D_{max} = 129 \times 520 + 32$, which yields 67,112 bits. Assuming the clock tolerance of commercial Ethernet

(0.01 percent), we get GuardDelay $> 2 \times 0.0001 \times 67112 = 13.4224$ bits. The nearest sensible value for GuardDelay is 16 bits, which is much larger than in the case of TCR but still quite reasonable and small compared to $2L$ or to the size of a typical packet.

Directory ETHER/DP in Examples contains an implementation of CSMA/CD-DP based on the reusable, generic tournament transmitter. The root process of this implementation is very similar to the root process of the second version of TCR (directory TCR2), and its discussion can be skipped. The reader may want to verify that the value of GuardDelay in the sample data set for the implementation of CSMA/CD-DP is safe.

8.3.2.4   Possible enhancements. One advantage of CSMA/CD-DP over TCR is the reduced number of collisions: each packet collides at most once. Consequently, under very heavy traffic conditions, less bandwidth is wasted for controlling the simple tournament, and the network tends to achieve a higher maximum throughput than TCR. For very light load, if there is only one station willing to transmit a packet, the network operates in the uncontrolled mode and the protocol incurs no access delay.

In the medium range of traffic conditions, the performance of CSMA/CD-DP is a bit disappointing. It takes little load to sustain the controlled mode indefinitely: it is enough if one station becomes ready every N slots, but this station has to wait for the average of $N/2$ slots to transmit its packet.

One can think of a different version of CSMA/CD-DP in which the controlled mode is exited a bit sooner. For example, following the end of a successful transmission, the stations need not reinitialize the tournament, but simply continue counting slots, assuming—as in TCR—that the transmission represents a virtual slot filled with a packet. Thus, after a successful transmission, the stations would decrement DeferCount, advancing the tournament towards its end. To ensure fair operation, the stations would switch their priorities after a collision rather than after a successful transmission. The reader is encouraged to experiment with this simple idea and investigate its merits in comparison with the original version of the protocol.

8.4   VIRTUAL TOKEN

Yet another variation on the tournament theme, aimed at improving the network performance for the medium range of traffic conditions, is a protocol dubbed Virtual Token (VT). This name results from a superficial resemblance to token protocols in which stations exchange a special packet (called the token). The station holding the token is authorized to transmit. As there is only one token in the network, this transmission in guaranteed not to collide with another transfer attempt.

The token in VT is virtual, which means that stations do not actually exchange any special packets. By virtue of counters, similar to those used in CSMA/CD-DP and updated in response to some events in the bus, the stations know their priorities. Talking about a (virtual) token, as opposed to dynamic priorities in CSMA/CD-

DP, makes sense, because the VT priority mechanism (at least in the basic version of the protocol) selects a single privileged station. The other stations are treated equally: they are all nonprivileged and their status is the same.

VT attempts to improve upon the idea of CSMA/CD-DP by shortening the duration of the tournament to the absolute minimum that gives a single station (the privileged one) a window of opportunity to transmit one packet successfully. As the notion of privileged station changes with time, every station gets its turn to become privileged, and the packet delay in VT is bounded.

8.4.1 The Protocol

As with the previous two solutions, the network starts in the uncontrolled mode with the transmission rules of Ethernet. A collision forces the stations to the controlled mode, whose duration is approximately one slot.

Each station maintains a counter, which, for analogy with CSMA/CD-DP, is called the station's Priority. As with CSMA/CD-DP, priorities of different stations are initialized to different values from 0 to $N-1$. They are updated in such a way that at critical moments of protocol operation priorities of different stations remain different. The station with priority 0 is privileged. We say that the station is in possession of the (virtual) token.

Assume that a collision occurs. All stations recognize the collision in due time, wait until it is cleared (as in TCR and CSMA/CD-DP), and mark the beginning of a virtual slot following the collision. Within that slot, the station with priority 0 is allowed to transmit. Other stations must wait until they determine whether the token-holding station has used its slot. Suppose that the privileged station was ready to transmit and it has done so in the virtual slot following the collision. This transmission is guaranteed to be successful, because all other stations delay their activities until they mark the end of this slot. Having sensed the transmission of the privileged station, all stations (including the privileged one) wait until the transfer is over. Then they switch their priorities in the following way:

```
Priority = (Priority - 1) % NStations;
```

Note that this formula is identical to the formula used by CSMA/CD-DP (section 8.3.1). For the basic version of VT discussed in this section, the only important property of the priority update operation is its cyclic nature: the virtual token circulates through all stations in the network.

Following the end of the packet transmitted by the token-holding station, a new station becomes privileged (gets the virtual token). All stations are now allowed to transmit their packets. If there is a collision, it will be handled as before, with a different station being authorized to transmit successfully in the next slot.

If the privileged station has no packet to transmit, the "slot of opportunity" will be empty, and it will be perceived as such by all stations in the network. Then the stations will also update their priorities (according to the preceding formula) and resume the normal mode of operation.

Note that the controlled mode only lasts for the one slot following a collision. With this approach, the tournament is only long enough to select a single winner, or to notify everybody that the winner does not want to take advantage of its privileged status. If there are multiple stations competing for access to the bus, they will keep on colliding until one of them gets hold of the virtual token. Then the privileged station will be allowed to transmit successfully and the remaining stations will collide again, until the next winner is selected. The contention resolution algorithm is split into a series of very short tournaments; thus, the network tends to return to the uncontrolled mode very fast and wastes little bandwidth under moderate contention.

8.4.2   The Implementation

The Virtual Token protocol just described can easily be implemented on the basis of the generic transmitter introduced in section 8.3.2.1. As with TCR and CSMA/CD-DP, the only interesting fragment of the protocol is the transmitter process, the remaining portions being directly transplanted from Ethernet. The VT transmitter can be defined as follows:

```
process Transmitter : CTransmitter (EtherStation) {
  int Priority;
  void onEndSlot () {
    if (++Priority == NStations) Priority = 0;
    TournamentInProgress = NO;
  };
  void onCollision () {
    TournamentInProgress = YES;
  };
  void onEOT () { onEndSlot (); };
  Boolean participating () {
    return Priority == 0 && S->ready (MinPL, MaxPL, FrameL);
  };
  void setup () {
    CTransmitter::setup ();
    Priority = S->getId ();
  };
};
```

The protocol-specific methods of the process are even simpler than in the case of CSMA/CD-DP. No counters are needed: the tournament consists of a single slot and ends when the process marks the end of this slot (by calling onEndSlot).

The maximum number of collisions suffered by a packet in VT is bounded by the number of stations N. In the worst case, when the station's priority is $N-1$ and all stations have packets awaiting transmission, the packet will collide exactly N times before it is eventually transmitted. Therefore, if we want to use

CObserver from section 8.2.2.4 to validate the protocol, its setup argument should be NStations.

Because of the very short tournament duration in VT, the protocol operates correctly with a very small value of GuardDelay. As an easy exercise, the reader may want to calculate this value for a sample network.

8.4.3   Possible Enhancements

Directory Examples/ETHER/VT contains an implementation of VT based on the transmitter described in the previous section. The reader may want to run the protocol to determine its delay-versus-throughput characteristics and compare it with the characteristics of the other protocols discussed in this chapter. Although VT performs better than TCR and CSMA/CD-DP for the medium range of traffic conditions, it still yields significantly to Ethernet. In VT, if two stations collide once, they will keep on colliding until one of them gets the virtual token. The backoff algorithm in Ethernet tends to disperse such simple contention scenarios much faster. After the first collision, the contenders have a good chance to be rescheduled in such a way that they will not collide again; with subsequent collisions, the probability of yet another collision decreases exponentially.

It is possible to devise a variant of VT whose performance under moderate load is only marginally worse than the performance of Ethernet. Under heavy load, because of its deterministic nature, the Virtual Token protocol will outperform Ethernet (and guarantee a bounded-time packet delivery), although it will prove slightly inferior to CSMA/CD-DP, because of higher collision overhead.

The author's experiments indicate that the most promising approach to reducing the overhead of VT for the medium range of traffic conditions is in alleviating the contention among the nonprivileged stations. The obvious idea, to introduce a randomized backoff algorithm similar to the backoff function in Ethernet, can be easily improved upon by using the station's Priority as an argument of the backoff function. With this approach, the role of Priority becomes more like an actual priority mechanism than a token-passing scheme. As long as the backoff delay is limited, the packet access time is still bounded, although the bound may be worse than for the pure version of the protocol.

As far as minimizing contention among nonprivileged stations, it is clear that the best results will be obtained when each nonprivileged station is assigned to a separate slot. However, this solution gets us too close to CSMA/CD-DP to be interesting. Whatever we gain this way by eliminating collisions, we will have to pay back with the increased waiting time for the scheduled transmission window. Thus, it seems that the right solution is a compromise: nonprivileged stations should be allowed to collide, but they should not be forced to collide all the way to a successful transmission.

The author experimented with the following simple and deterministic backoff function:

```
TIME backoff () {
  return (TIME) (Factor * Priority) * SlotLength;
};
```

where `Factor` is a floating-point number between 0 and 1. Value 0 of `Factor` corresponds to the "pure" version of VT. The other extreme value (1) gets us to a variant of CSMA/CD-DP. All the values in between represent a compromise. The reader is encouraged to try to find a good value for `Factor`. It may depend on the network configuration, especially the number of stations in the network.

8.5   PIGGYBACK ETHERNET

Besides the nondeterministic and unpredictable character of the backoff algorithm, the Ethernet protocol suffers from another painful drawback. Because of the requirement that all collisions must be recognized while the packets involved are still being transmitted, the protocol imposes a lower bound on the packet size (section 8.1.1.2).

The transmission time of the shortest packet in Ethernet must be at least twice as long as the propagation diameter of the network (L). The minimum packet length in the commercial network (576 bits) determines the maximum length of the Ethernet bus. Expressed in bits and rounded down to a safe value, this length is 256. To translate it into geographic terms, we need to divide it by the network transmission rate and multiply by the speed of signals in the medium. This gives us about 6 kilometers.

Now, imagine that you want to build a new Ethernet, ten times faster than its predecessor, i.e., a CSMA/CD network operating at 100 Mb/s. You have two choices: to increase the minimum packet length ten times or to reduce the maximum length of the network to 600 meters.[24] The first possibility seems rather unattractive. The minimum packet length in the commercial network is already a bit on the large side. Many popular applications involve short packets (e.g., character-oriented input/output, passing signals among multiple processes operating in a distributed environment). In such cases, the short packets must be inflated to the minimum legitimate size, which results in extremely poor utilization of the network bandwidth. Although 600 meters can still be an acceptable bound for the diameter of a local area network, it is somewhat short for campus-area environments or even for larger buildings.[25] One can still try to organize a larger network into a collection of shorter segments connected via gateways, but elegance, efficiency, and flexibility are not among the virtues that can be attributed to this approach.

---

[24]The third possibility, to increase ten times the signal propagation speed, cannot be treated seriously.

[25]Note that wires in a building are seldom laid along shortest paths between the nodes.

8.5.1   The Protocol[26]

Piggyback Ethernet attempts to relax the requirement that all packets must be inflated to $2L$. Yet the protocol is clearly a CSMA/CD protocol; its collision detection rules are the same as for the commercial network. The idea of the protocol is based on the following simple observation: if we know that a packet will not collide, the packet need not be inflated to $2L$ before it is transmitted. In other words, packets shorter than $2L$ can be transmitted safely and consistently if the protocol makes sure that they will never collide. Note that in VT the privileged station taking advantage of its reserved virtual slot following a collision can transmit a packet shorter than $2L$. All the other stations obey some rules to make sure that the reserved slot is not interfered with, and the privileged station knows that its packet will not collide. Similarly, in CSMA/CD-DP, stations transmitting in the controlled mode can transmit short packets, because these packets cannot collide (at least as long as the stations obey the protocol rules). Unfortunately, neither CSMA/CD-DP nor VT can be improved by relaxing the minimum packet length requirement for packets transmitted in the controlled mode. Although a successful transmission in a virtual slot filled with a short packet can be perceived by a station before the formal end of this slot is marked, the station must still wait for the formal end of this slot before it is allowed to mark the beginning of the next slot. Otherwise, if the station started a packet transmission too early, it would confuse other stations, which might qualify this activity to the previous slot.

Piggyback Ethernet assumes that the bus topology is strictly linear, i.e., it cannot operate on any tree-shaped broadcast bus. However, the bus is still fully broadcast and bidirectional. It can be viewed as a transition step between the general, ether-type, broadcast bus and the segmented, strictly linear, fiber-based bus discussed in chapter 9.

The protocol comes in two versions. We introduce the more complex, full version first and then show how the protocol can be simplified while retaining most of its advantageous properties.

8.5.1.1   The complete version.   The bus topology is strictly linear; thus, it makes sense to talk about two ends of the bus. For convenience, we refer to these ends as the left end and the right end. Of course, "left" and "right" are abstract concepts, so *the left end* will designate one end of the bus and *the right end* the other (opposite) end.

We assume that the stations are numbered in the order of their occurrence along the bus: the leftmost station has number 0, and the rightmost station is numbered $N-1$. Every station knows the bus location of all stations in the network. The bus location of a station s is given as the propagation distance from the leftmost station to s. Thus, each station maintains a table with N entries representing its distance to all stations. For uniformity, we assume that the distance table has an

---

[26]Fragments of this section have been reprinted from *Dobosiewicz, Gburzyński, and Rudnicki* (1993), with kind permission from Elsevier Science B.V., Amsterdam, The Netherlands.

entry describing the distance between the station and itself. Clearly, this entry contains zero.

The numbers reflecting the ordering of stations along the bus can be direct stations' addresses or, more reasonably, can be bound to the addresses via lookup tables. This way, each station would keep two tables: the distance table and the order table. In section 8.5.2.3 we sketch a method of filling these tables automatically during the network initialization phase.

The packet header includes one special bit, denoted by P, determining the so-called *piggyback direction*, which can be either left (i.e., toward the left end of the bus) or right (i.e., toward the right end). The protocol operates in two modes. In the uncontrolled mode, the standard rules of Ethernet are used. A station is allowed to transmit its packet immediately (having obeyed the packet spacing rules), provided that the bus is sensed idle. A station transmitting a packet in the uncontrolled mode sets its P bit at random and makes sure that the packet is no shorter than $2L$. Thus, packets transmitted in the uncontrolled mode are inflated to the minimum legitimate size—as in Ethernet. This way, the station is able to detect a possible collision while the packet is being transmitted. If a collision occurs, it is handled in the same way as in Ethernet, i.e., the participating stations abort their transfer attempts and reschedule them at a later time determined by the standard backoff function. In contrast to TCR, CSMA/CD-DP, and VT, the stations remain in the uncontrolled mode after a collision.

A successful packet transmission (recognized by all stations in due time) switches the network to the controlled mode. The station that was the last to transmit a packet is called the *leader*. A station s is allowed to append (piggyback) its packet at the end of the leader's packet, after a delay derived from the distance between s and the leader, and the value of the P bit in the leader's packet. When a station appends a packet to the leader's packet, it is guaranteed a successful transmission. At the end of this transmission, the station becomes a new leader.

Each end of a successful transmission triggers a synchronizing event, which is perceived by all stations in the network. The stations use this event to trace the location of a virtual marker that makes a "full circle" through the bus, visiting each station twice. The marker is launched at the leader, at the moment when the leader completes its successful transmission.

The controlled mode is exited after the marker has made the full circle through the stations and no station had a packet ready to transmit. Note that each transmission starts a new marker; therefore, as long as there is a continuous supply of traffic in the network, the controlled mode is never exited.

While a station s perceives the network as being in the controlled mode, it operates according to the following rules:

P1 Upon detecting the beginning of a packet transmission, s determines the sender of the packet (denoted by s_l) and the contents of the P bit (the piggyback direction). Then the station waits until the end of the transmission.

P2 Having sensed the end of a (necessarily successful) transmission, s computes three time delays $d_1(s_l, s)$, $d_2(s_l, s)$, and d_e (see later in this section).

P3 The station waits for $d_1(s_l, s)$ time units, and if a transmission is sensed during this interval, s resumes at *P1*. This transmission will be successful, and s will learn about the new leader and the new piggyback direction.

P4 If $d_1(s_l, s)$ time units have elapsed after the end of the leader's transmission, the bus is sensed idle, and s has a packet awaiting transmission, the station is allowed to transmit its packet. This transmission is guaranteed to be successful; thus, at its end s becomes the new leader and continues at *P2*.

P5 If s did not have a packet to transmit at the end of $d_1(s_l, s)$, it waits for $d_2(s_l, s) - d_1(s_l, s)$ time units (i.e., $d_2(s_l, s)$ time units after the end of the leader's transmission), and if a transmission is sensed during this waiting period, the station goes back to *P1*.

P6 If $d_2(s_l, s)$ time units have elapsed after the end of the leader's transmission, the bus is sensed idle, and s now has a packet ready for transmission, the station transmits the packet and continues at *P2* as the new leader.

P7 If s did not have a packet to transmit at the end of $d_2(s_l, s)$, it waits for $d_e - d_2(s_l, s)$ time units (i.e., d_e time units after the end of the leader's transmission), and if a transmission is sensed during this wait, the station goes back to *P1*.

P8 If d_e time units have elapsed after the end of the leader's transmission and the bus has been idle during that period, s switches to the uncontrolled mode.

The idea behind the three delays can be explained as follows. Let t_0 be the moment when s perceives the end of the packet transmitted by the leader s_l. At $t_0 + d_1(s_l, s)$ the virtual marker will visit s for the first time; at $t_0 + d_2(s_l, s)$ the marker will arrive at s for the second time; and at $t_0 + d_e$ the marker will disappear from the network.

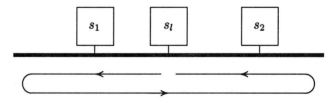

Figure 8.5 The order of turns in the controlled mode ($P = 0$)

Let us illustrate the operation of Piggyback Ethernet with a sample scenario. Assume that station s_l (see figure 8.5) transmits its packet successfully in the uncontrolled mode and that the P bit of the packet contains 0, which indicates the piggyback direction to the left. Station s_l becomes the leader. Consider the actions of two stations s_1 and s_2. Upon sensing the leader's packet, s_1 and s_2 recognize that it originated from s_l and that the P bit is 0. When s_1 and s_2 sense the EOT event, they switch to the controlled mode with s_l being the current leader. According to the piggyback direction determined by P, the virtual marker will visit s_1 before s_2. In fact, it will visit s_1 (and all stations located to the left of s_l) twice, then it will pass through the stations between s_l and s_2 (including s_l), next it will arrive at s_2, turn around the right end of the bus, visit s_2 for the second time and, eventually, reach s_l again. Theoretically, as soon as s_1 perceives the end of the leader's packet, it could transmit its own packet. Note, however, that the stations located between s_l and s_1 were visited by the marker before s_1. If any of them transmitted a packet, s_1 must be able to learn about this fact before it initiates its own transmission.

To avoid a collision, having heard the end of the packet transmitted by s_l, s_1 delays its transmission to learn whether the leader's packet is followed by another packet transmitted by one of the stations located between s_l and s_1. By sensing the bus during this delay s_1 avoids interfering with such a transmission. To make this idea work, a station s located between s_l and s_1 should use a shorter delay than s_1.

Assume that $P = 0$ and the piggyback direction is to the left, as in figure 8.5. The delay used by station s awaiting its turn to transmit should depend on the number of stations separating s from the leader. It is reasonable to postulate that this delay be quantized, i.e., allocated in units of fixed length. Thus, the immediate left neighbor of s_l could use one unit of delay, the next station to the left could delay its transmission by two units, and so on. If the station identifiers reflect the ordering of the stations along the bus, the delay used by station s_1 located to the left of s_l is equal to $(s_l - s_1) \times \delta$, where δ is the delay quantum.

In principle, the immediate left neighbor of the leader need not delay its transmission at all. However, the physical layer may need a packet space (similar to the packet space in Ethernet) making packet boundaries clear. In such a case, it may be reasonable to make δ coincide with the shortest packet space acceptable by the physical layer. As Piggyback Ethernet operating in the controlled mode is much better synchronized than Ethernet, δ can be much shorter than the minimum packet space in the commercial network.

In fact, s_1 computes three delays: $d_1^l(s_l, s_1)$, $d_2^l(s_l, s_1)$, and d_e (the superscript "l" reminds us that the piggyback direction is to the left). The first delay is equal to $(s_l - s_1) \times \delta$. The second delay simulates the path of the virtual marker to the left end of the bus and then back to s_1. It also includes additional delays needed for detection of a possible transmission started by a station located to the left of s_1. Note that each of these stations has two chances to transmit. Finally, the third delay simulates the path of the marker to the right end of the bus and back to s_l, including one unit of additional delay per every station visited along that path.

Similarly, station s_2 located to the right of the leader computes three delays $d_1^l(s_l, s_2)$, $d_2^l(s_l, s_2)$, and d_e. The values of these delays reflect the fact that all the stations located to the left of s_2 have a higher priority than s_2 (and some of them must be counted twice).

If a station awaiting one of its delays senses a packet, it waits for the EOT event triggered by this packet, recomputes the delays with respect to the new leader and new piggyback direction, and resumes waiting.

Assume that the wait period $d_1^l(s_l, s_1)$ elapses without a transmission having been sensed. At this moment, station s_1 gets its **first turn**, i.e., the first chance to transmit a packet. If s_1 has a packet awaiting transmission, it transmits the packet (this makes s_1 a new leader). The packet **is not inflated**. Its P bit is set in such a way as to retain the direction of the virtual marker. In this case (figure 8.5), if s_1 piggybacks its packet in the first turn, the P bit is set to 0 (the virtual marker continues moving to the left).

If s_1 has no packet to transmit at its first turn, it continues waiting, extending the delay period to $d_2^l(s_l, s_1)$. If no transmission is sensed during the second wait period, s_1 is given a second chance to transmit a packet, if one has become ready in the meantime. This is the station's **second turn**. This time s_1 sets the P bit of its packet to 1, as the virtual marker travels to the right.

If it happens that none of the stations located to the left of s_l has a packet to transmit, the stations located to the right of the leader are allowed to join the party, also having two turns each. The order in which these stations are given a chance to transmit is symmetric to the order in which the stations located to the left of s_l were getting their turns. In particular, station s_2 (figure 8.5) will piggyback its packet to the packet transmitted by s_l only if no station located to the left of s_2 is ready for transmission. If no station has a packet to transmit at one of its turns, the virtual marker makes a full circle through the network (visiting each station twice) and arrives unused back at the leader. Then the network switches to the uncontrolled mode of operation.

In summary, the transmission of s_l puts the network into the controlled mode and initiates a cycle in which all stations are given two chances (turns) to transmit their packets without a collision. One can think in terms of a virtual marker that is generated by the end of a successfully transmitted packet and that makes a circular trip through all the stations. The trip starts at the transmitter and visits each station twice. The direction of the cycle traveled by the virtual marker is determined by the P bit in the packet header, which is set by the leader. The first leader (initiating the controlled mode) sets P at random. Subsequent leaders sustaining the controlled mode by transmitting at their turns set the P bit according to the current direction of the virtual marker. A packet transmitted in controlled mode may be arbitrarily short: it need not be inflated, as its transmission is guaranteed to be successful.

The three delays are given by the following formulas (assuming station s_l is the leader and $P = 0$, i.e., the piggyback direction is to the left):

$$d_1^l(s_l, s) = \begin{cases} (s_l - s) \times \delta & \text{if } s_l > s \\ 2l(s_l) + (s_l + s + 1) \times \delta & \text{if } s_l \leq s \end{cases},$$

$$d_2^l(s_l, s) = \begin{cases} 2l(s) + (s_l + s + 1) \times \delta & \text{if } s_l > s \\ 2(L + l(s_l) - l(s)) + (2N + s_l - s) \times \delta & \text{if } s_l \leq s \end{cases},$$

$$d_e = 2L + 2N \times \delta,$$

where N is the number of stations in the network, L is the propagation length of the bus, $l(s)$ is the *location* of station s, i.e., the propagation distance of s from the left end of the cable, and δ is the delay quantum.

The formula for $d_1^l(s_l, s)$ when $s < s_l$ was already derived. To illustrate how to derive the remaining formulas, let us calculate $d_1^l(s_l, s)$ when $s_l \leq s$. If we ignore the additional delays for yielding to transmissions arriving from upstream, the virtual marker arrives at s $2l(s_l)$ time units after s perceives the end of the leader's packet. Indeed, if we imagine that the end of this packet bounces from the left end of the bus, it will reach s $2l(s_l) + l(s) - l(s_l)$ time units after it leaves s_l. However, s counts its waiting from the moment it perceives the end of the packet transmitted by s_l; hence, the imaginary "bounced" copy of this end will reach s $2l(s_l)$ time units after the (real) original. This waiting time must be augmented by the additional delay needed by s to yield to a possible transmission of a station preceding s in the virtual ring. One quantum of the additional delay must be added per each station visited by the marker. Each of the stations located to the left of s_l (including s_l) is visited twice and there are $s_l + 1$ such stations.[27] Then s has to yield to $s - s_l - 1$ stations between s and s_l (excluding s_l). This way we get $2(s_l + 1) + s - s_l - 1$, which combined with $2l(s_l)$ gives the value of $d_1^l(s_l, s)$ when $s_l \leq s$.

The calculation of d_e is simple: to complete its cycle, the virtual marker must cross the entire bus twice ($2L$ time units) and visit each station twice. Each visit at a station incurs an additional delay of δ.

The case when $P = 1$ is symmetric. The corresponding delays when the piggyback direction of the leader's packet is to the right, denoted by d_1^r and d_2^r, can be obtained from the preceding formulas by replacing s_l and s (on the right-hand side) by $N - s_l$ and $N - s$, respectively. Note that d_e does not depend on the piggyback direction.

Assume that station s is piggybacking its packet to a packet transmitted by s_l. Let P_l denote the contents of the P bit in the leader's packet. Note that P_l also identifies a direction: $0 = $ left, $1 = $ right. Station s sets the P bit of its packet according to the following rules:

$$P = \begin{cases} P_l & \text{if } s \text{ lies in direction } P_l \text{ from } s_l \text{ and the packet is piggybacked in the first} \\ & \text{turn, or } s \text{ lies in direction } \overline{P_l} \text{ from } s_l \text{ and the packet is piggybacked} \\ & \text{in the second turn;} \\ \overline{P_l} & \text{otherwise.} \end{cases}$$

By $\overline{P_l}$, we understand the direction opposite to P_l.

The piggyback direction of the packet transmitted by s coincides with the direction of the path traveled by the virtual marker. This way, the new cycle started by the packet transmitted by s can be viewed as a continuation of the previous cycle.

---

[27]Note that stations are numbered from zero.

8.5.1.2 The simplified version.   Some people may object to the requirement of Piggyback Ethernet that each station know the bus locations of all the other
stations. Although this knowledge need not (and cannot) be absolutely accurate,[28]
its acquisition requires a tricky initialization procedure (section 8.5.2.3).

In this section we describe a simplified version of Piggyback Ethernet in which
that requirement has been relaxed. Again, we assume that all stations in the network are assigned addresses from 0 to $N-1$, where N is the total number of stations,
in the increasing order of the station's distance from the left end of the (strictly
linear) bus. We no longer postulate that each station be aware of the bus locations
of the other stations. Bit P need not exist explicitly; its role can be played by
one predetermined bit of the packet. As the contents of this bit should be more or
less random, the least significant bit of the packet's CRC code (section 1.1.2.2) is a
natural candidate.

Like the complete protocol, the simplified protocol operates in two modes. In
the uncontrolled mode, it behaves in precisely the same way as the complete version.
When a station senses a successful transmission, it switches to the controlled mode.

In the controlled mode, some stations are allowed to append their packets to
the last-transmitted packet, in a certain order based on priorities. These priorities
are derived from the stations' positions with respect to the sender of the last packet.
As before, packets transmitted in the controlled mode never collide, and they need
not be inflated to $2L$.

Assume that a packet has been transmitted successfully by station s_l and the
end of this packet arrives at station s_1. Station s_l becomes the current leader. The
contents of the P bit of the leader's packet determine the piggyback direction. If
$P = 0$ and $s_1 < s_l$, or $P = 1$ and $s_1 > s_l$, we say that s_1 is *eligible* for piggybacking
its packet to the packet transmitted by s_l. Only the eligible stations are allowed to
piggyback their packets; all the other stations have to wait until the network returns
to the uncontrolled mode or until another transmission changes their eligibility
status. A station is eligible if its location relative to the leader coincides with the
piggyback direction (P) of the leader's packet.

An eligible station gets only one chance to piggyback its packet to the leader's
packet. The virtual marker triggered by the end of a successful transmission travels
only one section of the bus, in one direction—toward the end indicated by the
contents of P. As the stations do not have to simulate the return sweep of the
marker (the marker does not bounce off the end of the bus), they do not have
to know the propagation length of the segment traveled by the marker. Thus, an
eligible station s_1 is only obliged to yield to the stations located between s_l and s_1.
According to the rules described in the section 8.5.1.1, it waits for

$$d(s_l, s_1) = |s_l - s_1| \times \delta$$

time units, where δ plays the same role as in the complete version. If the bus has
been idle through this time, s_1 is allowed to start its transmission at $t + d(s_l, s_1)$,

---

[28]The uncertainty of the station location is compensated for by δ.

where t is the time when s_1 sensed the end of the leader's packet. The protocol guarantees that the transmission of s_1 will be successful; therefore, s_1 does not inflate its packet.

If the bus has become busy while s_1 has been waiting for its turn, it means that another eligible station, say s_2, located closer to the leader s_l had a packet to transmit. In such a case, s_1 waits for the end of the (necessarily successful) transmission of s_2 and uses the P bit of s_2's packet to determine its further actions. The P bit being random, noneligible stations may become eligible, and vice versa.

If after a successful transmission by s_l, there are no transmissions during the amount of time equal to

$$d_e(s_l) = 2L + \delta \times \left\{ \begin{array}{l} (s_l + 1) \text{ if } P = 0 \\ (N - s_l) \text{ otherwise} \end{array} \right. ,$$

all stations return to the uncontrolled mode. Note that the value of d_e gives the worst-case estimate on the time when the virtual marker falls off the end of the bus along the piggyback direction. This estimate can be improved, if the location of the leader is known to all stations. According to what we assumed at the beginning of this section, no such knowledge is available.

The P bit of a packet transmitted by one of the two extreme stations should be set deterministically to indicate the piggyback direction toward the populated end of the cable. This postulate is difficult to satisfy if the P bit is not explicit. Note however, that a station detecting the end of a successfully transmitted packet is able to recognize its transmitter. It may thus ignore the contents of P, if the packet happens to have been transmitted by an extreme station, and assume that the piggyback direction of such a packet is deterministic.

8.5.2   The Implementation

Discussing the implementation of Piggyback Ethernet, we restrict ourselves to the transmitter part of the protocol. The reception rules are the same as for Ethernet; thus, the receiver process can be borrowed directly from the commercial network (section 8.1.2.2).

8.5.2.1   The complete version.   The transmitter portion of the protocol is most naturally implemented with two processes. One process, called the Monitor, keeps track of the activities in the bus, detects transitions between modes, and notifies the other process (the Transmitter) when it is allowed to transmit. The transmitter acquires packets from the Client, transmits them (based on the *notices* received from the Monitor), and handles collisions. The two processes communicate via station attributes. The station structure for Piggyback Ethernet is as follows:

```
station PiggyStation : EtherStation {
    DISTANCE LDist, RDist;
    int PiggyDirection, Turn;
```

```
            Mailbox *Ready;
            Boolean Blocked;
            void setup ();
        };
```

This station type is an extension of the Ethernet station (section 8.1.2.1). The meaning of the additional attributes will become clear when we get to the code of the two processes. LDist and RDist give the station's distance (in ITUs) from the ends of the bus (left and right, respectively). These attributes (together with the mailbox) are initialized by the station's setup method, discussed in section 8.5.2.3. PiggyDirection and Turn are set by the monitor to indicate the piggyback direction of the leader's packet and the turn number (1 or 2). Based on these values, the transmitter sets the P bit of a packet transmitted in the controlled mode (i.e., piggybacked to the leader's packet). The mailbox is used by the monitor to send notices (alerts) to the transmitter indicating the moments when the station gets its turns to transmit in the controlled mode. Blocked is used to tell whether the station is operating in the controlled mode. If Blocked is equal to YES, it means that spontaneous transmissions are not allowed; the transmitter must wait for an alert from the monitor indicating one of the station's two turns to piggyback its packet to the leader's packet.

In a real-life implementation of the protocol, each station would have to maintain a distance table describing bus locations of all stations in the network. We avoid this table by letting a station (its monitor process) peek at the LDist and RDist attributes of other stations. This simplification does not affect the feasibility of our implementation. In a real network, the distance tables would be built during the network initialization phase, and their entries would contain copies of the LDist and RDist attributes of the corresponding stations (section 8.5.2.3). Let us look at the monitor process first. Its type is declared as follows:

```
process Monitor (PiggyStation) {
  DISTANCE LDist, RDist;
  Mailbox *Ready;
  TIME Delay1, Delay2, DelayX;
  Port *Bus;
  void setDelays ();
  void setup ();
  states {Waiting, Active, EndActivity, GoSignal, EndPacket, FTurn,
    STurn};
  perform;
};
```

Attributes LDist, RDist, Ready, and Bus provide local copies of the corresponding station attributes. Delay1, Delay2, and DelayX are the three delays described in section 8.5.1.1, which are computed by the process upon sensing the end of a successful transmission. In fact, DelayX (which corresponds to d_e—section 8.5.1.1) is constant and does not depend on the leader's location; thus, its value is precomputed by the process's setup method:

```
void Monitor::setup () {
  Bus = S->Bus;
  LDist = S->LDist;
  RDist = S->RDist;
  Ready = S->Ready;
  DelayX = 2 * L + 2 * NStations * DelayQuantum;
};
```

L and DelayQuantum are global variables representing the bus length and the delay quantum δ (section 8.5.1.1). Being constant and the same for all stations, DelayX could have been defined as a global parameter. However, by association with the other (dynamic) delays, we have decided to make it a station attribute.[29] These other delays, i.e., Delay1 and Delay2, are calculated by setDelays—the monitor's method called when the process detects the end of a successful packet transmission—in the following way:

```
void Monitor::setDelays () {
  Long Sender, SId;
  Sender = ThePacket->Sender;
  SId = S->getId ();
  if ((S->PiggyDirection = piggyDirection (ThePacket)) == Left) {
    if (SId < Sender) {
      Delay1 = (Sender - SId) * DelayQuantum;
      Delay2 = 2 * (LDist + SId * DelayQuantum) + DelayQuantum;
    } else {
      Delay1 = 2 * ((PiggyStation*) idToStation (Sender))->LDist +
        (SId + Sender + 1) * DelayQuantum;
      Delay2 = 2 * (RDist + (NStations - SId) * DelayQuantum) -
        DelayQuantum;
    }
  } else {
    if (SId > Sender) {
      Delay1 = (SId - Sender) * DelayQuantum;
      Delay2 = 2 * (RDist + (NStations - SId) * DelayQuantum) -
        DelayQuantum;
    } else {
      Delay1 = 2 * (((PiggyStation*) idToStation (Sender))->RDist)
```

---

[29]Note that in a realistic implementation there would be no global variables, and all parameters would have to be represented by station attributes. In our examples, we use global variables to emphasize the global nature of things expressed by them. From the protocol's perspective, all such variables are actually constants: their values can be computed at the network initialization phase, but they must not be changed while the protocol is running. Such global variables can be trivially replaced by constant station attributes.

```
      + (NStations + NStations - SId - Sender - 1) *
        DelayQuantum;
    Delay2 = 2 * (LDist + SId * DelayQuantum) + DelayQuantum;
  }
 }
};
```

The P bit of a packet is represented by one of the standard flags associated with type Packet (section 5.2.2). The macros

```
#define Left                 0
#define Right                1
#define piggyDirection(p)  (flagSet (p->Flags, PF_usr0))
#define setPiggyLeft(p)    (clearFlag (p->Flags, PF_usr0))
#define setPiggyRight(p)   (setFlag (p->Flags, PF_usr0))
```

provide simple tools for examining the contents of P and setting it appropriately. As a by-product of its operation, setDelays sets attribute PiggyDirection of the current station. Then it selects one of four possible cases based on the piggyback direction and the station's location with respect to the leader. We assume that stations' Ids directly reflect the order in which the stations are connected to the bus. The reader may want to verify that the delays are set according to the rules described in section 8.5.1.1. Note, however, that the value stored in Delay2 is the difference between the two delays, not the absolute value of the second delay. This way Delay2 gives the required waiting interval from the moment the station got its first turn rather than the time when it sensed the end of the leader's packet.

In a real-life implementation, the procedure for calculating Delay1 and Delay2 carried out by setDelays may prove too expensive. In such a case, a lookup table can be used that gives directly the values of the two delays based on the piggyback direction and the leader's Id. The entries in this table ($4N$ entries per station) will be precomputed and filled in at network startup.

Now we can look at the monitor's code:

```
Monitor::perform {
  state Waiting:
    Bus->wait (ACTIVITY, Active);
  state Active:
    S->Blocked = YES;
    Bus->wait (EOT, EndPacket);
    Bus->wait (SILENCE, EndActivity);
  state EndActivity:
    Timer->wait (TPSpace, GoSignal);
  state GoSignal:
    S->Blocked = NO;
    Ready->put ();
    proceed Waiting;
```

```
state EndPacket:
  setDelays ();
  Timer->wait (Delay1, FTurn);
  Bus->wait (ACTIVITY, Active);
state FTurn:
  S->Turn = 1;
  Ready->put ();
  Timer->wait (Delay2, STurn);
  Bus->wait (ACTIVITY, Active);
state STurn:
  S->Turn = 2;
  Ready->put ();
  Timer->wait (DelayX-Delay2-Delay1, GoSignal);
  Bus->wait (ACTIVITY, Active);
};
```

The process monitors all activities in the bus. Upon sensing an activity, the monitor moves to state Active, where it sets Blocked (to indicate that spontaneous transmissions are not allowed) and awaits further developments. If the activity ends with EOT, the process will wake up in state EndPacket. Otherwise, the activity results in a collision and the monitor will end up in state EndActivity.

Note that upon the end of a successful packet transmission, the two events awaited in state Active occur in the same ITU. The process assumes that they are prioritized in such a way that EOT is signaled before SILENCE, i.e., state EndActivity will not be entered if SILENCE is accompanied by EOT. This assumption agrees with the standard ordering of port events (section 6.2.12).

Assume that the activity sensed by the monitor in state Waiting has developed into a collision, i.e., the process has found itself in state EndActivity. Now it waits for the packet space interval (TPSpace ITUs) and then moves to state GoSignal. There the monitor clears the Blocked flag and sends a go signal to the transmitter by depositing an alert in the mailbox. Awakened by this signal, the transmitter will find that Blocked has been cleared, which means that the network remains in the uncontrolled mode.

To clean up after a collision, the protocol delays a transfer attempt by TPSpace time units after the perceived end of the last activity. The packet space interval in this case (assumed to be of the same order as in the commercial network) is represented by TPSpace rather than QuantumDelay.

Now suppose that the monitor wakes up in state EndPacket, which means that a packet has been transmitted successfully. The first thing that happens in this state is a call to setDelays. Note that ThePacket (used by the method) points to the packet triggering the EOT event. The rest of the code is simple. The process issues two wait requests: for Delay1 time units and for an activity in the bus. If no activity is heard before Delay1 elapses, the station gets its first turn to piggyback a packet. Then the monitor wakes up in state FTurn, where it sets Turn to 1 and notifies the transmitter (via mailbox Ready) that it is allowed to transmit. Having done this, the process waits for the second turn, which will occur Delay2 ITUs later, provided that no activity is sensed in the meantime.[30] The second turn is taken care of in state STurn.

If no bus activity has been sensed for DelayX time units after the end of the leader's packet, the controlled mode is to be abandoned. This happens DelayX − Delay2 − Delay1 ITUs after the monitor gets into state STurn. Then the process moves to state GoSignal, where it clears Blocked and notifies the transmitter that the bus is now available for spontaneous transmissions. We can now discuss the transmitter process. We start from its type definition, which, among other things, announces a few methods used by the process.

```
process Transmitter (PiggyStation) {
  Port *Bus;
  Packet *Buffer;
  int CCounter;
  Mailbox *Ready;
  void inflate (), deflate ();
  TIME backoff ();
  void setPiggyDirection ();
  void setup ();
  states {NPacket, WaitBus, Piggyback, XDone, Abort, EndJam,
    Error};
  perform;
};
```

Attributes Bus, Buffer, and Ready are pointers to the corresponding station attributes. They are set by the following simple setup method:

```
void Transmitter::setup () {
  Bus = S->Bus;
  Buffer = &(S->Buffer);
  Ready = S->Ready;
};
```

CCounter plays the same role as in the Ethernet transmitter (section 8.1.2.1): it counts collisions suffered by the packet currently being processed and is used as the argument of the backoff function (method backoff is borrowed from the Ethernet protocol—section 8.1.2.2). Methods inflate and deflate are called by the process to set the TLength attribute of the packet currently held in the station's Buffer.

```
void PTransmitter::inflate () {
  Buffer->TLength = Buffer->ILength + PFrame;
```

---

[30]Note that as long as the protocol functions correctly, this activity can only be a successfully transmitted packet, in particular, a packet transmitted by the cooperating transmitter process.

```
      if (Buffer->ILength < MinIPL)
        Buffer->TLength += (MinIPL - Buffer->ILength);
  };
  void PTransmitter::deflate () {
    Buffer->TLength = Buffer->ILength + PFrame;
  };
```

When a packet is about to be transmitted in the uncontrolled mode, it is **inflated** to make sure that its length is not less than the round-trip propagation delay of the bus. The global variable MinIPL gives the minimum inflated length of the information portion of a packet that may collide and therefore must not be shorter than the collision slot. Conversely, a piggybacked packet is **deflated** before transmission: its total length is set to the length of the information content augmented by the combined length of the header and trailer.

Before a packet is transmitted, regardless of the transmission mode, the packet's P bit (the piggyback direction) is set by the following method of the transmitter:

```
  void Transmitter::setPiggyDirection () {
    if (S->Blocked) {
      if (S->PiggyDirection == Left && S->Turn == 1 ||
        S->PiggyDirection == Right && S->Turn == 2)
          setPiggyLeft (Buffer);
      else
          setPiggyRight (Buffer);
    } else
      if (flip ())
        setPiggyLeft (Buffer);
      else
        setPiggyRight (Buffer);
  };
```

If Blocked is YES, it means that the transmission will be done in the controlled mode. Then the P bit of the packet is set based on the piggyback direction of the leader's packet and the piggyback turn, according to the rules given in section 8.5.1.1. Otherwise, the packet will be transmitted in the uncontrolled mode, and its piggyback direction is set at random (function flip was introduced in section 2.3.1).

Following is the code method of the transmitter:

```
  Transmitter::perform {
    state NPacket:
      if (S->ready (MinUPL, MaxUPL, PFrame)) {
        CCounter = 0;
        proceed WaitBus;
      } else
        Client->wait (ARRIVAL, NPacket);
```

```
    state WaitBus:
      if (S->Blocked)
        Ready->wait (NEWITEM, Piggyback);
      else {
        inflate ();
        setPiggyDirection ();
        Bus->transmit (Buffer, XDone);
        Bus->wait (COLLISION, Abort);
      }
    state Piggyback:
      if (S->Blocked) {
        deflate ();
        Bus->wait (COLLISION, Error);
      } else {
        inflate ();
        Bus->wait (COLLISION, Abort);
      }
      setPiggyDirection ();
      Bus->transmit (Buffer, XDone);
    state XDone:
      Bus->stop ();
      Buffer->release ();
      proceed NPacket;
    state Abort:
      Bus->abort ();
      Bus->sendJam (TJamL, EndJam);
    state EndJam:
      Bus->stop ();
      Timer->wait (backoff (), WaitBus);
    state Error:
      excptn ("Illegal collision for a piggybacked packet");
};
```

The process starts in state NPacket, where it acquires a packet for transmission from the Client and resets the collision counter (attribute CCounter). Then the transmitter moves to state WaitBus to check the network status. If Blocked is YES, it means that, according to the monitor's perception, the transmission cannot be started immediately. This may indicate a busy status of the bus (i.e., an activity currently perceived by the monitor on the station's port) or the controlled mode triggered by a valid packet transmission heard by the monitor a short while ago. In either case, the monitor will deposit an alert into the Ready mailbox at the nearest moment when the station becomes eligible for a transmission. Note that there are two possibilities. If an activity is currently sensed on the station's port, this activity will develop into a collision or into a successful transmission. In the former case, the monitor will clear `Blocked` and send the go signal `TPSpace` time units after sensing the nearest beginning of a silence period. In the latter case, the network (and also the station) will enter the controlled mode. `Blocked` will remain set for the entire duration of the controlled mode, and three alerts will be generated by the monitor. Two of those alerts will mark the moments when the station gets its two turns to piggyback a packet to the leader's packet, and the third alert will indicate the end of the controlled mode. Note that `Blocked` will be cleared when the third alert is delivered.

Assume that the transmitter gets to state `WaitBus` and finds `Blocked` to be YES. The process goes to sleep awaiting a monitor alert. Depending on the timing of its last state transition, the transmitter will be awakened in state `Piggyback` by one of the three monitor alerts. The capacity of mailbox `Ready` is zero (section 8.5.2.3); therefore, alerts inserted into the mailbox by the monitor are not queued and do not remain pending if the transmitter does not await them. In such a case, the go signal is ignored: although the station becomes eligible to transmit, no packet is available for transmission.

Note that somewhat contrary to the name of this state, if the transmitter has been restarted in state `Piggyback`, it does not necessarily mean that the station becomes eligible to piggyback a packet in the controlled mode. This is only the case if `Blocked` remains YES, which actually indicates the controlled mode. Then the process `deflates` the `Buffer` contents. Otherwise, the packet will be transmitted in the uncontrolled mode and it can legitimately collide; thus, it must be `inflated`. In either case, the piggyback direction of the packet is set appropriately (note that `setPiggyDirection` interprets `Blocked`) and the packet is transmitted. A collision detected during transmission in the uncontrolled mode is legal and is processed in the same way as in Ethernet (section 8.1.2.2). The transmitter also monitors the fate of piggybacked packets to detect their collisions. Of course, a packet transmitted in the controlled mode is not expected to collide. If it does, the process wakes up in state `Error`, where it diagnoses the problem and aborts the experiment.

When the process gets to state `WaitBus` and finds `Blocked` to be NO, the situation resembles a packet transmission in Ethernet. The carrier-sense part of the transmission protocol has been performed by the monitor (`Blocked == NO` means "bus idle, packet space obeyed"), and the transmitter is free to start a packet transmission. Of course, the packet must be inflated in this case. Its piggyback direction is set at random by `setPiggyDirection`.

8.5.2.2 The simplified version. Given the monitor/transmitter pair for the complete version of Piggyback Ethernet (section 8.5.2.1), the simplified version can be implemented with absolutely no effort. The new station type is just a simplification of the station type from section 8.5.2.1:

```
station PiggyStation : EtherStation {
  int PiggyDirection;
  Mailbox *Ready;
```

```
    Boolean Blocked;
    void setup ();
};
```

Attributes LDist, RDist, and Turn are not needed. According to the simplified protocol rules, the stations are not expected to know the distances on the bus. Moreover, each station gets at most one turn to piggyback its packet to the leader's packet, and there is no need to indicate which turn it is.

Notably, the transmitter process can be reused as is in the simplified version, except for method setPiggyDirection, which must be rewritten. To make the transmitter presented in section 8.5.2.1 shareable by the two versions of the protocol, we change the specification of setPiggyDirection. We also change the name of the process type to PTransmitter and use it as the base type for declaring two versions of the Transmitter type. This base type is declared as follows:

```
process PTransmitter (PiggyStation) {
  Port *Bus;
  Packet *Buffer;
  int CCounter;
  Mailbox *Ready;
  void inflate (), deflate ();
  TIME backoff ();
  virtual void setPiggyDirection () { };
  void setup ();
  states {NPacket, WaitBus, Piggyback, XDone, Abort, EndJam,
    Error};
  perform;
};
```

The only difference with respect to type Transmitter in section 8.5.2.1 is the virtual specification of setPiggyDirection. The default method has an empty body. Type PTransmitter is intentionally open and setPiggyDirection must be declared separately for each version of the protocol. The code method of PTransmitter is exactly as presented in section 8.5.2.1.

The specification of PTransmitter has been put into files ptransmitter.h and ptransmitter.c in IncludeLibrary. Directory ETHER/PiggyA contains the implementation of the complete version of Piggyback Ethernet. The transmitter type for this version is declared as follows:

```
process Transmitter : PTransmitter {
  void setPiggyDirection ();
};
```

where setPiggyDirection is defined exactly as shown in section 8.5.2.1. The transmitter process for the simplified version of the protocol (see directory ETHER/PiggyB) is declared in a similar way, except that setPiggyDirection has the following body:

```
void Transmitter::setPiggyDirection () {
  if (S->getId () == 0)
    setPiggyRight (Buffer);
  else if (S->getId () == NStations - 1)
    setPiggyLeft (Buffer);
  else
    if (flip ())
      setPiggyLeft (Buffer);
    else
      setPiggyRight (Buffer);
};
```

According to the protocol rules, the piggyback direction of a packet is set at random, except when the packet is sent by an extreme station.

In principle, the monitor process could have been redesigned to be shared by the two versions of the protocol, but this would involve a few additional (virtual) methods or flags modifying the behavior of its code method. Note that in the simpler version a station gets at most one turn; thus, some states of the monitor applicable to the complete version would be unused in the simplified version. Therefore, we decided to have two separate versions of type Monitor, with the simplified version defined as follows:

```
process Monitor (PiggyStation) {
  Mailbox *Ready;
  TIME DelayP, DelayX;
  Port *Bus;
  Boolean eligible ();
  void setup ();
  states {Waiting, Active, EndActivity, GoSignal, EndPacket,
    MyTurn};
  perform;
};
```

As before, DelayX represents d_e—the amount of time elapsing after the end of the leader's packet is heard at the station's port to the moment when the monitor proclaims the end of the controlled mode. In contrast to the complete version, where this delay is fixed, DelayX now depends on the leader's location and on the P bit of the leader's packet (the piggyback direction). Thus, this attribute cannot be preset in the monitor's setup method, whose exclusive role is now to initialize the local copies of the two station attributes:

```
void Monitor::setup () {
  Bus = S->Bus;
  Ready = S->Ready;
};
```

DelayP corresponds to Delay1 from the complete version. It marks the moment when the station gets its turn to piggyback a packet to the leader's packet. In the simplified version, a station must be *eligible* to get such a turn, i.e., it must lie on the piggyback direction from the leader. The eligibility status is determined by method eligible, which also computes the two delays:

```
Boolean Monitor::eligible () {
  Long Sender, SId;
  Sender = ThePacket->Sender;
  SId = S->getId ();
  if ((S->PiggyDirection = piggyDirection (ThePacket)) == Left) {
    if (SId < Sender)
      DelayP = (Sender - SId) * DelayQuantum;
    else
      DelayP = TIME_0;
    DelayX = 2 * L + (Sender + 1) * DelayQuantum;
  } else {
    if (SId > Sender)
      DelayP = (SId - Sender) * DelayQuantum;
    else
      DelayP = TIME_0;
    DelayX = 2 * L + (NStations - Sender) * DelayQuantum;
  }
  return DelayP != TIME_0;
};
```

The method calculates the two delays according to the rules outlined in section 8.5.1.2. DelayP == TIME_0 indicates that the station is not eligible; the method returns NO in such a case.

The simplified monitor process executes the following code:

```
Monitor::perform {
  state Waiting:
    Bus->wait (ACTIVITY, Active);
  state Active:
    S->Blocked = YES;
    Bus->wait (EOT, EndPacket);
    Bus->wait (SILENCE, EndActivity);
  state EndActivity:
    Timer->wait (TPSpace, GoSignal);
  state GoSignal:
    S->Blocked = NO;
    Ready->put ();
    proceed Waiting;
  state EndPacket:
```

```
                    if (eligible ())
                      Timer->wait (DelayP, MyTurn);
                    else
                      Timer->wait (DelayX, GoSignal);
                    Bus->wait (ACTIVITY, Active);
                  state MyTurn:
                    Ready->put ();
                    Timer->wait (DelayX-DelayP, GoSignal);
                    Bus->wait (ACTIVITY, Active);
          };
```

The reader may want to compare this code with the version discussed in section 8.5.2.1. There is only one turn state (**MyTurn**) entered when the station gets its single turn to piggyback a packet. In state **EndPacket**, the process determines the station's eligibility status. If the station is not eligible, the process waits for **DelayX** time units (until the controlled mode is exited) and then sends a go signal to the transmitter. Otherwise, when the station is eligible, the monitor sends the signal at the moment when the station gets its turn. The rest is the same as for the previous version of the monitor.

8.5.2.3 Initialization.   In our SMURPH implementation of Piggyback Ethernet, we ignore the relatively complex initialization phase of the protocol, especially in its complete version. The reader may look at files **root.c** in directories **ETHER/PiggyA** and **ETHER/PiggyB**, where the protocol programs are initialized. In particular, the station's setup method for the complete version is as follows:

```
void PiggyStation::setup () {
  int i;
  PiggyStation *ps;
  EtherStation::setup ();
  if (getId () == NNodes - 1) {
    for (i = 0; i < NNodes; i++) {
      ps = (PiggyStation*) idToStation (i);
      ps->RDist = ps->Bus->distTo (Bus);
    }
  }
  LDist = ((PiggyStation*) idToStation (0)) -> Bus -> distTo (Bus);
  Ready = create Mailbox (0);
  Blocked = NO;
};
```

This method assumes that stations' Ids directly reflect the ordering of the stations along the bus. Fortunately, the way the stations are connected to the linear link (files **lbus.h** and **lbus.c** in directory **IncludeLibrary**; see also section 8.1.2.4) automatically enforces the right order. The distance information is explicitly inserted into the stations after the last station (number NNodes − 1) has been created. This information is extracted from the bus link (section 3.3.3).

The station's setup method for the simplified version of the protocol is somewhat less involved:

```
void PiggyStation::setup () {
  EtherStation::setup ();
  Ready = create Mailbox (0);
  Blocked = NO;
};
```

However, the protocol still assumes that the Id attributes number the stations according to the order in which the stations have been connected to the bus. This is reflected in the monitor's method eligible (section 8.5.2.2), which calculates DelayP and DelayX based on this assumption.

It is unreasonable to postulate that the ordering of stations along the bus and the distance information (for the complete version) is known to the stations a priori, i.e., is hardwired into the stations. To be flexible, the protocol must be able to initialize itself dynamically during the network startup phase. We should assume that when the network is set up for the first time, the stations know nothing about their locations on the bus and the order in which they are connected. They also do not know the total length of the bus L, although they may all use some safe common upper limit on that length, which may be quite pessimistic.[31] However, we may assume that the stations are addressable, i.e., each station is assigned a *hardwired address*, which is different from the hardwired address of any other station. The hardwired addresses are not expected to obey any specific ordering.

We now sketch an initialization procedure based on the preceding assumptions. The stations start executing the initialization procedure in response to a startup signal, which may come as a special packet broadcast by the network monitor. During that procedure, the stations operate in the "Ethernet mode," i.e., all packets are inflated appropriately and collisions are recognized exactly as in the commercial network. The purpose of the initialization procedure is to inform every station about its position on the bus and, in the case of the complete version, also about the station's distance to all other stations. After the procedure has been completed, each station learns its "soft" address: a number from 0 to $N - 1$ reflecting the station's position from the left end of the bus. This address will be used during the "normal" operation of the protocol. Moreover, the station builds the address table identifying the other stations connected to the network. Each entry in the address table consists of the following items:

- Hardwired address
- Soft address,
- Distance from the station whose soft address is 0 (complete version only)

---

[31] Note that stations in commercial Ethernet do not know the actual length of the bus, but they all assume the same upper limit on this length (section 8.1.1.4).

Initialization Algorithm for the Complete Version. The algorithm consists of three phases. The purpose of the first phase is to single out the leftmost station on the bus. Of course, "leftmost" is an abstract concept. In fact, the first phase will choose one station that can be safely claimed to be located at one end of the bus. This end will be called the left end, and the opposite end will be called the right end.

Let L' denote the common bound on the bus length known by all stations at the beginning of the initialization procedure. Phase one operates as follows:

1. Every station attempts to manifest its presence in the network by broadcasting a packet. The first station that transmits successfully becomes a temporary coordinator.

2. Every station other than the coordinator sends a packet. This way the coordinator learns how many stations are connected to the network and the hardwired addresses of these stations. The coordinator assumes that all stations have identified themselves if the last end of a successfully transmitted packet is followed by a silence period of $2L'$. From now on, the stations other than the coordinator become silent. They only respond to explicit polling from the coordinator.

3. The coordinator polls every station in turn (by sending a packet explicitly addressed to the station) and awaits an immediate response. This way the coordinator learns about its distance to every other station in the network.

4. Let s_l be the most distant station from the coordinator. If there is more than one such station[32] (i.e., multiple most distant stations whose actual distances from the coordinator look the same), the one with the smallest hardwired address is selected. The coordinator broadcasts a packet informing all stations that s_l is the leftmost station in the network.

In the second phase, each station learns its location on the bus with respect to the leftmost station s_l selected in phase one. The second phase consists of the following steps:

5. Stations start to transmit polling packets to the leftmost station s_l. Eventually, one of them will succeed.[33] Let us denote this station by s_a (see figure 8.6).

6. The successful transmission of s_a is recognized by all stations. Having detected this transmission, every station (including s_a) starts to monitor the bus for the response of s_l. Let s be any station in the network, t_{s_a} the time when s hears the end of the packet transmitted by s_a, and t_{s_l} the time when s

---

[32]Note that it is legal for two or more stations to be connected to the same location on the bus. The protocol (both versions) will operate correctly with such stations, and their mutual ordering is irrelevant.

[33]Recall that the network operates in the Ethernet mode.

detects the response of the leftmost station s_l.[34] Station s **assumes** that its propagation distance from the left end of the bus is $(t_{s_l} - t_{s_a})/2$. Note that this assumption is valid for all stations located on the left side of s_a and also for s_a. For the remaining stations, the assumption is wrong: the estimated distance to the left end of the bus is too low. No station, with the exception of s_a, can be **certain** of its estimate at this moment.

7. All stations that are certain of their estimates retreat from the game. If there is any station that is yet uncertain, it attempts to poll station s_l. One of the uncertain stations eventually succeeds, and it learns its correct position on the bus,[35] as did s_a in the previous round. At the same time, all uncertain stations verify their estimates. If the new distance turns out to be larger than the previous estimate,[36] the station becomes certain and withdraws from the game.

8. The second phase of the initialization procedure ends when all stations are certain of their locations on the bus. The end of this phase is easily detectable by all stations. To recognize the moment when all stations know their distances from s_l, a station has to monitor the bus and detect packets sent by s_l. If the end of the last packet sent by s_l is followed by a long period of silence, e.g., $2L'$, the station may assume that phase two is over.

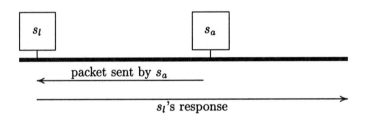

Figure 8.6 Initialization cycle (phase two) for the complete version of Piggyback Ethernet

In the last phase, the stations broadcast their locations. If the end of the last successfully transmitted packet is followed by $2L'$ bits of silence, the initialization procedure is complete. The leftmost station detects the end of the initialization procedure and broadcasts a short packet, whose successful end indicates the beginning of the normal operation of the protocol.

The soft addresses of stations are determined by the nondecreasing order of their distances from the left end of the bus. If two stations happen to occupy the

---

[34]In fact, to detect the response, the station must recognize a part of the packet header. We assume that t_{s_l} is the time when the beginning of the response packet is heard by the station.

[35]To reduce the chance for a collision, the stations may use their location estimates as parameters of the backoff function.

[36]Possibly incremented by a small tolerance margin.

same location (or two indistinguishable locations) on the cable, their order can be determined by comparing their hardwired addresses.

Initialization Algorithm for the Simplified Version.   Theoretically, to initialize the simplified version of Piggyback Ethernet, one could use the preceding algorithm and simply discard the irrelevant information. However, one objective of the simplified version was to eliminate the need for computing and maintaining exact distances between stations. Therefore, if there exists an algorithm for ordering the stations without measuring their distances from the end of the bus, such an algorithm will be deemed more appropriate for the simplified version.

Fortunately, there is a solution with the required property: the following algorithm orders the stations according to their occurrence along the bus without using any explicit distance information (the prerequisites are exactly as for the previous algorithm):

1. All stations play a tournament consisting of N games. The goal of a game is to select one station to be removed from the tournament. The removed station does not participate in subsequent games.

2. Upon detecting the initialization signal (a special packet), all stations start broadcasting their packets. Eventually, one of them will succeed. Let us denote this station by s_a (see figure 8.7).

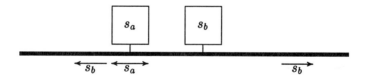

Figure 8.7   One step of the configuration algorithm for the simplified version of Piggyback Ethernet

3. Having transmitted successfully, s_a defers its further activities until it senses the end of the next successful transmission. All stations other than s_a continue their transfer attempts until one of them succeeds. Let us denote that second station by s_b.

4. Having recognized the end of the packet transmitted by s_b, s_a immediately follows it by its own packet. All other stations wait until they hear: first, the end of the packet transmitted by s_b, and next, the beginning of the packet transmitted by s_a.

5. Every station that finds the two packets to be (almost) adjacent assumes that it is located on the **left** side of s_a. If as perceived by a station, the two packets are separated by a clearly recognizable period of silence, the station assumes that it lies on the **right** side of s_a. Thus, after the first step, all stations are able to tell their relative locations with respect to s_a. Station s_a is called the *reference station* of the current game. The reference station transmits one

more packet and then is removed from the tournament—it will not contend
in subsequent games. However, as long as the tournament is still in progress,
all removed stations passively monitor the bus, to learn about their locations
with respect to subsequent reference stations.

6. All stations that have appeared to be located on the right side of the last
   reference station wait for $2L$[37] while the other (playing) stations contend to
   select a winner—the first station that broadcasts its packet successfully. If
   the contention does not start within the nearest $2L$ time units, the right-side
   stations will take over. Let us assume that there is a left-side station, say s_c,
   that wins.

7. Having detected the end of the packet transmitted by s_c, s_a responds with its
   own packet. Then s_c immediately appends another packet to the end of the
   packet transmitted by s_a. This way s_c becomes the new reference station, and
   the algorithm continues at step 5 with station s_c replacing s_a.

8. If there is no active station on the left side of the reference station, the stations
   on the right side detect that fact after $2L$ time units of silence following the
   last packet sent by the reference station. Then they start their contention to
   determine a winner. That winner becomes the next reference station. Note
   that the "orientation" of this new reference station will be different from the
   previous one. However, all stations monitoring the bus will recognize that the
   orientation has changed, and they will reverse their notion of sides (step 5).

9. The algorithm continues until there are no contending stations on both sides
   of the last reference station. This is recognized by all stations when they
   sense a $4L$ silence period following the end of the packet transmitted by the
   last reference station.

The obvious invariant of the algorithm is that every station removed from the
tournament knows its relative location with respect to all stations that have been
removed so far. With each game, one new station becomes removed. Thus, the
algorithm terminates and then all stations have been removed. Consequently, when
the algorithm stops, each station is able to tell its soft address on the bus.

A problem may occur when two (or more) stations are connected to the same
place on the bus, i.e., they are located too close to claim that one of them is clearly
on a side of the other. In such a case, the stations may play a randomized game to
determine their formal order; they may also use the order of their hard addresses.

8.5.2.4 The impact of clock tolerance on the delay quantum.   With Pig-
gyback Ethernet, the limited accuracy of clocks comes into play in two places. During the normal operation of the protocol, the monitor process calculates two or
three[38] delays following the perceived end of a leader's packet. These delays are

---

[37]Note that for the simplified version of the protocol, L is not computed by the initialization
algorithm but assumed to be preset to a safe boundary value, the same for all stations.

[38]In the complete version.

functions of the following parameters:

- δ (sections 8.5.1.1, 8.5.1.2), represented by `DelayQuantum` in the implementation (section 8.5.2.1)
- Locations of some stations on the bus (complete version only)
- Bus length L

Ultimately, the delays are computed with a certain tolerance depending on the clock accuracy. Note that the station's location (determined by the initialization algorithm) cannot be known with absolute precision. However, the imperfection of this knowledge is in direct proportion to the imperfection of clocks used by the stations. Consequently, we may assume that the stations know accurately their positions on the bus, but the clocks used to measure the delays needed by the protocol are a bit less accurate than in reality.

The delay quantum δ must be selected in such a way that piggybacked packets do not collide. Assume that the maximum clock deviation (section 4.5.2) is τ. This means that a time interval of length Δ to be measured by a station's clock may come out as any interval of length between $\Delta(1-\tau)$ and $\Delta(1+\tau)$. The maximum interval to be measured by a station is d_e, and the difference between the measurements of this interval for any two stations must be less than δ. To be on the safe side, we should postulate that the error be no bigger than a certain fraction of δ, e.g., $\delta/2$. With this assumption, even at the biggest possible error, the station still has $\delta/2$ time units to properly interpret the bus status. The postulate boils down to the following inequality:

$$d_e \times (1 + \tau) - d_e \times (1 - \tau) \leq \frac{\delta}{2} \ .$$

For the complete version of the protocol, this gives

$$(2L + 2N \times \delta) \times 2\tau \leq \frac{\delta}{2} \ ,$$

and in consequence

$$\delta \geq \frac{8L\tau}{1 - 8N\tau} \ .$$

As one might expect, δ depends on the propagation length of the bus and the number of stations in the network. As the right side of the inequality must be strictly positive, the condition

$$1 - 8N\tau > 0$$

restricts the maximum number of stations in the network for a given clock tolerance τ. To get an impression how serious this restriction is, assume that τ is equal to 0.0002, which is twice the maximum deviation of clocks in commercial Ethernet.[39] With this deviation, the maximum number of stations is bounded by

---

[39]The factor of 2 is intended to compensate for the errors in the location knowledge acquired during network initialization.

625. Conversely, assume that 50 stations are distributed along a 2000-bit bus (e.g., 400 meters of a 1 Gb/s medium). The minimum safe value of δ is then less than 2 bits.

For the simplified version of the protocol, the maximum value of d_e is $2L + N\delta$ and the previous calculations produce more favorable results. In particular, the condition for the maximum number of stations in the network becomes

$$1 - 4N\tau > 0 \; ,$$

which means that for a given clock deviation, the simplified version of the protocol can accommodate twice as many stations as the complete version.

8.5.3 Conclusions and Suggestions for Possible Enhancements

In contrast to the other "controlled" collision protocols discussed in this chapter, Piggyback Ethernet does not guarantee a bounded-time packet delivery. It retains the statistical nature of commercial Ethernet; its goal is to extend the Ethernet concept onto faster (and possibly longer) networks. The CSMA/CD protocol used in Ethernet requires that no packet be shorter than twice the propagation diameter of the bus. Piggyback Ethernet avoids this requirement by transmitting packets in a synchronized way, as long as there are enough of them to keep the network in the controlled mode. Packets are only inflated to $2L$ if the traffic is low. One can claim that the penalty of inflation is acceptable in such circumstances.

The reader is encouraged to experiment with our implementations of Piggyback Ethernet, which can be found in directories ETHER/PiggyA and ETHER/PiggyB of SMURPH Examples. In particular, a comparison with other versions of CSMA/CD, and also with the collision-free bus protocols discussed in the next chapter, may be interesting. There are several ways in which Piggyback Ethernet can be improved. One problem (with both versions) is the not-so-spectacular packet access time (and consequently packet delay) for packets transmitted in the uncontrolled mode. Such packets are inflated, and formally an inflated packet cannot be assumed to have been transmitted (or received) until its last bit has been transmitted (or received). If L is large compared to the size of an uninflated packet, the time spent on transmitting/receiving the packet's dummy portion may contribute a substantial delay to its performance measures. A natural solution to this problem is to put the dummy bits at the end of the packet preceded by the CRC for the valid (uninflated) portion. The recipient may assume that the packet has been completely received (and pass it to the upper protocol layers for further processing) without waiting for the end of the irrelevant dummy trailer. This approach poses a certain problem, however. Namely, it is possible that the sender of a packet that has been (or will be) successfully recognized and accepted by its recipient will detect a collision and assume that the packet has been destroyed. This will result in a retransmission, and eventually the recipient will get a duplicate of the previous packet. Fortunately, there is a simple method of detecting such duplicates and ignoring them. Having passed the packet for processing to the higher layers, the receiving station should monitor the reception of the dummy bits against a collision. Of course, there is no way to retract the packet when a collision is recognized in its dummy part. However, should such an event occur, the station may store a flag in its internal data structures (e.g., the address table) to indicate that the next packet arriving from the same sender is to be ignored. Another solution would be to send this information to the higher layers, so that the duplicate can be ignored after it is passed there. Notably, the protocol is able to cope with packet duplicates at the medium access level without furnishing the packets with sequence numbers.

The maximum throughput achieved by the simplified version of the protocol can be improved by making the P bit explicit and setting it in a biased way. Note that when a leader located close to the left end of the bus sets P to zero (indicating the piggyback direction to the left), the number of eligible stations is much smaller than it would be if the piggyback direction were opposite. We agreed in section 8.5.1.2 that the P bit of a packet transmitted by an extreme station should be ignored (only one piggyback direction is then sensible). Perhaps the distribution of the P bits should reflect the fact that the number of eligible stations on each side of the leader may be different. The reader may want to experiment with biased (nonuniform) distributions of P and investigate their impact on the maximum throughput achieved by the simplified version. One should be careful, however, not to compromise the fairness. By preferring the piggyback direction toward the more populated segment of the bus, one can easily starve the stations located close to its ends.

BIBLIOGRAPHIC NOTES

The concept of CSMA/CD originated with the ALOHA network developed at the University of Hawaii in 1971 (*Abramson* (1985)). Although the ALOHA network lacked the carrier-sense part of the protocols (collisions were detected by the absence of acknowledgments), it essentially followed the rules of CSMA/CD (spontaneous transmissions, randomized backoff). Commercial Ethernet is described in detail in many technical documents, in particular in *Ethernet* (1980). Less technical descriptions of the protocol and its underlying ideas can be found in *Metcalfe and Boggs* (1976), *Shoch et al.* (1982), *Shoch et al.* (1987), and in many books on local networks, e.g., *Tanenbaum* (1988) and *Stallings* (1987a; 1990). Numerous papers have appeared discussing various aspects of Ethernet performance, e.g., *Almes and Lazowska* (1979), *Tobagi and Hunt* (1980), *Bux* (1981), *Coyle and Liu* (1983; 1985), *Takagi and Kleinrock* (1985), *Gonsalves and Tobagi* (1988), and *Tasaka* (1986). The lack of an accurate analytical model of Ethernet caused quite a bit of confusion and, as has been demonstrated by *Boggs, Mogul, and Kent* (1988), some of the theoretical results on Ethernet performance must be treated with a grain of salt. A survey of analytical models of Ethernet and their confrontation with an accurate simulation model can be found in *Armyros* (1992).

Saulnier and Bortscheller (1994) discuss the issue of reusability of simulation models. This discussion may be relevant to our efforts to structure the implementation of Ethernet (section 8.1.2.4) in a way that would let us reuse its major components in other programs.

The Tree Collision Resolution protocol was originally described by *Capetanakis* (1979). *Berard, Gburzyński and Rudnicki* (1991) present a realistic implementation of TCR and show how observers helped to make this implementation correct. The implementation of TCR discussed in sections 8.2.2 and 8.3.2.1 is a modification of the program written by Marcel Berard as part of his M.Sc. thesis.

CSMA/CD-DP was introduced by *Kiesel and Kühn* (1983). The Virtual Token protocol was proposed by *Gopal and Wong* (1985) and investigated by *Gburzyński and Rudnicki* (1987; 1989d). In *Gburzyński and Rudnicki* (1989d), it is shown how to improve the performance characteristics of VT for the medium range of traffic conditions.

Both versions of Piggyback Ethernet were proposed by *Dobosiewicz and Gburzyński* (1990b) and *Dobosiewicz, Gburzyński, and Rudnicki* (1993). A collection of initialization procedures for bus protocols was discussed by *Dobosiewicz, Gburzyński, and Rudnicki* (1991). Among those procedures, the reader will find the startup algorithm for Piggyback Ethernet described in section 8.5.2.3.

Other attempts at improving various performance characteristics of CSMA/CD are discussed by *Kamal* (1987), *Dobosiewicz and Gburzyński* (1988; 1989), and *Molloy* (1985) (see also *Gburzyński and Rudnicki* (1989b)).

PROBLEMS

1. The granularity of time in the implementation of Ethernet (section 8.1.2) is one ITU per one bit insertion time. Reduce this granularity to 1000 ITUs per bit, and run both versions of the program. Are the performance results significantly different?

2. Rewrite the Ethernet transmitter in section 8.1.2.2 in such a way that no inquiries about the past are made. You may want to base your new version of the transmitter on the generic collision transmitter introduced in section 8.3.2.1.

3. Your boss asks you to produce statistics illustrating the average number of stations involved in a collision in Ethernet under a given network load. You argue that such a number is not well defined, but your boss needs these statistics anyway. Why is this number not well defined? Program an observer for Ethernet that would produce results satisfying your boss.

4. Modify the Ethernet transmitter in such a way that it yields to transmissions sensed while obeying the packet spacing rules. According to what we said in section 8.1.1.2, this version of Ethernet may be unfair. Examine the extent of this unfairness for a strictly linear bus.

5. Find closed formulas for the maximum packet access time in TCR, CSMA/CD-DP, and Virtual Token under extreme traffic conditions. How do the three protocols compare with respect to the maximum packet access time?

6. Program a variation of CSMA/CD-DP in which priorities are switched after a collision and the controlled mode ends after N slots. Compare the performance of this version

with the version presented in section 8.3.

7. Design and program detailed observers for CSMA/CD-DP and Virtual Token. These observers should be based on the same concept as the tournament observer for TCR (section 8.2.2.4), i.e., they should look like alternative specifications of the protocols.

8. Program the initialization procedure for Piggyback Ethernet discussed in section 8.5.2.3. Incorporate this procedure into the root process of the protocol implementation in directory ETHER/PiggyA. What is the complexity of the initialization procedure? How many packets must be transmitted before the initialization is complete?

9. Investigate the performance of the protocols presented in this chapter for a biased traffic pattern in which 95 percent of all packets either originate from or are addressed to one distinguished station. Program your traffic pattern in such a way that it can be added to the SMURPH include library (directory IncludeLibrary).

10. Program two bus configurations and put them into IncludeLibrary. With the first configuration, all stations are equally distant from each other. The bus is shaped like a star in which the segments connecting the stations to the center are all of the same length. The second configuration is strictly linear with the stations grouped into two clusters connected at the opposite ends of the bus. Use these configurations to experiment with the protocols discussed in this chapter. Note that Piggyback Ethernet cannot be coupled with a star-shaped bus. How do the protocols perform with your bus configurations?

9

Collision-free Bus Protocols

9.1 UNIDIRECTIONAL CHANNELS

All the protocols presented in this chapter operate on unidirectional channels. Fiber optics provide a natural means of implementing such channels. Unlike a wire that can be tapped into at several places without affecting its signal-passing properties, extracting information from a fiber-optic channel poses a bit of a problem. Although there exist methods of "stealing" a portion of the optical signal from such a channel and letting the rest pass undisturbed,[1] the most natural way to tap into a fiber cable is to cut it and reconnect using a signal repeater. Usually, such a repeater works in one direction only: it receives optical signals from the input segment of the channel, converts them into electric signals that are passed to the station, and uses these electric signals to drive a laser or light modulator that regenerates the input signal on the output segment of the channel. Thus, although there is nothing explicitly unidirectional in the nature of an optical fiber, the way of extracting signals from this medium predisposes it for information transfer in one direction.

We call connection of a station to a fiber-optic channel a tap and try to avoid confusing it with a port. Realistically, according to what we just said, such a connection is implemented using a pair of ports: the input port and the output port. We say that a tap is *passive* if it always relays verbatim whatever appears on its input port to the output port. Besides, a passive tap can be used to sense the input port and (perhaps somewhat contrary to the adjective) to insert a new signal into the output port. The inactive character of a passive tap does not mean

---

[1]Note that each connection of this sort attenuates the signal.

that the tap can only be used to sense the bus; it rather reflects the permanent status of the connection between the two channel segments. Thus, an *active* tap in our terminology is allowed to disconnect the input segment of the channel from the output segment. When required by the protocol, an active tap can be told not to relay the signals arriving on its input port to the output port. Taps of this sort are used in ring networks (discussed in chapter 10). For example, in FDDI, a station holding the token disconnects the ring, which can be viewed as a single, looped, unidirectional channel segmented with active taps.

Because of the built-in notion of a unidirectional link (section 3.2.1), passive taps can be modeled in SMURPH by single ports. This approach simplifies the implementation and relieves the implementor from the responsibility to program the tap's behavior. To remove unnecessary complexity from our programs, we represent undirectional channels with all-passive taps by unidirectional SMURPH links with a single port per tap. Unidirectional link types in SMURPH exist exactly for this purpose. The reader should keep in mind that they are merely convenient and innocent simplifications: the unidirectional nature of a real-life unidirectional channel is a consequence of the physics of taps, not an inherent property of the channel medium.

All the protocols discussed in this chapter are based on unidirectional channels in which all taps are passive. Consequently, in the SMURPH implementations of these protocols, each unidirectional channel is represented by a unidirectional link with one port per tap. Thus, for this chapter, we may agree to equate taps with ports. Unless said otherwise, the term *port* used to denote a tap refers to a pair of actual ports in a real-life implementation.

It should be noted that there exist networking concepts and workable solutions based on the purely optical approach to fiber-optic channels. With this methodology, channels are not segmented: the signal travels through the network as a light wave and is not converted back and forth at each tap. In particular, it is conceivable to use optical fibers as bidirectional, ether-type media, similar to the coaxial cable used in standard Ethernet. However, even those purely optical networks usually assume that fiber channels are unidirectional. As we will see, the unidirectional character of fiber-optic media is a powerful feature, which opens a completely new window of opportunity for MAC-level protocols. The first protocol discussed in this chapter is Expressnet, which well illustrates the advantageous properties of unidirectional channels.

9.2   EXPRESSNET

In chapter 8 we discussed a number of protocols for bus networks based on collision detection. We also demonstrated some limitations of these protocols, the most painful of them being the need to inflate short packets to a minimum size that makes all collisions detectable by the parties involved. Although Piggyback Ethernet (section 8.5) avoids inflation as long as the network remains in the controlled mode (i.e., there is an uninterrupted offered load of a sufficient intensity to provide a steady supply of leaders), packets transmitted in the uncontrolled mode must still be inflated. Besides, Piggyback Ethernet requires a relatively complicated and expensive initialization procedure that must be repeated whenever a new station is added to or disappears from the network. People generally agree that collision protocols are unsuitable for very fast networks, because of the unacceptable penalty of packet inflation. Therefore, other solutions must be sought for networks with the propagation diameter L significantly larger than the typical packet size.

9.2.1   The Protocol

In Expressnet all stations are connected to a single unidirectional bus. We say that this bus is single because it can be represented in SMURPH as a single unidirectional link. In reality, the bus is built of several segments separated with passive taps (and repeaters) at every station. Each station has two taps (ports) to the bus (see figure 9.1). Note that a network based on a single unidirectional bus could not get away with just one port per station. Each tap p on such a bus divides it into the upstream and downstream segments with respect to p. A tap can only receive information from upstream and can only transmit downstream. Thus, if all stations are to be reachable pairwise, the bus must visit each station at least twice in such a way that for every two stations s_1 and s_2, there is a tap belonging to s_2 located downstream from a tap belonging to s_1.[2] This is what happens in Expressnet. The bus in Expressnet (see figure 9.1) is usually presented as an S-shaped unidirectional link that visits all stations once, then turns and visits all stations once again, in the same order as before.

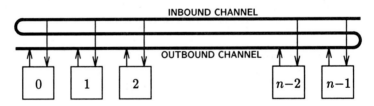

Figure 9.1   The topology of Expressnet

The bus is logically divided into two parts: the *outbound portion*, on which the stations transmit their packets, and the *inbound portion*, from which the packets are received. Of course, both portions are just fragments of the same single unidirectional bus, and the distinction is purely logical.

The protocol of Expressnet is based on the following hardware prerequisites, which imply a specific organization of the bus taps:

- All taps are passive, i.e., they always relay signals arriving from the upstream segment of the bus to the downstream segment.

---

[2]This statement must remain true when s_1 and s_2 are exchanged.

- A station must be able to receive packets from the tap connected to the inbound portion of the bus. Therefore, this tap must pass the relayed signals to the station.

- A station must be able to transmit packets on the tap connected to the outbound portion of the bus. Simultaneously, the station must detect signals arriving from the upstream segment of the tap. It is sufficient if the station can just learn whether there is a signal (transmission) arriving from upstream; there is no need to interpret such a signal.

A station willing to transmit a packet monitors its outbound port, i.e., the tap connected to the outbound portion of the bus. To be allowed to transmit, the station must sense the end of an activity in the outbound port. This event is denoted by EAC (for end of activity).[3] A station in Expressnet is not allowed to transmit spontaneously, e.g., upon sensing silence in the outbound port. Transmissions are only permitted at very specific moments marked by the EAC events on the outbound ports. Clearly, the protocol must guarantee a supply of such events, even in the absence of regular[4] traffic in the network.

Assume that a station s has just sensed EAC and decides to start a packet transmission. During some initial period of the transfer denoted by Δ_p, the station transmits a *preamble*, which contains no vital information and can be partly destroyed with no detrimental effect on the packet reception at the receiver. As in Ethernet (and other protocols discussed so far), the main role of the preamble is to tune the receiver's clock in such a way that it will properly strobe the individual bits of the packet (section 8.1.1.4). In Expressnet the preamble has a secondary purpose. If during the transmission of the preamble the station detects another activity arriving from the upstream segment of the outbound channel, it immediately aborts the preamble and defers the transfer attempt until the next EAC event on the outbound port.[5] In simple words, the station yields to transmissions arriving from upstream. Note that the preamble of a packet coming from upstream can be partially destroyed by an aborted transfer attempt of a downstream station. This happens because a station yielding to an incoming transmission needs some time to recognize the activity on its tap. The preamble bits arriving during that time will be damaged by the interfering preamble bits transmitted by the downstream station. Fortunately, a preamble can be damaged at most once; its damaged initial portion (although most likely useless for clock synchronization) will nonetheless be recognized as an activity by any subsequent downstream stations trying to come in

---

[3]Note that the EAC event does not correspond to any standard port event in SMURPH (section 6.2). Although SILENCE comes close to EAC (it occurs at the end of an activity that is followed by a silence period), SILENCE also occurs immediately if the inquired port has been silent for any period of time.

[4]Meaning "originating from the Client."

[5]A purist would notice that the two transfers actually *collide* and therefore Expressnet is a collision protocol. Because of the specific nature of this collision, which is much less destructive than a collision in a CSMA/CD protocol, we feel that Expressnet fits much better into the present chapter than into the previous one.

with their own preambles.

According to the simple yielding rules, the leftmost (i.e., most upstream—see figure 9.1) backlogged station having a packet ready to transmit preempts all the downstream stations. To keep the protocol fair, the winning station is allowed to transmit only one packet at a time. Then it has to wait until all the backlogged stations located downstream have been given an opportunity to transmit their packets. We say that a station that has transmitted its packet successfully must wait until the end of the current round before it is allowed to transmit its next packet.

Imagine that one station, say s, detects the EAC event in the outbound channel and transmits its packet without being preempted by an upstream station. The EAC event generated by the end of the packet propagates to the right (downstream), and the first backlogged station located downstream from s will append its packet immediately after the packet inserted by s. This scenario repeats until all backlogged stations situated downstream with respect to the first winner transmit their packets on the outbound channel. All these packets form a *train* of packets, which can be viewed as a single continuous activity.[6] Eventually, the train will reach the inbound channel and pass through it. Every station will hear all the packets of the train and receive the ones addressed to it. Moreover, every station will be able to detect the end of the train—a long enough period of silence[7] following the last packet.

In summary, the operation of the protocol consists in interpreting two types of events: EAC on the outbound channel and ETR (for end of train) on the inbound channel. Upon detection of EAC, a backlogged station is allowed to start inserting the preamble of its packet into the outbound port. The length of the preamble (Δ_p) should be sufficient to compensate for the worst-case latency of a station in responding to the EAC event and for the time required to detect an interfering activity arriving from upstream. Moreover, the undisturbed portion of a damaged preamble should be sufficiently long to fulfill its primary purpose, i.e., to prepare the receiver's clock for the packet reception. When the preamble has been transmitted with no interference from upstream, the station may assume that it has acquired access to the bus and its packet will be sent successfully.

After a successful transmission, the station waits for the ETR event on the inbound port. This event is triggered whenever an activity sensed on the port is followed by a sufficiently long period of silence (we denote it by Δ_t). This means that no more stations will append packets to the train; thus, a new round can be started.

To start a new round, the stations need an activity whose end will trigger the first EAC event. This activity can be provided in two ways. One possible solution is to have the most upstream station send a packet preamble, even if it has no packet

---

[6]Actually, the individual packets of the train can be separated by short silence periods (see the next footnote).

[7]If packets in the train are allowed to be separated by gaps, this period must be longer than the maximum gap duration.

to transmit. If the station happens to be backlogged, this preamble will be followed by a packet, which will constitute the "engine" of the new train. Otherwise, the end of the preamble will be perceived as *EAC* by the first downstream station having a packet ready to transmit. Note that if no station happens to be ready for the round, the end of the preamble inserted by the most upstream station will eventually arrive at the station's inbound port, where, in due time, it will trigger the *ETR* event. This scenario will repeat until a station becomes ready.

To avoid delegating one station as a round starter (which may have a negative impact on the network's reliability), all stations can play this role. Note that any station detecting the *ETR* event (on its inbound port) can insert a preamble (on the outbound port) to start a new round. Given a station *s*, all such preambles sent by the stations located upstream with respect to *s* will arrive at *s* at (approximately) the same time. At least, this is what will happen if the distances between ports in the outbound portion of the bus are the same as the corresponding distances in the inbound portion. With this approach, no station is singled out, and all stations execute exactly the same protocol. One exception is the initialization phase: the most upstream station still has to generate the startup activity that launches the very first round.

The resemblance of the train construction procedure in Expressnet to piggy-backing packets in Piggyback Ethernet (section 8.5) is impossible to miss. Both tricks are based on the concept of synchronizing transmissions to ends of activities in the bus. In Piggyback Ethernet, the bus is bidirectional, there is no notion of "upstream," and consequently the preemption of one transfer by another cannot be reasonably implemented by yielding while transmitting. In a network built on a bidirectional bus, an aborted preamble would propagate in both directions, and it could damage packets transmitted in the upstream segment of the bus long after it was aborted. Thus, stations in Piggyback Ethernet delay their transfer attempts to be able to yield in a nondestructive way—by sensing a higher priority transmission in advance, instead of interfering with it and backing off later. In Expressnet this is unnecessary because collisions are not destructive: there is always a winner to which the other parties yield on the fly.

9.2.2   The Implementation

Directory BUS/Expressnet in Examples contains an implementation of Expressnet, built according to the rules outlined in section 9.2.1. One element of this implementation that should be discussed first is the model of the S-shaped bus.

9.2.2.1   The bus. The protocol operates on a network whose backbone consists of an S-shaped bus (figure 9.1). To implement this bus topology using the modular approach introduced in section 8.1.2.4, we start by isolating the part of the station structure responsible for interfacing the station to the bus. This part has the following simple layout:

```
station SBusInterface virtual {
  Port *OBus, *IBus;
  void configure ();
};
```

The two ports will be built by `configure` upon the station's setup. Before the stations can be created, the root process must call a function (similar to `initBus` from section 8.1.2.4) that will build the link and initialize some variables needed by the subsequent invocations of `configure`. Following are these variables together with the function that prepares the ground for the dynamic configuration of the network backbone:

```
static Link *TheBus;
static RATE TR;
static DISTANCE D, Turn;
static int NP, NC;
static SBusInterface **Created;
void initSBus (RATE r, DISTANCE l, DISTANCE t, int np) {
  TheBus = create PLink (np+np);
  TR = r;
  D = l / (np-1);
  Turn = t;
  NP = np;
  NC = 0;
  Created = new SBusInterface* [NP];
};
```

The first argument of `initSBus` (r) gives the transmission rate (in ITUs per bit), which is the same for all outbound ports.[8] The second argument (1) specifies the bus length as the distance in ITUs between the two extreme stations. Thus, this is not the actual length of the link representing the bus, but rather the common length of the outbound channel and the inbound channel. Note that these parts must be of the same length if rounds are to be started independently by all stations (section 9.2.1). The specified length of the link is divided by the number of stations minus one, i.e., the number of segments in one channel. The result, which is stored in D, gives the length of one link segment separating a pair of neighboring stations. Argument t gives the length of the bus fragment connecting the outbound channel to the inbound channel, i.e., the turning segment of the link. The length of this segment may be the same as the common length of the two channels (if the stations are arranged linearly and the bus is actually laid as shown in figure 9.1), but generally it can be arbitrary. For example, the stations can be arranged into a ring with the extreme stations located very close to one another; in such a case, the turning

---

[8]The transmission rate of an inbound port is irrelevant, as no packets are ever transmitted on such a port.

segment will be very short. It is always possible to make it as short as the distance between two closest stations in the network.

The last argument of initSBus (np) specifies the number of stations that will be connected to the bus. The first statement of the function creates the link representing the bus; the number of ports in this link is equal to 2 × np. The transmission rate, the length of the turning segment, and the number of stations are saved in the global variables TR, Turn, and NP, respectively. Note that the link type is PLink, which forces a strictly linear topology of the link (sections 3.2.1, 3.3.3). D is set to the distance between two neighboring stations, which is assumed to be the same for all neighbors. Pointer Created represents an array of pointers to SBusInterface. This array will be used to locate the SBusInterface parts of all stations created so far, the number of these stations being kept in NC. The organization of the "network configuration" part of the protocol program follows the same lines as the linear bus interface discussed in section 8.1.2.4.

A station is configured into the network by calling the configure method of its SBusInterface; this operation will be performed by the station's setup method. The code of configure follows:

```
void SBusInterface::configure () {
  int i;
  SBusInterface *s;
  Created [NC++] = this;
  if (NC == NP) {
    for (i = 0; i < NP; i++) {
      s = Created [i];
      s->OBus = create (i) Port (TR);
      s->OBus->connect (TheBus);
      if (i > 0) Created [i-1] -> OBus -> setDTo (s->OBus, D);
    }
    for (i = 0; i < NP; i++) {
      s = Created [i];
      s->IBus = create (i) Port;
      s->IBus->connect (TheBus);
      if (i == 0)
        Created [NP-1] -> OBus -> setDTo (s->IBus, Turn);
      else
        Created [i-1] -> IBus -> setDTo (s->IBus, D);
    }
    delete Created;
    TheStation = idToStation (NP-1);
  }
};
```

As long as NC (the number of stations created so far) is less than NP, the method just keeps adding the pointers to the created stations (their SBusInterface parts) to `Created`. When the number of created station reaches NP, which means that all stations have been built, `configure` connects the stations to the bus. This operation is performed in two `for` loops. The first loop creates the outbound ports, connects them to the link representing the bus, and sets distances between these ports. Recall from section 3.2.1 that the order in which ports are connected to a unidirectional link determines the direction of the link segments separating these ports. Thus, station 0 is the most upstream station, and the station with the highest `Id` is located downstream with respect to all the other stations. As the link type is `PLink`, there is no need to define distances between all pairs of ports (section 3.3.3); therefore, only pairs of immediate neighbors are considered, and the distance between each such pair is set to D. The second `for` loop takes care of the inbound ports, which are processed in the same way as their predecessors. The distance from the last outbound port to the first inbound port is set to `Turn`, which represents the length of the "turning" piece of the bus.

After all ports have been processed, array `Created` (which was allocated dynamically by `initSBus`) is no longer needed, and the method deletes it. The last statement executed by the method may seem a bit strange. To understand why it is needed (or perhaps just may be needed), note that `configure` implicitly modifies the current station pointer. In fact, the method does it a number of times—whenever it executes `create` in one of the `for` loops—and, according to what we said in section 3.1.3, each such modification extends beyond the context of the corresponding `create`. Note that the `for` loops are only executed when the method is called for the last time; thus, before the first loop is entered, `TheStation` points to the station number NP − 1. To clean up after `configure` and make sure that `TheStation` is left intact when the method returns to its caller (i.e., the setup method of the last created station), we explicitly reset `TheStation` pointer to the original value.[9] Such tricks are quite legitimate (and sometimes necessary) during the network creation phase.

The interface to the S-shaped bus just described has been isolated from the protocol program and put into two library files `sbus.h` and `sbus.c`. These files are included by our implementation of Expressnet, which can be found in directory **BUS/Expressnet** of SMURPH **Examples**.

9.2.2.2 The protocol. All stations in Expressnet have an identical layout, described by the following data structure:

---

[9]By a fortunate coincidence, the last `create` operation executed in the second `for` loop implicitly sets `TheStation` to point to the last created station. Although by this coincidence the explicit recovery of the original value of `TheStation` becomes unnecessary, it is strongly recommended to perform this recovery habitually when the pointer is changed at all in a method or function called during the network creation phase. The function's caller does not see what the function is doing, and it may rely on the previous value of `TheStation` in an explicit or implicit way. For example, having called `configure`, the station's setup method in Expressnet (section 9.2.2.2) proceeds to initialize its `Client` interface portion. As part of this initialization, the station's packet buffer is created and implicitly assigned to the "current" station. Had the current station pointer been modified before the buffer creation, the buffer would have been assigned to the wrong station.

```
station ExStation : SBusInterface, ClientInterface {
  Packet Preamble;
  void setup () {
    SBusInterface::configure ();
    ClientInterface::configure ();
    Preamble.fill (NONE, NONE, PrmbL);
  };
};
```

The SBusInterface portion of the station type comes with the specification of the S-shaped bus. ClientInterface represents the traffic-specific fragment of the station's structure (section 8.1.2.4). The only local attribute of ExStation not inherited from the two interface classes is Preamble, a buffer holding a dummy packet representing the preamble. This buffer is filled by the station's setup method (operation fill—section 5.2.3), and its contents remain untouched throughout the entire protocol operation. Note that preambles in Expressnet play a special role (sometimes a preamble is transmitted alone, not followed by a packet), and it is necessary to separate them from packet headers.

Now we list the global variables representing the numerical parameters of the protocol. As viewed by the protocol, these variables are in fact constants. They are set by the root process before the protocol is started, and their values never change from then on.

```
Long MinPL, MaxPL, FrameL, PrmbL;
TIME EOTDelay;
```

The first three numbers are the standard packet acquisition parameters (e.g., section 8.1.2.2). Note that this time FrameL does not include the preamble length, which is stored separately in PrmbL. EOTDelay corresponds to Δ_t (section 9.2.1); it gives the length of the silence period needed to detect the end-of-train event on an inbound port. Having sensed that much silence after the end of a packet, a station may assume that the packet terminates the current train.

The receiver part of the protocol is not very interesting and, except for the difference in the station type and the name of the port pointer, equivalent to the receiver part of the Ethernet protocol (section 8.1.2.2). It may be worthwhile to look at the latter again, in its Expressnet-specific version. The type of the receiver process is defined as follows:

```
process Receiver (ExStation) {
  Port *Bus;
  void setup () { Bus = S->IBus; };
  states {WPacket, Rcvd};
  perform;
};
```

and its code method is a carbon copy of the Receiver code method from section 8.1.2.2:

```
Receiver::perform {
  state WPacket:
    Bus->wait (EMP, Rcvd);
  state Rcvd:
    Client->receive (ThePacket, ThePort);
    skipto (WPacket);
};
```

The transmitter part of Expressnet is organized into two processes: the end-of-train monitor (type EOTMonitor) responsible for detecting end-of-train events on the station's inbound port, and the transmitter (type Transmitter), which takes care of transmitting preambles and regular packets. If a copy of EOTMonitor runs at every station, we get the version of the protocol in which all stations behave identically and the responsibility for starting rounds is spread among all stations in the network. Alternatively, the monitor process can run in a single copy at the most upstream station, in which case the rounds will be started by this station only. The decision is left to the discretion of the Root process, to be made at the moment when the protocol processes are created and assigned to their stations. Let us start from the transmitter process. Its type is defined as follows:

```
process Transmitter (ExStation) {
  Packet *Preamble, *Buffer;
  Port *Bus;
  EOTMonitor *EOTrain;
  void setup (EOTMonitor *et = NULL) {
    Bus = S->OBus;
    Buffer = &(S->Buffer);
    Preamble = &(S->Preamble);
    EOTrain = et;
  };
  states {Wait, CheckBuf, Transmit, Yield, PDone, XDone, Error};
  perform;
};
```

As usual, the pointers to the relevant attributes of the station owning the process are copied by the process's setup method to private pointers. Note that Bus is set to point to the outbound port of the station: this is the only port accessed by the transmitter. The setup method defines an optional argument, which, if specified, should be a pointer to the train monitor process run at the station. This pointer is stored in EOTrain, from which it can be used to receive signals from the monitor. If EOTrain is NULL, no monitor is run at the station, and the transmitter should not await end-of-train events.[10] The code method of Transmitter is as follows:

---

[10]This can only happen in the protocol version, in which ETR events are handled exclusively by the most upstream station.

```
Transmitter::perform {
  state Wait:
    Bus->wait (EOT, CheckBuf);
    if (EOTrain != NULL)
      EOTrain->wait (SIGNAL, Transmit);
  state CheckBuf:
    if (S->ready (MinPL, MaxPL, FrameL))
      proceed Transmit;
    else
      skipto Wait;
  state Transmit:
    Bus->transmit (Preamble, PDone);
    Bus->wait (COLLISION, Yield);
  state Yield:
    Bus->abort ();
    skipto Wait;
  state PDone:
    if (S->ready (MinPL, MaxPL, FrameL)) {
      Bus->abort ();
      Bus->transmit (Buffer, XDone);
      Bus->wait (COLLISION, Error);
    } else {
      Bus->stop ();
      skipto Wait;
    }
  state XDone:
    Bus->stop ();
    Buffer->release ();
    skipto Wait;
  state Error:
    excptn ("Illegal collision");
};
```

The process starts in state Wait, where it awaits an EOT event on the outbound port, i.e., a moment when the station may try to transmit a packet. The *EAC* event required by the protocol (section 9.2.1) is represented by EOT. The implementation will make sure that all activities (packets) that are expected to trigger *EAC* are properly terminated with end-of-packet marks (section 6.1.2.1).

If the monitor process is running at the station (EOTrain is not NULL), the transmitter also awaits a signal from the monitor indicating that a new round is to be started. Assume first that the transmitter is awakened in state CheckBuf by an EOT event. If there is a message queued at the station (ready returns YES— section 8.1.2.4), the process continues in state Transmit. Otherwise, the transmitter moves back to Wait, where it awaits another EOT event or a signal to start a new round. As the transition from `Wait` to `CheckBuf` takes no time, the process must use `skipto` for the transition from `CheckBuf` to `Wait`, to make sure that the last EOT condition has disappeared from the port.

If the station has a ready packet when the EOT event occurs on its outbound port, the process transits from `CheckBuf` to `Transmit`. Another way for the transmitter to get to `Transmit` is to receive a signal from the end-of-train monitor in state `Wait`. In both cases, while in state `Transmit`, the process transmits a preamble and monitors the port for a collision. A collision means that another transmission (packet preamble) arrives from upstream and, according to the protocol rules, the station must yield to this transmission. In such a case, the process moves to state `Yield`, where it aborts the preamble and gets back to state `Wait` (via `skipto`). If the preamble has been transmitted successfully (state `PDone`), the transmitter calls `ready` to determine whether the station has a packet to transmit. Note that this need not be the case if state `Transmit` was entered in response to the end-of-train signal from the monitor. If there is a packet awaiting transmission, the process aborts the preamble and starts transmitting the packet. The preamble is aborted so that its end will not trigger EOT events on the outbound ports of the downstream stations. This role will be taken over by the end of the packet following the preamble. As a safety measure, while transmitting a packet, the process monitors the port for a collision. Such a collision is illegal and, if detected, is treated as an error condition (state `Error`).

If the station has no packet to transmit in state `PDone`, the role of the preamble is to start a new round. In such a case, the preamble must be properly terminated: its end must be perceived by downstream stations as the *EAC* event required by the protocol. Thus, the transmitter terminates the preamble by `stop` and moves back to state `Wait`. As the transmitter knows that it cannot take advantage of the current EOT (*EAC*) event (there is no packet to transmit), it uses `skipto` to ignore this event. Note that if multiple stations are authorized to start a new round, all the preambles except the one sent by the most upstream station will be aborted. Consequently, there will be only one *EAC* event starting the round.

A successful packet transmission results in a transition from state `PDone` to `XDone`. In state `XDone`, the process terminates the transmission, releases the packet buffer, and moves to state `Wait`.

The monitor process intercepts all EOT events on its station's tap and identifies those that correspond to *ETR* events, according to the protocol rules. The process is declared as follows:

```
process EOTMonitor (ExStation) {
  Port *Bus;
  void setup () {
    Bus = S->IBus;
  };
  states {Wait, Count, Signal, Retry};
```

```
        perform;
      };
```

and it executes the following code method:

```
      EOTMonitor::perform {
        state Wait:
          Bus->wait (EOT, Count);
        state Count:
          Timer->wait (EOTDelay, Signal);
          Bus->wait (ACTIVITY, Retry);
        state Signal:
          if (signal () != ACCEPTED)
            excptn ("End of train signal not accepted");
        transient Retry:
          skipto Wait;
      };
```

Whenever an EOT event appears on the station's inbound port, the process moves to state Count, where it waits for two events: a timeout of EOTDelay ITUs and an ACTIVITY on the port. If the Timer event is triggered before ACTIVITY, it means that the packet is followed by at least EOTDelay ITUs of silence. The end of such a packet should mark an *ETR* event. Thus, the monitor transits to state Signal, where it delivers the signal awaited by the transmitter. Note that if the protocol operates correctly, the signal must be awaited when it is deposited in the monitor's repository; this requirement is asserted by the process.

Packets separated by less than EOTDelay ITUs are assumed to belong to the same train. Consequently, if an activity is sensed on the port before the timeout expires, the monitor process will transit to state Retry and then to Wait, to await another EOT event. The detour transition via Retry is needed to skip the last EOT event (section 4.5.1) in the case when the activity immediately follows the previous packet.

9.2.2.3 The root process.

The reader may want to look at the files in directory BUS/Expressnet of SMURPH Examples to see how the different pieces of the Expressnet program have been put together. The last element of this program that deserves a few words of comment is the root process, whose complete definition is as follows:

```
      process Root {
        states {Start, Stop};
        perform {
          int NNodes, i;
          Long NMessages;
          DISTANCE BusLength, TurnLength;
          EOTMonitor *et;
```

```
state Start:
  readIn (TRate);
  setEtu (TRate);
  readIn (CTolerance);
  setTolerance (CTolerance);
  readIn (NNodes);
  readIn (BusLength);
  readIn (TurnLength);
  BusLength *= TRate;
  TurnLength *= TRate;
  initSBus (TRate, BusLength, TurnLength, NNodes);
  readIn (MinPL);
  readIn (MaxPL);
  readIn (FrameL);
  readIn (PrmbL);
  readIn (EOTDelay);
  EOTDelay *= TRate;
  initTraffic ();
  for (i = 0; i < NNodes; i++) create ExStation;
  for (i = 0; i < NStations; i++) {
    et = create (i) EOTMonitor;
    create (i) Transmitter (et);
    create (i) Receiver ();
    if (i == 0) et->signal ();
  }
  readIn (NMessages);
  setLimit (NMessages);
  Kernel->wait (DEATH, Stop);
state Stop:
  System->printTop ("Network topology");
  Client->printDef ("Traffic parameters");
  Client->printPfm ();
  idToLink (0)->printPfm ("Bus performance measures");
  };
};
```

The structure of this process resembles closely the structure of other root processes presented in chapter 8. The only fragment that may call for some explanation is the **for** loop creating the protocol processes. For each station, EOTMonitor is created first, its pointer saved in variable et, which is later passed as an argument to the Transmitter's setup method. This way, each station runs a copy of the monitor process, and new rounds are started by all stations. Note that the very first round must be started explicitly by Root. This is accomplished by depositing a signal (section 4.6.2.1) at the monitor process of station 0, which is the most upstream

station in the network. This way, when the transmitter of station 0 wakes up in
state Wait for the first time, it will receive an immediate end-of-train signal from
the monitor. By rewriting the for loop in the following way,

```
et = create (0) EOTMonitor;
et->signal ();
for (i = 0; i < NStations; i++) {
   create (i) Transmitter (et);
   et = NULL;
   create (i) Receiver ();
}
```

we can produce the alternative version of the protocol in which rounds are only
started by the most upstream station, i.e., station number zero.

9.3   FASNET

There exist several bus topologies applicable to networks built of unidirectional,
fiber-optic links. As we noticed in section 9.2.1, the straightforward, single-link
topology will not work for a unidirectional medium: each station must have at least
two taps if all stations are to be reachable from every station. In Expressnet there is
a single unidirectional link that folds and visits each station twice. Another common
solution is the dual-bus topology, i.e., a configuration of two separate unidirectional
links laid side by side as a single logical bus. The directions of the two links are
opposite. A station willing to transmit a packet selects the link that offers a path
to the destination. Thus, the station must know on which side of the (logical) bus
the recipient is located. The dual-bus topology is used in several networks, notably
in Fasnet and DQDB.

9.3.1   The Protocol

The topology of Fasnet, which is a typical dual-bus topology, is presented in figure 9.2. The stations are interconnected by a bus consisting of two unidirectional
links. We refer to these links as the *LR* channel (used for transfers from left to
right) and the *RL* channel (used for transfers in the opposite direction).[11] Each
station has two taps, one tap to each channel.

Fasnet is a slotted protocol. This means that packets can only be transmitted
within predefined frames that are inserted into the links at regular intervals. The
extreme stations, besides executing the same protocol as the other stations, are
responsible for generating slots. A slot is a special sequence of signals indicating that
whatever follows is a fixed-length silent frame where a packet can be accommodated.
Fixed-length packets placed into slot frames are sometimes called *segments*.

The leftmost station inserts slots into the *LR* channel; the other channel is
taken care of by the rightmost station. A slot starts with a slot marker, indicating

---

[11]Of course, *left* and *right* are just labels assigned to the two ends of the bus.

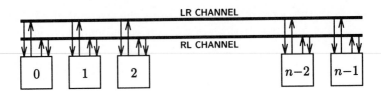

Figure 9.2 The topology of Fasnet

the beginning of the slot, followed by a header containing room for three binary flags. For two consecutive slots, the marker of the second slot is separated from the header of the previous one by a period of silence long enough to provide room for a segment together with its specific header and trailing checksum. The segment (viewed as a slot payload) is furnished with its own header, e.g., identifying the sender and the destination.

The network operates in a symmetric manner with respect to the direction of transfer. Thus, we only consider here transfers from left to right; transfers in the opposite direction are performed in exactly the same way, with the words *left* and *right* interchanged.

Consider the leftmost station on the bus, which inserts slots into the *LR* channel. These slots are organized into *cycles*. The purpose of one cycle is to give every backlogged station willing to transmit a segment to the right an opportunity to do so without interference. To ensure fairness, each ready station is allowed to transmit only one segment per cycle. This property makes the protocol somewhat similar to Expressnet, in which a station is allowed to transmit only one packet per round.   One of the three flags in the slot header is labeled *FULL*. Its role is to indicate whether the slot carries a segment (*FULL* = 1) or is empty and can accommodate a segment (*FULL* = 0). The other two flags are called *BOC* (for beginning of a cycle) and *SNC* (for start a new cycle). The only restriction on the order in which these flags occur in the slot header is that *BOC* must precede *FULL*.

When the protocol starts, station 0 (the leftmost station) generates the first slot with *BOC* set to 1 and the remaining two flags cleared. A station that has a ready segment addressed toward the right end of the bus awaits the arrival of a slot with the *BOC* flag set to 1. In other words, the station awaits the beginning of a cycle. From now on, the station monitors all subsequent slots and inserts the segment in the first empty slot (*FULL* = 0) that comes along. This empty slot can be the slot with the *BOC* flag set; hence the condition that *BOC* must precede *FULL* in the slot header. Having sensed the first slot with the *FULL* flag cleared, the station changes the contents of this flag to 1 and inserts the segment into the slot's frame. Technically, the search for an empty slot is performed in such a way that the station sets the *FULL* flag unconditionally to 1 in every slot passing by and simultaneously checks whether the overwritten value was 0.[12] This operation

---

[12]On a segmented, unidirectional fiber-optic channel, it is possible to perform these two steps

has no effect on a full slot. It changes the status of an empty slot to "full" and notifies the station that the slot has been found empty. Note that station 0 (the slot generator) also participates in the game. If station 0 is ready when it creates the first slot of a cycle (with $BOC = 1$), it will place its segment in this very slot.

Eventually, the starting slot of a cycle will arrive at the rightmost station. This station will see a train of full slots terminated by an empty slot. As each station is allowed to transmit only one segment per cycle, the maximum length of such a train is $N - 1$.[13] Having detected the first empty slot following the train of segments transmitted in the last cycle, the right end station concludes that the cycle is over. Then it signals the opposite end station that a new cycle should be started. This is accomplished by setting the SNC (start of cycle) flag in the next slot going to the left. When the leftmost station receives this slot, it will set the BOC flag in the next slot going to the right, effectively starting a new cycle.

Note that the SNC request is triggered by the first empty slot following BOC. In particular, if no station has a packet ready to transmit, the slot carrying the BOC flag will be empty, and the right end station will decide to send SNC as soon as it has examined the $FULL$ flag of this slot. Subsequent empty slots arriving at the rightmost station do not trigger SNC until the next slot with the BOC flag set is received. Starting from that moment, the station will monitor all slots, including the first slot of the new cycle, to detect the first empty slot marking the cycle's end.

The requirement that BOC precede $FULL$ in the slot header can be relaxed if stations are allowed to buffer fragments of slot headers and modify bits retroactively. We say that a protocol is delay-free, if no bits must be delayed at intermediate stations, e.g., to be modified based on some condition that can only be evaluated after some further bits have been looked at. Fasnet can be implemented in a delay-free manner, provided that the flags in the slot header are ordered properly. The operation of setting a single bit to 1 on the fly and simultaneously determining its previous contents is assumed to be delay-free.

9.3.2   The Implementation

Compared to the protocols discussed so far, Fasnet has two novel features. First, it is based on a dual-bus topology (figure 9.2), which has not been implemented yet. Second, the library files specifying the uniform traffic pattern shared by all previous implementations (`utraffic.h` and `utraffic.c`—section 8.1.2.4) need some adjustments before they can be incorporated into our implementation of Fasnet. This results from the fact that a Fasnet station runs two transmitters, each transmitter servicing one direction, and its `Client` interface consists of two buffers. Moreover, Fasnet is the first slotted protocol discussed in this book.

---

at the same time; clearly, the operation would not be feasible on an ether-type broadcast medium.

[13]As usual, N is the number of stations in the network. Note that the rightmost station never sends a segment to the right.

9.3.2.1   The dual bus.   By analogy to Expressnet, whose bus is said to be S-shaped, we use the letter "H" to identify the topology of Fasnet's backbone. Each station in Fasnet has two taps, one tap to each bus channel implemented as a single unidirectional link. As in Expressnet, which is also a delay-free protocol, each tap can be modeled by a single port (section 9.1).

The include library of SMURPH (IncludeLibrary) contains two files called hbus.h and hbus.c, which describe a parameterized configuration of the H-shaped bus with equally spaced stations. These files are used in two other protocols discussed later in the present chapter. The relevant portion of the ".h" file of this pair is as follows:

```
#define LRBus 0
#define RLBus 1
station HBusInterface virtual {
  Port *Bus [2];
  void configure ();
};
void initHBus (RATE, TIME, int);
```

The two symbolic constants identify bus channels and directions. They are used to index the two-element array of port pointers interfacing the station to the channels. As usual, the actual ports are brought into existence by configure when the station is created.

The other file, hbus.c, defines the configure method and the global function initHBus, which creates the bus links and prepares some variables for the subsequent invocations of configure. It has the following contents:

```
static Link *TheBus [2];
static RATE TR;
static DISTANCE D;
static int NP, NC;
static HBusInterface **Created;
void initHBus (RATE r, TIME 1, int np) {
  int i;
  for (i = 0; i < 2; i++) TheBus [i] = create PLink (np);
  TR = r;
  D = 1 / (np-1);
  NP = np;
  NC = 0;
  Created = new HBusInterface* [NP];
};
void HBusInterface::configure () {
  int i;
  HBusInterface *s;
  Created [NC++] = this;
```

```
  if (NC == NP) {
    for (i = 0; i < NP; i++) {
      s = Created [i];
      s->Bus [LRBus] = create (i) Port (TR);
      s->Bus [LRBus] -> connect (TheBus [LRBus]);
      if (i > 0)
        Created [i-1] -> Bus [LRBus] -> setDTo (s->Bus [LRBus], D);
    };
    for (i = NP-1; i >= 0; i--) {
      s = Created [i];
      s->Bus [RLBus] = create (i) Port (TR);
      s->Bus [RLBus] -> connect (TheBus [RLBus]);
      if (i < NP-1)
        Created [i+1] -> Bus [RLBus] -> setDTo (s->Bus [RLBus], D);
    };
    TheStation = idToStation (NP-1);
  };
};
```

All the global static variables are set by initHBus. TheBus is a two-pointer array identifying the unidirectional links that represent the bus channels. The number of ports on each channel is determined by the third argument of initHBus, which gives the number of stations. The first argument of the function specifies the common transmission rate of all ports. The second argument (1) tells the bus length in ITUs. This length is divided by np − 1 (the number of segments in a channel) to give the length D of a single segment separating two neighboring stations. Array Created (allocated dynamically by initHBus) is used by configure to store pointers to the HBusInterface portions of the stations created so far. The number of elements (pointers) currently stored in Created is kept in NC. This variable is incremented by configure each time the method is called, i.e., each time a new station is added to the network.

The actual operation of configuring the stations into a network is postponed until all the stations have been created (NC reaches NP). Then configure executes two for loops. The first loop connects the stations to the LR link, in the increasing order of their Id attributes. Thus, station 0 is the leftmost station (the most upstream station on the LR link), and the station with the highest Id is located at the right end of the bus (section 3.2.1). The second for loop traverses the stations in the reverse order of their Ids, i.e., from right to left, and connects them to the RL channel. Finally, array Created is deallocated and TheStation (affected by the loops) is reset to its original value, as it had been before the loops were entered (section 9.2.2.1).

9.3.2.2 The traffic pattern.
The library files describing our generic uniform traffic pattern used in all the protocol programs presented so far (utraffic.h

and `utraffic.c`—section 8.1.2.4) can be easily modified to meet the needs of our implementation of Fasnet. The modified files (stored in `IncludeLibrary`) are named `utraffic2.h` and `utraffic2.c`. The digit 2 indicates that the station's interface to the `Client` consists of two packet buffers. The contents of file `utraffic.h` specifying this interface are as follows:

```
#define Right 0
#define Left 1
station ClientInterface virtual {
  Packet Buffer [2];
  Boolean ready (int, Long, Long, Long);
  void configure ();
};
void initTraffic ();
```

The two symbolic constants represent transfer directions. According to the way the bus is created and configured (section 9.3.2.1), `Right` is the direction toward the station with the highest `Id`. `Right` and `Left` are used to index the two-element array of packet buffers.

Method `ready` has one additional argument (occurring at the first position of the argument list) identifying the buffer to be examined and possibly filled by the method. This argument can take two legitimate values: `Right` and `Left`. The role of `initTraffic` and `configure` is the same as before (section 8.1.2.4).

The second traffic description file (`utraffic2.c`) contains the full specifications of the two methods and the global function `initTraffic`, whose purpose is to read traffic parameters from the data file and create a traffic pattern according to these parameters. The code of `initTraffic` and `configure` is exactly the same as in `utraffic.c`, and we will not repeat it here. Method `ready` has been rewritten to account for its additional argument specifying the transfer direction of the packet to be acquired. The method is assisted by a *qualifying function* (section 5.4.1.2), passed as an argument to `getPacket`, in the following way:

```
static int Direction;
static int qual (Message *m) {
  return (Direction == Left && TheStation->getId () > m->Receiver)
    || (Direction == Right && TheStation->getId () < m->Receiver);
};
Boolean ClientInterface::ready (int d, Long mn, Long mx, Long fm) {
  Direction = d;
  return Buffer [d] . isFull () ||
    Client->getPacket (&(Buffer [d]), qual, mn, mx, fm);
};
```

The qualifying function cannot accept any arguments other than the message pointer;[14] therefore, the transfer direction is passed to `qual` in the global variable

---

[14]The configuration of arguments belongs to the function's type specification. The variant

`Direction`. This variable is set by **ready** to the value of its first argument (**d**). Note that when `Direction` is `Left`, the qualifying function will return `YES` if the `Id` of the message receiver is less than the `Id` of the inquiring (current) station. For the transfer direction to the `Right`, the condition describing the location of the receiver with respect to the current station is reversed.

Actually, `utraffic2.c` contains a bit more than this code. Besides the dual-bus networks discussed in this chapter, the file is reused in the implementation of Metaring (section 10.5.2.2), where a slightly trickier qualifying function is needed. Therefore, `utraffic2.c` allows the programmer to bypass the default qualifier and define its customized version. We return to this issue in section 10.5.2.2. Note that it is possible to have a pair of library files describing a uniform traffic pattern in which the station's interface to the `Client` is parameterized by the number of buffers and a user-supplied qualifying function for `getPacket`.

9.3.2.3   The protocol.   Fasnet is a slotted protocol. The most natural way to represent slot markers is to use special packets. The user portion of the `Flags` attribute of such a packet can store the flags carried by a slot marker. We start with the definition of the following symbolic constants:

```
#define SLOT NONE
#define BOC  PF_usr0
#define FULL PF_usr1
#define SNC  PF_usr2
```

`SLOT` identifies the packet type (the `TP` attribute—section 5.2.2) of the slot marker and is used to tell slot markers from segments, i.e., `Client` packets inserted into slot frames. As the packets representing slots are nonstandard, their `TP` attributes are `NONE`. The remaining three constants give the locations (bit numbers in `Flags`) of the three binary flags transported by a slot marker.

Following are four variables representing the global numerical parameters of the protocol:

```
Long SlotML, SegmPL, SegmFL;
TIME SegmWindow;
```

The first three of these variables store the packetization parameters. `SlotML` gives the total length (in bits) of the packet representing the slot marker. The interval between two consecutive slot markers is equal to `SegmWindow` ITUs. This interval can be filled with a segment, whose structure is the same as that of a regular packet. The length of the useful (payload) portion of this packet is given by `SegmPL`, and the length of the frame part, i.e., the header and trailer combined, is equal to `SegmFL`. Note that segments are of fixed length. The product of `SegmPL` + `SegmFL` and the network transmission rate (the common transmission rate of all ports) must

---

of `getPacket` accepting a qualifying function (section 5.4.1.2) only knows how to handle single-argument qualifiers.

not exceed `SegmWindow`. In fact, to account for clock errors, the interval separating two consecutive slot markers must be slightly longer than its minimum duration needed to accommodate a complete segment with its header and trailer.

Not all stations in Fasnet behave in the same way. The two extreme stations, besides running the same protocol as the other stations, are responsible for generating slots and inserting them into the channels. The structure of a regular station is defined in the following way:

```
station HStation : HBusInterface, ClientInterface {
  Mailbox *Strobe [2];
  void setup () {
    HBusInterface::configure ();
    ClientInterface::configure ();
    Strobe [LRBus] = create Mailbox (0);
    Strobe [RLBus] = create Mailbox (0);
  };
};
```

where `HBusInterface` and `ClientInterface` are taken from files `hbus.h` and `utraffic2.h` (sections 9.3.2.1, 9.3.2.2). An alert mailbox of capacity-zero is associated with each of the two ports interfacing the station to the bus. This mailbox is used to signal the beginning of an empty slot frame arriving at the corresponding port, i.e., a moment when the station can transmit a segment in a given direction.

First, let us focus on the protocol executed by a regular (nonextreme) station. Such a station runs three processes per each bus tap: the transmitter responsible for acquiring packets (segments) from the `Client` and transmitting them within slot frames, the strober monitoring slots passing through the taps and notifying the transmitter about the beginning of an empty frame, and the receiver detecting and receiving segments addressed to the station. The receiver is very simple and similar to the other receivers presented before. Its type can be defined as follows:

```
process Receiver (HStation) {
  Port *Bus;
  void setup (int dir) { Bus = S->Bus [dir]; };
  states {WPacket, Rcvd};
  perform;
};
```

and its code method can be copied directly from section 8.1.2.2. Upon creation, the process's setup method receives an integer argument that can be either `LRBus` or `RLBus` (0 or 1). This argument determines the direction of the receiver and is used to identify the port serviced by the process.

The other two processes, implementing the transmission portion of the protocol, cooperate with each other. The type definition of the transmitter is as follows:

```
process Transmitter (HStation) {
  int BusId;
```

```
          Port *Bus;
          Packet *Buffer;
          Mailbox *Strobe;
          void setup (int dir) {
            Bus = S->Bus [BusId = dir];
            Buffer = &(S->Buffer [dir]);
            Strobe = S->Strobe [dir];
          };
          states {NPacket, Transmit, XDone, Error};
          perform;
        };
```

As for the receiver, the setup argument determines the direction of the process, i.e., the port serviced by the transmitter, the buffer used to store packets acquired by the process from the Client, and the mailbox communicating the transmitter with its associated strober. The process executes the following code:

```
      Transmitter::perform {
        state NPacket:
          if (S->ready (BusId, SegmPL, SegmPL, SegmFL)) {
            signal ();
            Strobe->wait (NEWITEM, Transmit);
          } else
            Client->wait (ARRIVAL, NPacket);
        state Transmit:
          Bus->transmit (Buffer, XDone);
          Bus->wait (COLLISION, Error);
        state XDone:
          Bus->stop ();
          Buffer->release ();
          proceed NPacket;
        state Error:
          excptn ("Slot collision");
      };
```

The transmitter starts in state NPacket, where it attempts to acquire a packet (segment) going in the direction serviced by the process (BusId). If this attempt is unsuccessful, the process issues a wait request to the Client for a message ARRIVAL event and goes to sleep. Upon a message arrival to the station, the transmitter will be awakened in state NPacket, where it will reexecute ready. Note that a packet acquisition attempt following a message arrival event need not be successful; it may happen that the message goes in the direction opposite to the one serviced by the process.

If a packet has been acquired, the process sends a signal to itself (section 4.6.2.1) and awaits an alert from the strober marking the nearest moment when the segment can be transmitted. As we will shortly see, the transmitter's signal repository is monitored by the strober; a signal deposited there forces the strober to start inspecting the slots passing through the station's tap, to detect and reserve the first empty slot.

The remaining part of the transmitter's code method is simple and straightforward. In state `Transmit`, the process starts transmitting the segment and issues a wait request to the port for a collision. Of course, a segment transmitted within an empty slot frame cannot collide: the role of the port wait request is to make sure that the protocol operates correctly. When the segment has been transmitted entirely, the process wakes up in state `XDone`, where it terminates the transfer, empties the packet buffer, and moves back to state `NPacket` to take care of another packet.

Now let us look at the other process. Its type is declared as follows:

```
process Strober (HStation) {
  Port *Bus;
  Mailbox *Strobe;
  Transmitter *MyXmitter;
  void setup (int dir, Transmitter *pr) {
    Bus = S->Bus [dir];
    MyXmitter = pr;
    Strobe = S->Strobe [dir];
  };
  states {WaitReady, WaitEmpty, EmptyLoop, WaitBOC, BOCLoop};
  perform;
};
```

Besides the direction indication, the setup method takes another argument pointing to the transmitter process servicing the same direction as the strober. The strober needs access to the transmitter's signal repository. The code executed by the strober is as follows:

```
Strober::perform {
  state WaitReady:
    MyXmitter->wait (SIGNAL, WaitEmpty);
  state WaitEmpty:
    Bus->wait (EOT, EmptyLoop);
  state EmptyLoop:
    if (ThePacket->TP == SLOT && flagCleared (ThePacket->Flags,
      FULL)) {
      setFlag (ThePacket->Flags, FULL);
      Strobe->put ();
      skipto WaitBOC;
    } else
      skipto WaitEmpty;
```

```
    state WaitBOC:
      Bus->wait (EOT, BOCLoop);
    state BOCLoop:
      if (ThePacket->TP == SLOT && flagSet (ThePacket->Flags, BOC))
        proceed WaitReady;
      else
        skipto WaitBOC;
};
```

The strober remains dormant until it receives a signal from the transmitter indicating that there is a ready packet awaiting transmission in the direction serviced by the process. Then the strober starts awaiting the first marker of an empty slot, more specifically, the end of such a marker. The process accomplishes it by monitoring all EOT events on the port (state WaitEmpty) to detect the first such event triggered by the marker of a slot with the FULL flag cleared. All other EOT events are "skipped." Note that a slot marker is a special packet whose TP attribute is NONE.

Having found an empty slot in state EmptyLoop, the process reserves it by setting the FULL flag and immediately sends an alert to the transmitter. Note that at this moment the transmitter must be awaiting this alert. All this happens at the end of the slot marker; thus, the transmitter may start transmitting its packet right away.

According to the protocol (section 9.3.1), a station is allowed to transmit only once per cycle. Therefore, having sent the go signal to the transmitter, the strober does not consider sending another alert until it detects a slot with the BOC flag set. The process moves (via skipto) to state WaitBOC to skip the current slot and to examine the markers of subsequent slots until the first one with BOC set is found. When this happens, the strober transits to state WaitReady to await another signal from the transmitter. Note that a signal may be already pending at this moment (a packet may have arrived at the station while the strober was waiting for the beginning of a new cycle). In such a case, the current slot, i.e., the one starting the new cycle, will be reexamined in state EmptyLoop. The process uses proceed to transit from BOCLoop to WaitEmpty; thus, the EOT event triggered by the last slot seen in state BOCLoop still remains pending at WaitEmpty.

Now we can take care of the two extreme (head-end) stations, which, in addition to running the processes just presented, must generate slots and insert them into the channels. As a part of the slot generation procedure, an extreme station also sets the BOC and SNC flags, as described in section 9.3.1. Not surprisingly, the type of a head-end station is an extension of the regular station type:

```
        station HeadEnd : HStation {
          Packet SMarker;
          Mailbox *SendBOC, *SendSNC;
          void setup () {
            HStation::setup ();
```

```
                          SMarker.fill (NONE, NONE, SlotML);
                          SendBOC = create Mailbox (1);
                          SendSNC = create Mailbox (1);
                      };
                  };
```

SMarker is a packet buffer whose contents are preset by the station's setup method and remain the same during protocol execution. The packet kept in **SMarker** represents the slot marker.

The slot generation procedure is performed by two processes: the actual slot generator responsible for inserting slots into the channel serviced by the station, and the absorber process receiving slots from the other channel. The absorber detects end-of-cycle events and incoming *SNC* requests, and passes them to the slot generator via the two mailboxes owned by the head-end station. The type of the absorber process is declared as follows:

```
                  process Absorber (HeadEnd) {
                      Port *Bus;
                      Mailbox *SendBOC, *SendSNC;
                      Boolean WithinCycle;
                      void setup (int dir) {
                          Bus = S->Bus [dir];
                          SendBOC = S->SendBOC;
                          SendSNC = S->SendSNC;
                          WithinCycle = NO;
                      };
                      states {WaitSlot, SlotLoop};
                      perform;
                  };
```

As usual, the setup method saves pointers to the relevant station attributes in the process's local variables. Note that the slot generator process and its cooperating absorber service different directions and are associated with different ports of their station. This direction (**LRBus** or **RLBus**) is specified as the argument of the setup method when the process is created. The **Boolean** flag **WithinCycle** tells the absorber whether an empty slot arriving at the port serviced by the process should be interpreted as an event terminating the last cycle perceived on that port. Such an event will result in setting the SNC flag in the next slot inserted into the other port by the slot generator. The code run by the absorber is as follows:

```
Absorber::perform {
    state WaitSlot:
        Bus->wait (EOT, SlotLoop);
    state SlotLoop:
        if (ThePacket->TP == SLOT) {
            if (flagSet (ThePacket->Flags, BOC)) WithinCycle = YES;
```

```
            if (WithinCycle && flagCleared (ThePacket->Flags, FULL)) {
              WithinCycle = NO;
              SendSNC->put ();
            }
            if (flagSet (ThePacket->Flags, SNC)) SendBOC->put ();
          }
        skipto WaitSlot;
    };
```

The process monitors all slots arriving from the opposite end of the bus. Having detected a slot with the BOC flag set, the absorber sets WithinCycle to YES, to indicate that a cycle has started. An empty slot encountered during a cycle (while WithinCycle is YES) will be interpreted as the end of the cycle. The process will then deposit an alert in the SendSNC mailbox (to notify the slot generator that an SNC request should be send downstream) and set WithinCycle to NO, to make sure that subsequent empty slots will not trigger SNC requests until the beginning of a new cycle. Note that a cycle can end immediately, with the very slot starting it, if this slot happens to be empty.

If the SNC flag of an incoming slot is set, the slot generator should start a new cycle. The absorber notifies the other process about this event with an alert sent via the SendBOC mailbox.

The slot generator has the following structure:

```
              process SlotGen (HeadEnd) {
                Port *Bus;
                Mailbox *SendBOC, *SendSNC;
                Packet *SMarker;
                void setup (int dir) {
                  Bus = S->Bus [dir];
                  SMarker = &(S->SMarker);
                  SendBOC = S->SendBOC;
                  SendSNC = S->SendSNC;
                  SendBOC->put ();
                };
                states {Generate, XDone};
                perform;
              };
```

All its attributes are local pointers to the relevant attributes of the head-end station running the process. The last statement of the setup method deposits an alert into the SendBOC mailbox to initialize the slot generation procedure by starting the first cycle explicitly. Subsequent cycles will be started in response to the SNC requests arriving from the opposite end of the bus. The code method of the slot generator is as follows:

```
SlotGen::perform {
  state Generate:
    if (SendBOC->get ())
      setFlag (SMarker->Flags, BOC);
    else
      clearFlag (SMarker->Flags, BOC);
    if (SendSNC->get ())
      setFlag (SMarker->Flags, SNC);
    else
      clearFlag (SMarker->Flags, SNC);
    Bus->transmit (SMarker, XDone);
  state XDone:
    Bus->stop ();
    Timer->wait (SegmWindow, Generate);
};
```

At regular intervals, every SegmWindow ITUs, the process finds itself in state
Generate, where it transmits a new slot marker. Before the marker is inserted into
the port, its two flags BOC and SNC are set based on the status of the corresponding
mailboxes. Note that both SendBOC and SendSNC are capacity-1 mailboxes. The
status of a mailbox is determined by executing get (section 4.7.5), which empties
the mailbox if it contains a pending alert. The FULL flag of a new slot marker is
always zero. This flag was automatically cleared when SMarker was filled by the
station's setup method and it has not been changed after then.

9.3.2.4 The root process.   The complete code of our implementation of
Fasnet discussed in sections 9.3.2.1–9.3.2.4 is contained in directory BUS/Fasnet1
in SMURPH Examples. The portions related to the bus geometry (section 9.3.2.1)
and the traffic pattern (section 9.3.2.2) have been isolated and stored in
IncludeLibrary. File root.c of Fasnet1 contains the definition of the root process that builds the network, initializes the traffic generator, and starts the protocol
execution. The structure of this process is straightforward and similar to the other
root processes discussed in this book. The only fragment of the root's code method
whose meaning may not be obvious is the following:

```
for (i = 0; i < NNodes; i++)
  if (i == 0 || i == NNodes - 1)
    create HeadEnd;
  else
    create HStation;
for (i = 0; i < NNodes; i++) {
  pr = create (i) Transmitter (RLBus);
  create (i) Strober (RLBus, pr);
  pr = create (i) Transmitter (LRBus);
  create (i) Strober (LRBus, pr);
```

```
create (i) Receiver (RLBus);
create (i) Receiver (LRBus);
if (i == 0) {
  create (i) SlotGen (LRBus);
  create (i) Absorber (RLBus);
}
if (i == NNodes-1) {
  create (i) SlotGen (RLBus);
  create (i) Absorber (LRBus);
}
}
```

The first of the two **for** loops from this sequence creates the stations and implicitly connects them to the bus. According to our definition of direction (section 9.3.2.1), the order in which the stations are created imposes their ordering along the bus—from left to right. Thus, station 0 is the left head-end station and the last created station (numbered NNodes − 1) closes the bus from the right. The second loop creates and starts the protocol processes. For each station, including the head-end stations, six processes are started: two copies of the transmitter, strober, and receiver, each copy servicing a different port. The setup method of **Strober** takes two arguments, the second argument pointing to the cooperating **Transmitter**. Therefore, the transmitter process must be created first, its pointer saved and passed as an argument to the setup method of **Strober**. Then, additionally, if the station happens to be a head-end station, we create the two processes responsible for slot generation. The left extreme station (number 0) inserts slots into the *LR* bus; thus, the setup argument of its copy of **SlotGen** is LRBus. The absorber of the left-end station receives slots from the *RL* bus, and its setup argument indicates the direction opposite to the direction of **SlotGen**.

The reader may have noticed that each of the two extreme stations only needs one transmitter and one receiver. For example, the leftmost station never transmits anything to the left and never receives anything from that direction. Thus, its collection of processes (**Transmitter**, **Strober**, **Receiver**) servicing this direction is effectively unused and redundant. It makes no harm to create these processes, however. They go to sleep immediately after startup and remain dormant throughout the entire protocol execution.

9.4 UNSYNCHRONIZED PROTOCOLS

Both Expressnet and Fasnet operate in rounds, and their transmission rules are rather strict. To be allowed to transmit, a station must wait for its turn indicated by an explicit *synchronizing event*. In contrast to the collision protocols discussed in chapter 8, no spontaneous transmissions are possible. Even if the network is absolutely idle, a station getting a packet to transmit cannot do it immediately. Consequently, one may expect that Expressnet and Fasnet perform worse than the collision protocols for light traffic conditions. A natural question arises: What is the advantage of Expressnet and Fasnet (and other protocols of this sort) over the solutions proposed in the previous chapter?

9.4.1 Capacity-1 Protocols

It is not the objective of this book to carry out a detailed performance study of the protocols discussed here. But even without such a study, one property shared by all the bus protocols presented so far is almost obvious: their maximum achievable throughput tends to drop with the increasing propagation length (L) of the bus. For the collision protocols, which require that no packet be shorter than $2L$ (Ethernet, TCR, CSMA/CD-DP, Virtual Token), a large value of L results in a small fraction of the inflated packet being used to carry useful information. Ignoring the synchronization overhead, the maximum throughput of a network based on such a protocol must be bounded from above by

$$T_e = \frac{l_p}{\max(l_p + f, 2L)} \; ,$$

where l_p represents the average (or typical) length of an uninflated packet payload and f is the combined length of packet header and trailer. L is determined by the product of the network transmission rate r[15] and the geographic length of the bus L_g, in the following way:

$$L = \frac{rL_g}{v_p} \; ,$$

where v_p is the propagation speed of signals in the medium. For all practical purposes, we can assume that v_p is fixed (at about $0.8c$) and not flexible. Most physicists agree that there is no way to increase v_p beyond c; thus, all reasonable attempts to reduce L can only involve adjusting r and L_g.

The maximum throughput of an inflation-based CSMA/CD protocol improves when l_p is increased or L is decreased. In most cases, l_p is determined by the application profile of the network, and there is no sensible way to increase it. Similarly, the geographic size of the network is usually constrained and cannot be reduced. This brings us to the paradoxical conclusion that to improve the network's performance one has to **lower** its transmission rate. Of course, this cannot be true. The maximum throughput that we have in mind is normalized, i.e., expressed in bits of information per bit of time. With a higher transmission rate, the network passes bits faster and usually exhibits a higher absolute throughput expressed in bits per second. However, its normalized throughput may be worse than that achieved with a lower transmission rate. This tells us that the relation between the transmission rate and the absolute throughput is not linear. Although bits are passed faster and faster, the percentage of the network bandwidth used to transmit useful data is lower and lower. Consequently, it may happen that increasing the transmission

[15]Expressed in bits per second.

rate beyond a certain threshold makes no sense: the higher transmission rate brings no worthwhile improvement.

Many protocols, not only bus protocols, are affected by the same pattern of impact of l_p and L on network performance, although the extent of this impact varies from protocol to protocol. The ratio of L/l_p is denoted by a. Ethernet, and many other protocols, operate with a satisfying efficiency when a is not too big, i.e., L is not very large compared to l_p. For example, to avoid inflation in Ethernet, we need $a < 1/2$. Although the protocol may still operate reasonably well when $a = 1$, it is certainly not well suited for environments with $a \approx 100$. The problem of finding a protocol suitable for networks with a substantially larger than 1 is called the *Big-a* problem. A protocol whose maximum normalized throughput does not deteriorate with increasing a is called a *capacity-1* protocol. Such a protocol is able to utilize a fixed fraction (preferably close to 1) of the channel bandwidth, regardless of the propagation length of the network and the average size of packet payload.

Let us look at Piggyback Ethernet. Although this protocol alleviates the problems resulting from packet inflation in CSMA/CD, its maximum throughput still depends on L. Under heavy uniform load, i.e., assuming that all stations are constantly ready to transmit packets, the protocol never leaves the controlled mode of operation.[16] Assume that all stations have ready packets to transmit, and consider one round in which every station is given two chances to transmit a packet. As all stations are constantly backlogged, each station transmits twice in such a round. Thus, the number of packets transmitted in a round is $2N$, and the time needed to complete a round is $2L + 2N(\delta + l_p + f)$ (section 8.5.1.1). Consequently, the maximum throughput of the complete version of Piggyback Ethernet is given by the following formula:

$$T_p = \frac{2Nl_p}{2L + 2N(\delta + l_p + f)} \ .$$

Although packets are never inflated, the factor $2L$ is still present. Note that now, in comparison to Ethernet, this factor has been diluted among the N stations. This is why Piggyback Ethernet achieves a much higher throughput than inflation-based CSMA/CD protocols operating on long or fast networks; however, it is still not a capacity-1 protocol. The formula can be rewritten as

$$T_p = \frac{1}{\frac{a}{N} + \frac{\delta + f}{l_p} + 1} \ ,$$

which clearly demonstrates that the maximum normalized throughput of Piggyback Ethernet drops with increasing a.

Neither Expressnet nor Fasnet bring any improvement in this area. To calculate the maximum throughput of Expressnet, note that the time separating two consecutive fully loaded trains[17] is equal to $N(l_p + f) + L + L_t + \Delta_t$, where L_t is

---

[16]We are talking here about the complete version presented in section 8.5.1.1.

[17]As perceived by one distinguished station.

the length of the turning segment of the bus (section 9.2.1). Thus, the maximum throughput of Expressnet is equal to

$$T_x = \frac{Nl_p}{N(l_p + f) + L + L_t + \Delta_t}$$

or, equivalently,

$$T_x = \frac{1}{\frac{a}{N} + 1 + \frac{Nf + L_t + \Delta_t}{Nl_p}} \; ,$$

which is clearly a decreasing function of a. Similarly, the time separating two BOC requests sent by a slot generator in a heavily loaded Fasnet is at least equal to $N(s + f) + L$, where s is the slot payload length and f represents the combined overhead of slot markers, headers, and trailers. Assuming no packet-slot fragmentation (all packets fitting perfectly into slot windows), the maximum throughput of Fasnet is

$$T_f = \frac{2Ns}{N(s + f) + L} \; ,$$

The factor of 2 reflects the fact that the network consists of two channels operating in parallel. Converted to the a-dependent form, the formula takes the following shape:

$$T_f = \frac{2}{\frac{a}{N} + 1 + \frac{f}{s}} \; ,$$

which is very similar to the previous two results.

To answer the question posed in the introduction to this section, we have to conclude that the advantage of the synchronized protocols (including Piggyback Ethernet) over the inflation-based variants of CSMA/CD is in the reduced impact of a on network performance. However, neither Expressnet nor Fasnet eliminate this impact totally. Given a sufficiently long bus (or a sufficiently high transmission rate), the maximum normalized throughput of the network can be arbitrarily low. None of the protocols presented in this book so far is a capacity-1 protocol.

9.4.2 U-Net and H-Net

Let us return once again to Expressnet and try to understand why its maximum throughput depends on L and, consequently, on a. Expressnet operates in rounds, each round resulting in one train of packets being sent down the channel. The packets of a single train are adjacent to each other; thus, if the protocol were able to sustain a single train indefinitely, the utilization of the channel would be close to 1 and would not depend on L. Unfortunately, the length of a single train is limited to N packets. We can imagine that all trains are launched from the outbound port of the most upstream (leftmost) station. To be able to launch a new train, the leftmost station must see the end of the previous train on its inbound port. In the most optimistic implementation of Expressnet, the length of the turning segment of the bus is zero, and the distance between the two ports of the most upstream station is L. Therefore, the length of the shortest period of silence separating two consecutive trains is L, and this length determines the fraction of unused bandwidth.

Why are the trains limited to N packets each? The reason is simple: Expressnet wants to be fair and to offer a short response time to every station. If a single station were allowed to insert arbitrarily many packets during its turn, it could starve all the stations located downstream. Formally, there is nothing wrong with the idea of increasing the number of packets that a single station can append at the end of a train. As long as this number is limited, starvation is impossible and the maximum throughput achievable by the network is improved.

Besides the failure to become a capacity-1 protocol, Expressnet has another unpleasant drawback: its medium access time under light traffic conditions is nonzero. If there is absolutely no traffic in the network, the distance between two consecutive preambles starting empty trains is at least L.[18] In consequence, if a station gets a packet to transmit, its expected waiting time before the transfer can commence is $L/2$. Thus, by increasing L we worsen not only the normalized maximum throughput of the network; the average packet access time under light load is adversely affected as well.

Note that it is not difficult to come up with a protocol that formally fulfills the capacity-1 requirement. For example, a protocol that assigns the entire bandwidth of the network to one predefined transmitter is able to utilize the whole capacity of the channel, as long as the favored station has a continuous supply of messages to transmit. This is what could happen in Expressnet without the limit on the number of packets that a single station is allowed to contribute to the train in one cycle. Clearly, the maximum throughput achievable by such a protocol does not depend on L and formally the protocol belongs to the capacity-1 family. However, very few people would accept this idea as a practically useful solution, unless the application actually called for such a peculiar traffic pattern. This brings us to the following postulate:

> A capacity-1 protocol should be fair to deserve its classification. It is easy to produce unfair capacity-1 protocols with no practical value.

To demonstrate that the issue is far from trivial, let us consider the following simple modification of Expressnet. All trains are started by the leftmost (most extreme) station. Having started a train, i.e., having sent the starting preamble of the train, the station waits for $N \times (l_p^{max} + f)$ time units, where l_p^{max} is the maximum packet length, and starts another train. As before, each station is allowed to append at most one packet per train.

Modified this way, Expressnet becomes a capacity-1 protocol. Indeed, under heavy load, when all stations are constantly ready, the observed throughput of the network is of order $l_p/(l_p^{max} + f)$, which does not depend on L. Would we call this solution acceptable?

The problem with this idea is the fixed and pessimistically inflated train length.

---

[18]Assuming that the turning segment is of zero length.

Every station gets cyclically a "window of opportunity" to transmit a packet, which it can use or not. Windows unused by some stations cannot be claimed by other stations. For example, if only one station is ready to transmit a packet, the station will be allowed to do so every $N \times (l_p^{max} + f)$ bits of time. Consequently, the maximum throughput achievable in such circumstances is $1/N$ of the maximum throughput attainable under uniform heavy load. A situation like this is called a *fixed allocation* behavior. The network operates as if each station were assigned a fixed portion of the network bandwidth. This bandwidth is the private property of its owner and cannot be reused by other stations even if the owner is dormant. Clearly, protocols behaving this way cannot be considered flexible, and we are ready to form another postulate:

> To deserve its classification, a capacity-1 protocol cannot be based on fixed bandwidth allocation.

9.4.2.1 The protocol. In this section we introduce a very simple (one could even say naive) protocol that formally qualifies as a capacity-1 solution, although many people would object to treating it seriously. Namely, our protocol does not fulfill the "fairness" postulate: it is explicitly unfair and even starvation-prone. In section 9.4.3 we argue that this disadvantage need not be fatal. For many realistic traffic patterns occurring in real-life networks, the observed behavior of our protocol turns out to be more than acceptable.

The protocol occurs in a number of flavors. We will discuss two such forms resulting from the difference in the topology of the network backbone. Recall the "improvement" to Expressnet based on the idea of equally spaced trains started at regular intervals by the most upstream station. With this solution, inbound ports are only used for packet reception; there is no need to detect *ETR* events on the inbound ports. Consequently, the ordering of the inbound ports on the bus need not be the same as the ordering of the outbound ports. In particular, the protocol can be implemented on a U-shaped bus (figure 9.3) or on any other unidirectional bus shaped in such a way that all the outbound ports are visited before the inbound ports.

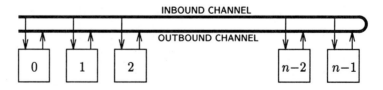

Figure 9.3 A U-shaped bus

Consider the U-shaped bus topology shown in figure 9.3 and a simple protocol, called U-Net, operating according to the following rules:

- A station having a packet to transmit monitors its outbound port. As soon as it detects silence in that port, the station starts transmitting the packet.

- While transmitting, the station monitors the outbound port to detect a possible collision caused by a packet arriving from upstream. As soon as a collision is detected, the station aborts its transmission and yields to the incoming activity.

- As in Expressnet, each packet is preceded by a short preamble, to give an active downstream station enough time to abort its transfer with no detrimental effect on the integrity of the packet arriving from upstream.

The preemption rules of U-Net are exactly the same as in Expressnet; however, in contrast to Expressnet, U-Net does not operate in cycles. There are no trains, and provided that the outbound portion of the bus is sensed idle, a station can start transmitting at any moment. Unlike Expressnet, U-Net incurs zero access delay under light load. Moreover, the maximum throughput of U-Net is close to 1 and, notably, it does not depend on a. Thus, formally, U-Net is a capacity-1 protocol.

Unfortunately, the protocol is unfair and starvation-prone. An upstream station having a continuous supply of packets to transmit may starve all stations located downstream. The severity of this problem depends on the network's application profile. One can hope (section 9.4.3) that under many realistic (correlated) traffic patterns actual starvation is not very likely, although it clearly occurs under heavy uniform load.

The same protocol can operate on an H-shaped network (figure 9.2). In this variant, dubbed H-Net, a station willing to transmit a packet must know whether the recipient is located on the left or right side of the bus—to select the proper channel for transmission. The remaining rules are the same as in U-Net: downstream transfer attempts yield to transmissions coming from upstream. The protocol favors stations located close to the ends of the bus transmitting toward the other end. One can think of two versions of H-Net, with one and two transmitters per station. In the double-transmitter version, each direction is serviced independently. There are two independent processes acquiring packets for transmission, each process handling packets that go in one direction. With one transmitter per station, the single process first acquires a packet for transmission and then, based on the packet's destination, decides in which direction (on which port) the packet should be sent. While the transmitter takes care of the packet, the other port is not serviced, although there may be ready packets going in the opposite direction. One would naturally expect that the double-transmitter protocol performs better than its tailored cousin; however, the single-transmitter version tends to be less unfair. This is not surprising: if a station is completely blocked while waiting to send a packet in one direction, it does not contribute to the traffic going in the opposite direction, and consequently does not starve the stations located downstream on the other channel. Of course, the extreme stations are still as potent as in the double-transmitter version: regardless of the protocol variant, each of them can only transmit in one direction and effectively use only one transmitter.

Both U-Net and H-Net can be turned into slotted protocols. In the slotted variant of U-Net, the most upstream station is responsible for generating empty slots and inserting them into the bus. A station having a packet (segment) awaiting transmission monitors the slots passing through its outbound port and grabs the first empty slot. The slot reservation mechanism is the same as in Fasnet (section 9.3.1). The *FULL* flag in the slot marker is the only flag required by the protocol. In slotted H-Net, slots are generated by the two extreme stations.

Regardless of whether the protocol is slotted or not, the network achieves its maximum throughput when the most upstream station (U-Net), or the two extreme stations (H-Net) is (are) constantly ready to transmit. The load offered to the other stations is then irrelevant: they are all delayed indefinitely. Compared to the unslotted variants, the slotted protocols exhibit better performance characteristics in the middle range of traffic conditions, where no stations are starved. This is because of the lack of collisions: no bandwidth is wasted for transporting useless initial fragments of aborted packets.

9.4.2.2 The implementation.   In this section we present the implementation of the unslotted variants of U-Net and H-Net. The user may find it entertaining to implement the slotted variants and compare them with their unslotted counterparts (see exercise 5 at the end of this chapter). The transmitters of both protocols operate according to the same rules; the only difference is in the procedure of packet acquisition. Therefore, it makes sense to isolate the shared parts of the two programs and put them into library files. The reader will find these files, named uprotocol.h and uprotocol.c, in IncludeLibrary. The shared fragments include the generic definitions of the transmitter and receiver. The types of the two processes are declared as follows:

```
process UTransmitter {
  Port *Bus;
  Packet *Buffer;
  virtual Boolean gotPacket () { return NO; };
  states {NPacket, WSilence, Transmit, XDone, Abort};
  perform;
};
process UReceiver {
  Port *Bus;
  states {WPacket, Rcvd};
  perform;
};
```

Note that neither process is explicitly associated with a specific station type. The two process types are intentionally incomplete: they will be used as base types to define actual process types for a specific protocol version. Therefore, neither UTransmitter nor UReceiver defines a setup method. This method can only be defined in a process subtype as it must know the type of the station owning the process to reference its relevant attributes. The gotPacket method of UTransmitter is virtual and is expected to be redefined in a subtype of UTransmitter. The role of this method is to perform all the operations related to packet acquisition from the Client.

Incomplete as they are, each of the two process types defines a code method. The code method of UReceiver has been borrowed directly from the Ethernet receiver (section 8.1.2.2):

```
UReceiver::perform {
  state WPacket:
    Bus->wait (EMP, Rcvd);
  state Rcvd:
    Client->receive (ThePacket, ThePort);
    skipto (WPacket);
};
```

The code run by UTransmitter is somewhat more involved:

```
UTransmitter::perform {
  state NPacket:
    if (gotPacket ())
      proceed WSilence;
    else
      Client->wait (ARRIVAL, NPacket);
  state WSilence:
    Bus->wait (SILENCE, Transmit);
  state Transmit:
    Bus->transmit (Buffer, XDone);
    Bus->wait (COLLISION, Abort);
  state XDone:
    Bus->stop ();
    Buffer->release ();
    proceed NPacket;
  state Abort:
    Bus->abort ();
    proceed WSilence;
};
```

The process starts in state NPacket, where it executes the subtype-specific method gotPacket to acquire a packet for transmission. The method is expected to return YES if a packet is available (in such a case, the packet has been stored in the station's buffer), and NO otherwise. If there is no packet to transmit, the transmitter issues a Client wait request, to be restarted in state NPacket upon the nearest message arrival to the station, and goes to sleep.

Having acquired a packet for transmission, the process gets to state WSilence, where it awaits a moment of silence in the channel. As soon as the port becomes silent (or if it is silent already), the transmitter proceeds to state Transmit, where it starts transmitting the packet. While the packet is being transmitted, the process monitors the port for a collision. If the packet has been transmitted completely without a collision, the process transits to state XDone, where the transmission is terminated (by stop) and the packet buffer is released. Upon a collision, the transfer is aborted (state Abort) and the transmitter moves back to state WSilence, to wait until the port becomes silent again.

Note that a collision is not destructive for the activity arriving from upstream. The downstream station (the one sensing the collision) aborts its transfer attempt and yields to the incoming activity. Unlike Expressnet (section 9.2.2.2), preambles in U-Net and H-Net have not been isolated from packets. This is unnecessary as preambles are never transmitted alone, nor are they used to trigger any special events. Of course, it is tacitly assumed that the preamble is long enough to afford sacrificing its few initial bits for collision detection latency.

File uprotocol.c also defines the following three variables:

```
Long MinPL, MaxPL, FrameL;
```

which represent the packetization parameters of the protocol. Although these parameters are not referenced explicitly by the code methods of the two generic processes, they are applicable to any actual protocol built on top of uprotocol.h and uprotocol.c.

To see how the generic process types just introduced can be incorporated into an actual protocol implementation, let us start with H-Net (directory BUS/H-Net1). The protocol is based on a bus topology whose implementation has been discussed already (section 9.3.2.1). File types.h of our implementation of H-Net includes three library files: hbus.h, utraffic2.h, and uprotocol.h. It also defines the following station type:

```
station HStation : HBusInterface, ClientInterface {
  void setup () {
    HBusInterface::configure ();
    ClientInterface::configure ();
  };
};
```

The protocol is so simple that no additional station attributes (other than the attributes defined in HBusInterface and ClientInterface) are needed. The actual process types for H-Net are defined as follows:

```
process Transmitter : UTransmitter (HStation) {
  int BusId;
  void setup (int dir) {
    Bus = S->Bus [BusId = dir];
    Buffer = &(S->Buffer [dir]);
  };
  Boolean gotPacket ();
```

```
};
process Receiver : UReceiver (HStation) {
  void setup (int dir) { Bus = S->Bus [dir]; };
};
```

Each of the two setup methods accepts one argument identifying the transfer direction serviced by the process. Note that each station will run a separate pair of the two processes, one pair for each channel of the dual bus. The only remaining element that must be provided to complete the protocol specification is the code of gotPacket. For H-Net, this code is as follows:

```
Boolean Transmitter::gotPacket () {
  return S->ready (BusId, MinPL, MaxPL, FrameL);
};
```

Recall that the ready method defined in utraffic2.h and utraffic2.c (section 9.3.2.2) requires a direction specification in its first argument. This specification is provided by the transmitter's attribute BusId set by the process's setup method.

A version of H-Net is possible in which there is only one transmitter process per station. This process acquires a packet for transmission in an unqualified way and then decides on which channel the packet should be sent. Only one direction is serviced at a time. While the transmitter is waiting to send a packet in a given direction, no attempt is made to find a packet going in the opposite direction—to be transmitted on the other port. A program implementing this version of the protocol can be found in directory BUS/H-Net2 of SMURPH Examples. The difference with respect to H-Net1 is in the declaration of the Transmitter type:

```
process Transmitter : UTransmitter (HStation) {
  void setup () { Buffer = &(S->Buffer); };
  Boolean gotPacket ();
};
```

which does not assign the process's Bus attribute to a predetermined port, and in gotPacket, which does this assignment dynamically upon a packet acquisition:

```
Boolean Transmitter::gotPacket () {
  if (S->ready (MinPL, MaxPL, FrameL)) {
    if (Buffer->Receiver < S->getId ())
      Bus = S->Bus [RLBus];
    else
      Bus = S->Bus [LRBus];
    return YES;
  } else
    return NO;
};
```

Of course, there is only one packet buffer per station. The traffic generator for the single-transmitter implementation of H-Net is based on files `utraffic.h` and `utraffic.c` (section 8.1.2.4).

We are not going to bore the reader with the discussion of the root processes of our implementations of H-Net. The structure and operation of these processes should be obvious. Instead, we will explain how to build U-Net using the building blocks of H-Net. Unfortunately, we are still one block short: we need a SMURPH specification of the U-shaped bus. There is no doubt that by now the reader has acquired enough familiarity with SMURPH to build this specification, e.g., using files `sbus.h` and `sbus.c` (section 9.2.2.1) as a starting point. Note that the station fragment representing the bus interface in U-Net (we call this fragment `UBusInterface`) has exactly the same layout as the bus interface in Expressnet (section 9.2.2.1). Also, the global function `initUBus`, which we will have to program, may look exactly like `initSBus`, except for the difference in the type name of the station fragment representing the bus interface. Following is an initial fragment of `ubus.c` (see `IncludeLibrary`). The reader may check that the matching ".h" file (`ubus.h`) has essentially the same contents as `sbus.h`.

```
static Link *TheBus;
static RATE TR;
static DISTANCE D, Turn;
static int NP, NC;
static UBusInterface **Created;
void initUBus (RATE r, TIME l, DISTANCE tl, int np) {
  TheBus = create PLink (np + np);
  TR = r;
  D = 1 / (np-1);
  Turn = tl;
  NP = np;
  NC = 0;
  Created = new UBusInterface* [NP];
};
```

Method `configure` of `UBusInterface` is very similar to its counterpart from `sbus.c`, although this time a difference can be noted:

```
void UBusInterface::configure () {
  int i;
  UBusInterface *s;
  Created [NC++] = this;
  if (NC == NP) {
    for (i = 0; i < NP; i++) {
      s = Created [i];
      s->OBus = create (i) Port (TR);
      s->OBus -> connect (TheBus);
```

```
      if (i > 0) Created [i-1] -> OBus -> setDTo (s->OBus, D);
    };
    for (i = NP-1; i >= 0; i--) {
      s = Created [i];
      s->IBus = create (i) Port (TR);
      s->IBus -> connect (TheBus);
      if (i < NP-1) Created [i+1] -> IBus -> setDTo (s->IBus, D);
    };
    Created [NP-1]->OBus -> setDTo (Created [NP-1]->IBus, Turn);
    delete Created;
    TheStation = idToStation (NP-1);
  };
};
```

The two for loops scan the stations in the opposite directions. In U-Net, the order in which stations are visited by the inbound channel is opposite to their ordering along the outbound channel.

In directory BUS/U-Net1 of SMURPH Examples the reader will find an implementation of U-Net based on the following library files: ubus.h/ubus.c, utraffic.h/utraffic.c, and uprotocol.h/uprotocol.c. File types.h of this program defines the following types:

```
station UStation : UBusInterface, ClientInterface {
  void setup () {
    UBusInterface::configure ();
    ClientInterface::configure ();
  };
};
process Transmitter : UTransmitter (UStation) {
  void setup () {
    Bus = S->OBus;
    Buffer = &(S->Buffer);
  };
  Boolean gotPacket ();
};
process Receiver : UReceiver (UStation) {
  void setup () { Bus = S->IBus; };
};
```

To make the protocol specification complete, we have to define the Transmitter's method gotPacket, which subsumes the virtual method of UTransmitter:

```
Boolean Transmitter::gotPacket () {
  return S->ready (MinPL, MaxPL, FrameL);
};
```

Each station in U-Net runs a single copy of UTransmitter and UReceiver. Thus, in contrast to H-Net, the setup methods of the two processes accept no arguments. The simple and straightforward definition of the root process is not listed here. The reader will find it in file root.c in the program's directory.

9.4.3   Uniform versus Correlated Traffic Patterns

Both U-Net and H-Net are unfair under heavy uniform load: given a continuous supply of packets to transmit, an upstream station persistently preempts all stations located downstream. This common shortcoming of the two protocols seems very serious and one could ask, Are these protocols of any practical value? An advocate of U-Net and H-Net can come up with the following two observations to reduce the apparent severity of the unfairness issue:

- Given a sufficiently long or fast network, a capacity-1 protocol will always outperform any protocol whose performance deteriorates with increasing L. Consider the maximum offered uniform load under which U-Net (H-Net) operates without starvation, in a manner perceived as fair. Let us denote this load, which does not depend on L, by λ. For any protocol that does not belong to the capacity-1 family, there exists L beyond which the protocol will saturate below λ.
- Real-life traffic patterns are never uniform. A protocol appearing unfair under uniform load may exhibit an acceptable behavior under a realistic traffic pattern.

From the first observation, it follows that U-Net (H-Net) may appear fair under uniform load exceeding the saturation threshold of another, absolutely fair, protocol. Consequently, talking about fairness makes more sense if the issue is related to the maximum throughput achievable by the network. A fair network may be pronounced worse than an unfair network, if the unfair network turns out to be fair under loads exceeding those that saturate the fair network.

The second observation is no less valid. Indeed, uniform and uncorrelated traffic patterns may be useful as abstractions of real traffic conditions, but their limitations should never be swept under the carpet. The role of a uniform traffic pattern is to minimize the number of parameters, make an analytical model feasible, or simply substitute for a real traffic pattern whose exact parameters are not known. It may be useful for arriving at meaningful conclusions regarding the global performance of a network, but a fairness study, requiring insight into the different behavior of individual stations, must take into account the correlation of the traffic among them. After all, the objective of a network is to **communicate** among the stations connected to it, as opposed to generating isolated messages at random. Thus, one should expect a real traffic pattern to be rather strongly correlated.

9.4.3.1   Measuring unfairness under uniform load. The reader may consider running some experiments with U-Net and H-Net to determine how unfair the networks are under uniform loads of varying intensity. One way to quantify unfairness under uniform traffic conditions is to look at message or packet access time (section 7.1.2.1) measured locally at individual stations-transmitters. The access times are better suited for this purpose than global delays (including the propagation time to the destination), as the latter may be biased by the bus geometry. Of course, the network shape may (and often does) introduce some unfairness into the medium access mechanism,[19] but we are not interested here in this kind of unfairness and would prefer to eliminate it from the scene. Message access time usually exhibits the same general tendency as the packet access time. As the message access time includes the queuing time at the sender, the observed variations in this measure at different stations will magnify the corresponding variations in the packet access time. Thus, we suggest measuring unfairness by comparing message access time at different stations.

Directory `Examples/BUS` contains versions of the protocol programs for U-Net and H-Net prepared especially for experiments aimed at investigating the unfairness of the two protocols. In subdirectory `U-Net2`, the reader will find essentially the same program as in `U-Net1` with one modification: the traffic pattern is described by the library files `utrafficl.h` and `utrafficl.c` instead of `utraffic.h` and `utraffic.c`. Similarly, in the implementation of H-Net in subdirectory `H-Net3`, the library files `utraffic2.h` and `utraffic2.c` have been replaced with `utraffic2l.c` and `utraffic2l.h`. The new traffic files specify the same uniform traffic pattern as their previous versions (section 8.1.2.4), augmented by additional code for measuring message access time (section 7.1.2.1) at individual stations. These modifications are briefly described here.

File `utrafficl.h` defines the following nonstandard traffic type:

```
traffic UTraffic {
  void pfmMTR (Packet*);
  exposure;
};
```

which is used later to create the uniform traffic pattern. The nonstandard traffic type is needed to respecify the virtual method `pfmMTR` defined in class `Traffic` (section 7.1.2.3). We use this method to monitor all situations when a message becomes completely transmitted. With every event of this kind, we add a sample to a random variable associated with the station sending the message. This sample will give the message access delay, i.e., the amount of time elapsing after the message arrived at the station until it has been transmitted (which happens at the moment when `pfmMTR` is called).

A random variable pointer has been added to `ClientInterface`—the station's fragment representing the interface to the traffic generator. This fragment now is as follows:

---

[19]For example, Ethernet implemented on a linear bus is slightly unfair. On the average, stations located close to the middle of the bus perceive events in the medium sooner than stations connected close to the ends.

```
station ClientInterface virtual {
  Packet Buffer;
  RVariable *MAT;
  Boolean ready (Long, Long, Long);
  void configure ();
};
```

The actual random variable will be created by the station's `configure` method when the station itself comes into existence.

Note that type `UTraffic` announces a private exposure method (section 7.3.2). This method (its contents are discussed later) makes it possible to write the message access delays at individual stations to the output file, or display them via DSD (appendix A). The last addition to `utraffic.h` is the announcement of the following global function:

```
void printLocalMeasures ();
```

which calls the nonstandard paper exposure (sections 7.3.1, 7.3.2.1) of the traffic pattern to include the list of local message access delays in the output file. Intentionally, `printLocalMeasures` is to be called from the root process when the simulation experiment has been completed.

The actual behavior of the traffic generator is described by the contents of `utraffic1.c`. Let us look at an initial portion of this file:

```
static UTraffic *UTP;
static ClientInterface *CInt [MAXSTATIONS];
void initTraffic () {
  double mit, mle;
  int i;
  readIn (mit);
  readIn (mle);
  UTP = create UTraffic (MIT_exp+MLE_exp, mit, mle);
  for (i = 0; i < MAXSTATIONS; i++) CInt [i] = NULL;
};
```

The array of pointers to `ClientInterface` segments (absent in `utraffic.c`) is now needed by the `pfmMTR` method of the traffic pattern to access the `MAT` attributes of the stations. Unlike similar arrays used in network geometry description files (section 8.1.2.4), `CInt` is declared statically,[20] because `initTraffic` does not know the number of stations in the network and cannot create the array dynamically with the right size. To keep the function compatible with its `utraffic.c` version, we decided not to use an argument (which would have been useless in the `utraffic.c` version of the function). The contents of `CInt` are needed for the entire duration of a simulation run, not just during initialization.

---

[20]The constant `MAXSTATIONS` is defined in `utraffic1.h` as 256.

ClientInterface defines two methods: ready, which is exactly the same as before, and configure, which has been extended as follows:

```
void ClientInterface::configure () {
  UTP->addSender (TheStation);
  UTP->addReceiver (TheStation);
  MAT = create RVariable, form ("MAT %3d", TheStation->getId ());
  Assert (TheStation->getId () < MAXSTATIONS,
    "Too many stations, increase MAXSTATIONS in utrafficl.h");
  CInt [TheStation->getId ()] = this;
};
```

In addition to its previous version, the new method creates the random variable to be used for measuring the local message access time and stores the pointer to the station's ClientInterface segment in CInt. Note the nickname (sections 2.4.2, 2.4.7) specified with the create operation, incorporating the Id of the station owning the random variable. This nickname will be useful for identifying the random variable on the window menu of DSD (section A.7.2).

Each time an entire message is transmitted by some station, pfmMTR is called to update the access delay statistics of the transmitting station. This happens when the station executes release for the last packet of a message (section 7.1.2.3). Following is the code of pfmMTR:

```
void UTraffic::pfmMTR (Packet *p) {
  double d;
  d = (double) (Time - p->QTime) * Itu;
  CInt [TheStation->getId ()] -> MAT -> update (d);
};
```

The access time is calculated as the difference between the current time (the contents of Time) and the time when the message was queued at the station (attribute QTime of the packet being transmitted). This difference is multiplied by Itu (section 2.2.2), which operation converts it from ITUs to ETUs.

Note that to access the random variable pointed to by the MAT attribute of the station, pfmMTR must make this reference via CInt. The method belongs to the traffic pattern (not the station), and the station completing the message transmission can only be identified by TheStation (section 3.1.3). As ClientInterface is a virtual subclass of the actual station type (which is not even known to the method), TheStation cannot be simply *cast* to ClientInterface (see also section 8.1.2.4).

Similar modifications have been applied to files utraffic2.h and utraffic2.c (section 9.3.2.2) to produce files utraffic21.h and utraffic21.c used in a revised implementation of H-Net (directory BUS/H-Net3). Both traffic generators share the same nonstandard exposure method for UTraffic. This method is defined in the library file lmatexp.c included from utrafficl.c and utraffic21.c. This definition is as follows:

```
UTraffic::exposure {
  int i, NS; Long count;
  double X [MAXSTATIONS], Y [MAXSTATIONS], min, max, mom [2], Max;
  Boolean First;
  Traffic::expose;
  onpaper {
    exmode 4:
      if (Hdr == NULL) Hdr = "Local message access times";
      print (Hdr);  print ("\n\n");
      for (i = 0, First = YES; i < NStations; i++)
        if (CInt [i] != NULL)
          if (First) {
            CInt [i] -> MAT -> printACnt ();
            First = NO;
          } else
            CInt [i] -> MAT -> printSCnt ();
      print ("\n");
  };
  onscreen {
    exmode 4:
      for (i = 0, NS = 0, Max = 0.0; i < NStations; i++) {
        X [i] = (double) i;
        if (CInt [i] != NULL) {
          NS = i;
          CInt [i] -> MAT -> calculate (min, max, mom, count);
          if ((Y [i] = mom [0]) > Max) Max = Y [i];
        } else
          Y [i] = 0.0;
      }
      startRegion (0.0, (double) NS, 0.0, Max * 1.05);
      displaySegment (022, NS+1, X, Y);
      endRegion ();
      for (i = 0; i <= NS; i++) {
        display (i);
        display (Y [i]);
      }
  }
};
```

At the very beginning, the method calls the standard exposure method associated with type Traffic; this way, the standard exposure is also available for type UTraffic (section 7.3.2.2). The nonstandard exposure defines one new display mode (number 4) for both forms.[21] The paper form of the new exposure mode

---

[21] Note that modes 0–3 are taken by the standard exposure for type Traffic (section 7.3.5.6).

consists of a header followed by the list of statistics representing message access times for all individual stations. Only the stations equipped with `ClientInterface` (`CInt[i] !=NULL`) are accounted for. Note that in general the network may consist of several classes of stations, and some stations may not accept messages from `UTraffic`. Such stations have no `MAT` attributes and should not be included in the exposure. Before the stations are created, `initTraffic` presets `CInt` to all `NULL`s. Thus, the entries that remain `NULL` after all stations have been built (see the `configure` method of `ClientInterface`) indicate the stations that should be ignored by our exposure method.

A single entry of the exposure list is obtained by exposing the random variable of the corresponding station. The first random variable is exposed with `printACnt` rather than `printSCnt` (section 7.3.5.4); this way, the first line of the list will be automatically preceded by a caption.

The screen form of the nonstandard exposure mode for type `UTraffic` consists of a region (section 7.3.3.3) followed by the list of pairs: the station `Id` and the average message access time measured at the station. The region displays the average access time graphically. Points on the horizontal axis represent station locations on the bus, and the vertical axis tells the average message access time observed at a given station. Preprocessing is required before the display information can be sent to DSD. The first `for` loop prepares the region contents. Array `X` is filled with station Ids, i.e., integer numbers from 0 to `NStations` $- 1$. For each station equipped with `ClientInterface`, the parameters of the random variable pointed to by `MAT` are calculated (section 7.1.1.2). The only parameter of interest is the mean value of the random variable (returned by `calculate` in `mom[0]`), which is stored in array `Y` at the index corresponding to the given station. At the same time, the maximum of the mean values for all stations is computed in `Max`. This maximum value is used to scale the vertical axis of the region. The range of the vertical coordinate is from zero to slightly more than the maximum of the average access delays for all stations.

File `lmatexp.c` also contains the full specification of `printLocalMeasures`, which can be used to request the paper form of our nonstandard exposure in a transparent way. This specification is as follows:

```
void printLocalMeasures () { UTP->printOut (4); };
```

To take advantage of the screen form of the exposure, we need a window template (sections 7.3.3.1, A.6) describing the window layout for the list of items sent by the exposure method to DSD. File `lmat.t` in subdirectory `Templates` of SMURPH `Examples` contains such a template. The reader may want to modify this file (according to the rules described in section A.6) to change the window layout. The ways of making the template file visible to the display program are discussed in sections A.4 and D.4.

9.4.3.2   Remote procedure call.   Now we would like to present models of two simple correlated traffic patterns representing typical distributed applications run in a LAN environment. The reader is encouraged to experiment with these traffic patterns in the context of U-Net and H-Net, to determine how unfair these simple protocols are when faced with correlated communication scenarios. We promise that the results will be quite surprising!

As one abstraction of a realistic correlated traffic pattern we propose the uniform *remote procedure call* model. In this model, each station runs two tasks: a *customer* process[22] performing some hypothetical computations, and a *server* process that offers some remotely accessible service to other stations. Every now and then, the customer issues an RPC request to a remote server at another station. The process issuing the request is blocked until a response arrives from the remote server. This response represents the results returned by the remote procedure. In the uniform RPC model, we assume that all stations are homogeneous, i.e., the profile of their activities is statistically the same. Whenever a station issues an RPC request, the server station for that request is determined at random in such a way that all stations except the sender have equal chances for being selected. While the customer process of a given station is suspended awaiting an RPC result, the server at the same station is allowed to run and process the incoming RPC requests. These requests are queued at the station in FIFO order. We assume that there is only one transmitter process at each station and that responses sent by the server part have priority over requests of the customer process.

The structure of station activities in the RPC model is shown in figure 9.4. An instance of the uniform RPC model is characterized by the following four parameters:

- Mean *request interarrival time*, which says how often RPC requests are generated by a customer process
- Mean *request message length*
- Mean *request service time*, which determines the amount of time spent by the server process on servicing a request
- Mean *response message length*

We assume that the requests arrive according to the Poisson distribution. However, in contrast to uncorrelated traffic scenarios, a process may be waiting for a response, in which case its time does not flow. The exponentially distributed interval until the next request generation is measured from the response arrival for the previous request. Consequently, a customer process may have at most one outstanding RPC request at a time. The distributions of the remaining parameters (message lengths and service time) are also assumed to be exponential.

The RPC traffic generator is contained in files `rpctraffic.h` and `rpctraffic.c` in IncludeLibrary. The first of these files defines the following data types:

```
traffic RQTraffic {
    void pfmMRC (Packet*);
```

---

[22]We prefer not to use the word *client* to avoid confusion with the `Client` AI.

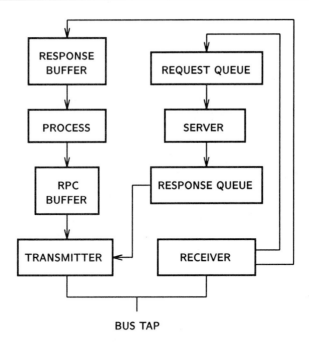

Figure 9.4 The RPC model

```
    exposure;
};
traffic RPTraffic {
  void pfmMRC (Packet*);
};
mailbox RQMailbox (Long);
station ClientInterface virtual {
  Packet Buffer;
  TIME StartTime;
  RVariable *RWT;
  RQMailbox *RQ;
  Mailbox *RPR;
  Boolean ready (Long, Long, Long);
  void configure ();
};
process RQPilot {
  ClientInterface *S;
  Mailbox *RPR;
  void setup (ClientInterface *s) {
    S = s;
```

```
                    RPR = S->RPR;
                  };
                  states {Wait, NewRequest};
                  perform;
                };
                process RPPilot {
                  ClientInterface *S;
                  RQMailbox *RQ;
                  Long RQSender;
                  void setup (ClientInterface *s) {
                    S = s;
                    RQ = S->RQ;
                  };
                  states {Wait, Done};
                  perform;
                };
                void initTraffic ();
                void printLocalMeasures ();
```

The first of the two traffic types (RQTraffic) represents RPC requests; the other traffic type (RPTraffic) is used to generate responses. Both types redefine the virtual method pfmMRC (declared in class Traffic) to intercept message reception events. Type RQTraffic declares a private exposure method. The role of this method is to display the response time statistics at individual stations. The discrepancy in the service time observed for different customers can be viewed as a measure of network unfairness.

Attributes StartTime and RWT of ClientInterface are used exclusively for measuring performance. The latter is a random variable pointer; this random variable accumulates the local response time statistics for the station's customer. The mailbox pointed to by RQ stores incoming requests awaiting service at the station. Each such request is represented by a station Id identifying the request sender, i.e., the station that will get the response when the request has been processed. The other mailbox, pointed to by RPR, is an alert repository used to signal "request processed" events. Each such event results in a response message's being generated and queued at the station for transmission to the request sender. Methods ready and configure have the same meaning as in the other traffic generators discussed in this book.

The traffic generator is driven by nonstandard pilot processes (section 5.3.5) belonging to types RQPilot (request generation) and RPPilot (response generation). A separate pair of pilot processes exists for each station involved in the RPC traffic. Formally, each process of such a pair is owned by a specific station, and it may use the attributes of its owner to communicate with the other processes run by the station. Note, however, that neither of the two process type declarations specifies the owning station type. Consequently, the S attribute is not defined automatically, and it must be declared explicitly and also set explicitly by the process's setup method. The reason it must be done this way is in the virtual character of type `ClientInterface` and in the postulate that the traffic generator should be kept independent of the actual station type. As we will shortly see, the pilot processes are generated by the `configure` method of `ClientInterface`, which is only aware of the `ClientInterface` portion of the station. Although at the moment of station creation `TheStation` points to the complete data structure representing the entire station, there is no way for `configure` (or anything created by `configure`) to use `TheStation` to reference the `ClientInterface` segment of the current station without knowing the complete station type. In consequence, the automatic setting of the `S` attribute (as a pointer to the complete station structure) would render this pointer useless for the pilot processes, which are not (and should not be) aware of the complete type of their owning station. Note that the following, apparently natural, solution would not work:

```
process RQPilot (ClientInterface) {
  Mailbox *RPR;
  void setup () {
    RPR = S->RPR;
  };
  states {Wait, NewRequest};
  perform;
};
```

`S` points to the complete station structure, whereas its actual type is `ClientInterface`. There is no way to *cast* the complete station type to a virtual supertype without knowing the complete type (see also sections 8.1.2.4, 9.4.3.1). Therefore, `S` is set explicitly by the process's setup method to point to the `ClientInterface` segment of the owning station. A pointer to this segment is passed to the setup method by `configure`—as an argument.

Two global functions are announced in `rpctraffic.h`: `initTraffic`, providing the usual initialization interface to the root process, and `printLocalMeasures`, also used by `Root`—to invoke the nonstandard paper exposure of type `RQTraffic`. Similar global functions were declared in file `utraffic1.h` (section 9.4.3.1).

The behavior of the RPC traffic generator is described by the functions contained in file `rpctraffic.c`. This file starts with the following declarations:

```
static RQTraffic *RQTP;
static RPTraffic *RPTP;
static RVariable *RWT;
static ClientInterface *CInt [MAXSTATIONS];
```

All these pointers are initialized by the global function `initTraffic`:

```
void initTraffic () {
  double rqit, rqle, srvt, rple;
```

```
    int i;
    readIn (rqit);   // Mean request interarrival time
    readIn (rqle);   // Mean request message length
    readIn (srvt);   // Mean service time
    readIn (rple);   // Mean response message length
    RQTP = create RQTraffic (MIT_exp+MLE_exp+SCL_off, rqit, rqle);
    RPTP = create RPTraffic (MIT_exp+MLE_exp+SCL_off, srvt, rple);
    RWT = create RVariable;
    for (i = 0; i < MAXSTATIONS; i++) CInt [i] = NULL;
};
```

The function reads the four parameters of the RPC traffic listed at the beginning of this section and then creates two traffic patterns representing the request and response portions of the traffic. The standard pilot processes of the Client are switched off for the two traffic patterns (option SCL_off). As each station involved in the RPC traffic runs a private copy of the pilot process for RQTraffic, the mean request interarrival time is interpreted on a per station basis. This means that the global mean interarrival time of requests to the network is equal to $rqit/N$, where N is the number of stations generating the requests. However, as a station waiting for a response to its last request does not count the time until the next request arrival, the concept of a global request interarrival time does not make much sense.

The mean request service time (srvt) is stored as the mean interarrival time of the second traffic pattern. This way, an instance of service time can be obtained by calling the genMIT method of RPTraffic.[23] There is no danger of this parameter being interpreted as an actual message interarrival time, as the two traffic patterns are exclusively driven by the user-supplied pilot processes.

The global random variable pointed to by RWT and created by initTraffic is used to collect the total response delay statistics for all stations combined. Random variables keeping track of local response delays are defined at individual stations. Array CInt plays the same role as in utrafficl.c (section 9.4.3.1), i.e., it converts station Ids to ClientInterface pointers. As before, the size of this array is determined statically by the symbolic constant MAXSTATIONS defined in rpctraffic.h. The pointers in CInt are preset to NULLs by initTraffic and set by configure whenever a new station equipped with ClientInterface is created. The code of configure is as follows:

```
  void ClientInterface::configure () {
    RQTP->addSender (TheStation);
    RQTP->addReceiver (TheStation);
    RWT = create RVariable, form ("RWT %3d", TheStation->getId ());
    RQ = create RQMailbox (MAX_long);
    RPR = create Mailbox (0);
```

---

[23]Note that both rqit and srvt are expressed in ETUs (section 5.3.4). Most likely, but depending on the definition of the ETU by the root process, one ETU is equivalent to the insertion time of a single bit. Of course, this is the case in both H-Net and U-Net.

```
    Assert (TheStation->getId () < MAXSTATIONS,
      "Too many stations, increase MAXSTATIONS in rpctrafficl.h");
    CInt [TheStation->getId ()] = this;
    create RQPilot (this);
    create RPPilot (this);
};
```

Every station equipped with `ClientInterface` is added to the sender and receiver sets of the request traffic pattern. All stations have equal chances for being selected as senders and receivers, and their potential contribution to the traffic is statistically the same. No explicit set of senders or receivers is defined for the response traffic pattern (pointed to by RPTP). Messages of this traffic pattern are generated deterministically in response to the request messages.

The method also creates two mailboxes. The request mailbox (pointed to by the station's `RQ` attribute) is of unlimited capacity. In principle, the number of pending requests queued at a station can be arbitrary. The capacity of the other mailbox (RPR) is zero; this mailbox is used to pass simple alerts to the pilot process of the request traffic pattern. Finally, the method stores the pointer to the station's `ClientInterface` part in CInt and creates the two pilot processes.

As we said earlier, the response traffic takes priority over the request traffic generated by the same station. This is reflected in the code of the **ready** method:

```
Boolean ClientInterface::ready (Long mn, Long mx, Long fm) {
    if (Buffer.isFull () || RPTP->getPacket (&Buffer, mn, mx, fm))
      return YES;
    else if (RQTP->getPacket (&Buffer, mn, mx, fm)) {
      StartTime = Buffer.QTime;
      return YES;
    } else
      return NO;
};
```

If the packet buffer is empty, the method tries first to acquire a packet from the response traffic pattern and then, only if this attempt is unsuccessful, the method consults the request traffic pattern. In the latter case, if a request packet has been acquired, the station's attribute `StartTime` is set to the queued time of the packet. The contents of this attribute will be used to calculate the response delay for the request represented by the packet. This delay is equal to the amount of time elapsing after the request message was queued at the sending station until the matching response message is completely received by the same station.

Depending on the packetization parameters of the protocol, a single request message can be split into a number of request packets, and a single response message can be split into several packets as well. A request is assumed to have been received completely (and then its processing is started) when the last packet of the request message has been received. Similarly, the request generation process of a station awaiting a response to its last request remains dormant until the station receives the last packet of the response message. Whenever a request message (meaning the last packet of this message) is received by a station, an item is stored in the request mailbox of the receiving station. This is accomplished by method pfmMRC of the request traffic pattern (section 7.1.3.2), which is defined as follows:

```
void RQTraffic::pfmMRC (Packet *p) {
  CInt [p->Receiver] -> RQ -> put (p->Sender);
};
```

As pfmMRC belongs to RQTraffic rather than to ClientInterface, the request mailbox is accessed via CInt, in a way that does not depend on the complete station type. The item stored in the mailbox[24] identifies the sender of the request and is used to address the response message when the request has been processed.

A similar, although a bit more involved, method of the response traffic pattern is invoked at each arrival of a response message to a station:

```
void RPTraffic::pfmMRC (Packet *p) {
  double d;
  ClientInterface *CI;
  (CI = CInt [p->Receiver]) -> RPR -> put ();
  d = (Time - CI->StartTime) * Itu;
  CI->RWT->update (d);
  RWT->update (d);
};
```

The method deposits an alert in the RPR mailbox of the receiving station to wake up the pilot process responsible for request generation (the process has been inactive during the request processing). Then the method calculates the response delay, converts it to ETUs, and updates two random variables: the local variable of the receiving station and the global variable that keeps track of the total response delay measured for all stations combined.

The code method of the request generation process follows. Recall that a separate copy of the process runs at every station equipped with ClientInterface.

```
RQPilot::perform {
  state Wait:
    Timer->wait (RQTP->genMIT (), NewRequest);
  state NewRequest:
    if (RQTP->isSuspended ()) {
      RQTP->wait (RESUME, Wait);
      sleep;
    }
    RQTP->genCGR (TheStation);
```

---

[24]Note that the capacity of the request mailbox is unlimited.

```
      RQTP->genMSG (TheStation->getId (), RQTP->genRCV (),
        RQTP->genMLE ());
      RPR->wait (NEWITEM, Wait);
  };
```

The process loops through state Wait, where it generates a message interarrival interval and sleeps for that interval before proceeding to NewRequest. In state NewRequest, if the traffic pattern is not suspended (sections 5.5.1, 5.5.3), the process generates a message addressed to a randomly selected receiver. Otherwise, it waits until the traffic pattern is resumed and then it starts again from state Wait.

To exclude the generating station from the receiver set of RQTraffic, the pilot process calls genCGR (section 5.5.2) before genMSG. The argument of genCGR identifies the current station, i.e., the station generating the request. This affects the behavior of genMSG as if the current station were selected as a sender by a previous call to genSND. This way, the process makes sure that the current station will not be generated by genRCV as the receiver of the request message. Having generated a message, the pilot process suspends itself until it receives an alert on the RPR mailbox. This alert will be delivered by the pfmMRC method of RPTraffic when a response to the request message has been received by the station. Note that the alert is always awaited when it arrives; thus, the capacity of the mailbox pointed to by RPR can be zero.

The other pilot process runs the following code:

```
RPPilot::perform {
  state Wait:
    if (RQ->empty ())
      RQ->wait (NONEMPTY, Wait);
    else {
      RQSender = RQ->get ();
      Timer->wait (RPTP->genMIT (), Done);
    }
  state Done:
    RPTP->genMSG (TheStation->getId (), RQSender, RPTP->genMLE ());
    proceed Wait;
};
```

In state Wait, the process examines the request queue represented by the mailbox pointed to by RQ. If the request queue turns out to be empty, the process suspends itself until the queue becomes nonempty, in which case state Wait will be reentered. If the request mailbox is nonempty, the process extracts the first item from the mailbox and stores it in RQSender. This item is an integer number (Id) identifying the request sender. Then the pilot process generates the service time for the request. This is done by calling the genMIT method of the response traffic pattern. Note that when this traffic pattern was created by initTraffic, the service time distribution was disguised as the interarrival time distribution. In state Done, where the pilot process gets after the service time interval, the response message is generated and addressed explicitly to the request sender. Then the process moves back to state Wait, where it continues extracting requests from the request mailbox as long as more requests are pending.

The nonstandard exposure method of RQTraffic is defined in a separate file (lrwtexp.c) in IncludeLibrary. This file, which is reused in the *file server* traffic pattern discussed in the next section, also defines the global function printLocalMeasures. Its contents are very similar to the contents of file lmatexp.c (section 9.4.3.1).

Directory BUS/H-Net4 in SMURPH Examples contains the implementation of H-Net coupled with the RPC traffic pattern. The reader will find it interesting to compare the unfairness of H-Net under RPC traffic with the unfairness of the same network operating under uniform uncorrelated load.

9.4.3.3 File server.

Another traffic pattern that can be viewed as a generic abstraction of real-life communication scenarios occurring in local networks is a single-server model with one station offering a global service to all other stations. A canonical example of such a setup is the *file server* traffic pattern, which can be perceived as a biased version of the RPC model in which all requests are addressed to one distinguished station. This station (the server) generates no requests of its own; its sole role in the network is to provide the file service to its customers. Our model of the file server traffic is based on the following assumptions:

- There are two types of requests to the file server: a request to read a file page and a request to write (flush) a file page. The ratio of reads to writes is a parameter of the traffic pattern.

- Messages exchanged between the server and the regular stations (customers) are of two types, the fixed length of messages of a given type being a parameter of the traffic pattern. A page read request is represented by a (supposedly short and fixed-length) *page identifier* message sent by a customer to the server. In response, the server sends a fixed-length page to the customer. A write request consists of a file page sent from a customer to the server. The server responds with a *confirmation* message, whose fixed length is the same as the length of a page read request.

- The request processing time at the server is exponentially distributed. The mean value of this time is a parameter of the traffic pattern. For simplicity, we assume that the processing time does not depend on the request type, i.e., the same mean value is used to generate the processing time for read and write requests.

- All requests are of the same priority. The server queues the incoming requests and processes them sequentially in FIFO order.

- Similarly to the uniform RPC scenario, the request interarrival time is exponentially distributed with the mean value specified as a parameter of the traffic pattern. The request type is determined upon a request arrival at the sender. A customer station with an outstanding request is blocked: its request generation process remains dormant until the request has been satisfied.

Files `fstrafficl.h` and `fstrafficl.c` in `IncludeLibrary` contain a SMURPH implementation of the file server traffic pattern based on these assumptions. This implementation has been derived from the RPC model discussed in section 9.4.3.2. We focus here on the differences between the two models.

The following data types are defined in `fstraffic.h`:

```
traffic RQTraffic {
  virtual void pfmMRC (Packet*);
  exposure;
};
traffic RPTraffic {
  virtual void pfmMRC (Packet*);
};
class Request {
 public:
  Long SId;
  Boolean Write;
  Request (Long, Boolean);
};
mailbox RQMailbox (Request*);
station ClientInterface virtual {
  Packet Buffer;
  TIME StartTime;
  Boolean Write;
  RVariable *RWT;
  Mailbox *RPR;
  Boolean ready (Long, Long, Long);
  void configure ();
};
process RQPilot {
  ClientInterface *S;
  Mailbox *RPR;
  void setup (ClientInterface *s) {
    S = s;
    RPR = S->RPR;
  };
  states {Wait, NewRequest};
  perform;
};
process RPPilot {
  ClientInterface *S;
  Request *LastRq;
```

```
    states {Wait, Done};
    perform;
};
void initTraffic ();
void printLocalMeasures ();
```

Types RQTraffic, RPTraffic, and RQPilot have exactly the same layouts as their counterparts from rpctraffic.h (section 9.4.3.2). There are two modifications to ClientInterface: the RQ attribute representing the request queue is missing, and another attribute, Write of type Boolean, appears in its place. In the file server model, the request queue occurs in exactly one instance that formally belongs to the server station. For easy access, the pointer to the request queue will be declared in fstrafficl.c as a global static variable. The role of Write is to indicate the type of the last request generated by the station. If Write is YES, the last request was a write request; otherwise, it was a read request. As at most one outstanding request can be issued by a customer station at a time, Write can be viewed as an additional attribute of the request message queued at the station. The server station does not use this attribute.

In the declaration of RPPilot, attribute RQSender (of type Long) has been replaced by LastRq (of type Request*). The reason for this substitution is the more complex representation of requests in the file server model. Whereas in the RPC model, the only relevant attribute of a pending request is the Id of its sender, a request in the file server model is additionally characterized by its type (read/write), which is determined upon the request generation at the sender. A pending request queued at the server for processing is described by a data structure of type Request, which, besides the station Id of the customer (attribute SId) carries a Boolean flag (Write) telling write requests from read requests. Consequently, the item type of the request mailbox (RQMailbox) is Request*, i.e., the mailbox stores pointers to request structures. One of the Flags of a request packet (section 5.2.2) is used to differentiate between packets carrying read and write requests. File fstrafficl.h defines the following symbolic constant:

```
#define WRITE_FLAG PF_usr0
```

which associates the write flag with the user flag number zero (section 5.2.2). If this flag is set, the packet represents a write request.

File fstrafficl.c declares the same global static variables as rpctrafficl.c and the following additional variables:

```
    static Long PageLength, StatLength, TheServer;
    static double WriteProbability;
    static RQMailbox *RQ;
```

All these variables are set by initTraffic; the first two define the page length and the length of the page request/confirmation message, respectively. TheServer tells the Id of the server station and WriteProbability gives the probability that a randomly chosen request is a write request. RQ stores the global pointer to the server's request queue. The code of initTraffic, which initializes the global variables of the traffic generator, is as follows:

```
void initTraffic () {
  double rqit, srvt;
  int i;
  readIn (PageLength);
  readIn (StatLength);
  readIn (rqit);      // Mean request interarrival time
  readIn (srvt);      // Mean service time
  readIn (WriteProbability);
  readIn (TheServer);
  RQTP = create RQTraffic (MIT_exp+SCL_off, rqit);
  RPTP = create RPTraffic (MIT_exp+SCL_off, srvt);
  RWT = create RVariable;
  for (i = 0; i < MAXSTATIONS; i++) CInt [i] = NULL;
};
```

As before, the mean service time (which is the same for read and write requests) is disguised as the mean interarrival time for the response traffic pattern. Both traffic patterns are driven by nonstandard pilot processes (very similar to the processes listed in the previous section). In contrast to the RPC model, each station runs only one pilot process. A customer station runs a single copy of RQPilot. Thus, the mean request interarrival time is again interpreted on a per customer basis. The server station executes an instance of RPPilot. All the pilot processes are created by the following configure method of ClientInterface:

```
void ClientInterface::configure () {
  Long Id;
  if ((Id = TheStation->getId ()) != TheServer) {
    RQTP->addSender (TheStation);
    RWT = create RVariable, form ("RWT Sttn %3d", Id);
    RPR = create Mailbox (0);
    create RQPilot (this);
    Assert (TheStation->getId () < MAXSTATIONS,
      "Too many stations, increase MAXSTATIONS in rpctrafficl.h");
    CInt [Id] = this;
  } else {
    RQTP->addReceiver (TheServer);
    create RPPilot;
    RQ = create RQMailbox (MAX_long);
  }
};
```

Each customer (i.e., a station whose Id is different from TheServer) is added to the senders set of the request traffic pattern. The receiver set of this traffic pattern consists of a single station—the server. Response messages are generated and addressed explicitly upon every completion of request processing, and the response traffic pattern (RPTP) needs neither a senders nor a receivers set.

Each customer is also furnished with a random variable (RWT) collecting the response time statistics for the station. No such variable is created for the server, which generates no requests. As the server station is not included in CInt (CInt[TheServer] == NULL), it will not be examined by the exposure method of RQTraffic (section 9.4.3.2) when the local response delay statistics are produced. Although the request mailbox is pointed to by a global variable (RQ), the mailbox is created in the context of the server station and formally is owned by the server. The server has no RPR mailbox, whose purpose is to wake up the request generation process at a customer.

The ready method of ClientInterface is copied from the RPC model (section 9.4.3.2) with a simple modification:

```
Boolean ClientInterface::ready (Long mn, Long mx, Long fm) {
  if (Buffer.isFull () || RPTP->getPacket (&Buffer, mn, mx, fm))
    return YES;
  else if (RQTP->getPacket (&Buffer, mn, mx, fm)) {
    if (Write) setFlag (Buffer.Flags, WRITE_FLAG);
    StartTime = Buffer.QTime;  // Start counting waiting time
    return YES;
  } else
    return NO;
};
```

If a request packet acquired for transmission represents a write request (station's attribute Write is YES), the packet's write flag is set. The Write attribute of a customer station is set by the pilot process responsible for generating request messages. Formally, the request type specification belongs to the request message. In this case, however, taking advantage of the fact that at most one outstanding request can be queued at a single customer station at a time, we can represent the type of this request by a Boolean flag associated with the station. This way we avoid introducing a nonstandard message type, which would unnecessarily complicate our traffic generator.

Following is the code method of the request generator process. Recall that a separate instance of this process runs at every customer station.

```
RQPilot::perform {
  Long ml;
  state Wait:
    Timer->wait (RQTP->genMIT (), NewRequest);
  state NewRequest:
```

```
        if (RQTP->isSuspended ()) {
          RQTP->wait (RESUME, Wait);
          sleep;
        }
        if (rnd (SEED_traffic) < WriteProbability) {
          S->Write = YES;
          ml = PageLength;
        } else {
          S->Write = NO;
          ml = StatLength;
        }
        RQTP->genMSG (TheStation->getId (), TheServer, ml);
        RPR->wait (NEWITEM, Wait);
      };
```

In state Wait, the process generates an interarrival interval and sleeps for that interval before proceeding to state NewRequest. Then the request type is determined at random, and the message length and the station's Write attribute are set accordingly. Note that the process properly handles suspend/resume status changes of the traffic pattern (section 5.5.1). It does not generate a request if the traffic pattern has been suspended but waits for the RESUME event and restarts from state Wait.

Finally, the request message is generated and queued at the station. Before moving back to state Wait, the pilot process awaits an alert on the RPR mailbox. Upon reception of a response message from the server, this alert will be delivered by the pfmMRC method of RPTraffic, whose code is exactly the same as in the RPC model (section 9.4.3.2).

Whenever a request packet is received at the server, the following method of RQTraffic is automatically called:

```
            void RQTraffic::pfmMRC (Packet *p) {
              RQ -> put (new Request (p->Sender,
                flagSet (p->Flags, WRITE_FLAG)));
            };
```

The only statement of this method creates a new request structure and stores a pointer to this structure in the request mailbox. The constructor for type Request (used implicitly by the new operator) is defined as follows:[25]

```
            Request::Request (Long sid, Boolean wf) {
              SId = sid;
              Write = wf;
            };
```

---

[25]A constructor in C++ is a special method that is called automatically upon object creation. A single class type may declare a number of constructors with different configurations of arguments. This explanation is addressed to those readers who are not well versed in C++.

The pilot process running at the server examines the request queue and extracts from it requests for processing. The code method of this process is listed below.

```
RPPilot::perform {
  Long ml;
  state Wait:
    if (RQ->empty ())
      RQ->wait (NONEMPTY, Wait);
    else {
      LastRq = RQ->get ();
      Timer->wait (RPTP->genMIT (), Done);
    }
  state Done:
    ml = LastRq->Write ? StatLength : PageLength;
    RPTP->genMSG (TheServer, LastRq->SId, ml);
    delete LastRq;
    proceed Wait;
};
```

If the request queue is found nonempty, the first request is extracted from the mailbox, its pointer stored in LastRq. Then the process sleeps for the interval corresponding to the request processing time (the distribution of this time poses as the interarrival time distribution for the response traffic pattern) and moves to state Done, where a response to the request is generated. Based on the request type (attribute Write), the length of this response is either StatLength (write request) or PageLength (read request). The response message is addressed to the request sender pointed to by the SId attribute of the request structure. Finally, this structure is deallocated by the standard C++ operator delete.

The pilot process loops through states Wait and Done as long as more requests are available. When the request mailbox is found empty, the process suspends itself until a new request put in the mailbox (by the pfmMRC method of RQTraffic) changes its status.

The nonstandard exposure method for type RQTraffic is shared by the RPC and file server models. This method is defined in file lrwtexp.c in IncludeLibrary; this file is included by fstrafficl.c.

Subdirectory U-Net3 in Examples/BUS contains an implementation of U-Net with the file server model used as the traffic generator. The sample data set in U-Net3 describes a network configuration in which the server is located in the least privileged (i.e., most downstream) position on the bus. Somewhat paradoxically, with this setup the network turns out to be almost perfectly fair.[26] The reader may want to investigate how the network fairness is affected when the server is moved to other locations.

[26]You may have a hard time explaining to your boss that the most important station in the network should be connected in the least favorable place on the bus.

9.5   DQDB

Both H-Net and U-Net can occur in slotted versions (section 9.4.2.1). It is possible to enhance the slotted versions of the protocols by introducing a slot request mechanism that, without sacrificing the capacity-1 property, eliminates starvation. The DQDB protocol is based on this idea. The acronym stands for Distributed Queue Dual Bus and reflects the underlying concept of the protocol according to which the network maintains a distributed queue of backlogged stations. Each single station keeps enough information to avoid starving its downstream successors on the channel. Because of the distributed character of the queue, the protocol is not based on a centralized feedback mechanism, and its maximum achievable throughput is independent of the propagation length of the bus.

9.5.1   The Protocol

The MAC-level protocol of DQDB can be implemented on an H-shaped as well as a U-shaped bus. The H-shaped network (figure 9.2), which is the standard configuration of DQDB, is discussed first.

The two head-end stations are responsible for inserting empty slots into the respective channels of the bus. The slot marker in DQDB carries two binary flags: the ubiquitous *FULL* flag needed by all slotted protocols, and another flag labeled *RQST* (for slot reservation request). A new slot marker inserted into the network by a head-end station has both flags cleared. In addition to generating slots, the head-end stations run the same protocol as the other (regular) stations. A head-end station is the first station to examine the slots generated by itself.

Each station maintains a pair of integer counters for each transfer direction. These counters are denoted by RQ (the request counter) and CD (the countdown counter). Initially, when the protocol is started, both counters are preset to zero. The operation of the protocol is direction-symmetric; therefore, we can focus on one transfer direction. Let us consider transfers from left to right and an arbitrary station s. Assume that s has no packet to transmit towards the right end of the bus. Then the request counter for the LR direction at s is

- Incremented by 1 whenever a slot with the $RQST$ flag set is seen by s on the RL channel (i.e., the channel going in the opposite direction).

- Decremented by 1 (but not below zero) whenever an empty slot ($FULL = 0$) is relayed by s on the LR channel. Note that s has no packet to transmit to the right; thus, it relays all empty slots received from the left to its right neighbor.

Now suppose that s becomes ready to transmit a packet (segment) to the right. It copies the request counter (RQ) to the countdown counter (CD) and resets RQ to zero. At the same time, the station queues a request to set the $RQST$ flag in the first slot going to the left (on the RL channel) in which $RQST$ is zero. This operation is performed in exactly the same way as slot reservation, i.e., the station unconditionally sets the $RQST$ bit in all slots arriving from the right and simultaneously checks whether the previous contents of $RQST$ were zero (section 9.3.1). From now on, i.e., from the moment the station becomes ready to transmit, until the segment gets transmitted, the station behaves as follows:

- Whenever an empty slot is seen on the LR channel, the station checks if CD contains zero. If this is the case, s reserves the empty slot by setting its $FULL$ bit and transmits the segment within the reserved slot. Otherwise, s decrements CD by 1 and lets the empty slot go by.
- Whenever a slot with the $RQST$ flag set arrives from the right (on the RL channel), the station increments the RQ counter. Note that RQ is not decremented along with CD.

The role of the request counter is to notify s how many downstream stations have pending segments awaiting transmission. Based on the current value of RQ, a station getting a segment to transmit determines how many empty slots it should let go by to make sure that the downstream stations are not starved. Note that if the network is devoid of traffic, RQ is zero and, consequently, the medium access delay for a station getting a segment to transmit is also zero.[27] To argue that DQDB is a capacity-1 protocol, we can observe that under extremely heavy uniform load (all stations have a continuous supply of segments to transmit), all slots reaching the terminal ends of the channels are full. The propagation length of the bus has no impact on this phenomenon.

A station becoming ready to transmit joins a virtual queue of stations waiting for bus access. The station manifests its presence in the queue by setting the $RQST$ flag in a slot traveling in the direction opposite to the intended direction of transfer. This way, every single station is able to learn the number of backlogged stations located downstream from it. Note that although no single station knows the identity of the downstream contenders, the complete configuration of backlogged stations can be reconstructed from the RQ counters and from the $RQST$ flags in the slot markers being in transit. In this sense, the set of all RQ counters describes the network's notion of the *distributed queue* of stations competing for bus access. This explains the protocol's name.

A station s that has acquired a segment for transmission moves the contents of RQ to CD, storing in CD the current count of downstream backlogged stations. The request counter RQ is then zeroed, and it will not be decremented while the station is waiting to transmit the segment. However, RQ will count all new slot requests arriving from downstream, keeping track of the stations that will become backlogged while s is waiting for medium access. According to the protocol, s is only expected to yield to those downstream stations that had been logged into its RQ before the station became ready to transmit. In the perception of s, the stations that have been counted by RQ have requested bus access before s and, to ensure

---

[27]To be exact, we should say that the mean access time under light load is half of the slot length.

fair network operation, s should postpone its transmission until it makes sure that those stations have been given the opportunity to do the same.

Unfortunately, although DQDB is starvation-free, it is not absolutely fair. The reason for this is in the distributed character of the request queue. At any moment, the contents of RQ at station s reflect the number of those backlogged stations located downstream from s that have managed to report their status to s, but the stations whose requests have not yet made it to s are, of course, unaccounted for. Thus, s does not really know how many downstream stations have become backlogged before s, it only knows how many backlogged stations had reported their status before s itself became backlogged. The discrepancy between the two notions becomes larger with the increasing propagation length of the bus.

For example, consider two stations s_1 and s_2 connected as shown in figure 9.5. Assume that each of the two stations has a continuous supply of segments addressed toward the right end of the bus and no other station is ready to transmit in this direction. Being the nearer ready station to the slot generator, s_1 is able to use all slots except the slots requested by s_2. Note, however, that the situation of s_2 is not very favorable, especially if the propagation distance between s_1 and s_2 is substantial. Having sent a slot request on the RL bus, s_2 must wait until this request arrives at s_1. Then s_1 will skip one empty slot, this slot will eventually reach s_2, the station will transmit one segment and send another request down the RL bus. It is not difficult to see that s_2 will be getting one empty slot every $2d(s_1, s_2)$ slots, where $d(s_1, s_2)$ is the distance between s_1 and s_2 expressed in slots. All the other slots reaching s_2 will be filled with segments transmitted by s_1. Although s_2 is not starved, the bandwidth allocation in this scenario is unfair, the unfairness being proportional to the distance between s_1 and s_2. Thus, although DQDB is a capacity-1 protocol, it may exhibit unfair behavior in some circumstances. The seriousness of this problem tends to increase with increasing a.

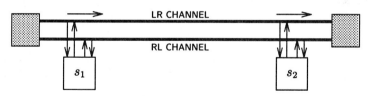

Figure 9.5 A malicious communication scenario for DQDB

Numerous attempts have been made (see Bibliographic Notes at the end of this chapter) to eliminate the unfairness of DQDB. None of the proposed solutions turns DQDB into an absolutely fair protocol, although a significant improvement has been achieved for many malicious traffic scenarios. One simple enhancement that has been incorporated into the DQDB standard is the *bandwidth balancing* (BWB) mechanism. With this solution, a backlogged station will skip an empty slot every now and then, even if its CD counter contains zero.

Although the original version of DQDB was devised for the H-shaped bus, the protocol can easily be adapted for the U topology (figure 9.3). In this variant of DQDB, each station is equipped with only one pair of counters. The most upstream station generates empty slots and inserts them into its outbound port. As far as slot requests are concerned, the most natural solution is to insert the request bits on the inbound ports, which approach affects the purely inbound character of these ports. The protocol, i.e., the rules of updating the counters and accessing the bus are exactly the same as in the "H" version.

A purist who prefers to retain the passive character of the inbound ports can think of a variant of the protocol in which request bits are inserted on the outbound ports. With this solution, the rules for updating the RQ counter must be changed. Namely, each station has to count the $RQST$ flags arriving at its outbound port as well as the inbound port. For each slot request arriving at the outbound port, the station should ignore one request arriving at the inbound port—to account for the fact that some requests arrive from upstream and are addressed to upstream stations.

One of the standard recommendations for a DQDB installation is to use a looped topology in which the two head-end stations "touch" each other. This way the network looks like a ring, although in fact it is still a dual bus terminated on both ends with slot generators. The advantage of the looped topology is the possibility of combining the slot generation functions and other administrative duties performed by the end stations within a single physical station. Of course, logically, the network remains a dual-bus network with two separate head-end stations on each end of the bus.

9.5.2   The Implementation

In this section we present an implementation of DQDB for the H-shaped bus. This implementation has some common features with the implementation of Fasnet discussed in section 9.3.2. Thus, we return for a while to Fasnet and try to figure out the best way to recycle its fragments in DQDB.

9.5.2.1   Fasnet revisited.
Clearly, the receiver process of Fasnet can be used directly in DQDB. To modify the transmitter process of Fasnet in such a way that it can be reused in DQDB, note that there is exactly one place where the process's code method must be changed. Namely, after a segment acquisition from the Client (the ready method of ClientInterface), the process should move the contents of the station's RQ counter to CD and then zero out RQ. As a matter of fact, we can make a somewhat more general observation that the transmitter of Fasnet can be reused in many slotted protocols. The process performs rather elementary actions related to medium access, and the protocol-specific operations are implemented in the Strober process, which drives the transmitter. Thus, it may make sense to build a generic process type based on type Transmitter of Fasnet (section 9.3.2) with the intention of using it to create specific transmitter types for slotted protocols. Fasnet is a relatively simple protocol, and it requires no special

actions to be performed upon a segment acquisition, but this need not be the case in general. Therefore, it may be reasonable to provide a virtual method associated with the generic transmitter type, which would take care of this end.

Directory BUS/Fasnet2 in SMURPH **Examples** contains a modified version of the protocol program from BUS/Fasnet1 (section 9.3.2) in which the reusable fragments have been set aside and stored in library files. There are two such files: sprotocol.h and sprotocol.c; they define two generic types: STransmitter and SReceiver representing a transmitter and a receiver for a slotted protocol. Except for the different type name, type SReceiver is defined exactly as type UReceiver presented in section 9.4.2.2 (the different name of this type reflects the slotted character of the generic protocol). The other process type is announced in **sprotocol.h** as follows:

```
process STransmitter {
  Port *Bus;
  Packet *Buffer;
  Mailbox *Strobe;
  virtual Boolean gotPacket () { return NO; };
  states {NPacket, Transmit, XDone, Error};
  perform;
};
```

Attributes Bus and Buffer play the standard role. The mailbox pointed to by Strobe will be used by the strober process (this process is expected to assist the transmitter) to indicate the beginnings of slot frames whence the transmitter is allowed to insert a segment (section 9.3.2.3). The generic transmitter type is not parameterized by a station type, and it declares no setup method. The owning station type, as well as the setup procedure, depend on the ultimate type of the transmitter, and they will be specified within that type.

The virtual method gotPacket is intended to be called instead of **ready**, to acquire a segment from the Client.[28] The default version of this method is void: it is assumed that the subtype of STransmitter will define the pertinent protocol-specific version of gotPacket.

The code method of STransmitter (defined in sprotocol.c) is as follows:

```
STransmitter::perform {
  state NPacket:
    if (gotPacket ()) {
      signal ();
      Strobe->wait (NEWITEM, Transmit);
    } else
      Client->wait (ARRIVAL, NPacket);
  state Transmit:
```

---

[28]The same approach was taken in U-Net and H-Net (section 9.4.2.2).

```
        Bus->transmit (Buffer, XDone);
        Bus->wait (COLLISION, Error);
    state XDone:
        Bus->stop ();
        Buffer->release ();
        proceed NPacket;
    state Error:
        excptn ("Slot collision");
};
```

The reader will notice that except for the call to gotPacket (which replaces the call to ready), this method is identical to the code method of Fasnet Transmitter (section 9.3.2.3).

Let us now look at the revised implementation of Fasnet. We discuss only those elements of this implementation that have changed with respect to the version discussed in section 9.3.2. One obvious difference is the inclusion of sprotocol.h in types.h. Moreover, the following process types in types.h are defined differently:

```
process Transmitter : STransmitter (HStation) {
    int BusId;
    void setup (int dir) {
        Bus = S->Bus [BusId = dir];
        Buffer = &(S->Buffer [dir]);
        Strobe = S->Strobe [dir];
    };
    Boolean gotPacket ();
};
process Receiver : SReceiver (HStation) {
    void setup (int dir) { Bus = S->Bus [dir]; };
};
```

The only missing fragment of the transmitter is the definition of gotPacket, which in its Fasnet version is as follows:

```
Boolean Transmitter::gotPacket () {
    return S->ready (BusId, SegmPL, SegmPL, SegmFL);
};
```

The other parts of the implementation, including the specifications of Strober, SlotGen, and Absorber, are exactly as before.

9.5.2.2 DQDB. Our implementation of DQDB is built along the same lines as the implementation of Fasnet discussed in sections 9.3.2 and 9.5.2.1. The station type for DQDB contains additional attributes representing the counters needed by the protocol:

```
station HStation : HBusInterface, ClientInterface {
  Mailbox *Strobe [2];
  int CD [2], RQ [2];
  void setup () {
    int i;
    HBusInterface::configure ();
    ClientInterface::configure ();
    for (i = 0; i < 2; i++) {
      Strobe [i] = create Mailbox (0);
      CD [i] = 0;
      RQ [i] = 0;
    }
  };
};
```

A separate pair of counters (CD, RQ) is needed for each transfer direction; thus, each of the two counters is declared as a two-element array indexed by the direction ordinal (LRBus, RLBus). Besides creating two instances of the Strobe mailbox (to be used for the same purpose as in Fasnet), the station's setup method initializes both pairs of counters to zero.

The two head-end stations are objects belonging to a subtype of HStation, whose one additional attribute is the fixed-contents packet buffer representing the slot marker. This subtype is declared as follows:

```
station HeadEnd : HStation {
  Packet SMarker;
  void setup () {
    HStation::setup ();
    SMarker.fill (NONE, NONE, SlotML);
  };
};
```

The setup method of HeadEnd invokes the setup method of the supertype and prefills the marker buffer. SlotML is a constant representing the length of the slot marker in bits. As DQDB is an industrial standard, it makes sense to encapsulate its relevant numerical parameters into a library file. This file, named dqdb.h, is as follows:

```
#define SlotML 8                       // Slot marker length in bits
#define SegmPL 384                     // Segment payload length in bits
#define SegmFL 32                      // Segment header length in bits
#define SegmWL (SegmPL+SegmFL+2)       // Segment window length in bits
#define CTolerance  0.0001             // Clock tolerance
#define SLOT NONE
#define FULL PF_usr0
#define RQST PF_usr1
```

As a matter of fact, only the first three constants from this list are mentioned by the standard. They represent, respectively, the length of the slot marker in bits, the length of the payload portion of the segment, and the length of the segment header. Note that although the marker has room for eight binary flags, only two of these flags are used by the basic version of the protocol introduced in section 9.5.1.[29]

DQDB can be implemented on the basis of several physical and virtual media, e.g., standard digital virtual channels offered by telephone companies. Such channels may offer a built-in slotting mechanism on which DQDB slots can be imposed. Our implementation is based on simple raw unidirectional links, which provide no underlying timing protocol to support the physical layer of DQDB. In this context, SegmWL denotes the length of the segment window in the slot area, i.e., the length of the silence period following the slot marker in an empty slot. This window should be large enough to accommodate a segment with its header; thus, its minimum length is SegmPL + SegmFL. In a realistic implementation, some safety margin should be added to this minimum—to compensate for the limited accuracy of clocks at the head-end stations. The margin of two bits included in SegmWL is "a bit" exaggerated. With the assumed clock tolerance (constant CTolerance), the maximum absolute deviation of the slot length is less than 0.1 bit.

The remaining three constants define convenient symbols for identifying packets and their flags. SLOT is the TP attribute of a dummy packet representing a slot marker (this type is NONE, as slot markers are preset by fill—section 5.2.3). FULL and RQST identify two packet flags (section 5.2.2), applicable to slot markers, used to represent the *FULL* and *RQST* bits carried by the markers.

Each regular station runs three processes: the transmitter, responsible for acquiring segments from the Client and inserting them into slot windows; the strober, implementing the protocol rules and notifying the transmitter about transmission opportunities; and the receiver, responsible for detecting and receiving segments addressed to the station. The receiver process is exactly the same as in Fasnet (section 9.5.2.1), and we do not discuss it here. The type of the transmitter process is declared as follows:

```
process Transmitter : STransmitter (HStation) {
  int BusId, *CD, *RQ;
  void setup (int dir) {
    Bus = S->Bus [BusId = dir];
    Buffer = &(S->Buffer [dir]);
    Strobe = S->Strobe [dir];
    CD = &(S->CD [dir]);
    RQ = &(S->RQ [dir]);
  };
```

---

[29]Some of the other bits are used in the refined commercial version of DQDB. We do not discuss the full commercial version here, as its refinements add no interesting features at the medium access control level. The reader will find more details about the commercial protocol in one of the texts mentioned in Bibliographic Notes at the end of this chapter.

```
        Boolean gotPacket ();
    };
```

The transmitter's setup method is called with an int-type argument that identifies the transfer direction serviced by the process. The direction ordinal is stored in the process's local attribute BusId. The remaining two local attributes of **Transmitter** are pointers to the station's counters (CD and RQ) corresponding to the transfer direction serviced by the process. Being shared and modified by both the transmitter and the strober, the counters are accessed by the processes via pointers.

Type **Transmitter** is derived from the library type **STransmitter** representing the generic transmitter process for slotted bus protocols. Consequently, the DQDB transmitter inherits the attributes of **STransmitter** (Bus, Buffer, Strobe) and its code method (section 9.5.2.1). The virtual method **gotPacket** referenced by that code method describes the operations that must be performed by the protocol upon a segment acquisition from the Client:

```
    Boolean Transmitter::gotPacket () {
        if (S->ready (BusId, SegmPL, SegmPL, SegmFL)) {
            *CD = *RQ;
            *RQ = 0;
            return YES;
        } else
            return NO;
    };
```

If a segment is available for transmission (**ready** returns YES), the method moves RQ to CD (as required by the protocol) and clears RQ. Then **gotPacket** returns YES to notify the caller that a segment has been acquired and stored in the station's buffer indicated by the direction ordinal BusId. Otherwise, if no segment is available, the method returns NO. The remaining part of the bus access protocol of DQDB is implemented by the strober process, which identifies the slots that can be used by the transmitter to insert a segment. The type definition of the strober is as follows:

```
    process Strober (HStation) {
        Port *Bus;
        Mailbox *Strobe;
        Packet *Buffer;
        Transmitter *OtherXmitter;
        int *MyRQ, *OtherRQ, *MyCD;
        void setup (int dir, Transmitter *pr) {
            Bus = S->Bus [dir];
            OtherXmitter = pr;
            Strobe = S->Strobe [dir];
            Buffer = &(S->Buffer [dir]);
```

```
        MyRQ = &(S->RQ [dir]);
        MyCD = &(S->CD [dir]);
        OtherRQ = &(S->RQ [1-dir]);
    };
    states {WaitSlot, WaitLoop};
    perform;
};
```

Attributes Bus, Strobe, and Buffer are set by the process's setup method to point to the corresponding attributes of the owning station, according to the direction serviced by the process (this direction coincides with the transfer direction of the cooperating transmitter). The pointer to the other transmitter process running at the station, i.e., the transmitter servicing the opposite direction, is stored in OtherTransmitter. Note that the setup method of Strober takes two arguments. The pointer to the opposite transmitter will be passed to the method (together with the direction ordinal) when the strober process is created. The strober uses the signal repository of OtherTransmitter to decide whether a slot request should be sent down the bus. Note that STransmitter deposits a signal in its own repository after each segment acquisition from the Client (section 9.5.2.1).

MyRQ and MyCD are pointers to the RQ and CD counters for the direction serviced by the process, and OtherRQ points to the other RQ counter, associated with the opposite direction. According to the protocol, slot requests received by the strober affect the request counter pointed to by OtherRQ.

The code method of the strober consists of just two states:

```
Strober::perform {
    Packet *p;
    state WaitSlot:
        Bus->wait (EOT, WaitLoop);
    state WaitLoop:
        p = ThePacket;
        if (p->TP == SLOT) {
            if (flagSet (p->Flags, RQST))
                (*OtherRQ)++;
            else if (OtherXmitter->erase ())
                setFlag (p->Flags, RQST);
            if (flagCleared (p->Flags, FULL)) {
                if (Buffer->isFull ()) {
                    if (*MyCD == 0) {
                        setFlag (p->Flags, FULL);
                        Strobe->put ();
                    } else
                        (*MyCD)--;
                } else {
                    if (*MyRQ > 0) (*MyRQ)--;
```

```
            }
          }
        }
        skipto WaitSlot;
    };
```

The process monitors all slots passing by, interprets, and sometimes sets the flags in their markers. At the beginning of a slot window in which the station is allowed to insert a segment, the strober deposits an alert in the `Strobe` mailbox, to notify the transmitter about the opportunity. Let us take a closer look at these actions.

The sequence of statements following the first `if` in state `WaitLoop` is executed at the end of every slot marker traveling in the direction serviced by the process, with `p` pointing to the packet representing the slot marker. If the request flag of the marker is set, the request counter for the opposite direction (`OtherRQ`) is incremented. Otherwise, the process executes `erase` on the signal repository of the opposite transmitter. If `erase` returns `YES`, it means that the repository was nonempty, which indicates a pending slot request. In such a case, the strober sets the `RQST` flag of the current slot. The signal repository of the opposite transmitter is automatically emptied and becomes ready to accommodate another slot request.

If the slot is empty (its `FULL` flag is cleared), the strober checks whether the station is ready to transmit in the serviced direction (the buffer contains a segment awaiting transmission). If this happens to be the case, the process further checks whether the `CD` counter is zero (note that `RQ` was copied into `CD` at the moment of segment acquisition). If `CD` contains zero, the strober reserves the slot by setting the `FULL` flag in the marker and deposits an alert in `Strobe` to notify the transmitter that the segment can be transmitted immediately. Note that the marker flags are examined at the end of the dummy packet representing the marker (event `EOT`); thus, the transmitter receives the alert at the beginning of the slot window. If `CD` is nonzero, the counter is decremented and the empty slot travels undisturbed down the bus.

An empty slot arriving when the station is not ready to transmit in the direction serviced by the strober is skipped, but the request counter for this direction is decremented, provided that it is not already zero. Having completed the processing cycle of one slot marker, the process skips to state `WaitSlot` to await the next `EOT` event. Although all such events move the process to state `WaitLoop`, the events caused by segment packets are ignored by the strober (they do not satisfy the `if` condition).

Each of the two head-end stations runs the same collection of processes as a regular station, plus one additional process responsible for generating slots. The type of the slot generator process is declared as follows:

```
        process SlotGen (HeadEnd) {
          Port *Bus;
          Packet *SMarker;
```

```
void setup (int dir) {
  Bus = S->Bus [dir];
  SMarker = &(S->SMarker);
};
states {Generate, XDone};
perform;
};
```

and its simple code method is listed below.

```
SlotGen::perform {
  state Generate:
    Bus->transmit (SMarker, XDone);
  state XDone:
    Bus->stop ();
    Timer->wait (SegmWindow, Generate);
};
```

Every SegmWindow ITUs the slot generator visits the state Generate, where it transmits a new slot marker. SegmWindow is the length of the segment window in the slot area expressed in ITUs. This length is precomputed (by the root process) as the product of SegmWL and the network transmission rate (common for all ports).

Directories DQDB1 and DQDB2 in Examples/BUS contain two DQDB programs for the H-shaped bus with different traffic patterns. The program in DQDB1 is driven by the uniform traffic pattern with two buffers per station and nonstandard access delay statistics collected individually for each station (library files utraffic21.h and utraffic21.c). In the other program (DQDB2), the protocol is coupled with the file server traffic pattern introduced in section 9.4.3.3. The reader may want to run these programs to determine how unfair DQDB is for the two traffic scenarios. As it turns out, DQDB is only marginally unfair under uniform undersaturated loads, even if the traffic is uncorrelated.

BIBLIOGRAPHIC NOTES

The reader will find more information on the technology and properties of fiber-optic channels in *Lee, Kang, and Lee* (1993). Expressnet was proposed by *Fratta, Borgonovo, and Tobagi* (1981; 1983). Fasnet was introduced by *Limb and Flores* (1982). The performance of the two protocols was further investigated by *Tobagi and Fine* (1983) (see also *Dobosiewicz, Gburzyński, and Rudnicki* (1993)). *Ali and Vastola* (1994) discuss the ways of increasing the maximum throughput achieved by Expressnet (without compromising fairness) by introducing multiple cycle types and allowing a station to transmit more than one packet during one cycle.

The Big-*a* problem, formulated by *Kleinrock and Levy* (1987), is based on the premise that no signals can propagate faster than light in vacuum. Very few physicists question this elementary consequence of Special Relativity, but the reader interested in attacking the Big-a problem from this end will find a few promising suggestions in *Herbert* (1988).

U-Net and H-Net were formally classified by *Maxemchuk* (1988) as LCSMA-CD/U/P and analyzed under uniform correlated traffic patterns by *Dobosiewicz and Gburzyński* (1990a; 1991a; 1991b). In *Dobosiewicz and Gburzyński* (1991b), the reader will also find the models of correlated traffic patterns discussed in section 9.4.3.

The general issue of fairness in bus networks was investigated by *Marsan* (1982), *Maciejewski* (1990), and *Dobosiewicz, Gburzyński, and Maciejewski* (1990; 1992) (see also *Maciejewski, Dobosiewicz, and Gburzyński* (1990)). The fairness model used by Dobosiewicz, Gburzyński, and Maciejewski is based on the "point of view" approach. It turns out that a network unfair from one point of view can be absolutely fair from another point of view (see also *Dobosiewicz and Gburzyński* (1991c)). *Mukherjee and Meditch* (1988) proposed a method for improving the fairness of protocols in the U-Net and H-Net class for uniform uncorrelated traffic patterns. This method is based on the so-called p-persistent behavior of stations, with different persistence factors (p) used by different stations. A station ready to transmit may decide to postpone its transmission for some randomized amount of time (dependent on the station's location on the bus) to yield some bandwidth to downstream stations.

DQDB has been described in many books and articles. Besides the standard document *DQDB* (1990), which is very technical and difficult to read, we recommend the text by *Kessler and Train* (1991), which contains essentially all information on the protocol standard (and more) presented in a reader-friendly fashion. *Mukherji and Bisdikian* (1991) give an excellent survey of literature on DQDB, including reports on the numerous efforts to alleviate the inherent unfairness of the protocol.

Hundreds of papers have been published on the performance of DQDB with a stress on its unfairness and suggestions for improvement, e.g., *Wong* (1929), *Hahne, Choudhury, and Maxemchuk* (1990), *Karol and Gitlin* (1990), *Conti, Gregori, and Lenzini* (1991), *Davids and Martini* (1990), *Mukherjee and Banerjee* (1991), *Cheung* (1992), *Kumar and Bovopoulos* (1992), *Sharon and Segall* (1994), *Hassanein, Wong, and Mark* (1994). *Dobosiewicz and Gburzyński* (1991c) describe an implementation of DQDB on a double-U-shaped bus (the so-called UU topology) and show that such a network tends to be fair under uniform uncorrelated load.

The bandwidth balancing mechanism mentioned in section 9.5.1 is described and analyzed by *Hyun and Han* (1991). *Kamal, Wong, and Hassanein* (1992) and *Pach, Palazzo, and Panno* (1992) discuss techniques for increasing the maximum throughput achievable by the network based on reusing full slots whose segments have been already received. *Karvelas, Papamichail, and Polyzos* (1991; 1992) discuss a possible enhancement to DQDB based on periodically rotating the slot generator in a looped topology. This solution aims in the same direction as the pretzel ring and DPMA, which are presented in the next chapter (section 10.6).

PROBLEMS

1. Devise and implement a variant of Expressnet for the U-shaped bus (figure 9.3). Can you suggest a simple recovery procedure for the failure of the most upstream station (responsible for starting trains)?

2. In Fasnet, an *SNC* request is sent after the first empty slot of the last cycle is received by the end station. Consider a modification of Fasnet in which *SNC* is sent in response to every empty slot reaching the end of the bus. Implement this protocol and compare its performance to the performance of standard Fasnet. What can you say about the fairness of the modified protocol?

3. Devise and implement a slotted version of Expressnet and an unslotted version of Fasnet. Determine the performance curves (throughput versus delay) of these protocols and compare them with the performance curves of the standard versions.

4. Passive taps (section 9.1), used by all protocols discussed in this chapter, are emulated in SMURPH by single ports connected via unidirectional links. Program a process describing the behavior of a passive tap implemented as two ports—the way it is done in real life. Reimplement Expressnet using your new taps and bidirectional links interfacing pairs of adjacent taps. Run the program, and compare its behavior (including the execution time) to the behavior of the implementation of Expressnet discussed in section 9.2.2 (directory BUS/Expressnet).

5. Implement the slotted variants of H-Net and U-Net, and compare the performance curves (throughput versus delay) of the slotted variants with the curves for the unslotted variants. Explain the difference in the shape of these curves.

6. Determine the maximum uniform uncorrelated load of H-Net and U-Net under which no stations are starved. Check if this load depends on the propagation length of the bus. Decide on some reasonable packetization parameters, and determine the minimum bus length for which a 32-station starvation-free U-Net outperforms a 32-station Expressnet in terms of the maximum achievable throughput.

7. Under the file server traffic, U-Net exhibits an almost perfectly fair behavior, if the server is located in the least privileged (i.e., most downstream) position. Determine experimentally how the network fairness is affected when the server's location is different. In particular, how unfair does the network become when the server is moved to the most upstream position?

8. Devise a reasonably general malicious traffic scenario for DQDB, and implement a traffic pattern generating messages according to this scenario. Propose a measure of unfairness that will be automatically calculated and exposed by your traffic pattern.

9. At the end of section 9.5.1, we mention briefly two possible ways of implementing DQDB on a U-shaped bus. Implement both versions of DQDB for the U topology, and investigate their fairness in relation to the fairness of the standard version. Use the traffic generator from the previous exercise.

10. Design and implement an Expressnet-like protocol for a network built on a bidirectional broadcast bus (as in Ethernet) with a strictly linear geometry.

10

Ring Protocols

10.1 A CRITIQUE OF BUS TOPOLOGY

So far, the search for an absolutely fair capacity-1 protocol for a bus network has been unsuccessful. Although some refined variants of DQDB come close to absolute fairness, this fairness is never perfect, and usually it only holds if the offered traffic fulfills some criterion of reasonableness.

To achieve fairness, a bus protocol must employ some kind of synchronization mechanism that accounts for all stations in the network. A station willing to transmit a packet must base its decision to access the medium on the status of all the other stations. If multiple stations are ready at the moment, the decision procedure must come up with a fair ordering of the contenders in a way that neither explicitly nor statistically discriminates against any stations.

The accuracy of the decision to transmit with respect to fairness remains in conflict with the objective of maximizing the bus utilization. To transmit in a way that guarantees absolute fairness, a station must wait until its decision to access the medium has gained the acceptance of all the other stations. This is the modus operandi of most of the protocols discussed in the previous two chapters.[1] A medium access strategy based on this premise involves the exchange of explicit or implicit signals across the network, and its efficiency drops (its time cost grows) with the increasing propagation length of the bus. As a moral from this simple observation, we can draw the following conclusion:

> It is impossible to build a capacity-1 protocol in which decisions to transmit are based on complete knowledge of the current status of all stations in the network.

---

[1] All protocols except U-Net, H-Net, and DQDB.

Note that this conclusion is valid for all networks, not only for bus networks. It triggers a natural question: Is it possible at all to build a fair capacity-1 protocol?

Let us take a closer look at DQDB, which is a capacity-1 protocol whose fairness is questionable. Although DQDB is unfair, the operation of every single station in DQDB is driven by feedback from other stations. The protocol uses this feedback to avoid starvation. How does it happen that DQDB retains its capacity-1 status despite negotiating medium access across the network? The answer is in the delayed character of the feedback. A station is allowed to access the medium in advance while waiting for the consent of the other contenders. It may turn out later, after the station has transmitted a number of segments, that it was in fact supposed to share the bandwidth with other ready stations. In such a case, the station tries to fulfill the needs of those other stations before proceeding with its next transmission.

Note that there is no alternative to delaying the processing of the feedback information if the protocol is supposed to possess the capacity-1 property. Neither is there an alternative to taking advantage of the feedback information if the protocol is to be fair. Therefore, methodologically, DQDB aims in the right direction. However, because of the lack of station symmetry, the feedback processing in DQDB is skewed. The location of a station with respect to the slot generator determines how soon the station can inspect new slots inserted into the network and also how fast the station can respond to slot requests arriving from upstream.

By the very meaning of the word *delayed*, feedback signals[2] from different stations may reach the station receiving these signals at different moments, not necessarily in the same order in which they have been sent. Consequently, once we agree on the delayed feedback, it is quite natural and acceptable for the network to appear temporarily unfair, in the sense that during some (supposedly short) periods of time certain stations are favored over others. Under these circumstances, a protocol will be considered fair if it exhibits a long-term station symmetry, stated as follows:

> During appropriately long time intervals, the average processing time of feedback signals emitted by a station does not depend on the location of this station.

Note that DQDB violates this long-term symmetry. The average processing time of a slot request grows with the distance of the station issuing the request from the slot generator.

As the performance of a capacity-1 protocol should be independent of the medium length, it seems that the station symmetry requirement (as stated) implies topology symmetry with respect to every station. Note that DQDB would be fair if the slot generators were allowed to move along the bus in such a way that every station enjoyed the privilege of being an end station for the same amount of time. Unfortunately, DQDB cannot be easily modified along these lines. The inherently station-asymmetric bus topology makes it impossible by definition to locate an end station in the middle of the bus.

---

[2]These signals can be explicit or implicit.

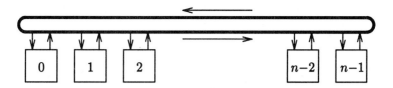

Figure 10.1 A single unidirectional ring

The most natural station-symmetric topology is the ring (see figure 10.1). Ring topologies occur in several versions, including single unidirectional rings (figure 10.1), dual counter-rotating or co-rotating rings (figure 10.4), pretzels (figure 10.5), and so on. All these topologies are discussed in the following sections as the backbones for the protocols introduced there. They are all station-symmetric. In section 10.6 we present a fair capacity-1 protocol built on the basis of a ring topology.

In most protocols for ring networks, stations are allowed to disconnect the ring temporarily. Thus, ring ports are generally active, in contrast to the ports in bus networks based on unidirectional channels (section 9.1). Consequently, a single linear bus can be viewed as a special case of a ring that is permanently disconnected in exactly one place. Similarly, the dual-bus configuration of DQDB can be treated as a pair of counter-rotating rings, both rings being permanently disconnected at the same station. Thus, the ring topology is more general than the bus topology; no wonder that it opens a whole range of new possibilities for medium access protocols.

10.2 RESPONSIBILITIES OF A RING PROTOCOL

Consider the single-ring topology shown in figure 10.1 in which information travels in one direction, e.g., counterclockwise. Each station is directly connected to two neighbors: its immediate predecessor and its immediate successor on the ring. The station receives packets from the predecessor, possibly interprets them, and relays them to the successor. A medium access protocol for such a network should establish a collection of rules for the following two elements of the station's behavior:

- Transmission rights, i.e., when a station is allowed to transmit
- Cleaning duties, i.e., how packets are removed from the ring

As the ring forms a closed structure, the cleaning rules are needed to make sure that packets inserted into the ring by transmitting stations eventually disappear from the network.

10.2.1 Cleaning Rules

A station willing to transmit a packet waits until the transmission rules are obeyed (whatever they are) and then transmits the packet on the outbound port. The packet will be passed from one station to another until it reaches the destination. Having recognized its address in the packet header, the recipient station will receive the packet. Here we arrive at the first dilemma: Should the recipient relay the received packet to its successor or not? At first sight, it might seem that the obvious answer to this question is "of course not." The packet has been received, the network has fulfilled its obligation with respect to the transmitter, and there is no point in relaying the packet any further. It turns out, however, that the issue is bit trickier than it seems. Essentially, there are at least three reasons why in many ring protocols a received packet continues to be relayed past its destination:

- To be able to erase the packet completely, the recipient must buffer at least a portion of the packet. Note that the station does not know where the packet is addressed until it has examined the fragment of the packet's header containing the destination address. Buffering packets at intermediate stations increases the packet delay and adds to hardware complexity.
- If the destination is dormant (e.g., switched off), the packet will not be removed. Thus, the protocol cannot rely exclusively on destination cleaning, which reduces the attractiveness of this approach.
- By letting the packet go by, the recipient can pass some message to the sender (e.g., by setting a flag in the trailer) related to the quality of reception. Many ring protocols use this technique for acknowledging received packets.

Although there exist protocols based on destination cleanup, this approach is always treated with due reservation. It is more common to erase packets at their senders (source cleaning). This way, each packet makes a full circle through the ring. Note, however, that the situation of the sender that has to recognize the arrival of its own packet is only slightly better than the situation of the receiver. The station has to recognize its own address in the sender address field of the packet header before it can start erasing the packet. One way to implement full source cleaning is to use a clock to predict the exact moment when the packet will arrive back at the sender. This only works if the round-trip delay of the ring is a stable quantity, i.e., the operation of relaying a packet at a station always takes the same amount of time. Generally, this solution is considered infeasible because it requires very accurate clocks and assumes extremely predictable behavior by all the stations on the ring. On the other hand, complete source reuse can be easily implemented in slotted protocols, where the transmitter can locate its segment by counting the slots passing by its tap since the moment of transmission.

In most ring protocols, the ring is temporarily disconnected in various places at various moments, which operation dynamically turns the ring into a bus (or a collection of buses). The disconnection is logical: the tap at which the ring becomes disconnected ceases to relay signals from the input channel to the output channel. A station disconnecting the ring assumes cleaning duties by removing from the network all traffic reaching it on the tap of disconnection.

10.2.2   Transmission Rules

Assume that a station gets a packet to transmit. At the moment when this happens, the station's tap may be busy relaying a packet down the ring. Clearly, the station cannot transmit its own packet while another packet is being inserted into the output channel. According to the general guidelines of a MAC-level protocol, which takes the responsibilities of the network layer (section 8.1.1.2), the station should never destroy transient packets before they reach their destinations. This way, we arrive at the first universal transmission rule:

> Never transmit into a channel that is currently busy relaying a packet that has arrived from upstream.

Thus, a station becoming ready must wait with its packet at least until the output channel becomes idle.

Now assume that a station has started transmitting its own packet. What is going to happen if the station receives a packet from upstream to be relayed down the ring? Essentially, there are three ways of handling this problem:

- The incoming transmission is buffered and will be relayed when the station is done with its own packet. This technique is called *buffer insertion.*
- The station aborts its transmission immediately and relays the packet arriving from upstream. A similar technique is used in several bus protocols, e.g., Expressnet, U-Net, and H-Net.
- The protocol rules make it impossible for a transmitting station to be confused by a packet arriving from upstream. For example, a transmitting station may be required to disconnect the ring before transmission.

In the last case, the protocol must guarantee that all packets discarded from the ring at the point of disconnection have been already received at their destinations. This guarantee may result from a combination of transmission rules and cleaning rules. A station willing to transmit a packet may have to postpone its transmission if it knows that the ring may be disconnected in a way that obstructs the packet's path to the destination. This brings us to the second general transmission rule:

> Do not transmit if you suspect that your packet may not make it to the destination because of a ring disconnection along its path.

In many protocols, this rule is not stated explicitly. It is often hidden among the explicit transmission rules, which guarantee implicitly that every transmitted packet is seen by its destination before being erased from the ring. Nonetheless, it is important to realize the importance of the rule, which is obeyed by all ring protocols, regardless of their specific explicit rules.

10.3   FDDI

FDDI, which stands for Fiber Distributed Data Interface, is a commercially available ring network aimed at campus-area environments. The network operates at 100 Mb/s, which is exactly one order of magnitude above the transmission rate of Ethernet. In fact, FDDI is intended to replace Ethernet in the environments where the configuration of the computing equipment has reached the limits of Ethernet's capacity. It can also be used to interconnect smaller (local area) networks (e.g., Ethernets) of a large institution spread over an area comparable to a university campus. The maximum reasonable length of the FDDI ring is claimed to be about 100 km. It is thus conceivable to use FDDI for metropolitan networking, although some negative properties of the MAC protocol (discussed later) discourage such applications.

Somewhat contrary to the acronym, FDDI need not be based on fiber-optic channels. Versions of the network connected via twisted-pair cables are commercially available. Notably, these economy clones of FDDI operate at the full speed of 100 Mb/s. The only penalty for substituting wire for fiber is the reduced maximum distance between a pair of neighboring stations.

A real-life installation of FDDI is usually based on two independent rings laid side by side. However, only one of these rings is active at a time; the second ring is a safety measure to be evoked in case of a segment failure (disconnection) in the first ring. As we do not discuss here the ring reconfiguration procedure of FDDI employed to recover from such failures, we can safely assume that FDDI is a single-ring network. The medium access protocol of FDDI is clearly a single-ring protocol.

The original FDDI standard has been recently revised, and a new version of the protocol has been proposed. This new version, dubbed FDDI-II, purports to solve (or at least to alleviate) some of the problems of the original protocol, especially the way of handling synchronous (real-time) traffic. In our discussion we confine ourselves to the original FDDI (sometimes called FDDI-I), as the new incarnation introduces no essentially novel features at the MAC level.

10.3.1   Token-Passing Schemes

FDDI is a member of the family of protocols based on token passing. Token passing is a simple synchronization tool applicable to any distributed system consisting of a number of agents accessing a shared resource with mutual exclusion. The idea consists in having a single copy of a special attribute, called the token, that is passed among the agents, e.g., in a circular fashion. An agent willing to access the shared resource must wait until it receives the token. Then it holds the token for the duration of the critical operations and releases the token when these operations are completed. As there is only one token in the system, this simple mechanism guarantees that only one party can access the shared resource at a time.

One can think of using token passing as a medium access mechanism in bus networks. In this scheme, the stations pass around a special packet representing the token. The token packet travels cyclically, visiting all stations during one full cycle. Each station knows the identity of its successor, i.e., the next station to receive the token. The succession relation imposes a logical ring structure onto the network. Of course, this structure need not have anything in common with the way the stations are connected to the bus. A station willing to transmit a packet waits until it receives the token. Then the station *seizes* the token (does not pass it immediately to the successor) and transmits its own packet instead. Having completed the transmission of its own packet, the station *releases* the token, i.e., transmits the token packet, addressing it to the next station on the logical ring.

Ring networks are naturally predisposed to token-based access schemes. The ring notion of circular succession simplifies the operation of passing the token as well as the structure of the token itself. In a bus network, the token packet must be explicitly addressed to the next station that should receive it. Moreover, the token recipient must recognize its own address in the destination field of the token's header before it can claim the token. In a ring network, each station has a direct link to its successor and a direct link from its predecessor. Thus, the token need not be addressed, and its structure can be extremely simple. In some ring protocols, the token is just a special signal (a pulse) without any structure whatsoever.

The simplest description of a token-passing protocol for a ring network is as follows. Upon initialization, one station generates a token packet and inserts it into the network. From now on, the token circulates in the ring. A station receiving the token (on the input channel) and having no packet ready to transmit should pass the token immediately on the output channel. This is the normal default behavior of a station, which relays down the ring all traffic reaching it from upstream. A station having a packet awaiting transmission waits until it receives the token. Then the station seizes the token (does not relay it on the output channel), disconnects the ring (ignoring any activities arriving from upstream), and inserts its own packet into the output channel. Having finished transmitting the packet, the station follows it with the token and reconnects the ring. It is not difficult to see that a station seizing the token can disconnect the ring safely. At any moment when the token is physically present in the ring, it follows the last transmitted packet. Therefore, a station receiving the token knows that all packets arriving after the token have made a complete circle through the ring and consequently must have been seen by their destinations.

This description ignores a number of details, e.g., the actual representation of the token and the mechanism of capturing it. Note that this mechanism need not be trivial. If the token is represented as a special packet, then it seems that at least some portion of a packet arriving on the input channel must be buffered before the packet can be relayed on the output channel. How could it be otherwise possible to capture the token without letting it go down the ring—to the next station? If a special signal is used to represent the token, then it may be possible to retain the simple no-delay retransmission policy for regular packets at the expense of complicating the physical layer.

There exist token ring protocols in which the token, besides playing its synchronizing symbolic role, provides a placeholder for a (typically fixed-size) packet (segment). Such a token looks like a slot marker: a flag in the marker tells whether the placeholder carries a segment or is empty. A station willing to transmit a segment waits until the token arrives at the station. Then, using the familiar trick (section 9.3.1), the station examines the status of the placeholder associated with the token and, if the placeholder happens to be empty, reserves it and fills with the segment to transmit. The simplest way to empty the placeholder is to do it at the sender after the token has made a full circle through the ring.[3] Note that with this scheme, it is possible to have multiple tokens (provided that the ring is long enough), although the cleanup procedure becomes then a bit trickier (the sender must count tokens to find the one to be emptied).

The difference between token packets and token markers followed by placeholders can be bridged logically by interpreting the operation of reserving a placeholder as capturing the token. Indeed, one can say that by modifying a bit in the token marker the station changes the token's shape and thus captures it. What propagates down the ring is a packet preceded by the modified token mark, which will not be interpreted as an attribute that grants the transmission privilege. The token is rebuilt (inserted back) by the sender when the packet returns to the station, which approach also makes sense in "pure" token protocols. Despite these similarities, we prefer not to call the "marker + placeholder" concept a token-passing scheme. This way, we avoid putting all slotted ring protocols under the same umbrella. As we will see later, some of these protocols are actually based on token passing (and then the token is something different from the slot marker), while some others clearly fall into other categories (despite the presence of slot markers and *FULL* flags).

10.3.2 The Packet Format in FDDI

FDDI is a classic token-passing protocol, which means that the token (represented as a special packet) governs both the cleaning and transmission rules. The token's structure is essentially the same as the structure of a regular packet. The packet layout in FDDI is shown in figure 10.2.

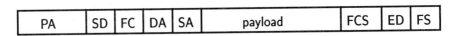

Figure 10.2 The packet layout in FDDI

The physical layer of FDDI uses the so-called 5b4b encoding, in which four information bits are transformed into five "actual" bits that are inserted into a channel. For the logical presentation of the protocol, and also for the purpose of modeling it in SMURPH, we could have ignored the fact that bits are encoded

---

[3]Destination cleanup is possible, but it requires buffering the token and a portion of the segment header before they can be relayed.

in a special way (we have been doing so successfully until now). Unfortunately, some traces of the bit-encoding scheme are visible at the MAC level of FDDI. Each configuration of four bits representing a nibble (half-byte) of a packet payload is mapped into a five-bit physical *symbol*. Clearly, there are more different possible five-bit symbols than four-bit nibbles; consequently, some symbols can be made special. Such special symbols occurring in FDDI packets are easily distinguishable from "valid" logical information carried by packet payloads. They are used as delimiters, packet type indicators, and various status flags associated with packets.

A packet in FDDI starts with a *preamble* (*PA*) consisting of at least 16 *IDLE* symbols. A station must be prepared to correctly receive a packet whose preamble contains as few as 12 *IDLE* symbols or is longer than the standard 16 symbols. In physical terms, the standard length of a packet preamble (16 symbols) translates into 80 "actual" bits. Logically, expressed as the amount of the useful bandwidth occupied by the preamble, this length is 64 "information" bits. From the user's perspective, it makes more sense to measure all lengths in information bits. After all, these are the bits that determine the effective capacity of the network. Therefore, it makes sense to say that the standard length of a preamble in FDDI is 64 bits, although the purists should perhaps stick to the symbol concept, which circumvents the need for discriminating between the two kinds of bits.

The preamble is followed by two consecutive symbols constituting the so-called *starting delimiter* (*SD*). The starting delimiter terminates the preamble and marks the beginning of the proper packet. The packet type is determined by the next pair of symbols denoted by *FC* (for *frame control*). In particular, the token packet is identified by a special value of *FC*.

In a regular packet (which carries a payload), the frame control field is followed by two station addresses, each address occupying 48 logical bits (i.e., 12 symbols). The first address (*DA*) identifies the station to receive the packet. The address format (not discussed here) offers multicast and broadcast capabilities. The second address (*SA*) identifies the packet's original sender.

The next portion of the packet is the variable-length payload. FDDI sets the maximum length of a single packet payload at 4500 bytes, which translates into 36,000 logical bits or 9000 symbols. The minimum length of the payload portion is zero, i.e., it is legal for a packet to carry no information other than its header and trailer. The payload is ended by a 32-bit *frame check sequence* (*FCS*) field, which is just another name for a CRC checksum used to assess the packet's integrity at the recipient's end. The *FCS* sequence is followed by the *ending delimiter* (*ED*) consisting of one special symbol. Formally, the end of the payload portion of a packet is triggered by an occurrence of the *ED* symbol. Then the receiver has to remove the last two bytes of the payload and use it as a checksum that covers the proper payload as well as the *FC*, *DA*, and *SA* fields. The packet ends with the *frame status* (*FS*) indicator, which typically consists of three symbols. These symbols can be used by the recipient to indicate whether it has recognized its address and received correctly the packet's payload. As we will shortly see, a packet in FDDI is guaranteed to return to its originator; thus, the *FS* field can be used by the recipient to pass an acknowledgment to the sender.

The token format is essentially the same as the format of a regular packet. The natural difference is the lack of the address fields (DA and SA) and the payload portion. Also, the FS indicator does not occur in the token. Its three symbols are replaced by an additional (second) ED delimiter. Thus, the ED field of the token packet consists of two symbols, not one.

To build a logical model of FDDI in SMURPH, we need not be concerned with the actual layout of the packet headers and trailers, but we have to know their lengths, as well as the limitations on the payload size. The reader may want to verify that the combined length of the header and trailer of a regular packet (excluding the preamble) is 160 bits, whereas the token length (also without the preamble) is 24 bits.

10.3.3   The MAC-level Protocol of FDDI

The protocol of FDDI consists of the initialization phase, during which the stations manifest their presence and negotiate how much bandwidth each of them should get from the network, and the proper operation phase, during which the network offers its communication service to the users. Occasionally, the network may enter a subset of the negotiation phase during normal operation, e.g., after a failure (lost token) or when a new station becomes active. We only briefly mention the initialization phase and focus our attention on the normal operation phase, which is driven by the actual medium access protocol of FDDI.

The basic idea of the protocol is generic to all token protocols for ring networks. At the risk of irritating the reader, we rephrase it once again using the terminology of FDDI.

A station willing to transmit a packet waits for the token. The station recognizes the token by the specific contents of the FC field and grabs the token by failing to relay this field on the output channel. In principle, the operation of capturing the token can be performed smoothly, without buffering the incoming packet, using the ubiquitous flip-one-bit-on-the-fly technique described in section 9.3.1. The last physical bit of FC for a valid token packet must be zero. Thus, a station can destroy the token by unconditionally setting this bit to 1 and simultaneously determining its previous value (to make sure that the token has not been destroyed by an upstream station). In the commercially available incarnations of FDDI, stations buffer a number of incoming symbols before relaying them on the output channels. This way the operation of destroying the token is simplified: the entire FC field of the token can be examined and stripped explicitly as desired.

Having captured the token, the station is allowed to transmit one or more packets (the exact rules are explained later) and, finally, it should create a new token and insert it into the network. The protocol rules guarantee that, as long as there are no failures, there is exactly one token packet, which at any given moment is either held by some station or is in transit somewhere in the ring.

A token-holding station erases from the ring all packets arriving on the input port of the station's tap. Besides, each station has to recognize and strip the packets that it transmitted. As this is only possible after an initial portion of a packet has been relayed down the ring, unstripped packet leftovers continue circulating in the network until they are eventually absorbed by a token-holding station.

At first sight, the partial source cleanup feature of FDDI seems to be merely a courtesy of the sender. The fragmented periods of silence reclaimed this way cannot be used to transmit packets, as the transmission rights are restricted to the station that holds the token. A transmitting station always removes from the ring all the packets arriving from upstream, and it does not care whether these packets have been already partially stripped by their senders or not. The role of source cleanup is to make sure that the same packet is never received more than once. If a transmitting station releases the token before its packet completes a full circle through the ring, the packet will be seen twice (or perhaps even more times) by the same potential receivers. By stripping the packet before it embarks on its second trip through the ring, the station makes sure that the packet will not be received again.

Up to this point, FDDI looks like a generic token-passing protocol with a specific packet format. The most important element of the medium access control mechanism of FDDI is the collection of token-holding rules that determine for how long every station is allowed to keep the token. The protocol attempts to be flexible with bandwidth allocation. Consequently, the amount of the token-holding time per station varies dynamically with the changing pattern of network load.

For reasons that will become clear shortly, the traffic in the network is divided into two classes:

- Synchronous traffic with a reasonably well-bounded maximum access time. This traffic class represents real-time applications requiring guaranteed fast service.

- Asynchronous traffic with a reasonable average access time under light and moderate loads, but with possibly large and generally unpredictable delays under heavy traffic conditions.

During the initialization procedure, all stations determine how much of the synchronous portion of the network bandwidth each of them will get. For each station s_i, its share of the synchronous bandwidth is described by a time interval S_i negotiated during the startup phase. A station s_i receiving the token is always allowed to grab and hold it for the negotiated interval S_i, and use this time for transmitting synchronous packets. The sum of the synchronous shares over all stations in the network

$$S = \sum_{i=0}^{N-1} S_i \ ,$$

gives the upper limit on the amount of time that the network can spend transmitting synchronous packets during one full rotation of the token.

Each station is guaranteed its negotiated synchronous share every time it sees the token. Note, however, that synchronous shares unused by some stations (because these stations had no synchronous traffic to offer when they were visited by the token) cannot be reused by other stations. The asynchronous traffic class is handled in a more flexible way. The startup procedure determines a single global numerical parameter A, which tells for how much time all stations can transmit asynchronous packets during one token rotation. Unlike the synchronous bandwidth, this portion of the network capacity is not preallocated to individual stations, but it can be claimed on demand—within the global limit. The sum $S + A$ gives an estimate of the maximum combined token-holding time during one round trip of the token through the ring. The stations operate in a manner that attempts to obey this estimate.

Given the propagation length of the ring L, the maximum interval between two consecutive token arrivals to the same station (the so-called *target token rotation time*) is estimated by the following formula:

$$TTRT = L + S + A + \Delta,$$

where Δ represents the sum of the repeater delays at all stations.

Each station is equipped with two timers called TRT (for *token rotation timer*) and THT (for *token-holding timer*). Whenever a station receives the token, it resets TRT to zero, and from then on the timer is incremented at the clock rate. At any moment, TRT tells the amount of time that has elapsed after the token last arrived at the station.

Before resetting TRT to zero, a station receiving the token calculates the allowed token-holding time $THT = TTRT - TRT$. If THT is greater than zero, the timer starts decrementing at the clock rate. According to the protocol, the station is allowed to transmit asynchronous packets as long as its THT timer is greater than zero.

If at the moment when the token arrives at a station TRT is less than $TTRT$, we say that the token is early; otherwise, the token is late. In the latter case, the station cannot transmit any asynchronous packets: a late token is interpreted as an indication that the entire asynchronous bandwidth associated with the current round of the token has been used. In any case, even if the token is late, a station receiving it can grab it and transmit the station's allotted share of synchronous packets. If the token arrives early and the station has both synchronous and asynchronous packets awaiting transmission, it should start with the synchronous packets and then, if THT is still greater than zero, proceed with the asynchronous packets until either THT runs down to zero or the station runs out of packets to transmit. More specifically, a token-holding station can start transmitting a new asynchronous packet if THT is still nonzero.[4] It can thus extend its token-holding

---

[4]It is possible to use a priority scheme in which different priority classes of asynchronous packets use different non-negative values representing different thresholds of THT. A packet transmission can be started if THT is greater than the packet's threshold value. Note that lower thresholds correspond to higher priorities.

time up to the maximum packet length—which FDDI sets at 36,000 bits—beyond
the late-token limit. Note that a token arriving late at a station can leave it even
later and become more late when it arrives at the next station. This happens if the
station receiving a late token has synchronous packets awaiting transmission. In
the most extreme case, when all stations are able to fill their synchronous quota,
the maximum interval between two consecutive token arrivals at the same station
can slightly exceed $TTRT + S$. As S is bounded from above by $TTRT$, the longest
round trip of the token in FDDI is bounded by $2\,TTRT$.

10.3.4   The Implementation

In most commercial installations of FDDI, S is zero, i.e., no bandwidth is set aside
for critical, time-sensitive applications. Network managers do not like the synchronous traffic concept of FDDI, owing to its lack of flexibility, and use it only
when absolutely necessary. The asynchronous bandwidth is more flexible, but the
upper bound on the access time for an asynchronous packet is very poor. This
problem is discussed in section 10.3.5.

In our implementation of FDDI, we ignore the synchronous portion of the
traffic. We also assume that all stations are homogeneous and all packets have the
same priority. It will not be difficult to enhance our program by including all the
features of FDDI that have been left out. The reader is encouraged to do it as an
exercise.

10.3.4.1   The single-ring topology.
FDDI is the first protocol discussed in
this book that uses a ring topology. It is reasonable to assume that this topology
is generic enough to be useful in other protocol programs; therefore, we put its
definition in the include library (files `sring.h` and `sring.c`). This definition follows
the same pattern as the other topology descriptions presented in previous chapters.
Thus, file `sring.h` contains the following declarations:

```
station SRingInterface virtual {
  Port *IRing, *ORing;
  void configure ();
};
void initSRing (RATE, TIME, int);
```

The virtual type `SRingInterface` describes the ring interface portion of the
station structure. `IRing` and `ORing` are pointers to the input and output port,
respectively. These ports will be built by the `configure` method when the station
is created.

The global function `initSRing` will be called from the root process, to create
the ring channels and define their attributes. The complete function is defined in
file `sring.c`, whose initial fragment is as follows:

```
static PLink **Segments;
static RATE TR;
```

```
static DISTANCE D;
static int NP, NC;
static SRingInterface **RStations;
void initSRing (RATE r, TIME l, int np) {
  int i;
  NP = np;
  Segments = new PLink* [NP];
  for (i = 0; i < NP; i++) Segments [i] = create PLink (2);
  TR = r;
  D = l / NP;
  NC = 0;
  RStations = new SRingInterface* [NP];
};
```

All the static global variables declared in the header of sring.c are initialized by initSRing. The function sets NP to the number of stations (passed as the third argument), which coincides with the number of links in the ring. Data structures representing these links will be pointed to by the elements of Segments, which is an array of link pointers. As all the links are simple point-to-point unidirectional channels, they are best represented by type PLink (section 3.2.1).

The second argument of initSRing gives the total propagation length of the ring in ITUs. This length is divided by NP—the number of ring segments—to produce the length of a single channel (stored in D). This length is the same for all channels, and the network is absolutely station-symmetric.

The first argument of the function specifies the network transmission rate. This rate is stored in R to be used by the configure method of SRingInterface as the setup argument for creating output ports. The dynamically allocated array pointed to by RStations, together with NC representing its element count, will also be used by configure—to store pointers to the SRingInterface segments of the stations that have been created so far. The complete definition of configure is as follows:

```
void SRingInterface::configure () {
  int i, j;
  IRing = create Port;
  ORing = create Port (TR);
  RStations [NC++] = this;
  if (NC == NP) {
    for (i = 0; i < NP; i++) {
      j = (i+1) % NP;
      RStations [i] -> ORing -> connect (Segments [i]);
      RStations [j] -> IRing -> connect (Segments [i]);
      RStations [i] -> ORing -> setDTo (RStations [j] -> IRing, D);
    }
    delete RStations;
```

```
        delete Segments;
    }
};
```

The method starts by creating the two ports interfacing the station to the ring. Note that the transmission rate of IRing (the input port) is undefined: this port is never used to transmit anything. Then the pointer to the station's SRingInterface portion is added to RStations, and the method checks whether all stations have been built, i.e., all slots in RStations have been filled in. If this happens to be the case, the stations are configured into the network, and the two dynamic arrays RStations and Segments (not needed anymore) are deallocated. The operation of configuring the network consists in connecting the ports to the proper links and assigning distances between the end ports on the same links. Link number i connects stations i and $i + 1$ mod NP (NP is the number of stations connected to the ring).

10.3.4.2   The protocol.   As FDDI is a commercial standard, its fixed numerical parameters should be treated as constants. These constants have been set aside and stored in the include library (file fddi.h) to be shared by other implementations of the protocol, e.g., the ones to be designed and programmed by the reader. The contents of fddi.h are as follows:

```
#define MaxPL       36000
#define FrameL        160
#define PrmbL          64
#define TokL           24
#define CTolerance 0.0001
```

The maximum packet length in FDDI (constant MaxPL) is 36,000 bits, which translates into 4500 bytes (octets) or 9000 FDDI symbols. The protocol imposes no minimum packet length; in particular, the payload portion of a packet can be empty. Constant FrameL gives the combined length of the header and trailer for a regular packet, excluding the preamble. Preambles in our program will be separated from packets and represented as jamming signals (section 6.1). The standard length of a preamble (constant PrmbL) is 64 bits. The preamble length is the same for regular packets and the token, whose total length (excluding the preamble) is 24 bits (constant TokL). The last constant (CTolerance) defines the tolerance of clocks. This parameter is not specified in the protocol standard; its role in our program is to make the implementation more realistic.

All stations in our simple model of FDDI have the same layout and run identical configurations of processes. The station type is declared as follows:

```
station FStation : SRingInterface, ClientInterface {
  TIME TRT, THT;
  void setup () {
    SRingInterface::configure ();
    ClientInterface::configure ();
```

```
    TRT = THT = TIME_0;
  };
};
```

TRT and THT are the two timers discussed in section 10.3.3. In our implementation, they are not exactly timers (although we will continue calling them this), because they do not "tick" automatically at the clock rate. Instead, they are used to store clock readings and compare them later with other readings.[5] Both timers are initialized to zero by the station's setup method. Once the token has made its first round trip through the ring, at any moment afterwards, the value of TRT tells the time when the station was last visited by the token.

Each station permanently runs two processes: the relay process and the receiver. The receiver, which is very simple and standard (section 8.1.2.2), is not discussed here. Additionally, whenever a station becomes eligible to transmit,[6] its relay process spawns a single transmitter process that remains alive for as long as the station can legitimately continue transmitting packets.

The initialization procedure of FDDI is not modeled by our program. It is assumed that all stations are homogeneous and that they use the same preassigned value of $TTRT$, which is decided upon by the root process and stored in a global variable. However, a tiny fragment of the protocol setup phase must be present in our implementation. Namely, one station must generate the token and insert it into the ring. In our program, this task is assumed by station 0; it is performed by a special process created at station 0 by Root. The type of this process has the following definition:

```
process Starter (FStation) {
  Port *ORing;
  Packet *Token;
  void setup () { ORing = S->ORing; };
  states {Start, PDone, Stop};
  perform;
};
```

The short life of Starter lasts only as long as it takes to transmit the token. Having created the token packet and inserted it into the station's output port (ORing), the process disappears forever. Its simple code method is as follows:

```
Starter::perform {
  state Start:
    Token = create Packet;
```

---

[5]Note that the actual timers in a real network could be implemented this way. The timers in FDDI are used to compare clock readings at some critical moments rather than going off and triggering some events automatically.

[6]According to the protocol rules, this happens when a backlogged station receives an early token.

```
                    Token->fill (NONE, NONE, TokL);
                    ORing->sendJam (PrTime, PDone);
                 state PDone:
                   ORing->stop ();
                   ORing->transmit (Token, Stop);
                   delete Token;
                 state Stop:
                   ORing->stop ();
                   terminate;
           };
```

In its first state, the process creates a raw packet structure and then fills it
(section 5.2.3) with the attributes identifying the token. The token packet has no
sender and no explicit receiver. Its total length, determined by constant TokL, is 24
bits. This length does not cover the preamble, which, as we said at the beginning
of this section, is generated as a separate activity—a jamming signal. The time
needed to transmit the preamble (PrTime) has been precomputed by Root and
expressed in ITUs as the product of PrmbL (64 bits) and the transmission rate.
Having inserted the preamble into the station's output port (ORing), the process gets
to state PDone, where it terminates the preamble and starts transmitting the token.
Note that the data structure representing the token can be (and is) immediately
deallocated (operation delete) as soon as the transmission is started. According to
the semantics of transmit (section 6.1.2.1), the packet structure is copied into the
activity structure that is actually inserted into the port; thus, the original object
is no longer needed. In state Stop, the Starter completes the token transmission,
terminates itself, and ceases to exist.

The heart of the implementation is the relay process, which implements the
token-passing rules and the cleaning rules. The relay process is responsible for
detecting the token packet, intercepting it, spawning an instance of the transmitter
process (if the protocol rules allow the station to capture the token), regenerating
the token, and inserting it back into the ring. Its type definition is as follows:

```
           process Relay (FStation) {
             Port *IRing, *ORing;
             Packet *Relayed;
             void setup () {
               IRing = S->IRing;
               ORing = S->ORing;
               Relayed = create Packet;
             };
             states {Mtr, SPrm, EPrm, Frm, WFrm, EFrm, MyTkn, IgTkn,
               PsTkn, PDone, TDone};
             perform;
           };
```

The process is responsible for relaying packets arriving from the input port

(IRing) to the output port (ORing). The data structure representing the packet currently being relayed is kept in the packet buffer pointed to by **Relayed**. Upon a token reception, the process determines whether the station should hold the token. If this is the case, the token is captured and the ring is disconnected, i.e., the process ceases to relay the incoming packets to the output port. Then the transmitter process is spawned and it continues to exist for as long as the station has packets to transmit and the token-holding time is still within the limits imposed by the protocol. Finally, the token is inserted back into the ring, and the ring is reconnected. All these operations are performed by the following code method:

```
Relay::perform {
  Transmitter *Xmitter;
  state Mtr:
    IRing->wait (BOJ, SPrm);
  state SPrm:
    ORing->startJam ();
    IRing->wait (EOJ, EPrm);
  state EPrm:
    ORing->stop ();
    IRing->wait (BOT, Frm);
  state Frm:
    *Relayed = *ThePacket;
    if (Relayed->Sender == S->getId ())
      Relayed->Receiver = NONE;
    ORing->startTransfer (Relayed);
    skipto WFrm;
  state WFrm:
    IRing->wait (ANYEVENT, EFrm);
  state EFrm:
    if (IRing->events (EOT)) {
      if (Relayed->TP == TOKEN)
        proceed MyTkn;
      else
        ORing->stop ();
    } else
      ORing->abort ();
    proceed Mtr;
  state MyTkn:
    S->THT = Time - S->TRT;
    S->TRT = Time;
    if (S->ready (0, MaxPL, FrameL) && S->THT < TTRT) {
      ORing->abort ();
      Xmitter = create Transmitter;
      Xmitter->wait (DEATH, PsTkn);
```

```
    } else
      proceed IgTkn;
  state IgTkn:
    ORing->stop ();
    proceed Mtr;
  state PsTkn:
    ORing->sendJam (PrTime, PDone)
  state PDone:
    ORing->stop ();
    ORing->transmit (Relayed, TDone);
  state TDone:
    ORing->stop ();
    proceed Mtr;
};
```

State Mtr, where the process starts its operation, is the entry point of a main loop, whose one turn takes care of one packet arriving from upstream. Each packet must start with a preamble; therefore, the only event awaited in state Mtr is BOJ (section 6.2.7), which indicates the beginning of a preamble announcing a new packet. Upon the occurrence of this event, the process moves to state SPrm, where it starts replicating the preamble (a jamming signal) on the output port. This operation continues for as long as the source preamble is being perceived on IRing. When it ends, the process moves to state EPrm to terminate the copy of the preamble propagated to the output port and to await the beginning of the packet that should normally follow the preamble.

In state Frm, the arriving packet is copied to the intermediate buffer. Note that formally this operation is not allowed in a realistic model of the protocol. At the moment when we just sense the beginning of a packet arriving at the inbound port we do not have enough information to make a complete copy of the packet. Therefore, we do not treat the contents of Relayed as a complete structure. We assume that it is just a scratch variable representing the packet in transit, and we tacitly agree to perform only such operations on this variable that would make sense in real life. To contradict our intentions, the first operation performed on Relayed in state Frm does not seem very realistic. We examine the Sender attribute of the packet, although it will not be available until some initial portion of the packet's header has arrived at the station. This is a simple and innocent trick played to simulate source cleanup. Recall from section 10.2.1 that a station in FDDI is expected to strip from the ring the packets that it created. This stripping is partial and has no impact on protocol performance; it is just a courtesy of the sender, except for one thing: it makes sure that the same packet is never received twice by its destination. It would be possible to model in SMURPH the exact type of source cleanup implemented in real FDDI. This might be valuable as an exercise, but the net effect would be hardly commensurate with the effort. Thus, we settle for a simple solution that has the desired effect and avoids the burden of introducing several additional states to the relay process, which would unnecessarily inflate its already long code method. With our solution, a station recognizing itself in the Sender field of a relayed packet changes the Receiver attribute of the packet to NONE. Such a packet will be ignored by all receivers until it hits the token-holding station and disappears from the network. Note that exactly the same fate would await the stripped remnant of a packet in a real-life FDDI ring.

Having examined the Sender attribute of the relayed packet (and possibly modified its Receiver attribute), the relay process starts retransmitting the incoming packet on the output port. Then it moves to state WFrm (using skipto) to await the moment when the retransmission will be complete. This can happen in two ways: either the incoming packet will be terminated properly and it will trigger the EOT event, or the packet will arrive aborted and another event (SILENCE, BOJ) will be triggered instead. The second scenario is only possible for the token packet.[7] To determine what exactly happens, the process awaits ANYEVENT (section 6.2.9) and when an event is triggered (state EFrm), it checks whether the event is EOT (indicating a complete packet) or anything else (indicating an aborted token). Note that to issue a sensible wait request for ANYEVENT, the process must have arrived at state WFrm via skipto rather than proceed. Otherwise, ANYEVENT would have been triggered immediately, by the still pending BOT event that caused the previous transition to state Frm.

If in state EFrm the relay process concludes that the incoming packet does not terminate properly, it aborts the retransmission of this packet on the output port. Otherwise, the packet type is checked to detect the token. Note that a standard receiver process is monitoring the input port at the same time. Thus, there is no need for the relay process to detect packets addressed to its station. If the incoming packet is not the token, its retransmission on the output port is terminated normally (by stop). With this operation, the packet retransmission cycle is completed and the process moves back to state Mtr to await another packet arrival from upstream. If the packet turns out to be the token, before its terminator is inserted into the output port, the process transits to state MyTkn to determine whether the token should be captured. The station attribute TRT tells the time when the station was last visited by the token. By subtracting this value from the current time (Time), the process obtains the total rotation time of the token measured from the moment of its previous arrival at the station. This is equivalent to reading the value of the *TRT* timer, according to the protocol specification in section 10.3.3. The perceived token rotation time is stored in the station's THT attribute. The station is allowed to transmit if there is a packet awaiting transmission (method ready) and THT is less than TTRT. If these two conditions hold simultaneously, the relay process decides to capture the token. Thus, it aborts the token retransmission on the output port, creates the transmitter process, and suspends its own activity until the transmitter terminates. The responsibility to use the token according to the protocol rules rests

---

[7]As we will see, the operation of intercepting the token is modeled by aborting the token retransmission. To be valid, the token packet must be terminated properly.

now with the transmitter.

Note that the aborted token packet will not be recognized as the token by another copy of the relay process at a downstream station. Before the process even starts looking at the packet type (state EFrm), it must recognize the valid end-of-packet mark. Logically, this method of capturing the token is equivalent to the mechanism postulated in the protocol specification (section 10.3.3).

When the transmitter concludes that it is done with its share of packets, it terminates itself, and the relay process regains control in state PsTkn. Then the process inserts a new token into the ring (states PsTkn, PDone, and TDone) and resumes the monitoring of the input port in state Mtr.

Now it is time to have a look at the transmitter process. Its type is defined as follows:

```
process Transmitter (FStation) {
  Port *ORing;
  TIME TStarted;
  void setup () { ORing = S->ORing; };
  states {Xmit, PDone, EXmit};
  perform;
};
```

The only attribute whose purpose is not immediately obvious is TStarted. It is used as a temporary variable for counting the accumulated transmission time and monitoring the token-holding interval. The code method of Transmitter is as follows:

```
Transmitter::perform {
  state Xmit:
    TStarted = Time;
    ORing->sendJam (PrTime, PDone);
  state PDone:
    ORing->stop ();
    ORing->transmit (S->Buffer, EXmit);
  state EXmit:
    ORing->stop ();
    S->Buffer.release ();
    if (S->ready (0, MaxPL, FrameL) &&
      (S->THT += Time - TStarted) < TTRT)
      proceed Xmit;
    else
      terminate;
};
```

The process gets to state Xmit each time it decides to transmit a new packet. At the time when the transmitter is created, it is known that there is a least one packet queued at the station and, according to the protocol rules, the station is allowed to transmit at least one packet. The process sets `TStarted` to the current time and inserts a preamble into the output port. Attribute `TStarted` will be used to measure the time spent by the process on transmitting the packet together with its preamble. When the transmitter is done with the preamble (state `PDone`), it terminates the preamble and transmits the contents of the station's packet buffer. Note that this buffer was initially filled by the relay process (in state `MyTkn`) when the decision to capture the token was made.

The transmitter transits to its last state (`EXmit`) when the entire packet has been transmitted. Then it stops the transmission, releases the packet buffer, and determines whether the token should be held for another transmission. This is the case if the station has more packets to transmit and it has not reached its limit on the token-holding time. The first part of this condition is checked by calling `ready`. If the method returns `NO`, it means that the message queue is empty and the transmitter has accomplished its task. Otherwise, the transmitter adds to the station attribute `THT` the difference between the current time and `TStarted`, i.e., the amount of time spent on transmitting the last packet. `THT` was set by the relay process to the perceived token rotation time at the moment when the token was captured by the station. Thus, if the updated value of `THT` ends up being less than `TTRT`, the station is still allowed to transmit. In such a case, the transmitter transits back to its first state to insert into the ring another preamble followed by another packet. If no further transmissions are possible, the process just terminates itself.

We do not discuss here the structure of the `Root` process, which is standard and straightforward. The reader will find the complete FDDI program in directory `RING/FDDI` of SMURPH `Examples`.

10.3.4.3 FDDI observers.   Token protocols for ring networks are often used as examples for demonstrating formal methods of protocol verification. The correctness of a token protocol can be easily asserted by expressing some simple dynamic properties of the token, which is a convenient single and tangible object governing the behavior of the entire distributed system. Our implementation of FDDI in directory `RING/FDDI` incorporates two observers (files `observers.h` and `observers.c`) describing simple statements about the token that must be fulfilled by a correct implementation of the protocol. One of these observers, `TokenMonitor`, makes sure that the token is never lost or duplicated. In other words, at most one station at a time is given transmission rights and the protocol is "alive," i.e., every now and then the token is perceived by some station. The type of `TokenMonitor` is declared in the following way:

```
observer TokenMonitor {
  TIME TokenPassingTimeout;
  states {Resume, Verify, Duplicate, Lost};
  void setup () {
    TokenPassingTimeout = TTRT + TTRT;
  };
```

```
    perform;
};
```

To detect a lost token, the observer imposes a limit on the maximum amount of time that can legitimately elapse between two moments when the token is seen at a station. This limit is set at $2 \times TTRT$ and stored in `TokenPassingTimeout`—a local attribute of `TokenMonitor`. The code method executed by the observer is as follows:

```
TokenMonitor::perform {
  state Resume:
    inspect (ANY, Relay, MyTkn, Verify);
    timeout (TokenPassingTimeout, Lost);
  state Verify:
    inspect (TheStation, Relay, PsTkn, Resume);
    inspect (TheStation, Relay, IgTkn, Resume);
    inspect (ANY, Relay, MyTkn, Duplicate);
    timeout (TokenPassingTimeout, Lost);
  state Duplicate:
    excptn ("Duplicate token");
  state Lost:
    excptn ("Lost token");
};
```

The observer starts in state `Resume`, where it issues one inspect request followed by a timeout request. The inspect request describes a situation when the relay process at any station wakes up in state `MyTkn`. This corresponds to the token being perceived by the station and must happen before the timeout expires. Otherwise, the observer will transit to state `Lost`, where it will display a pertinent message and abort the simulator (section 2.3.5).

When a token is perceived at a station, there are two possible legal continuations of the network's global state:

- The token may be captured by the station. In this case, the relay process will eventually get to state `PsTkn` to release the token.

- The station may not be able to use the token. Then the relay process will transit to state `IgTkn`.

These legitimate transitions are described by the first two inspect requests issued by the observer in state `Verify`. Note that this time the first argument of inspect is `TheStation`, as the expected transitions must occur at the same station that has noticed the token. The third inspect request is used to detect a scenario in which the token is seen again at some station before one of the expected transitions has taken place. Such a configuration of events will be interpreted as a duplicate token (state `Duplicate`). The last possibility (or should we rather say *impossibility*) accounted for by the observer is the scenario in which none of the sequences described by the three inspect requests occurs for the timeout interval. This happens when the station that saw the token last did not release it on time; such a situation is diagnosed as a lost token.

Although `TokenMonitor` is able to detect the lost-token condition, it does not guarantee that the token, while present, fulfills its primary purpose, which is allocating the network bandwidth equally to all stations. The absolute fairness property of FDDI may be difficult to assert formally,[8] but we may be willing to settle for a reasonable approximation. If it operates correctly, FDDI imposes an upper bound on the packet access delay. This bound is estimated in section 10.3.5 as a function of the numerical parameters of the network. We can easily program an observer to verify that no packet is postponed by more than the "official" bound on the packet access time. This property is not equivalent to fairness (according to any sensible definition), but it is a bit stronger than the lack of starvation. The type of our observer is declared as follows:

```
observer FairnessMonitor {
    TIME MaxDelay;
    void setup (TIME md) { MaxDelay = md; };
    states {Resume, CheckDelay};
    perform;
};
```

The setup argument passed to the observer upon its creation gives the bound on the maximum packet access time. This bound is stored by the setup method in attribute `MaxDelay`, which is referenced by the observer's code method:

```
FairnessMonitor::perform {
    Packet *Buf;
    TIME Delay;
    state Resume:
        inspect (ANY, Relay, IgTkn, CheckDelay);
    state CheckDelay:
        Buf = &(((FStation*)TheStation)->Buffer);
        if (Buf->isFull ()) {
            Delay = Time - Buf->TTime;
            Assert (Delay <= MaxDelay, "Starvation");
        }
        proceed Resume;
};
```

The observer monitors all situations when a relay process decides not to capture the arriving token and passes it immediately to the next station on the ring. This happens whenever the relay process finds itself in state `IgTkn`. Then the

---

[8]Especially since no generally accepted definition of fairness is known to the author.

observer wakes up in state CheckDelay, where it examines the contents of the station's packet buffer. If the buffer turns out to contain a packet, the observer asserts that the packet's waiting time (the difference between the current time and the time when the packet became ready for transmission—sections 5.2.2, 7.1.2.1) is not greater than the upper bound.

Note that if the relay process does not transit through state IgTkn after a token arrival at the station, it means that the token has been captured and it will be held for at least one packet transmission. Regardless of whether the token is captured or not, the process attempts to fill the station's packet buffer (state MyTkn); thus, the status of the packet buffer examined by the observer in state CheckDelay reflects correctly the ready status of the station. To demonstrate that FairnessMonitor actually asserts the lack of starvation, we should prove that one of the two critical states of the relay process, IgTkn and PsTkn, is visited at definite time intervals. This can be assumed to be a corollary from the statement asserted by the previous observer.

10.3.5   Shortcomings of FDDI

FDDI is a reasonably simple and effective protocol for ring networks. Because of the station symmetry of the ring topology, the protocol is fair; however, the maximum throughput of FDDI tends to deteriorate with the increasing propagation length of the ring. Consequently, FDDI is not a capacity-1 protocol. Besides, FDDI incurs access delays proportional to L, even under light traffic conditions. This stems from the fact that before it is allowed to transmit, a station must acquire the token first. The average waiting time for the token is half of the ring length (assuming that no other stations are ready to transmit). Under heavy load, the maximum packet access time for asynchronous traffic, although formally bounded from above, can be huge. To illustrate this, let us discuss the following example.

Example

Let us assume for simplicity that S is zero and the stations are numbered according to their succession along the ring. Thus, A represents the total token-holding time per one round of the token. Imagine that the token starts at station s_0 at time t_0 and makes an idle turn through the ring (i.e., no station is ready to transmit). Each station s_i, $0 < i < N$, is visited by the token at time

$$t_i = t_{i-1} + d(s_i, s_{i-1}),$$

where $d(s_i, s_{i-1})$ is the propagation length of the ring segment connecting s_i to s_{i-1}. In particular, the token arrives back at station s_0 at time $t_0 + L$.

Suppose that one station, say s_3, gets a bunch of packets to transmit. When the token arrives at s_3 for the second time, which happens at time $t_3 + L$, it is early by A, and s_3 can use the entire asynchronous bandwidth of the token. If s_3 happens to have enough packets to transmit for A time units, the token released by s_3 will be late when it arrives at s_4. In fact, the token will continue to be late at all subsequent stations, until it gets back to s_3 (where it will be late as well) and is released by s_3

again. Then the token will arrive early at s_4. If s_4 has acquired in the meantime enough packets to hold the token for A time units, the scenario will repeat. Thus, s_5 will receive a late token and will have to wait for an entire turn before it can transmit a packet.

This example shows that the packet access time in a heavily loaded FDDI network can be huge. The way the protocol allocates the asynchronous bandwidth, a single station can utilize the entire remaining bandwidth associated with the current round of the token. Consequently, all the stations located downstream are forced to wait until the token completes its round and returns to the greedy station. Under extreme conditions, each station is allowed to use the token once per N rounds, the maximum duration of a round being of order $TTRT$.

In fact, a single round can take more than $TTRT$, even in the absence of asynchronous traffic, as a station is allowed to start transmitting a packet (possibly a huge one) as long as the token is formally not late. The actual maximum duration of a single round is thus $TTRT + l_p^{max}$, where l_p^{max} is the maximum packet length. If synchronous traffic is present, this figure must be augmented by S.

The possibility of huge access delays for asynchronous traffic was the primary reason for introducing in FDDI the concept of synchronous traffic and treating such traffic in a special way. The penalty paid for the lower access delays incurred by FDDI for synchronous packets is the low flexibility of bandwidth allocation in the synchronous region. Unlike the asynchronous portion of the network bandwidth, the synchronous bandwidth unused by one station cannot be claimed by its successor. This lack of flexibility makes the synchronous traffic option not very attractive; not surprisingly, it is avoided if not absolutely necessary.

The maximum throughput of FDDI is easy to derive formally. The amount of time taken by one round trip of the token is equal to the sum of the token-holding time at all stations and the propagation length of the ring. The portion of this time spent on inserting traffic into the network is equal to the token-holding time. Thus, the maximum throughput achievable by the network is roughly equal to

$$T_f = \frac{TTRT - L}{TTRT} \ .$$

As the denominator in this formula includes L (which does not occur in the numerator), the maximum throughput of FDDI decreases linearly with the increasing propagation length of the ring. Consequently, FDDI is not a capacity-1 protocol.

One may naively suggest that the maximum throughput achievable by FDDI can be pushed arbitrarily close to 1 by increasing the token-holding time, i.e., $TTRT - L$. Obviously, this approach has severe limitations. First, it assumes unrealistically that all stations have a sufficient number of packets to fill the large token-holding window. Second, increasing the token-holding time increases the bound on the packet access time, which is already a problem in FDDI. In consequence of these drawbacks, the idea of FDDI cannot be extrapolated onto networks substantially faster than 100 Mb/s, which is the nominal transfer rate of the commercial network.

10.4 THE INSERTION RING

The weak spots of FDDI result from the restrictive role of the token. Token-passing protocols in which transmission rights are restricted to the token-holding station (e.g., FDDI) are called *strong-token protocols*. In a strong-token protocol, the time while the token is in transit is wasted, as no station is allowed to transmit during that time. During one round trip of the token, L time units are wasted for passing the token through the links separating the neighboring stations. Clearly, the performance of a strong-token protocol is bound to deteriorate with the increasing propagation length of the ring.

10.4.1 The Protocol

An obvious alternative to a strong-token protocol is a token-less access scheme in which stations can transmit spontaneously. One problem with implementing such a scheme is the need for a mechanism to prevent the destruction of packets arriving from upstream while a station is inserting its own traffic into the ring. Moreover, as there is no natural and safe way to disconnect the ring, the cleaning responsibilities must now be clearly assigned either to the source (sender) or to the destination (receiver).

The second issue complicates a bit the operation of relaying the traffic at intermediate stations. Regardless of whether packets are erased by their senders or recipients, they must be erased entirely. Otherwise, as the ring is never disconnected, there would be no way to expunge the leftovers of partially stripped packets. Therefore, each station must buffer at least an initial fragment of every incoming packet before it starts to relay the packet on the output port.

Once we put up with the mandatory buffering of packets at intermediate stations, we can use the same mechanism to implement a safe medium access scheme. Assume that a station s has decided to insert its own packet into the ring. Even if the station has sensed the ring idle before starting the transfer, a packet may arrive from upstream at any moment while s is transmitting its own packet. One thing the station should not do is to destroy the incoming packet: its sender wants to believe that a packet transmitted without problems will reach the destination in good shape (section 8.1.1.2). What other options are there?

It is possible to force s to abort its own transmission and yield to the packet arriving from upstream. This way, the station will create a partial unterminated packet that will have to be erased by some station. To be erasable, the packet must be equipped with at least the portion of its header that contains the identifier of the station responsible for stripping it.[9] This can be easily accomplished if s inserts

---

[9]Depending on whether source or destination erasure is implemented, the recognizable portion of the partial packet must contain either the source or the destination address.

its own packet through the relay buffer. If a packet arrives from upstream before
the first bit of the packet transmitted by s has left the buffer, the entire contents of
the buffer are erased and no fragment of the packet generated by s ever appears in
the ring. Consequently, nothing has to be stripped in this case. Otherwise, the size
of the relay buffer guarantees that the packet contains all the information needed
by the eraser to fulfill its obligation. In such a case, the packet is aborted and the
buffer emptied normally. Its contents will be inserted into the ring followed by the
packet that has arrived from upstream.

Under heavy load, aborted packets may become a nuisance, and they may
take a substantial portion of the network throughput. Note that an aborted packet
may abort other packets on its way downstream, before it eventually reaches the
station that will absorb it. Fortunately, with the relay buffers already present,
another solution is possible in which packets are never aborted. This way, the network can operate without bandwidth wastage and achieve a spectacular throughput
unbeatable by other solutions.

The solution consists in making the size of the relay buffer variable. The
current size of the buffer is indicated by a dynamic pointer (see figure 10.3). The
incoming traffic passes through a short fixed portion of the buffer, called the *hallway*, where it is determined whether a packet should be erased by the station or
relayed further down the ring. Then the traffic to be relayed is inserted into another
fragment of the relay buffer (the so-called *insertion buffer*) at the location determined by the dynamically adjustable pointer. Initially, as shown in figure 10.3, the
pointer is set to the beginning of the insertion buffer and the incoming traffic "cuts
through" the buffer. Any contents of the insertion buffer preceding the pointer location are automatically inserted into the output port at the network transmission
rate.

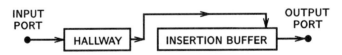

Figure 10.3 The relay buffer in the insertion ring

Assume that a station gets a packet to transmit. There are two possible
strategies to transmit a packet without disrupting the traffic arriving from upstream:

Strategy 1. The station waits until the output port is silent, i.e., no incoming traffic is relayed to the output port. Then, if the amount of space remaining
in the insertion buffer is sufficient to accommodate the station's packet, the station
starts transmitting its packet directly to the output port. Any traffic arriving from
upstream while the station is transmitting is stored in the insertion buffer, and the
buffer pointer is adjusted appropriately. This way, the buffer is inserted into the
ring: it makes the ring longer and delays the arrival of the incoming traffic at the
output port. When the station is done with its packet, it resumes emptying the

contents of the insertion buffer. The buffer will return to its "cut-through" status as soon as no traffic will have arrived at the buffer for the duration of the station's transmission time.

Strategy 2. The station checks if there is enough room in the insertion buffer to accommodate its packet. If so, the station puts the packet into the buffer. If no incoming packet is currently being inserted into the buffer, the buffer pointer is updated to point to the end of the portion occupied by the station's packet. The contents of the buffer will immediately start to be transferred to the output port. This way, the station's packet is inserted into the ring: the ring length is virtually increased by the occupied portion of the insertion buffer. Otherwise, to avoid disrupting the incoming traffic, the buffer pointer is not adjusted immediately, but after the nearest end of packet perceived on the input port.

The two strategies are practically identical in their behavior. Note that with strategy 1, the station is allowed to start its own transmission at the nearest packet boundary in the traffic arriving from upstream, provided that there is enough room in the buffer to store the incoming traffic while the station is transmitting. With both strategies, if the ring is silent and the insertion buffer is empty, the station can start transmitting immediately. The minimum size of the insertion buffer must be at least equal to the maximum packet length, including all headers and trailers.

10.4.2   The Implementation

Our SMURPH implementation of the insertion ring is based on the second of the two strategies described in section 10.4.1. To make the presentation a bit easier, we introduce two simplifications, which can be easily eliminated by the reader as an exercise (see exercise 3 at the end of this chapter). First, we assume that the clock tolerance is zero, which, in this particular case, boils down to the postulate that all stations always use the same exact transmission rate. Second, the time is measured directly in bits, i.e., the internal transmission rate of all output ports is 1. The relaxation of the first simplification must be preceded by an analysis of the buffering problems incurred by uneven transmission rates at different stations. As this analysis has no direct connection to the medium access protocol of the insertion ring, we prefer to postpone it until the next section. The second simplification is a natural consequence of the first one: as all transmission rates are absolutely accurate, there is no reason to complicate things by quantizing the time below the bit insertion interval. The removal of this simplification is pretty straightforward: it would just obfuscate a bit the formula used by the following **free** method of PQueue and affect one statement in the code method of the transmitter process. The modification results from the need to convert time to bits while calculating the amount of free space in the buffer.

The most tricky and novel fragment of the program presented in this section is the structure of the insertion buffer. This buffer is implemented as a mailbox of the following type:

```
mailbox PQueue (Packet*) {
  Long MaxLength, CurLength;
  TIME TSTime;
  void setup (Long l) {
    MaxLength = l;
    CurLength = 0;
    setLimit (MAX_long);
  };
  Long free () {
    return CurLength == 0 ? MaxLength :
      MaxLength - CurLength + (Long) (Time - TSTime);
  };
  void inItem (Packet *p) {
    if (CurLength == 0) TSTime = Time;
    CurLength += p->TLength;
  };
  void outItem (Packet *p) {
    CurLength -= p->TLength;
    TSTime = Time;
    delete p;
  };
};
```

The mailbox stores packet pointers identifying the packets currently transiting through the insertion buffer. The two Long attributes represent the total buffer length in bits (MaxLength) and the length of its currently used portion (CurLength). In fact, CurLength gives the combined total length of all packets currently present in the buffer and is only updated when a packet is added to or removed from the buffer. Consequently, the actual length of the used buffer portion may be less than CurLength, as the first packet in the buffer may have been partially inserted into the output port and removed from the buffer. To be able to determine the exact amount of free space in the buffer at any moment, we maintain another attribute, TSTime, which is set to the time when the station started to insert into the output port the first packet from the buffer. The setup method initializes MaxLength to a user-specified value. CurLength is set to zero, which denotes the cut-through status of the buffer.

Although the mailbox capacity is set by the setup method to virtual infinity (operation setLimit—section 4.7.5), the actual amount of free space in the buffer is determined by the free method. If CurLength is zero, which means that the buffer is empty, the method returns MaxLength to indicate that the entire buffer is free and available. Otherwise, according to what we said above, the length of the used portion of the buffer is equal to CurLength minus the length of the already transmitted portion of the first packet. Time being measured in bits, the length of the transmitted fragment of the first packet is obtained by subtracting TSTime (the

moment when the station started to relay the front packet to the output port) from
the current time (Time).

Recall from section 4.7.2 that inItem and outItem are two standard methods of a mailbox, which are called automatically when a new item is stored in
(inItem) or removed from (outItem) the mailbox. We use these methods to update CurLength and TSTime. Whenever a new packet is added to the buffer, inItem
is called with the packet pointer passed as the argument. If CurLength turns out to
be zero (which means that the buffer is empty), TSTime is set to the current time.
A packet stored into an empty insertion buffer immediately starts to be flushed to
the output port. In any case, CurLength is incremented by the total length of the
packet. If a packet is removed from the buffer (which happens when the packet has
been entirely inserted into the output port), outItem is called, and it decrements
CurLength by the total length of the removed packet and resets TSTime to the current time. The second operation indicates that the next packet in the buffer (if
there is any) will start to be retransmitted on the output port within the current
ITU. The last operation performed by outItem is delete, which deallocates the
packet data structure. The explicit deallocation is necessary, as the pointers stored
in the mailbox point to copies of packet structures created by the process servicing
the input port.

Our implementation of the insertion ring is based on the single-ring topology
introduced in section 10.3.4.1. A station in the insertion ring descends from the
same library subtypes as an FDDI station:

```
station IStation : SRingInterface, ClientInterface {
  PQueue *IBuffer;
  Boolean Blocked;
  void setup (Long bufl) {
    SRingInterface::configure ();
    ClientInterface::configure ();
    IBuffer = create PQueue (bufl);
    Blocked = NO;
  };
};
```

The station's setup argument gives the capacity of the insertion buffer in bits.
This argument is passed directly to the setup method of the mailbox. Attribute
Blocked is a Boolean flag indicating whether an incoming packet arriving from
upstream on the input port is currently being stored in the insertion buffer. In such
a case, we say that the insertion buffer is *blocked*. According to the second strategy
described in section 10.4.1, a ready station is allowed to insert its packet into the
buffer as soon as there is enough room in the buffer to accommodate the packet.
However, to avoid disrupting the traffic being relayed, the station does not adjust
the buffer pointer until the buffer is unblocked, i.e., no traffic to be relayed arrives
from upstream. Before the buffer pointer is adjusted to include the station's packet,
the insertion of this packet into the buffer is formally irrelevant. The station could

as well delay storing the packet until the buffer becomes unblocked. This is how it is done in our implementation: a backlogged station waits until the nearest moment when the following two conditions are fulfilled simultaneously:

- The insertion buffer is unblocked, i.e., no incoming traffic is currently being pumped in the buffer.
- There is enough free space in the buffer to accommodate the station's packet.

Then the station stores the packet in the buffer and immediately adjusts the buffer pointer. Note that the pointer is not explicitly present in the data structure representing the buffer (mailbox PQueue). If packets are always inserted into the buffer when the buffer is unblocked, the implicit location of the pointer is at the end of the buffer contents.

Each station runs three processes. The Input process receives packets from the input port, determines their fate, and stores the packets to be relayed at the end of the insertion buffer (at the current location of the imaginary pointer). The Relay process services the output port. It extracts packets from the output end of the insertion buffer and inserts them into the output port. Finally, the Transmitter process takes care of the packets generated by the station. Depending on the buffer status, the transmitter inserts such packets into the insertion buffer.

The type definition of the input process is as follows:

```
process Input (IStation) {
  Port *IRing;
  PQueue *IBuffer;
  Transmitter *Xmitter;
  Packet *Pkt;
  void setup (Transmitter *pr) {
    Xmitter = pr;
    IRing = S->IRing;
    IBuffer = S->IBuffer;
  };
  states {WaitBOT, NewPacket, CheckRcv, Receive, Drop};
  perform;
};
```

Attributes IRing and IBuffer are pointers to the corresponding attributes of the station owning the process. Xmitter points to the transmitter process running at the same station. The input process uses this pointer to signal the transmitter when the status of the insertion buffer changes from blocked to unblocked. Pkt is just a temporary variable to store a pointer to the packet being currently extracted from the input port. The process runs the following code:

```
Input::perform {
  state WaitBOT:
    IRing->wait (BOT, NewPacket);
```

```
                  state NewPacket:
                    Pkt = ThePacket;
                    Timer->wait (HdrL, CheckRcv);
                  state CheckRcv:
                    if (Pkt->isMy ()) {
                       IRing->wait (EOT, Receive);
                    } else {
                       Packet *p;
                       p = create Packet;
                       *p = *Pkt;
                       S->Blocked = YES;
                       IBuffer->put (p);
                       IRing->wait (EOT, Drop);
                    }
                  state Receive:
                    Client->receive (Pkt, IRing);
                    proceed WaitBOT;
                  state Drop:
                    S->Blocked = NO;
                    Xmitter->signal ();
                    proceed WaitBOT;
                };
```

The process starts in state WaitBOT, where it sleeps until a packet arrives at the input port. Then, in state NewPacket, the process determines the packet's fate. This state models the passage of the incoming packet through the hallway buffer (section 10.4.1), where it is determined whether the packet should be removed from the network. The pointer to the packet is stored in Pkt and the process sleeps for the amount of time determined by HdrL (header length). This numerical parameter of the implementation gives the delay needed for the recognition of the relevant portion of the packet header. This delay is equal to the length of the hallway buffer. In our implementation of the insertion ring, packets are erased by their destinations. For a given format of the packet header, HdrL should be set to the length of an initial fragment of this header including the destination address, possibly augmented by a few bits of safety margin.

When the input process gets to state CheckRcv, the packet's fate has been determined. At this moment, the first bit of the packet is about to come out of the hallway buffer, and the process must decide whether the packet should be relayed on the output port. If the packet happens to be addressed to the station (packet's method isMy returns YES—section 6.2.13), it should be received by the station and removed from the ring. In such a case, the process awaits the EOT event on the input port, which will result in a transition to state Receive. In that state, the input process will receive the packet and move back to state WaitBOT, to await another packet arrival from upstream.

If the packet must be relayed, it is stored in the insertion buffer. To accomplish this, the process creates a copy of the packet and stores a pointer to this copy in the mailbox representing the insertion buffer.[10] Then the process waits until the end of the relayed packet appears on the input port. When this happens, the process wakes up in state Drop, where it clears the blocked status of the insertion buffer and notifies the transmitter about the status change via a signal. Finally, the input process moves back to state WaitBOT to await another incoming packet.

The type declaration of the relay process is as follows:

```
process Relay (IStation) {
  Port *ORing;
  PQueue *IBuffer;
  void setup () {
    ORing = S->ORing;
    IBuffer = S->IBuffer;
  };
  states {WaitPacket, XDone};
  perform;
};
```

The process just empties the packets from the insertion buffer one by one to the output port. This is accomplished by the following code method executed by Relay:

```
Relay::perform {
  state WaitPacket:
    if (IBuffer->first () == NULL)
      IBuffer->wait (NONEMPTY, WaitPacket);
    else
      ORing->transmit (IBuffer->first (), XDone);
  state XDone:
    ORing->stop ();
    IBuffer->get ();
    proceed WaitPacket;
};
```

In its initial state (WaitPacket) the process checks whether the insertion buffer contains a packet. Operation first (section 4.7.5) returns the first element from its mailbox (a packet pointer in this case), or NULL if no element is available. If the

---

[10] A copy is needed because the original activity carrying the packet will be deallocated when it leaves the output port (sections 3.2.2, 6.1.1). An alternative solution would be to assign a nonzero archival time to the links representing the ring segments and use pointers to original packets. This archival time should be longer than the length of the insertion buffer. One additional modification needed with this approach is the removal of the delete statement from the outItem method of PQueue.

mailbox (insertion buffer) is empty, the process waits until an item is stored there (event NONEMPTY—section 4.7.4) and then repeats the sequence at state WaitPacket.

Having found a packet in the buffer, the relay process initiates its transmission and transits to state XDone when the transfer is complete. Then the process stops the transfer and executes get on the mailbox (section 4.7.5) to remove the packet from the buffer. Note that in consequence of calling get the outItem method of the mailbox will be automatically invoked. Finally, the process moves back to state WaitPacket to take care of the next packet in the buffer.

The last interesting element of the protocol program is the transmitter process. Its role is limited to monitoring the buffer status and inserting packets into the buffer, according to the rules described earlier. The type of the transmitter process is defined as follows:

```
process Transmitter (IStation) {
  PQueue *IBuffer;
  Packet *Buffer;
  void setup () {
    IBuffer = S->IBuffer;
    Buffer = &(S->Buffer);
  };
  states {Acquire};
  perform;
};
```

The process is so simple that it only has one state. The complete code method of Transmitter is as follows:

```
Transmitter::perform {
  Long f;
  state Acquire:
    if (S->Blocked)
      wait (SIGNAL, Acquire);
    else if (S->ready (MinPL, MaxPL, FrameL)) {
      if ((f = IBuffer->free ()) >= Buffer->TLength) {
        Packet *p;
        p = create Packet;
        *p = *Buffer;
        IBuffer->put (p);
        Buffer->release ();
        proceed Acquire;
      } else
        Timer->wait (Buffer->TLength - f, Acquire);
    } else
      Client->wait (ARRIVAL, Acquire);
};
```

If the insertion buffer is blocked, the process sleeps in its only state awaiting a signal from the input process. When the signal arrives (meaning that the buffer has been unblocked), the transmitter attempts to acquire a packet for transmission. If the acquisition is successful, the process determines whether the amount of free space in the buffer makes it possible to store there the acquired packet. If so, a copy of the packet is created and the pointer to the copy is deposited (put) in the mailbox representing the insertion buffer. The buffer is immediately released and becomes ready to accommodate another packet from the Client.[11] Then the transmitter moves back to the beginning of its state.

If the amount of free space in the insertion buffer is insufficient to accommodate the packet, the process determines for how long it has to wait before a next try can sensibly be made. The waiting time is equal to the difference between the required amount of space and the number of bits available. As time is measured in bits, this formula[12] gives the amount of time required by the relay process to flush to the output port a sufficient number of bits from the buffer to create room for the new packet. Note, however, that the required amount of space will only be freed if no traffic arrives from upstream in the meantime. The transmitter has no guarantee that when it tries again later, the packet will be accommodated.

When it turns out that the insertion buffer is unblocked but no Client packet is available for transmission, the process suspends itself until the nearest ARRIVAL event.

The complete implementation of the insertion ring protocol presented here, including the definition of the root process (omitted from our discussion), is contained in directory RING/Insertion of SMURPH Examples.

10.4.3   Problems with the Insertion Ring

In comparison with token-based ring access schemes, the insertion ring concept is very attractive, as it attempts to organize the network operation without introducing a single synchronizing agent. This way, multiple stations can transmit in parallel and the ring bandwidth can be utilized much better than, say, in FDDI. Indeed, formally, the insertion ring is a capacity-1 protocol. Assuming destination cleaning and uniform traffic distribution, an average packet has to travel one-half of the ring before it is removed from the network. As stations are allowed to transmit whenever they perceive the ring silent, this means that, irrespective of the propagation length of the ring medium, two packets can be inserted into the ring simultaneously at any time. Consequently, the maximum throughput achievable by the insertion ring is 2. Even under unfriendly traffic conditions (each packet is addressed to the destination immediately preceding the sender) or, equivalently, assuming source cleanup, the maximum throughput of the protocol is 1, and it also does not depend on the propagation length of the ring.

---

[11] Note that the station can store a number of packets in the insertion buffer at once, provided that there is enough free space available.

[12] It will have to be changed if a lower granularity of time is used.

Despite the formal capacity-1 property, the insertion ring falls short of becoming the ideal protocol for ring networks. Its drawbacks can be stressed in the following points:

- The protocol is starvation-prone. A station may have to wait indefinitely to insert its own packet into the network if a continuous stream of traffic to be relayed arrives from upstream.
- Because of the dynamically adjustable size of the insertion buffers at stations, the effective propagation length of the ring is variable. The prominence of this phenomenon increases with the number of stations.
- The lack of an ultimate cleaning agent (like a token-holding station in FDDI) introduces a potential for the presence of "orphaned" packets in the network. Special measures must be taken to deal with such packets.
- The implementation of the insertion buffer is tricky (especially for very high transmission rates), and it adds to the hardware cost of a station.

Malicious traffic scenarios for insertion rings, resulting in explicit starvation, are not difficult to conceive. Any station having a continuous supply of packets addressed to a destination located further than one hop down the ring starves all the intermediate stations-relays located on the path to the destination. Although each station-relay is allowed to expedite its own packet into the insertion buffer at the nearest packet boundary in the incoming traffic, once the insertion buffer becomes full, it can only be emptied while the input port is silent.

The variability of the effective propagation length of the ring contributes to so-called *jitter*, i.e., the irregularity of packet arrivals at the destinations, even if those packets were sent at very regular intervals by their source stations. Some real-time applications, e.g., voice and video transmission, may require the jitter to be well-bounded from above. Although a high jitter may result from several properties of a medium access scheme, the jitter incurred by the insertion ring protocol is inherent: it occurs regardless of the sender's efforts to transmit the packets at regular intervals.

In the insertion ring, packets are erased from the network by stations that explicitly recognize their cleaning duties with respect to the packets. Assume that an insertion ring network uses a destination-cleaning scheme and imagine that a packet is transmitted to a nonexistent destination, e.g., a station that has been switched off. Such a packet will never be removed from the network; at least it will not be removed if the destination-cleaning scheme is the only means of packet stripping. At first sight, it may seem that switching to source cleaning (or implementing a dual cleaning scheme in which packets that have not been erased by their destinations are recognized and removed by their senders) solves the problem, but this is not the case. What happens if a station transmits a packet and then goes down before the packet completes its tour around the ring? What happens if the packet's header is damaged in such a way that no station is able to assume cleaning duties with respect to the packet? In token-based protocols, these problems are trivial: after all, any activity will eventually reach a token-holding station and be removed from the network, but in a token-less ring, orphaned packets may circulate indefinitely, permanently impairing (or even killing) the network.

To detect orphaned packets and get rid of them, insertion ring networks must take special measures. To account for damaged packets, which cannot be claimed by their official erasers, these measures are usually implemented in special monitoring stations that keep track of all activities passing through the ring and recognize those that have not been claimed for two or more turns.

The second and fourth drawbacks from the preceding list can be eliminated by implementing the insertion ring protocol in a slotted fashion. With this approach, the ring is filled at the initialization phase with slots (appropriately spaced slot markers) that from then on circulate in the network indefinitely. The header of each slot carries the usual *FULL* flag, which is handled in the way typical of a slotted protocol (section 9.3.1). A station willing to transmit a packet (segment) waits until it gets an empty slot from upstream. Then the station reserves the slot by flipping its *FULL* bit and inserts the segment into the slot's payload area. The slot will be emptied by the destination (assuming destination cleaning), which, having recognized its address in the segment header, will clear the *FULL* bit. Note that the hallway buffers at stations (section 10.4.1) are still needed to implement the erasure, but they are fixed, incur constant delay, and have no adverse impact on the jitter.

Slotting eliminates yet another problem with the insertion ring, which is not really a drawback of the protocol (it was not mentioned in the list) but it must be accounted for in a realistic implementation. Because of the slightly different transmission rates used by different stations, it is possible that the insertion buffer will overflow while receiving traffic from upstream. This may happen at a station-relay whose clock is slightly slower than the clock of an upstream transmitter generating a continuous stream of packets to be relayed downstream. At least two solutions to this problem are possible. One way is to separate packets by interpacket spaces. A station detecting that its insertion buffer has crossed the "high-water mark" decreases the length of the interpacket spaces and effectively increases its transmission rate.[13] Another solution is to use the reception rate of the incoming packets to strobe the station's transmitter whenever a packet is arriving from upstream. This way, the buffer will never overflow because for each bit inserted into the buffer at the input end, one bit leaves the buffer at the output end. Depending on the signal-encoding method, slight variations in the transmission rate may be acceptable. Typically, these variations do not exceed 0.01 percent. This solution also eliminates the underflow problem, which occurs when a relaying station transmits slightly faster than the traffic to be relayed arrives from upstream. The underflow problem is generally less serious than the overflow problem: a station detecting the buffer underflow condition may transmit a dummy symbol that will be ignored and

---

[13]In the slotted version of the protocol, the role of the interpacket spaces is played by the safety margin included in the distance between two consecutive slot markers.

stripped by the receiver. The second solution attempts to equalize the transmission rate across the entire network; thus, our simplified implementation discussed in section 10.4.2 approximates it well.

The most serious problem with the insertion ring protocol is the potential for starvation. In this respect, the protocol is reminiscent of U-Net and H-Net (section 9.4.2), which (formally) are also capacity-1 protocols. Both U-Net and H-Net, as well as the insertion ring, trade fairness for the capacity-1 property. In contrast to the insertion ring, the unfairness of U-Net and H-Net results from the nonsymmetry of the bus topology (although the starvation in the two networks can only occur under suitable traffic conditions). The unfairness of the insertion ring, which is a station-symmetric network, is solely the consequence of malicious traffic scenarios.

10.5 METARING

The ring access protocol presented in this section can be viewed as an attempt to refine the insertion ring concept and eliminate its most painful disadvantage—the starvation potential. Unfortunately, this attempt is only partly successful and yields a compromise: the resulting protocol is starvation-free, but its capacity-1 property is not preserved.

10.5.1 The Protocol

The Metaring protocol consists of two conceptually disjoint parts: a dual insertion ring operating according to the principles discussed in the preceding sections, and a control mechanism, called SAT, imposed on the insertion ring. The role of the control mechanism is to avoid starvation. The SAT part can be switched off, in which case the network operates as a pure starvation-prone insertion ring.

10.5.1.1 The dual insertion ring.
The dual insertion ring part of Metaring implements essentially the same protocol that was discussed in section 10.4. The additional trick consists in using two counter-rotating rings (see figure 10.4). A station willing to transmit a packet selects the ring that offers fewer hops to the destination. As the rings are counter-rotating, the maximum number of hops separating two stations is $\lfloor N/2 \rfloor$, where N is the total number of stations. If N is odd, the most distant destination can be reached equally well on either ring. In such a case, the ring used for a transmission to the most distant destination can be selected at random. The protocol employs destination cleanup.

Note that a station in Metaring must associate an attribute with each potential destination, identifying the ring via which the destination should be reached. These attributes can be assigned to stations during the network initialization phase.

The advantage of two counter-rotating rings versus a single insertion ring is in at least quadrupling the maximum throughput achievable by the network. One would naturally expect that the maximum throughput of a dual-ring network would

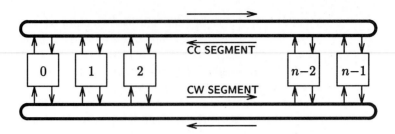

Figure 10.4 A dual counter-rotating ring

be twice as high as the maximum throughput of a similar network based on a single ring. Because of the spontaneous character of transmissions in an insertion ring, the gain from doubling the network hardware is significantly higher than the natural linear improvement.

The maximum transmission distance in Metaring is one-half of the ring circumference. Under uniform traffic conditions, an average packet travels only one-fourth of the ring, and four packets can be inserted into each ring segment simultaneously at any moment. Consequently, the maximum throughput achieved by the dual insertion ring is 8, which is an absolute upper limit on any dual-ring network in which each ring segment constitutes a single channel. This spectacular figure can be improved even further in a large network in which traffic exhibits some locality patterns, i.e., most packets are addressed to not-so-distant destinations. Note that locality patterns are generally not advantageous for a single insertion ring. In a single ring, if the distance from station s_1 to s_2 involves few hops, say k, the distance from s_2 to s_1 involves many hops, namely $N - k$. Therefore, geographic proximity coincides with propagation proximity only in one direction, whereas in the opposite direction it implies propagation remoteness. This is not the case in a dual counter-rotating ring, which can take full advantage of the traffic locality and use it to increase the maximum throughput achievable by the network.

Not surprisingly, Metaring comes in two versions: unslotted and slotted, selectable upon network initialization. Regardless of the version, the protocol is starvation-prone (for the same reasons as the single-ring buffer insertion protocol—section 10.4.3) unless the SAT mechanism is in effect.

10.5.1.2 The SAT mechanism. In section 10.1 we suggested that the trade-off between fairness and high bandwidth utilization is a typical phenomenon, regardless of the network topology and protocol organization. A natural method of enforcing fairness in a ring network is to pass a token among stations. This way, we can easily make sure that every station gets its fair share of the network bandwidth, but we cannot guarantee that the stations can transmit whenever bandwidth is available. In "pure" Metaring presented in the previous section, the opposite statement is true: all bandwidth of the dual ring is always usable by the stations, but there is no way to guarantee that every station can access that bandwidth in a predictable time.

The SAT mechanism imposed on Metaring is in fact a token-passing scheme. The basic idea is fairly simple. A special message, called SAT,[14] circulates in the network. A station can transmit at any time, but there is a bound on the number of packets that a single station can transmit between two consecutive arrivals of a SAT message to the station. A station that cannot get enough bandwidth to become "satisfied" grabs the SAT message and holds it until the incoming traffic dies out and the station can transmit its packet quota. Then the station inserts the SAT message back into the ring.

The complete algorithm for passing SAT messages is presented in section 10.5.2.5 as part of the Metaring implementation. To discuss it in more detail, let us focus on a single transfer direction. The operation of the two ring segments is perfectly symmetric, also with respect to the SAT portion of the protocol.

During the network initialization phase, each station is assigned two integer constants (per each ring segment) describing the station's bandwidth requirements. If all stations have the same requirements, the values of these constants are the same for all stations. The first constant, denoted by k, gives the maximum number of packets that the station is allowed to transmit before it receives a SAT message. The other constant, denoted by l, specifies the number of packets that the station needs to transmit between two consecutive SAT arrivals to become "satisfied." More specifically, we say that a station is satisfied if either it has been able to transmit l packets since it last saw a SAT message, or its packet queue is empty (i.e., the station has nothing to transmit). To keep track of its transmission rights, each station maintains a counter (we denote it by *count*) that is incremented by 1 with every packet transmission. The SAT-passing algorithm can be outlined in the following points:

1. Upon network initialization, a single SAT message (per ring segment) is created and inserted into the ring. Each station is assigned the values of k and l, and its *count* variable is cleared.

2. Whenever a satisfied station receives a SAT message, it forwards the message immediately to the next station in the ring. If the station is not satisfied, it holds the SAT message until either its *count* reaches l or its packet queue becomes empty, i.e., until the station becomes satisfied. In either case, having forwarded the SAT message, the station resets its *count* to zero.

3. A station can only transmit its own packets for as long as *count* remains less than k. Note that *count* is incremented by 1 after each packet transmission.

4. To account for the possibility of a lost SAT message, each station maintains a timer that is reset after every reception of SAT. If the timer goes off before a SAT message has been received, the station behaves exactly as if a SAT message actually arrived.

Point 4 introduces the possibility of multiple SAT messages circulating in the

---

[14]SAT stands for "satisfied."

network, which can happen when multiple stations detect a lost SAT at approximately the same time. This is not harmful, because multiple SAT messages tend to be merged into one. An unsatisfied station will hold all the incoming SAT messages until it becomes satisfied, and then the station will release a single copy of SAT. As no station can hold a SAT message indefinitely, the unsatisfied station will eventually get its share of the ring bandwidth, regardless of how many copies of SAT are present in the network. Clearly, the SAT timeout interval should be set to a safe value, somewhat higher than the maximum legitimate SAT interarrival time.

The SAT-based access control mechanism described here does not mention the direction in which the SAT messages are passed. It may seem natural to pass the messages on the same ring segment as the traffic controlled by them. As the SAT messages are very simple and have no structure,[15] they can be passed as special short signals between packets. In the slotted version of the protocol, a special flag in the slot header can be reserved to represent a SAT message.

It turns out that the SAT mechanism operates much better (the network achieves a higher maximum throughput) if the SAT messages are passed in the direction opposite to the traffic direction, i.e., on the opposite ring segment. The explanation of this phenomenon is simple: a released SAT message is destined for the upstream neighbors of the releasing station, and its purpose is to notify those neighbors that they can resume their operation. Clearly, the fastest way to reach your upstream neighbor is to send the message upstream, against the incoming traffic. To make this idea work without unnecessary delays, it has been proposed that the SAT messages be imposed on the regular traffic as special symbols[16] recognizable by the receivers. A SAT symbol can occur in the middle of a packet; it will be stripped by the receiver before the packet is stored in the insertion buffer or passed to the higher protocol layers.

10.5.2   The Implementation

Directory RING/Metaring1 in SMURPH Examples contains an implementation of the pure variant of Metaring without the SAT mechanism. This implementation is a straightforward extension of the insertion ring program discussed in section 10.4.2, and we do not describe it here. Instead, we focus on the full implementation of Metaring (in its unslotted version), including the upstream SAT mechanism.

10.5.2.1   The ring.

Although possible, the exact implementation of the SAT messages interleaved with regular packets is tricky. Therefore, we have decided on an innocent and natural simplification: the SAT messages are passed via separate channels doubling the regular channels used for passing normal packets. The simplification does not seem very serious for two reasons:

---

[15]This is why we do not call them *packets*. Unfortunately, the term *message* is not much better.

[16]Such special symbols may be naturally available if the 5b4b encoding scheme is employed (section 10.3.2).

- SAT messages are separated from the regular traffic at the boundary of the physical and data-link layers. Therefore, these messages are in fact transmitted over a separate logical channel that, for economic reasons, has been combined with the channel carrying the regular traffic.

- SAT messages are very short (a few bits), and their impact on the packet transmission time is negligible.

Our simplification makes it easier to program the Metaring protocol, but it complicates a bit the topology of the network backbone. The ring consists of four segments, not just two. Following are the contents of the library file mring.h, which defines the layout of the station's interface to the network:

```
#define CWRing 0
#define CCRing 1
station MRingInterface virtual {
  Port *IRing [2], *ORing [2], *ISat [2], *OSat [2];
  void configure ();
};
void initMRing (RATE, TIME, int);
```

The two symbolic constants identify the transfer directions: CWRing stands for the clockwise segments and CCRing denotes the counterclockwise segments. Of course, the notions of "clockwise" and "counterclockwise" are purely abstract. In particular, the way the two rings are drawn in figure 10.4 makes them both look clockwise, although in fact they operate in opposite directions. It is assumed that the stations are numbered in the order of their occurrence along the clockwise ring.

The station's interface to the ring consists of eight ports represented by Port pointers grouped into four arrays. Array IRing stores pointers to the input ports from the ring segments carrying the regular traffic. IRing[CWRing] points to the input port from the clockwise segment, and IRing[CCRing] stores the pointer to the input port from the counterclockwise segment. Similarly, array ORing contains two pointers identifying the output ports to the regular-traffic segments of the ring. The remaining two arrays, ISat and OSat, store pointers to the input and output ports of the ring segments representing the virtual channels for passing SAT messages.

The configure method of MRingInterface will be called by the station's setup method when a station object is created. Its role is to configure the station into the network. The global function initMRing should be invoked by the root process to define the numerical parameters of the ring. The arguments of initMRing have the same meaning as the arguments of function initSRing discussed in section 10.3.4.1.

The complete definition of initMRing, as well as the code of the configure method of MRingInterface, is contained in file mring.c in IncludeLibrary. This file starts with the following declarations:

```
static PLink **REG [2], **SAT [2];
static RATE TR;
```

```
static DISTANCE D;
static int NP, NC;
static MRingInterface **RStations;
void initMRing (RATE r, TIME 1, int np) {
  int i, j;
  NP = np;
  for (j = 0; j < 2; j++) {
    REG [j] = new PLink* [NP];
    SAT [j] = new PLink* [NP];
    for (i = 0; i < NP; i++) {
      REG [j][i] = create PLink (2);
      SAT [j][i] = create PLink (2);
    }
  }
  TR = r;
  D = 1 / NP;
  NC = 0;
  RStations = new MRingInterface* [NP];
};
```

The two-element arrays REG and SAT indexed by the direction ordinal (CWRing, CCRing) contain pointers to four lists of links describing the ring segments. For example, the links in REG[CWRing] constitute the clockwise ring carrying regular traffic. Similarly, SAT[CCRing] contains pointers to the links of the counterclockwise ring used for passing SAT messages. The other global variables have their counterparts in already discussed network configuration files. In particular, RStations identifies a temporary array storing pointers to the MRingInterface fragments of the stations that have been built so far during the network creation phase.

The three arguments of initMRing specify, respectively, the common transmission rate of all output ports (in ITUs per bit), the total propagation length of the ring (in ITUs), and the number of stations to be connected to the ring. The first and third arguments are directly stored in the global variables TR and NP, respectively. The total propagation length of the ring is divided by NP to produce the length of a single link separating a pair of neighboring stations. This length, which is the same for all links, is stored in D. The arrays of link pointers are created dynamically, the size of each array being equal to NP (the number of links in each of the four rings coincides with the number of stations in the network). The outer for loop goes through the transfer directions (0 and 1 corresponding to CWRing and CCRing), and the inner loop creates all the links for the pair of rings oriented in the given direction. Each link is a simple unidirectional point-to-point channel. The total number of links is $4 \times NP$.

As usual, NC is initialized to zero. This variable will count the number of stations already configured into the network. The last statement of the function creates the RStations array, whose size is naturally also NP.

Whenever a new station is created, the `configure` method of its `MRingInterface` fragment is invoked to interface the station to the ring. The code of this method is as follows:

```
void MRingInterface::configure () {
  int i, j;
  for (i = 0; i < 2; i++) {
    IRing [i] = create Port;
    ORing [i] = create Port (TR);
    ISat [i] = create Port;
    OSat [i] = create Port (TR);
  }
  RStations [NC++] = this;
  if (NC == NP) {
    for (i = 0; i < NP; i++) {
      j = (i+1) % NP;
      RStations [i] -> ORing [CWRing] -> connect (REG [CWRing][i]);
      RStations [j] -> IRing [CWRing] -> connect (REG [CWRing][i]);
      RStations [i] -> ORing [CWRing] ->
                    setDTo (RStations [j] -> IRing [CWRing], D);
      RStations [i] -> OSat [CCRing] -> connect (SAT [CCRing][i]);
      RStations [j] -> ISat [CCRing] -> connect (SAT [CCRing][i]);
      RStations [i] -> OSat [CCRing] ->
                    setDTo (RStations [j] -> ISat [CCRing], D);
      j = (i+1) % NP;
      RStations [j] -> ORing [CCRing] -> connect (REG [CCRing][i]);
      RStations [i] -> IRing [CCRing] -> connect (REG [CCRing][i]);
      RStations [j] -> ORing [CCRing] ->
                    setDTo (RStations [i] -> IRing [CCRing], D);
      RStations [j] -> OSat [CWRing] -> connect (SAT [CWRing][i]);
      RStations [i] -> ISat [CWRing] -> connect (SAT [CWRing][i]);
      RStations [j] -> OSat [CWRing] ->
                    setDTo (RStations [i] -> ISat [CWRing], D);
    }
    delete RStations;
    for (i = 0; i < 2; i++) {
      delete REG [i];
      delete SAT [i];
    }
  }
};
```

The method starts with creating the eight ports, four per each direction. The transfer rate of all output ports is set to TR; the transfer rate of the input ports, being irrelevant, is left unspecified. Then the pointer to the station's `MRingInterface` portion (this) is stored in RStations, and NC is incremented by 1. The remaining code of the method is executed only once, when NC reaches NP, i.e., when all stations have been created. The first for loop under the if statement goes through all stations and connects station number i to its clockwise successor, i.e., station number j = i + 1 mod NP. The body of the for loop consists of four blocks, each block taking care of one ring segment, in the following order:

- Clockwise segment carrying the regular traffic.
- Counterclockwise SAT segment. Note that SAT messages passed on this segment control the regular traffic in the clockwise ring.
- Counterclockwise segment carrying the regular traffic.
- Clockwise SAT segment. SAT messages circulating in this segment control the traffic in the counterclockwise ring.

Having accomplished the task of configuring the network, the configure method deallocates all the dynamic arrays that were created by initMRing.

The program implementing the pure variant of Metaring without SAT (directory RING/Metaring1) uses the same geometry description files as the full implementation, i.e., mring.h and mring.c. Only two ring segments of the network backbone are used by the SAT-less variant: the SAT-passing rings are ignored.

10.5.2.2   The traffic pattern.   In section 9.3.2.2 we discussed the implementation of a uniform traffic pattern with two packet buffers per station (files utraffic2.h and utraffic2.c in IncludeLibrary). At the end of section 9.3.2.2 we hinted at some modifications of that traffic pattern needed to make it usable in the Metaring program. These modifications involve the qualifying function for getPacket (section 5.4.1.2) used to select packets addressed in specific directions.

As presented in section 9.3.2.2, the traffic pattern is applicable to dual-bus networks with the concept of direction described by the following qualifying function:

```
int qual (Message *m) {
  return (Direction == Left && TheStation->getId () > m->Receiver)
    || (Direction == Right && TheStation->getId () < m->Receiver);
};
```

where Direction is set by the ready method of ClientInterface before calling getPacket. With this qualifying function, we assume that the stations are numbered according to their occurrence on the bus from left to right. Thus, a station with a smaller Id is located to the left of a station with a bigger Id.

In Metaring the selection of the proper ring for transmission should be based on a slightly different idea of direction. A packet should be transmitted in the direction (clockwise or counterclockwise) that offers the smaller number of hops to the destination. Assuming that the stations are numbered clockwise in the increasing order of their Ids, this criterion can be expressed by the following qualifier:

```
int qual (Message *m) {
  Long d;
  d = m->Receiver - TheStation->getId ();
  if (Direction == CCRing) d = -d;
  return (NStations + d) % NStations <= NStations/2;
};
```

where `Direction` is set to either `CWRing` or `CCRing`. Note that a message addressed to the destination equally distant from the source in both directions[17] will qualify to `CWRing` as well as to `CCRing`.

The only modification in the traffic pattern from section 9.3.2.2 required to make it applicable in the Metaring implementation is the replacement of the qualifying function. In fact, file `utraffic2.c` has been prepared for this modification by embedding the declaration of the standard qualifying function (for dual-bus networks) in the following conditional construct:

```
#ifdef PrivateQualifier
extern int Direction;
int qual (Message*);
#else
static int Direction;
int qual (Message *m) {
  return (Direction == Left && TheStation->getId () > m->Receiver)
    || (Direction == Right && TheStation->getId () < m->Receiver);
};
#endif
```

By defining the symbol `PrivateQualifier` before including `utraffic2.c`, the user will eliminate the default qualifying function. The function will be announced as implicitly external rather than `static`, so that it can be specified in a user-supplied program file. At the same time, variable `Direction` (to be referenced by the qualifying function) is declared as `extern`[18] to be accessible from the outside of `utraffic2.c`.

10.5.2.3   The station structure.   Having been built as an extension of the insertion ring implementation, our Metaring program heavily borrows from its predecessor. In particular, the mailbox type `PQueue` used to implement the insertion buffer is exactly the same as in the previous program. The station structure, however, is a bit more complicated, although it can still be viewed as an extension of the station structure from the insertion ring:

```
station MStation : MRingInterface, ClientInterface {
  PQueue *IBuffer [2];
```

---

[17] This can only happen if the number of stations in the network is odd.

[18] Note that `Direction` is also accessed by the **ready** method of `ClientInterface` defined in `utraffic2.c`.

```
        Boolean Blocked [2], SATFlag [2];
        Packet SATPkt;
        int Count [2];
        void setup (Long bufl) {
          int i;
          MRingInterface::configure ();
          ClientInterface::configure ();
          for (i = 0; i < 2; i++) {
            IBuffer [i] = create PQueue (bufl);
            Blocked [i] = NO;
            SATFlag [i] = NO;
            Count [i] = 0;
            SATPkt.fill (NONE, NONE, SATLength);
          }
        };
      };
```

Some of the differences are obvious. The two-element array of PQueue pointers represents two insertion buffers required for the two transfer directions in Metaring. Similarly, the Blocked flag occurs in two copies organized into a two-element Boolean array. The additional pair of flags (SATFlag) is used to mark the "SAT received" status of the station. Whenever a SAT message is received by the station from a given ring segment, the SATFlag for the direction of that segment is set to YES and remains set until the station releases the message. SAT messages are represented by special packets (SATPkt). The length of a SAT packet is determined by SATLength—a numerical parameter of the protocol read by the root process from the input data file.

The SAT mechanism requires three additional station attributes per each transfer direction, corresponding to the constants k and l, and the variable $count$ introduced in section 10.5.1.2. We assume that the values of k and l are the same for all stations; thus, the two parameters have been made global (variables K and L). The transmission counters are represented by the two-element integer array Count, each element serving as the transmission counter for one direction.

The station's setup method initializes all attributes in an obvious way. As for the insertion ring (section 10.4.2), the single setup argument specifies the length of the insertion buffer in bits. Note that when the network starts up, two SAT messages (one per each transfer direction) must be inserted into the ring. This will be accomplished by the root process (section 10.5.2.6), which will explicitly set both SATFlag indicators at station 0.

Each station runs five processes for each transfer direction, which yields the total of ten processes per station. Three of the five processes we are already familiar with; they are the input process, the relay process, and the transmitter from the insertion ring program. The remaining two processes implement the SAT mechanism.

10.5.2.4   The insertion ring part.   The two parts of the protocol, i.e., the insertion ring and the SAT mechanism, are well separated from each other, and they can be discussed individually. In fact, the three processes implementing the insertion ring part of the protocol are practically direct copies of their counterparts from section 10.4.2. As far as the input process and the relay process are concerned, the only difference is in the setup methods, which select the proper collection of the station's attributes based on the transfer direction to be serviced by the process. In particular, the setup method of the input process is as follows:

```
void setup (int dir) {
  IRing = S->IRing [dir];
  IBuffer = S->IBuffer [dir];
  Blocked = &(S->Blocked [dir]);
};
```

When an instance of the input process is created, the setup argument identifies the transfer direction (CWRing or CCRing). A similar modification is required for the setup method of the relay process:

```
void setup (int dir) {
  ORing = S->ORing [dir];
  IBuffer = S->IBuffer [dir];
};
```

The transmitter process has changed a bit more, but its close relation to the insertion ring transmitter is evident. The type of the Metaring transmitter is defined as follows:

```
process Transmitter (MStation) {
  PQueue *IBuffer;
  Packet *Buffer;
  Boolean *Blocked;
  int *Count;
  SATSender *SATSnd;
  int Direction;
  void setup (int dir) {
    Direction = dir;
    IBuffer = S->IBuffer [dir];
    Buffer = &(S->Buffer [dir]);
    Blocked = &(S->Blocked [dir]);
    Count = &(S->Count [dir]);
  };
  states {Acquire};
  perform;
};
```

Three attributes of the process are new: the Count pointer linked to one copy of the station's transmission counter, SATSnd pointing to the process responsible for sending SAT messages on the opposite ring, and Direction identifying the transfer direction serviced by the process. SATSnd is not initialized by the process's setup method: it will be set explicitly by the root process (section 10.5.2.6). The transmitter will use this pointer to send signals to the SAT sender.

The new code of the transmitter is a straightforward extension of the transmitter code listed in section 10.4.2:

```
Transmitter::perform {
  Long f;
  state Acquire:
    if (*Blocked || *Count >= K)
      wait (SIGNAL, Acquire);
    else if (S->ready (Direction, MinPL, MaxPL, FrameL)) {
      if ((f = IBuffer->free ()) >= Buffer->TLength) {
        Packet *p;
        p = create Packet;
        *p = *Buffer;
        IBuffer->put (p);
        Buffer->release ();
        ++(*Count);
        SATSnd->signal ();
        proceed Acquire;
      } else
        Timer->wait (Buffer->TLength - f, Acquire);
    } else
      Client->wait (ARRIVAL, Acquire);
};
```

Upon entry to its only state, the process checks whether a transmission is allowed. According to the insertion ring part of the protocol, the station can store its own packet into the insertion buffer if the buffer is not blocked (section 10.4.2) and there is enough room in the buffer to accommodate the packet. The SAT rules (section 10.5.1.2) additionally specify that the station should refrain from transmitting if it has reached its quota (the transmission counter has reached k) without receiving a SAT message in the meantime. If the buffer is blocked or the station has exhausted its transmission quota, the transmitter waits for a signal to be deposited in its own signal repository. This signal will be sent either by the input process (as in section 10.4.2) or by the SAT sender (section 10.5.2.5) upon the departure of a SAT message from the station. When the signal arrives, the transmitter will reexecute the if statement in state Acquire. The body of that statement is essentially the same as in the insertion ring program (section 10.4.2), except for two additional statements:

```
++(*Count);
SATSnd->signal ();
```

executed after the process has stored a packet in the insertion buffer. The first statement increments the transmission counter (section 10.5.1.2) needed to implement the SAT rules, and the second signals the SAT sender process (section 10.5.2.5) to check if the new value of Count makes the station satisfied. If this is the case and a SAT message is being held by the station, the message will be released immediately.

10.5.2.5   The SAT part.   The SAT-passing mechanism is implemented by two processes (per transfer direction) run at every station. One of these processes (the SAT receiver) absorbs SAT messages, and the other (the SAT sender) inserts them back into the network. The type definition of the SAT receiver is as follows:

```
process SATReceiver (MStation) {
  Port *ISat;
  Boolean *SATFlag;
  SATSender *SATSnd;
  void setup (int dir) {
    ISat = S->ISat [dir];
    SATFlag = &(S->SATFlag [dir]);
  };
  states {WaitSAT, Receive};
  perform;
};
```

SATSnd is a pointer to the SAT sender process servicing the same direction as the SAT receiver. Note that this pointer is not initialized by the process's setup method; it will be assigned explicitly by the root process (section 10.5.2.6). Attributes ISat and SATFlag provide references to the corresponding station attributes for the direction serviced by the process. ISat points to the input port from the SAT channel, and SATFlag refers to the Boolean flag indicating the presence of a SAT message (for the given direction) at the station. The SAT receiver runs the following code:

```
SATReceiver::perform {
  state WaitSAT:
    ISat->wait (BOT, Receive);
    Timer->wait (SATTimeout, Receive);
    wait (SIGNAL, WaitSAT);
  state Receive:
    *SATFlag = YES;
    SATSnd->signal ();
    skipto WaitSAT;
}
```

Whenever a packet arrives from the SAT channel (such a packet can only be a SAT message) or the SAT timer goes off, the process transits to state `Receive`, which corresponds to the reception of a SAT message. The role of the signal wait request (the third statement at state `WaitSAT`) is to reset the SAT timer after a SAT departure from the station. It is not difficult to guess that the signal awaited with this request by the SAT receiver will be delivered by the SAT sender process upon a SAT transmission.

In state `Receive`, the process sets `SATFlag` to indicate that a SAT message is currently held by the station. Note that a single `Boolean` flag is used for this purpose. Consequently, subsequent SAT messages arriving at the station (including SAT timeouts) while a SAT message is being held will be ignored. Having received a SAT message, the receiver signals the SAT sender process. It is possible that the station is immediately satisfied (e.g., it has no packets to transmit), in which case the SAT message will be instantly retransmitted on the output SAT channel. Finally, the process moves back to state `WaitSAT` to await another SAT arrival. Operation `skipto` is used for this purpose—to make sure that the `BOT` event from the last SAT message has disappeared from the port (section 4.5.1).

Now let us look at the SAT sender process. Its type is declared as follows:

```
process SATSender (MStation) {
  Port *OSat;
  Boolean *SATFlag;
  int *Count, Direction;
  Transmitter *Xmitter;
  SATReceiver *SATRcv;
  Packet *SATPkt;
  void setup (int dir) {
    Direction = dir;
    OSat = S->OSat [dir];
    SATFlag = &(S->SATFlag [dir]);
    Count = &(S->Count [1 - Direction]);
    SATPkt = &(S->SATPkt);
  };
  states {WaitSend, CheckSend, XDone};
  perform;
};
```

Attributes `XMitter` and `SATRcv` are pointers to the other processes of the co-hort servicing the same transfer direction. Recall that SAT messages for a given transfer direction circulate in the opposite direction; thus, the `Count` attribute referenced by the SAT sender is taken from the opposite direction ($1 - $ `Direction`). With the convention assumed in assigning station attributes to directions, the direction of an attribute always means the direction of the ring channel associated with the attribute. As the `Count` attribute is related to packet transmission, its direction ordinal is determined by the transfer direction of regular packets. On the other hand, SATFlag is internal to the SAT-passing mechanism, and its direction ordinal is induced by the SAT-passing direction. Of course, any other consistent convention could be used. Note that SATPkt (i.e., the preset packet buffer representing the SAT message) occurs in a single copy at each station. This packet looks the same at each station regardless of the direction, and its structure is constant.

Following is the code method of the SAT sender:

```
SATSender::perform {
  state WaitSend:
    wait (SIGNAL, CheckSend);
  state CheckSend:
    if (*SATFlag && (*Count >= L ||
      !S->ready (1-Direction, MinPL, MaxPL, FrameL))) {
      OSat->transmit (SATPkt, XDone);
      *SATFlag = NO;
      *Count = 0;
      Xmitter->signal ();
      SATRcv->signal ();
    } else
      proceed WaitSend;
  state XDone:
    OSat->stop ();
    proceed WaitSend;
}
```

The condition for emitting a SAT message is examined upon the reception of the signal awaited by the SAT sender in its first state (WaitSend). The signal is ignored, and the process returns to its initial state, if the condition is not fulfilled. The signal awaited in state WaitSend may arrive either from the transmitter process (after a packet transmission) or from the SAT receiver (when a SAT message has been received). In the first case, the signal indicates that Count has been incremented; thus, it is possible that the station has become satisfied. According to the SAT-passing rules described in section 10.5.1.2, if a station is holding a SAT message, it should release this message as soon as it becomes satisfied. In the second case, a SAT message just arrives at the station. If the station has no own packet to transmit, it is automatically satisfied and should release the SAT message immediately.

The SAT-passing condition is described by the argument of the if statement in state CheckSend. This condition reads: a SAT message should be sent on the SAT output channel (OSat) if the station is currently holding a SAT message (SATFlag is set) and the station is satisfied (i.e., either Count has reached L or there are no packets awaiting transmission). Having initiated the operation of passing the SAT message (by starting the transmission of SATPkt), the sender clears SATFlag and resets Count to zero. The process also sends two signals: one to the transmitter process (to indicate new transmission opportunities resulting from Count having

become zero) and to the SAT receiver (to reset the SAT timer). Having completed
the transmission of the SAT message (in state XDone) the SAT sender terminates
the transfer and returns to its initial state.

10.5.2.6   The root process.   The only interesting fragment of the root process for our Metaring program is the loop that creates processes and assigns them
to stations. As we remember from the previous two sections, all processes except
the output process use pointers to other processes to pass them signals. It turns
out to be more convenient to assign these pointers explicitly in the root process,
rather than passing them as setup arguments. If a process pointer is passed as an
argument of the setup method of another process, the first process must be created
before the second process. This poses obvious problems when two processes (e.g.,
the SAT sender and SAT receiver) require pointers to each other.

The relevant fragment of the root process code is as follows:

```
for (i = 0; i < NNodes; i++) create MStation (BufferLength);
for (i = 0; i < NNodes; i++) {
  Transmitter *tr;
  SATSender *ss;
  Input *in;
  SATReceiver *sr;
  for (j = 0; j < 2; j++) {
    tr = create (i) Transmitter (j);
    in = create (i) Input (j);
    create (i) Relay (j);
    ss = create (i) SATSender (1-j);
    sr = create (i) SATReceiver (1-j);
    tr -> SATSnd = ss;
    in -> Xmitter = tr;
    sr -> SATSnd = ss;
    ss -> SATRcv = sr;
    ss -> Xmitter = tr;
    if (i == 0) {
      *(ss->SATFlag) = YES;
      ss->signal ();
    }
  }
}
```

Variables NNodes and BufferLength, as well as several other numerical parameters of the program, are read from the input data file. The first for loop creates
the stations, and the second loop starts the processes and assigns them to their owners. The inner loop is executed twice, once for each ring direction,[19] and takes care

---

[19]The loop index j assumes values 0 and 1, which correspond to CWRing and CCRing (section 10.5.2.1).

of the process cohort implementing the packet transfer protocol in the given direction. Note that the SAT-passing processes (i.e., `SATSender` and `SATReceiver`) of a given cohort belong to the ring direction opposite to the direction of the processes handling the regular traffic.

Once the five processes have been created, their pointers are available and can be assigned to the interested parties. This is accomplished by the five assignment statements following the last `create` operation.

To start up the protocol, the root process creates one SAT message per each direction and assigns it to station number zero. This operation consists in setting the station's `SATFlag` attribute (to indicate the presence of a SAT message at the station) and sending a signal to the SAT sender process—in the same way as after a regular SAT arrival from the ring (section 10.5.2.5). Note that the initialization of the SAT mechanism performed by `Root` is not absolutely necessary. Had it not been done, the SAT processes would have generated SAT messages in response to the SAT timeout events. Although most likely multiple SAT messages would have appeared in the network this way, they would eventually have merged into one SAT message per direction, as described in section 10.5.1.2.

The protocol program implementing the Metaring protocol can be found in directory `RING/Metaring2` of SMURPH `Examples`. Directory `RING/Metaring1` contains essentially the same program with the SAT mechanism removed. The same effect can be achieved in the full version of the protocol by setting K to a huge value (approximating infinity).

10.5.3   Problems with Metaring

Although Metaring comes close to an ideal ring access protocol, it inherits some of the disadvantages of the insertion ring discussed in section 10.4.3. One exception is the starvation potential, which in Metaring has been turned into a trade-off between fairness and high bandwidth utilization.

Notably, the token-passing apparatus of Metaring (disguised as the SAT-passing mechanism) is much less strict than its counterpart in FDDI: a station in Metaring does not have to hold the token (the SAT message) to transmit a packet, provided that it fulfills certain token-induced criteria. This way, in contrast to FDDI, the protocol incurs zero access delay under light load. Nonetheless, it can be easily shown that the maximum throughput of Metaring (under uniform load) is determined by the following formula:

$$T_m = min\left(\frac{2Nk}{L}, 8\right)   .$$

Thus, Metaring is not a capacity-1 protocol unless k is infinite, i.e., the SAT mechanism is disabled. On the other hand, for a given propagation length of the ring L and the number of stations N, there exists a minimum value of k ($k = \lceil 4L/N \rceil$) for which the maximum throughput of the network is 8 despite the SAT mechanism being active. Note, however, that a single heavily loaded station may still not be able to get the full bandwidth of the ring medium, even in the absence of other backlogged stations. Having transmitted k packets, the station should hold its further transfers until it receives a SAT message. If no other station is ready to transmit, the SAT message will not be held during its trip through the ring, but this trip will still take L time units. Without SAT, the maximum throughput of Metaring is 8, irrespective of L and N;[20] however, the protocol is then starvation-prone.

The advantageous properties of Metaring with respect to the strong-token protocols (like FDDI) indicate that the weakening of the token's role in controlling access to the medium is the right direction toward a fair, capacity-1 protocol for ring networks.

10.6 DPMA AND THE PRETZEL RING

DPMA is a fair capacity-1 protocol for ring networks based on the concept of passing a weak token. The token in DPMA is weak (as in Metaring), because its possession by a station is not a necessary condition for starting a packet transmission. The protocol can be compared to U-Net (section 9.4.2.1), in which the head station is shifted cyclically. This way, a station can start transmission at any moment, with the upstream stations enjoying a privilege over the downstream stations. The current location of the token determines the position of the most upstream station (the token-holding station disconnects the ring) and, as the token circulates in the network, different stations assume this role at different moments. This way, the network achieves fairness.

10.6.1 The Pretzel Ring Topology

Simple as it sounds, the preceding idea must be refined a bit to be turned into something original and useful. As the station holding the token disconnects the ring, another station willing to initiate a spontaneous token-less transmission must account for the possibility that its packet will reach the token-holding station (and be erased from the ring) before arriving at the destination. Even if we could somehow guarantee that token-less transmissions magically reach their destinations without crashing into the token, the only advantage we would get from weakening the token's role would be zero access delay under light load. Under heavy load, the only successful transmissions would be performed by token-holding stations (they would preempt all spontaneous transfer attempts) and the protocol would degenerate to a strong-token protocol. We know what this means: the maximum throughput under heavy uniform load would deteriorate with the increasing propagation length of the ring.

The first step to transform our idea into a capacity-1 protocol is a simple modification of the ring topology. Later it will turn out that this modification is

---

[20]Ignoring the packetization overhead.

not absolutely necessary: it is possible to have a capacity-1 version of DPMA on a regular single-loop unidirectional ring; however, the full benefits of the protocol crop up in its implementation on the so-called *pretzel ring*.

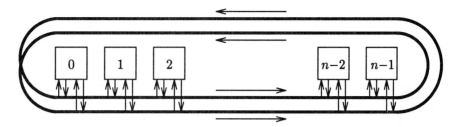

Figure 10.5 The pretzel ring

The pretzel ring is a dual ring connected as shown in figure 10.5. Essentially, the ring consists of a single unidirectional segment that loops twice through the network but, to make our presentation easier, we treat the two loops as separate segments. The pretzel ring resembles a Möbius tape with one surface. Assuming that the ring is not disconnected, an activity inserted into any place on the ring will pass through both segments before arriving back at the point of insertion.

Each station is connected to the pretzel ring in two places, once to each segment. The two connections are identical: every station perceives the same topology of the network from each connection.

The merits of the pretzel ring will become clear in the next section, where we discuss DPMA—the protocol operating on the pretzel ring topology. At this moment, we can only hint at these merits. Assume that there is only one token circulating in the ring and the station holding the token disconnects the ring at the tap at which the token has arrived. A station willing to carry out a spontaneous (token-less) transmission knows one thing: regardless of the token location, a packet transmitted on one of the two taps will reach its destination without damage. The safe tap for a token-less transmission is the one that was earlier visited by the token.

10.6.2   The Protocol

DPMA, which stands for Distributed Pretzel Multiple Access, is a token-passing protocol for the pretzel ring topology. The protocol occurs in several versions, some slotted and some unslotted. In this section we discuss the basic slotted version of DPMA. Later, in section 10.6.2.6, we hint at a few possible modifications of the protocol.

10.6.2.1 Basic prerequisites. As in most ring networks, a station connected to the pretzel ring is expected to relay the traffic arriving from its upstream neighbor to the downstream successor. Being connected to two segments of the ring, the station has to duplicate this labor on both connections. Each station has two separate receiver processes independently monitoring its two taps for packets addressed to the station. No destination cleaning is used; therefore, packets need not be buffered before they are relayed. The protocol, especially the slotted version, can be implemented with a minimum collection of hardware prerequisites. It is sufficient if a station is able to change one bit in the slot marker on the fly, e.g., as in Fasnet (section 9.3.1).

The number of transmitters at a station is flexible and can be either one or two. The protocol does not rule out the possibility of two simultaneous transmissions by the same station, although it may be reasonable to postulate otherwise, e.g., to preserve the packet ordering at destinations. In our implementation of DPMA, we assume that it is legal for a single station to transmit two packets at the same time.

In its slotted version, DPMA requires two binary flags in the slot header. One of these flags is the standard *FULL* bit used to tell a used slot from an empty one. The other flag, called *TOKEN*, is used for token passing. A station must be able to perform the following operations on these flags:

- Set the flag unconditionally to 1 and determine its previous value
- Unconditionally reset the flag to zero (no interest in the previous value)

The minimum retransmission delay at a station-relay is determined by the complexity of these operations. Clearly, the second operation is trivial. Any station must be able to insert anything into the ring, e.g., its own segment. In section 9.3.1 we argued that the first operation can be performed on the fly without incurring any retransmission delay.

During the network initialization phase, the ring is filled with empty slots; from then on, the slots circulate in the network indefinitely. The operation of stripping a segment (erasing a slot payload) consists in resetting the *FULL* bit in the slot marker to zero.

Like every MAC-level protocol for a ring-like topology, DPMA has two main responsibilities:

- To determine when a station is allowed to transmit (insert its own segment into a slot) and—as there are two possible transmitting taps—from which tap
- To determine how slots are emptied (the cleaning rules)

A token-passing mechanism is used to single out the station that logically disconnects the ring: the ring is disconnected by the token-holding station at the tap at which the token was captured.[21] The disconnection is logical, and the slot markers arriving from upstream are relayed through the disconnection tap. However, all slots crossing this tap are stripped, their *FULL* flags unconditionally reset to zero. As there is only one token, at any moment the pretzel can be disconnected in at most one location.

---

[21] As it makes a difference from which tap of a station the token is received, we will sometimes say that the token is held by a tap rather than a station.

Normally, when a station relays a slot marker on the output port of its tap, it sets the *TOKEN* bit of this marker to 1. This means that the token is *not* passed within the slot. A station holding the token and willing to pass it down the ring clears the *TOKEN* flag in the next slot marker to be relayed. Any station receiving a slot marker on the input port sets the *TOKEN* flag to 1 and determines its previous value. If the original value of the flag was 0, it means that the station has captured the token. Every station that recognizes an arriving token must capture the token and hold it for an amount of time equal to the value of *THT*—a constant associated with the station. As in FDDI, priorities can be implemented by assigning different values of *THT* to different stations, although the relation between the actual priority of a station and the value of its *THT* is less straightforward than in FDDI.[22] For simplicity, we may assume that all stations use the same value of *THT*.

10.6.2.2   Timing.   In contrast to FDDI, stations do not release the token early if they have nothing to transmit; they must hold it for the whole amount of time assigned to them. As the protocol is slotted, the token-holding time (and other time intervals measured by the stations) are expressed in slots. The stations measure these intervals by counting slots passing by their taps. The minimum token-holding time is clearly one slot per station.

As each station holds the token for a fixed amount of time, the time that elapses between two consecutive token captures by the same station is constant and the same for all stations. Preserving the terminology of FDDI, we denote this time by *TTRT*, which in the case of DPMA stands for *total token rotation time*. The value of *TTRT* is given by the formula

$$TTRT = L + \sum_{i=0}^{N-1} THT_i \ ,$$

where THT_i is the token-holding time at station number i. If all stations use the same token-holding time, *TTRT* is equal to $L + N \times THT$.

If for technical reasons the repeaters at stations incur nontrivial retransmission delays, these delays are assumed to have been included in L, i.e., they inflate the propagation length of the ring. Note that *TTRT* is expressed in slots and its value is accurate.

Each station is equipped with a counter called the *token rotation timer* (*TRT*), which counts the time (the number of slots) elapsed from the moment the station last acquired the token. Unlike its FDDI counterpart, DPMA's *TRT* is not used for synchronous traffic (in fact, no explicit notion of synchronous traffic is needed in DPMA—section 10.6.2.5) but as a pointer to estimate the token position. Whenever a station acquires the token, it resets its *TRT* to zero. Then the counter is

---

[22]The reason for this is the fixed token-holding time at every station, regardless of whether the station has segments to transmit or not. The value of *THT* assigned to station *s* affects not only the priority of *s* but also, to some extent, the priorities of stations following *s* on the ring. Thus, the problem of allocating *THT* in a way that would reflect a known bias in the load profile of different stations boils down to solving a set of linear equations.

incremented by 1 with each slot passing through the station's tap. The station expects to receive the token when the value of *TRT* reaches *TTRT*.

The role of the token is different in DPMA and in FDDI: in FDDI it is used to inform the station about the available bandwidth left by the other stations during the current token cycle, while in DPMA the token is used solely for synchronizing long-term clocks. Formally, there is no need for an explicit token, as each station knows exactly in which slot the token will arrive. Thus, in principle, following the initialization phase in which all stations are informed about the starting location of the token, the network can operate without the token being actually passed. It seems, however, that the token flag explicitly passed among stations is useful for implementing certain network management operations, e.g., a dynamic addition of a new station to the network. As the cost incurred by the tangible presence of the token in the network is just a single bit in the slot marker, there is no reason to advocate frugality in this case.

10.6.2.3 Cleaning rules. The cleaning rules of DPMA are practically identical to those of FDDI. First, the token-holding station logically disconnects the ring at the tap at which the token was acquired. This means that the station empties all slots arriving at the input port of that tap. Besides this natural token-based cleaning rule, each station is expected to empty the slots that it filled with its own segments, after they have made one full loop through the ring. To accomplish this task without buffering the slot headers before they are relayed, a station filling a slot with a segment stores the time of this operation expressed in slots. The station expects this slot to arrive at its other tap L slots later; thus, it can be ready to clear the *FULL* bit of the slot at the moment when the slot marker passes through the tap. As a station can transmit a sequence of segments before the first segment of this sequence makes a full circle through the ring, it has to maintain a queue of numbers describing the intervals separating the expected arrivals of these slots back at the station.

Alternatively, to simplify the slot-counting operation and make it foolproof, one can consider augmenting the slot marker format with an extra numeric field. With this solution, all slots are permanently tagged during the initialization phase in such a way that different slots are assigned different tags, e.g., consecutive integer numbers from zero to $2L-1$. A station inserting its own segment into a slot puts the tag value of this slot into a queue. As slots pass by, the station compares their tags with the tag stored in the top element of the queue. When the tag of an incoming slot matches the top tag in the queue, the station resets the *FULL* bit of this slot and removes the top element from the queue. To make this idea work, the location of the tag field in the slot marker should precede the location of the *FULL* bit.

10.6.2.4 Transmission rules. The two taps of each station are dynamically labeled "yellow" and "green." Let N be the number of stations. The protocol is initialized in such a way that the first N taps following the tap holding the token are labeled "yellow" and the remaining N taps are labeled "green." This statement is turned into a protocol invariant by the following rule:

> Whenever a station releases the token, it labels the tap on which the token is released "yellow." At the same time, the other tap is labeled "green."

Consequently, at any moment of the protocol operation, the token divides the pretzel into two continuous and contiguous segments. The next N taps to be visited by the token, including the tap at which the token is being held, are colored "green." The last N taps visited by the token, excluding the tap at which the token is being held, are painted "yellow."

The rules for transmitting are very simple. A station willing to transmit a segment is allowed to do so:

- In the first empty slot sensed on the "green" tap
- In the first empty slot sensed on the "yellow" tap, provided that the condition $TRT \geq TTRT - L$ holds

To understand the merit of these rules, imagine the pretzel divided by the token into the two differently painted zones. A station transmitting in the "green" zone knows that its segment will visit all other stations in the network (and return to the sender on the other tap) before it has a chance to be absorbed by a token-holding tap. On the other hand, a station transmitting on a "yellow" tap knows that the token is located less than N taps downstream. Therefore, as the token moves slower than a slot, there is a possibility that the transmitted segment will catch up with the token and be cleaned out before reaching its destination. The condition in the transmission rule for a "yellow" tap says that the token is far enough down the ring not to be reached by the segment before it has visited at least N taps. Indeed, the total amount of time needed by the token to visit N taps (i.e., to make a full round-trip through the ring) is $TTRT$. The same trip made by a segment takes only L time units. Consequently, if TRT has reached $TTRT - L$, i.e., the token departed from the tap no less than $TTRT - L$ time units ago, the segment will not catch up with the token before it has been seen by all stations in the ring.

Note that the "yellow" tap condition can be weakened, if the transmitting station knows how many stations separate it from the destination and for how long the token is going to be held at these stations. In its present pessimistic form, the condition guarantees that the segment will safely return to the destination; thus, it can be used to transmit broadcast segments.[23]

The transmission rules never mention the token, and it is clear that token possession has little to do with transmission rights. The token-holding station enjoys a momentary priority over all other stations in acquiring empty slots for transmission. Also a station stripping its own segment from a full slot can immediately reuse this slot to transmit another segment, unless the slot is stripped in the "yellow" zone and the transmission condition does not hold.

---

[23] One can also implement an acknowledgment scheme based on a flag inserted into the segment trailer by the recipient.

It is not difficult to show that DPMA is a capacity-1 protocol. The reader can easily verify (see exercise 7 at the end of this chapter) that at any moment two taps in the network, possibly belonging to different stations, are guaranteed successful transmission. Therefore, ignoring the overhead on slot markers and fragmentation, the maximum throughput achieved by DPMA is 2, regardless of the propagation length of the ring. DPMA is also fair, because the rotating token makes the long-term behavior of the protocol indifferent to the station location.

10.6.2.5 Synchronous traffic.

Unlike FDDI, DPMA need not explicitly differentiate between synchronous and asynchronous traffic. With each turn of the token, every station gets a guaranteed share of the bandwidth at fixed time intervals, which it can use as it pleases. Essentially, there exist three possible transmission strategies as far as synchronous traffic is concerned:

Transmit only during token possession. This strategy offers the lowest possible jitter (practically zero) and should be used if low jitter is the primary concern. Each station has a guaranteed synchronous bandwidth equal to $THT/TTRT$. Bandwidth guaranteed for synchronous traffic, but unused, may be used freely for transmitting other segments. The maximum synchronous throughput is limited to $(TTRT - L)/TTRT$.

Transmit at all opportunities. If the volume and structure of synchronous traffic are not static or exceed the guaranteed upper bound of $THT/TTRT$, a higher *maximum* bandwidth for synchronous traffic may be obtained by allowing the transmission of synchronous packets from every tap—at the expense of a nonzero jitter. With this strategy, synchronous traffic is given priority over asynchronous traffic, but the two types of traffic are treated in the same way in all other respects. This approach results in maximum bandwidth availability for synchronous traffic, but the jitter is also high because of the possibly irregular access intervals. Also, it is possible for synchronous traffic to completely preempt asynchronous traffic.

Transmit during token possession and slot reuse. This strategy is a compromise between the other two. Synchronous transmissions are allowed during token possession and at predictable transmission windows by stations stripping and reusing their own segments. Note that if a station transmits m segments at time t from a "green" port, it is guaranteed to get a transmission window of m frames at time $t + L$. It can be shown that if the sum of the token-holding times at stations is a divisor of $2L$, these transmission windows are not only predictable but also occur at highly regular intervals.

The last approach seems to be particularly well suited for synchronous traffic organized into sessions of more or less constant intensity. A station willing to sustain the regularity of its transmission windows should make sure that it reuses all its segments. Sometimes it might be reasonable to reserve a slot (i.e., mark it as full) without transmitting any data—just to keep it booked for the next round. Note that the second option is not applicable to FDDI, i.e., one cannot simply postulate that excess synchronous traffic be transmitted at any opportunity, preempting the asynchronous traffic. The huge upper bound on the packet access time for asynchronous traffic makes this idea worthless. After all, this was the primary reason for introducing a separate synchronous traffic class in FDDI.

In contrast to FDDI (and strong-token protocols in general), the maximum throughput achieved by DPMA does not depend on THT—the token-holding time. From the point of view of predictability and short-term fairness, the token-holding time should be as short as possible. The minimum value of THT is one slot per station; this should also be the standard recommended value.

10.6.2.6   Other variants of DPMA.   DPMA has a number of advantageous properties: it is fair, its maximum throughput does not depend on the propagation length of the ring, it incorporates synchronous traffic in a natural way—without introducing a separate access mechanism for this purpose. In comparison with other token protocols, e.g., FDDI, certain network management operations in DPMA are also simplified. For example, the lost-token diagnosis and recovery is trivial: every station knows exactly when the token is supposed to arrive, so the token can be claimed even in its physical absence. One can say that the behavior of DPMA is *predictable*. This property is usually associated with low jitter, but it also implies that abnormal events, e.g., errors requiring a recovery action, can be diagnosed fast and repaired promptly.

One can think of several ways to improve DPMA. By weakening the "yellow" tap condition (as suggested in section 10.6.2.4), the maximum throughput of the protocol can be pushed beyond 2. This will be caused by the fact that not all segments will have to make a full circle through the ring before being stripped/reused. Consequently, under heavy traffic conditions, statistically more than two stations will be able to transmit their segments at the same time. It is also possible to introduce a destination-reuse mechanism into the protocol (and increase the maximum throughput even further), but this would require relay buffers—something we would prefer to avoid.

Notably, the pretzel topology of the DPMA ring is not an absolute must, as far as the capacity-1 property is concerned. It is possible to implement a variant of the protocol for a regular single-loop ring to which each station is connected only once. All the protocol rules are the same as before, except for the tap-painting rules, which become redundant. All taps are always "yellow"; thus, the "yellow" tap rule (section 10.6.2.4) applies to all transmissions. One can easily show that the maximum throughput achieved by the single-loop variant of DPMA is no less than

$$max \left(\frac{L}{TTRT}, 1 - \frac{L}{TTRT} \right) \ .$$

Although this expression depends on L, its value does not decrease to zero when L becomes large. In fact, it is never less that $1/2$, regardless of the values of

L and *TTRT*. One disadvantage of the single-loop version of DPMA is a nonzero
access delay under light load resulting from the fact that stations are not allowed
to transmit in the (global and permanent) "yellow" zone.

An unslotted variant of the protocol can be implemented; its throughput will
tend to be slightly lower than 2, but still independent of L.[24] In the unslotted
version of DPMA, slot reservation is replaced by a collision mechanism borrowed
from Expressnet (section 9.2) or unslotted U-Net/H-Net (section 9.4.2.1). A station
willing to transmit a packet waits for a period of silence on one of its taps. The
station can start transmitting on the "green" tap at any moment whenever the tap
is perceived idle. The "yellow" tap can only be used for transmission if, in addition
to being silent, it also satisfies the inequality introduced in section 10.6.2.4. As the
time is now unslotted, all intervals are measured by clocks rather than slot counters.
An explicit token packet is necessary to synchronize clocks at different stations.

A transmitting station can be legitimately preempted by another transmission
arriving from upstream. In such a case, the station must abort its transfer attempt
and yield to the incoming activity. As with Expressnet, each packet (including
the token packet) is preceded by a preamble, whose role, besides synchronizing
the receiver to the incoming packet, is to absorb collisions and give the preempted
stations ample time to abort their transmissions without affecting the integrity of
the incoming packet.

A station holding the token disconnects the pretzel on the tap on which the
token was captured and ignores any activities arriving on that tap from upstream.
As in the slotted version, the token is held for a prescribed amount of time (measured by a clock) and then inserted back into the ring. The limited accuracy of
independent clocks poses no problems from the viewpoint of transmission rules.
The "yellow" tap condition can be evaluated with a safety margin accounting for
a nonzero tolerance of the *TRT* timer. The most serious implementation problem
with the unslotted variant of DPMA is packet stripping. DPMA employs destination cleaning, and there are two possible ways for a station to recognize its own
packet that should be stripped:

- The station reads a portion of the packet header and recognizes its own address
  in the sender field.
- The station knows exactly when the packet is going to arrive at one of the
  station's taps, and it disconnects that tap for the packet's duration.

With slots, the second solution could be implemented easily. By counting
the slots passing through its taps, a station is able to determine exactly which slot
contains its previously transmitted segment, and it can be ready to clear the *FULL*
bit in the slot marker when it arrives. In unslotted DPMA, a station can in principle
set up a timer when it starts a packet transmission and expect the packet to arrive
at the other tap *L* time units later. This time, however, we are talking about an

---

[24]Depending on the traffic profile, the maximum effective throughput of the unslotted version
may be actually higher than in slotted DPMA, owing to the lack of slot/packet fragmentation.

estimate of the packet arrival time rather then exact knowledge. The problem is aggravated by the presence of aborted packet fragments that can be arbitrarily short and that must also be stripped by their senders to avoid bandwidth wastage. In summary, we have to conclude that it is unrealistic to postulate full packet stripping at destinations in the unslotted variant of the protocol, unless relay buffers are used.

Note, however, that even with complete stripping, the reclaimed period of silence can seldom be reused in its entirety. Packets being of variable length, it is unrealistic to expect that a station transmitting in a stripped packet frame will fit its packet precisely to the length of the available silence period. A station reusing its own frame is in a slightly better position than other stations, as it can know the length of the frame and can tailor its packet to this length. Other stations can only guess. If a guess is overoptimistic, the transmission will be preempted by a packet following the stripped frame, and the frame will be filled with garbage for one complete trip through the ring.

One idea that works reasonably well consists in putting up with partial stripping. A station recognizes its own packet after some initial portion of the packet header has been relayed down the ring. This portion includes an additional field specifying the length of the payload portion of the packet. From that field, a station trying to reuse the stripped frame can deduce a safe length of a packet that can fit into the reclaimed silence period. This way, packets transmitted in reused frames tend to be shorter than the original packets, but they have better chances for not being preempted. Note that a frame can be reused a number of times before its unstrippable remnants are eventually absorbed by a token-holding station; thus, it pays to locate the sender identification at the beginning of the packet header—to reduce the size of these remnants.

Another possibility is to abort the preempted packets gracefully. A station transmitting a packet and sensing another packet arriving from upstream terminates the transmitted packet with a complete trailer. The untransmitted portion of the packet will be sent as another packet in the next period of silence. To be able to terminate the packet properly, i.e., to insert the CRC code and the terminal sequence of symbols, the station must delay the incoming transmission for a short while (a few octets). Thus, this solution requires a modest hallway buffer attached to the input port.

The last interesting idea that we would like to mention is a compromise between the fully slotted protocol and its totally unslotted version with variable-size packets. In the proposed *semislotted variant* of DPMA, all packets are of the same length, but no explicit slot markers are inserted into the ring. Thus, a packet can be transmitted spontaneously, according to the timing rules of the protocol, if the station perceives one of its taps silent. As in the fully unslotted version, collisions are possible and transmissions can be preempted, resulting in aborted packet fragments circulating in the network. However, with the packet length being fixed, one can think of implementing a safe full-reuse mechanism without resorting to relay buffers. Let l_p be the fixed packet length. To be able to strip its packet entirely, a transmitting station records the time t when it started the packet transmission and begins to expect the arrival of this packet at its next tap a while before $t + L$, e.g., at time $t + L - l_p/2$. Starting at this moment, when the station senses a starting packet boundary, it can freely remove the incoming packet. As no valid packet can be shorter than l_p, the station knows that any activity shorter than l_p (that initially appears like a packet) can be freely stripped without destroying anything important. By the same token, any stripped frame can always be fully reused.

The token (a special packet) is absorbed by the station in the same way, i.e., it is removed entirely. Timing is based on the value of the TRT clock. Note that while absorbing the packet containing the token, the station reads the contents of the packet to make sure that the packet actually is the token (e.g., to diagnose a lost-token condition).

Note that a station reusing the frame of its own packet can start its new transmission before the old packet actually arrives at the station. Formally, the reuse can start a short while after $t + L - l_p$. As we said before, whatever activity shorter than l_p precedes the awaited frame, it cannot be a valid packet. In reality, depending on the accuracy of stations' clocks, some safety margin should be added to the minimum theoretically safe reuse time.

10.6.3   The Implementation

We now present a SMURPH program implementing the slotted variant of DPMA. As usual, we start by introducing the network geometry description module specifying the configuration of the pretzel ring.

10.6.3.1   The pretzel ring.   There are few tricky things in the part of our implementation describing the pretzel ring geometry. One nonstandard item on the short checklist is the monitoring station. This time we would like to include this station explicitly in the network configuration. Its primary role will be to fill the pretzel with slots during the initialization phase. Then the station will provide an elastic insert into the pretzel, making sure that the medium accommodates an entire (and always the same) number of slots, regardless of its actual propagation length. The reader may find some other uses for the monitoring station, in particular, experimenting with recovery algorithms from abnormal situations.

Owing to the presence of the monitoring station, whose interface to the ring is different from the interface of a regular station, two virtual station classes are declared in the header file of the geometry module (see file `pring.h` in `IncludeLibrary`):

```
station PRingInterface virtual {
  Port *IRing [2], *ORing [2];
  void configure ();
};
station PMonitorInterface virtual {
  Port *IRing, *ORing;
```

```
    void configure ();
};
```

As we can see, the monitoring station has only one tap (two ports) to the ring. Notably, with the pretzel topology, the station will be able to monitor both segments of the ring (i.e., see all activities passing through the network) via this tap. The port-naming convention is the same as in FDDI (section 10.3.4.1) and Metaring (section 10.5.2.1), i.e., IRing stands for an input port and ORing identifies an output port. In the case of PRingInterface, a pair of ports indicated by the same index value (0 or 1) represents one tap.

File **pring.h** also announces the following global function:

```
    void initPRing (RATE, TIME, int);
```

which is to be used by the root process to specify the numerical parameters of the pretzel. From left to right, the arguments stand for the transmission rate (common for all output ports), the propagation length of the pretzel (a single segment), and the total number of regular stations (the monitor station excluded) connected to the network.

The way the network is configured is described in file **pring.c** in IncludeLibrary. A starting fragment of this file, whose layout closely resembles the layout of all geometry files discussed so far, is as follows:

```
static PLink **Segments;
static RATE TR;
static DISTANCE D;
static int NP, NC;
static PRingInterface **RStations;
void initPRing (RATE r, TIME l, int np) {
  int i, nl;
  NP = np;
  Segments = new PLink* [nl = NP+NP+1];
  for (i = 0; i < nl; i++) Segments [i] = create PLink (2);
  TR = r;
  D = (l + l) / NP;
  NC = 0;
  RStations = new PRingInterface* [NP];
};
```

The meaning of the global variables is standard. TR is set by initPRing to the network transmission rate (in ITUs per bit). NP gives the total number of regular stations to be connected to the ring, and NC will be used by configure to count how many stations have been created so far. Pointers to the PRingInterface fragments of these stations will be stored in array RStations, which is created dynamically by the function. Another dynamically created array, Segments, keeps pointers to the individual links connecting pairs of adjacent stations. The number of these links

is 2NP + 1: two links per each regular station and one additional link for the ring
monitor. The distance separating two connected taps of two neighboring regular
stations is given by D, which is set to the ratio of the ring length (specified as an
argument to `initPRing`) and the number of stations. This distance is the same for
all adjacent station pairs.

The remaining portion of `pring.c` defines the `configure` methods for
`PRingInterface` and `PMonitorInterface`. The first of these methods (the one
for a regular station) is defined as follows:

```
void PRingInterface::configure () {
  int i;
  for (i = 0; i < 2; i++) {
    IRing [i] = create Port;
    ORing [i] = create Port (TR);
  }
  RStations [NC++] = this;
};
```

The method just creates the station's ports and adds the pointer to the station's `PRingInterface` fragment to array `RStations`. It is assumed that the monitor station will be created last, after all regular stations have been built. Thus, the
job of configuring the network is delegated to the second method:

```
void PMonitorInterface::configure () {
  int i, LN;
  Port *p1, *p2;
  Assert (NC == NP, "Monitor must be created last");
  IRing = create Port;
  ORing = create Port (TR);
  for (LN = 0, i = 0; i < NP-1; i++, LN++) {
    (p1 = RStations [i] -> ORing [0]) -> connect (Segments [LN]);
    (p2 = RStations [i+1] -> IRing [0]) -> connect (Segments [LN]);
    p1->setDTo (p2, D);
  };
  (p1 = RStations [NP-1] -> ORing [0]) -> connect (Segments [LN]);
  (p2 = RStations [0] -> IRing [1]) -> connect (Segments [LN]);
  p1->setDTo (p2, D);
  for (LN++, i = 0; i < NP-1; i++, LN++) {
    (p1 = RStations [i] -> ORing [1]) -> connect (Segments [LN]);
    (p2 = RStations [i+1] -> IRing [1]) -> connect (Segments [LN]);
    p1->setDTo (p2, D);
  };
  (p1 = RStations [NP-1] -> ORing [1]) -> connect (Segments [LN]);
  IRing -> connect (Segments [LN]);
  p1->setDTo (IRing, D/2);
```

```
  LN++;
  ORing -> connect (Segments [LN]);
  (p2 = RStations [0] -> IRing [0]) -> connect (Segments [LN]);
  ORing->setDTo (p2, D/2);
  delete Segments;
  delete RStations;
};
```

With its first statement, the method makes sure that all regular stations have already been created. Then it builds the two ports owned by the monitor station and proceeds to connect all stations to the links that were previously created by initPRing. This operation is performed in the following stages:

1. The first for loop takes care of the first loop of the pretzel, demarcated by the 0-labeled taps of the regular stations. It creates a chain of connected stations starting at the output port of station 0 and ending at the input port of station $NP-1$. The propagation distance between a pair of directly connected stations is set to D.

2. The 0-labeled output port of station $NP-1$ is connected to the 1-labeled input port of station 0. This is the first turning link of the pretzel, constituting a continuation of the chain built in the previous stage. The length of this link is also D.

3. The second for loop continues chaining the stations via their 1-labeled taps. The chain built by this loop starts from the output port of station 0 and ends at the input port of station $NP - 1$. Again, the propagation length of every link is set to D.

4. The pretzel is closed with two links connected by the monitor station. First, the 1-labeled output port of station $NP - 1$ (the current end of the chain) is connected to the input port of the monitor. Then the monitor's output port is connected to the 0-labeled input port of station 0. This way the end of the tap chain meets its beginning. The length of each of the two links interfacing the monitor station to the ring is $D/2$; thus, the propagation distance between the output port of station $NP - 1$ and the input port of station 0 is still D.[25]

Having completed the configuration procedure, the method releases the two arrays that were previously allocated by initPRing. These arrays are no longer needed.

10.6.3.2   Protocol organization.   A SMURPH program implementing the slotted variant of DPMA can be found in directory RING/Pretzel of SMURPH Examples. The traffic pattern used by this program is the simple uniform traffic pattern (files utraffic.h and utraffic.c) introduced in section 8.1.2.4. Although

---

[25] Assuming no delay at the monitor station. Later we see that the monitor in fact introduces a certain delay.

the client interface described in this traffic pattern defines only one packet buffer per station, a single station will be able to transmit two packets at the same time.

Besides the parameters describing the network configuration (the three numbers passed as arguments to `initPRing`—section 10.6.3.1), the protocol is parameterized by the following numerical values:

```
Long SlotML, SegmPL, SegmFL;
TIME SegmWindow;
int THT;
```

initialized by the root process from the input data file. The first four numbers describe the slot and segment size. `SlotML` stands for the length of the slot marker in bits, and `SegmWindow` gives the time duration of the slot's segment area, i.e., the space between two consecutive slot markers. The segment size is bits is equal to the sum of `SegmPL` (the payload portion of a segment) and `SegmFL` (the combined length of segment header and trailer). It is understood that this sum translated into time units is slightly less than `SegmWindow`—to provide a safety margin accounting for the limited accuracy of clocks. `THT` is the token-holding interval, which is assumed to be the same for all stations. This interval is expressed in slots and therefore it is an object of type `int`. The protocol, specifically the relay process (section 10.6.3.4), uses a global variable declared as follows:

```
int TZLength;
```

and preset by `Root` to the product of `THT` and the number of stations. The value of `TZLength`, called the *token zone length*, represents $TTRT - L$, i.e., the right-hand side of the inequality occurring in the "yellow" tap transmission rule (section 10.6.2.4).

Slot markers are modeled as special packets that do not belong to the `Client`'s traffic pattern. Our implementation of destination cleaning assumes that slot markers carry numerical identifiers assigned to them by the monitor station during the protocol initialization phase (section 10.6.2.3). The following packet type represents slot markers:

```
packet SMarker {
    int Number;
};
```

where `Number` is the numerical tag of the slot. The remaining two attributes of a slot marker (the binary flags *FULL* and *TOKEN*) are encoded into two packet flags (section 5.2.2) identified by the following symbolic constants:

```
#define FULL  PF_usr0
#define TOKEN PF_usr1
```

One more constant:

```
#define SLOT  NONE
```

is an alias for the value of the TP attribute of a slot marker and is used to tell slot markers from regular packets.

Each regular station maintains a queue of tags identifying the slots that must be cleaned by the station (section 10.6.2.3). In fact, there are two such queues per station, one for each tap. They are represented by mailboxes of the following type:

```
mailbox SList (int);
```

Following is the complete type declaration of a regular station:

```
station PStation : PRingInterface, ClientInterface {
  SList *Purge [2];
  Boolean Yellow [2];
  void setup () {
    int i;
    PRingInterface::configure ();
    ClientInterface::configure ();
    for (i = 0; i < 2; i++) Purge [i] = create SList (MAX_long);
    Yellow [0] = NO;
    Yellow [1] = YES;
  };
};
```

Besides the tag queues, the only other station attribute not defined in the interface modules included from the library is a pair of Boolean flags indicating which of the two taps is currently "yellow" and which is "green." At any moment, only one of the two Yellow flags can be YES, the other must be NO.

The station's setup method calls the configure methods of the interface portions; then it creates the two mailboxes[26] and initializes the Yellow flags. When the protocol is started, the token is released by the monitor station, whose location on the pretzel precedes the location of the 0-th tap of station 0. Thus, this tap will be first to receive the token. Consequently, all 0-labeled ports are initially green (they are in front of the token) and the remaining (1-labeled) ports are yellow.

The monitor station also uses a mailbox. Its role is to provide an elastic relay buffer between the two ports serviced by the station, which guarantees that the ring contains an entire number of slots, even if the spacing between slot markers, as they are relayed by the stations, is subject to slight fluctuations. The monitor station absorbs these fluctuations by repeating the incoming slots at the standard rate on the output port of its tap. The type of the mailbox used by the monitor station for this purpose is as follows:

```
mailbox DBuffer (Packet*) {
    void outItem (Packet *p) { delete p; };
```

---

[26]Although the mailboxes are created with infinite capacity, the maximum number of slot tags stored in a mailbox is bounded by L (expressed in slots).

```
        void setup () { setLimit (MAX_long); };
    };
```

The mailbox stores pointers to copies of packets (slot markers and segments)
arriving on the input port. Method `outItem`, called automatically whenever a
packet pointer is extracted from the mailbox (section 4.7.2), is responsible for deallocating the packet data structure. Clearly, the mailbox capacity need not be infinite; it can be reasonably bounded for any specific values of clock tolerance and
L.

The type of the monitor station is declared as follows:

```
        station PMonitor : PMonitorInterface {
          DBuffer *DB;
          void setup () {
            PMonitorInterface::configure ();
            DB = create DBuffer;
          };
        };
```

Note that the station has no interface to the `Client`, as it generates no traffic
of its own.

10.6.3.3 The processes of the monitor station.

We start the presentation
of the protocol processes from the cohort of processes run by the monitor station.
The protocol has a distinct initialization phase, during which the pretzel is filled
with slot markers, and the behavior of the monitor station during that phase is
different from its behavior during normal operation. There are three processes
associated with the monitor station: the input process (type `IConnector`), the
output process (type `OConnector`), and the slot generator (type `SlotGen`). The
role of the input process is to receive packets from the input port and deposit
them in the mailbox representing the relay buffer. The output process retrieves
the packets from the mailbox and retransmits them on the output port, respacing
the slot markers according to the station's clock. The third process is only active
during the initialization phase. It generates slot markers and inserts them at proper
intervals into the output port. The slot generator disappears as soon as the entire
pretzel has been filled with slot markers, which is recognized by the nonempty status
of the relay buffer. The type of the slot generator is declared as follows:

```
        process SlotGen (PMonitor) {
          Port *ORing;
          DBuffer *DB;
          SMarker *SMark;
          int SCount;
          void setup () {
            ORing = S->ORing;
            DB = S->DB;
```

```
      SMark = create SMarker;
      SMark->fill (NONE, NONE, SlotML);
      setFlag (SMark->Flags, TOKEN);
      SCount = 0;
    };
    states {GenSlot, XDone};
    perform;
  };
```

The process references two attributes of the monitor station: the output port (ORing) and the relay buffer (mailbox DB). The local pointers to these attributes are set by the setup method. The setup method also creates and fills a packet representing the slot marker and initializes an integer counter (SCount) to be used for tagging the slot markers with unique identifiers. The slot marker has its TOKEN flag set. According to section 10.6.2.1, this means that the token **is not passed** in the slot marker, which situation can be viewed as the default. The other flag, FULL, is cleared automatically by create (section 5.2.3), so a default marker announces an empty slot. The process executes the following code:

```
SlotGen::perform {
  state GenSlot:
    if (DB->nonempty ())
      terminate;
    else {
      SMark->Number = SCount;
      ORing->transmit (SMark, XDone);
    }
  state XDone:
    ORing->stop ();
    ++SCount;
    Timer->wait (SegmWindow, GenSlot);
};
```

State GenSlot is assumed whenever the process wants to insert a new slot marker into the output port. At the beginning, the slot generator checks whether the relay mailbox is nonempty, which means that the first slot marker inserted by the process has circled the pretzel twice and arrived back at the station. In such a case, the process assumes that it has accomplished its task and terminates itself. As explained in section 10.6.3.5, the output process is not active during the initialization phase; thus, there is no danger that it will empty the mailbox before the slot generator has had a chance to detect its nonempty status.

Before a new slot marker is transmitted on the output port, its Number attribute is set to SCount, representing the current tag value to be assigned to the marker. SCount is incremented in state XDone after the marker has been transmitted. Then the process sleeps for SegmWindow ITUs, to provide a period of silence for a segment, and moves back to state `GenSlot` to insert another slot marker into the network.

Let us now look at the input process of the monitor station, whose type declaration is as follows:

```
process IConnector (PMonitor) {
  Port *IRing;
  DBuffer *DB;
  void setup () {
    IRing = S->IRing;
    DB = S->DB;
  };
  states {WaitBOT, Activity};
  perform;
};
```

The code method of `IConnector` is as follows:

```
IConnector::perform {
  SMarker *sm;
  Packet *pk;
  state WaitBOT:
    IRing->wait (BOT, Activity);
  state Activity:
    if (ThePacket->TP == SLOT) {
      sm = create SMarker;
      *sm = *((SMarker*)ThePacket);
      DB->put (sm);
    } else {
      pk = create Packet;
      *pk = *ThePacket;
      DB->put (pk);
    }
    skipto WaitBOT;
};
```

The process sleeps in its initial state `WaitBOT` until it detects a packet arriving from upstream on the input port (`IRing`). Then `IConnector` moves to state `Activity`, where it determines the packet type and, based on this information, creates a data structure to accommodate a copy of the packet. The incoming packet is then copied and the pointer to the copy is placed into the relay mailbox. Finally, the process moves back to state `WaitBOT` to await another packet arrival. Operation `skipto` is used for this transition to make sure that the beginning of the previous packet has disappeared from the input port.

The other end of the station's relay buffer is serviced by the output process, whose type is declared as follows:

```
process OConnector (PMonitor) {
  Port *ORing;
  DBuffer *DB;
  TIME LastSlot;
  void setup () {
    ORing = S->ORing;
    DB = S->DB;
    LastSlot = TIME_0;
    assert (DB->nonempty (), "OConnector -- ring not filled");
    clearFlag ((DB->first ())->Flags, TOKEN);
  };
  states {Startup, NextPacket, XDone};
  perform;
};
```

Besides the pointers to the two station's attributes referenced by the process, OConnector declares variable LastSlot of type TIME, which will be used to store the departure time of the last slot marker. To make sure that the amount of space between two consecutive slot markers is sufficient to accommodate a segment, the process will schedule the transmission of a new marker no sooner than SegmWindow ITUs after the end of the previous marker, i.e., at time SegmWindow + LastSlot.

The output process is started after the pretzel has been filled with slot markers, at the end of the protocol initialization phase. The setup method verifies that the process is not started prematurely by asserting that the relay mailbox is nonempty. Note that the nonempty status of the mailbox is also used by the slot generator process to detect the completion of the initialization phase.

The setup method of OConnector clears the TOKEN flag in the first slot to be sent to the output port (the top slot marker in the relay mailbox). This way, the first slot marker that leaves the monitor station will carry the token, which will be subsequently received by station 0 on its 0-labeled tap. LastSlot is initially set to zero, which practically means that the first slot marker can leave the relay mailbox as soon as the initialization phase is over.

The output process runs the following code:

```
OConnector::perform {
  TIME d;
  state NextPacket:
    if (DB->nonempty ()) {
      if ((DB->first ())->TP == SLOT && (d = Time - LastSlot) <
      SegmWindow)
        Timer->wait (SegmWindow - d, NextPacket);
      else
        ORing->transmit (DB->first (), XDone);
    } else
      DB->wait (NONEMPTY, NextPacket);
```

```
  state XDone:
    ORing->stop ();
    if ((DB->first ())->TP == SLOT) LastSlot = Time;
    DB->get ();
    proceed NextPacket;
};
```

In state `NextPacket`, the process checks whether the relay mailbox contains a packet. If it does not, the process waits until the mailbox becomes NONEMPTY and tries again. Otherwise, if the top packet in the mailbox is a slot marker and the amount of time elapsed after the departure of the previous slot marker (`Time − LastSlot`) is less than `SegmWindow` (i.e., the amount of space required to accommodate a segment), the process waits until the intermarker gap becomes large enough. In any other case, the packet is immediately transmitted on the output port. When the transfer is complete, the process will wake up in state `XDone`.

Note that a regular packet, i.e., a segment, must directly follow a slot marker and cannot arrive unexpectedly. Thus, there is no need to check or adjust the timing of a regular packet: it can be sent to the output port as soon as it appears in front of the relay mailbox.

If it turns out that the top packet is a slot marker and cannot be relayed immediately, the process waits for the proper amount of time (`SegmWindow − (Time − LastSlot)`) and reexecutes the sequence of statements in state `NextPacket`. The next time around, the condition of the second-level `if` statement in this state will evaluate to false and the process will transmit the slot marker. The code of `OConnector` could be organized in such a way that following the timer wait request in state `NextPacket` the process would transmit the top packet from the mailbox directly, without having to reexecute the two `if` statements. That, however, would require introducing an extra state that would unnecessarily complicate the code method.

Having completed the retransmission of the current top packet to the output port (state `XDone`), the process terminates the transfer and, if the packet was a slot marker, sets `LastSlot` to the current time. This way the intermarker gap is measured from the end of the previous marker to the beginning of the next one. Then the process executes `get` on the mailbox to remove the top packet that has just been relayed to the output port. Note that the mailbox defines an `outItem` method (section 10.6.3.2) that automatically deallocates the packet data structure when its pointer is removed from the mailbox. Finally, the output process moves back to its first state to take care of the next incoming packet.

10.6.3.4 The relay process. The medium access protocol of DPMA is implemented by one process running in two copies at every regular station. Each copy services one tap and takes care of everything: it relays incoming packets (slot markers and segments) to the output port, receives packets addressed to the station, monitors token arrivals, releases the token, and transmits the packets (segments) arriving to the station from the `Client`. Not surprisingly, the process is rather long, although its logic is fairly simple. Following is its type declaration:

```
process Relay (PStation) {
  Port *IRing, *ORing;
  SList *MyPurge, *YourPurge;
  Packet *SBuffer, *LBuffer;
  Long TCount;
  Boolean HoldingToken, Erasing, Transmitting, *IAmYellow,
    *YouAreYellow;
  void setup (int segment) {
    IRing = S->IRing [segment];
    ORing = S->ORing [segment];
    MyPurge = S->Purge [segment];
    YourPurge = S->Purge [1-segment];
    SBuffer = &(S->Buffer);
    LBuffer = create Packet;
    TCount = 0;
    HoldingToken = Erasing = Transmitting = NO;
    IAmYellow = &(S->Yellow [segment]);
    YouAreYellow = &(S->Yellow [1-segment]);
  };
  states {WaitSlot, NewSlot, MDone, WaitEOT, RDone, XDone};
  perform;
};
```

Attributes `IRing` and `ORing` are pointers to the two ports describing the tap serviced by the process. The two `SList` pointers provide references to the queues of slot tags identifying the slots to be stripped by the station. `MyPurge` points to the queue of tags for the present copy of the relay process (i.e., indicating the slots to be emptied by this process), and `YourPurge` refers to the other queue, handled by the other copy of `Relay`. `SBuffer` is a local copy of the station's packet buffer defined in the `ClientInterface` portion of the station structure (section 8.1.2.4). The `ClientInterface` buffer pointed to by `SBuffer` will only be used for packet acquisition from the `Client`. As soon as a packet (segment) is acquired into the station's buffer, it will be copied into a local packet buffer associated with the process. This local buffer, pointed to by `LBuffer`, is created by `Relay`'s setup method.

The integer variable `TCount` is a dual-purpose timer counting the slots arriving at the process's tap from upstream. If the process is holding the token, `TCount` calculates the token-holding time; otherwise, it simulates TRT—the token rotation timer needed to implement the "yellow" tap transmission rule (sections 10.6.2.2, 10.6.2.4).

The three `Boolean` flags: `HoldingToken`, `Erasing`, and `Transmitting`, complement the process's state structure by describing certain conditions of the tap recognized by the process. One can notice that such flags are formally superfluous, as they can be replaced with more process states. In many cases, however, it is more natural to use flags (de facto multiplying process states) rather than create several explicit states to express the different conditions described by the flags. Generally, it is up to the programmer to draw a line between the two approaches. In some cases, the different states must be perceptible by observers (section 7.2.2), which makes the decision simpler.

Attributes IAmYellow and YouAreYellow point to the station's flags describing the "yellow" status of the taps. The flag pointed to by IAmYellow is YES when the tap serviced by the process is "yellow" (section 10.6.2.4). The other pointer references the status flag of the tap handled by the other copy of Relay.

All the attributes of the relay process are initialized by the setup method, which accepts one argument specifying the tap index (0 or 1). All relay processes are created at the beginning of the protocol initialization phase. Clearly, they are needed during this phase to propagate the slot markers inserted into the pretzel by the monitor station. The behavior of a relay process during the initialization phase is the same as during normal operation. The following code method of Relay makes no distinction between the two modes:

```
Relay::perform {
  SMarker *SMark;
  state WaitSlot:
    Erasing = Transmitting = NO;
    IRing->wait (BOT, NewSlot);
  state NewSlot:
    assert (ThePacket->TP == SLOT, "Slot marker expected");
    SMark = (SMarker*) ThePacket;
    ++TCount;
    if (MyPurge->nonempty () && MyPurge->first () ==
     SMark->Number) {
      Erasing = YES;
      MyPurge->get ();
    }
    if (HoldingToken) {
      if (TCount == THT) {
        clearFlag (SMark->Flags, TOKEN);
        *IAmYellow = YES;
        *YouAreYellow = NO;
        TCount = 0;
        HoldingToken = NO;
      } else
        Erasing = YES;
    } else if (flagCleared (SMark->Flags, TOKEN)) {
      setFlag (SMark->Flags, TOKEN);
```

```
          HoldingToken = YES;
          Erasing = YES;
          TCount = 0;
        }
        if (Erasing)
          clearFlag (SMark->Flags, FULL);
        if (flagCleared (SMark->Flags, FULL) &&
          (!(*IAmYellow) || TCount >= TZLength) &&
          S->ready (SegmPL, SegmPL, SegmFL)) {
          *LBuffer = *SBuffer;
          clearFlag (SBuffer->Flags, PF_full);
          setFlag (SMark->Flags, FULL);
          Transmitting = YES;
          YourPurge->put (SMark->Number);
        };
        ORing->startTransfer (SMark);
        IRing->wait (EOT, MDone);
      state MDone:
        ORing->stop ();
        if (Transmitting)
          ORing->transmit (LBuffer, XDone);
        else if (Erasing)
          skipto WaitSlot;
        else if (IRing->events (BOT)) {
          ORing->startTransfer (ThePacket);
          skipto WaitEOT;
        } else
          proceed WaitSlot;
      state WaitEOT:
        IRing->wait (EOT, RDone);
      state RDone:
        ORing->stop ();
        if (ThePacket->isMy ()) Client->receive (ThePacket, IRing);
        proceed WaitSlot;
      state XDone:
        ORing->stop ();
        LBuffer->release ();
        proceed WaitSlot;
  };
```

The process operates in a loop, which starts its every turn with a transition from WaitSlot to NewSlot, whenever a new slot marker arrives on the input port of the tap serviced by the process. This transition is triggered by the BOT event awaited in state WaitSlot, where Relay moves after every completion of a one-slot service cycle. Each new cycle starts with flags `Erasing` and `Transmitting` both reset to `NO`. The third flag, `HoldingToken`, is initially `NO`—it has been cleared by the setup method—but it becomes `YES` when the process receives the token and remains set for the entire token-holding interval.

In state `NewSlot`, the process verifies that the incoming packet actually is a slot marker, which should normally be the case. Then it saves the pointer to the marker (returned in `ThePacket` by the `BOT` event—section 6.2.11) in a temporary local variable `SMark` and increments `TCount` by 1. The role of `TCount` is to count the slots passing through the tap. The counter is reset to zero on two occasions: when the tap receives the token and when the token is released. Thus, if the tap is holding the token, `TCount` tells the elapsed token-holding time; otherwise, it implements the *TRT* timer (section 10.6.2.4), i.e., gives the interval after the last token departure from the tap.

If the queue of tags identifying the slots that must be stripped by the process (pointed to by `MyPurge`) is nonempty, the process compares the first tag from the queue with the `Number` attribute of the incoming slot. If the two numbers match, the slot must be emptied. In such a case, `Erasing` becomes `YES` and the top element is removed from the tag list. The actual cleaning operation will be performed later.

If the tap is holding the token, the process checks whether the token should be passed in the current slot. This will happen if `TCount` has reached `THT`. In such a case, the `TOKEN` flag in the slot marker is cleared,[27] the current tap is painted "yellow," and the other tap is painted "green," according to the rules outlined in section 10.6.2.4. `TCount` is then reset to zero (from now on it will be used as *TRT*) and `HoldingToken` is set to `NO` to indicate that the tap is no longer in possession of the token. If the token held by the port is to stay for the current slot, `Erasing` is set to `YES` to indicate that the slot must be stripped unconditionally, whether it was filled by the current station or not.

In the `else` part of the outer `if` statement, executed when the tap is not holding the token, the process checks whether the token arrives in the current slot. If this is the case, the process grabs the token by setting the `TOKEN` flag in the slot marker, sets `HoldingToken` to `YES`, and resets `TCount` to zero—to start calculating the token-holding time. Note that `Erasing` is also set to `YES`: when the slot carrying the token is being processed, the tap **is already holding the token** and the slot should be stripped unconditionally.

The next `if` statement checks the final setting of the `Erasing` flag. If the slot is to be stripped, the `FULL` flag of its marker is cleared. After all these operations, if the slot turns out to be empty,[28] it can be used to transmit a packet (segment) queued at the current station. A transmission from the "green" tap is always legal, but the "yellow" tap must fulfill the following condition (section 10.6.2.4): `TCount` (read: *TRT*) is not less than `TZLength` (read: the sum of token-holding times at

---

[27]Once again we remind the reader that the cleared flag actually means that the token **is passed** in the slot.

[28]It either arrived empty from upstream or became stripped at the tap.

all stations). Finally, the station must be ready to transmit, i.e., method **ready** defined in its **ClientInterface** part must return YES, filling the station's packet buffer as a side effect.

The contents of the station's single "official" buffer (pointed to by **SBuffer**) are immediately copied to the local buffer of the relay process. Then the station's buffer is marked as empty and becomes ready to accommodate another packet. This way, the two copies of **Relay** operating at the same station share the single packet buffer, yet they can transmit in parallel.

The actual transmission of the segment acquired from the **Client** must be postponed until the slot marker has been fully inserted into the output port. At this moment, the process only learns that the station will transmit its own segment within the slot when the right time comes. This is indicated by setting the **Transmitting** flag. The process also reserves the current slot—by setting the FULL flag in its marker—and appends the slot's tag (the **Number** attribute) at the end of the tag queue examined by the other copy of **Relay**. This way, when the slot arrives at the other tap of the station (having made a full circle through the ring), it will be stripped (and possibly reused) by the other process.

The last two statements in state **NewSlot** relay the incoming slot marker on the output port. When the process gets to this stage, the flags of the incoming slot have been fully recognized and its new flags have been prepared. The clock for transmitting the slot marker is strobed by the input rate; thus, when the EOT event occurs on the input port, the slot marker is assumed to have been entirely transmitted. Then the process moves to state **MDone**.

At **MDone**, the marker transmission is terminated and the process determines whether the marker should be followed by a segment. Three outcomes are now possible:

- The station wants to transmit its own segment in the slot. In such a case, the contents of **LBuffer** are transmitted to the output port.
- The station strips the slot without transmitting anything. Then the process executes **skipto** to state **WaitSlot** to await another slot marker arriving from upstream.
- The slot should be relayed "as is."

In the second case, the **skipto** operation guarantees that a segment possibly following the slot marker will be ignored. A segment in a full slot is always transmitted immediately after the slot marker: the EOT event caused by the marker coincides with the BOT event triggered by the segment. This way, a stripped segment will never trigger a BOT event in state **WaitSlot**.

To detect whether the current slot marker is followed by a segment to be relayed, the process invokes the **events** method of the input port (section 6.3.1) with BOT passed as the argument. If the method returns a nonzero value (it can only return 0 or 1 in this case), it means that the EOT event triggered by the marker (that caused the transition to state **MDone**) coalesces with the BOT event of an incoming segment. In such a case, the segment is transmitted to the output port, and the process moves to state `WaitEOT` to clock this transmission, i.e., to await an `EOT` event on the input port. When this event finally occurs, the relay process finds itself in state `RDone`, where it terminates the retransmission of the segment. At this moment it makes sense to check whether the segment was addressed to the current station, in which case it must be received. This way, `Relay` assumes momentarily the duties of a receiver, and no separate process is needed to perform these duties. In any case, having completed the operation of relaying the segment to the output port, the relay process moves back to state `WaitSlot`.

The last state, `XDone`, is entered when the station's own segment has been entirely transmitted. The process terminates the transfer, releases the contents of its local buffer, and transits to state `WaitSlot` to complete its processing cycle.

10.6.3.5   The root process.   The root process of our DPMA program differs a bit from the other root processes that have been discussed so far. Owing to the distinct initialization phase of the protocol, it is natural to build the root process for DPMA around three states rather than the typical `Start`, `Stop` pair. The complete definition of DPMA's `Root` is as follows:

```
process Root {
  PMonitor *PM;
  states {Start, Running, Stop};
  perform {
    int NNodes, i, j;
    Long NMessages;
    TIME RingLength;
    RATE TRate;
    double CTolerance;
    SlotGen *SG;
    state Start:
      readIn (TRate);
      setEtu (TRate);
      readIn (CTolerance);
      setTolerance (CTolerance);
      readIn (NNodes);
      readIn (RingLength);
      RingLength *= TRate;
      initPRing (TRate, RingLength, NNodes);
      readIn (SlotML);
      readIn (SegmPL);
      readIn (SegmFL);
      readIn (SegmWindow);
      SegmWindow *= TRate;
      readIn (THT);
      TZLength = THT * NNodes;
```

```
                    initTraffic ();
                    readIn (NMessages);
                    setLimit (NMessages);
                    for (i = 0; i < NNodes; i++) create PStation;
                    PM = create PMonitor;
                    Client->suspend ();
                    for (i = 0; i < NNodes; i++)
                      for (j = 0; j < 2; j++) create (i) Relay (j);
                    SG = create (PM) SlotGen;
                    create (PM) IConnector;
                    SG->wait (DEATH, Running);
                  state Running:
                    create (PM) OConnector;
                    Client->resume ();
                    Kernel->wait (DEATH, Stop);
                  state Stop:
                    System->printTop ("Network topology");
                    Client->printDef ("Traffic parameters");
                    Client->printPfm ();
              };
          };
```

Most of the code in state Start is straightforward: the process reads a few input numbers, converts some of them from bits to ITUs, defines the numerical parameters of the pretzel (initPRing—section 10.6.3.1), initializes the traffic pattern (initTraffic—section 8.1.2.4), and builds the stations. NNodes regular stations (type PStation) are created, followed by the monitor station of type PMonitor. Then the process executes the Client's suspend method (section 5.5.1) to avoid traffic generation during the initialization phase.

Two copies of the relay process are created for each station, the tap index (0 or 1) is passed as the argument to the process setup method. Then the root process creates the slot generator and the input process of the monitor station, and goes to sleep until the slot generator terminates itself, which event marks the end of the initialization phase. As we said in section 10.6.3.3, the output process (OConnector) of the monitor station is not created until the initialization phase is over.

In state Running, where the root process moves after completing the initialization phase, the output process of the monitor station comes to life and the network starts normal operation. The pilot processes of the Client are resumed, and the stations start to receive messages for transmission. As usual, the root process suspends itself awaiting the dummy Kernel termination event (section 4.8) that is triggered when one of the simulation exit conditions (section 4.9) is met. When this happens, the process will wake up in its final state Stop, where it will expose some objects (print out the simulation results) and cease to exist.

BIBLIOGRAPHIC NOTES

A complete description of FDDI, including the physical layer, the medium access control protocol, and the initialization phase, can be found in *FDDI* (1987). This document may be hard to read in spots, but it gives the most exhaustive, general documentation of the concept. The protocol is presented in a more legible (although less complete) way in several articles and books, notably *Ross* (1989), *Karol and Gitlin* (1990), *Dykeman and Bux* (1988); also *Stallings* (1987a; 1987b; 1990), *Tanenbaum* (1988), and *Martin* (1989). While the journal articles, besides introducing FDDI, discuss some performance aspects of the protocol, the book sections only sketch the basic operation principles of the medium access scheme. *Bertsekas and Gallager* (1992) give a formal definition of the medium access protocol of FDDI and analyze the worst-case access delay. *Kessler and Train* (1991) devote a substantial part of their book to FDDI, and that book can be recommended as a user-friendly alternative to *FDDI* (1987). *Jain* (1989) studies the impact of various parameters of FDDI, including *TTRT*, on network performance and suggests how these parameters should be tailored to suit application needs. Several issues related to the reliability of FDDI and the ways of enhancing it by modifying the network topology are investigated by *Willebeek-LeMair and Shahabuddin* (1994), *Yin and Silio* (1994), and *Kamat, Agrawal, and Zhao* (1994).

Other protocols for ring networks, including token rings and insertion rings, are discussed in the preceding books and in *Derfler and Stallings* (1986) (IBM token ring), *Hopper, Temple, and Williamson* (1986) (various token rings and insertion rings), *Huber, Steinlin, and Wild* (1983) (a buffer insertion ring), *Hopper and Williamson* (1983) (the Cambridge Ring). For a performance study of token ring networks, including FDDI, see *Bux* (1989).

Methods of improving the performance of token rings by introducing multiple tokens are discussed by *Cohen and Segall* (1992) and *Kamal* (1990). *Todd* (1994) introduces the concept of a token grid network consisting of interconnected rings synchronized by multiple tokens.

Metaring was introduced by *Cidon and Ofek* (1989; 1990) and further analyzed by *Wu, Ofek, and Sohraby* (1992) and *Chen, Cidon, and Ofek* (1993). *Cidon et al.* (1994) propose a number of improvements to the SAT scheme based on the same idea of allocating transmission quotas to stations.

Problems related to the stability of ring networks based on destination cleaning and reuse have been identified and analyzed by *Georgiadis, Szpankowski, and Tassiulas* (1993) and *Tassiulas and Georgiadis* (1994). The results obtained from these studies suggest that ring networks with destination cleaning tend to behave in a stable manner without sophisticated access control mechanisms. Several access schemes for such rings, including Metaring, are compared by *Breuer and Meuser* (1994).

The pretzel ring and DPMA were presented by *Dobosiewicz and Gburzyński* (1992; 1994). Several versions of the protocol in its generalization for the so-called spiral ring topologies are discussed in *Dobosiewicz and Gburzyński* (1993).

The last paper also compares DPMA with Metaring and DQDB.

PROBLEMS

1. Implement a token bus protocol, i.e., a medium access protocol for a broadcast-type (ether) bus based on passing an explicit token packet. The protocol should have a distributed startup phase during which the stations determine the optimum way of token passing (the successor relation) and elect the station that generates the token.

2. Discuss the possible ways of enhancing FDDI in such a way that packets are stripped completely by their sources. Is there a way of taking advantage of full packet stripping in FDDI?

3. The implementation of the insertion ring protocol presented in section 10.4.2 is based on a few simplifying assumptions. Remove these simplifications, and implement a realistic version of the protocol. Prove formally that your packet spacing, buffer size, and possibly other numerical parameters needed by your implementation are safe for the given number of stations and clock tolerance.

4. Implement a slotted variant of the insertion ring protocol.

5. Calculate the minimum safe value of the SAT timeout in a Metaring network as a function of the number of stations, the ring length, K, L, and the maximum packet size.

6. Consider a simplified version of DPMA operating on a regular single-loop ring in which all ports are always "yellow." What is the maximum throughput achieved by this version? What is the average packet access delay under light load? Implement your protocol by modifying the program introduced in section 10.6.3, and investigate its performance.

7. Show formally that DPMA is a capacity-1 protocol.

8. Assume that a dormant station that was ignored by the initialization phase of DPMA becomes alive and it wants to join the protocol. Devise and implement in SMURPH a foolproof procedure for this operation that will never result in a packet loss. How about a similar procedure for a station going down?

9. Implement the semislotted variant of DPMA with fixed-length packets (section 10.6.2.6). How would one cope with the limited accuracy of independent clocks? Assuming that the message length is exponentially distributed with a given mean, what is the optimum fixed packet length? Calculate this optimum analytically, and measure it experimentally.

10. The trick of sharing the same single packet buffer by two relay processes in our implementation of DPMA affects some performance measures of the packet, i.e., these measures are not calculated correctly. Which measures are they? How can the problem be fixed without changing the station's interface to the Client?

11

Switched Networks

11.1 HUBNET

By a *switched network* we understand a network in which at least some stations have to make *routing decisions*. A station makes routing decisions if it relays incoming packets on several output channels. Whenever a packet arrives at the station, the station has to decide on which output port (or ports) the packet should be retransmitted. Usually, the primary premise of a routing decision is to move the packet closer to the destination.

One can argue that a ring network (e.g., one of the networks discussed in the previous chapter) is a degenerate switched network. A ring station relays the incoming packets, and its primary objective is to move them closer to their destinations, but it has no choice as to the output port on which a given packet will be relayed. Thus, its routing decisions are trivial and nobody would seriously classify a ring network as a switched network.[1] The first MAC-level protocol discussed in this chapter operates on a switched network, which is also degenerate in some sense; nonetheless, its switching character is indisputable.

11.1.1 The Network Backbone

Hubnet is a clear-cut case of a *star network* (see figure 11.1). The central station in Hubnet, called the *hub*, is different from the other stations and behaves like a fairly simple switching device. Each regular station is connected to the hub via

---

[1]Note that even a station in Metaring or pretzel ring (which has two output ports) relays packets without making any nontrivial routing decisions.

two channels, the *selection channel* and the *broadcast channel*, and has two ports, one port to each channel (see figure 11.1). The selection channel is a unidirectional point-to-point link used by the regular station to send a packet to the hub. This link ends at the hub with a *selection port*, which the hub can use to sense an incoming packet.

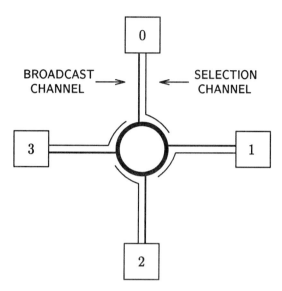

Figure 11.1   The backbone of Hubnet

The broadcast channels operate in the opposite direction, and their purpose is to transfer data from the hub to the regular stations. Unlike the selection channels, which are separate, all the broadcast channels are connected into a single, uniform, broadcast-type medium. The hub has a single port to this medium (called the *broadcast port*); whatever activity is inserted into this port by the hub will reach all the regular stations in due time.

The broadcast channel being single, each transmission relayed by the hub to the broadcast port propagates to all stations. Consequently, the network can effectively transmit only one packet at a time.

11.1.2   The Protocol

The medium access scheme of Hubnet is even simpler than its topology. A station having a packet to transmit just inserts it into the selection port. The packet eventually reaches the hub, which can be in one of two states:

- If the hub is *idle*, it marks itself as busy and connects the selection port on which the packet arrives to the broadcast port. This way, the packet will propagate to all stations, in particular to its intended recipient. When the packet has been relayed entirely (the selection port becomes silent), the hub marks itself back as idle.

- If the hub is *busy*, it simply ignores the incoming packet.

A transmitting station that wants to learn the fate of its packet must listen to its broadcast port for a prescribed amount of time starting from the moment it initiated the transfer. If the packet eventually arrives back at the station on the broadcast port, it means that the transmission was successful; otherwise, the packet has not made it through the hub and must be retransmitted.

The minimum amount of time that the transmitter should wait for the echo of its packet before concluding that the packet has been rejected by the hub is equal to the round-trip propagation delay between the station and the hub augmented by the length of the packet header portion that contains the sender address. In a realistic implementation, a tolerance margin compensating for the limited accuracy of the station's clock should be added to this minimum.

A sender that does not receive its own packet after the prescribed delay can retransmit the packet immediately. Note that when the hub receives two or more packets simultaneously (or almost simultaneously) it selects one of those packets nondeterministically and rejects the others. Although the network may suffer from some fairness problems, e.g., when greedy stations are located close to the hub and they can use short timeouts, it is usually starvation-free. The protocol is statistical in nature (e.g., like Ethernet), and it offers no bound on the maximum packet access time under heavy load. Note, however, that unlike Ethernet the packet payload in Hubnet can be arbitrarily short without the throughput degradation characteristic of the collision protocols. As each station in Hubnet can transmit at most one packet per $2L$ time units (where L is the propagation distance separating the station from the hub), the maximum throughput achieved by the network is bounded by

$$T_h = \frac{N \times l_p}{2L} \, ,$$

where N is the number of stations and l_p is the (average) packet length. Thus, Hubnet is not a capacity-1 protocol.

11.1.3   Hubnet Hierarchies

Multiple hubs can be connected into a single hierarchical Hubnet with lower-level hubs attached as regular stations to higher-level switches. To make this possible, the hub should be organized as shown in figure 11.2.

The modification consists in isolating the hub's broadcast port from the broadcast channel and providing two separate taps: one to the broadcast channel, the other from the broadcast port. In a single-switch network (like the one shown in figure 11.1), the two taps are connected and the broadcast port is permanently coupled to the broadcast channel. By separating them, one can build a network like that shown in figure 11.3, where two second-level switches are connected to

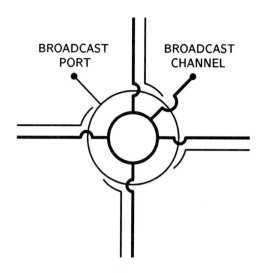

Figure 11.2 The hub structure for hierarchical interconnections

the central hub. The output port of a second-level switch is treated by the central switch as a selection port of a regular station. Note that the broadcast channel still forms a single and uniform medium interconnecting all stations in the network.

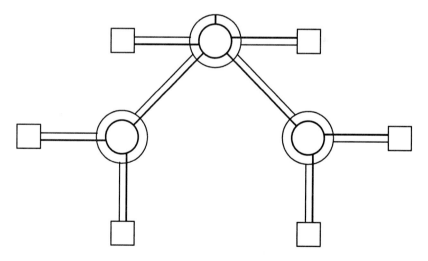

Figure 11.3 A hierarchical Hubnet

A station connected to the central hub is serviced as before: the broadcast port of the central switch is connected to the broadcast channel, and whatever packets are relayed by the hub reach all stations in the network. When a station attached to a secondary hub transmits a packet, this packet has first to make it through the secondary switch. If this switch is busy, the packet will be rejected and ignored. Otherwise, it will be retransmitted on the broadcast port of the secondary hub and will reach the central switch on one of its selection channels. Then the medium access procedure for the packet will enter the second stage. The packet will be relayed to the broadcast link, provided that the central hub is idle; otherwise, it will be ignored and forgotten, although it has passed successfully through the second-level switch. In general, higher-level switches reduce the amount of traffic arriving at lower-level switches by trimming it to the volume that can be passed through a single channel. High-priority stations can be connected directly to the central hub, whereas less critical stations can access the network via higher-level switches. One can also imagine a network in which no stations are attached directly to the central switch, which is used solely to process the input from second-level hubs.

11.1.4   The Implementation

In directory SWITCH/Hubnet of SMURPH Examples the reader will find a program implementing the single-switch variant of Hubnet. As usual, we start presenting this implementation from the network geometry module.

11.1.4.1   The network backbone. Although the Hubnet backbone is not reused in any other protocol program in Examples, the SMURPH description of this backbone has been isolated into two independent files, hub.h and hub.c, and put into IncludeLibrary. The network interface of a regular station is specified in the following virtual type defined in hub.h:

```
station HubInterface virtual {
  Port *SPort, *BPort;
  void configure ();
};
```

where SPort is the station's port to the selection link and BPort is the port to the broadcast channel. The hub is implemented as a special station interfaced to the network via the following class:

```
station HubStation virtual {
  Port **SPorts, *BPort;
  void configure ();
};
```

Now SPorts is an array of port pointers, each port from this array representing the end of one selection link from a regular station. Like a regular station, the hub has only one port to the broadcast channel—pointed to by BPort.

As usual, the network is built by the root process, and this operation is initiated by calling a global function that sets the numerical parameters of the configuration. For Hubnet, this function has the following header:

```
                    void initHub (RATE, TIME, int);
```

The three arguments, from left to right, denote the network transmission rate (ITUs per bit), the propagation distance (the number of ITUs) from a regular station to the hub, and the number of regular stations in the network. The function is fully defined in hub.c, whose initial fragment is as follows:

```
            static TIME MLL;
            static int NP, NC;
            static HubInterface **HStations;
            void initHub (RATE r, TIME l, int np) {
              NP = np;
              HStations = new HubInterface* [NP];
              TR = r;
              MLL = l;
              NC = 0;
            };
```

Variables NP and NC have the standard meaning: NP is set by initHub to the total number of regular stations, and NC (initialized to zero) will be used by configure to count the number of stations that have been created so far. Array HStations will be used to keep pointers to the HubInterface fragments of these stations. Variable MLL, set by initHub to the value of its second argument, gives the propagation distance between a regular station and the hub. This value is interpreted either as an absolute and deterministic length of a selection channel, in which case the star structure of the network is perfectly symmetric, or as a mean length, in which case the actual length of a selection channel is generated as an exponentially distributed random number. With both options, the resulting length of a given selection channel is the same as the length of the corresponding broadcast link.

The hub station is created last, and when this happens, all the regular stations are ready to be configured into the network. The configure method of HubInterface is very simple:

```
              void HubInterface::configure () {
                SPort = create Port (TR);
                BPort = create Port;
                Assert (NC < NP, "Too many stations");
                HStations [NC++] = this;
              };
```

The method just creates the two ports and adds the station pointer to HStations, incrementing NC by the way. The real job, i.e., the operation of connecting the ports to the links, is performed by the configure method of HubStation:

```
        void HubStation::configure () {
          int i, j;
```

```
    Link *lk;
    TIME *lg;
    Assert (NC == NP, "The hub must be created last");
    SPorts = new Port* [NP];
    for (i = 0; i < NP; i++) SPorts [i] = create Port;
    BPort = create Port (TR);
    lg = new TIME [NP];
    for (i = 0; i < NP; i++) {
      lk = create Link (2);
      HStations [i] -> SPort -> connect (lk);
      SPorts [i] -> connect (lk);
#ifdef SameLinkLength
      lg [i] = MLL;
#else
      lg [i] = tRndPoisson (MLL);
#endif
      setD (HStations [i] -> SPort, SPorts [i], lg [i]);
    }
    lk = create Link (NP + 1);
    BPort->connect (lk);
    for (i = 0; i < NP; i++) {
      HStations [i] -> BPort -> connect (lk);
      setD (HStations [i] -> BPort, BPort, lg [i]);
    }
    for (i = 0; i < NP-1; i++)
      for (j = i+1; j < NP; j++)
        setD (HStations[i]->BPort, HStations[j]->BPort, 2 * lg[i]);
    delete lg;
    delete HStations;
}
```

With its first statement, the method asserts that the hub is indeed being created as the last station, i.e., all the regular stations have been created already. Then it builds the array of port pointers (SPorts) interfacing the switch with the selection links. The second for loop goes through all regular stations and for each station creates a selection link connecting the station to the hub. The link is then furnished with two ports, one from the regular station and the other from the hub, and the distance between the two ports is assigned. The length of a selection link is determined in one of two ways, depending on whether the symbolic constant SameLinkLength is defined or not. If the constant is defined, all selection links are assumed to be of the same length, given by MLL. Otherwise, the length of a selection link is generated as an exponentially distributed random number and MLL specifies the mean value of this distribution. In either case, the link length is stored in a local array (lg) to be used later for describing the geometry of the broadcast channel. One spoke of the broadcast channel connecting the hub to a regular station is assumed to be of the same length as the selection channel of this station.

The number of ports of the broadcast channel is equal to the number of regular stations plus 1 (NP + 1). The first of these ports is the broadcast port of the hub, and the remaining ports are assigned to the regular stations. The distance between the hub's broadcast port and the broadcast port of a regular station is set to the corresponding entry of lg, i.e., to the length of the selection link between the station and the hub. To complete the description of the broadcast channel, we have to specify the distances between all pairs of stations, not just the distances between the regular stations and the central switch. This is accomplished by the last for loop, which makes sure that the distance between a pair of broadcast ports of two regular stations is equal to the sum of the lengths of the selection links connecting these stations to the hub.

11.1.4.2   The protocol.   We start presenting the protocol implementation from the behavior of the hub station. The type of this station is defined as follows:

```
station Hub : HubStation {
  Boolean Busy;
  void setup () {
    HubStation::configure ();
    Busy = NO;
  };
};
```

Note that the hub has no Client interface part, and consequently it never transmits any packets of its own. The only attribute of the hub that does not belong to the interface class HubStation is the Boolean flag Busy telling whether the switch is currently relaying a packet (arriving on one of the selection ports) to the broadcast channel.

The hub station runs NP identical processes, each process listening to its dedicated selection port. The type declaration of the hub process is as follows:

```
process HubProcess (Hub) {
  Port *SPort, *BPort;
  void setup (int sn) {
    BPort = S->BPort;
    SPort = S->SPorts [sn];
  };
  states {Wait, NewPacket, Done};
  perform;
};
```

The argument of the setup method identifies the selection port (an element of array SPorts defined in HubStation) serviced by the process. Each copy of HubProcess handles one private selection port, but all copies share the same single broadcast port. The Busy flag of the hub station can be viewed as a semaphore guarding access to the broadcast channel. The process executes the following code:

```
HubProcess::perform {
    state Wait:
        SPort->wait (BOT, NewPacket);
    state NewPacket:
        if (S->Busy) skipto Wait;
        S->Busy = YES;
        BPort->transmit (ThePacket, Done);
    state Done:
        BPort->stop ();
        S->Busy = NO;
        proceed Wait;
};
```

Each HubProcess starts in state Wait, where it issues a wait request for the only interesting event—a packet arrival on the selection port. When the beginning of a packet is sensed, the process transits to state NewPacket, where it attempts to get hold of the broadcast channel. If the Busy flag is set, meaning that another copy of HubProcess is relaying a packet to the broadcast port, the process just ignores the incoming packet and transits back to Wait, to expect another packet arrival. This transition involves skipto rather than proceed (section 4.5.1) to make sure that the BOT event has disappeared from the port.

If the Busy flag is not set, the broadcast channel is available. In such a case, the process reserves the channel by setting Busy to YES and transmits the incoming packet on the broadcast port. When the transmission is complete, the process transits to state Done, where it terminates the transfer and clears the Busy flag to mark the broadcast channel as free. Finally, the process cycles back to its initial state Wait to await another packet arrival on the selection port.

The behavior of a regular station is a bit more complicated. A regular station is described by the following type:

```
station HStation : HubInterface, ClientInterface {
    Mailbox *StartEW, *ACK, *NACK;
    void setup () {
        HubInterface::configure ();
        ClientInterface::configure ();
        StartEW = create Mailbox (1);
        ACK = create Mailbox (1);
        NACK = create Mailbox (1);
    };
};
```

Besides the attributes hidden in the interface subclasses, the station defines three mailboxes, which pass alerts among the processes run by the station.

The traffic module bound to the program (files `utraffic.h` and `utraffic.c`—section 8.1.2.4) describes a simple uniform traffic pattern with one packet buffer per station. The station runs three permanent processes and occasionally spawns an additional temporary process, which disappears after a while. One of the three processes is the standard receiver (section 8.1.2.2 or section 9.2.2.2) hooked up to the station's broadcast port. The other two processes are the `Transmitter`, responsible for transmitting and retransmitting packets on the selection port, and the `Monitor`, detecting the echo of the station's own packets on the broadcast port and notifying the transmitter about the success or failure of its transfer attempts. The type definition of the transmitter process is as follows:

```
process Transmitter (HStation) {
  Port *SPort;
  Packet *Buffer;
  Mailbox *StartEW, *ACK, *NACK;
  void setup () {
    SPort = S->SPort;
    Buffer = &(S->Buffer);
    StartEW = S->StartEW;
    ACK = S->ACK;
    NACK = S->NACK;
  };
  states {NewPacket, Retransmit, Done, Confirmed, Lost};
  perform;
};
```

The three mailboxes communicate the process with the monitor. Having started a packet transmission, the transmitter sends an alert to the monitor via the `StartEW` (start echo wait) mailbox. Then it expects to receive back an alert from the monitor. If the monitor's alert arrives on the `ACK` mailbox, it is interpreted as a positive acknowledgment signal, and the transmitter assumes that the packet has made it through the hub. Otherwise, when the monitor detects a timeout, it sends the alert via `NACK`, in which case the transmitter has to retransmit the packet. These operations are performed by the following code method run by the transmitter:

```
Transmitter::perform {
  state NewPacket:
    if (S->ready (MinPL, MaxPL, FrameL))
      proceed Retransmit;
    else
      Client->wait (ARRIVAL, NewPacket);
  state Retransmit:
    SPort->transmit (Buffer, Done);
    StartEW->put ();
```

```
        NACK->wait (RECEIVE, Lost);
    state Done:
        SPort->stop ();
        NACK->wait (RECEIVE, Retransmit);
        ACK->wait (RECEIVE, Confirmed);
    state Confirmed:
        Buffer->release ();
        proceed NewPacket;
    state Lost:
        SPort->abort ();
        proceed Retransmit;
};
```

The transmitter sleeps in state `NewPacket` until it is able to acquire a packet from the `Client`. Then the process moves to state `Retransmit`, where it starts transmitting the packet. At the same time, the transmitter deposits an alert in `StartEW` to notify the monitor that it should start awaiting the packet's echo on the broadcast port.

Note that if the packet is long or the distance between the station and the hub (and consequently the echo waiting timeout) is short, the monitor's alert may arrive while the packet is still being transmitted. If this alert carries a positive acknowledgment, the packet should be transmitted entirely and released. Otherwise, the transmitter may want to abort the transfer early—it makes no sense to continue transmitting the packet that has been already rejected by the hub—and start it again from the beginning. Therefore, the last statement executed in state `Retransmit` is a wait request to the `NACK` mailbox, whose purpose is to detect an early negative acknowledgment alert arriving from the monitor. If this alert arrives, the transmitter transits to state `Lost`, where it aborts the transfer and immediately moves back to `Retransmit` to start the transmission from scratch.

When the transmission has been completed (and no negative acknowledgment alert has arrived from the monitor), the transmitter finds itself in state `Done`. Then the process terminates the transfer and awaits the arrival of any alert from the monitor. It may happen that a positive acknowledgment alert is already pending in the `ACK` mailbox. Such an alert arriving while the packet is still being transmitted is not lost (note that the mailbox capacity is 1); it will be immediately detected by the transmitter in state `Done`, and the process will transit directly to state `Confirmed`.

While in state `Done`, the transmitter knows for sure that sooner or later exactly one of the two mailboxes `ACK` or `NACK` will become nonempty (if `ACK` is not nonempty already). Upon the reception of a positive acknowledgment, the process moves to state `Confirmed`, where it releases the current packet and transits back to `NewPacket` to acquire another one. If the negative acknowledgment alert is received after the packet has been completely transmitted, the transmitter moves directly to state `Retransmit` to transmit the packet again.

Now let us look at the second process. Its type is declared as follows:

```
process Monitor (HStation) {
  Port *BPort;
  Mailbox *StartEW, *ACK, *NACK;
  Packet *Pkt;
  TIME EchoTimeout;
  AClock *AC;
  void setup () {
    BPort = S->BPort;
    StartEW = S->StartEW;
    ACK = S->ACK;
    NACK = S->NACK;
    EchoTimeout =
      (BPort->distTo (((Hub*)idToStation (NStations-1))->BPort) +
        SndRecTime) * 2;
  };
  states {WaitSignal, WaitEcho, Waiting, NewPacket, CheckEcho,
    NoEcho};
  perform;
};
```

The process services the broadcast port and references the same three mailboxes as the transmitter. Attribute Pkt is a temporary variable to store a pointer to the packet perceived by the monitor on the broadcast port. EchoTimeout gives the waiting time for the packet echo. The echo waiting time is measured from the moment the monitor receives an alert on the StartEW mailbox. If no packet echo arrives within the EchoTimeout interval, the monitor sends a negative acknowledgment to the transmitter (deposits an alert in the NACK mailbox). Needless to say, a positive acknowledgment is sent as soon as the packet shows up on the station's broadcast port.

The minimum value of EchoTimeout equals twice the distance between the station and the hub, augmented by the delay needed by the station to recognize its address in the packet header. This additional delay is a numerical parameter of the protocol represented by the global variable SndRecTime. As calculated by the setup method,[2] the timeout includes SndRecTime twice—to provide a safety margin compensating for the limited accuracy of the station's clock.

When it receives a startup alert from the transmitter, the monitor spawns a simple process of type AClock that models an alarm clock. A pointer to this process is stored in the monitor's attribute AC. The alarm clock is set for EchoTimeout ITUs, and when it goes off it deposits a signal in the monitor's signal repository. This way the monitor is relieved from the task of measuring the time elapsed after the arrival of the transmitter's alert. The complete definition of the alarm clock process follows:

---

[2]Method distTo was introduced in section 3.3.3.

```
process AClock (HStation, Monitor) {
  TIME Delay;
  void setup (TIME d) { Delay = d; };
  states {Start, GoOff};
  perform {
    state Start:
      Timer->wait (Delay, GoOff);
    state GoOff:
      F->signal ();
      terminate;
  };
};
```

Upon creation, the process receives a setup argument specifying the time interval for which the alarm clock is to be set. In its initial state, the process issues a timer wait request for that interval and goes to sleep until the timer event is triggered. Then, in state GoOff, the process deposits a signal in the repository of its parent (accessed via the standard attribute F—section 4.2) and terminates itself.

Now we can look at the code method of the monitor:

```
Monitor::perform {
  state WaitSignal:
    StartEW->wait (RECEIVE, WaitEcho);
  state WaitEcho:
    AC = create AClock (EchoTimeout);
    proceed Waiting;
  state Waiting:
    BPort->wait (BOT, NewPacket);
    TheProcess->wait (SIGNAL, NoEcho);
  state NewPacket:
    Pkt = ThePacket;
    Timer->wait (SndRecTime, CheckEcho);
    TheProcess->wait (SIGNAL, NoEcho);
  state CheckEcho:
    if (Pkt -> Sender == S->getId ()) {
      if (erase () == 0)
        AC -> terminate ();
      ACK->put ();
      proceed WaitSignal;
    } else
      proceed Waiting;
  state NoEcho:
    NACK->put ();
    proceed WaitSignal;
};
```

The process remains dormant until it receives an alert from the transmitter (via StartEW). Then, in state WaitEcho, the monitor creates the alarm clock process and sets it for EchoTimeout ITUs. Next, the process moves to state Waiting, which can be viewed as the entry point of a loop in which the monitor awaits the packet's echo on the broadcast port. Two wait requests are issued in state Waiting: one for a BOT event on the broadcast port, the other for a signal arrival to the process's own repository. The latter event is equivalent to the timer going off. When it occurs, the monitor moves to state NoEcho, where it sends a negative acknowledgment to the transmitter by depositing an alert in the NACK mailbox.

Upon detection of a packet arriving at the broadcast port, the process moves to state NewPacket to examine the sender field in the packet header. Formally, this can be accomplished no sooner than SndRecTime ITUs after the BOT event triggered by the packet arrival. The monitor models this waiting time by a delayed transition from NewPacket to CheckEcho. Before issuing a timer wait request in state NewPacket, the process saves the packet pointer (returned by the BOT event) in the temporary variable Pkt, so that this pointer is still available in state CheckEcho. While waiting for the transition to occur, the monitor also awaits a signal from the alarm clock process. If the alarm clock goes off before the monitor gets to the sender field of the packet, the waiting is aborted and a negative acknowledgment alert is sent to the transmitter.

In state CheckEcho, the monitor compares the packet's Sender attribute with the Id of the station owning the process. If the packet happens to have been sent by another station, it is ignored: the process moves immediately to state Waiting to await another BOT event. Otherwise, the packet has been transmitted by this station. In such a case, the monitor terminates the alarm clock process and deposits an alert in the ACK mailbox, which is interpreted by the transmitter as a positive acknowledgment. Then the process moves to state WaitSignal to await another startup alert from the transmitter.

The termination request to the alarm clock process is issued conditionally, based on the result of the erase operation (section 4.6.2.1) performed on the monitor's signal repository. This way, the monitor protects itself against the unlikely (but not explicitly impossible) scenario in which the alarm clock goes off within the same ITU when it is to be terminated. Should this happen, the terminate operation would be illegal, as the alarm clock process would not be alive any longer. Besides, the monitor's signal repository would be left in a "full" state—polluted with a pending signal that has not been received by the monitor. Next time around, this signal would be misinterpreted as a premature timeout. The if statement preceding terminate takes care of both ends.

11.2   FLOODNET

In contrast to Hubnet, the network presented in this section has no inherent topology and it can be configured into arbitrary graphs. Despite the meshed and switched architecture, Floodnet is a close cousin of Ethernet (section 8.1) and can be viewed as a refinement of CSMA/CD. One problem with the bus architecture of Ethernet is that each packet fills the entire network and is de facto received by all stations. The idea of Floodnet is to reduce the amount of network resources occupied by one packet transmission to the path from the source to the destination. This postulate is not difficult to fulfill in a switched network, if the intermediate nodes are allowed to interpret the packet header and make smart routing decisions directing the packet along a single (possibly the shortest) path to the recipient. A Floodnet switch, however, never interprets the header of a relayed packet, nor does it attempt to guess where the packet is heading. The confinement of the path traveled by a packet is the result of negative feedback from the stations to which the packet is not addressed.

11.2.1   The Protocol

Floodnet consists of a number of switches interconnected via point-to-point channels (see figure 11.4). Each channel is duplex, which means that it can transfer data in both directions at the same time. In SMURPH, such a channel can be modeled as a pair of unidirectional links going in opposite directions.

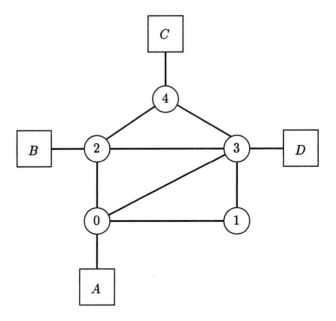

Figure 11.4   A sample configuration of Floodnet

Although one could postulate that some or all switches are also hosts that originate or absorb the network traffic, it is more convenient to assume that the hosts are special stations interfaced with the switches via duplex channels. This way, the network is organized according to the standard OSI view that separates the communication subnet from the hosts (figure 1.2). In principle, any number of hosts, in particular zero, can be connected to a single switch.

Different switches may have different connectivity, i.e., different numbers of neighbors connected to them via (duplex) channels. We assume that a single host can be connected to only one switch; thus, the connectivity of a host is always exactly 1.

The medium access protocol of Floodnet operates as follows.

A host having a packet to transmit is allowed to start the transmission at any time, provided that it senses no activity on the input port of its channel. If an activity shows up on the input port while a packet is being transmitted, the host aborts the transfer, backs off, i.e., sleeps for a randomized period of time, and tries again. These are the complete transmission rules for a host.

A switch relays activities from its input ports to the output ports. When a switch wants to relay an activity from one of its input ports to an output port, it just connects the input port to the output port. As a switch never interprets the structure of an activity arriving at its input port, there is no need to call these activities packets. In fact, besides packets, the protocol uses *dummy activities*, which, like the jamming signals of Ethernet (section 8.1.1.3), need not have any structure.

A switch can be in one of two states: *busy*, if it is relaying an activity from one of its input ports to at least one of its output ports, or *idle* otherwise. Assume that an activity arrives at an idle switch. The activity arrives on an input port representing one of the channels connecting the switch to its neighbors. This channel is called the *source channel*, and the neighbor sending the activity is called the *source neighbor*. The switch marks itself as busy and connects the source input port to all the output ports except for the output port of the source channel. This way, the incoming activity is relayed to all the neighboring switches except for the source neighbor.

Now suppose that an activity arrives at a busy switch. The activity arrives on channel c, which is different from the source channel. In such a case, the switch ignores the incoming activity, but it disconnects the output port of channel c from the input port of the source channel. In short, an interfering activity arriving at a busy switch is treated as a negative feedback signal advising the switch to stop relaying the source activity in the direction of the incoming activity.

A busy switch may stop relaying the source activity before the activity has disappeared from the source port. This will happen if the switch has received negative feedback from all channels other than the source channel. Then the switch sends a dummy activity on the output port of the source channel to pass the negative feedback to the source neighbor. If the source activity has been completely relayed on at least one output port, the switch returns to its idle state.

A host receiving a packet addressed to some other host (having recognized the wrong recipient address in the packet header) sends a dummy activity on the output port. This activity will be treated by the host's switch as a negative feedback signal, and the switch will stop relaying the packet to the host.

Let L be the propagation diameter of the network.[3] The protocol assumes that the minimum length of a valid packet (dummy activities excluded) is at least equal to $2L$ plus the amount of time needed by a host to recognize the recipient address in the packet header. Under this assumption, when a source host completes a packet transmission, it can claim that the packet has made it to the destination. Indeed, if the last bit of a packet is transmitted and no negative feedback has been received from the network, it means that there is an alive path connecting the source host with another host that has recognized its address in the sender field of the packet header.

To illustrate the operation of the protocol, consider the network shown in figure 11.4 and assume that host A sends a packet addressed to host D (the other hosts are idle). When the packet reaches switch number 0, it is relayed to switches 1, 2, and 3. Starting from this point, the detailed behavior of the network depends on the propagation length of the channels. For example, if channel 0–3 is shorter than the paths 0–1–3 and 0–2–3, switch 3 will first receive the packet from channel 0–3. Then it will relay the packet to switches 1, 2, and 4, and also to host D. The activities arriving at switch 3 from channels 1–3 and 2–3 will be blocked; they will disappear after a while, when switches 1 and 2 receive negative feedback from switch 3. Upon the reception of an activity from channel 1–3, switch 1 will send a dummy activity to switch 0 and become idle. Switch 4 will most likely receive its first copy of the packet via channel 2–4. The second copy arriving from channel 3–4 will be blocked, and in a while switch 3 will stop relaying the packet to switch 4. Having received a dummy activity from host C (the packet is addressed to D), switch 4 (having no way to relay the packet) will send a dummy activity to switch 2 and become idle. Eventually, switch 2 will get negative feedback from host B and switch 3; then it will send a dummy activity to switch 0 and turn idle. Finally, the only remaining active path will be A–0–3–D, which will remain active until the packet is transmitted.

Note that if path 0–1–3 happens to be shorter than channel 0–3, switch 3 will first receive the packet via channel 1–3. Then the final path taken by the packet will be A–0–1–3–D.

Floodnet operates at its best if most packets are substantially longer than $2L$. Then the flooding phase of a transmission takes a small fraction of the total transmission time and the network can handle multiple simultaneous transfers. If many packets are shorter than $2L$ (and must be inflated), the performance of Floodnet deteriorates drastically.

In contrast to regular packets, dummy activities can be arbitrarily short, provided that they can still be recognized as activities by the receiving parties. To make sure that activities (including aborted packets) are never ignored, the protocol must impose a minimum length on the duration of an activity. For example, if an aborted packet were shorter than the minimum acceptable activity duration, its

---

[3]The propagation diameter of a mesh network is the amount of time needed for a signal to travel between two most distant hosts.

transmission would have to be sustained until the minimum duration was reached.

Generally, a host failing to transmit its packet should delay the retransmission by a randomized amount of time of order at least $2L$. To see why a randomized backoff is needed, assume that host B (from the network shown in figure 11.4) wants to send a packet to D and, at the same time, host C wants to send a packet to A. Depending on the timing and the lengths of channels, it is possible that both transmissions will be stopped. If they are retried at the same (or almost the same) time, the scenario will repeat itself, resulting in an indefinite lock-out.

11.2.2   The Implementation

Despite the apparent simplicity of the Floodnet switch, an event-driven description of its behavior is not trivial. As the name suggests, flooding is essentially an analogous phenomenon, and its best models are built of pipes and valves. Nonetheless, our implementation of Floodnet, which we discuss in this section, is reasonably short and presentable.

11.2.2.1   Defining general meshed network configurations.   We start by introducing a library module that can be applied to generate practically any meshed network backbone. This module (files `mesh.h` and `mesh.c` in `IncludeLibrary`) are reused in two other case studies included in this chapter.

The station interface to a mesh network is described by the following virtual type defined in `mesh.h`:

```
station MeshNode virtual {
  Port **IPorts, **OPorts;
  Long *Neighbors;
  int Order;
  void configure (int);
};
```

Different stations may have different connectivity. The connectivity of a station is determined by its `Order` attribute, which gives the number of input and output ports defined in `MeshNode`. These ports are represented by two dynamically created arrays of pointers: `IPorts` (for the input ports) and `OPorts` (for the output ports). Each array contains `Order` port pointers.

`Neighbors` is another array of size `Order` that gives the Ids of the neighbors connected to the station via its output ports. If `Neighbors[i] ==n`, it means that `OPorts[i]` points to a port whose link is connected to station number n, i.e., this station owns the output port attached to the opposite end of the link. It is legal to have several links (ports) to the same neighbor. The module does not assume that all connections are symmetric, i.e., a link from station s_1 to s_2 does not automatically imply a link from s_2 to s_1. If the channels are to be duplex (as in Floodnet), the user must make sure that they are built this way.

A number specifying the station's connectivity must be passed to the `configure` method of `MeshNode` when the station is created. The user is responsible for providing a function that describes how the stations are connected. This function can be viewed as a dynamic representation of the incidence matrix of the network graph. The network creation procedure is initiated by calling a global function with the following header:

```
void initMesh (RATE, CFType, Long);
```

where, as usual, the first argument specifies the common transmission rate of all output ports and the last argument gives the number of stations to be configured into a mesh. The middle argument is a pointer to the incidence function programmed by the user. The header of this function should comply with `CFType`, which is declared in `mesh.h` as follows:

```
typedef int (*CFType) (Long, Long, DISTANCE&);
```

For example, it may look like this:

```
int incFun (Long F, Long T, DISTANCE &D);
```

F and T are integer numbers representing station `Ids`. The function is expected to return the number of links from station F to station T. If this number is nonzero, D (which is passed by reference) should be set by the function to the length of the connection in ITUs. If there are multiple links from station F to T, all these links must be of the same length D.

Examples

The following incidence function describes a fully connected network without the diagonal, i.e., each station is connected to all other stations but not to itself:

```
int FullMesh (Long i, Long j, DISTANCE &d) {
  d = Dist;
  return i != j;
};
```

All links have the same length determined by `Dist`, which is a global variable.

Following is another incidence function. This time, it defines a simple ring network with the length of each segment read from the input data file:

```
int Ring (Long i, Long j, DISTANCE &d) {
  if ((i + 1) % NStations == j) {
    readIn (d);
    return 1;
  } else
    return 0;
};
```

The ordering of stations along the ring is the same as in our FDDI model (section 10.3.4.1). The reader may want to reimplement FDDI using the mesh module

to describe the ring topology. Although less frugal in terms of memory requirements, the mesh version is more flexible, as it allows different links of the ring to be
of different length.

Note that the incidence function from the second example only works under
the assumption that it is called exactly once per each pair of adjacent stations i and
j. The function has a side effect consisting in a number being read from the input
file. Clearly, the user wants to provide a single number per each link. Moreover, he
or she would like to know the order in which the links will be examined, to prepare a
sensible input data set. Fortunately, the way an incidence function is invoked by the
mesh module is very systematic and deterministic. Before we get there, let us look
at the initial fragment of file mesh.c, which defines the global function initMesh:

```
static CFType Connectivity;
static Long NP, NC;
static RATE TR;
static MeshNode **Nodes;
void initMesh (RATE r, CFType cn, Long np) {
  TR = r;
  NP = np;
  NC = 0;
  Connectivity = cn;
  Nodes = new MeshNode* [NP];
};
```

As usual, the function saves the values of its arguments in static global variables, from which they can be accessed by the configure method of MeshNode and
its associated functions. Array Nodes will store pointers to the MeshNode parts of
stations as they are created. Variable NC, initialized to zero, will tell the number
of stations that have been created so far. The code of the configure method is as
follows:

```
void MeshNode::configure (int order) {
  int i;
  Order = order;
  IPorts = new Port* [Order];
  OPorts = new Port* [Order];
  Neighbors = new Long [Order];
  for (i = 0; i < Order; i++) {
    IPorts [i] = NULL;
    OPorts [i] = NULL;
    Neighbors [i] = NONE;
  }
  Nodes [NC++] = this;
  if (NC == NP) {
```

```
   buildMesh ();
   checkConnectivity ();
   delete Nodes;
   TheStation = idToStation (NP-1);
  }
};
```

The method builds the dynamic arrays of port pointers, but it does not create the ports. All entries in the arrays and in Neighbors are set to special values (NULL and NONE) indicating that the station is not connected yet to any neighbor. Then the station is added to Nodes, and NC is incremented by one. When the counter reaches NP (meaning that all stations have been created), the method calls two global functions: buildMesh, to create the channels prescribed by the user-supplied incidence function, and checkConnectivity, to verify that the connections built by the previous function exhaust all port slots at all stations. This means that the situation when an entry in a port pointer array (IPorts or OPorts) remains unspecified is treated as an error. Finally, the method deallocates the Nodes array and cleans up after buildMesh by resetting TheStation to its original value (section 9.2.2.1).

Function buildMesh does most of the work needed to configure the network. It examines all station pairs and for each pair determines whether the stations are to be connected and with how many links. The complete code of buildMesh is as follows:

```
void buildMesh () {
  Long i, j, nc;
  int fp1, fp2;
  MeshNode *S1, *S2;
  DISTANCE lg;
  PLink *lk;
  Port *p1, *p2;
  for (i = 0; i < NP; i++) {
    S1 = Nodes [i];
    for (j = 0; j < NP; j++) {
      for (nc = Connectivity (i, j, lg); nc; nc--) {
        S2 = Nodes [j];
        lk = create PLink (2);
        for (fp1 = 0; fp1 < S1->Order; fp1++)
          if (S1->OPorts [fp1] == NULL) break;
        Assert (fp1 < S1->Order,
          form ("Station %1d: no more output ports", i));
        for (fp2 = 0; fp2 < S2->Order; fp2++)
          if (S2->IPorts [fp2] == NULL) break;
        Assert (fp2 < S2->Order,
          form ("Station %1d: no more input ports", j));
        p1 = S1->OPorts [fp1] = create (i) Port (TR);
```

```
                    p2 = S2->IPorts [fp2] = create (j) Port;
                    p1 -> connect (lk);
                    p2 -> connect (lk);
                    p1 -> setDTo (p2, lg);
                    S1 -> Neighbors [fp1] = j;
                }
            }
        }
    };
```

The first two for loops scan all station pairs i and j, including i == j. In some networks, e.g., in MNA (section 11.4), a station can be legitimately connected to itself; thus, the diagonal of the incidence matrix cannot be excluded explicitly. The third, innermost loop is only executed if the user-supplied incidence function returns nonzero, meaning that there is at least one link from station i to j. The actual number of links is returned by the incidence function and stored in nc. The loop executes nc times, creating all these links and the ports interfacing them to the stations. Only the output ports are assigned a transmission rate. As an input port is never used for a transmission, its transmission rate is irrelevant.

The port slots are allocated on a first-free basis. As the link is assumed to go from station i to station j, the function scans the OPorts array at station i (pointed to by S1) and selects the first unused entry from this array to store the pointer to the output port of the link. Similarly, the first unused entry from IPorts at station j is used to store the input port pointer. If no free port slot is available at either of the two stations, the connection cannot be made and the function diagnoses the problem. This means that the station's connectivity (Order) is inconsistent with the incidence matrix of the network graph. The link length (the distance from the input port to the output port) is set to lg, which was passed as the third (reference) argument to the incidence function (and was set by the function to the distance between the two stations).

Finally, the Id of the target station (j) is stored in the Neighbors array of station i, at the same index that the pointer to the input port was stored in IPorts. The role of Neighbors is to give the station a means to identify its neighbors and know via which ports they can be reached. The Floodnet protocol makes no use of this information, but it may become useful in protocols in which stations have to make nontrivial routing decisions.

The last step in configuring the network is to check whether all port slots at all stations have been used. Note that buildMesh detects the situations when the number of port slots available at a station is insufficient to satisfy the requirements of the incidence function, but it does not verify that no port slots are left dangling after all connections have been made. This end is served by the following function:

```
void checkConnectivity () {
    Long i;
    int p;
```

```
MeshNode *S;
for (i = 0; i < NP; i++) {
  S = Nodes [i];
  for (p = 0; p < S->Order; p++) {
    Assert (S->IPorts [p] != NULL,
      form ("Station %1d, input port %1d left dangling", i, p));
    Assert (S->OPorts [p] != NULL,
      form ("Station %1d, output port %1d left dangling", i, p));
  }
}
};
```

which simply scans all stations and their port arrays to detect unassigned entries.

11.2.2.2   Global parameters and station types.

The SMURPH program implementing Floodnet is parameterized by several numerical values and the user-supplied incidence function (section 11.2.2.1). The numerical parameters of the protocol are represented by the following variables set in the root process:

```
Long MinPL, MaxPL, FrameL, NoiseL;
TIME MinActTime, RcvRecDelay, FloodTime, PSpace;
RATE TRate;
```

The first three values are the standard packetization parameters used for packet acquisition. NoiseL gives the length in bits of a dummy activity used by a switch or host to send an explicit negative feedback signal to its neighbor. Dummy activities are represented by special nonstandard packets. MinActTime describes the minimum duration of a recognizable activity. Whenever a switch or host is forced to abort a packet transmission because of negative feedback from its neighbors, it makes sure that the packet has been transmitted for at least MinActTime ITUs. The length of a dummy activity (NoiseL) expressed in ITUs should not be less than MinActTime. RcvRecDelay is the amount of time elapsing from the moment a packet arrives at a host (triggering a BOT event) until the host is able to decode the packet's destination address from the header. FloodTime is twice the estimated propagation diameter of the network, the worst-case time needed by a host to flood the network with a packet transmission and receive a negative feedback signal. This parameter corresponds to TwoL in the Ethernet program (section 8.1.2) and is used exclusively by the backoff function. The protocol assumes that the total length of the shortest legitimate packet, i.e., MinPL + FrameL, is greater than FloodTime.

A switch should avoid mistaking two consecutive packet transmissions for a single activity. Note that a switch may need to change its state on the boundary between two such packets. Therefore, consecutively transmitted packets should be separated by silence periods analogous to interpacket spaces in Ethernet, although playing here a slightly different role. The length of an interpacket space is given by PSpace. The last numerical parameter of the implementation, TRate, is the common transmission rate of all output ports.

The implementation is based on two station types: hosts and switches. The host type is substantially simpler than the switch type:

```
station Host : MeshNode, ClientInterface {
  Packet Noise;
  void setup () {
    MeshNode::configure (1);
    ClientInterface::configure ();
    Noise.fill (NONE, NONE, NoiseL);
  };
};
```

Besides the mesh interface, the host station is also equipped with a Client interface and receives messages for transmission. Our implementation makes use of the simple uniform traffic pattern defined in the library files utraffic.h and utraffic.c (section 8.1.2.4). Buffer Noise, filled by the station's setup method, holds a dummy packet to be used for sending explicit negative feedback signals on the output port.

The switch type is somewhat more involved:

```
station Switch : MeshNode {
  Mailbox *IdleSignal, *RelaySignal, *StopSignal, *AbortSignal,
    *BlockSignal;
  int NActive, NBouncing;
  Boolean Idle;
  Packet Noise, *RPacket;
  void setup (int order) {
    MeshNode::configure (order);
    IdleSignal  = create Mailbox (0);
    RelaySignal = create Mailbox (0);
    StopSignal  = create Mailbox (0);
    AbortSignal = create Mailbox (0);
    BlockSignal = create Mailbox (0);
    Idle = YES;
    Noise.fill (NONE, NONE, NoiseL);
  };
};
```

although it has no Client interface part (switches generate no traffic of their own). Attribute Noise has the same definition and purpose as in a host station. RPacket stores the pointer to the source packet being processed by the switch. The meaning of the remaining attributes will become clear when we get to the processes run by the switch; now we just briefly announce their purpose. The switch executes Order copies of the same process (type PortServer), each copy servicing one channel (port pair) of the switch. The port servers of the same switch communicate via the five capacity-0 mailboxes. In particular, when a packet arrives to an idle switch (whose

`Idle` attribute is `YES`), the process servicing the port on which the packet is sensed deposits an alert in `RelaySignal` to notify the other processes that they should relay the incoming packet on the output ports of their channels. `StopSignal` and `AbortSignal` are used to terminate a packet retransmission normally and abnormally. The purpose of `IdleSignal` is to help the processes reach a consensus as to the exact moment when the switch gets into the idle state. Finally, `BlockSignal` receives an alert when all port server processes relaying an incoming packet to their output ports have sensed activities on their input ports. Recall from section 11.2.1 that such a scenario is interpreted as a negative feedback signal from the network. The mailbox is monitored by the process servicing the source input port, which, upon the reception of an alert, sends a dummy activity up the source channel and aborts the retransmission procedure.

`NActive` and `NBouncing` are integer counters keeping track of the number of server processes engaged into the relaying operation. When the switch starts retransmitting a source packet on all channels other than the source channel, `NActive` is set to `Order − 1`, i.e., the number of server processes effectively relaying the packet. Each time a process drops off in consequence of negative feedback from its channel, `NActive` is decremented by 1. This way, the process that drops off last can recognize the blocked state of the operation (`NActive` becomes zero) and deposit an alert in `BlockSignal`. The other counter is used to count the processes that have terminated all activities related to the last retransmission and have determined that both ports of their channels are idle. If all processes have reached this state, `NBouncing` becomes equal to `Order` and the switch can resume its idle state.

11.2.2.3   The port server process.   Each channel of a Floodnet switch (perceived by the switch as a pair of ports) is monitored by one copy of the port server process. All port servers run identical code; however, during the operation of relaying a packet through the switch, they behave in a nonsymmetric way. One process receives the source packet on the input port of its channel, and the other processes retransmit this packet on their output ports.

The type declaration of the port server process is as follows:

```
process PortServer (Switch) {
  Port *IPort, *OPort;
  TIME RStarted;
  int Order;
  Packet *Noise;
  Mailbox *IdleSignal, *RelaySignal, *StopSignal, *AbortSignal,
    *BlockSignal;
  void setup (int p) {
    Order = S->Order;
    IPort = S->IPorts [p];
    OPort = S->OPorts [p];
    Noise = &(S->Noise);
```

```
      IdleSignal  = S->IdleSignal;
      RelaySignal = S->RelaySignal;
      StopSignal  = S->StopSignal;
      AbortSignal = S->AbortSignal;
      BlockSignal = S->BlockSignal;
   };
   states {Idle, GrabIt, Relaying, Stop, Abort, Bouncing, Bounce,
      NDone, DAbort, Quit, WaitEOT, CheckEOT, Blocked};
   perform;
};
```

All attributes of PortServer except RStarted are copies of the station attributes that the process wants to reference. The setup argument identifies the channel to be serviced by the process and determines the entries from the port arrays to be assigned to IPort and OPort. The role of RStarted is to save the starting time of an activity inserted into the output port (OPort). When this activity is later terminated (aborted), the process can check its duration against the minimum legal duration of a recognizable activity (MinActTime). If this activity turns out to be too short, the process delays its termination until the minimum duration time is met. Now we discuss in detail the following code method of PortServer:

```
PortServer::perform {
  TIME t;
  state Idle:
    if (!S->Idle) proceed Relaying;
    IPort->wait (BOT, GrabIt);
    RelaySignal->wait (NEWITEM, Relaying);
  state GrabIt:
    if (S->Idle) {
      S->RPacket = ThePacket;
      S->Idle = NO;
      RelaySignal->put ();
      S->NBouncing = 0;
      S->NActive = Order - 1;
      skipto WaitEOT;
    }
  transient Relaying:
    RStarted = Time;
    OPort->startTransfer (S->RPacket);
    StopSignal->wait (NEWITEM, Stop);
    AbortSignal->wait (NEWITEM, Abort);
    IPort->wait (ACTIVITY, DAbort);
  state Stop:
    OPort->stop ();
    proceed Bouncing;
```

```
    state Abort:
      OPort->abort ();
    transient Bouncing:
      if (++(S->NBouncing) == Order) {
        S->Idle = YES;
        IdleSignal->put ();
        proceed Idle;
      }
      IdleSignal->wait (NEWITEM, Idle);
      IPort->wait (BOT, Bounce);
    state Bounce:
      if (S->Idle) proceed Idle;
      S->NBouncing--;
      OPort->transmit (Noise, NDone);
    state NDone:
      OPort->abort ();
      proceed Bouncing;
    state DAbort:
      if ((t = Time - RStarted) < MinActTime) {
        Timer->wait (MinActTime - t, Quit);
        sleep;
      }
    transient Quit:
      OPort->abort ();
      if (--(S->NActive) == 0) BlockSignal->put ();
      proceed Bouncing;
    state WaitEOT:
      IPort->wait (ANYEVENT, CheckEOT);
      BlockSignal->wait (NEWITEM, Blocked);
    state CheckEOT:
      if (IPort->events (EOT)) {
        assert (S->NActive, "Late block");
        StopSignal->put ();
      } else
        AbortSignal->put ();
      proceed Bouncing;
    state Blocked:
      OPort->transmit (Noise, NDone);
};
```

When the process wakes up in state Idle for the first time, the Idle flag of the switch is YES and the immediate transition to state Relaying is not executed. As long as the switch is idle, all its port servers sleep in state Idle awaiting two events: BOT on the input port and NEWITEM on the RelaySignal mailbox. The first process that detects a packet arrival on its input port (is awakened by the BOT event) transits to state GrabIt, where it claims the switch for its packet. Among the operations performed in state GrabIt, the claiming process deposits an alert in RelaySignal to force the other processes to state Relaying, where they will retransmit the source packet on their output ports. The only problem with these natural and apparently simple transitions is that they have to account for the unlikely, but not impossible, scenario in which two or more port servers try to claim the switch within the same ITU. To make sure that only one process can effectively take control of the switch at a time, the switch resource must be guarded by a critical section.

A process waking up in state GrabIt cannot simply set the Idle flag to NO and assume that it has acquired the switch for its source packet. If another process receives a BOT event within the same ITU, it may also end up in state GrabIt believing that its packet is the one to be relayed by the switch. Therefore, the Idle flag is treated as a semaphore. In state GrabIt, the process checks if Idle is still NO, and it claims the switch only if no other process has done it already. Otherwise, the process falls through to state Relaying (defined as transient—section 4.4.3), as if it responded to the other event awaited in state Idle.

The following actions are performed by the process that has successfully claimed the switch:

1. The pointer to the arriving packet is saved in RPacket. As RPacket is a station attribute, the source packet will be accessible to the remaining processes run by the switch.

2. The switch status is changed to busy by setting the Idle flag to NO. This operation also locks the critical section guarding the switch resource.

3. An alert is deposited in RelaySignal to force the other processes to state Relaying. In that state, a process retransmits the packet pointed to by RPacket on its output port.

4. NBouncing is set to zero and NActive is set to Order − 1. According to what we said earlier, NActive tells the number of channels on which the source packet is being relayed. The packet is initially retransmitted on all the output channels except the source channel. At the same time, NBouncing gives the number of port servers that have concluded that the relaying operation has completed and the switch should get back to the idle state. Clearly, no process should be arriving at such conclusions at this moment.

5. The source process moves to state WaitEOT to await a normal or abnormal termination of the source packet, or another event that will force the process to abandon the retransmission procedure.

The claiming procedure is completed within one ITU. When it is over, the successful claimant (from now on, we call it the *source process*) is making a transition to WaitEOT (the skipto operation takes one ITU) and the other processes find themselves in state Relaying. A relaying process simply starts transmitting the packet pointed to by RPacket on the output port. The starting time of the transfer is saved in `RStarted` to measure the effective duration of the packet activity in case it will have to be prematurely aborted. The retransmission can terminate:

- Normally, by the source process, if it detects an `EOT` event on its input port. In such a case, the source process deposits an alert in `StopSignal`.
- Abnormally, by the source process, if the source packet is incomplete, i.e., it has been aborted by its sender.
- Abnormally, by the relaying process, if it receives a negative feedback signal (an activity) from the input port.

In the first two cases, the process does not have to check the duration of the relayed activity against the minimum legal duration (`MinActTime`). If the packet terminates normally, it is a complete packet, whose minimum length certainly obeys the rule. If the packet arrives aborted, whoever aborted it made sure that the packet activity was no shorter than `MinActTime`. The only problem is when the process aborts the retransmission in consequence of an activity appearing on its input port.

A relaying process that receives negative feedback from its input port transits to state `DAbort`, where it calculates the duration of the packet's relayed portion. If this duration is all right, the process falls through to state `Quit`; otherwise, it delays the transition to `Quit` by the minimum amount of time needed to make the activity inserted into the output port long enough. Then, in state `Quit`, the process aborts the retransmission and decrements `NActive` to indicate that one of the relaying processes has dropped off the game. If `NActive` ends up being zero, the process deposits an alert in `BlockSignal` to notify the source process that it should send a negative feedback signal up the source channel.

Regardless of how a relaying process terminates the retransmission of the source packet, it eventually gets to state `Bouncing`, which plays the role of a "waiting room" before state `Idle`. This waiting room is needed, because different processes may terminate their activities at different moments, but the `Idle` state can only be assumed if all ports of the switch are consistently silent. For as long as the switch is not formally `Idle`, any new activity appearing on an input port should meet with a negative feedback activity sent on the corresponding output port. Note that the switch may remain in the busy state for a while after the source packet has been completely relayed;[4] thus, this statement concerns the source channel as well.

A process entering state `Bouncing` perceives no activity on its input port and inserts no activity into its output port. Thus, its portion of the switch is idle. The way `NBouncing` is updated, it tells the number of processes currently waiting in the `Bouncing` state. If `NBouncing` reaches `Order`, meaning that all processes of the switch perceive the switch as idle, they are all allowed to enter the `Idle` state. To force this global transition consistently, the process detecting that `NBouncing` has reached `Order` changes the `Idle` flag to `YES` and deposits an alert into mailbox `IdleSignal`. The other processes waiting in state `Bouncing` will respond to the

---

[4]For example, some processes may still be sending negative feedback activities on their output ports.

NEWITEM event triggered by this operation and transit to state `Idle`.

To be absolutely foolproof, the mechanism needs one additional bolt. Besides awaiting the `NEWITEM` event on `IdleSignal`, a bouncing process must also respond to activities (packets) arriving on its input port. Thus, it is possible that a process will miss the mailbox alert, because a `BOT` event occurs on its port at the very moment when `NEWITEM` is triggered. To protect itself against this mishap, once it gets to state `Bounce` in response to the `BOT` event, the process examines the `Idle` flag, which once again is used as a semaphore. If `Idle` is `YES`, meaning that the switch has been forced into the idle state while the process was making its last transition, the process moves directly to `Idle`, ignoring the `BOT` event. The event will be taken care of in state `Idle`—as described before.

In state `Bounce`, if the switch has not changed its state to idle, the process transmits the `Noise` packet (a dummy activity) on the output port. But before starting the transfer, the process decrements `NBouncing` by 1 to indicate its temporary absence from the bouncing pool. This way, until the process transmits the packet and enters the `Bouncing` state again, the switch is guaranteed to remain busy. The transmission of the dummy activity is completed in state `NDone` by abort rather than stop—to accentuate the dummy character of the packet.[5]

Now for an easy exercise: what is the purpose of the `if` statement in state `Idle`? Is it possible at all that a process entering the `Idle` state may find the switch busy? Unfortunately, the answer to this question is yes. Although all processes transit from `Bouncing` to `Idle` within the same ITU, they do it in a nondeterministic order. It may thus happen that one process, say P_1, will get to state `Idle`, find the `BOT` event already pending on the input port, and move to `GrabIt` before another process, say P_2, is given the opportunity to enter `Idle` and issue the mailbox wait request. Should this happen, P_2 will not perceive the alert deposited by P_1 and will not know that the switch has been claimed already.[6] The `if` statement is the simplest way to remedy the problem. If a process entering the `Idle` state finds that the switch is not idle any more, this can only mean that a source process has already claimed the switch. In such a case, the process moves directly to state `Relaying`—exactly as it should have in response to the missed mailbox event.

The only fragment of `PortServer`'s code method that has not been discussed yet is the sequence of the last three states. Having notified all the remaining processes about the source packet to be relayed, the source process moves from `GrabIt` to `WaitEOT`, to await the termination of the incoming packet. As the process cannot know whether the packet is complete or aborted, it waits for `ANYEVENT` on the input port. At the same time, the process monitors the `BlockSignal` mailbox, which will receive an alert when the last process of the relaying cohort gets a negative feedback signal from its channel. Should this happen, the process will wake up in state `Blocked`, where it will send a dummy activity up the channel and transit to `NDone`.

---

[5]The transmission could be terminated by `stop` without affecting the protocol behavior.

[6]Note that all mailboxes are capacity-0.

Having received ANYEVENT from its input port, the process transits to state CheckEOT to determine the status of the incoming packet. Depending on whether the transition has been caused by EOT or any other event, the process deposits an alert into StopSignal or AbortSignal. Then it concludes its part by moving to state Bouncing to await the global transition of all processes to state Idle.

11.2.2.4 The host processes.

Two processes are run by each host station: the transmitter and the receiver. The transmitter acquires packets from the Client and transmits them on the output port. While a packet is being transmitted, the process monitors the input port for an incoming activity that will be interpreted as a signal to abort the transfer. Such a situation is treated like a collision in Ethernet (section 8.1.1.3): the transmitter backs off for a randomized period of time depending on the number of times the packet has been blocked and tries again. The type declaration of the transmitter is as follows:

```
process Transmitter (Host) {
  Port *IPort, *OPort;
  TIME TStarted;
  Packet *Buffer;
  TIME backoff ();
  int BlockCount;
  void setup () {
    IPort = S->IPorts [0];
    OPort = S->OPorts [0];
    Buffer = &(S->Buffer);
  };
  states {Acquire, Waiting, XDone, Abort, Quit};
  perform;
};
```

Attributes IPort, OPort, and Buffer are pointers to the corresponding attributes of the host station. TStarted serves the same purpose as RStarted in the port server process (section 11.2.2.3). It is used to determine whether a packet to be aborted has been transmitted long enough to satisfy the shortest activity requirement (MinActTime). Whenever a packet is aborted in consequence of a negative feedback signal arriving from the channel, BlockCount is incremented by 1. This counter is used in the same way as CCounter in Ethernet (section 8.1.2.1), i.e., as the implicit argument of the backoff function. The process executes the following code:

```
Transmitter::perform {
  TIME t;
  state Acquire:
    if (!S->ready (MinPL, MaxPL, FrameL)) {
      Client->wait (ARRIVAL, Acquire);
```

```
      sleep;
    }
    BlockCount = 0;
transient Waiting:
  if (IPort->busy ()) {
    IPort->wait (SILENCE, Waiting);
    sleep;
  }
  if (OPort->busy ()) {
    OPort->wait (SILENCE, Waiting);
    sleep;
  }
  TStarted = Time;
  OPort->transmit (Buffer, XDone);
  IPort->wait (ACTIVITY, Abort);
state XDone:
  OPort->stop ();
  Buffer->release ();
  Timer->wait (PSpace, Acquire);
state Abort:
  if ((t = Time - TStarted) < MinActTime) {
    Timer->wait (MinActTime - t, Quit);
    sleep;
  }
transient Quit:
  OPort->abort ();
  BlockCount++;
  Timer->wait (PSpace + backoff (), Waiting);
};
```

Having acquired a packet from the Client, the transmitter resets BlockCount to zero and falls through from Acquire to Waiting. Then it checks whether both ports are silent, i.e., the channel is idle. Clearly, the process should not start a transfer if an activity is currently arriving on the input port. First, the incoming activity is already a negative feedback signal, so the transfer would have to be aborted immediately. Second, the transfer could be interpreted as a negative feedback signal by the sender of the incoming activity. The transmitter also checks the output port. As we will see, upon the reception of a packet addressed to another host, the receiver process uses the output port to send a negative feedback signal up the channel. By checking the port status before transmission, the processes make sure that only one of them gets hold of the port at a time.

The transmitter loops in state Waiting until both ports are idle, and then it inserts the Client's packet into the output port. The starting time of the transmission is saved in TStarted. While the packet is transmitted, the process awaits an activity on the input port. If the packet has been transmitted without problems, the transmitter wakes up in state XDone, where it stops the transfer and releases the packet buffer. Then the transmitter moves back to its initial state, Acquire, but delays this transition by PSpace ITUs. This way, the process makes sure that at least PSpace ITUs of silence will separate two consecutive packets transmitted by the host.

If the transmission is interrupted by an activity on the input port, the process transits to state Abort, where it checks whether the transmitted portion of the packet is shorter than MinActTime. If so, the transfer continues until its duration (measured from TStarted) reaches MinActTime; otherwise, the transmitter moves directly to Quit. Then the process aborts the transmission, increments BlockCount by 1, and goes to sleep for the amount of time determined by the backoff function. The value returned by backoff is augmented by PSpace; thus, the minimum waiting time before a retransmission attempt in state Waiting is PSpace ITUs.

The right shape of the backoff function for Floodnet is difficult to guess. The frequency and destructiveness of collisions, or rather blocking scenarios, depend on the network geometry and traffic distribution. It is rather obvious that an exponential backoff function (e.g., borrowed from Ethernet—section 8.1.1.3) would be an overkill; therefore, we have decided on the following simple linear formula:

```
TIME Transmitter::backoff () {
    return toss (BlockCount) * FloodTime;
};
```

The resultant delay is an integer multiple of FloodTime—the round-trip propagation time through the entire network—drawn from a uniform distribution. The actual multiplier is between 0 and BlockTime − 1, inclusively. Thus, when a packet is blocked for the first time, the backoff function returns zero and the retransmission delay is just PSpace. Of course, this does not mean that the host will actually try to retransmit the packet that soon (the channel may remain busy for some time).

11.2.2.5   A sample Floodnet.   Being a mesh network, Floodnet does not restrict the geometry of its implementations in the same way as, for instance, Ethernet, FDDI, or DQDB. Therefore, we have decided to treat the protocol specification of Floodnet (sections 11.2.2.2, 11.2.2.3, 11.2.2.4) as a library module. This module consists of two files: floodswitch.h, containing the declarations of station and process types, and floodswitch.c, defining the process code methods and the global variables representing protocol parameters. The two files have been put into IncludeLibrary. They #include the respective files of the mesh module (section 11.2.2.1) and are this way self-contained.

Directory SWITCH/FloodTorus of SMURPH Examples contains a sample implementation of Floodnet. As the protocol is completely described elsewhere (in the library files floodswitch.h and floodswitch.c), the program only consists of the root process and the incidence function (section 11.2.2.1) describing the network geometry. Both items have been put into file root.c, which begins with the following two lines:

```
#include "utraffic.c"
#include "floodswitch.c"
```

Consequently, our implementation makes use of the simple uniform traffic pattern introduced in sections 8.1.2.3 and 8.1.2.4.[7] File `floodswitch.c` includes `floodswitch.h`, `mesh.h`, and `mesh.c` from `IncludeLibrary`; thus, the program sets to work all the pieces that we presented in sections 11.2.2.1–11.2.2.4.

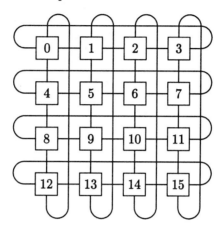

Figure 11.5 A torus network

The incidence function describes a two-dimensional torus topology, shown in figure 11.5 for sixteen stations. Each switch is connected to four neighbors and the network is symmetric with respect to the switch location. By definition of Floodnet, each channel between a pair of neighboring switches is a pair of unidirectional links going in opposite directions. The number of switches to form a complete symmetric torus must be a square.

Before we discuss the incidence function, let us look at the complete definition of the root process, together with four global variables set by the process and used by the incidence function:

```
static DISTANCE SwitchLinkLength, HostLinkLength;
static int NSwitches;
static int D;
process Root {
  states {Start, Stop};
  perform {
    int i, j;
    Long NMessages;
```

---

[7]Note that `utraffic.c` includes `utraffic.h`.

```
    double CTolerance;
    state Start:
      readIn (TRate);
      setEtu (TRate);
      readIn (CTolerance);
      setTolerance (CTolerance);
      readIn (NSwitches);
      for (D = 1; D * D < NSwitches; D++);
      Assert (D * D == NSwitches,
        "The number of switches must be a square");
      readIn (SwitchLinkLength);
      SwitchLinkLength *= TRate;
      readIn (HostLinkLength);
      HostLinkLength *= TRate;
      initMesh (TRate, Connected, NSwitches + NSwitches);
      readIn (MinPL);
      readIn (MaxPL);
      readIn (FrameL);
      readIn (RcvRecDelay);
      RcvRecDelay *= TRate;
      readIn (PSpace);
      PSpace *= TRate;
      readIn (NoiseL);
      readIn (MinActTime);
      readIn (FloodTime);
      MinActTime *= TRate;
      FloodTime *= TRate;
      initTraffic ();
      for (i = 0; i < NSwitches; i++) create Switch (5);
      for (i = 0; i < NSwitches; i++) create Host;
      for (i = 0; i < NSwitches; i++)
        for (j = 0; j < 5; j++)
          create (i) PortServer (j);
      for (i = NSwitches; i < NSwitches + NSwitches; i++) {
        create (i) Receiver;
        create (i) Transmitter;
      }
      readIn (NMessages);
      setLimit (NMessages);
      Kernel->wait (DEATH, Stop);
    state Stop:
      System->printTop ("Network topology");
      Client->printDef ("Traffic parameters");
      Client->printPfm ();
```

```
  };
};
```

The only nontrivial fragment of the root process is a portion of the code method in state **Start**. The first two values read by the process from the input file are the transmission rate (common for all output ports) and the tolerance of clocks (section 4.5.2). The experimenter time unit (ETU—section 2.2.2) is set to the transmission rate; as usual, the time used to interpret traffic parameters and display the standard performance measures will be expressed in bits.

The third input number is the number of switches in the network (**NSwitches**). The process verifies that this number is a square and stores the square root of **NSwitches** in D. Thus, D gives the number of rows and columns in the torus. We assume that each switch has a host station connected to it. Consequently, the total number of stations in the network (**NStations**) will be a double square, e.g., 8, 18, 32, 50, 72, and so on. Given a switch **Id**, the **Id** of the host connected to this switch is obtained by adding **NSwitches** to the switch **Id**.

The total number of channels attached to a switch is five: four channels interface the switch to its torus neighbors and the fifth channel connects the switch to its host. The next two numbers read from input give the length of an interswitch channel and the length of a switch-to-host channel, respectively. The program assumes that these lengths are specified in bits and converts them to ITUs.

The call to **initMesh** specifies **Connected** as the incidence function. The function will be used by **buildMesh** no sooner than after the last station has been created (section 11.2.2.1). This will happen in the last turn of the second **for** loop following the call to **initTraffic**.

The rest of the root code is rather straightforward. The variables set between the call to **initMesh** and the **for** loops are numerical parameters of the protocol, and they were all discussed in sections 11.2.2.2–11.2.2.4. The setup argument of a switch station (section 11.2.2.2) specifies the switch connectivity (the **Order** attribute—section 11.2.2.1). This is also the number of copies of the port server process (section 11.2.2.3) running at a single switch. The setup argument of a port server identifies the channel serviced by the process.

The only piece missing from our program is the following incidence function:

```
int Connected (Long a, Long b, DISTANCE &d) {
  Long ra, ca, rb, cb;
  if (a < NSwitches && b < NSwitches) {
    d = SwitchLinkLength;
    ra = a / D; ca = a % D;
    rb = b / D; cb = b % D;
    if (ra == rb) {
      if ((ca -= cb) < 0) ca = -ca;
      return ca == 1 || ca == D - 1;
    } else if (ca == cb) {
      if ((ra -= rb) < 0) ra = -ra;
```

```
                    return ra == 1 || ra == D - 1;
                } else
                    return 0;
            } else {
                d = HostLinkLength;
                return a == b + NSwitches || b == a + NSwitches;
            }
        }
```

When the function is called, the first two arguments identify a potential pair of stations to be connected by a unidirectional link (section 11.2.2.1). As every two stations in our network are connected by at most one duplex channel, the function returns 1 if there is a link from switch a to switch b, and 0 otherwise. In the former case, the link length must be stored in d.

If both stations are switches (the if condition holds), d is set in advance to SwitchLinkLength and the function calculates the row and column positions of a and b. Assuming that the switches are numbered by rows, the row number of a switch is obtained by dividing its Id by D and taking the integer part of the result. Similarly, the column number can be determined by taking the switch Id modulo D. The if statements following these calculations check if the two switches are neighbors. This happens when they share a row or a column and are located one hop apart along the other coordinate. The second part of the condition is a bit tricky owing to the wraparound property of the torus.

If at least one Id identifies a host, the function checks whether one Id can be obtained from another by adding NSwitches to it. This means that one station (the one with the lower Id) is a switch and the other is the host connected to the switch. The link length stored in d in that case is HostLinkLength.

The incidence function assumes that all links of the same type are of the same length. Of course, the reader is free to try other ideas. For example, it is possible to randomize link lengths using the input parameters as the mean values. With this approach it may be reasonable to store the generated lengths in an array to make sure that they are the same in both directions.

11.3 THE MANHATTAN STREET NETWORK

Although Floodnet attempts to contain the amount of network resources needed to sustain a single transmission to the path from the sender to the destination, the operation of negotiating these resources takes an amount of time proportional to the network diameter. During that time, the entire network is filled with the packet, which must be significantly longer than $2L$ if the benefits of the resource containment during the post-flooding stage of the transmission are to be observable. Thus, although Floodnet is an interesting case study, its properties hardly make it competitive in modern real-life applications. An approach that does not require short packets to be inflated to twice the flooding time of the network has much better chances for finding applications in a high-performance environment.

Having completed transmitting a (possibly short) packet, a sending station would like to believe that the intermediate switches will successfully relay the packet to the destination using a reasonable fraction of network resources. To implement this idea, we have to equip the switches with more wisdom than the simple feedback capability of a Floodnet switch. A packet arriving at a switch should be looked at and, based on its destination, relayed on the appropriate output channel with the intention of moving it closer to the recipient. Ideally, the switch should relay each incoming packet on the best output channel, i.e., the channel that offers the shortest path to the destination. One can list several problems with this obvious idea:

- There may be a continuous supply of packets (from several input channels) that should be relayed via the same output channel. Thus, the switch must buffer the incoming packets that cannot be relayed immediately. No safe limit on the length of the buffer can be explicitly imposed and, unless some special steps are taken, packets can be lost.

- Persisting biases in the traffic pattern will tend to overutilize some regions of the network and leave other regions underutilized. In some cases, a packet might be able to reach the destination faster via an alternative (and apparently not best) route, because the best route happens to be congested.

- To be able to route packets optimally, each switch must have complete knowledge of the network geometry. This knowledge may be difficult to maintain, especially if the network undergoes frequent reconfigurations.

The first two problems are typically solved by taking advantage of alternative routes and employing backpressure mechanisms to reduce the rate of incoming packets when the buffer space becomes short. The backpressure mechanisms are usually based on sending explicit signals to the neighbors (via backward links) notifying them when they should decrease or increase the rate at which packets are being sent. With the most complex network layer protocols for wide area networks, each switch (*node*) maintains a dynamically updated database including the routing tables, i.e., the ranked lists of output channels for each destination, the congestion status of the neighbors, and some statistical data describing measured packet delivery time along different routes. Special status report packets are passed among the switches to keep their databases up to date.

The third problem can be eliminated or alleviated in two ways. If the network is regular and the stations obey some addressing rules, it may be possible to obtain the routing information by comparing the destination address with the address of the current switch. If the network is not regular but is large, the exact routing information for distant destinations may be unnecessary. Instead, without much impact on the protocol performance, the switch may route all packets addressed to a distant cluster of stations (a domain) treating the entire cluster as a single station. This way, the amount of routing information kept at a switch can be greatly reduced.

In local and metropolitan area networks, one favors simple solutions that take advantage of the uniformity, regularity, and high reliability of the network backbone. The Manhattan Street Network (MSN) is an example of a high-performance switched network with an uncomplicated uniform architecture driven by a simple protocol described by a collection of localized routing rules. The amount of routing information kept at a single switch is very limited and independent of the network size.

11.3.1   The Network Architecture

Imagine a rectangular array of stations interconnected via unidirectional point-to-point links, as shown in figure 11.6. The edges of the rectangle are wrapped up, as in the torus configuration of Floodnet discussed in section 11.2.2.5. Unlike the Floodnet torus, the MSN grid is built of unidirectional connections. Their structure resembles the layout of one-way streets and avenues in Manhattan. It is assumed that both the number of rows (streets) and the number of columns (avenues) are even, although these numbers can be different (i.e., the rectangle does not have to be a square).

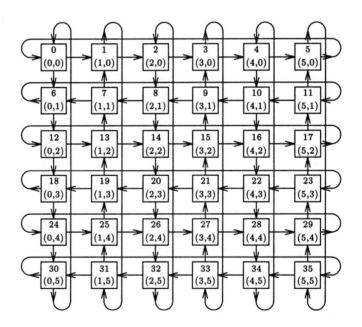

Figure 11.6 A 6 × 6 Manhattan Street Network

MSN operates in a slotted fashion. At approximately fixed intervals each station emits a pair of slot markers on both its output ports. Each of the two slots may be empty, or it may carry a segment. A segment inserted by a station within the payload window of an outgoing slot may be a copy of an incoming segment (which is relayed by the station on its way to the destination), or it may be the station's own segment. It is possible that only a subset of stations generate own traffic while the other stations are just switches that relay segments arriving from the network. In principle, any station can insert its own segments into the network, and both the network geometry and protocol rules are indifferent to the station location.

A segment arriving at an input port of a station either is addressed to the station or must be relayed on one of the two output ports. In the latter case, based on the destination address in the segment header, the station determines the preferred output port for the segment and attempts to relay the segment on its preferred port. Because of the slotted nature of the protocol, the station operates in cycles, one cycle resulting in the insertion of a pair of slots into the output channels. A pair of slots arriving at the two input ports is aligned in such a way that both incoming slots are available when the station is about to issue a pair of outgoing slots. Thus, in one cycle, the station absorbs two input slots, determines their preferred output channels, and relays the slots on the output ports attempting to fulfill their preferences. Assume that the station does not generate its own traffic. The following scenarios are then possible:

- Both incoming slots are empty. In such a case, the station emits two empty slots. Clearly, no routing decisions are needed.

- One incoming slot is empty and the other slot is full. The segment carried by the full slot is retransmitted on the preferred output port, the other slot emitted by the station is empty.

- Both incoming slots are full, but their segments choose different preferred output channels. In such a case, both segments are retransmitted on their preferred channels.

- Both incoming slots are full and their segments bid for the same preferred output channel. In this scenario, one incoming segment is relayed via its preferred link and the other is *deflected*, i.e., relayed via the other channel.

The exact routing rules are presented in the next section. Several versions of these rules are possible, but they all assume the same general guidelines. A routing scheme operating according to these guidelines is called *deflection routing*.

A station having its own segment to transmit awaits a cycle in which at least one incoming slot is empty. Then the station substitutes its own segment for the empty slot and proceeds as if the segment had just arrived from the network. Note that the station can transmit two own segments in one cycle if both incoming slots happen to be empty.

The intention of deflection routing is to avoid buffering transient packets at intermediate stations. The role of the buffer is played by the entire network, which automatically reroutes packets via alternative paths if their preferred paths are unavailable. As each station has the same number of input and output ports, no segments are ever lost, as long as all stations are operable.

One tricky problem with MSN is the alignment of incoming slots at the beginning of a routing cycle. Generally, different stations may generate slots at slightly different rates, which may result in two possible mismatch scenarios:

- The incoming slots are (or one of the incoming slots is) not available when the station is about to emit the next pair of output slots.
- The incoming slots arrive faster than the station is able to retransmit them on the output ports.

One can think of several methods of coping with these problems. The most refined solutions employ backpressure signals sent to the upstream neighbors via special backward links. If the clock rates at different stations are not excessively out of line, one can get away with elastic *alignment buffers* attached to the input ports. Note that such buffers are needed, even if all clocks are perfect, for two reasons:

- Even if all slots are issued at very regular intervals, the beginnings of slots at different input ports may show up at different moments, the maximum difference being the slot length.
- At least a portion of an incoming segment must be buffered before the segment can be relayed. This is needed because the station must recognize the recipient address in the segment header and perform some calculations to determine the preferred output port for the segment.

With the proposed solution, each input port is connected to one end of an elastic buffer that absorbs slots arriving from the network. These slots can be extracted from the other end of the buffer as they are needed. It is assumed that the extraction rate will approximately match the arrival rate.

Having emitted a pair of slots on the output ports, the station waits until a pair of incoming slots is available. This means that both input buffers are nonempty and each of them contains a sufficient fragment of a segment to decode its destination and determine its preferred output port. If the buffers are not in this state when the station is ready to issue a new pair of outgoing slots, the station delays the slot generation until both incoming slots are handy. This way, the slot generation rate of the station is synchronized to the slot arrival rate from the network. The network is filled with slot markers during the initialization phase and, once this phase is over, the number of slots in the network does not change. Thus, regardless of the clock tolerance at different stations, the amount of input buffer space can be limited. This amount can be further reduced by introducing flexible slot spacing, along the lines suggested in section 10.4.3 for unslotted Metaring.

During the initialization phase, each station executes its normal protocol with an additional pair of processes hooked up to the input ports. Each such process generates empty slots at the normal slot arrival rate and inserts them into the input buffer of the port associated with the process. These slots are extracted from the other end of the buffer, according to the mechanism described previously. The procedure stops, and the startup process terminates itself, as soon as it detects a slot marker on the input port. The last slot generated by the process may partially overlap with the slot arriving from the network; in such a case, the overlapping portion will be stored in the buffer. Note that the same technique can be used to recover from lost slot markers, e.g., after a temporary malfunction of a station. A station failing to detect a slot marker on one of its input ports after a certain timeout may summon the startup process to supply empty slots until the channel resumes normal slot delivery from the network.

11.3.2   The Routing Rules

The Manhattan Street Network forms a regular directed graph. Ignoring the possible differences in the propagation lengths of particular links, we measure the cost of the path traveled by a segment on its way to the destination by the number of hops, i.e., different links constituting this path. For any intermediate station visited by the segment, one can determine the shortest possible path from that station to the destination. The output port offering this path is the segment's preferred port. In many cases, the same-length shortest path is available via both output ports; then the segment can be relayed on both ports with the same opportunities. For each MSN configuration, port preferences can be precomputed and stored at stations as static arrays. Such an array may have N entries, corresponding to N stations in the network, each entry indicating the preferred port for a given destination.[8] In section 11.3.4.7 we show how this can be done using the well-known all-shortest-paths algorithm by Floyd (see Bibliographic Notes at the end of this chapter).

The regular structure of MSN makes it possible to determine the preferred port locally, by comparing the destination address with the address of the station making the routing decision. We show a localized algorithm for selecting the preferred port that produces the same results as the all-shortest-paths method based on global knowledge. One disadvantage of the local algorithm is its high "static complexity" manifested in the large number of conditions that must be checked to produce the answer. This number can be reduced by making the rules simpler and less accurate. The simplification can be carried out in a number of ways exhibiting a trade-off between complexity and accuracy. Another disadvantage of the localized rules is their dependence on the regular structure of the network. In real-life applications, it is unrealistic to assume that the number of stations in MSN will be always rectangular with an even number of rows and columns. The global method of ranking the output ports of a routing station works for any graph, in particular, for a degenerate MSN in which some rows, columns, or just individual stations are missing. Although there exist localized algorithms for incomplete MSN configurations, they are only approximate, which means that in some cases the relayed segment may be directed through a suboptimal path.

---

[8]The careful reader has noticed that only $N - 1$ entries are needed, as the current station cannot be a legitimate destination for any routing decision. However, to simplify indexing, one would be inclined to ignore this saving.

The localized algorithm discussed here only works for complete regular configurations of MSN.[9] Assume that the number of stations N is equal to $N_c \times N_r$, where N_c is the number of columns and N_r is the number of rows. Both N_c and N_r are even. The stations are numbered by rows, as shown in figure 11.6. A station address i can be converted to a pair of coordinates $[c(i), r(i)]$, representing the column and row positions of the station in the rectangle, in the following way:

$$c(i) = i \bmod N_c \, ,$$
$$r(i) = \lfloor i/N_c \rfloor \, .$$

Similarly, given a pair of coordinates $[c, r]$ representing a station location in the network, the station address can be obtained as follows:

$$i = r(i) \times N_c + c(i) \, .$$

With this simple transformation, we assume that the row/column coordinate pairs offer a natural alternative way of identifying stations.

Suppose that a station $[c, r]$ relays a segment addressed to another station $[c_d, r_d]$. The problem of deciding which of the two ports of the relaying station is preferred can be presented in a canonical form that depends on the location of the relaying station with respect to the destination but not on the absolute locations of the two stations in the network rectangle.

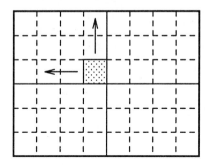

Figure 11.7   The canonical location of the destination.   (Adapted with permission from *Maxemchuk* (1987), © 1987 IEEE)

We transform the network rectangle in such a way that the destination station is located in the center, as shown in figure 11.7. Actually, as the numbers of columns and rows are even, the destination cannot be located exactly in the center; thus, we assume that the central station is positioned above and to the left of the geometric center of the rectangle. Moreover, we postulate a specific orientation of the column and row of the central station, namely, up and left. The station is assigned coordinates $[0, 0]$; the coordinates of the remaining stations are determined by the natural

[9]In Bibliographic Notes at the end of this chapter, the reader will find references to approximate algorithms for irregular configurations.

order from left to right and from top to bottom. In particular, both coordinates of a station located above and to the left of the central station are negative. For example, figure 11.8 shows the transformed network from figure 11.6, assuming that the destination station has coordinates [3, 4] in the original grid. The numbers in round parentheses give the original coordinates, and the numbers in square brackets show their transformed versions.

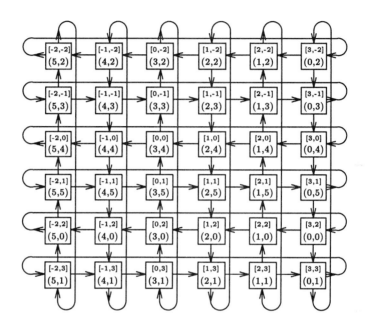

Figure 11.8 The 6 × 6 Manhattan Street Network after coordinate transformation

The reader will find it an easy exercise to verify that the transformation described above is defined formally by the following formulas:

$$c_t = \frac{N_c}{2} - \left(\frac{3N_c}{2} + \delta(r_d) \times (c_d - c)\right) \bmod N_c ,$$

$$r_t = \frac{N_r}{2} - \left(\frac{3N_r}{2} + \delta(c_d) \times (r_d - r)\right) \bmod N_r ,$$

where

$$
\begin{aligned}
[c_d, r_d] \quad &= \quad \text{original coordinates of the destination,} \\
[c, r] \quad &= \quad \text{original coordinates to be transformed,} \\
[c_t, r_t] \quad &= \quad \text{transformed coordinates,} \\
\delta(k) \quad &= \quad +1 \text{ if } k \text{ is odd, and } -1 \text{ otherwise.}
\end{aligned}
$$

The factor δ is needed to reverse the orientation of the row and column if the transformed orientation of the destination's row/column is different from the original orientation. The transformation formulas assume that the original orientation of row zero and column zero is right and down, respectively.

In its canonical form, the problem of selecting the preferred output link for a segment addressed to the centrally located destination is illustrated graphically in figure 11.9. The arrows indicate the preferred directions that offer the shortest possible paths to the destination. In many cases, two or more directions are preferred. From two stations (the left top and right bottom corners), the segment can be relayed in any direction and always gets closer to the destination.[10] If from a given station the segment can be relayed in two of the preferred directions, both output ports have the same preference. Similarly, if neither output channel goes in a preferred direction, both output ports offer the same opportunities, and they are deemed equally preferred.

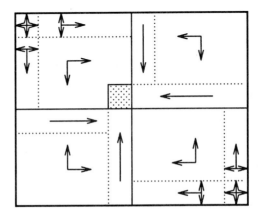

Figure 11.9   Direction preference in the canonical routing problem. (Adapted with permission from *Maxemchuk* (1987), © 1987 IEEE)

It can be shown formally that the preference arrows in figure 11.9 always indicate the best possible routes to the destination and that they exhaust all the possibilities of such routes. In other words, a station following the prescription imprinted in figure 11.9 is able to make the same quality routing decisions as a station using preference tables based on the global knowledge of all-pairs shortest paths.

The actual algorithm executed by a routing station to determine the preference of its output ports can be outlined in the following points:

1. The station decodes the destination address of the segment to be relayed and, based on this address, transforms its own address to the canonical form.

2. The station determines its location in the diagram shown in figure 11.9 and the preferred relay directions.

---

[10]Note that in any specific configuration only two arrows per station are actually applicable. For the two corner stations, these effective arrows have opposite orientations.

3. The station examines its two output ports and for each port it checks whether the output channel connected to the port goes in one of the preferred directions. If so, the port is marked "preferred"; otherwise, it is marked "not preferred."

The last step is a bit tricky. To be able to tell the direction of its output channels in the transformed network, the station must know the transformed coordinates of its neighbors reachable via these channels. Thus, for each segment to be relayed, the station must perform three transformations and test a number of conditions to locate its region in the routing diagram.

In general, the routing problem deals with two segments that must be relayed simultaneously. The routing rules are randomized to explore statistically all alternative routes that offer the same opportunities to the relayed segments. Specifically, these rules are as follows:

- If there is only one segment to be relayed, the segment is relayed via the port with the higher preference. If both ports have the same preference, one of them is chosen at random.
- If there are two segments and neither of them prefers exactly one of the two ports, the segments are relayed at random.
- If there are two segments and both prefer exactly one same output port, the segments are relayed at random. Note that this way one of the two segments will follow its preferred route and the other will be deflected.
- If there are two segments, one of them preferring a single output port and the other without a preference, the first segment is relayed on its preferred port and the other segment is relayed on the other port.

It has been demonstrated (see Bibliographic Notes) that the routing rules must be randomized to avoid so-called *live-locks*, i.e., situations when segments are deflected indefinitely, via the same circular paths, without a chance of ever reaching their destinations.

11.3.3   Problems with the Manhattan Street Network

One common problem shared by all deflection networks, including MSN, is the possibility that segments belonging to the same message can be shuffled on their way to the destination. As different segments may take different routes (with different numbers of hops), they may arrive at the destination in an order that differs from the order in which they were originally sent. Consequently, the destination must use a reassembly buffer if the segments belong to a stream-type traffic in which the preservation of packet ordering is essential.

Manhattan Street Networks are also starvation-prone, although owing to the regular station-symmetric topology, they are not explicitly unfair. A station in MSN can only transmit its own segment in a routing cycle in which at least one incoming slot is empty. The supply of empty slots arriving at a station is controlled by its upstream neighbors; if these neighbors fill all their outgoing slots, the station will wait forever. Feedback-based backpressure mechanisms have been proposed to avoid starvation in MSN, but they are contrary to the spirit of high-speed networking, where bandwidth negotiation across the network should be avoided at all cost.

The localized routing algorithm is quite complicated and requires several calculation steps involving multiplication and division. The complexity of the routing algorithm is critical, because it determines the amount of the hallway buffer space needed to accommodate an initial portion of the incoming segment while its fate is being determined. One can think of several ways of reducing the computation time by using lookup tables of size proportional to N. For example, the values produced by the two transformation formulas can be precomputed for all possible configurations of arguments and stored in four lookup tables with $2 \times (N_r^2 + N_c^2)$ entries. With this solution, however, the advantages of the local approach will practically disappear. With much less lookup storage (N two-bit entries per station),[11] each station can store precomputed port preferences for all possible destinations. It may make sense to precompute these preferences with the localized algorithm, but it seems more reasonable to use the all-shortest-paths approach based on the global knowledge of the network geometry. With the latter solution, the network can be irregular (it need not even resemble a torus) and the routing algorithm will still be optimal and efficient. Note that the postulate of locality of the routing algorithm is very difficult to fulfill in any real network, even if its actual geometry happens to be perfectly regular. Generally, it is unreasonable to expect that station addresses are consecutive integer numbers nicely arranged by the rows of the MSN rectangle. Thus, to make sense of the network regularity, the stations will have to be able to convert absolute (and possibly irregular) station addresses into their coordinates in the MSN grid. The only feasible way of implementing this conversion is to use an address table of size N. The cost of adding two additional bits to each entry in this table seems rather insignificant compared to the complexity of the localized routing algorithm. It would be an interesting exercise to devise a distributed procedure for calculating the all-shortest-paths preferences on the fly. With this solution, the network might start with a rough approximation of the optimal preferences and refine them dynamically as the stations acquire more knowledge about the actual geometry of the network.

11.3.4   The Implementation

We discuss two SMURPH programs modeling regular MSN configurations. The two programs are identical, except for the part of the routing algorithm that determines the preference of the output ports. In the first implementation (directory SWITCH/Manhattan1), the output ports are ranked based on the localized approach that consists in converting the routing problem to its canonical form and then applying the diagram from figure 11.9. The routing algorithm in the second program (di-

---

[11] Two bits are required, because three different preference values are needed: two to indicate a preference of one specific port, and a third to say that both ports are equally preferred.

rectory SWITCH/Manhattan2), uses precomputed lookup tables that tell directly the port preference for each routing station and each possible destination. The lookup tables are filled in before the protocol is started, according to the all-shortest-paths information extracted from the network graph.

11.3.4.1 The traffic pattern. Our implementation of MSN uses a variation of the uniform traffic pattern with two packet buffers per station. The two buffers are needed, because a single station can transmit two segments in one slot generation cycle, if both slots arriving from the network happen to be empty. One could easily adopt for our present program the uniform traffic pattern introduced in section 9.3.2.2 (files utraffic2.h and utraffic2.c) by overwriting its default qualifier function (section 10.5.2.2) with a trivial qualifier returning always YES. This way the direction attributes of the buffers would be ignored and the buffers would become equivalent, i.e., each of them could accommodate any segment, regardless of its destination.

It so happens, however, that need a uniform traffic pattern with n equivalent buffers per station (section 11.4.3). Therefore, we may as well introduce that traffic pattern here and notice that two is a special case of n.

The traffic pattern in question is described in files utrafficn.h and utrafficn.c in IncludeLibrary. It assumes that the number of buffers per station is flexible, in particular, different stations may have different numbers of buffers. The ClientInterface portion of a station is described in file utrafficn.h by the following virtual station type:

```
station ClientInterface virtual {
  Packet **Buffer;
  Boolean ready (int, Long, Long, Long);
  void configure (int);
};
```

As the number of packet buffers is not known a priori, the buffers are represented as a dynamically created array of pointers to packet buffers.[12] The buffers, as well as the array itself, will be created by the configure method of ClientInterface, whose argument specifies the actual number of buffers for the particular station. The first argument of the ready method identifies the packet buffer via its number, which must be between zero (inclusively) and the value that was passed to configure (exclusively). The remaining arguments of ready have the standard meaning (e.g., section 8.1.2.4).

---

[12]The reader may wonder why we use an array of pointers to packet buffers rather than an array of packet buffers. As we remember from section 5.2.3, a packet buffer can only be declared statically (within a station structure) or created dynamically by the create operator. It is thus illegal to have a dynamically created array of packet buffers. There is simply no way to force such buffers to be built by create when the array comes into existence. On the other hand, static arrays of packet buffers declared as station attributes are perfectly legitimate, but unfortunately we do not know the number of buffers in advance.

The two methods of `ClientInterface` are defined in file `utrafficn.c`. This file also defines the global function `initTraffic`, which is used by the root process to initialize the traffic pattern. The complete contents of `utrafficn.c` are as follows:

```
static Traffic *UTP;
void initTraffic () {
  double mit, mle;
  readIn (mit);
  readIn (mle);
  UTP = create Traffic (MIT_exp+MLE_exp, mit, mle);
};
void ClientInterface::configure (int nb) {
  int i;
  Buffer = new Packet* [nb];
  for (i = 0; i < nb; i++) Buffer [i] = create Packet;
  UTP->addSender (TheStation);
  UTP->addReceiver (TheStation);
};
Boolean ClientInterface::ready (int b, Long mn, Long mx, Long fm) {
  return Buffer [b] -> isFull () ||
    Client->getPacket (Buffer [b], mn, mx, fm);
};
```

There is hardly anything to explain in this code, which is a straightforward modification of the code from `utraffic.c` (section 8.1.2.4). One can make a simple observation that the single-buffer traffic pattern described in files `utraffic.h` and `utraffic.c` is a special case of our new traffic pattern (nb = 1 for all stations).

11.3.4.2   Global parameters and data types.   We start our presentation from the local implementation of MSN, which uses the transformation-based localized routing rules introduced in section 11.3.2. MSN operates in a slotted fashion with the slot structure described in the same way as in Fasnet (section 9.3.1), by the following global values announced in file `types.h` of the program:

```
Long SlotML, SegmPL, SegmFL;
TIME SegmWindow;
```

`SlotML` gives the length of the slot marker, `SegmPL` specifies the length of the segment payload area, and `SegmFL` tells the combined length of the segment header and trailer (the frame information). When slot markers are inserted into a channel, the time duration of the gap separating the beginning of a slot marker from the end of the previous marker is at least equal to `SegmWindow`. Thus, the sum of `SegmPL` and `SegmFL` expressed in ITUs (i.e., multiplied by the network transmission rate) must be less than `SegmWindow`.

As in Fasnet, slot markers are modeled by special packets with the type attribute (TP) equal to `NONE` (section 9.3.2.3). The symbolic constant

```
#define SLOT NONE
```

represents symbolically the value of the TP attribute of a slot marker. The MSN protocol needs only one flag in the slot marker—to tell the full/empty status of the slot. The role of this flag is played by one of the `Flags` bits (section 5.2.2) of the marker packet. One more symbolic constant,

```
#define FULL PF_usr0
```

provides a convenient alias for the location of this flag in the `Flags` attribute of the marker.

To be able to carry out their routing duties, all stations must know the shape of the network rectangle, namely, the number of columns and rows. These parameters are stored by the root process in the following global variables:

```
Long NCols, NRows, NCols05, NRows05, NCols15, NRows15;
```

Besides the number of columns and rows (`NCols` and `NRows`), the list includes the precomputed halves of these values (`NCols05` and `NRows05`) and 3/2 of them (`NCols15` and `NRows15`). A quick look at the transformation formulas in section 11.3.2 explains why all these values are useful. The last global parameter of the protocol, represented by variable `TRate` of type `TIME`, is the common transmission rate of all output ports.

The following macrooperations offer shortcuts for a few simple arithmetic operations used by the transformation procedure:

```
#define col(n)  ((n) % NCols)
#define row(n)  ((n) / NCols)
#define odd(n)  ((n) & 1)
#define evn(n)  (!odd (n))
```

The first two macros decode the column and row number from a station address (the `Id` attribute). The remaining two operations are predicates telling whether the argument (interpreted as an integer number) is odd or even.

All stations in MSN are of the same type. In our program, we assume that every station is interfaced to the `Client` (section 11.3.4.1) and, besides relaying incoming segments, is able to contribute its own segments to the network traffic. The station type is as follows:

```
station MStation : MeshNode, ClientInterface {
  DBuffer *DB [2];
  Packet SMarker;
  void setup () {
    int i;
    MeshNode::configure (2);
    ClientInterface::configure (2);
    for (i = 0; i < 2; i++) DB [i] = create DBuffer (MAX_long);
```

```
        SMarker.fill (NONE, NONE, SlotML);
    };
};
```

Type DBuffer is declared as

```
                mailbox DBuffer (Packet*);
```

and represents the elastic buffer used to align the slots arriving on the two input
ports, to make them appear as if they had arrived at the same time. In contrast to
a similar mailbox type introduced in section 10.6.3.2, the present mailbox has no
outItem method that would automatically deallocate the packet structure pointed
to by the retrieved pointer. Clearly, whoever extracts packets from the mailbox is
responsible for deallocating them explicitly. Attribute SMarker is a special packet
representing the slot marker. The contents of this packet are filled by the station's
setup method.

The geometry part of the implementation is based on the mesh module introduced in section 11.2.2.1 (files mesh.h and mesh.c). The argument of configure
for MeshNode is 2, which means that the station has two input and two output ports.
The way these ports are connected to the network is determined by the incidence
function (section 11.3.4.6).

11.3.4.3 The input processes and slot generators.

Each station runs two
input processes extracting incoming slots from the input ports and inserting them
into the alignment buffers, and one relay process that retransmits the slots on the
output ports. During the initialization phase, each station runs two additional
processes that generate empty slots and deposit them in the mailboxes representing
the alignment buffers. Each of the slot generators disappears as soon as the input
port connected to the alignment buffer serviced by the process becomes active. From
then on, the slots arrive from the network and there is no need to generate them
explicitly. The role of the slot generator is then taken over by the corresponding
input process.

As the role of a slot generator is similar to the role of an input process, the
two processes also look very similar. Let us start with the slot generator, whose
type declaration is as follows:

```
                process SlotGen (MStation) {
                  DBuffer *DB;
                  Port *IPort;
                  Packet *SMarker;
                  void setup (int d) {
                    DB = S->DB [d];
                    IPort = S->IPorts [d];
                    SMarker = &(S->SMarker);
                  };
                  states {GenSlot, Exit};
```

```
    perform;
  };
```

All three local attributes of the process are pointers to the corresponding station attributes. The process services one alignment buffer (pointed to by DB) and listens to the input port associated with that buffer. The index of the buffer, and of the associated input port, is passed to the process's setup method when the slot generator is created. The process executes the following code:

```
SlotGen::perform {
  Packet *pk;
  state GenSlot:
    clearFlag (SMarker -> Flags, FULL);
    pk = create Packet;
    *pk = *SMarker;
    DB->put (pk);
    Timer->wait (SegmWindow + (SMarker->TLength) * TRate, GenSlot);
    IPort->wait (BOT, Exit);
  state Exit:
    terminate;
};
```

The slot generator loops through its initial state GenSlot until it senses a BOT event on the input port. Then the process moves to state Exit, where it terminates itself. In state GenSlot, the process creates a packet, fills it with the image of an empty slot, and deposits a pointer to this packet in the alignment mailbox. Then it waits for the amount of time corresponding to the full length of the slot, including the marker and, if no slot arrives at the input port in the meantime, moves back to state GenSlot.

For as long as its port is idle, the slot generator behaves exactly as the input process would behave if it were receiving from the port empty slots at regular intervals. From the point of view of the relay process, it makes no difference whether the empty slots that appear at the output end of the alignment buffer have arrived from the network or have been produced by the slot generator. Therefore, the initialization phase need not be distinguished from the normal operation of the protocol. In fact, this phase has no clear boundary, as different copies of the slot generator may accomplish their tasks (and disappear) at different moments.

Following is the type declaration of the input process:

```
process Input (MStation) {
  DBuffer *DB;
  Port *IPort;
  void setup (int d) {
    DB = S->DB [d];
    IPort = S->IPorts [d];
  };
```

```
    states {WaitSlot, NewSlot, Receive, RDone};
    perform;
};
```

The two attributes are the same as for the slot generator. The input process has no use for SMarker, as it only deals with slots that arrive from the network (via IPort). The code method run by the process is slightly more complicated than the code method of the slot generator:

```
Input::perform {
  Packet *pk;
  state WaitSlot:
    IPort->wait (EOT, NewSlot);
  state NewSlot:
    if (ThePacket->TP == SLOT) {
      pk = create Packet;
      *pk = *ThePacket;
      DB->put (pk);
      if (IPort->events (BOT)) {
        assert (flagSet (pk->Flags, FULL) && ThePacket->TP != SLOT,
          "Slot marker followed by garbage");
        if (ThePacket->isMy ()) {
          clearFlag (pk->Flags, FULL);
          skipto Receive;
        } else {
          pk = create Packet;
          *pk = *ThePacket;
          DB->put (pk);
        }
      }
    }
    skipto WaitSlot;
  state Receive:
    IPort->wait (EOT, RDone);
  state RDone:
    assert (ThePacket->isMy (), "My packet expected");
    Client->receive (ThePacket, IPort);
    skipto WaitSlot;
};
```

The reason for this complication is that the input process has to deal with nonempty slots (such slots are represented by two consecutive packets), and it also has to assume the role of the receiver, i.e., it has to recognize segments addressed to the current station and remove them from their slots.

The process starts in state WaitSlot, where it awaits the end of a slot marker appearing on the input port. It is more convenient to respond to the EOT event triggered by the end of an incoming slot marker than to the BOT event caused by the beginning of this marker. If the slot happens to be full, the segment carried by the slot immediately follows the slot marker. This means that the EOT event triggered by the marker overlaps with the BOT event announcing the beginning of the segment. Consequently, both the marker and the segment are available at the same moment.

Having sensed an EOT event on its port, the input process moves to state NewSlot. Then it checks whether the packet triggering the event is actually a slot marker. As we will see, the EOT event can also be caused by the end of a previously processed segment, in which case it should be skipped and ignored. If the packet happens to be a slot marker, the process makes a copy of it and deposits this copy in the alignment mailbox.[13] Then it checks whether a BOT event is pending on the input port, which can only mean that the slot marker is followed by a segment. If this is the case, the process asserts that the FULL flag in the slot marker is set (only a full slot can carry a segment) and checks whether the segment[14] is addressed to the current station. In such a case, the FULL flag of the slot marker is cleared (the segment will be extracted from the slot) and the process moves to state Receive to simulate packet reception.

The careful reader may object to the way the input process recognizes that the segment is addressed to the current station. At the moment when the process discovers this fact, only the beginning of the segment is present on the input port. Realistically, the process should wait for some initial portion of the segment header before claiming that it knows the segment's recipient. This would require a hallway buffer (similar to the hallway buffer used in the insertion ring—section 10.4.1) separating the input port from the alignment buffer. Note, however, that the hallway buffer can be modeled by increasing the length of all channels by the same amount. Without affecting the realistic status of the model, we can imagine that besides the "official" input port, the input process has another tap connected to the input channel before the input port. This invisible tap allows the process to know the destination of an incoming segment at the moment when the beginning of that segment appears on the "official" port.

In state Receive, the input process waits for the EOT event caused by the end of the segment. When this event occurs, the process wakes up in state RDone, where it receives the segment and transits to state WaitSlot to await the next slot arrival on the input port. The transition is made with skipto, to remove the EOT event from the port, although there would be no harm if proceed were used instead. EOT events caused by segment packets are ignored in state NewSlot.

If the slot marker is followed by a segment, but the segment is not addressed to the current station, the segment is stored in the alignment buffer following its

---

[13]Of course, the reader remembers why the slot marker must be copied. The original packet structure pointed to by ThePacket will be automatically deallocated as soon as the packet disappears from the input channel.

[14]Note that the **events** operation has reset ThePacket to point to the segment packet.

slot marker. In such a case, the process does not wait for the end of the segment
before transiting back to state `WaitSlot`: it just executes `skipto` to avoid being
restarted by the same pending EOT event caused by the last slot marker. In consequence, the end of the segment will trigger a transition from `WaitSlot` to `NewSlot`.
This transition will have no effect, however, as the condition of the outermost `if`
statement in state `NewSlot` will not hold.

11.3.4.4   The router process.   Besides the input processes and (temporarily) slot generators, each station runs a single copy of the router process. In one
cycle, the router process absorbs two input slots from the alignment buffers, optionally fills one or both of them with own segment(s) acquired from the `Client`,
determines via which output ports the slots should be routed, and transmits them
synchronously on the output ports. As both outgoing slots are emitted at exactly
the same time, all these operations can be performed by a single process. The type
of the router process is declared as follows:

```
process Router (MStation) {
  DBuffer **DB;
  Port *OPorts [2];
  Packet **Buffer, *SMarker, *OP [2];
  int OS [2];
  TIME RTime;
  void route ();
  void setup () {
    DB = S->DB;
    Buffer = S->Buffer;
    SMarker = &(S->SMarker);
  };
  states {Wait2, SDone, PDone};
  perform;
};
```

The process services both output ports of its owning station and extracts
incoming slots from both alignment mailboxes; thus, most of its attributes are two-
element arrays. Attributes `DB`, `Buffer`, and `SMarker` are assigned by the setup
method to point to the corresponding station attributes. One may guess that the
role of `OPorts` is to identify the output ports of the station; however, this attribute
is not initialized in the setup method. At the moment when a pair of outgoing slots
is about to be emitted, `OPorts[i]` ($i = 0, 1$) points to the output port on which
the slot that arrived on input port number i is to be relayed. Thus, the `OPorts`
attribute is set by the routing algorithm each time the process emits a new pair of
outgoing slots.

Array `OP` stores pointers to the segments extracted from the current pair of
incoming slots. `OP[i]` points to the segment that arrived on the input port number
i. The status of the incoming slots and their segments is described by `OS`, whose

entries may contain the following values:

```
#define FREE       0
#define OWN        1
#define INCOMING   2
```

Value FREE indicates that the corresponding slot has arrived empty (or its segment has been received and removed by the station), but the station has no own segment to fill the slot. Consequently, the slot will be relayed as empty to the output port. Value OWN tells that the slot has arrived empty and has been filled by the station's own segment. The last value describes a slot that has arrived full and whose segment must be relayed further.

The purpose of RTime is to guarantee that slots inserted by the process into the output ports are spaced properly. The process stores in this attribute the time when the segment window of the currently emitted slot began and makes sure that the next slot marker is issued no sooner than SegmWindow ITUs later.

The routing algorithm has been isolated from the process code method and put into a separate method (route) to be easily exchangeable. This has also reduced the complexity of the code method, which is quite long.

In the first step of a slot generation cycle, the router extracts a pair of slots from the alignment buffers and determines whether they are full or empty. For each empty slot, the process attempts to fill it with the station's own segment acquired from the Client. Then the slots are presented to the routing algorithm, which sets OPorts according to the rules described in section 11.3.2. All these operations are performed in the following code method executed by the router:

```
Router::perform {
  int i;
  Packet *sm, *pk;
  state Wait2:
    for (i = 0; i < 2; i++)
      if (DB [i] -> empty ()) {
        DB [i] -> wait (NONEMPTY, Wait2);
        sleep;
      }
    for (i = 0; i < 2; i++) {
      sm = DB [i] -> get ();
      assert (sm -> TP == SLOT, "Slot marker expected");
      if (flagSet (sm -> Flags, FULL)) {
        assert (DB [i] -> nonempty (), "Missing payload");
        pk = DB [i] -> get ();
        assert (pk -> TP != SLOT, "Payload expected");
        OP [i] = pk;
        OS [i] = INCOMING;
      } else {
```

```
        if (S->ready (i, SegmPL, SegmPL, SegmFL)) {
          OP [i] = Buffer [i];
          OS [i] = OWN;
        } else
          OS [i] = FREE;
      }
      delete sm;
    }
    route ();
    for (i = 0; i < 2; i++) {
      if (OS [i] == FREE)
        clearFlag (SMarker -> Flags, FULL);
      else
        setFlag (SMarker -> Flags, FULL);
      OPorts [i] -> transmit (SMarker, SDone);
    };
  state SDone:
    RTime = Time;
    for (i = 0; i < 2; i++) {
      OPorts [i] -> stop ();
      if (OS [i] == FREE)
        Timer->wait (SegmWindow, Wait2);
      else
        OPorts [i] -> transmit (OP [i], PDone);
    }
  state PDone:
    for (i = 0; i < 2; i++) {
      if (OS [i] != FREE) {
        OPorts [i] -> stop ();
        if (OS [i] == OWN)
          OP [i] -> release ();
        else
          delete OP [i];
      }
    }
    Timer->wait (SegmWindow - (Time - RTime), Wait2);
}
```

Most actions of the process apply simultaneously to a pair of slots. Each such an action is encapsulated in a for loop, whose body is executed twice, for $i = 0$ and 1. Upon the entry to its initial state, the router determines the status of the alignment mailboxes. If at least one mailbox turns out to be empty, the process sleeps until the mailbox becomes nonempty and tries again. The second for loop in state Wait2 extracts a pair of slots from the mailboxes. If the slot being extracted happens to be full, another packet is retrieved from the mailbox, its pointer stored in the corresponding entry of OP. This packet represents the segment carried by the slot. At the same time, the slot status (OS) is set to INCOMING to indicate that the slot carries a segment that has arrived from the network. For an empty slot, the router attempts to acquire a segment from the Client into the station's buffer whose index is equal to the index of the slot being processed. If this attempt succeeds, the buffer pointer is stored in OP. This way the acquired segment appears as if it had arrived from the network. The slot status is set to OWN to indicate that this is actually not the case (the reason we have to know the difference will become clear shortly). If the incoming slot is empty and there is no segment to fill it, the slot status is set to FREE. Such a slot will be relayed as empty. The last statement under the for loop deallocates the data structure representing the slot marker. Eventually, any packet inserted into one of the alignment mailboxes has to be deallocated. Note, however, that the segment structure (for a slot that arrived nonempty) cannot be deallocated at this moment, as the segment will have to be transmitted on one of the output ports.

When the execution of the second loop in state Wait2 has been completed, both slots are ready to be relayed. The process invokes now the routing algorithm (method route) to set the entries of OPorts to the proper output port pointers. Then the router transmits two slot markers on the output ports, and the FULL flags of these markers are set according to the status of the slots being relayed. After the slot markers have been fully emitted, the process transits to state SDone.

In state SDone, the router starts by setting RTime to the current time, to mark the beginning of the segment window of the emitted slots. Then, for each of the two slots, it terminates the transmission of the marker and either sleeps for SegmWindow ITUs (if the slot is going to be empty) or transmits the segment that is to be carried by the slot. Note that when the process completes the sequence of statements in state SDone, it may end up waiting for SegmWindow ITUs on the Timer and for the end of a segment transmission. This will happen if one of the slots is empty and the other is full. In fact, the two events are both timer events and, as the segment transmission time is slightly shorter than the segment window, the end-of-transmission event will be triggered first and the process will wake up in state PDone.

If both outgoing slots are empty, the process will transit from SDone directly to Wait2, SegmWindow ITUs after the slot markers were inserted into the output ports. If at least one slot is nonempty, the router will find itself in state PDone at the moment when the segment transmission is complete. Then it will go through the slots once again and terminate the segment transmission (or transmissions, if both slots are nonempty). Now we come to the point where the difference between an OWN segment and an INCOMING segment that has arrived from the network becomes important. The former must be released after the transmission, because the current station is its original sender and the latter must be deallocated, because it was extracted from a mailbox. Having terminated the segment transmission, the router sleeps for a short while, to make sure that the next pair of slot markers will be inserted into the output ports no sooner than `SegmWindow` time units after the end of the previous pair. Finally, the router transits to state `Wait2` to begin a new cycle.

11.3.4.5 The routing algorithm.

The routing decision regarding the fate of each pair of slots processed by the router is made by method `route`. Given a pair of outgoing slots, the method must make a binary decision, selecting one of two possible ways of relaying these slots on the output ports. The method starts by encoding the preference of the two slots into a four-bit integer value, which is later used to index the possible cases. The first (more significant) two-bit nibble of the preference pattern describes the preference of slot number 0. If the left (more significant) bit of this nibble is 1, it means that the route offered by output port number 0 lies along a direction that is preferred by the slot. Similarly, the right (less significant) bit of the nibble tells the preference status of the route offered by port number 1. In the same way, the second (less significant) two-bit nibble describes the preference of the other slot. Note that nibble patterns 00 and 11 are equivalent: they both say that the slot represented by the nibble will be equally happy to be relayed via either output port.

The code of `route` is as follows:

```
void Router::route () {
  int i, prf;
  prf = 0;
  for (i = 0; i < 2; i++) {
    if (OS [i] != FREE)
      findPreferred (S -> getId (), OP [i] -> Receiver,
        S -> Neighbors, prf);
    else
      prf <<= 2;
  }
  switch (prf) {
    case  0:  // 00 00   0 --> ANY    1 --> ANY
    case  3:  // 00 11   0 --> ANY    1 --> BOTH
    case  5:  // 01 01   0 --> 1      1 --> 1
    case 10:  // 10 10   0 --> 0      1 --> 0
    case 12:  // 11 00   0 --> BOTH   1 --> ANY
    case 15:  // 11 11   0 --> BOTH   1 --> BOTH
              OPorts [i = flip ()] = S->OPorts [0];
              OPorts [1 - i]       = S->OPorts [1];
              break;
    case  1:  // 00 01   0 --> ANY    1 --> 1
    case  8:  // 10 00   0 --> 0      1 --> ANY
    case  9:  // 10 01   0 --> 0      1 --> 1
    case 11:  // 10 11   0 --> 0      1 --> BOTH
    case 13:  // 11 01   0 --> BOTH   1 --> 1
```

```
                    OPorts [0] = S->OPorts [0];
                    OPorts [1] = S->OPorts [1];
                    break;
    case   2:   // 00 10    0 --> ANY     1 --> 0
    case   4:   // 01 00    0 --> 1       1 --> ANY
    case   6:   // 01 10    0 --> 1       1 --> 0
    case   7:   // 01 11    0 --> 1       1 --> BOTH
    case  14:   // 11 10    0 --> BOTH    1 --> 0
                    OPorts [0] = S->OPorts [1];
                    OPorts [1] = S->OPorts [0];
                    break;
    default:
                    excptn ("Illegal preference pattern");
    }
}
```

The preference pattern (variable prf) is built by two calls to function findPreferred, each call storing in the pattern one nibble corresponding to one outgoing slot. Before we look at this function, let us try to understand what happens in route. The method clears prf and then examines the two slots starting from slot number 0. If the slot is full, findPreferred is called to determine the slot preferences and add a nibble to prf. As we will see, the nibble is added onto the least significant two bits of prf with the previous contents of the pattern shifted two binary positions to the left. Consequently, after both slots have been examined, the two nibbles occupy the four least significant bits of prf, with the more significant nibble corresponding to slot number 0. If a slot happens to be empty, its nibble is simply skipped and left to be two zeros (an empty slot has no port preference).

In the second stage, the value of the preference pattern determines the way the slots are mapped to the output ports. There are three possibilities:

- The mapping is random, i.e., it is straightforward or reverse with probability 1/2. This happens if neither slot has a clear port preference or if both slots prefer the same single output port.
- The mapping is straightforward. This mapping is selected if at least one slot prefers the single port whose index is the same as the slot index, and the other slot prefers the other port or has no clear preference.
- The mapping is reverse. The reverse mapping is chosen if at least one slot prefers the single port whose index is opposite to the slot index, and the other slot prefers the other port or has no clear preference.

Now we are ready to discuss the operation of findPreferred. The function accepts the following four arguments in the listed order:

- The Id of the station making the routing decision, i.e., the current station.
- The destination Id.

- A two-element array specifying the Ids of the neighbors connected to the station via its output ports. Such an array is a standard attribute of any station equipped with the MeshNode interface (section 11.2.2.1).
- The preference pattern to be augmented by a new nibble. This argument is passed by reference, because it will be modified by the function.

The function transforms the routing problem to the canonical form and then determines the location of the current station in the diagram shown in figure 11.9. The code of findPreferred is as follows:

```
static void findPreferred (Long s, Long d, Long n [2], int &prf) {
  Long i, sc, sr, dc, dr, nc [2], nr [2];
  sc = col (s);
  sr = row (s);
  dc = col (d);
  dr = row (d);
  transform (sc, sr, dc, dr);
  for (i = 0; i < 2; i++) {
    nc [i] = col (n [i]);
    nr [i] = row (n [i]);
    transform (nc [i], nr [i], dc, dr);
  }
  if (sc <= 0) {                    // Left half
    if (sr <= 0) {                  // Left upper quadrant
      if (sc > -NCols05+1) {        // Not the leftmost column
        if (sr > -NRows05+1)        // Not the upmost row
          setpref (NO, YES, NO, YES);
        else                        // Upmost row
          setpref (NO, YES, YES, YES);
      } else if (sr > -NRows05+1)   // Not the left upper corner
        setpref (YES, YES, NO, YES);
      else                          // Left upper corner
        setpref (YES, YES, YES, YES);
    } else {                        // Left bottom quadrant
      if (sc < 0) {                 // Not the destination column
        if (sr > 1)                 // Not the first row
          setpref (NO, YES, YES, NO);
        else                        // First row
          setpref (NO, YES, NO, NO);
      } else                        // Destination column
        setpref (NO, NO, YES, NO);
    }
  } else {                          // Right half
    if (sr <= 0) {                  // Right upper quadrant
      if (sr < 0) {                 // Not the first row
```

```
            if (sc > 1)              // Not the first column
              setpref (YES, NO, NO, YES);
            else                     // First column
              setpref (NO, NO, NO, YES);
          } else                     // First row
            setpref (YES, NO, NO, NO);
        } else {                     // Right bottom quadrant
          if (sc < NCols05) {        // Not the last column
            if (sr < NRows05)        // Not the last row
              setpref (YES, NO, YES, NO);
            else                     // Last row, not the last column
              setpref (YES, NO, YES, YES);
          } else {                   // Last column
            if (sr < NRows05)        // Not the right bottom corner
              setpref (YES, YES, YES, NO);
            else                     // Right bottom corner
              setpref (YES, YES, YES, YES);
          }
        }
      }
    }
  }
```

Except for i, which is a loop index, the local variables used by the function have the following meaning:

sc, sr   the column and row of the station making the routing decision

dc, dr   destination column and row

nc, nr   neighbor column and row

The last two variables are two-element arrays, as there are two neighbors connected to the station via its output ports.

The function starts with converting station Ids to column/row coordinates and transforming the coordinates of the routing station and its neighbors according to the formulas given in section 11.3.2. For clarity, the transformation formulas have been covered with a simple function defined as follows:

```
void transform (Long &c, Long &r, Long cd, Long rd) {
  c = NCols05 - (NCols15 + (odd (rd) ? cd - c : c - cd)) % NCols;
  r = NRows05 - (NRows15 + (odd (cd) ? rd - r : r - rd)) % NRows;
};
```

The neighbor coordinates are needed to tell the direction of the routes offered by the output ports. These coordinates are transformed, in the same way as the coordinates of the routing station, to make sure that the notion of direction is interpreted in the canonical rectangle. The list of if statements following the transformation of coordinates determines the location of the transformed coordinates of the routing station in the direction diagram (figure 11.9). These statements can be viewed as a decision tree whose leaves correspond to the distinct regions of the diagram. When the region has been located, the preference nibble is set according to the direction arrows of that region. This is accomplished by macro `setpref`, whose four arguments represent the four possible preference directions: left, right, up, and down, in this order. Value YES or NO appearing on the position of a given direction tells whether the region has an arrow pointing in that direction. In particular, for the upmost row of the left upper quadrant without the left upper corner, `setpref` is invoked with the arguments (NO,YES,YES,YES), meaning that the region has arrows in all directions except to the left. The macro is defined in the following way:

```
#define geq(a,b) ((a) != (b) - 1 && (a) <= (b) + 1)
#define leq(a,b) ((a) != (b) + 1 && (a) >= (b) - 1)
#define setpref(l,r,u,d) \
  for (i = 0; i < 2; i++) \
    prf = (prf << 1) | ((l || geq (nc [i], sc)) && \
                        (r || leq (nc [i], sc)) && \
                        (u || geq (nr [i], sr)) && \
                        (d || leq (nr [i], sr))    )
```

Predicates `geq` and `leq` define the relations $\geq$ and $\leq$ between the coordinates of the routing station and those of its neighbors. In particular, `geq(a,b)` returns nonzero if and only if `a` is greater than or equal to `b` in the coordinate metrics of the transformed rectangle. To understand the logic behind the not-so-obvious definition of `geq` imagine a routing station s_r located somewhere inside the transformed network rectangle (figure 11.8) and assume that we are interested in comparing the column coordinate of s_r with the column coordinate of its neighbor s_n. We say that the column coordinate of s_n is less than the column coordinate of s_r if s_n can be reached from s_r by going one hop to the left. If s_r does not touch the rectangle boundary, this condition is equivalent to the column coordinate of s_n being equal to the column coordinate of s_r minus 1. Now, if s_r is located on the left edge of the rectangle, one hop to the left gets us to the opposite right edge. In such a case, the column coordinate of the left neighbor of s_r is greater than the column coordinate of s_r by more than 1 (if it were greater just by 1, s_n would be the right neighbor of s_r). Thus, the condition for the column coordinate of s_n to be less than the column coordinate of s_r is as follows:

$$\text{col}(s_n) = \text{col}(s_r) - 1 \quad || \quad \text{col}(s_n) > \text{col}(s_r) + 1 .$$

As the `geq` condition is a negation of "less," the formula used in the macro is a simple negation of the preceding formula. The definition of `leq` can be explained using similar reasoning. One should note that the two macros only work for the coordinates of neighboring stations; fortunately, we do not expect them to work in any other circumstances.

The mechanism of `setpref` is now easy to explain. The `for` loop executes twice, once for each of the two bits of the preference nibble. Each bit is set to 1 only if the corresponding neighbor lies on a preferred path from the routing station. As before, we negate the condition that we want to explain and ask the following question: What does it mean that the path to a given neighbor is not preferred by the slot? Clearly, the path is not preferred if, for instance, the slot does not want to go to the left, but the neighbor is located to the left of the routing station. Or the slot does not want to go down, but the path to the neighbor is directed down, and so on. If any such alternative for one of the four directions happens to be true, the port leading to the neighbor must be deemed "not preferred." Note, however, that the neighbor must be located in some direction from the routing station. Therefore, if all the alternatives are false, it means that the direction of the neighbor is preferred by the slot. The formula used by `setpref` to determine the contents of one bit of the preference nibble is just a negation of these alternatives. Consequently, the nibble bit corresponding to a given output port is set to 1 if the route offered by the port is preferred.

11.3.4.6   The incidence function.   The root process of our protocol program for MSN is straightforward and thus not discussed here. Although the protocol has an equivalent of an initialization phase, this phase need not be separated from the normal operation, and there is no trace of it in the state structure of the root process. The only portion of the root module that may be of some interest is the code of the incidence function that defines the unidirectional torus geometry of the MSN grid. This function is as follows:

```
int Connected (Long a, Long b, DISTANCE &d) {
  Long ra, ca, rb, cb, t;
  d = LinkLength;
  ra = row (a); ca = col (a);
  rb = row (b); cb = col (b);
  if (ra == rb) {
    if (odd (ra)) {
      t = ca; ca = cb; cb = t;
    }
    cb -= ca;
    return cb == 1 || cb == 1 - NCols;
  } else if (ca == cb) {
    if (odd (ca)) {
      t = ra; ra = rb; rb = t;
    }
    rb -= ra;
    return rb == 1 || rb == 1 - NRows;
  } else
```

```
        return NO;
    };
```

Given a pair of station identifiers a and b, the function returns 1 if and only if b is an upstream neighbor of a, i.e., b can be reached from a in a single hop. To check whether this is the case, the function converts the station Ids to the column/row coordinates and locates the stations in the MSN grid. First of all, to be neighbors, the stations must share the same row (ra == rb) or the same column (ca == cb). Assume that the stations belong to the same row. If the number of that row is odd, the row is oriented to the left; otherwise, it is oriented to the right. In the first case, the function exchanges the values of ca and cb, effectively reversing the row orientation. What remains to be determined is whether cb is equal to ca + 1 mod NCols. Exactly the same calculations, related to row numbers rather than column numbers, are performed if the stations share the same column.

The function assumes that all links in the MSN grid are of the same length. This length, represented by the global static variable LinkLength of type DISTANCE, is initialized by the root process from the input data file.

11.3.4.7 Global routing.   In this section, we show how to modify the protocol program presented in sections 11.3.4.1–11.3.4.6 to take advantage of precomputed preference tables.   The large number of if statements in function findPreferred (section 11.3.4.5) looks certainly discouraging to anyone contemplating a realistic implementation of the MSN concept. As we said in section 11.3.3, it may be more reasonable to base the routing algorithm on precomputed preference tables that would directly describe the port preference for each possible destination.

To modify our protocol program along these lines, we start by augmenting the station type with one additional attribute representing the preference table:

```
    station MStation : MeshNode, ClientInterface {
      DBuffer *DB [2];
      Packet SMarker;
      unsigned char *Pref;
      void setup () {
        int i;
        MeshNode::configure (2);
        ClientInterface::configure (2);
        for (i = 0; i < 2; i++) DB [i] = create DBuffer (MAX_long);
        SMarker.fill (NONE, NONE, SlotML);
      };
    };
```

The preference table will be allocated and filled by a special function called from the root process after all stations have been created. The required size of the array is NStations entries, each entry storing two bits of information. These two bits directly represent the preference nibble for a given destination (section 11.3.4.5).

In the localized version of the routing algorithm, the nibble was painstakingly re-calculated each time it was needed. Now it will be computed once and stored in the preference table, from which it can be accessed many times without excessive calculations.

Having created all stations, the root process calls the following function:

```
void assignPortRanks () {
  short **IM, t1, t2, t;
  Long i, j, k;
  MStation *S;
  IM = new short* [NStations];
  for (i = 0; i < NStations; i++) IM [i] = new short [NStations];
  for (i = 0; i < NStations; i++) {
    for (j = 0; j < NStations; j++)
      IM [i][j] = (i == j) ? 0 : MAX_short;
    S = (MStation*) idToStation (i);
    for (j = 0; j < 2; j++)
      IM [i][S->Neighbors [j]] = 1;
  }
  for (k = 0; k < NStations; k++)
    for (i = 0; i < NStations; i++) {
      if ((t1 = IM [i][k]) < MAX_short)
        for (j = 0; j < NStations; j++)
          if ((t2 = IM [k][j]) < MAX_short &&
          (t = t1 + t2) < IM [i][j])
            IM [i][j] = t;
    }
  for (i = 0; i < NStations; i++) {
    S = (MStation*) idToStation (i);
    S->Pref = new unsigned char [NStations];
    for (j = 0; j < NStations; j++)
      if ((t1 = IM [S->Neighbors [0]][j]) <
      (t2 = IM [S->Neighbors [1]][j]))
        S->Pref [j] = 2;
      else if (t1 > t2)
        S->Pref [j] = 1;
      else
        S->Pref [j] = 0;
  }
  for (i = 0; i < NStations; i++) delete IM [i];
  delete IM;
};
```

The first for loop of the function creates and initializes array IM, which will be used to calculate the length of the shortest paths from each station to every other station. The array is a square matrix with NStations rows and columns. At the end of the shortest-paths algorithm, entry [i][j] of IM will tell the minimum number of hops from station i to station j. The array is initialized according to the incidence relation of the network graph. The diagonal entries are set to zero (as each station can be reached from itself in zero hops), all entries representing immediate hops (channels to neighbors) are set to 1, and all the remaining entries are set to a huge value simulating infinity.

The three nested for loops intermixed with two if statements implement the well-known all-shortest-paths algorithm by Floyd. It is important to notice that this algorithm works for any graph, and the regular structure of the MSN grid is of no advantage here. Thus, the global version of the protocol will operate correctly on any mesh network in which every station has two input and two output ports.

With the shortest path information in hand, the function proceeds to create and fill the port preference tables. The outer loop (indexed by i) goes through all stations. For each station, the preference array is allocated and filled by the inner loop (indexed by j), which examines all possible destinations. For each destination, the function determines the number of hops needed to reach the destination from the current station via each of the two output ports. For example, if port 0 offers a shorter path than port 1, the resulting nibble value is 2 (section 11.3.4.5). Note that value 3 is not used, as we are not able to tell the difference between the cases when both ports are preferred and when they are both not preferred. Fortunately, these scenarios are completely equivalent from the viewpoint of the routing algorithm. Having created the preference tables at all stations, the function deallocates the IM array, which is no longer needed.

The routing algorithm can now be substantially simplified and implemented as a trivial prelude to the switch statement in function route (section 11.3.4.5). We list just this prelude, hoping that the reader will find it easy to fill in the details:

```
prf = 0;
for (i = 0; i < 2; i++) {
  prf <<= 2;
  if (OS [i] != FREE) prf |= S->Pref [OP [i] -> Receiver];
}
```

As before, the preference pattern is built of two nibbles, but this time the nibbles are extracted directly from the precomputed preference table. The number of case values in the switch statement can be reduced to nine, as there are only three legal values of each nibble. Of course, there are still three different ways of mapping the outgoing slots to the output ports.

11.4   THE MULTIGRID NETWORK ARCHITECTURE

The Manhattan Street Network operates in a slotted and synchronized fashion. The need to enforce slot alignment at a routing station complicates the station hardware and, in a large network, may require a backpressure mechanism to keep the slot arrival rate approximately even. Is it really necessary that the incoming slots be aligned before they can be relayed? One can think of a variant of MSN in which an incoming packet is relayed as soon as it arrives at the station and its destination address has been determined. If its preferred port happens to be occupied by another packet, the incoming packet is deflected, i.e., relayed on the other, unpreferred port. With this approach, explicit slots are not needed and, in principle, packets can be of arbitrary length. What suffers is the quality of the routing decision. Clearly, it is much better to make such a decision if both incoming packets are subject to it at the same time. For example, assume that two packets P_0 and P_1 arrive at a station on its input ports. Suppose that P_0 has no port preference but P_1 prefers to be relayed via one specific port, e.g., port number 0. If both packets are available when the station is making the routing decision, it will relay packet P_1 via port 0 and packet P_0 via port 1. Imagine, however, that the network operates in an asynchronous manner (packets are relayed individually) and packet P_0 arrives at the station slightly ahead of P_1. As P_1 is not available when the station is making the routing decision regarding P_0, the station is free to choose either of the two output ports, in particular port number 0. Now, when P_1 becomes ready to be relayed, it will be forced to go via its unpreferred route, although, had the station known the preferences of both packets before relaying them, it would have directed them both to their preferred ports. One can conceive of an even worse scenario in which all packets arriving at a station are perpetually deflected, i.e., none of them follows its preferred route. As a continuation of the previous thought experiment, imagine that another packet, say P_2, arrives while P_1 is being relayed via its unpreferred port. Suppose that P_2 wants to be relayed on port 1, i.e., the same port that is currently occupied by P_1. Of course, P_2 will be deflected, and if P_1 terminates before P_2 does, another packet may arrive at the station while P_2 is being transmitted and share the fate of P_2. This scenario may continue indefinitely, if the preference pattern of the arriving packets is sufficiently inopportune.

The benefits of asynchronous deflection routing are too tempting to be discarded on such grounds, however. The Manhattan Street Network may not be well suited for asynchronous routing because of the small number of options (just two output ports), resulting in a relatively high likelihood of unfortunate scenarios. But in a network with a station connectivity significantly larger than two, the situation may be quite different. For example, if each packet has eight output ports to choose from and the preference ranks of these ports have several levels, the likelihood of really malicious no-progress scenarios may be reduced to an acceptable level. After all, in pure CSMA/CD, it is theoretically possible that two packets will collide for several hours, but nobody seems to consider this disastrous possibility a serious treat to Ethernet's reliability.

11.4.1   The MNA Switch

The Multigrid Network Architecture (MNA) is a high-speed networking concept based on a fast switching device whose logical structure is presented in figure 11.10. The MNA switch is equipped with a number of input ports and the same number of output ports. Typically, this number (the switch connectivity) is 8 or 16.

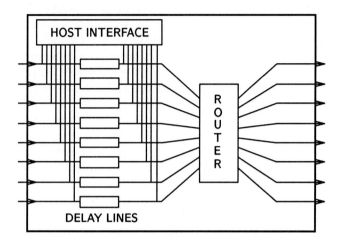

Figure 11.10   The MNA switch

The switch operates as a fast asynchronous routing device. Based on the destination address encoded in the header of a packet arriving on an input port, the switch ranks the output ports according to the packet's preference. The packet is relayed on the most preferred of the idle output ports.

Packets are not buffered before they are relayed, except for a short hallway portion needed to decode the destination address from the packet header. Consequently, packets are not aligned at the switch, and each routing decision deals with one packet at a time.

The switch is capable of relaying all incoming packets in parallel. Thus, if packets arrive on all the input ports at (almost) the same time, all these packets will be relayed to the output ports. Multiple MNA switches can be configured into networks (e.g., see figure 11.11). Not all ports of a switch must be used, but if some ports are left disconnected, then the number of connected output ports must not be less than the number of connected input ports. As this rule is enforced for all switches in the network, one can easily see that the actual input connectivity of a switch must be equal to its output connectivity. It makes perfect sense to connect an output port of a switch to one of its own input ports. Such a link can be viewed as a local buffer for a packet that cannot be relayed via its preferred route.

A switch can be equipped with a host interface, in which case it is capable of inserting its own traffic into the network. Besides, such a switch has to recognize

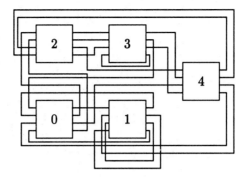

Figure 11.11 A sample MNA network

packets addressed to the host and receive them, i.e., forward them to the host instead of relaying them to the output ports. A packet generated by the host is routed by the switch in the same way as if it had arrived from the network on one of the input ports. However, before the switch decides to use an output port to relay the host packet, it must know that the output port will not be needed to relay a network packet before the host packet has been entirely transmitted. Note that the switch must be able to relay all packets arriving on the input ports; thus, at moments, it may need all its output ports to relay the network traffic. To deal with host packets, the switch tries to "predict the future" of the network input ports for the interval of one packet transmission. This is accomplished by inserting a delay line before each input port. The delay line has a sensing tap at a distance slightly more than one maximum-length packet before the port. If the tap has been sensed idle for the time interval corresponding to the packet transmission, the "free slot" of this input port can be used to insert a host packet into the network. Thus, for a host packet transmission, the host is temporarily connected to one of the network input ports that is going to be idle for the duration of the transfer. If no such port exists at the moment, the host's packet is blocked until an input port becomes available. Otherwise, the packet appears as if it had arrived from the network and is routed in the same way as any other packet. A switch that is not interfaced to a host need not be equipped with delay lines and additional sensing taps.

Packets in MNA can be of variable length, but a maximum (not excessive) packet length should be imposed to limit the length of a delay line at a switch connected to a host. The network does not suffer from the alignment problems of MSN. As a transient packet is practically not buffered during its transition through a switch, it seems natural to synchronize the retransmission rate to the arrival rate of the packet.

In contrast to Floodnet, and like MSN, MNA is a capacity-1 network, as its maximum throughput does not depend on the propagation length of the links. As a matter of fact, the network was designed with very high transmission rates in mind, of order 1 Gb/s per channel. It is tacitly assumed that the length of a delay line (and thus the maximum packet length) is relatively short in comparison to the length of a typical link connecting two switches.

11.4.2   The Routing Rules

As each packet in MNA is relayed individually, the routing rules of MNA are much simpler than in the Manhattan Street Network. MNA switches can be configured into any, possibly very irregular, configurations, as long as they preserve the same connectivity of input and output ports at every switch. It is postulated that all connections be bidirectional, i.e., a link from switch s_1 to switch s_2 should be accompanied by a link from s_2 to s_1. This property, although not directly required by the routing mechanism, is advantageous in case of a switch failure. If all connections are bidirectional, the failure of a switch does not violate the balance of alive input and output ports at its neighbors. Thus, unless the network becomes disconnected, it can still operate without packet loss, provided that all neighbors of the dead switch are aware of its absence. Each switch maintains a two-dimensional fixed routing table indexed by station numbers along one dimension and by output port numbers along the other. Let k denote the switch connectivity. For a given destination address d, the routing table produces k numbers $r_0(d), \ldots, r_{k-1}(d)$ representing the cost ranks of the output ports $p_0, \ldots, p_{k-1}$. The most natural way of ranking the ports is to make $r_i(d)$ equal to the minimum number of hops to the destination d offered by port p_i. The routing tables are precomputed based on the results of the all-shortest-paths algorithm applied to the network graph.

Assume that a packet arrives at a switch on one of its input ports. According to what we said in the previous section, there is no need to treat packets arriving from the host connected to the switch in a different way than packets arriving from the network. Having determined the destination address d of the packet, the switch fetches from the routing table the row of k numbers $r_0(d), \ldots, r_{k-1}(d)$ representing the cost ranks of the output ports for destination d. All entries corresponding to the output ports that are currently busy relaying some packets are erased from the row, e.g., by setting them to infinity. Then the switch selects the idle output port with the minimum value of r_i. If several idle ports have the same lowest cost, one of these ports is chosen at random.

The routing algorithm is randomized (as in MSN—section 11.3.2) to reduce the likelihood of a live-lock. Because of the possibly irregular topology and asynchronously-made routing decisions, it is impossible to rid MNA of live-locks absolutely. However, the high connectivity of an MNA switch combined with the randomization of the routing rules makes live-locks unlikely to the extent of rendering them practically negligible. The observed performance of MNA does not suffer much if the routing tables are simplified by assigning the same cost ranks to less eligible output ports and ignoring small differences in their actual eligibility. This approach has two advantages: it reduces the size of the lookup tables and increases the randomization of the routing algorithm, which in turn decreases the likelihood of a live-lock.

11.4.3   The Implementation

Like Floodnet switches (section 11.2.2.5), MNA switches can be configured
into practically arbitrary, possibly irregular, meshes. Therefore, the geometry-
independent part of our MNA implementation has been turned into a library module
(files `mnaswitch.h` and `mnaswitch.c`) and stored in `IncludeLibrary`, from which
it can be included by programs implementing specific network configurations.

11.4.3.1   Station types.   An MNA configuration may consist of stations of
two types. The basic station type is `Switch`, which describes a host-less switch with
no `Client` interface. A station of this sort generates no traffic of its own; it just
relays packets arriving from the network. Type `Switch` is defined as follows:

```
station Switch : MeshNode {
  unsigned char **PRanks;
  Boolean *Idle;
  int route (Packet*);
  virtual Port *iPort (int i) { return IPorts [i]; };
  void setup (int order) {
    int i;
    MeshNode::configure (order);
    Idle = new Boolean [order];
    for (i = 0; i < order; i++) Idle [i] = YES;
  };
};
```

The network backbone of our implementation is derived from the mesh module introduced in section 11.2.2.1; thus, type `Switch` descends from `MeshNode`. The
`MeshNode` part of `Switch` defines two arrays of port pointers: `IPorts` and `OPorts`,
representing the collections of input and output ports of the switch. The two arrays are of the same size determined by the argument of `configure`. The value
of this argument (the switch connectivity) is stored in attribute `Order` defined in
`MeshNode`. In principle, a single configuration of MNA may include switches of
different connectivity. Therefore, the switch connectivity is specified as the setup
argument, individually for every switch.

Attribute `PRanks` represents the two-dimensional static routing table specifying output port ranks for every destination. The table is not created by the setup
method of the switch; it will be built and initialized by a special function called
from the root process, in a similar way as the static preference table in an MSN
station (section 11.3.4.7).

The status of each of the output ports is indicated by its entry in the `Boolean`
array `Idle`. If `Idle[i]` is `YES`, it means that the output port number `i` is free and
can be used to relay a packet. The port status is changed to busy (`Idle[i]` becomes

NO) when the port is selected by the routing algorithm to relay an incoming packet. A busy output port will become idle again as soon as the packet being inserted into the port has been terminated.

Method `route` implements the routing algorithm. It is called with a packet pointer passed as the argument and returns the index of the output port on which the packet should be relayed. To understand the role of method `iPort`, we have to look at the other station type, representing a switch interfaced to a host:

```
station Host : Switch, ClientInterface {
  Port **NDelay, **XDelay;
  int *Used;
  Mailbox *FreePort;
  Port *iPort (int i) { return XDelay [i]; };
  void setup (int order, DISTANCE delay) {
    int i;
    PLink *lk;
    Switch::setup (order);
    ClientInterface::configure (order);
    NDelay = new Port* [order];
    XDelay = new Port* [order];
    Used = new int [order];
    FreePort = create Mailbox (0);
    for (i = 0; i < order; i++) {
      NDelay [i] = create Port (TRate);
      XDelay [i] = create Port (TRate);
      lk = create PLink (2);
      NDelay [i] -> connect (lk);
      XDelay [i] -> connect (lk);
      NDelay [i] -> setDTo (XDelay [i], delay);
      Used [i] = 0;
    }
  };
};
```

The `ClientInterface` portion of a Host switch comes from the traffic module discussed in section 11.3.4.1. Note that the argument of `configure` for `ClientInterface` is equal to the station's connectivity (order). Thus, the number of packet buffers owned by the station is the same as the number of port pairs.

Type `Host` inherits the structure of `Switch` and adds to this structure a few new attributes. Recall from section 11.4.1 that a switch interfaced to a host must be equipped with delay lines that allow it to predict the future of the input ports for the maximum duration of a packet transmission. The simplest way to implement a delay line would be to add one extra port to the interstation link, before the standard input port. Unfortunately, the library module used to describe the backbone of our implementation (section 11.2.2.1) predefines all interstation links as having two ports each. Thus, we have to settle for the second-best solution and model the delay lines as separate unidirectional links inserted between the input ports and the routing module. Delay line number i is represented by a pair of ports pointed to by `NDelay[i]` (the entry port) and `XDelay[i]` (the exit port). All delay lines at one station have the same length, which is passed to the station via the second setup argument. As in the case of a host-less switch, the first setup argument specifies the switch connectivity, which of course determines also the number of delay lines.

Array `Used`, whose size is equal to the switch connectivity, keeps track of the status of the delay lines. Whenever an activity (a packet) is inserted into delay line number i, `Used[i]` is incremented by 1. When a packet leaves a delay line, the corresponding entry in `Used` is decremented by 1. This way if `Used[i]` is zero, it means that no packet is currently passing through the i-th delay line. In such a case, the station can transmit its own packet simulating its arrival on the i-th input port. Mailbox `FreePort` plays the role of a signaling device for restarting blocked transmission attempts from the host. An alert is deposited into this mailbox whenever an entry in `Used` is updated from 1 to 0.

Regardless of whether the switch is equipped with the host interface or not, its routing responsibilities are the same. This end is served by a collection of processes accepting incoming packets and relaying these packets on the best available output ports. In a host-less switch, the packets to be relayed arrive directly on the input ports (array `IPorts` defined in `MeshNode`—section 11.2.2.1). In a host switch, the role of the input ports is taken over by the exit ports of the delay lines, and the input ports become sensing taps for monitoring the contents of the delay lines. This is where method `iPort` becomes handy. The role of this method is to provide a transparent way of accessing the ports that deliver packets arriving from the network to the routing processes. Depending on whether it is invoked on a host-less switch or on a switch equipped with delay lines, `iPort(i)` returns either `IPorts[i]`, i.e., the pointer to the i-th input port, or `XDelay[i]`, i.e., the pointer to the exit port of the i-th delay line. As the routing processes run at the `Switch` level and do not see the attributes specific to type `Host`, the `iPort` method is declared as `virtual` in `Switch`. This way, the `Host` version of the method is always used on a host switch even if referenced as a `Switch` attribute.

11.4.3.2   The routing protocol.

The routing portion of the MNA protocol is executed at the `Switch` level and is the same for both switch types. Each switch, regardless of its type, runs `Order` copies of the routing process, whose type definition is as follows:

```
process Router (Switch) {
  Port *IPort, *OPort;
  int  OP;
  void setup (int p) { IPort = S->iPort (p); };
  states {Waiting, NewPacket, WaitEnd, EndPacket, WaitRcv, Rcv};
```

```
  perform;
};
```

Each copy of Router services one "input" port (IPort), whose number is passed to the process upon its creation via the setup argument p. The word *input* has been put in quotation marks and it can only be taken literally if we are on a host-less switch. Otherwise, the "input" port serviced by the process is in fact the exit port of the delay line number p. This is guaranteed by method iPort (section 11.4.3.1), which provides a transparent way of identifying the ports that deliver packets to the routing processes.

Attributes OPort and OP are not initialized by the setup method. The process assigns them dynamically while making a routing decision, i.e., selecting one of the output ports to relay an incoming packet. Then OP is set to the index of the output port in OPorts, and OPort is assigned the port pointer.

Following is the code method of Router:

```
Router::perform {
  state Waiting:
    IPort->wait (BOT, NewPacket);
  state NewPacket:
    if (ThePacket->isMy ()) skipto WaitRcv;
    OP = S->route (ThePacket);
    OPort = S->OPorts [OP];
    S->Idle [OP] = NO;
    OPort->startTransfer (ThePacket);
    skipto WaitEnd;
  state WaitEnd:
    IPort->wait (EOT, EndPacket);
  state EndPacket:
    OPort->stop ();
    S->Idle [OP] = YES;
    proceed Waiting;
  state WaitRcv:
    IPort->wait (EOT, Rcv);
  state Rcv:
    Client->receive (ThePacket, IPort);
    proceed Waiting;
};
```

State Waiting is the idle state, in which the process awaits a packet arrival on its input port. When this happens, the router gets to state NewPacket, where it first checks if the packet is addressed to the current station. If so, the process transits to state WaitRcv to simulate the packet reception—in the standard way. Otherwise, the station's route method is invoked to find the output port on which the packet should be relayed.

The careful reader has noticed that we play here the same trick that we played for the Manhattan Street Network in section 11.3.4.3. Namely, we assume that the destination address of an incoming packet is known immediately, at the very moment when the packet triggers the BOT event. In a real-life implementation of MNA, we would have to pass the packet through a (conceivably short) hallway buffer to achieve this effect. As before, we can safely claim that the hallway buffer can be modeled by increasing the length of all interstation links by the same amount.[15]

The value returned by route is an index into OPorts. The process stores this index in OP and sets OPort to the output port pointer (the appropriate entry from OPorts). Then it marks the selected output port as busy (by setting Idle[OP] to NO) and initiates the transmission of the incoming packet on the output port. Finally, the router skips to state WaitEnd to await an EOT event on the input port, i.e., the termination of the incoming packet. When this happens, the process transits to state EndPacket, where it terminates the transfer, resets the status of the output port to Idle, and returns to state Waiting to await another packet arrival.

The reader may wonder why the transition from state NewPacket to WaitEnd is done with skipto rather than proceed. As packets in MNA need not be separated by silence periods, it is possible that the BOT event that caused the transition from Waiting to NewPacket coincides with the EOT event marking the end of a previous packet that arrived on the same input port. Should this happen, and if proceed were used instead of skipto, the process would sense in state WaitEnd the EOT event pertaining to the previous packet. This error would result in an infinite loop through states Waiting, NewPacket, WaitEnd, and EndPacket, in which the simulated time would remain frozen.

The actual routing decision is made by the route method declared as an attribute of Switch. The role of this method is to find the index of an idle output port with the minimum value of the cost rank for a given destination Id extracted from the packet header. This is accomplished in the following way:

```
#define MAXORDER 256
int Switch::route (Packet *p) {
  int P [MAXORDER], R [MAXORDER], NP, r, min, i, j;
  Long rcv;
  rcv = p -> Receiver;
  for (min = MAX_int, i = NP = 0; i < Order; i++) {
    if (Idle [i]) {
      r = PRanks [i][rcv];
      if (r <= min) {
        P [NP] = i;
        R [NP] = r;
        min = r;
        NP++;
```

---

[15]In the case of a host switch, adding an extra passive tap to the delay line would solve the problem.

```
          }
        }
      }
    assert (NP, "route: can't relay packet");
    for (i = 0, j = 0; i < NP; i++)
      if (R [i] == min) P [j++] = P [i];
    return (j > 1) ? P [toss (j)] : P [0];
  };
```

The method extracts the **Receiver** attribute of the packet to be relayed and uses its value as an index into the routing table (**PRanks**). The row of **PRanks** pointed to by the destination **Id** gives the cost ranks of the station's output ports. The first **for** loop goes through all these ports and determines the minimum cost among all the output ports that are idle. The indexes of the ports that qualify as potential candidates are stored in array P; the other array (R) stores their cost ranks.

Note that the method cannot just select the first idle port with the minimum cost. If there are other idle ports with the same cost, one of them must be chosen at random in such a way that no port is privileged or discriminated against. Thus, the **for** loop collects into the two local arrays all output ports that are idle and whose costs are less than or equal to the current minimum. When the loop terminates, NP gives the number of ports that have been collected this way. According to the connectivity rules, this number must be nonzero: the protocol guarantees that all packets arriving at the switch can be relayed on-line. Generally, not all ports represented by the indexes in P have the same lowest cost and not all entries in R are the same. The arrays describe just a subset of the idle output ports, including all the idle ports with the lowest cost equal to min. The second **for** loop eliminates from P all the indexes corresponding to ports with a higher than minimum cost. If more than one index remains in P after this operation, one index is selected at random (section 2.3.1).

The routing tables are initialized before the protocol is started, in essentially the same way as in the global version of MSN. The only difference between the MNA version of **assignPortRanks** and the version discussed in section 11.3.4.7 is in the following code fragment:

```
        for (i = 0; i < NStations; i++) {
          S = (Switch*) idToStation (i);
          S->PRanks = new unsigned char* [S->Order];
          for (j = 0; j < S->Order; j++) {
            S->PRanks [j] = new unsigned char [NStations];
            for (k = 0; k < NStations; k++)
              S->PRanks [j][k] = IM [S->Neighbors [j]][k];
          }
        }
```

which creates the routing tables in MNA based on the all-shortest-paths matrix built by the Floyd's algorithm. As before, IM[i][j] gives the minimum number of hops from switch i to switch j. Given a switch number i, the cost rank of port j for destination k is determined as the length of the shortest path to the destination from the neighbor of switch i connected to it via port j.

11.4.3.3   The transmission protocol.

The only processes run by a host-less switch are the cohort of routers extracting packets from the input ports and relaying them on the output ports. A switch equipped with the host interface (and the delay lines) executes three more processes per each input port. Two of these processes handle the delay line attached to the port and keep track of its status. The third process acquires packets from the Client and submits them to the routers, pretending that they have arrived from the network.

All packets arriving from the network on the input ports must pass through the delay lines before they are seen by the routers. Therefore, on a host switch, the routers extract packets from the exit ports of the delay lines rather than directly from the input ports. Each delay line is fed by a dedicated process that relays packets from the corresponding input port into the entry port of the delay line. The type of this process is declared as follows:

```
process InDelay (Host) {
  Port *IPort, *NPort;
  int MP;
  void setup (int p) {
    IPort = S->IPorts [MP = p];
    NPort = S->NDelay [MP];
  };
  states {Waiting, In, WaitEOT, RDone};
  perform;
};
```

The setup argument of InDelay gives the index of the input port serviced by the process, which is also the index of the corresponding delay line (its entry port). The setup method stores pointers to these ports in the local attributes IPort and NPort, and also saves the index value in MP. The code method of InDelay is as follows:

```
InDelay::perform {
  state Waiting:
    IPort->wait (BOT, In);
  state In:
    NPort->startTransfer (ThePacket);
    S->Used [MP] ++;
    skipto WaitEOT;
  state WaitEOT:
```

```
              IPort->wait (EOT, RDone);
          state RDone:
            NPort->stop ();
            proceed Waiting;
      };
```

Having sensed the beginning of a packet on the input port, the process moves from state Waiting to state In to initiate a retransmission of the incoming packet on the entry port of the delay line. At the same time, it increments Used[MP] to indicate that one more packet is currently transiting through the delay line number MP. As explained in section 11.4.3.1, the role of Used is to keep track of the occupied/free status of the delay lines. Finally, the process skips to state WaitEOT to await the termination of the incoming packet. When this happens, the process will transit to state RDone, where it will stop the retransmission and move back to its initial state Waiting.

The exit port of a delay line is monitored by another simple process, whose sole purpose is to count the packets leaving the delay line. Its type declaration is as follows:

```
          process OutDelay (Host) {
            Port *XPort;
            int MP;
            Mailbox *FreePort;
            void setup (int p) {
              XPort = S->XDelay [MP = p];
              FreePort = S->FreePort;
            };
            states {Waiting, Out};
            perform;
          };
```

As in InDelay, attribute MP stores the port index identifying the entry of Used to be updated when the process detects a packet leaving the delay line. The mailbox pointed to by FreePort receives an alert whenever the new value of this entry is zero. All these operations are performed by the following simple code method, which requires no further explanation:

```
OutDelay::perform {
  state Waiting:
    XPort->wait (EOT, Out);
  state Out:
    assert (S->Used [MP], "Port should be marked as 'used'");
    if (--(S->Used [MP]) == 0) FreePort->put ();
    skipto Waiting;
};
```

Each host switch executes **Order** copies of the transmitter process responsible for inserting station's own packets into the network. Unlike the other processes run by the switch, the transmitters are not explicitly associated with any ports. Their number coincides with the number of input (and output) ports, because, under favorable circumstances, a single switch can transmit that many own packets simultaneously. The type declaration of the transmitter process is as follows:

```
process Transmitter (Host) {
  Port *XPort;
  int BF, XP, Order;
  Packet *Buffer;
  Mailbox *FreePort;
  void setup (int b) {
    Buffer = S->Buffer [BF = b];
    Order = S->Order;
    FreePort = S->FreePort;
  };
  states {NewMessage, RetryRoute, EndXmit, Error};
  perform;
};
```

Attributes **Buffer**, **Order**, and **FreePort** are local references to the corresponding attributes of the station owning the process. The setup argument (b) has the same range as a port index, but instead of a port it identifies a packet buffer. The index of the buffer serviced by the transmitter is stored in attribute BF to be passed to the **ready** method of **ClientInterface** (section 11.3.4.1) upon a packet acquisition. Attributes **XPort** and **XP** are not initialized by the setup method. They will be set dynamically to identify the delay line (its exit port) selected by the transmitter to submit its packet to the router. The process executes the following code:

```
Transmitter::perform {
  state NewMessage:
    if (!S->ready (BF, MinPL, MaxPL, FrameL)) {
      Client->wait (ARRIVAL, NewMessage);
      sleep;
    }
  transient RetryRoute:
    for (XP = 0; XP < Order; XP++)
      if (!S->Used [XP]) break;
    if (XP == Order) {
      FreePort->wait (NEWITEM, RetryRoute);
    } else {
      S->Used [XP] ++;
      XPort = S->XDelay [XP];
```

```
                      XPort->transmit (Buffer, EndXmit);
                      XPort->wait (COLLISION, Error);
                    }
            state EndXmit:
              XPort->stop ();
              Buffer->release ();
              proceed NewMessage;
            state Error:
              excptn ("Transmitter: illegal collision");
         };
```

The transmitter remains dormant in state NewMessage until it acquires a Client packet for transmission. When this happens, the process finds itself in state RetryRoute, where it tries to locate an empty delay line, i.e., the line whose transient packet count is zero. If no such line can be found at the moment, the transmitter suspends itself awaiting the NEWITEM event on the FreePort mailbox. Every time an OutDelay process sets its entry in Used to zero, it also deposits an alert in FreeDelay with the intention of awakening the transmitters waiting for an empty delay line. When the process is restarted by the mailbox event, it reexecutes the search loop in state RetryRoute. Note that despite the go signal indicating the apparent availability of an empty delay line, the search need not be successful, as several copies of the transmitter may be competing for the same scarce commodity. In such a case, only one process will get the line and the others will fail again.

Having found an empty delay line, the process reserves it by raising its Used count. This way the line will not be perceived as empty by the other copies of the transmitter. Immediately afterwards the process starts transmitting its packet on the exit port of the delay line. Thus, in fact, Used is telling the truth: one packet is transiting through the line, although that packet was not inserted into the line's entry port. Note that during the transfer the process awaits a collision—to make sure that the empty status of the delay line has been recognized correctly. Of course, collisions are impossible unless there is a problem with the protocol.

The rest is simple. The transmitted packet will be perceived by the router process servicing the exit port and relayed in the same way as a packet arriving from the network. When the transfer is over, the transmitter will move to state EndXmit, where it will terminate the transmission and release the packet buffer. Note that the process need not reset Used[XP] to zero. This will be done by the OutDelay process monitoring the exit port when it perceives the EOT event triggered by the packet.

11.4.3.4 Sample MNA configurations.

Directories MNA1 and MNA2 in Examples/SWITCH contain two sample programs implementing specific configurations of MNA. The network from directory MNA1 is a hypercube with the geometry described by the following incidence function (section 11.2.2.1):

```
int Connected (Long a, Long b, DISTANCE &d) {
  register Long p, i;
  p = (a | b) & ( a | b);
  for (i = 1; i < p; i += i);
  d = LinkLength;
  return i == p;
}
```

The right-hand side of the first assignment statement produces the "exclusive bitwise or" of a and b. Thus, the binary representation of p has 1's on those and only those positions on which a and b differ. The for loop following the assignment statement calculates in i the minimum power of 2 not less than p. The function decides that switches a and b should be connected by a link if i is equal to p, which simply means that p is a power of 2, i.e., its binary representation contains a single 1. Expressed in terms of a and b, this property says that the binary representations of the two numbers differ in exactly one binary position. If the total number of switches N is a power of 2, the network connected according to this rule forms a regular hypercube with $log_2(N)$ links going out and coming into every switch. Note that the incidence relation is symmetric, i.e., a link from a to b implies a link from b to a.

Hypercubes are very popular architectures for interconnecting multiple processors of tightly coupled distributed computers. Because of the simple and very regular structure of a hypercube network, routing decisions can be performed locally and are trivial. The maximum diameter of a hypercube expressed as the number of hops separating two most distant switches grows as a logarithmic function of the total number of switches in the network.

From the viewpoint of MNA, hypercubes are somewhat less attractive, mainly because the switch connectivity depends on the number of switches in the network. Moreover, if the network is to be regular, the total number of switches must be a power of 2. The second constraint is not very serious as, owing to the global table-driven routing, MNA configurations need not be regular. Thus, the unused ports in an incomplete MNA hypercube can be connected arbitrarily.

The root process for the hypercube configuration of MNA (directory MNA1) illustrates no novel features, and we do not discuss it here. All switches in the network are equipped with the host interface, which means that all stations are created as objects of type Host with all their associated processes. The sample data file in directory MNA1 describes a hypercube with 32 switches, which implies five link pairs per switch.

The second program (directory MNA2) implements an MNA network based on the Manhattan Street topology described in section 11.3.4.6. The incidence function used to describe the geometry of the network backbone has been copied directly from the MSN program (directory Manhattan1). Each switch has only two input and two output ports.

Although the MNA concept is not well suited for low-connectivity networks, the MSN variant of MNA can be useful to determine how much the network performance suffers when the synchronous routing algorithm of MSN is replaced with the asynchronous rules of MNA. The reader is encouraged to conduct experiments along these lines.

The code method of the root process for the MSN variant of MNA follows:

```
Root::perform {
  int NNodes, i, j;
  Long NMessages;
  DISTANCE DelayLineLength;
  double CTolerance;
  state Start:
    readIn (TRate);
    setEtu (TRate);
    readIn (CTolerance);
    setTolerance (CTolerance);
    readIn (NCols);
    readIn (NRows);
    Assert (evn (NCols) && evn (NRows),
      "The number of rows/columns must be even");
    NNodes = NCols * NRows;
    readIn (LinkLength);
    LinkLength *= TRate;
    initMesh (TRate, Connected, NNodes);
    readIn (MinPL);
    readIn (MaxPL);
    readIn (FrameL);
    readIn (DelayLineLength);
    DelayLineLength *= TRate;
    initTraffic ();
    for (i = 0; i < NNodes; i++)
      if (evn (col (i)) && evn (row (i)))
        create Host (2, DelayLineLength);
      else
        create Switch (2);
    assignPortRanks ();
    for (i = 0; i < NNodes; i++) {
      if (evn (col (i)) && evn (row (i))) {
        for (j = 0; j < 2; j++) {
          create (i) Router (j);
          create (i) InDelay (j);
          create (i) OutDelay (j);
          create (i) Transmitter (j);
        }
```

```
        } else {
          for (j = 0; j < 2; j++)
            create (i) Router (j);
        }
      }
      readIn (NMessages);
      setLimit (NMessages);
      Kernel->wait (DEATH, Stop);
    state Stop:
      System->printTop ("Network topology");
      Client->printDef ("Traffic parameters");
      Client->printPfm ();
  };
```

Following the usual preamble defining the clock accuracy and the transmission rate of the network, the process reads the number of columns and rows in the MSN grid. Then it verifies whether both these numbers are even[16] and sets the number of stations to be equal to the product of the number of rows and columns. The network backbone is configured exactly as for MSN. All interstation links are of the same length (LinkLength), which is read from the input data file and converted from bits to ITUs. The root process also reads from the input file the length of a delay line at a host switch (DelayLineLength), to be passed as the second setup argument of all host stations. Expressed in bits, this length must be greater than the total size of the longest packet, including its header and trailer.

Only the stations located at intersections of even-numbered rows and even-numbered columns are equipped with host interface. These stations are created as objects of type Host; all the other stations are host-less switches that just relay the network traffic. A host-less switch runs only a collection of Router processes, one process per every input port. Each of the host switches is additionally supported by the cohort of processes implementing the transmission part of the protocol (section 11.4.3.3).

BIBLIOGRAPHIC NOTES

Hubnet was introduced by *Lee and Boulton* (1983) and also presented by *Hopper, Temple, and Williamson* (1986). The latter authors also describe the concept of Floodnet, which was originally introduced by *Petitpierre* (1984). The prototype Hubnet built at the University of Toronto operated at the nominal transfer rate of 50 Mb/s per link. The performance of Hubnet was analyzed by *Kamal and Hamacher* (1986), *Kamal* (1986), and *Lee, Boulton, and Thomson* (1988). *Hassanein and Kamal* (1993) investigate an interesting anomaly in Hubnet behavior resulting from a correlation between the echo waiting time and the packet length.

---

[16]Macros evn, odd, row, and col are inherited from the original MSN implementation (section 11.3.4.2).

The Manhattan Street Network driven by a synchronous deflection-routing scheme was proposed and investigated by *Maxemchuk* (1985; 1987; 1989; 1991). In *Maxemchuk* (1991) the reader will find a discussion of several problems that may occur in MSN, including live-locks and starvation, and the motivation behind the randomization of the routing rules. The localized routing algorithm described in section 11.3.2 is based on *Maxemchuk* (1987). In that paper, it is also shown formally that for a complete MSN grid the localized procedure produces the same results as an algorithm based on the all-shortest-paths approach. Moreover, the reader will find there other variants of the routing rules, including simplified rules for complete grids as well as approximate localized rules for irregular incomplete networks.

MNA was introduced by *Maitan, Walichiewicz, and Wealand* (1990b; 1990a) and *Gburzyński and Maitan* (1993). The latter paper presents an analytical model for calculating the performance of regular MNA configurations under uniform traffic conditions. A working prototype of the MNA switch was built in the Palo Alto Lockheed Lab in California.

The all-shortest-paths algorithm used to precompute the static routing tables in sections 11.3.4.7 and 11.4.3.2 was originally proposed by *Floyd* (1962). This algorithm can also be found in practically any textbook on algorithm design, in particular in *Aho, Hopcroft, and Ullman* (1974).

PROBLEMS

1. Imagine a Hubnet in which different stations are connected to the hub via links of drastically different length. Discuss the merits of the following two solutions regarding the echo timeout used by different stations:

   - The echo timeout used by a station is equal to twice the propagation length of the link connecting the station to the hub, plus the necessary margin for recognizing the station's address in the packet header.
   - All stations, regardless of their distance from the hub, use the same echo timeout determined by the longest link in the network.

2. Write a SMURPH program implementing the hierarchical Hubnet discussed in section 11.1.3.

3. Devise and analyze a lock-out scenario for Floodnet. Can you propose a method of preventing such scenarios that would not be based on a randomized backoff?

4. Implement a hypercube version of Floodnet with 64 switches, in which every switch is connected to exactly one host. Compare the performance of this network to the performance of a torus Floodnet with the same number of switches and the same diameter.[17] Make sure that the average packet in your experiments is at least eight times longer than the network diameter. Explain your results.

---

[17]The maximum distance between a pair of stations.

5. Calculate the upper bound on the alignment buffer length in MSN as a function of clock tolerance and network size.

6. Devise a distributed initialization algorithm for MSN and MNA. With your algorithm, each station will build its routing table individually, based on the feedback from other stations.

7. Imagine a variant of MSN operating in a store-and-forward fashion. A segment that cannot be relayed along its single preferred route is buffered until the preferred output port becomes available. The only situation when a segment must be deflected is when a station runs out of its limited buffer space. Devise a buffering strategy for this protocol. Is it better to have a single global segment buffer per station or a separate buffer for each output port? Implement this variant of MSN, and determine its maximum achievable throughput as a function of the buffer size.

8. Using the program in directory `Examples/SWITCH/MNA1`, draw the performance curve (throughput versus packet delay) for a hypercube configuration of MNA with 128 stations. Explain what happens when the offered uniform load exceeds the saturation point of the network.

9. Implement a slotted synchronous variant of MNA in which the incoming segments are aligned at the switch and routed all at the same time. Such a network can be viewed as a generalization of the MSN concept onto arbitrary meshes with arbitrary switch connectivity. Devise a routing strategy that will minimize the penalty of the deflected segments. How can you randomize this strategy to avoid lock-out scenarios? Compare the maximum throughput achieved by the synchronous variant of MNA with the maximum throughput of the asynchronous network.

10. Consider a complete Manhattan Street Network in which all connections are bidirectional. Each station has four input and four output ports, and all rows and columns offer paths in both directions. Devise a collection of localized routing rules for this network. Your rules must be optimal, i.e., they must offer the same choice of routes as the global rules based on all-shortest-paths information.

Appendixes

A

DSD: The Dynamic Status Display Program

A.1 BASIC PRINCIPLES

DSD is a stand-alone program for monitoring simulation experiments in SMURPH on-line. In principle, the display program is exchangeable. For example, one version of the program may take care of displaying things on a regular terminal with a cursor addressing capability while another version may do it via X-Windows on a graphic terminal. The program described here works for regular ASCII terminals with the cursor addressing capability.

SMURPH communicates with DSD by receiving requests from the display program and responding with some information in a device-independent format. The display program and the simulator need not execute on the same machine; therefore, the information sent between these two parties is also machine-independent.

A typical unit of information comprising a number of logically related data items is a *window*. At the simulator's end, a window is represented by the following parameters:

618

- Standard name of the exposed object (section 2.4.2).
- Number specifying the window exposure mode (section 7.3.1).
- Id of the station to which the information displayed in the window is to be related. This attribute is generally optional and may not apply to some windows (section 7.3.5). In any case, if the station Id is absent, it is assumed that the window is global, i.e., not related to any particular station.

These elements correspond to one mode of the screen exposure associated with the object, or rather, with the object's type (section 7.3.4.1). Additionally, this exposure mode can be made station-relative. Whenever the contents of a window are to be updated (refreshed), the corresponding exposure mode is invoked.

The graphical layout of the exposure's window built by DSD is of no interest to SMURPH. The display program organizes its windows based on window templates associated with object types and their exposure modes (section 7.3.1). The simulator only knows which data items are to be sent to DSD to fill the window's dynamic fields. These data items are sent periodically by the simulator in response to a prior request from the display program indicating that the window has been summoned to the screen. This request specifies the three parameters of the window, which are used by SMURPH to identify the exposure (the object to be exposed), its mode, and the station to which the exposure is to be related.

From now on, we assume that a window is something intentionally displayable, described on SMURPH's end by the combination of the object's standard name, exposure mode, and an optional station Id. Although SMURPH does not really deal with windows, it has its own perception of window contents. For the simulator, a window is a sequence of items sent to the display program by invoking one of the screen forms of an exposure method (section 7.3.1).

A window can be put into a step mode, in which the simulator will update the window after processing every event that "has something to do with the window contents." For example, for a window corresponding to a station exposure, it means "every event that awakes one of the processes owned by the station." After each screen update in the step mode the simulator becomes suspended and an explicit user action is needed to continue its execution until the next stepped event.

At any moment during a simulation run, SMURPH may be connected to DSD (then we say that the display is active), or it may not. While the display is active, the simulator maintains the list of active windows, whose contents are periodically sent (section 7.3.3.1) to the display program by invoking the corresponding exposures. Note that SMURPH sends to the display program only raw data representing the information described by the object's exposure specification.

The display program may wish to activate a new window, in which case SMURPH adds it to the active list, or to deactivate one of the active windows, in which case the window is removed. The simulator alone never makes any decisions as to which windows are to be active/inactive. Its internal window list is updated exclusively in response to requests from the display program.

Upon the initial communication setup, SMURPH sends to the display program the layout of the hierarchy of all displayable objects. This hierarchy is a tree reflecting the relation of "belonging to." Every displayable object handled by the simulator belongs to some other object.[1] In some cases, this relationship is obvious (e.g., a packet buffer belongs to the station owning it); in other cases it is enforced (e.g., observers belong to the Root process) to make sure that every object has its place in the ownership hierarchy. To simplify things, it is assumed that each displayable object belongs to exactly one other object. This assumption is generally reasonable, although, e.g., a port naturally belongs to two objects: a station and a link. In this case, it is assumed that ports belong to stations, as this relationship is usually more relevant from the user's point of view.

Objects (the nodes of the object ownership tree) are represented by their standard names, supplemented by nicknames wherever they are defined. The display program transforms the ownership hierarchy into a hierarchy of menus for locating individual exposable objects.

Whenever the simulator creates a new exposable object, it notifies DSD about this fact and the display program updates its internal description of the ownership hierarchy. Whenever an exposable object ceases to exist and consequently should be removed from DSD's database, SMURPH also sends a pertinent message to the display program.[2] A typical operation performed by the user of DSD is a request to display a window associated with a specific object. Using the menu hierarchy (reflecting the object ownership structure), the user locates the proper object and issues a pertinent command. This request is turned by DSD into a window description understandable by SMURPH. This description is then sent to the simulator, which adds the requested window to its internal list of active windows. From now on, the dynamic information representing the window contents (a sequence of items—section 7.3.3) will be periodically sent to the display program every `DisplayInterval` events (section 7.3.4.2). The default value of `DisplayInterval` is 5000 events; the user can change this default by pressing the 'i' key in DSD (section A.8.5).

A.2   THE MONITOR

The simulator and DSD need not run on the same machine. It is assumed that simulation experiments are performed in the environment of UNIX machines interconnected into a local area network. One of these machines is designated to be the SMURPH *monitor host*. The most natural candidate for this machine is the personal workstation owned by the SMURPH user. Different users of SMURPH may (but do not have to) use different monitor hosts.

The identity of the monitor host is established during SMURPH installation

---

[1] As we will see, this hierarchy is a tree rooted at station System (section 3.1.2); thus, the system station does not belong to any other object. However, the system station is not a displayable object (it defines no screen exposure modes—section 7.3.5.12), so this sentence remains universally true.

[2] To minimize overhead, these notifications take place at the nearest moment when the window contents are sent to the display program.

(section B.1). A special program called `monitor` is then created; this program should constantly run in the background on the SMURPH monitor host.

The purpose of the monitor is to keep track of all simulation experiments started by the user who owns the monitor. Whenever a simulator instance is started (on any machine connected to the local network), it reports to the monitor; when the simulation run terminates, the monitor also learns about this fact and removes the experiment description from its data structures. This way, at any moment, the monitor knows about all simulation runs that are in progress on all machines in the local network. The following items of information are stored by the monitor for each experiment:

- Name of the host on which the experiment is running
- Simulator call command, i.e., the program name and the call arguments
- Date and time when the simulator was started
- Process `id` of the simulator
- Description of a logical channel[3] connecting the monitor to the simulator

The first four elements can be inspected by the user (they identify individual experiments); the last item makes it possible for the monitor to pass requests to the simulator.

A.3   LIST MODES OF DSD

The display program has three modes of execution. The first two modes are called *list modes*: they are used to list some short, general information without establishing a display session with a simulator instance. When called with:

```
dsd -l
```

DSD displays information about all simulator instances currently running. This information is produced by connecting to the monitor and displaying the contents of its internal database. One line of text is written for each active simulation run; it contains the first four items from the monitor's description of the experiment (section A.2). A somewhat more verbose output is produced by calling

```
dsd -s
```

With this call, two lines are displayed for each active simulation experiment. The first line contains exactly the same data as in the previous case, and the second line lists the following items:

- Total number of messages `received` so far (section 7.1.2.2)
- Simulated time in ITUs
- CPU time used in seconds

---

[3]This "channel" is a UNIX socket.

These data are obtained by connecting to the monitor and asking it to poll the running simulators for their status information.

A.4 ESTABLISHING A DISPLAY SESSION

To establish a display session with an active simulator instance, DSD should be called in the following way:

dsd [-t *stfname*] [-u *utfname*]

The two arguments are optional: the first specifies a nonstandard system template file, the second, an additional template file for user-defined windows. Window templates are discussed in section A.6.

When called this way, DSD connects to the monitor and receives from it the list of active simulation experiments. If this list is empty, the program produces the message:

No active smurphs

and exits immediately. Otherwise, it displays the list of active simulator instances on the terminal screen (in a manner similar to a list call—section A.3) and expects the user to select one experiment to which to connect.

The terminal cursor is initially located at the first entry of the experiment list, which can be selected by default. The user can change the selection by moving the cursor down (the 'j' key) or up (the 'k' key). Finally, when the selection has been made, the user hits the 'x' key (for *exit*), and the program will attempt to establish connection with the selected simulator instance.

The connection is established by asking the monitor to send a connect request to the simulator. Having received such a request, the simulator creates a communication channel[4] and returns the parameters of this channel to the monitor. The monitor in turn passes these parameters to DSD, which can use them to establish a direct communication link with the simulator.

This scenario assumes that the simulator is already active (running) when the display connection is established. In some cases, the user would like to establish a display session before the simulator has started, e.g., to trace its behavior from the very beginning. It is possible to call the simulator in such a way that it stops immediately after the protocol initialization phase (section 4.8), before commencing the simulation run (section B.3). It is also possible to stop the simulation at any moment from the protocol program (e.g., when the program detects an abnormal or interesting situation) and wait for a display connection from DSD (section 7.3.4.2).

Once established, the display session is terminated upon an explicit request from DSD or when the simulation run is terminated (completed or aborted).

---

[4]A UNIX socket.

A.5 MENUS: GENERAL CONCEPTS

The user communicates with the display program via a collection of menus. The collection of windows displayed on the screen can be viewed as a special case of a menu. Most commands for navigating through menus and selecting items are single-character strokes. The following command characters have a standard meaning (all departures from this standard and additional commands are described individually for specific menus):

?   Displays a help screen for the current menu, i.e., the collection of legal commands and their meaning

r   Redisplays the screen, e.g., after its contents have been messed up. `Ctrl-L` has the same effect

k   Moves the cursor one item up

j   Moves the cursor one item down

h   Moves the cursor one item to the left

l   Moves the cursor one item to the right

n   Displays the *next* portion of the menu

p   Displays the *previous* portion of the menu

x   Exits the menu

q   Terminates the display session and exits DSD

The interpretation of *next* and *previous* portions depends on the menu. Generally, if the list of objects to be presented in a menu does not fit into a single screen image, it is split into a number of portions, and the user can browse through these portions using the 'p' and 'n' keys.

For each menu being displayed, the notion of the *current* item is defined. The current item is pointed to by the cursor; its identifier is also displayed in the left bottom corner of the screen. The four corners of the screen have standard purposes, as follows:

- The left bottom corner of the screen identifies the current item. It is also used as the input field for the commands that require line input.
- The right bottom corner is used to display messages, e.g., about errors.
- The left top corner contains the menu title.
- The right top corner displays the text "Hit '?' for help."

The 'x' command exits the current menu and *transfers* DSD to another menu. For example, exiting the startup menu (with the list of active experiments), the display program moves to the *object* menu, from which the user can select windows to be displayed.

By hitting 'q', the user terminates the display session and exits DSD. The simulation experiment is continued, unless the user requested its termination (section A.8).

A.6 WINDOW TEMPLATES

The material in this section is not absolutely necessary for a user who merely wants to use DSD for viewing standard exposures. It may be useful, however, if the user would like to define a nonstandard screen exposure (section 7.3.2), which requires a matching window template on DSD's side (section 7.3.3.1) to become functional. This section will also help the reader understand how the information sent by the simulator to the display program is turned into windows displayed on the screen.

The layout of a window is determined by the *window template*, which is a textual pattern supplied to DSD in one of two template files. One template file contains templates of standard windows corresponding to the displayable types predefined by SMURPH, i.e., the standard subtypes of *Object* (section 2.4.1). The other file is provided by the user and contains templates of nonstandard user-defined windows. It may also contain templates that override some of the standard templates. This way, the user may define customized layouts for standard windows.

The system template file, called `stemplates`, resides in DSD's source directory (section B.1). This file is used automatically by the program, unless the user changes this default with the `-t` call option (section A.4).

A template file contains a sequence of template definitions: each template describes one window layout associated with a combination of the object type, the exposure mode, and a designator that determines whether the window should or should not be station-relative.

A.6.1 Template Identifiers

A template definition starts with the template identifier, which consists of up to three parts. Whenever the user requests a specific window to be added to the window menu (section A.7.2), DSD attempts to find a template identifier matching the requested parameters of the window. A request to add a window to the window menu specifies an object, a display mode, and (optionally) a station to which the window is to be related. These three items are reflected in the following general format of the template identifier:

typename mode station

The first (mandatory) part of the template identifier should be the type name of an *Object* type (section 2.4.2). The template will be used to expose objects belonging to the given type, or objects whose *base type* (section 2.4.2) coincides with the given type.

The second part specifies the display mode of the template. If this part is missing, the default mode 0 is assumed. Thus, the first two components of a template identifier select an exposure method and one `exmode` fragment of its screen portion (section 7.3.2.1), i.e., the piece of code that sends the window information to the display program.

The third (and last) item, if present, indicates whether the window can be made station-relative. If this part is absent, the window is global, i.e., the template cannot be used to display a station-relative version of the exposure.[5] An asterisk ('*') appearing in that place defines a station-relative window template. Such a template can only be used for a station-relative exposure, i.e., besides the object to be exposed and its display mode, the user request must specify a station (any station) to which the exposure should be related.

The last legitimate alternative for the third component of a template identifier is the sequence of two asterisks ('**'), which means that the window represented by the template can (but does not have to) be station-relative. Such a template can be used for any exposure matching the first two parts of the template identifier, irrespective of whether the exposure is station-relative or not.[6]

When the user requests addition of a new window to the window menu (section A.7.2), the templates are searched in the order of their occurrence in the template file, for the first template whose identifier matches the parameters of the request. If found, this template will be used to determine the window layout. The user-supplied template file takes precedence over the standard file: this way, user template definitions can override standard definitions. Formally, the search procedure for a matching template can be described in the following way:

1. The two template files, i.e., the user template file and the standard template file, are logically concatenated into a single template file in such a way that the user part precedes the standard part. If no user template file was specified when DSD was called (section A.4), only the standard file is used.

2. The template file is searched sequentially from the beginning. First, an attempt is made to find a template whose identifier satisfies the following properties:

   a. The *typename* part of the identifier matches the type name (section 2.4.2) of the object to be exposed.

   b. The *mode* part of the identifier matches the requested exposure mode.

   c. The third component of the identifier agrees with the station-relative status of the requested exposure. More specifically, if the requested exposure is global, this component must be either empty (global template) or '**' (flexible template). If the requested exposure is station-relative, the third component of the template identifier must be either '*' or '**'.

3. If a template is found whose identifier satisfies these criteria, the search terminates, and the found template will determine the window layout.

4. Otherwise, the object's base type name (section 2.4.2) is used instead of its

---

[5]Note that the exposure code identified with the first two arguments may send different items to the display program, depending on whether the exposure is global or station-relative (section 7.3.2.1).

[6]No standard (system) template has this property. All the standard exposures that can be made station-relative send different information in their global and station-relative versions. Thus, these versions require different templates.

type name, and the search is repeated.

Example

To illustrate how the template search is carried out, suppose that the user declares two station types, say Hub and Node. Assume that the user provides a nonstandard exposure method for type Hub and a matching collection of window templates for this method (in the user template file), but no nonstandard exposure is defined for type Node. Now, if the user requests a screen exposure for a Hub object with an exposure mode corresponding to one of the modes defined in the Hub's exposure method, the corresponding user-supplied template will be selected. On the other hand, standard Station templates will be used for exposing objects of type Node. The first part of the template search to expose a Node-type station will fail (no templates are defined specifically for type Node), then DSD will perform the second part of the search with type Station (the base type of Node) used instead of Node. This will result in selecting one of the standard templates for type Station (assuming that the requested exposure mode coincides with one of the standard modes).

Note that if the user-supplied exposure method for type Hub does not override all standard exposure modes for type Station, these standard modes are still available for exposing stations of type Hub. For the first part of the template search to be successful, all attributes of the exposure request must match the corresponding portions of the template identifier. Thus, the standard exposure modes not covered by the user-provided templates for type Hub remain associated with the standard templates for type Station.

A.6.2   Template Structure

Templates are quite easy to define. The simplest way to define a nonstandard template is to modify one of the standard templates from file **stemplates** in DSD's source directory. Also, the best way to understand how templates are built is to look at a specific example. The template presented in figure A.1 resembles the standard template describing the layout of the mode 0 Timer window (section 7.3.5.2).

As we have said, a template definition starts with the identifier (section A.6.1), whose first field is mandatory. The template from figure A.1 is global (its window cannot be made station-relative), because the third field of the identifier is empty.

The second line of a template definition is a quoted string describing briefly the window's purpose. This description will identify the template on the menu used to select the object's exposure mode. The description string must not contain newline characters.

Any text following the closing quotation mark of the description string and preceding the first line starting with 'B' or 'b' is assumed to be a comment and is ignored. Similarly, all empty lines, i.e., those containing nothing except possible blanks or **tab** characters are always skipped.

The next relevant line of the template, starting with the letter 'B,' begins the description of the window format. The first and the last nonblank characters from this line are removed, and the length of whatever remains determines the width of

```
Timer 0
"Wait requests (global)"
// Displays Timer wait requests coming from all stations
B012345678901234567890123416789012345678101234567190123456789011345678901 2+B
|######~Time~~~St~~~Process/Idn~~~~TState~~~~~~~AI/Idn~~~~~Event~~~~~State|r
|%%%%%%%%%%%&  %%% %%%%%%%%%/&&&  %%%%%%%%% %%%%%%%/&&&  %%%%%%%%% %%%%%%%%%|
*                                                                         |
*                                                                         |-
*8                                                                        |+
**                                                                        |
E0123456789012345678901234567890123456789012345678901234567890123456789012E
```

Figure A.1   A sample template

the window. All characters other than '|' and '+' are just counted to the window width and have no special meaning. Characters '|' and '+' are also counted, but they are special: they describe the legitimate ways of clipping the window along its width (the x-axis). Each vertical bar, and also the optional '+' character, indicates a position at which the window can be truncated. The user (or the program, e.g., if there is not enough room on the screen to accommodate the full version of the window) may select any of the legal truncations. The clipping column pointed to by '|' or '+' will be included in the truncated version of the window. The plus sign indicates the recommended default clipping. Only one plus character may occur in the B-line: there can be only one default width for a window.

For the template shown in figure A.1, the default horizontal clipping corresponds to the full window width. In this case, the plus sign could be omitted: if it does not occur within the B-line, its implicit position is at the end of this line—just in front of the closing 'B.'

The line starting with 'B' does not belong to the window frame, and it does not contribute to the window height. Similarly, the closing line of the template (the one starting with 'E') is not considered to be part of the window frame. In fact, only the first character (the letter 'E') from the closing line is relevant, and the rest of this line is ignored.

Note.   The case of all special letters occurring in the template definition is ignored. Thus, 'B' can be replaced by 'b', and 'E' can be replaced by 'e.' This does not apply to the strings representing fixed pieces of text (captions) to appear in the window. Such strings stand for themselves, and they are not interpreted by DSD.

All nonempty lines (not beginning with 'X' or 'x') occurring between the starting and closing lines describe the window contents. Each such line should begin with '|' or '*'. A line beginning with '|' is a *format*, or *layout, line*: it specifies the layout of the corresponding line in the window. A layout line terminates with a matching vertical bar. The two bars do not count in the layout: they are just delimiters, like the two letters 'B' encapsulating the width line. The terminating bar can be followed by additional information, which does not directly belong to the layout but may associate certain attributes with the items defined within the line.

A.6.3 Special Characters

Within the layout portion of a template line, some characters have special meaning. All nonspecial characters stand for themselves, i.e., they will be displayed directly on the positions they occupy within the template. Following are all the special characters and their meanings:

A contiguous string of these characters indicates the place where the window *title* will be displayed.

~   This character stands for a virtual blank and will be displayed as a blank within the window. Regular blanks are also displayed as blanks; however, two items separated by a sequence of regular blanks are considered separate, in the sense that each of them has an individually definable set of attributes (section A.6.8). Items separated by strings of virtual blanks are assigned attributes globally—as if they were a single item.

%   A sequence of '%' characters reserves room for one simple data item sent by the simulator to be displayed in the window (section 7.3.3.2). If the received item is shorter than the reserved field, it will be right-justified.

&   A sequence of ampersands also reserves room for one simple data item, but the item will be left-justified if it does not fill the entire field.

@   This character is used to define a *region* boundary. Regions (sections 7.3.3.3, A.6.7) are rectangular areas within windows that are filled with semigraphic contents.

The window title displayed in the area marked with a sequence of '#' characters consists of the standard name of the exposed object, followed by the exposure mode number, followed in turn by the Id attribute of the station to which the window is related. The last item only occurs if the exposure is station-relative; it is absent in a global exposure. If the object's nickname is defined (section 2.4.2), the standard name is replaced by the nickname. The program will attempt to fit the title in such a way as to fill the entire title field. The title will be truncated if the field is too short to contain it all. If more than one title area is specified, the title will be replicated in all these areas.

Nonblank fields separated by sequences of virtual blanks ('~') appear as different items, but all these fields are assigned the same set of attributes—as a single item. Moreover, the separating sequence of virtual blanks receives the same attributes as the fields it separates. For example, the header line of the template from figure A.1 contains a number of items separated by virtual blanks. The letter 'r' occurring after the terminating bar of the header line is a field attribute: it says that the first field from the line will be displayed in *reverse video*. Since all items of the header line are separated by virtual blanks, they are assigned attributes as a single field; thus, the entire line will be displayed in reverse video.

A sequence of '%' characters reserves a field to contain a single data item sent to DSD by the simulator as part of the information representing the object's exposure (section 7.3.3.2). The data type of this item is irrelevant from the viewpoint of the template specification and will be determined upon the item's arrival. The program will attempt to contain the item within its field. The item will be truncated (from the left) if it is longer than the field, and right-justified if it happens to be shorter than the field. The only difference between '&' and '%' is that an item displayed in a field marked by a sequence of ampersands is left-justified if it does not fill the field entirely.

Data items arriving from the simulator are assigned to their fields in the order in which they arrive. The order of fields is from left to right within a line, and when the line is filled completely, DSD switches to the next line. If there are more data items than fields in the template, the superfluous items are ignored by the display program.

A.6.4   Exception Lines

A special character can be *escaped*, i.e., turned into a nonspecial one in a way that does not affect the visible length of the layout line. Any layout line can be preceded by an *exception line* starting with the letter 'X' or 'x'. The exception line does not count in the window layout; it just marks some positions in the layout line that follows it. If a position in the exception line is marked by '|', the character occupying that position in the next layout line will be treated as a regular character, irrespective of what this character actually is.

Sometimes two data fields that should contain two different items arriving from the simulator are adjacent, i.e., they appear as a single continuous field in the layout line. An exception line can be used to separate such fields. If a position marked with '+' in an exception line occurs in the middle of a data field in the next layout line, the field is split into two separate fields: the first field ends at the position marked by the '+' (but includes this position), and the second starts at the position immediately following the mark. Any other characters (except newline) occurring in an exception line are treated in the same way, i.e., as fillers used to advance the position counter.

Consider for example the template presented in figure A.1. The first two fields from the second layout line of this template are adjacent. According to the description of the mode 0 global exposure for the Timer (section 7.3.5.2), the first field will contain a time value, and the second field will receive a single-character flag. In this case, taking advantage of two different field types, we can define the two adjacent fields without resorting to escape lines. Note that the justification mode for the second field is irrelevant: it is one character long, and the item displayed there is always a single character.

The layout line in question could have been defined in the following way:

```
X            +                                                                           X
|%%%%%%%%%%% %%% %%%%%%%%/&&& %%%%%%%% %%%%%%%/&&& %%%%%%%% %%%%%%%%|
```

Now, although the sequence of '%' characters starting the layout line looks like a single data field, the '+' in the preceding exception line splits this sequence into two fields, as they are defined explicitly in the original version of the layout line.

Note that fields number 4 and 5 (also 7 and 8) are not adjacent. They are separated by '/', which is a regular character standing for itself, and DSD has no problems recognizing them as separate fields.

A single layout line can be preceded by a number of exception lines, the effect of the multiple exception lines being cumulative.

A.6.5   Replication of Layout Lines

Sometimes the same layout line has to be replicated a number of times. In some cases, this number is quite arbitrary, i.e., depending on the amount of space available on the screen, the program may decide to allocate more or fewer rows to the window. Such a situation occurs with the Timer window (figure A.1), which is actually a table (section 7.3.5.2) consisting of multiple rows with exactly the same format (the header line is an obvious exception). Many other standard exposures are arranged in a similar fashion (section 7.3.5). A template line starting with an asterisk stands for a replication of the last regular layout line. The asterisk can be followed by a positive integer number specifying how many replications are needed. If the number is missing, the default replication count of 1 is assumed. A double asterisk means that the number of replications is undefined: the program is free to assume any non-negative number.

A replication line need not contain any characters other than the asterisk possibly followed by a number, or two asterisks. For uniformity, replication lines (like regular layout lines) are usually terminated with a closing bar. A replication line may contain a vertical clipping indicator, i.e., '–' or '+', specifying a legal height of the window—in the same way as for horizontal clipping (section A.6.2). In such a case, the replication line must terminate with a vertical bar and the clipping indicator should follow that bar.

A.6.6   Window Height and Vertical Clipping

The window height is determined by the number of proper layout lines, excluding the B line, the E line, empty lines, and exception lines. As well as in width, windows can be clipped in height, by cutting some rows from the bottom. A layout line whose contents part terminates with a vertical bar can include a clipping indicator that should immediately follow the terminating bar. This indicator can be either '–' (minus) or '+'. As with the vertical bar for width clipping, '–' points to one of the legal clipping rows (the row containing the '–' will be included in the displayed portion of the window) and '+', which may appear only once (i.e., at the end of at most one layout line), specifies the default clipping. If the '+' indicator does not occur, the default number of rows to be displayed is equal to the number of layout lines in the template, including replications.

Owing to the replication lines, vertical clipping is a bit trickier than horizontal clipping. In particular, if a replication line with undefined count appears in a template, the actual number of layout lines is impossible to tell. The following rules explain how such cases are handled by DSD:

- A clipping indicator occurring at a replication line with a definite replication count (the line starts with a single asterisk) is associated with the last line of this count.

- An implicit '-' indicator is associated with each replication generated by a line starting with '**'. In simple words, the window can be legitimately clipped at any line resulting from an unlimited replication.

- A '+' indicator appearing at a '**' line or past this line is ignored, i.e., default clipping cannot be defined at a line whose exact location in the window cannot be inferred from the template.

- If the window height is unlimited and the default height indicator ('+') does not occur within the part preceding the '**' line, the default height of the window is equal to the maximum height available at the time when the window is requested. In such a case, the height will be determined by DSD at the moment when the window is opened.

Example

Let us revisit the `Timer` template presented in figure A.1. A window described by this template starts with a header line (including the window title and item captions) followed by several data rows with the same layout. The minimum window height is 4 lines, the default height is 12 lines, and the maximum height of the window is unlimited. DSD can display the window with any height greater than three lines (each of the layout lines generated by the unlimited replication is a legitimate clipping line).

A.6.7   Regions

A region is a rectangular fragment of a window used to display graphic information. Region data sent by the simulator to DSD consist of one or more segments (section 7.3.3.3). Each segment is a sequence of points to be displayed within the region. Depending on the segment attribute pattern, these points can be loose, they can be connected with lines, or they may represent tops of histogram stripes extending to the bottom of the region rectangle. In the last two cases, the lines are displayed as sequences of characters.

Within the template, the region rectangle is described by marking each of its four corners with '@'. For example, figure A.2 shows the standard template for exposing random variables with mode 0. According to the specification of this exposure (section 7.3.5.4), the first item to be displayed is a region with one segment presenting graphically the history of 24 last exposed mean values of the random

```
RVariable 0
"Full contents"
B----------------------B
|######################|  r
|@                    @|  '*'
|                      |
|                      |
|                      |
|                      |
|                      |
|                      |
|                      |
|                      |
|@                    @|-
|----------------------|  r
|Count:  %%%%%%%%%%%%%%|- h n
|Min:    %%%%%%%%%%%%%%|- h n
|Max:    %%%%%%%%%%%%%%|- h n
|Mean:   %%%%%%%%%%%%%%|- h n
|StDev:  %%%%%%%%%%%%%%|+ h n
X     |                    X
|CI95%:  %%%%%%%%%%%%%%|- h n
|        %%%%%%%%%%%%%%|- n
**                     |
E----------------------E
```

Figure A.2 Mode 0 `RVariable` template

variable. The first layout line of the template contains the window title field spread across the entire row. The region rectangle starts in the second line and occupies 11 rows and 24 columns. Note that the corners marked by '@' belong to the region rectangle. Except for the corner characters, the rest of the rectangle representing the region within the template is ignored, i.e., any characters appearing there, possibly including special characters different from '@', are treated as a comment.

A single template may define a number of regions. Regions must not overlap, and they must be perfectly rectangular. The ordering of regions among themselves and other fields (important for the correct interpretation of the data items arriving from SMURPH) **is determined by the positions of their left top corners.**

A.6.8 Field Attributes

A layout line terminated by '|' can specify attributes to be attached to the fields defined within the line. The optional specification of these attributes should follow the clipping indicator, if one is associated with the line.

If more than one attribute specification is addressed to the same field (this only makes sense for regions), all these specifications must be encapsulated in parentheses "(...)." Specifications for different fields are separated by blanks. The correspondence between specifications and fields is determined by the order of their occurrence from left to right. Note that regions are represented for this purpose by their left top corners; thus, an attribute specification for a region must be appended to this row of the template that specifies the first line of the region rectangle. Superfluous specifications are ignored. Fields without specifications are assigned default attributes.

For a nonregion field, the attribute specification is very simple and restricted to a single letter describing the display style. The following letters are applicable:

n Normal display (the default)

r Reverse video

h Highlighted (extra bright) display

b Blinking display

For a terminal that does not support a given display style, the style specification is ignored and the default normal style is assumed.

Four attributes are applicable to a region. Note that parentheses must be used if more than one attribute specification is given. A region attribute determines one of the following properties:

- Region display style. This attribute is specified in the same way as for a regular field.

- Point display character, i.e., the character used to represent points displayed within the region.

- Line display character, i.e., the character used to draw line segments connecting points, if the points are to be connected with lines.

- Region scaling, i.e., how the point coordinates sent by SMURPH are to be transformed into character locations within the region.

The two display characters are specified as one item encapsulated between single quotation marks. For example, "'o.'" defines 'o' as the point display character and '.' (the period) as the line display character. If only one character appears between the quotation marks, the other is assumed to be the same. If no display character is explicitly associated with a region, both display characters default to the asterisk ('*').

The scaling attribute of a region is specified as a sequence of four floating-point numbers separated by commas. Their meaning and order are the same as for the arguments of startRegion (section 7.3.3.3). Automatic scaling is assumed if no explicit scaling is assigned to the region, unless the region data sent by SMURPH contain their own scaling parameters.[7] Scaling requested by the simulator always

---

[7]This is the case for all regions displayed by standard exposures.

takes precedence over the scaling attribute assigned to the region by the template.

Example

Figure A.3 shows an example of a window template with two regions and several other fields. The first layout line of this template defines three fields: the fixed string "Station," a right-justified data field, and the title field. As these fields are separated by virtual blanks (section A.6.3), they are assigned attributes as a single field. Thus, the entire first row of the window will be displayed highlighted.

```
Mytype 0 **
"Just an example"
B                               |                    B
|Station~%%%~~~~~~~~~~~~~~~~~~~~~##################| h
|@                        @  Number~of~packets: %%%%%%%| (r '@') n b
|                            Number~of~bits:    %%%%%%%| n b
|                            Acknowledgments:   %%%%%%%| n h
|                            Retransmissions:   %%%%%%%| n n
|                            Errors:            %%%%%%%| n b
|                            Average~delay:     %%%%%%%| n h
|                            ==========================| r
|@                   @  @                 @  Status| h r
|=======Variance========                    A %%%%|-r h n
|Hits:       %%%%%%%%%%%                     B %%%%| h n h n
|Misses:     %%%%%%%%%%%                     C %%%%| h n h n
|Total:      %%%%%%%%%%%                     D %%%%| h n h n
|Successes:  %%%%%%%%%%%                     E %%%%| h n h n
|Failures:   %%%%%%%%%%%                     F %%%%| h n h n
|Total:      %%%%%%%%%%% @                 @ G %%%%| h n h n
|Fairness:   %%%%%%%%%%% =======Mean======== H %%%%| h n r h n
|~~~~~~~~~~~~~~~~~~~~~~~~~~~~~~~~~~~~~~~~~~~~~~~~~~~~| r
E                                                   E
```

Figure A.3 Sample template with two regions

The second layout line defines five fields: a region, three fixed strings separated by virtual blanks, and a right-justified data field. The region will be displayed in reverse video with '@' used to draw both points and lines. The three words "Number of packets" will be displayed normally (note that they all receive attributes as a single field), and the data item will appear blinking (provided that the terminal offers this capability).

The remaining fields and attributes are easy to comprehend. Recall that a portion of a region rectangle does not count as a field, except for its first line. In particular, layout line number 9 has two fields, not three.

A.7   THE OBJECT MENU

The object menu is entered automatically by DSD when the user leaves the startup menu (section A.4) by hitting the 'x' key. The object menu allows the user to browse through the hierarchy of exposable objects and select the windows to be included in the window menu, i.e., displayed on the screen (section A.8).

A.7.1   The Hierarchy of Exposable Objects

All exposable objects known to the simulator and to the display program are organized into a tree reflecting their *ownership* relation. The root of this tree is the System station (section 3.1.2), which is assumed to own (directly or indirectly) all exposable objects. The structure of the ownership tree is shown in figure A.4. The ordering of subnodes in the figure reflects the order in which the identifiers of objects represented by the subnodes appear in the object menu.

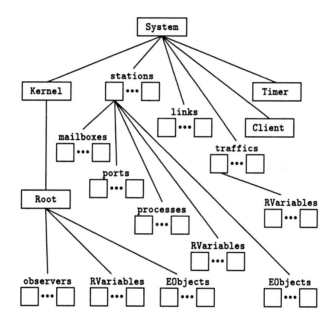

Figure A.4 The ownership hierarchy of exposable objects

The first object owned by System is Kernel—the root of the process hierarchy (section 4.8). Note that the parent-child relationship of processes need not coincide with the ownership hierarchy, e.g., protocol processes created (and thus parented) by Root are owned by their stations.

The System station owns all regular stations of the network. These stations constitute a flat structure: they are all direct descendants of System. Similarly, links, traffic patterns, and the two global dæmons Client and Timer also belong to the System station.

A regular station owns its mailboxes and ports. It also owns all regular processes, RVariables, and EObjects that were created by Root in the context of the station (section 4.3). The rules for determining the ownership of such objects created while the protocol is running are different.

Each traffic pattern owns its standard collection of random variables that keep track of various performance measures (section 7.1.2.1). A nonstandard random variable created in a user-defined traffic pattern, by its setup method, is also owned by the traffic pattern.

The Kernel process owns the user-defined Root process responsible for initialization (section 4.8) and all system processes. The system processes are invisible to the user (and they do not appear in the object menu), unless the simulator has been called with the -s option (sections 7.3.5.1, B.3).

The Root process is the owner of all observers (section 7.2.2). It also owns any RVariables and EObjects that were created by Root outside the context of any regular station, i.e., with TheStation containing NULL or pointing to the System station.

There are three categories of exposable objects that can be created (and possibly destroyed) dynamically by the protocol after the initialization phase, namely, processes, random variables, and EObjects. Such an object is owned by the process directly responsible for creating it. Thus, the ownership relation of processes created by other protocol processes (not by Root) coincides with the parent-child relationship.

A.7.2   Adding New Windows to the Window Menu

The object menu can be entered in two ways: from the startup menu and from the window menu. Initially, the collection of windows to be displayed on the screen is empty. Thus, exiting the startup menu, DSD enters the object menu so that the user can specify the windows that should appear on the screen. Later, the user may return to the object menu from the window menu to add more windows. When the object menu is entered, the simulator is halted and its ownership tree is frozen: the configuration of exposable objects does not change while the user is browsing through the object menu.

The object menu consists of object identifiers linked according to the object ownership hierarchy (figure A.4). An object identifier is obtained from combining the object's nickname with its standard name. If the object has no nickname, just the standard name is used. Standard names of ports and mailboxes are stripped of their station parts (sections 3.3.1, 4.7.3). As we mentioned in section A.7.1, ports and mailboxes appear under their owning stations in the object menu. Consequently, the station parts of their standard names are redundant.

While the object menu is active, DSD displays in the left top corner of the screen the name of the owner (also called the parent) of the current collection of objects. Initially, immediately after the menu is entered, the current parent is System and the screen contains the names of the objects owned by the System station, in the order shown in Figure A.4. Using the keys 'h', 'j', 'k', and 'l' (section A.5) the user can navigate through the objects from the current collection, including the owner. The current object is pointed to by the cursor; its identifier is also displayed in the left bottom corner of the screen.

If not all object names of the current collection fit into the screen at once, the keys 'n' and 'p' can be used to switch to the *next* and *previous* pages of object names.

By pressing 'c' the user moves one level down in the ownership hierarchy: the current object becomes the new owner, and the screen is filled with the first (or only) page of its successors. The 'f' key does the opposite: it moves the menu one level up, i.e., the new owner is assumed to be the owner of the current owner. In either case, the screen is filled with the identifiers of the objects belonging to the new owner.

The 'a' key is used to add a new window to the pool of windows to be presented on the screen (the window menu). By hitting this key, the user indicates that the current object, i.e., the object whose identifier is pointed to by the cursor, is to be exposed. If, based on the list of available templates (section A.6), DSD concludes that there are more than one exposure modes (section 7.3.1) available for the object, or, although there is just one exposure mode, it admits station-relative windows, the program prompts the user for more information. The object menu is temporarily abandoned, and DSD presents the *mode selection menu.*

The mode selection menu is the list of all possible exposure modes for the object. This list is built based on the collection of templates matching the object's type name (section A.6.1). Each template corresponds to one entry in the menu. The entry consists of the mode number and the template description string (section A.6.2). The user can browse through the entries of the mode selection menu using the keys 'j', 'k', 'n', and 'p', as described in section A.5.

The entry pointed to by the cursor is assumed to be the current entry. If this entry describes a mode (template) that requires or admits a station identifier (i.e., the window must or can be station-relative), a station Id prompt appears in the left bottom corner of the screen. The window indicated by the current entry can be added to the window menu in one of the following ways:

- If no station Id is required for the window, the user can hit 'a' or the *return* key. The window will be added immediately.

- If a station Id is required (or it is optional but the user wants to specify a station Id), the user should enter the station number.

In the second case, as soon as the user types the first digit, the cursor will move to the prompt area in the left bottom corner of the screen and the digit will be echoed in that area. The UNIX "character kill" and "line kill" characters can be used to control typing. The "line kill" character gets the user back to the mode selection menu with the cursor left at the last current item. Having entered the station Id, the user hits the *return* key. The new window is added to the active set of windows and DSD remains in the mode selection menu. The user can add more windows for the current object (e.g., using other modes or relating the windows to other stations) or hit 'x' to move to the object menu.

DSD refuses to add the new window if the window is already active, or if there is no room on the screen to accommodate the window. In such a case, a pertinent message is displayed in the right bottom corner of the screen.

The program attempts to fit the new window into the configuration of windows already present in the window menu. These windows are not allowed to overlap, yet all of them must be fully contained within a single screen image at the same time. If the window, with its default size, cannot fit into the existing collection of windows, the program will try to reduce the window size according to the clipping information associated with the window template (section A.6).

DSD executes a rather tricky (perhaps unnecessarily tricky) algorithm to accommodate the new window on the screen in such a way as to minimize screen fragmentation. Once displayed, the window can be moved to another location on the screen by a user command (section A.8.3).

The normal way to exit the object menu is to press the 'x' key. The program will then move to the window menu (section A.8) and display the selected collection of windows on the screen. By hitting 'q' while in the object menu the user abandons the display session and terminates DSD.

A.8　THE WINDOW MENU

The window menu is entered when the user exits from the object menu (section A.7) by pressing the 'x' key. The current configuration of selected windows is initially displayed with empty contents and the program awaits a user command to proceed. The simulator is still halted: it will not resume its operation until the user hits the *return* key.

Unlike the other menus, the window menu treats the top line as a regular line: it is not reserved to display special information. The bottom line, however, is still special: the left bottom corner displays the identifier of the *current window* and the right bottom corner is used to present exceptional (error) messages.

As for all other menus, '?' is the help key. When pressed, it displays the list of available command keys with a brief description.

A.8.1　General Commands

Typically, the contents of the windows displayed by the window menu are refreshed every specific number of simulation events (section 7.3.4). Only the dynamic part of a window is refreshed, i.e., the parts described in the window template by data items and regions (section A.6); the titles, fixed fields, and so on, are displayed once—when the window menu is entered or resumed.

A number of command keys are available in the window menu. Any key hit by the user while the menu is in the periodic update mode, even before the key is interpreted as a possible command, forces the simulator to refresh the contents of the active windows and halt. Then the character is interpreted and, if it happens to represent a valid command, the command is executed.

Some commands leave the simulator suspended. This way, the user may execute a number of commands before SMURPH is allowed to change the simulation state. In such a case, by pressing the *return* key the user exits the frozen state and forces the simulator to proceed. When SMURPH is halted and awaits a user response to continue, the text "HOLDING" is displayed in the right bottom corner of the screen.

At every moment while the window menu is presented, the notion of the *current window* is defined: the identifier of the current window appears in the left bottom corner of the screen. Some commands, described in the following sections, apply to the current window. The user can change the current window by using the keys 'h', 'j', 'k', and 'l', as described in section A.5.

When the user exits the window menu by pressing the 'x' key, DSD abandons the current display session and moves to the startup menu. By hitting 'q' the user terminates DSD.

Normally, when a display session is terminated, the simulator resumes its normal execution. It is possible to terminate the simulator from the window menu by pressing the 't' key. Because this command is potentially unsafe, the program asks for confirmation before sending the termination request to SMURPH.

At any moment the user may attempt to add new windows to the window menu. The 'w' key leaves the window menu temporarily and moves DSD to the object menu, from which new windows can be added. By exiting the object menu ('x') the user moves back to the window menu. The simulator is blocked while the object menu is active.

A.8.2   Removing Windows

A window can be removed by making it the current window and then hitting the 'd' key (for *delete*). The removed window is erased from the screen and from the pool of windows maintained by SMURPH. No more update information regarding this window will be sent by the simulator.

A.8.3   Moving Windows

A window can be moved to another free location on the screen that is large enough to accommodate the window in its present shape. To move a window, the user should first make it the current window and then press the 'm' key (for *move*). The user will be asked to move the cursor (using the keys 'h', 'j', 'k', and 'l') to the new location of the left top corner of the window. Locations that cannot possibly accommodate the window are automatically skipped.

By hitting the *return* key the user accepts the new location. The window is erased at its previous location and redisplayed in the new place.

The 'a' key can be used to abort the *move* command without affecting the screen layout.

A.8.4   Resizing Windows

A window can be resized, according to the clipping information associated with the window template (section A.6), provided that there is enough room to accommodate the resized window at its present location. To resize the current window the user should press the 'c' key (for *clip*). DSD will display the cursor in the right bottom corner of the window and ask the user to move the cursor (using the keys 'h', 'j', 'k', and 'l') to the new location of this corner. The cursor is only allowed to visit the legal coordinates for the right bottom corner, determined by the clipping indicators of the window template.

By hitting the *return* key the user accepts the new size of the window. The window is erased and redisplayed with the new size.

The 'a' key aborts the *clip* command without affecting the window shape.

Note.   When a window is resized, the display program sends to the simulator a number that determines how many data items are to be sent when the window contents are refreshed. This indication restricts the volume of data passed between SMURPH and DSD and increases the communication speed. However, irrespective of the actual horizontal clipping, SMURPH cannot be aware of the window width (it is assumed that the simulator has absolutely no knowledge of the window layout). Thus, when DSD informs the simulator about the number of items in the window, it assumes the maximum possible window width. In consequence, the items that are clipped off owing to the reduced width will actually arrive from the simulator: they will be ignored and skipped by DSD. The moral of this story is that by reducing the window width alone, the user does not reduce the volume of data sent by the simulator to the display program.

A.8.5   Changing the Display Interval

The global variable `DisplayInterval` maintained by SMURPH (section 7.3.4.2) tells how often the screen contents are to be refreshed. Every `DisplayInterval` simulation events, the simulator sends to DSD the new values of the data items (including regions) to be displayed within active windows. When a display session is started, `DisplayInterval` is set to 5000 events.[8] By hitting the 'i' key while in the window menu, the user can change the contents of `DisplayInterval`. DSD will prompt the user for the new value in the left bottom corner of the screen. Having entered the new value, the user should hit the *return* key to complete the operation. "Character kill" and "line kill" characters are available while the new value is entered. By hitting the "line kill" character, the user aborts the operation and retains the previous value of `DisplayInterval`.

---

[8]This only applies to the UNIX version of the package.

A.8.6   The Step Mode

The window menu can be put into the so-called *step mode*, in which the simulator is stopped whenever a specific event occurs. An explicit user action is then required to resume the execution. This way a simulation experiment can be traced by monitoring selected events that may be of interest to the user.

The step mode is associated with windows, i.e., we say that a window or a set of windows is being *stepped*. If a window is stepped, the simulator is halted whenever an event occurs that is somehow related to the window. Then the contents of the window reflect the state of the simulation **after** the stepping event has been processed.

Multiple windows can be stepped at the same time. The occurrence of any event related to any of the stepped windows suspends the simulator.

The following rules describe what we mean by "an event related to a window":

- If the object exposed in the window is a station, the related event is any event waking any process owned by the station.
- If the object is a process, the related event is any event waking the process. One exception is the `Kernel` process. It is assumed that all events are related to `Kernel`; thus, by stepping a `Kernel` window, the user intercepts all events, effectively stepping the entire simulator.
- If the object is a random variable or an exposable object of a user-defined type, the related event is any event related to the object's owner (section A.7.1).
- If the object is an observer, the related event is any waking event that results in restarting the observer.
- If the object is an AI not previously mentioned, the related event is any waking event triggered by the AI.

To put a window into the step mode the user should first make it the current window and then hit the 's' key. DSD will prompt the user for a number representing the earliest time in ITUs when the window can be stepped. The user can respond in three ways:

- By entering a non-negative number terminated by the *return* key.
- By hitting the *return* key (without typing any number), which is equivalent to entering 0. This way, the window will be stepped immediately.
- By hitting the "line kill" character, which will abort the step command.

The possibility of stepping a window after some specific moment is useful for debugging. For example, to trace the sequence of events leading to an error, the user records the (simulated) time of the error occurrence. Then the simulator is started again under control of DSD (with the -d option—section B.3). Before it is allowed to proceed, some windows, e.g., one of the `Kernel`'s windows, can be stepped a while before the error is bound to occur. After the simulator has halted, the user can monitor all events, or perhaps just some of them (depending on which windows are stepped), display additional windows to get some insight into the problems, and so on.

While in the step mode, whenever an event related to one of the stepped windows occurs, the simulator updates the window contents and halts. The text "STEP" is then displayed in the right bottom corner of the screen. The user is free to execute any commands that are legal in the regular (periodic update) mode. The *return* key (or the space bar) can be used to advance the simulation. When pressed, it results in a go message being sent to the simulator: in response to this message, SMURPH will proceed until the next occurrence of a stepping event.

By hitting the 'u' key the user *unsteps* the current window. The capital letter 'U' exits the step mode globally, by unstepping all windows. Unstepping all windows does not automatically force the simulator to the periodic update mode. SMURPH is left suspended until the user hits the *return* key.

Note. No periodic screen update is done in the step mode, i.e., the windows displayed on the screen are only updated when a stepping event is intercepted by SMURPH or when the user hits a key (any key) on the terminal.

A.9   TIMEOUTS

Both DSD and the simulator use timeouts to detect the disappearance of the other party. If the simulator has been halted for 15 minutes without any user action, it disconnects from the display program and resumes normal execution. If the display program sends a request to the simulator and receives no response within 30 seconds, it assumes that the connection has been broken and aborts the display session. Normally, the simulator responds to such requests immediately—by reacting to asynchronous i/o on the channel[9] connecting it to the display program.

No connection timeout is detected when SMURPH has been called with the -d option (section B.3) and is waiting for DSD to come in. In such a case, the simulator will be waiting indefinitely for the display program.

BIBLIOGRAPHIC NOTES

Only superficial familiarity with UNIX is needed to use DSD. In this appendix we try to avoid technical terminology related to UNIX. The whole idea of implementing DSD as a separate program was aimed at relieving the simulator of the OS-specific issues. To understand better the nature of communication between the simulator and the display program, the reader may consult some books on UNIX, e.g., *Stevens* (1992), *Anderson* (1991), or *Rochkind* (1985). Sockets, which provide a vehicle for communicating the simulator with the monitor and DSD, are explained in a popular article by *Côté and Smith* (1992).

---

[9]The socket.

B

SMURPH Under UNIX

B.1 INSTALLATION

SMURPH can be obtained via anonymous `ftp`, e.g., from `ftp.cs.ualberta.ca`.[1] It comes as a single compressed file named `smurph.`*xxx*`.tar.gz`, where *xxx* stands for the version number (which will change in subsequent revisions of the program). This file unpacks[2] into two subdirectories: `SMURPH` (its contents are described in this appendix) and `SERDEL`, containing an independent program (introduced in appendix C) for supervising batches of simulation experiments executed in the domain of a local network.

In principle, the package can be installed on any machine running a BSD-compatible UNIX clone,[3] equipped with the GNU C++ compiler. In particular, SMURPH runs under Linux on various PC-compatible computers. The package has been also successfully installed with the AT&T `Cfront` compiler on Sun workstations (Sun-3 and SPARC machines), on SGI computers running BSD-compatible versions of System V, and on the 64-bit Digital Alpha machine running OSF. One hardware-dependent feature of SMURPH is *checkpointing* (section B.4): the checkpointing code must be written separately for each machine type. Fortunately, this feature is not essential: SMURPH can be used without it, although for large experiments involving many simulation runs, checkpointing (explored by SERDEL—appendix C) may be very useful. It is hoped that the checkpointing facility will

---

[1] You can use `archie` (or `xarchie`) to find the most convenient `ftp` site that offers the package.

[2] The UNIX command needed to unpack the file is "`zcat smurph.`*xxx*`.tar.gz | tar -xvf -.`"

[3] Sockets are required to make the simulator communicate with the monitor and DSD.

be gradually extended to cover the variety of equipment on which SMURPH can be installed (it works on all the machines just mentioned).

SMURPH feels somewhat more comfortable with the GNU compiler than with AT&T Cfront. In particular, the Cfront version of C++ may occasionally generate warning messages during compilation. In many cases, these messages are spurious (Cfront tries to be smarter than it can be), but they should always be looked at carefully, as sometimes they may hint at potential problems. The most painful disadvantage of Cfront (version 2.0) is the inability to compile nontrivial in-line functions. Some versions of the compiler even generate incorrect code without any warning! Therefore, it is recommended that **perform** methods of processes and observers be always expanded outside the declarations of their owning types.

The package comes as a collection of files organized into the directory structure presented in figure B.1. The root directory of this structure contains the following items:

MANUAL   This is a directory that includes a self-contained LaTeX version of the SMURPH manual.

SOURCES   This directory contains the complete source code of the package.

Examples   This directory contains the protocol programs that were introduced in chapters 8–11.

README   This file contains the copyright notice and the log of changes introduced to the package since version 0.9.

scopy   This is a shell script used to create copies of the package (for different users) by linking them to the original.

In order to produce a copy of the manual, you should move to the MANUAL directory and execute **make**. Ignore any warnings generated by LaTeX. The manual will be written to file **manual.dvi**, from whence it can be converted to a device-dependent format, according to the locally established rules. There is a subdirectory of MANUAL called REPORT that contains a short introductory document about SMURPH.

The vital parts of the package are contained in directory SOURCES, which consists of the following entries:

SIMULATOR   This is a directory that contains the source code of the simulator part. These files are used to create SMURPH libraries that are configured with user-supplied protocol files into stand-alone simulators.

MONITOR   This directory contains the source files of the monitor used to keep track of active simulation runs and to connect the simulator to the display program (section A.2).

DSD   This directory contains the source code of the display program DSD (appendix A), together with a document describing the protocol used by the display program to communicate with the simulator.

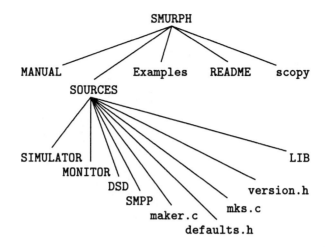

Figure B.1 The structure of SMURPH directories

SMPP	This directory contains the source code of the SMURPH preprocessor smpp that is run (automatically) before the C++ compiler to turn SMURPH constructs into C++ code.
LIB	This directory contains the source code of the basic C++ i/o library (in its SMURPH version) and the memory allocator.
maker.c	This is the source code of **maker**—the program used to configure the package.
defaults.h	This file contains definitions of default values to be used by the configuration program **maker**.
version.h	This file contains the version number of the package and the code for recognizing the C++ compiler version.
mks.c	This is the source code of **mks**—the program used to create simulator instances for user-supplied protocol programs.

To install the package, the user should copy the SMURPH directory tree to his/her file system, into any location reachable from the home directory. A single copy of the package can be shared by a number of users. In such a case, instead of copying all the files, the user should perform the following two steps:

1. Create the SMURPH directory and move (**cd**) there. This directory can be assigned any name.

2. Execute the **scopy** script by entering

$$prfx/\texttt{scopy}$$

where *prfx* is the path to the **scopy** script in the original SMURPH directory.

In consequence of these operations, a copy of the SMURPH directory tree will be built without duplicating most of the files. Then the user should move to the SOURCES subdirectory and compile the maker program by executing

cname -o maker maker.c

where *cname* stands for the name of the C++ compiler (e.g., g++). Note that the program must be compiled with the same C++ compiler that will be used for creating simulators.

Having created maker, the user is ready to configure SMURPH. This is done by executing

maker

and responding to a few questions asked by the program. In most cases, the default answers (indicated by maker) make sense and are recommended. The program asks about the following things, in the listed order:

1. The name of the C++ compiler. The default is "g++" if maker has been compiled with the GNU compiler, and "CC" otherwise.

2. Whether type LONG should be equivalenced with long long rather than long (sections 2.2.1, 2.2.3). This option is applicable to machines/compilers that offer the extended integer type.

3. The path to the SOURCES directory, i.e., to the directory containing the source files of the package.[4] The default is the current directory.

4. Whether SMURPH's private versions of C++ i/o and memory allocation programs should be used instead of the standard programs that come from C++ libraries (see the note at the end of section 2.3.2). This question is only asked if SMURPH is configured with the GNU compiler. With the AT&T compiler, the package automatically uses its private library.

5. The path to the directory where binary libraries of the simulator modules will be kept. These libraries will be linked with user-supplied protocol programs to build simulator instances. The default path is "../LIB," i.e., the libraries will be kept in subdirectory LIB in the root directory of the package.

6. The maximum number of versions of the binary library to be kept in the library directory (the role of this parameter is explained in section B.2). The default number is 5.

7. The path to the directory containing #include files for protocol programs. This directory will be searched automatically for any files #included by a protocol program and not found in the protocol program's directory. The default path is "../Examples/IncludeLibrary," which points to the include library used by the programs discussed in chapters 8–11.

---

[4] It is possible to keep the actual SOURCES subdirectory somewhere else, i.e., the location of maker does not have to coincide with the location of SOURCES.

8. The name of the host running the SMURPH monitor (section A.2). The default is "no host," meaning that the monitor, the simulator, and DSD will always be running on the same machine—in a local environment. By specifying a host name, the user selects a "network" installation of SMURPH and declares that the three parties will communicate via network-domain (AF_INET) sockets. In such a case, they can all run on different machines with the monitor attached to the designated host. Otherwise, UNIX-domain (AF_UNIX) sockets will be used, and the monitor will not be visible outside the machine on which it is run.

9. The number of the monitor socket port or the path to the directory used by the monitor to store its master socket node. If a host name was specified in the previous step, the master socket used by the monitor to accept connections from its clients (simulator instances and DSD) is a network-domain (AF_INET) socket. Such sockets are identified via port numbers unique within the host domain. The default port number is 3991. This number can be changed if it happens to collide with an already used port. For a local installation (no host name was specified in the previous step), the user can specify the directory that will include the dummy file representing the UNIX-domain master socket created by the monitor. The default directory for this purpose is the same as the source directory of the monitor.

10. The name to be assigned to the simulator builder program, i.e., the program that will be used to create simulator instances. The default name is "mks."

11. The directory where mks is to be put. The default is "~/bin," where "~" stands for the user's home directory.

12. Whether the monitor is to be created. If the answer is yes (which is the default), maker will create the binary version of the monitor and put it into directory MONITOR.

13. Whether DSD is to be created. If the answer is yes (which is the default), an executable version of DSD (file dsd) will be created and put into directory DSD.

14. Whether the executable display program should be put into the same directory as mks. If the answer is yes (the default), maker will ask for the name to be assigned to the program (the default name is "dsd") and move the program from DSD to the directory where mks was put.

When maker is done, it updates the contents of file version.h in directory SOURCES to reflect some of the user's selections.

The library directory (LIB) stores the linkable binary files obtained from the simulator sources in SOURCES/SIMULATOR, possibly in multiple versions resulting from different configurations of arguments for mks. In the next section we explain what this means. Initially, when the package is installed for the first time, this directory is empty. New versions of simulator's binary files will be added there by mks—as needed to build executable simulator instances.

It is possible that the LIB directory exists and contains something when maker is called. This may happen when **maker** has been called for a previously installed package, e.g., to reinitialize it with another version of the C++ compiler. In such a case, the directory will be erased.

The maximum number of library versions tells how many different versions of the binary files (corresponding to different configurations of **mks** parameters) can be kept simultaneously in **LIB**. The bigger this number, the less time it takes on average to generate a new simulator instance,[5] at the expense of disk space.

The monitor should be created and run on one designated host. Most naturally, it is a workstation owned by the user, but it can be any machine visible in the local network via UNIX IPC tools. The executable version of the monitor is put into file **monitor** in directory **MONITOR**. The user should move there and run the monitor in the background by executing

```
monitor &
```

The monitor should be running all the time. It uses a negligible amount of system resources, and its impact on the workstation's performance is absolutely imperceptible.

There is a small chance that the monitor will exit immediately with the following diagnosis:

```
port probably taken, rebuild with another socket port
```

which means that the monitor failed to open an **AF_INET** domain socket to make itself visible across the network as a server.[6] Such a problem may occur if the port number assigned by **maker** to the socket is in use. The user should then execute **maker** once again, selecting another port number. Typically, legal values are between 2000 and 9000.[7]

With the operation of starting the monitor, the installation of the package is essentially complete. The user may want to maintain different versions of the package for different types of machines available in the network. If the network is not homogeneous, the different versions of SMURPH can be produced by cloning a single version, using **scopy** to minimize disk overhead. With **scopy**, the new SMURPH directory is produced by linking to the "original" and physically copying only those files that are modified by **maker** or later by **mks**. Such files must occur in different versions for different machine types. Note that DSD need not be available on all the different machines in the network. Typically, the user only cares about running DSD on his/her private computer.[8] Thus, **maker** asks specifically whether DSD is to be created.

---

[5]Since there is a better chance that the right versions of the binary files are present in **LIB** and **mks** does not have to recompile the sources.

[6]This problem can only occur in a network installation of the package.

[7]Consult your manual or ask the system administrator for legitimate values usable by non-privileged users.

[8]Note that it does not have to be the machine running the monitor.

Example

Here we present a sample SMURPH installation transcript. Prompts coming from the system or mks are in the standard (Roman) font, and user entries are in *italics*.

> *mkdir MySmurph*
> *cd MySmurph*
> *˜smowner/SMURPH/scopy*

This sequence of user entries creates a SMURPH directory and links it to an existing (original) SMURPH directory owned by user *smowner*. The sequence that follows could have been executed in the original SMURPH directory as well:

> *cd SOURCES*
> *g++ −o maker maker.c*
> *strip maker*

At this moment, the SMURPH maker program is ready. We assume that the GNU C++ compiler (**g++**) will be used with the package. In the following dialogue with **maker**, user responses with the *return* key (to select the default option recommended by the program) are represented by long dashes "———."

> *maker*

Hi, this is SMURPH version 1.82. You will be asked a few simple questions. By hitting RETURN you select the default answer indicated in the question. Note that in the vast majority of cases the default answers are fine.

What is the name of your C++ compiler? (g++):
———
Assuming g++

If your machine supports 64-bit **long** arithmetic (type **long long**), you may want to use this feature in the implementation of type **BIG** (**TIME**). If the 64-bit operations are performed in (or at least assisted by) hardware, this option may offer a significant improvement. Note that on machines that inherently use 64-bit representation for type **long** (e.g., DEC Alpha), this will be taken care of automatically. Do you want to use type **long long** instead of **long** to implement **BIG** numbers? (n)
———
Type **LONG** will be defined as **long**

Give me the path to SMURPH sources (at least from your home directory). If the path starts with '/', it will be assumed to be absolute; otherwise, it will be interpreted relative to your home directory. The default path is:

> /home/pawel/MySmurph/SOURCES

which is the current working directory.

─────
Assuming /home/pawel/MySmurph/SOURCES

Do you want SMURPH to use its own version of i/o library and memory allocator/deallocator? If you answer 'no', the standard i/o library and memory allocator (malloc) will be used. The SMURPH version (default) is more efficient, but it only contains the essential subset of the i/o operations. (y)

─────
Assuming private library

Please give the path to the directory where you want to keep binary libraries. This directory need not exist at present, but if it exists, IT WILL BE CLEARED. The default path is:

  /home/pawel/MySmurph/LIB

which is equivalent to ../LIB

─────
Assuming /home/pawel/MySmurph/LIB

Specify the maximum number of versions of the binary library to be kept simultaneously. Whenever the configuration of options of the SMURPH make program requests a new library version to be created, and the current number of library versions is equal to the maximum, the least recently used library will be removed. The default limit is 5.

─────
Assuming 5

Give me the path to the include library (absolute or relative to your home directory). The default path is:

  /home/pawel/MySmurph/Examples/IncludeLibrary

which is equivalent to ../Examples/IncludeLibrary

─────
Assuming /home/pawel/MySmurph/Examples/IncludeLibrary

Specify the host running the SMURPH monitor. The default is "no host" meaning that the simulator, the monitor, and DSD will all be running on the same machine.

sheerness

Specify the number of the monitor socket port on the host that will be running the SMURPH monitor. The default port number is 3991.

─────
Assuming 3991

Specify the name of the SMURPH make program (mks):

―――

Assuming mks

Specify the path to the directory that is to contain the make program. The default path is:

/home/pawel/bin

BIN

Creating i/o library + malloc ...
Creating mks ...
Creating smpp ...
Should I create the monitor? (y):

n

Should I create the terminal display program DSD? (y):

―――

Creating dsd ...
DSD has been written to file DSD/dsd.
Should I move it to /home/pawel/BIN? (y)

―――

Specify the name of the program (dsd):

―――

Done.

As we can see, conversation with **maker** is quite simple and straightforward. Note that the monitor has not been created. It is possible that the host running the monitor (*sheerness*) is of a different type than the current host on which the dialogue is taking place. In such a case, another **maker** session should be carried out on *sheerness*.

B.2 CREATING SIMULATOR INSTANCES

Although we often say that SMURPH is a simulator, it merely provides an environment for building problem-oriented simulators, which, once created, may exist independently of the package. An actual simulator is created by compiling the user-supplied protocol program and linking it with the simulator libraries.

The protocol program may consist of a number of C++ files, the name of a file ending with the suffix ".c"[9] or ".cc."[10] All these files should be kept in one directory. They may #include some user-created ".h" files; some of those

---

[9]With the AT&T compiler, a protocol file must not end with "..c."

[10]The suffix ".C" (formally accepted by the GNU C++ compiler) is reserved for **smpp**.

"includes" may come from the "include" library declared when the package was installed (section B.1). To create an executable simulator for a given protocol program, the user should move to the directory containing the protocol files and execute mks (we assume that the default name of mks has not been changed at installation). The argument list of mks may specify the source files to be compiled. In such a case, only the indicated files will be compiled and put together with library modules. Otherwise, if no source files are indicated explicitly, mks will process all the files in the current directory that end with the proper suffixes. Besides the optional file names, the program accepts the following arguments (in an arbitrary order):

-a   All references to assert (section 2.3.5) are turned into empty statements. This may speed up the simulation a little at the expense of some potential errors passing undetected. If this argument is not used, instances of assert are active.[11]

-b   This argument must be followed by a single decimal digit indicating the selected precision of type BIG (section 2.2.3). The number should be separated from "-b" by a space. Value 0 means that BIG numbers will be represented using type double. The default precision of type BIG is 2.

-d   Type DISTANCE (section 2.2.6) will be defined as BIG. If this argument is not used, type DISTANCE is equivalent to LONG.

-f   The C++ compiler will be called with the optimization option. The default is no optimization.

-g   This argument indicates that a debug version of the simulator is to be created. The C++ compiler will be called with the debugging option[12] and protocol tracing (section 7.2.1) will be enabled.

-i   Type BITCOUNT (section 2.2.6) will be defined as BIG. If this argument is not used, type BITCOUNT is equivalent to LONG.

-m   Error checking for operations on BIG numbers, for precision higher than 1, will be suppressed (section 2.2.4). Using this argument may slightly reduce the simulation time at the price of missing some possible arithmetic errors.

-n   Clock tolerance (section 4.5.2) will be set to 0, irrespective of the specification of the protocol program. This argument effectively removes all code for randomizing time delays and makes all local clocks absolutely accurate.

-p   This option enables the three-argument variants of wait requests. Without "-p," wait requests may not specify the order argument (sections 4.1, 4.4.1), and all requests are implicitly assumed to be of the same order 0.

-q   This option enables the message queue size limit checking described in section 5.3.7. By default, this checking is disabled.

---

[11] Note that Assert operations (section 2.3.5) cannot be deactivated.

[12] Making the protocol program traceable by the UNIX debugging tools, e.g., dbx and gdb (the latter applicable to the GNU compiler).

-z   This option enables "faulty links" described in section 6.4. By default "faulty links" are disabled, i.e., all links are error-free.

-o   This argument must be followed by a file name (separated from "-o" by a space). The created simulator executable will be written to the specified file. The default file name, assumed in the absence of "-o," is smurph.

-r   Type RATE (section 2.2.6) will be defined as BIG. If this argument is not used, type RATE is equivalent to LONG.

-u   The standard pilot processes of the Client are permanently disabled, i.e., no traffic will be generated automatically, regardless of how the traffic patterns are defined (section 5.3).

-v   Observers are disabled, i.e., they are never started, and they do not monitor the protocol operation. This argument can be used to speed up the protocol execution without having to remove the observers (section 7.2.2).

-t   The protocol files are recompiled even if their binary (.o) versions are up-to-date. This option can be used after a library file included by the protocol program has been modified, to force the recompilation of the protocol files, even if they appear unchanged.

-8   This option replaces the SMURPH internal random number generator with a generator based on the UNIX rand48 family. The rand48-based generator is slightly slower than the SMURPH generator, but it has a longer cycle.

In consequence of running mks, the protocol files[13] are compiled and merged with SMURPH files. The program operates similarly to the standard UNIX utility make,[14] i.e., it only recompiles the files whose binary versions are not up-to-date. The resulting executable protocol simulator is written to file smurph (in the current directory), unless the user has changed this default with the -o option.

Note. In determining the list of protocol program files to be recompiled, mks only looks at the files appearing on its argument list. Thus, if a file included by one of those files has been modified, the program will not force the recompilation of the including file, unless it has been modified also. In such a case, it is recommended to use the -t option, which instructs mks to recompile all user-supplied protocol files.

Formally, the standard simulator files of SMURPH should be combined with the user-supplied protocol files, then compiled, and finally linked into the executable program. Note that it would be quite expensive to keep all the possible binary versions of the standard files: each different configuration of mks arguments (except "-o" and "-t") needs a separate binary version of practically all files.[15] Thus, only a few most recently used versions are kept. They are stored in directory LIB; each

---

[13]Note that these files do not have to actually reside in the current directory, i.e., the directory from which mks is called. They can be located anywhere as long as their names on the mks argument list are specified relative to the current directory.

[14]In fact, make is called at the last stage of processing.

[15]The total number of combinations is 163,840.

version has a separate subdirectory there, labeled with a character string obtained from a combination of mks arguments. When the user requests creation of a simulator instance with a combination of arguments that has no matching subdirectory in LIB, mks recompiles the standard files and creates a new LIB subdirectory. If the total number of subdirectories exceeds the declared limit (section B.1), the least recently used subdirectory is removed from LIB before the new one is added.

Note. It may be unsafe to run concurrently multiple copies of mks within the domain of a single copy of the package, even if these copies reference different input/output files. Although the program uses file locks trying to ensure the consistency of LIB subdirectories, these locks are ineffective across NFS.

B.3   RUNNING THE SIMULATOR

A simulator instance created by mks is a self-contained, directly executable program for modeling the behavior of the user-defined network and protocol. This program accepts a number of arguments:

-r   This argument should be followed by at least one and at most three non-negative integer numbers defining the seed values for the random number generators. The three numbers are assigned (in this order) to SEED_traffic, SEED_delay, and SEED_toss (section 2.3.1). If not all three numbers are specified, only the first seed is (or the first two seeds are) set. A seed that is not explicitly initialized is assigned a default value, which is always the same.

-d   When this argument is used, the simulator will suspend its execution immediately after Root completes the initialization phase (section 4.8). The program will wait for a connection from DSD (section A.4) before proceeding.

-t   This argument indicates that protocol tracing should be switched on (section 7.2.1). Two non-negative integer numbers can optionally follow "-t." The first number, if present, indicates the simulated time (in ITUs) when the tracing should commence. If the number is absent, time 0 is assumed, i.e., the tracing is active from the very beginning. The time argument is available to the protocol program via the global variable TracingTime of type BIG. This variable contains BIG_INF if "-t" has not been used. The second number optionally specifies the station (its Id) to which the tracing should be restricted. This number is stored in the global variable TracedStation of type Long (section 7.2.1). Note that automatic protocol tracing is only performed if the simulator has been created with "-g" (section B.2).

-f   This argument can be used together with "-t" to switch on the *full* tracing (section 7.2.1). It is illegal to specify "-f" if "-t" has not appeared earlier in the argument list. The presence of "-f" is indicated to the protocol program by the contents of the global variable FullTracing of type int. This variable contains YES if "-f" has been selected, and NO otherwise.

-o If this argument is used, SMURPH will write to the output file the description of the network configuration and traffic. The simulator does it by calling

```
System->printTop ();
Client->printDef ();
```

(sections 7.3.5.5, 7.3.5.12) immediately after the network initialization phase.

-c This argument affects the interpretation of the message number limit (section 4.9.1).

-u When this argument is specified, the standard client is disabled and will not generate any messages, regardless of how the traffic patterns are defined. Note that the client can be disabled permanently, when the simulator is created, by the -u option of mks (section B.2).

-s This argument indicates that information about internal (system) events should be included in exposures (section 7.3.5.1).

-k This argument must be followed by exactly two numbers: a non-negative double number less than 1.0 and a small non-negative integer number. These values will be used as the default clock tolerance parameters, i.e., deviation and quality (section 4.5.2).

-m If this option is specified, SMURPH will write a message to the console (/dev/console) whenever it is started, terminated, aborted, checkpointed (section B.4), or resumed from a checkpoint file.

The first argument from the left that does not start with "-" is assumed to be the name of the input data file. Similarly, the second parameter with this property is interpreted as the output file name. If the input file name is "." (a period) or if no file name is specified at all, SMURPH assumes that input data is to be read from the standard input. If no output file is specified, the results will be written to the standard output.

Examples

Let us look at a few sample call lines for the simulator:

```
smurph -r 11 12 datafile -d outfile
```

In this example, smurph is called with SEED_traffic and SEED_delay (section 2.3.1) initialized to 11 and 12, respectively. The simulation data are read from file datafile, and the results are written to outfile. Before the protocol execution is started, the simulator will suspend itself awaiting connection from the display program.

```
smurph . out
```

With this simple configuration of arguments, the simulation data will be read from the standard input, and the results will be written to file out.

```
smurph -k 0.000001 3 < data > out1234
```

In this case, the clock tolerance parameters are set to 0.000001 (`deviation`) and 3 (`quality`). The input data is read from file `data`, and the simulation results are written to file `out1234`.

B.4 CHECKPOINTING

Potentially, a single simulation run may take a substantial amount of time, in some cases even a few days. For a program running for so long, it may be useful to interrupt it at certain moments and save its state in a file. Such an operation is called *checkpointing*, and the file used to store the complete information about the state of a program at some stage of its execution is called a *checkpoint file*.

The checkpoint file can be used to restart the program at a later time and continue its execution from the moment when the program was checkpointed. One obvious benefit of this feature is the possibility of recovering a substantial amount of the program's work after a system crash. In case of such a mishap, the program need not be run from the beginning, but its execution can be resumed from the last checkpoint.

In a LAN environment consisting of multiple homogeneous machines running UNIX, checkpointing offers yet another interesting possibility. Namely, a program running on one computer can be checkpointed and moved to another computer of the same type. In particular, by moving programs from overloaded machines to ones that are less heavily used, the user may balance the system load and speed up the execution of these programs. In appendix C, we present SERDEL—a tool for automated supervision of multiple simulation experiments. SERDEL uses checkpointing to move the experiments among different (but homogeneous) hosts.

Checkpointing in SMURPH has been implemented in a reasonably simple way. In the general case, there usually are problems with preserving the contents and status of various partially read or written files used by the checkpointed program. In most cases, once a simulation run has started, there is only one file whose contents must be saved at a checkpoint—the output file. The output file is opened at the beginning of the program execution and may be partially written when the simulator is checkpointed. The simple idea employed here is to write the information describing the program state into the output file past any partial results already present there. A special non-ASCII sentinel is used to separate the two parts of the output file so that they can be identified and interpreted properly upon a restart. This way the complete information about the state of the checkpointed simulator and its environment is contained in one easily identifiable file. One disadvantage of this approach is that the checkpointed program cannot be continued directly: it is exited and must be restarted from the checkpoint (output) file. A copy of the file must be made if the checkpoint state information is to be saved.

To checkpoint a SMURPH simulator the user has to send it the `SIGUSR1` UNIX signal (number 30 under the BSD system, or 16 under System V). This signal will be ignored if the simulator is currently in a state that makes checkpointing impossible, e.g., connected to the display program. Otherwise, the information about the state of the program is written to the current output file, and the simulator terminates.

Note.   Checkpointing a simulator that uses a nonstandard data file (or a number of such files) may have a disastrous effect: the simulator may not be restartable.

A checkpointed simulator is resumed in the following way:

```
smurph -R outfile
```

where `outfile` is the output file containing the checkpoint information. The version of the simulator called with the -R option must be **exactly the same** as the checkpointed version. The program will be restarted and continued from the moment when the checkpoint was made. All the original call parameters will be restored with the exception of the output file name, which will be changed to the name of the checkpoint file.

Example

With the following sequence of commands,

```
smurph infile out_1 -c -r 4 5 6
kill -30 "smurph process id"
cp out_1 out_2
smurph -R out_2
```

the simulator will be checkpointed and then restarted as if it were originally called

```
smurph infile out_2 -c -r 4 5 6
```

One thing that may be somewhat confusing is the way a restarted program appears on the process list produced by the UNIX command **ps**. Namely, its program call line will look exactly like the original call line with the old output file name. The reason for this glitch is that the image of the call line is taken by **ps** from the program's stack area, which is restored to its original contents by the restart procedure. To avoid confusion, it is recommended to restart the simulator with the original output file name.

Example

The following sample sequence of commands is suggested as a method of saving the program state and continuing its execution:

```
smurph infile outfile ...
kill -30 "smurph process id"
cp outfile savedstate
smurph -R outfile
```

File **savedstate** can be used as a backup checkpoint file. If the simulator is to be restarted, **savedstate** can be copied or renamed to **outfile** so that the original output file name is always used.

BIBLIOGRAPHIC NOTES

Several general books on UNIX can be recommended to the reader who is interested in learning more about the interface between SMURPH and the operating system, e.g., *Wang* (1987) or *Stevens* (1992). The way SMURPH implements checkpointing is not really described anywhere, but the reader may get some insight into these issues from *Bach* (1986) and *Leffler et al.* (1989). The code for checkpointing was in fact inspired by an example from *Bach* (1986). This book is recommended for a reader interested in extending the checkpoint feature to other machines, not mentioned at the beginning of this chapter. *Litzkow and Solomon* (1992) present CONDOR, a package for migrating processes on UNIX, which uses checkpointing. Although the way SMURPH does checkpointing is somewhat different from that adopted in CONDOR, the paper of Litzkow and Solomon brings up a few interesting points related to checkpointing in general.

C

SERDEL: Organizing Multiple Experiments

C.1 PURPOSE

SERDEL, which stands for Supervisor for Executing Remote Distributed Experiments on a LAN, is a program for automated distribution of multiple simulation experiments in SMURPH over a local network of more or less homogeneous computers. An institution of the size of a computing science department typically owns quite a few powerful workstations whose CPUs are idle most of the time. Usually, such a workstation sits on somebody's desk, and although one is often tempted to take advantage of its wasted power, it is not always easy to do without upsetting the rightful owner of the machine.

Despite difficulties in programming distributed network simulators, network simulation is an easily and naturally distributable computation. Typically, a network is simulated to determine its performance under varying parameters, i.e., traffic conditions, medium length, number of stations. Multiple simulation experiments are usually required to obtain a sufficient number of points of a smooth performance curve. These experiments are independent. Thus, a collection of independent (but interconnected) workstations can potentially provide a simulation environment comparable to that of a supercomputer. The only synchronization problem is allocation of experiments to machines. Moreover, as we want to be able to use computers that may physically and formally belong to specific users, we would like to make sure that the simulator will disappear from a machine as soon as its owner shows up.

The purpose of SERDEL is to allocate different simulation experiments, described by a user-provided list, to available machines described by a host database. The host availability is determined by a configuration of dynamic parameters, and it may change over time. SERDEL periodically monitors the experiments and hosts. Upon detecting that a new host has become available, the program may decide to use it to start a new experiment. When SERDEL discovers that a host that is currently running an experiment has become unavailable (e.g., a user logged on to it), the program will checkpoint (section B.4) and swap out the experiment (or experiments) run on the host. No trace of the swapped-out experiments will be left on the machine that has become unavailable. A swapped-out experiment will be resumed as soon as its last host or another machine of the same type becomes available.

The hosts described in the SERDEL's database need not be absolutely homogeneous. It is assumed that they all run a BSD UNIX clone (or a System V UNIX with BSD compatibility) and that they share files via NFS. The list of machine types is limited by SMURPH's checkpoint facility (section B.1). It can be declared that on selected hosts SMURPH should be run without checkpointing. Experiments will not be swapped out from such hosts: once started, an experiment will run to completion (or abortion).

C.2   INSTALLATION

SERDEL's installation is very simple—almost trivial. In fact, the program need not be installed: it is just compiled and becomes ready for execution. Directory SERDEL (which comes with the SMURPH directory in the same package) contains all the files needed by the program. By executing **make** in that directory, the user creates an executable version of SERDEL, which is written to file **serdel**. This file can be freely renamed, moved to other directories, and so on. The program is nonprivileged, and it runs happily in the regular user mode.

Besides running **make** to create **serdel**, the user should compile the simple program in file **guard.c** into a separate executable version for each host type (section C.5). This can be accomplished by simply calling the C compiler in the following way:

```
cc -o guard guard.c
```

Note that both SERDEL and the **guard** program are written in plain C.

File **serdel.h**, in its initial part, contains definitions of a few constants that can be redefined by the user before executing **make**. These definitions are commented, and they will be easily understood by the user after reading this appendix.

C.3   PROGRAM ORGANIZATION AND OPERATION

By an *experiment session* we mean the execution of a batch of experiments described by the user-supplied list. During an experiment session supervised by SERDEL, the program is run constantly at one dedicated machine. This machine may have its description in the host database, i.e., it may be one of the hosts eligible for running the simulator, or it may be a "special" machine that does not run any experiments by itself. SERDEL uses few resources, and it can run alone on a slow computer or share a faster machine with the simulator.

The program accepts two input files and (optionally) produces a report from its activities. The input files are expected to reside in the directory from which SERDEL has been called. Their names are Hosts and Experiments. The first file contains the host database identifying the collection of machines to be used for running the experiments. The second file describes the batch of simulation experiments to be executed. The report is written to the UNIX standard error stream, which can (and should) be assigned to a file when SERDEL is started.

SERDEL can be called with at most one parameter that specifies the range of the report output. When the parameter is absent, no report is produced except for information about serious errors. If the parameter is "v" (lower-case), a short report is generated. This short report contains information about all experiments that have been started, swapped out (checkpointed), resumed, or completed, as well as about any problems (not necessarily serious) encountered by SERDEL during the experiment session. If SERDEL is called with parameter "V" (upper-case), a long report is produced. In addition to the items of information produced in the short report, the output will include transcripts of SERDEL's communication with the hosts. The report has the form of a "dayfile," i.e., all messages are tagged with the time of their generation.

The program operates in cycles. At the beginning of a cycle SERDEL wakes up and reads the two input files. Then it examines and possibly updates the configuration of active experiments. The program may decide to start new experiments, swap out some active experiments, and so on. Finally, when the cycle processing is finished, SERDEL goes to sleep for 150 seconds. After this delay the program will start its next cycle.

The status of the experiments as perceived by the program is kept in the Experiments file, whose updated version is written at the end of a cycle.[1] Between cycles, the Experiments file contains the complete status description of the experiment session. In particular, if SERDEL is killed (e.g., by a system crash or reboot), it can be restarted with the existing Experiments file, and the session will be continued consistently. This way, the impact of the centralized session control on the reliability of the distributed system is very small. Note that a killed or crashed SERDEL can be resumed on another machine.

The Experiments file can be updated by the user on the fly, e.g., the user may add there new experiments or change manually the status of some existing experiments. To make sure that the file is consistently interpreted by SERDEL, such an operation should be performed according to the following prescription:

1. Change the name of the Hosts file (using mv). The file will become unavailable

---

[1] The file is not written if no experiment status has changed during the cycle.

to SERDEL, and the program will not be executing its normal cycles until the Hosts file appears back in the program's home directory.

2. Make sure that SERDEL is not in the middle of a cycle. Usually, this can be checked by executing "ps" two or three times. Within a cycle, the program spawns processes that communicate with the hosts. If a cycle is in progress, the user has to wait until it is completed, which normally takes less than a minute.

3. Edit the Experiments file.

4. Change the name of the Hosts file back to Hosts. This will resume the normal execution of cycles.

This mechanism, although somewhat clumsy, has proved so far to be quite adequate. A better solution may be thought of in the future. The reader is encouraged to devise and implement a collection of simple tools for modifying the Experiments file in a safe and consistent way.

As a rule, the lack (or disappearance) of any of the two input files will stop SERDEL. As the Hosts file is never written into by the program, it is always safe to copy this file or update it while the program is running.

If the program detects a formal error in the Hosts file or in the Experiments file, it will write a message to the standard error and will not execute the cycle. This message will reappear at the beginning of each subsequent cycle until the problem is fixed.

C.4   STRUCTURE OF THE HOSTS FILE

The Hosts file consists of a number of entries describing the hosts to be monitored by SERDEL. A line starting with "#" in the first position is assumed to be a comment line. Comment lines are entirely ignored by the program. One host is described by 11 items separated by white spaces (i.e., spaces, tabs, newline characters) or commas. Multiple adjacent white space characters are equivalent to a single white space. A comma delimiting an item can be preceded or followed by an arbitrary number of white space characters, the whole sequence standing for a single delimiter.

The 11 items constituting the description of a single host are not separated from the previous or next description in any special way. Although it is natural to organize the Hosts file into lines, each line describing one host, the newline ("\n") characters are treated by SERDEL as regular delimiters. Thus, if one or more items are missing from one description, the corresponding number of initial items from the next description will be used. This will surely result in an error, and SERDEL will not interpret the contents of the Hosts file until they are fixed.

If a textual item must contain spaces or commas (which otherwise would be interpreted as delimiters), then either the entire item should be put in double quotation marks or each of the spaces or commas should be preceded by a backslash ("\"). A backslash can be forced to be interpreted as a regular character by preceding it with another backslash.

Following are the items describing a single host in the order in which they should appear in the file:

1. Host name.

2. Host type. This can be any character string assigned by the user to a particular machine/operating system configuration. Two hosts with the same type are assumed to be indistinguishable as far as their programming environment is concerned. In particular, an experiment checkpointed on one host can be restarted on another host of the same type.

3. Character string giving the syntax of the `ps` command to produce the list of all processes owned by the user, including any possible processes detached from the terminal. For a host running a standard BSD system, it should be `"ps -x"`. Note that this string contains a space, so the quotation marks are its integral part.

4. Floating-point number specifying the host's *startup threshold load*. This load corresponds to the first of the three load indicators produced by the UNIX `uptime` command. If the host's load is below the specified value, it is legal to start an experiment on the host.

5. Floating-point number specifying the host's *swap-out threshold load*. When the host's load rises above this value, any experiments running on the host will be checkpointed and removed.

6. Integer number giving the priority at which experiments are to be run on the host. This number should be non-negative and will be turned into a negative parameter of `nice` (0 represents the highest priority, 20 the lowest).

7. Integer number specifying the maximum number of experiments to be run on the host simultaneously.

8. Character string YES or NO telling whether the appearance of an interactive user should force all experiments running on the host to be checkpointed and removed. If this parameter is YES, no experiments will be started on the host as long as an interactive user is present (section C.5).

9. Character string identifying the *guard program*. This parameter is meaningful only if the value of the previous parameter is YES. The role of the guard program is explained in section C.5.

10. Character string YES or NO telling whether experiments executed on the host are to be periodically checkpointed, even if the host does not change its availability status. Periodic checkpointing makes sense for long simulation runs, as in the case of a host crash, the aborted experiment (or experiments) can be restarted[2] from the last checkpoint file. If this parameter is YES, SERDEL will be checkpointing an experiment running on the host every six hours, unless the experiment has been checkpointed in the meantime for another reason.

11. Piece of text specifying the hours when the host is available.

---

[2]The program does it automatically.

In general, the string describing the host's availability hours can be long and complicated: different hours can be specified for different days of the week, and several time intervals can be defined within a single day. Consider the following sample string

MWF0800-1200/2200-2400/0200-0400TR0000-0800AS0000-0000

which says that the host will be available on Mondays, Wednesdays, and Fridays between 8:00 and noon, between 22:00 and midnight, and between 2:00 and 4:00 in the morning. On Tuesdays and Thursdays the host is available from midnight until 8:00 and all around the clock on Saturdays and Sundays.

Each day of the week is uniquely identified by a single code letter. These letters are "S," "M," "T," "W," "R," "F," "A," from Sunday to Saturday. A sequence of adjacent code letters tells that the following interval specification applies to all the indicated days. Multiple interval specifications for the same day (or days) are separated by slashes ("/"). If an interval specification is followed by a letter, it indicates the beginning of a description for another day (or a group of days).

An interval specification consists of a pair of numbers separated by a hyphen ("-"). Each number of this pair denotes an hour (the first two digits) and a minute (the last two digits) in the 24-hour notation. The first number can be greater than the second, e.g., 2200-0400 represents a time interval starting at 10 p.m. and ending at 4 a.m. Note, however, that at midnight SERDEL will start looking at the interval description of another day.

If the day code of an interval specification is missing (note that it is legal for the first specification only), it is assumed that the specification refers to all days of the week. For example, the availability definition

1600-0800

is legal and says that the host is available from 4 p.m. until 8 a.m. through all days of the week.

An experiment can only be started on a given host within one of its availability intervals. When the host becomes unavailable, all the experiments running on it are checkpointed and swapped out.

C.5   DETECTING INTERACTIVE USERS

If parameter number 8 of a host description (section C.4) is YES, SERDEL will detect the presence of an interactive user on the host. In the remainder of this section, we consider only hosts with this property. The operations described here are not performed for a host if the eighth parameter of its description is NO.

A host is considered to be used interactively if it has a logged-in user whose idle time (produced by the UNIX w command) is less than 20 minutes. No experiment will be started on a host that is being used.

The first stage of each SERDEL's cycle consists in examining all experiments that, according to the status information in the Experiments file, are in execution.

As a part of this operation, SERDEL issues a w command to each host running an experiment. If the output of this command indicates that the host is currently being used, the experiment (or experiments) run on the host are checkpointed. The time interval between two consecutive cycles is typically of the order of 4–5 minutes. Generally, this interval cannot be decreased without increasing the overhead of SERDEL to a visible level. Yet, the delay of a few minutes in recognizing the presence of an interactive user may be annoying to the workstation's owner. Therefore, together with each experiment SERDEL starts a special tiny process called guard, which executes on the same host and knows the identity of the guarded experiment process. Every ten seconds the guard process monitors the status of the host's tty devices and upon detecting a user activity, it immediately sends the checkpoint signal to the experiment process.

The guard program is very simple and short, and its overhead is completely negligible. The program should be compiled separately for each machine type (section C.2) and put into a directory visible from both its target host and the machine running SERDEL. The path to the guard program is specified as item number 9 of the host description (section C.4). SERDEL will try to run the guard process by issuing an rsh command with this item given as a parameter.

If an empty string ("") is given as the path to the guard program, no guard process will be started on the host. However, SERDEL will still be able to detect the presence of an interactive user—in the slower way.

Note that with the guard process experiments will disappear from machines that become used, even if the SERDEL process dies, e.g., after a crash of its host.

Example

Following are sample contents of the Hosts file.

```
# HOST     TYPE   PSCMND      SIT SOT PR CN INT GUARD          CHKP AVAILABLE
radway    sparc  "ps -x"     0.7 2.1 10  1  YES BIN/SUN4/guard YES  1800-0800
warspite  sparc  "ps -x"     0.7 2.1 10  1  YES BIN/SUN4/guard YES  2200-0700
bellis    sparc  "ps -x"     0.7 2.1 10  1  YES BIN/SUN4/guard YES  0800-2400
innisfree sgi    "ps -u pawel" 8.0 35.0 00  1  NO  ""             NO   0000-2400
```

Note that no checkpointing is ever performed on the last host, at least as long as its load remains below 35.

Note. The two threshold loads (columns labeled SIT and SOT in the preceding example) should be set in such a way as to avoid swapping loops. If the difference between the swap-in and swap-out thresholds is too small, then the following scenario is possible. An experiment is started and then, a while later, because of the higher load caused by the new process, it is checkpointed. After a few minutes, as the load drops below the swap-in threshold, the experiment is swapped back in. Then the load increases above the swap-out threshold, and so on.

One should remember that each experiment started on a host increases the host's load by at least one unit. Thus, the minimum sensible difference between the two threshold values is equal to the maximum experiment count for the given host (column CN). To be on the safe side, the actual difference should be somewhat larger than this absolute minimum.

C.6 STRUCTURE OF THE EXPERIMENTS FILE

Experiments described by the contents of the Experiments file are organized into groups. The number of groups can be arbitrary; in particular, there can be just a single group. One group identifies a directory that is expected to contain the executable code of the simulator (or, possibly, a number of versions of this code—for different machine types) and the data files to be used in the experiments.

The rules for delimiters are the same as for the Hosts file. Comments may also appear in the Experiments file; however, they will be removed from it by SERDEL when the original file is overwritten by its updated version. Each group description starts with a header in the following format:

directory [*mtype pname*] ... [*mtype pname*] *params*

The first nonblank character must be an asterisk, which is followed by the path name of the group's directory. This path is relative to the user's home directory, unless it starts with "/." It is recommended to use absolute paths, unless the user's home directory is the same on all hosts listed in the Hosts file.

The directory name is followed by a sequence of pairs of items enclosed in square brackets. The first item of a pair identifies a host type—it should match one of the host types in the Hosts file. The second item is the file name identifying the executable simulator version appropriate for the given host type. This file name is interpreted relative to the group's directory. Not all host types mentioned in the Hosts file have to appear in the list at the group header. If some host types are not mentioned there, the hosts of those types will not be used to run the experiments described by the group.

The last item, denoted by *params*, is optional. If present, it will be appended to the simulator's call line; thus, its purpose is to specify the call options of the simulator (section B.3). If it contains blanks (which is rather typical), either the entire item must be enclosed in double quotation marks or each of the blanks must be "escaped" with a backslash ("\"). Two call parameters, the names of the input and output files, are included by SERDEL automatically in the simulator's call line.

The group header is followed by a sequence of run descriptions, each description having the following form:

@ *datafile outputfile*

where *datafile* is the name of an existing data file and *outputfile* identifies the output file to be created in the simulation run. Both these file names are interpreted relative to the group's directory. If the output file already exists when the experiment is started, it will be erased.

The list of run descriptions terminates with the end of the Experiments file or at the beginning of the next group (indicated by an asterisk).

Example

Following are sample contents of the Experiments file.

```
* BUS/DQDB/Uniform [sparc smurph_sp] [sgi smurph_sg]
    @ data1 output1
    @ data2 output2
    @ data3 output3

* RING/FDDI/FServer [sparc smurph] "-r 1 2 3"
    @ dt01 out01
    @ dt02 out02
    @ dt03 out03
    @ dt04 out04
```

Note that the header of the second group specifies only one host type. Thus, the experiments described in this group will only be executed on machines of type **sparc**. For each experiment in the second group, the string "-r 1 2 3" will be appended to the simulator call line. For example, the third experiment from this group will be executed as

```
smurph RING/FDDI/FServer/dt03 RING/FDDI/FServer/out03 -r 1 2 3
```

SERDEL will perform this call by issuing the UNIX **rsh** command to an available remote host (of type **sparc**) and substituting all file names with their full paths obtained by prepending to them the group's directory path.

C.7   PROGRESS STATUS

The Experiments file is updated by SERDEL at the end of each cycle in which the status of at least one experiment has changed. The experiment status information is kept as part of the experiment's description, after the name of the output file. The status part of an experiment description is initially blank (section C.6); this means that the experiment has not started yet. After the experiment has been started, its description line may be as follows:

```
@ dt03 out03 - bellis 11567 676700359
```

Generally, the character following the name of the output file determines the experiment status; the configuration of the items following this character depends on the status. If the output file name is not followed by anything other than "@" (indicating the beginning of the next sample description) or "*" (starting the next group header), it means that the experiment has not started yet.[3] Otherwise, one of the following status characters may appear there:

---

[3]Blanks and newline characters have no meaning; they are just delimiters.

- This character indicates that the experiment is currently being executed. Three items follow (in this order): the name of the host on which the experiment is running, the UNIX process id of the experiment, and the encoded time when the experiment was last checkpointed.

+ The experiment has been completed. The only item following the "+" character is the name of the host on which the experiment was last run.

! The experiment has been checkpointed and swapped out. Two items follow: the name of the host on which the experiment was last run and the time when the experiment was checkpointed.

? The experiment status could not be determined in the last cycle, because the host on which the experiment is supposedly running did not respond. If the situation persists for five consecutive cycles, SERDEL will assume that the host is dead and the experiment has been aborted. If a checkpoint file exists, the experiment status will be changed to "checkpointed." This way, the experiment will be automatically restarted from the last checkpoint file, as soon as a suitable host becomes available. Otherwise, i.e., if no checkpoint file is available, the experiment status will be changed to "not started," so that its execution will commence from scratch.

At the beginning of each cycle, SERDEL determines the status of the experiments that were last perceived as being "in execution." This is done by executing remotely the **ps** command (the third item of the host description—section C.4) and looking up the experiment process id in the list produced by **ps**. If the experiment process has disappeared, SERDEL checks the output file. If this file is complete, i.e., it ends with the line

> @@@ End of output

the experiment status is changed to "completed." Otherwise, the program checks whether the output file contains checkpoint information, which means that the experiment has been checkpointed (by SERDEL—in the previous cycle—or by the guard process). If it is not the case, the experiment is assumed to have been aborted.

In the second stage of a cycle, SERDEL attempts to restart experiments that have been marked as "checkpointed." A checkpointed experiment can only be restarted on a host of the same type as the host on which the experiment was started.

At the end of a cycle, the program tries to start new experiments that have not been executed yet.

When SERDEL decides to checkpoint an experiment, it merely sends to the simulator process the checkpoint signal and does not change its perception of the experiment status. The checkpointed status of the experiment will be detected in the next cycle: normally, the process will have disappeared by then, and its output file will contain the checkpoint information. Nothing wrong will happen, however, if the experiment is still alive when SERDEL gets to examine it for the second time. Note that while SMURPH is connected to DSD it ignores checkpoint signals. Therefore, by establishing a display session with an experiment, the user locks it temporarily on its current host.

Before restarting a checkpointed experiment, SERDEL creates and saves a copy of the output file with the checkpoint information. The original information is discarded from the output file by the simulator when the experiment is restarted. The saved copy will be used to restart the experiment if it gets lost for any reason, e.g., because of a crash of its current host. Having detected that an experiment has been aborted, SERDEL determines whether a saved checkpoint file exists that can be used to restart the experiment. If so, the checkpoint file is simply copied to the output file, and the experiment status is changed to "checkpointed." Otherwise, the only alternative is to start the experiment from scratch; in such a case, its status is changed to "not started."

While an experiment is in progress (i.e., as long as its status is different from "not started" and "completed"), SERDEL keeps in the group's directory two files, which are removed after the experiment completes. The names of these files are obtained by prefixing the output file name by "**errors_**" and "**checkp_**" The first file contains whatever the simulator has written to its standard output and standard error. When SERDEL detects that the experiment has completed, it copies this file to the report file (section C.3) and then destroys it. The second file contains the last copy of the output file with checkpoint information.

C.8 PITFALLS

SERDEL is a simple but surprisingly powerful and reliable tool. There are, however, a few problems that it cannot cope with in a reasonable way. For example, if an experiment crashes internally (e.g., the executable file or the data file does not exist) without producing an output file that looks complete, SERDEL will keep on trying to restart the experiment in each cycle. Fortunately, problems of this kind do not occur too often. SMURPH tries to produce a complete-looking output as long as the data file exists.

Sometimes it may happen that an experiment gets aborted while it is checkpointing itself, which may result in a corrupted checkpoint file. This in turn may cause a restart loop, i.e., the experiment is restarted and crashes immediately, then SERDEL detects that the checkpoint file exists, so it is used to restart the experiment, which crashes again, and so on. The full turn of this loop takes two cycles.

These problems can be detected by monitoring the report file (section C.3). One sure way to clear the status of a misbehaving experiment is to edit the **Experiments** file by hand.

BIBLIOGRAPHIC NOTES

A similar but more general tool named CONDOR is available from the University of Wisconsin (see *Litzkow, Livny, and Mutka* (1988) and *Litzkow and Solomon* (1992)). SERDEL is not meant to compete with CONDOR. From the viewpoint of the specific application for which it was written, SERDEL has some advantages over CONDOR. For example, CONDOR does not allow the supervised program to use IPC tools, which are essential for the operation of DSD. Moreover, no system changes are required to use SERDEL. The program leaves absolutely no trace of its past or intended future activity on a "leased" machine, and the machine's owner has no sensible reason to object to this activity.

D

SMURPH on the Mac

D.1 STRUCTURE OF THE PACKAGE

In this appendix we describe the differences between the Macintosh version of the package and its UNIX version. We assume that the reader has become acquainted with the contents of appendix B. The present appendix supplements appendix B and focuses on the differences between the Macintosh version of SMURPH and the standard UNIX version, which will be used here as a reference. All features of SMURPH described in chapters 1–7 and appendixes A and B, and not mentioned explicitly in this appendix, are present in the Macintosh version of the package.

The Macintosh version of SMURPH requires the Macintosh Programmer's Workshop (MPW) version 3.2 or later, which is distributed separately by Apple. This document assumes that the reader has basic knowledge of MPW. The package has been developed and tested under System 7 on a PowerBook 140 with 8 MB of main memory. SMURPH may not compile on a PowerBook with less memory unless virtual memory is switched on.

As with the UNIX version, the user receives the complete source code of the package, including the auxiliary programs and the run-time library for turning the simulator into a Macintosh application. The package is organized into a collection of folders and files presented in figure D.1.

File Notes contains a modified version of this appendix; CLICKME is a copy of the README file from the UNIX version of the package. Note that the SMURPH manual is not included with the package. Folder LIB is initially empty. As in the UNIX version, it will be used to keep different binary versions of the simulator's

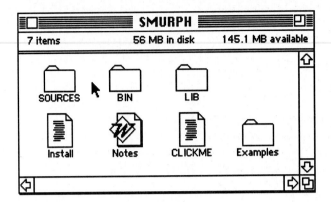

Figure D.1   The contents of the SMURPH folder

files (section B.2). Folder BIN contains initially a single file—the mks script[1] used
to create simulator instances. Intentionally, this folder is to be used for storing
SMURPH-related executables callable directly as MPW scripts or tools.

As in the UNIX version of the package, folder Examples contains the protocol
programs that were presented in chapters 8–11. The contents of folder SOURCES are
listed in figure D.2.

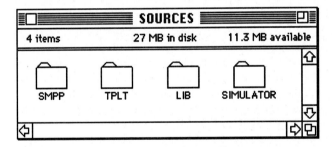

Figure D.2   The contents of the folder SOURCES

The most important difference with respect to the UNIX version is the lack of
an explicit DSD folder (the display program has been combined with the simulator)
and the presence of TPLT. The MONITOR folder is also absent: the concept of a
SMURPH monitor does not make much sense on the Macintosh. The TPLT folder
contains DSD window templates and a special program called tplt for turning these
templates into Macintosh resources.

---

[1]In the Macintosh version of the package, mks is implemented as an MPW script.

D.2   INSTALLATION

The installation of SMURPH is very simple (much simpler than for the UNIX version). The SMURPH folder from the installation diskette should be copied (preferably to the hard disk). Its name and location can be arbitrary, but the structure of internal folders must not be changed. Then the user should move to the target copy of the SMURPH folder (whatever its name and location) and execute `Install` as an MPW script (in the MPW worksheet window). The installation script will compile a few programs, create some resources, put them into proper locations within the SMURPH folder hierarchy and, if everything goes well, display a completion message. Following are the actions performed during installation, in the order in which they are executed:

1. The `mks` script is edited, its header modified to reflect the name and location of the SMURPH folder.

2. Any existing contents of `LIB` are erased. In the release copy of SMURPH, `LIB` is empty, so this action is void.

3. The SMURPH i/o library is built, and the standard resources are created. These resources do not include DSD templates, which are taken care of separately. The created files are put into `SOURCES:LIB`.

4. The template resource file (to be used by DSD) is built from the template source file (`SOURCES:TPLT:templates`) and stored in file `SOURCES:TPLT:res.r`. As the first step of this operation, program `tplt` is compiled and linked, and its executable version is put into `BIN`. The program can be called by the user to create resources for nonstandard window templates.

5. The SMURPH preprocessor (`smpp`) is compiled and linked. The preprocessor's executable is stored in `SOURCES:SMPP`.

The installation procedure can be performed at any moment on an already installed and working copy of the package—to reinitialize the package and make sure that all its parts are in good shape. If the `LIB` folder happens to be nonempty at the moment when `Install` is called, its contents will be erased.

It is reasonable to add SMURPH's `BIN` folder to the list of folders searched by MPW for a tool or script for execution. This way `mks` will be callable directly as a standard tool or script. To do so, the user should edit the `UserStartup` script of MPW and add there (e.g., at the very end) the following line:

$$\texttt{Set Commands \{Commands\}, }\textit{smurphpath}\texttt{:BIN:}$$

where *smurphpath* is the path to the SMURPH folder.

The user may also wish to look at the header of the `mks` script in folder `BIN`. Some constants defined in this header can be modified by the user. One example of such a constant is the maximum number of libraries to be kept in `LIB`. The default value (5) is the same as for the UNIX version.

D.3   CREATING SIMULATOR INSTANCES

In the Macintosh version of SMURPH, mks has been turned into a script. This script accepts a configuration of parameters (most of them are the same as in the UNIX version) and generates a Makefile that will build the specified simulator instance. In contrast to the UNIX version, this makefile is not automatically executed: the user has to run it explicitly—by selecting an item from the Build menu of MPW or by calling make. The primary reason for this solution is the relatively slow execution speed of mks. Once the makefile has been prepared, it can be (re)used many times without having to go through the time-consuming process of creating it.

A simulator instance can be created in one of three versions:

- Full application, including the DSD part (incorporated into the application).
- Abridged application, without DSD. The progress of simulation can still be monitored on the *status window*.
- MPW tool. The simulator can only be run under control of MPW, without the possibility of monitoring its execution on-line.

The MPW tool version offers the smallest overhead in terms of the code size and processing time. However, it requires the presence of MPW during the simulation run. The user has little control over the simulator. The only thing he or she can do is to abort the experiment. The abort event (the Macintosh *command* key and "." pressed together) is intercepted by the simulator—in the same way as in the UNIX version—and SMURPH aborts gracefully. The MPW tool version is recommended for multiple simulation runs that are to be organized into batches driven by MPW scripts.

The abridged application version is the recommended version for individual simulation runs that do not have to be monitored by the user, except possibly for some rudimentary status information. The simulation run can be suspended and later resumed, also aborted or forcefully terminated. With the full application version, the user gets the full advantage of DSD, including the possibility of stepping the simulator through selected windows.

As with the UNIX version of the package, the protocol code may occupy a number of separate files. The name of such a file must end with the suffix ".c" or ".cp". Most of the parameters of the UNIX version of mks are applicable to the Macintosh script. In particular, the options -a, -d, -f, -g, -i, -n, -m, -p, -q, -r, -u, -v, -z have precisely the same meaning as in the UNIX version (section B.2). Following are the additional options of the Macintosh mks script and those standard options (available in the UNIX version) whose meaning is different in the Macintosh version:

-b   Precision of type BIG. This argument should be followed by a space followed in turn by a single decimal digit specifying the precision of BIG numbers. Precision 0 (i.e., BIG implemented as double) **cannot be used** on the Macintosh.

-o   Selects the full application version of the simulator and (optionally) spec-
         ifies the name of the file to contain the executable simulator. This argu-
         ment can be optionally followed by the file name (separated from "-o"
         by a space). If the name is absent, the simulator will be written to file
         smurph. The name of the simulator file is also the target of the make-
         file constructed by **mks**. "Full application" is the default simulator type
         assumed if no type is indicated explicitly. Note that to specify a non-
         standard simulator file (other than **smurph**) one has to indicate explicitly
         the simulator type.

-oa   Equivalent to "-o." Exists for compatibility with the next two options.

-os   This option, if used instead of "-o" (or "-oa") selects the abridged ap-
         plication version of the simulator.

-ot   With this option, used instead of "-o" ("-oa") or "-os," the simulator
         will be built as an MPW tool.

-rs   Specifies an additional template resource file to be included in the re-
         source fork of the created application. This parameter must be followed
         by a file name (preceded by a space) and cannot be used together with
         "-os" or "-ot."

-sade   With this argument, **mks** will generate a symbol file for SADE—the sym-
         bolic debugger. Note that "-g" does not force the SADE symbol table to
         be generated. In most cases "-sade" is used in conjunction with "-g."

An argument ending with ".c" or ".cp" is interpreted as a source file name.
An arbitrary number of such files can be specified anywhere in the argument list.
The files will be processed in the order in which they are specified. If no source file
is explicitly specified, all files with the proper suffixes found in the current folder
will be processed.

Each source file is first preprocessed by **smpp** into a C++ file. The result is
written into a temporary file named as the source file with "@" added in front, as
the first character of the file name. Then the C++ compiler is called with the
temporary file given as the input file; finally, the temporary file is deleted. Any
possible errors listed by the C++ compiler (or **smpp**) refer to the original source
file and specify correct line numbers within that file. If the -sade option is used,
the "@" files are not removed. SADE does not recognize SMURPH constructs; thus,
symbolic debugging can only be performed on the C++ source files produced by
smpp. With "-sade," the errors listed by the compiler refer to the "@" files, rather
than to the original source files.

The default memory size of a simulator application is 1 MB. This size may
be insufficient for bigger models. The user can increase this size by selecting the
application icon, choosing **Get Info** from the Finder's File menu and entering a
new size into the proper box of the information window. One can also edit the SIZE
resource (file SOURCES:LIB:resources or its compiled version SOURCES:LIB:res.r)
to increase the standard size permanently for all simulators to be created.

D.4 CREATING TEMPLATE RESOURCE FILES

The UNIX version of DSD reads window templates from two files: the "system" file containing templates for the standard exposures, and the optional "user" file specifying templates for user-defined windows (section A.4). In the Macintosh version of the package, templates must be turned into *resources* before they can be accessed by DSD (which is integrated with the simulator application). Standard templates are turned into resources automatically when the package is installed. User templates require simple preprocessing before they can be made accessible to the simulator.

The structure of a template file was described in section A.6. The standard template file for the Macintosh version of SMURPH (TPLT:stemplates) is just a copy of the UNIX template file with one global modification: the title fields (section A.6.3) have been removed from all templates. No title fields are needed in the Macintosh version: the title is automatically displayed in the window's title bar. It is still possible to use title fields, but they are redundant.

Another redundant element of a template specification is the definition of region display characters (section A.6.8), which is ignored. On the Macintosh, regions are displayed graphically with points represented by black squares. The following two fields of the segment attribute argument (passed to startSegment— section 7.3.3.3) are interpreted (we assume that bits are numbered from the least significant position starting from 0):

bits 0–1   The display mode. Value 0 means that the segment will be displayed as a loose collection of points. Value 1 indicates that the points should be connected with lines. Value 2 selects histograms, i.e., vertical stripes extending from the points down to the bottom of the region rectangle. The default display mode is 0.

bits 2–5   The pen thickness for drawing points and lines. This value (expressed in pixels) is incremented by 1 before it is used as a pen size (so that thickness 0 actually stands for 1). The default value of the thickness field is 4 (which corresponds to the pen size of 5).

The list of clipping rows and columns associated with a window template is ignored (the window can be rescaled to any reasonable size), except for the default clipping specification, which retains its meaning: it specifies the initial size of the window. When the window is opened, its initial size is determined by the default clipping.

To convert a template file into a resource file, one should use the tplt tool created when SMURPH was installed (section D.2). If the MPW Commands list includes the BIN folder of SMURPH, tplt can be called directly, as a standard tool, in the following way:

tplt templatefile resourcefile

where *templatefile* is the file containing templates and *resourcefile* is the output file that will contain the template resources. Resources of two types are written to *resourcefile*: TPLL representing a bundle (list) of templates corresponding to one object type, and TPLT describing individual templates. TPLL resources are "named": the resource name coincides with the object type name. It is possible to override a standard template (by including its definition in the user template file), but then all the templates for the given object type (the entire template bundle) will be overridden. Thus, if the user template list for the object type does not cover all exposure modes, the uncovered modes will not be available.

By default, the resources generated by `tplt` are assigned small numbers starting from 128. The resources corresponding to standard templates are assigned bigger numbers—starting from 16,384. This way a user TPLL resource (with a small number) subsumes the standard TPLL resource with the same name and all the TPLT resources (actual templates) pointed to by the TPLL resource. By specifying a third parameter to `tplt` (which can only be "`-sys`") the user can force the resource numbers to start from 16,384. The `tplt` tool is called this way by `Install`—to create the standard template resource file.

To include a nonstandard template resource file created by `tplt` in the resource fork of the simulator, the user should specify the `-rs` option of `mks` (section D.3). This only makes sense for the full application version of the simulator.

D.5   RUNNING THE SIMULATOR

The MPW tool version of the simulator is called in practically the same way as on UNIX. The processing of options and the interpretation of file names are identical. Two options from the UNIX version, `-d` and `-m` (section B.3), are not applicable to the Macintosh version and cannot be specified. All the other options are valid and retain their meaning.

Because of the somewhat restricted concept of signal processing under MPW, SMURPH cannot react properly to some errors. Memory overflow is usually handled gracefully, i.e., the simulator is able to terminate itself in a controlled way and produce the output file, but other errors, e.g., illegal memory reference, may abort the operating system. This also applies to the application versions of the simulator. SADE (the symbolic debugger) is usually quite helpful in locating tricky bugs.

A tool version of the simulator can be aborted by the user—in the same way as any other MPW tool. Note, however, that the abort condition is only examined during a *system check*, when the tool passes control to the system—by rotating the ball cursor. A simulator tool does it every 256 simulation events. If the protocol hits a loop in which no events are processed, the simulator will not be abortable.

The check interval for the tool version of the simulator can be redefined at the moment when the tool is called by specifying the `-i` option (no such option is available in the UNIX version). This option should be followed by a space, followed in turn by a positive integer number not greater than 4096 specifying the number of simulation events separating two consecutive system checks.

D.5.1   Launching the SMURPH Application

An application version of the simulator, like any Macintosh application, is launched
by double-clicking the simulator's icon. The parameters are entered via a dialogue
box, which is displayed immediately after the application is started. The initial
contents of this box are presented in figure D.3.

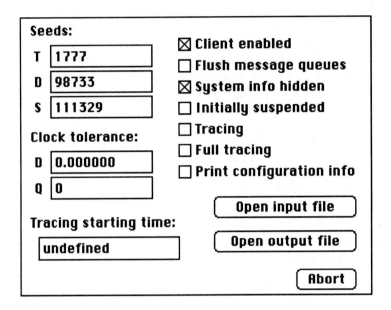

Figure D.3   The startup dialogue box

The meaning of the particular fields from the startup box should be clear. The
three "seed" boxes can be used to change the standard values of the seeds for the
random number generator. "T" stands for SEED_traffic, "D" for SEED_delay, and
"S" for SEED_toss (section 2.3.1). The clock tolerance parameters (deviation—
D and quality—Q) are only meaningful if the simulator was not created with
"-n"; otherwise, the two boxes do not appear in the dialogue. The box marked
Tracing starting time is associated with the checkbox labeled Tracing. Putting
a value into the former text box automatically checks the Tracing checkbox; conversely, checking the Tracing checkbox results in value 0's appearing in the Tracing
time box. These boxes, together with Traced station and Full tracing, correspond to options -t and -f of the tool version. Recall that standard tracing is only
effective if the simulator was created with "-g"; however, the boxes defining the
tracing parameters appear in the startup dialogue irrespective of this option. The
protocol program can interpret the value of the global variables TracingTime and
TracedStation (section 7.2.1), even if the simulator was not created with "-g."

The checkboxes from the startup dialogue can be easily associated with the following options of the UNIX version: -u, -c, -s, -d, -t, -f, -o, in order from top to bottom (section B.3). Note that "-d" does not apply to the tool version. In the application version, this option suspends the simulator before the first protocol event is executed, but after the initialization phase (section 4.8). It is useful if the user wants to open some windows immediately at the beginning of the simulation run, e.g., to step the protocol (section A.8.6). A suspended simulator can be resumed by selecting `Resume` from the `File` menu (section D.5.2).

The two buttons for opening files are used to identify the input data file and the output file. They invoke the standard system dialogue boxes for browsing through the folder hierarchy and selecting files. As soon as a file is (successfully) selected, the corresponding button disappears from the startup dialogue. If the button does not go away, it means that the selected file could not be opened by the simulator. If both files have been opened, both file selection buttons disappear from the dialogue, and another button labeled `Done` appears besides `Abort`. By clicking the `Done` button the user dismisses the startup dialogue and the simulation run is started. Clicking the `Abort` button, which can be done at any stage of filling the startup dialogue, aborts the simulator.

D.5.2   Controlling the Application

The following discussion describes the interface of a full SMURPH application. The interface of an abridged application is a simple subset of this interface. The menu bar of a simulator application consists of five items (see figure D.4). The *apple* menu has the standard meaning. The `File` menu is used to control the execution status of the simulation. The item list of this menu is presented in figure D.5.

| **★   File   Edit   DSD   Windows** |

Figure D.4   The menu bar of a SMURPH application

The `Resume` item is initially disabled, unless the simulator has been started with the "suspend" option (section D.5.1), in which case `Resume` is highlighted and `Suspend` is disabled. By selecting `Suspend` the user suspends the simulator; then it can be restarted by `Resume`. `Stop` forces normal termination of the simulation experiment, irrespective of whether the exit conditions (section 4.9) have been met. This is accomplished by setting the message number limit to zero. Thus, the simulator is terminated as if the declared number of messages to be received has been reached (section 4.9.1). By selecting `Abort`, the user forces abnormal termination of the simulation run. In either case, the simulator application remains alive, in particular, it is possible to open and close DSD windows. To exit the simulator application, the user should select `Quit` from the `File` menu. If `Quit` is selected and the simulator has not been terminated (i.e., it is running or suspended), an alert is displayed and user confirmation is required. If confirmed, the operation aborts the simulator immediately, and the SMURPH application disappears.

```
 File
   Suspend              ⌘S
   Resume               ⌘R

   Stop                 ⌘T

   Abort                ⌘A

   Quit                 ⌘Q
```

Figure D.5 The File menu

The Edit menu is not used by the simulator; it exists for the desk accessories that may coexist with the simulator application. The DSD menu controls the DSD part of the application. Its layout is presented in figure D.6.

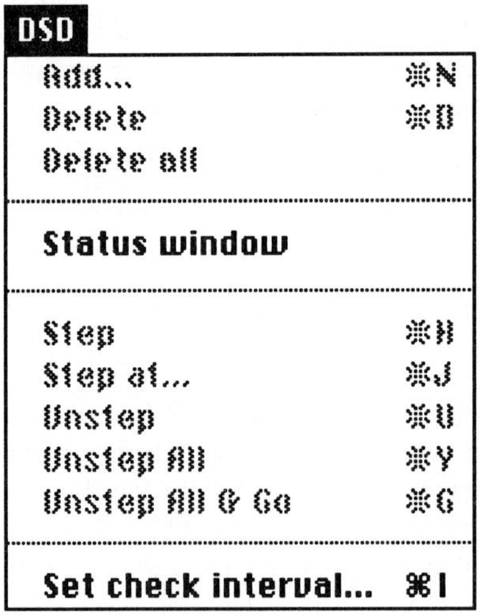

```
 DSD
   Add...               ⌘N
   Delete               ⌘D
   Delete all

   Status window

   Step                 ⌘R
   Step at...           ⌘J
   Unstep               ⌘U
   Unstep All           ⌘Y
   Unstep All & Go      ⌘G

   Set check interval...  ⌘I
```

Figure D.6 The DSD menu

All items except Status window and Set check interval... are initially dimmed. The Add... item becomes highlighted immediately after the initialization phase is over. Starting from this moment, it is possible to open DSD windows. Recall that if the simulator was started with the "suspend" option, it will be suspended at this very moment. By selecting the Add... item from the DSD menu, the user may open some windows and then resume the simulator (item Resume from the File menu). The simulator does not have to be suspended in order for the Add... item to be selectable.

The Add... item displays a dialogue that can be used to browse through the hierarchy of displayable objects and their templates, and select the windows to appear on the screen.

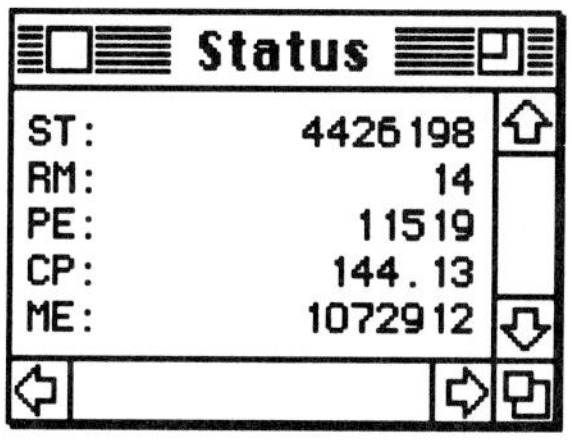

Figure D.7   The status window

The status window displaying a few basic parameters of the simulation run is selectable directly by the Status window item from the DSD menu. The layout of this window is presented in figure D.7. The numbers displayed in the status window denote the following:

ST   Simulated time in ITUs

RM   Number of messages received so far

PE   Number of processed simulation events

CP   CPU time spent on simulation (the system overhead is subtracted)

ME   Amount of free memory (in bytes) available for dynamic allocation

By default, the simulator interprets system events (e.g., mouse clicks) every 256 simulation events. This number (the so-called check interval) can be reset by the user to any value between 1 and 4096. This is done by selecting Set check interval... from the DSD menu and setting a *control* in a simple dialogue. Note that if the check interval is long, the simulator may be slow in responding to user events, sometimes even very slow. On the other hand, using very short check intervals (a few simulation events) may slow down the simulation considerably. To alleviate this problem, after certain user events the simulator remains for a while (about 3 seconds) in the system event processing loop. This way consecutive user events are processed smoothly, even if the check interval is long. The check interval is equivalent to the *display interval* available to the protocol program via the global variable `DisplayInterval` (section 7.3.4.2). Before checking for a pending system event, the simulator application refreshes the contents of the windows displayed on the screen.

D.5.3   Controlling Windows

The dialogue displayed by the `Add...` item allows the user to traverse the object ownership hierarchy described in section A.7.1. The layout of the `Add...` dialogue (with sample contents) is presented in figure D.8.

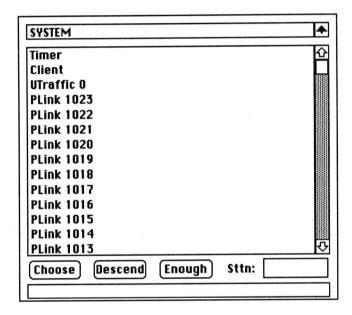

Figure D.8   The `Add...` dialogue

The text displayed in the top box of the dialogue identifies the object whose descendants are listed in the scrollable selection box below. The descendants of `System`, which is the root of the object ownership hierarchy, are initially displayed in this box. To descend one level, the user should select an object in the selection box and then push the `Descend` button. The selected object will appear in the top box, and the list of its descendants will be displayed in the selection box. If the selected object has no descendants, a message will appear in the bottom (message) box and the dialogue will remain at its previous place in the object hierarchy.

To move up in the hierarchy, the user should click in the top box or in the up arrow located to the right of that box. To display a window belonging to the exposure of a specific object, the user should select that object in the selection box and push `Choose` (double-clicking the object has the same effect). The list of templates available for the selected object will then appear in the selection box. A window is added by selecting its template and pushing `Choose` (or double-clicking the template). For a station-relative template, the user should fill the `Sttn` box with the station number (`Id`) before choosing the template. Hitting `Enough` (at any moment) dismisses the `Add...` dialogue. All the windows selected while the dialogue was present will be added to the collection of displayed windows.

The windows present on the screen are updated every "check interval" simulation events (section D.5.2). Additionally, if some windows are stepped (section D.5.4), all windows are updated whenever the earliest step condition is met.

If the amount of information to be displayed in a window exceeds the current window size, the window's scroll bars become highlighted. These scroll bars can be used to select the portion of the window contents to be actually presented in the window. For the sake of time efficiency, the absolute limit of 512 rows is imposed on the total length of what can be displayed in a window. This limit applies to the standard windows that produce lists of rows with the same layout, e.g., the list of wait requests addressed to an activity interpreter (section 7.3.5.2). If such a list is longer than 512 rows, only the first 512 rows can ever be scrolled into the window's display area.

A displayed window is brought to the front by clicking in its contents. The user can make a window invisible by clicking in its "go-away" box. An invisible window is not removed from the display pool. It can be brought back to the screen by choosing its title from the `Windows` menu. The menu is initially empty. Whenever a window is added to the display, its title is also added to the `Windows` menu. For a visible window, clicking its title in the `Windows` menu has the same effect as clicking in the window's contents, i.e., the window becomes the front window. The status window does not appear in the `Windows` menu. To bring it to the front, the user has to click in its contents or select `Status window` from the DSD menu.

To remove a window permanently from the display pool, the user has to make it the front window and select `Delete` from the DSD menu. This also applies to the status window. `Delete all` removes all windows, including the status window. The title of a removed window disappears from the `Windows` menu.

In the abridged application version of the simulator, most menu items are disabled. It is still possible to display (and hide) the status window, to modify the value of the check interval, and to use all the items from the `File` menu.

D.5.4   Stepping

Any window, except the status window, can be stepped. When a window is stepped, the simulator stops after processing the nearest event associated with the object exposed in the window. The semantics of stepping were described in section A.8.6. Multiple windows can be stepped simultaneously.

To step a window, the user should bring it to the front and select `Step` or `Step at...` from the DSD menu. In the first case, the window is stepped immediately. In the second case, the user can specify the moment when the window is to become stepped, in the dialogue presented in figure D.9.

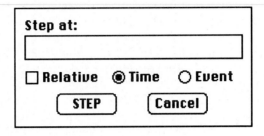

Figure D.9 The Step at... dialogue

The moment when the window will become stepped can be identified either by the time (in ITUs) or the simulation event number.[2] The entered value can be absolute or relative to the current moment. In the latter case, the specified time or event number will be added to the current time or event number.

Whenever a stepping condition occurs for one of the displayed and stepped windows, the simulator updates all the windows and suspends itself. To proceed to the next step condition, the user should press any key while the cursor is within one of the simulator's windows. It is recommended to keep the cursor in the front window, as then the cursor's shape reflects the status of the simulator.

To unstep a window, the user should bring it to the front and select Unstep from the DSD menu. If the step condition is currently present on the window, the user will have to hit any key on the keyboard to continue simulation. Unstep all unsteps all the stepped windows; Unstep all & go does the same thing and immediately resumes simulation.

D.5.5 Cursor Shapes

While the cursor is kept in the front window (including the status window), its shape tells the simulation status. All the cursor shapes used by a SMURPH application are listed in figure D.10.

Figure D.10 Cursor shapes

The first two cursor shapes from the left are toggled while the simulator is running. Their alternating pattern indicates the frequency with which the simulator

---

[2]Both these values are printed by the simulator when it hits an error.

checks for system events. The third shape is used while the simulator is suspended. The fourth shape indicates a step condition (a key must be pressed to continue simulation), and the fifth is used as a pointer in dialogues.

D.5.6   Changes in the SMURPH–DSD Interface

The semantics of some of the functions interfacing the protocol program with the display program have changed slightly with respect to the UNIX version. Specifically, the following changes are to be noted:

- In the full-application version of the simulator, `DisplayActive` (section 7.3.4.2) is preset to 1 (the display program is assumed to be permanently connected to the simulator). In the abridged application version and in the tool version, `DisplayActive` is preset to 0.

- In both application versions, `requestDisplay` (section 7.3.4.2) forces immediate screen update and has no other effect. In the tool version, `requestDisplay` does nothing. The function always returns 1 (`ERROR`).

- In both application versions, `displayNote` (section 7.3.4.2) presents an alert, which must be dismissed by the user to continue the experiment. In the tool version, the function writes the message to the standard error. The function always returns `NULL`.

- In both application versions, `refreshDisplay` (section 7.3.4.2) forces immediate screen update. In the tool version, the function does nothing.

Besides the standard (and somewhat restricted) region drawing functions described in section 7.3.3, the graphic apparatus of the Macintosh can be used to fill the contents of a region. Following `startRegion`, the current graphics port is set to the port representing the region's window. Between `startRegion` and `endRegion`, the exposure method can call all the drawing operations from the Macintosh *toolbox*. One thing the method should not do is to change the origin coordinates of the region's graphics port. These coordinates are set to the left top corner of the region area, which excludes a small margin separating this area from the region boundary. By calling the global function

```
void getRegionSize (short &x, short &y);
```

the exposure method can get the size of the region's rectangle (x gives the width and y the height) in pixels.

Generally, a protocol program prepared for the UNIX version of SMURPH should run without any modifications with the Macintosh version. In some cases, the user will have to rearrange the "include" structure of the protocol files. The C preprocessor of MPW does not accept paths as arguments of the `#include` operation, i.e., these arguments must be simple file names. It is possible, however, to specify "include" directories (folders) to be searched automatically for the included files.

BIBLIOGRAPHIC NOTES

This appendix uses quite a bit of Macintosh jargon. This jargon is explained in many books, notably by *Chernicoff* (1991a; 1991b). These two books contain practically all the information needed to understand SMURPH's interface with the Macintosh system. The six volumes of *Inside Macintosh* (*Apple* (1991)) provide a complete reference to Macintosh internals, but they are somewhat difficult to study without a more friendly introductory reading (as in Stephen Chernicoff's books).

Macintosh Programmer's Workshop (MPW) is sold by Apple with extensive documentation. The user is advised to purchase SADE (the symbolic debugger), which is handy for tracing malicious bugs.

References

ABRAMSON, N. 1985. Development of the ALOHANET. *IEEE Transactions on Information Theory IT-31*, 119–123.

AHO, V., J. HOPCROFT, AND J. ULLMAN. 1974. *The Design and Analysis of Computer Algorithms*. Addison-Wesley.

AHRENS, J., AND U. DIETER. 1972a. Computer methods for sampling from gamma, beta, Poisson and binomial distributions. *Computing 12*, 223–246.

————. 1972b. Computer methods for sampling from the exponential and normal distributions. *Communications of the ACM 15*, 873–882.

————. 1980. Sampling from binomial and Poisson distributions: a method with bounded computation times. *Computing 25*, 193–208.

————. 1982a. Computer generation of Poisson deviates from modified normal distributions. *ACM Transactions on Mathematical Software 8*, 163–179.

————. 1982b. Generating gamma variates by a modified rejection technique. *Communications of the ACM 25*, 47–54.

AHRENS, J., AND K. KOHRT. 1981. Computer methods for efficient sampling from largely arbitrary statistical distributions. *Computing 26*, 19–31.

ALI, I., AND K. S. VASTOLA. 1994. The shifting cycle-gated SCG protocol for high speed bus networks. In *Proceedings of IEEE INFOCOM'94* (Toronto, June), 1112–1119.

ALMES, G., AND E. LAZOWSKA. 1979. The behaviour of Ethernet-like computer communication networks. In *Proceedings of the 7th Symposium on Operating Systems Principles* (Asilomar, CA, December), ACM SIGCOMM, 66–81.

ANDERSON, B. 1991. *UNIX Communications.* Howard W. Sams & Co.

APPLE COMPUTER, INC. 1991. *Inside Macintosh, Volumes I-VI.* Addison-Wesley.

ARMYROS, S. 1992. On the behavior of Ethernet: are existing analytic models adequate? CSRI-259, Computer Systems Research Institute, Toronto, Ontario, Canada.

AYACHE, J. M., P. AZÉMA, AND M. DIAZ. 1979. Observer: a concept for on-line detection of control errors in concurrent systems. In *Proceedings of the 9th Symposium on Fault-Tolerant Computing* (Madison, WI, June), 1–8.

BACH, M. 1986. *The Design of the UNIX Operating System.* Prentice-Hall.

BARTEE, T. 1985. *Data Communications, Networks, and Systems.* Howard W. Sams & Co.

———. 1986. *Digital Communications.* Howard W. Sams & Co.

BARTLETT, K., R. SCANTLEBURY, AND P. WILKINSON. 1969. A note on reliable full-duplex transmission over half-duplex lines. *Communications of the ACM* 12(5), 260–265.

BERARD, M., P. GBURZYŃSKI, AND P. RUDNICKI. 1991. Developing MAC protocols with global observers. In *Proceedings of Computer Networks'91* (Wrocław, Poland, June), 261–270.

BERTAN, B. R. 1989. Simulation of MAC layer queuing and priority strategies of CEBus. *IEEE Transactions on Consumer Electronics 35* (August), 557–563.

BERTSEKAS, D., AND R. GALLAGER. 1992. *Data Networks.* Prentice-Hall.

BIRTHWISTLE, G. 1979. *Demos—Discrete Event Modelling in Simula.* Macmillan.

BIRTHWISTLE, G., O. DAHL, B. MYHRHAUG, AND K. NYGAARD. 1973. *Simula Begin.* Studentlitteratur, Oslo.

BOESCH, F. 1968. Properties of the distance matrix of a tree. *Quarterly of Applied Mathematics 26,* 607–609.

BOGGS, D., J. MOGUL, AND C. KENT 1988. Measured capacity of an Ethernet: myths and reality. WRL research report 88/4, Digital Equipment Corporation, Western Research Laboratory, 100 Hamilton Avenue, Palo Alto, CA.

BRATLEY, P., B. FOX, AND L. SCHRAGE. 1987. *A Guide to Simulation.* Springer-Verlag.

BREUER, S., AND T. MEUSER. 1994. Enhanced throughput in slotted rings employing spatial slot reuse. In *Proceedings of IEEE INFOCOM'94* (Toronto, June), 1120–1129.

BRINCH HANSEN, P. 1973. *Operating Systems Principles.* Prentice-Hall.

BUDKOWSKI, S., AND P. DEMBINSKI. 1987. An introduction to ESTELLE, a specification language for distributed systems. *Computer Networks and ISDN Systems 14,* 3–23.

BUX, W. 1981. Local-area subnetworks: a performance comparison. *IEEE Transactions on Communications 28*, 4 (April), 612–624.

———. 1989. Token-ring local-area networks and their performance. In *Proceedings IEEE 77* (February), 238–256.

CAPETANAKIS, J. 1979. Tree algorithms for packet broadcast channels. *IEEE Transactions on Information Theory 25*, 505–515.

CHEN, J., I. CIDON, AND Y. OFEK. 1993. A local fairness algorithm for gigabit LANs/MANs with spatial reuse. *IEEE Journal on Selected Areas in Communications 11*, 8 (October), 1183–1192.

CHERNICOFF, S. 1991a. *Macintosh Revealed, Volume One: Unlocking the Toolbox.* Hayden Books.

CHERNICOFF, S. 1991b. *Macintosh Revealed, Volume Two: Programming with the Toolbox.* Hayden Books.

CHEUNG, S. 1992. Controlled request DQDB: Achieving fairness and maximum throughput in the DQDB network. In *Proceedings of IEEE INFOCOM'92* (Florence, Italy, May), 180–189.

CHOW, Y., AND H. ROBBINS. 1965. On the asymptotic theory of fixed-width sequential confidence intervals for the mean. *Annals of Mathematical Statistics 36*, 457–462.

CIDON, I., L. GEORGIADIS, R. GUERIN, AND Y. SHAVITT. 1994. Improved fairness algorithms for rings with spatial reuse. In *Proceedings of IEEE INFOCOM'94* (Toronto, June), 1103–1111.

CIDON, I., AND Y. OFEK. 1989. METARING—a ring with fairness and spatial reuse. Technical report, IBM T.J. Watson Research Center.

———. 1990. A full-duplex ring with fairness and spatial reuse. In *Proceedings of IEEE INFOCOM'90*, 969–981.

COHEN, R., AND A. SEGALL. 1992. Multiple logical token rings in a single high-speed ring. *Technion technical report 738.*

CONTI, M., E. GREGORI, AND L. LENZINI. 1991. A methodological approach to an extensive analysis of DQDB performance. *IEEE Journal on Selected Areas in Communications 9*, 1 (January), 76–87.

CÔTÉ, R., AND B. SMITH. 1992. Tapping into sockets. *Byte 17*, 3 (March), 261–266.

COVENEY, P., AND R. HIGHFIELD. 1991. *The Arrow of Time.* Fawcett Columbine.

COYLE, E., AND B. LIU. 1983. Finite population CSMA/CD networks. *IEEE Transactions on Communications 31*, 11 (November), 1247–1251.

———. 1985. A matrix representation of CSMA/CD networks. *IEEE Transactions on Communications 33*, 1 (January), 53–64.

CRANE, M., AND A. LEMOINE. 1977. *An Introduction to the Regenerative Method for Simulation Analysis.* Springer-Verlag.

CULBERSON, J., AND P. RUDNICKI. 1989. A fast algorithm for constructing trees from distance matrices. *Information Processing Letters 30*, 4 (February), 215–220.

DAHL, O., B. MYHRHAUG, AND K. NYGAARD. 1970. Common base language. Publication s-22, Norwegian Computing Center, Oslo.

DAHL, O., AND K. NYGAARD. 1967. Simula: A language for programming and description of discrete event systems. Introduction and user's manual, 5th ed., Norwegian Computing Center, Oslo.

DAVIDS, P., AND P. MARTINI. 1990. Performance analysis of DQDB. In *Proceedings of IEEE IPCCC* (Phoenix, AZ), 548–555.

DAVIDSON, J., et al. 1977. The arpanet TELNET protocol: its purpose, principles, implementation, and impact on host operating system design. In *Proceedings of the Fifth Data Communications Symposium* (Snowbird, Utah, September), ACM, IEEE, 4-10–4-18.

DAVIES, P. 1992. *The Mind of God.* Simon & Schuster.

DAY, J., AND H. ZIMMERMANN. 1983. The OSI reference model. In *Proceedings of the IEEE* (December), 1334–1340.

DEITEL, H. 1990. *An Introduction to Operating Systems.* Addison-Wesley.

DERFLER, F., AND W. STALLINGS. 1986. The IBM Token-ring LAN. *PC Magazine* (March).

DEVROYE, L. 1981. The computer generation of Poisson random variables. *Computing 26*, 197–207.

DIJKSTRA, E. 1971. Hierarchical ordering of sequential processes. *Acta Informatica 1*, 115–138.

DOBOSIEWICZ, W., AND P. GBURZYŃSKI. 1988. Ethernet with segmented carrier. In *Proceedings of IEEE Computer Networking Symposium* (Washington, DC, April), 72–78.

———. 1989. Improving fairness in CSMA/CD networks. In *Proceedings of IEEE SICON'89* (Singapore, July).

———. 1990a. Issues of fairness in fast LANs under realistic traffic conditions. In *Proceedings of MILCOM'90* (Monterey, CA, September), 41–45.

———. 1990b. Performance of Piggyback Ethernet. In *IEEE IPCCC'90* (Scottsdale, AZ, March), 516–522.

———. 1991a. A fault-tolerant capacity-1 protocol for very fast local networks. In *Proceedings of SPIE's International Symposium on Optical Engineering and Photonics in Aerospace Sensing* (Orlando, FL, April), 123–133.

————. 1991b. On the apparent unfairness of a capacity-1 protocol for very fast local area networks. In *Proceedings of the Third IEE Conference on Telecommunications* (Edinburgh, Scotland, March).

————. 1991c. The topology component of protocol performance. In *The 16th IEEE Annual Conference on Local Computer Networks* (Minneapolis, MN, October), 582–588.

————. 1992. A new topology for MANs: the pretzel ring. In *Proceedings of IEEE INFOCOM'92* (Florence, Italy, May), 2408–2414.

————. 1993. DSMA: a fair capacity-1 protocol for ring networks. In *Proceedings of the Second International Symposium on High Performance Distributed Computing* (Spokane, WA, July), 92–99.

————. 1994. An alternative to FDDI: DPMA and the pretzel ring. *IEEE Transactions on Communications 42*, 1076–1083.

DOBOSIEWICZ, W., P. GBURZYŃSKI, AND V. MACIEJEWSKI. 1990. Behaviour of unidirectional broadcast LANs in a file server model. In *Proceedings of ICCS* (Singapore, November), 1138–1142.

————. 1992. A classification of fairness measures for local and metropolitan area networks. *Computer Communications 15*, 295–304.

DOBOSIEWICZ, W., P. GBURZYŃSKI, AND P. RUDNICKI. 1991. Dynamic recognition of the configuration of bus networks. *Computer Communications 14*, 4 (May), 216–222.

————. 1993. On two collision protocols for high speed bus LANs. *Computer Networks and ISDN Systems 25*, 11 (June), 1205–1225.

DQDB. 1991. Distributed queue dual bus subnetwork of a metropolitan area network. IEEE Std. 802.6-1990, July.

DYKEMAN, D., AND W. BUX. 1988. Analysis and tuning of the FDDI media access protocol. *IEEE Journal on Selected Areas in Communications 6* (July), 997–1010.

ETHERNET. 1980. The Ethernet, a local area network, data link layer and physical layer specifications. Digital Equipment Corporation, Intel Corporation, Xerox Corporation, Version 1.0.

FDDI. 1987. Fiber Distributed Data Interface (FDDI)—Token ring media access control (MAC). American National Standard for Information Systems, Doc. No. X3, 139-1987.

FELLER, W. 1971. *An Introduction to Probability Theory and its Applications.* Wiley.

FISHMAN, G. 1990. *Principles of Discrete Event Simulation.* Wiley.

FISHMAN, G., AND L. MOORE. 1986. An exhaustive analysis of multiplicative congruential random number generators with modulus $2^{31} - 1$. *SIAM Journal on Scientific and Statistical Computing 7*, 24–45.

FISZ, M. 1963. *Probability Theory and Mathematical Statistics.* Wiley.

FLOYD, R. 1962. Algorithm 97: shortest path. *Communications of the ACM 5,* 6 (June), 345.

FRANTA, W. 1977. *The Process View of Simulation.* North-Holland.

FRATTA, L., F. BORGONOVO, AND F. TOBAGI. 1981. The Express-net: A local area communication network integrating voice and data. In *Proceedings of International Conference on Performance of Data Communication Systems and Applications* (Paris, September).

FREEMAN, R. 1989. *Telecommunication System Engineering.* Wiley.

FREUND, J. 1992. *Mathematical Statistics.* Prentice-Hall.

FRITZSCH, H. 1984. *The Creation of Matter.* Basic Books.

FROST, V. S., AND B. MELAMED. 1994. Traffic modeling for telecommunications networks. *IEEE Communications Magazine 32,* 3 (March), 70–81.

GBURZYŃSKI, P., AND J. MAITAN. 1993. Deflection routing in regular MNA topologies. *Journal of High Speed Networks 2,* 2, 99–131.

GBURZYŃSKI, P., AND P. RUDNICKI. 1987. A better-than-token protocol with bounded packet delay time for Ethernet-type LAN's. In *Proceedings of Symposium on the Simulation of Computer Networks* (Colorado Springs, CO, August), IEEE, 110–117.

———. 1989a. The LANSF protocol modeling environment, version 2.0. University of Alberta, Department of Computing Science, TR 89-19, Edmonton, Canada.

———. 1989b. A note on the performance of ENET II. *IEEE Journal on Selected Areas in Communications 7* (April), 424–427.

———. 1989c. On formal modelling of communication channels. In *Proceedings of IEEE INFOCOM'89,* 143–151.

———. 1989d. A virtual token protocol for bus networks: correctness and performance. *INFOR 27,* 183–205.

———. 1991. LANSF: a protocol modelling environment and its implementation. *Software Practice and Experience 21,* 1 (January), 51–76.

GEORGIADIS, L., W. SZPANKOWSKI, AND L. TASSIULAS. 1993. Stability analysis of scheduling policies in ring networks with spatial reuse. In *Proceedings of 21st Annual Allerton Conference on Communication, Control, and Computing* (Allerton, IL), 1109–1119.

GONSALVES, T. A., AND F. A. TOBAGI. 1988. On the performance effects of station locations and access protocol parameters in Ethernet networks. *IEEE Transactions on Communications 36,* 4 (April), 441–449.

GOPAL, P., AND J. WONG. 1985. Analysis of a hybrid Token-CSMA/CD protocol for bus networks. *Computer Networks and ISDN Systems 9,* 131–141.

GRIBBIN, J. 1988. *The Omega Point.* Bantam Books.

GROZ, R. 1986. Unrestricted verification of protocol properties in a simulation using an observer approach. In *Proceedings of the IFIP WG 6.1 6th Workshop on Protocol Specification, Testing, and Verification* (June), 255–266, North-Holland.

HAHNE, E., A. CHOUDHURY, AND N. MAXEMCHUK. 1990. Improving the fairness of DQDB networks. In *Proceedings of IEEE INFOCOM'90* (San Francisco, June), 175–184.

HAKIMI, S., AND S. YAU. 1964. Distance matrix of a graph and its realizability. *Quarterly of Applied Mathematics 22*, 305–317.

HASSANEIN, H., AND A. KAMAL. 1993. A study of the behaviour of Hubnet. *IEE Proceedings-E 140*, 2 (March), 134–144.

HASSANEIN, H. S., J. W. WONG, AND J. W. MARK. 1994. An effective erasure node algorithm for slot reuse in DQDB. In *Proceedings of IEEE INFOCOM'94* (Toronto, June), 1302–1309.

HENSHALL, J., AND A. SHAW. 1985. *OSI Explained: End to End Computer Communication Standards.* Ellis.

HERBERT, N. 1988. *Faster than Light.* New American Library.

HEYMAN, D. P., AND T. V. LAKSHMAN. 1994. Source models for VBR broadcast-video traffic. In *Proceedings of IEEE INFOCOM'94* (Toronto, June), 664–671.

HIDEKI, I. 1990. *Error-Control Coding Techniques.* Academic Press.

HOLZMANN, G. 1991. *Design and Validation of Computer Protocols.* Prentice-Hall.

HOPPER, A., S. TEMPLE, AND R. WILLIAMSON. 1986. *Local Area Network Design.* Addison-Wesley.

HOPPER, A., AND R. WILLIAMSON. 1983. Design and use of an integrated Cambridge ring. *IEEE Journal on Selected Areas in Communications 1*, 5 (November), 775–784.

HUBER, D., W. STEINLIN, AND P. WILD. 1983. SILK: an implementation of a buffer insertion ring. *IEEE Journal on Selected Areas in Communications 1*, 5 (November), 766–774.

HYMAN, H. 1966. Comments on a problem in concurrent programming control. *Communications of the ACM 9*, 3, 45.

HYUN, I., AND K. HAN. 1991. Dynamic bandwidth balancing mechanism for improving DQDB performance. In *Proceedings of IEEE ICC'91* (Denver, June), 1345–1349.

IGLEHART, D. 1978. The regenerative method for simulation analysis. In *Software Engineering*, vol. 3, ed. K. Chandy and R. Yeh. Prentice-Hall.

ISO. 1979. *Reference Model of Open Systems Interconnection.*

JAIN, R. 1989. Performance analysis of FDDI token ring networks: effect of parameters and guidelines for setting TTRT. Technical report DEC-TR-655, Digital Equipment Corporation.

JERUCHIM, M., P. BALABAN, AND K. SHANMUGAN. 1992. *Simulation of Communication Systems*. Plenum Press.

KAMAL, A. 1986. A performance model for a star network. In *Proceedings of GLOBECOM'86*, 12–18.

———. 1987. A CSMA/CD bus network protocol with resolution of multiplicity-two collisions. University of Alberta, Department of Computing Science, Edmonton, Canada. Unpublished.

———. 1990. On the use of multiple tokens on ring networks. In *Proceedings of IEEE INFOCOM'90* (San Francisco, June), 15–22.

KAMAL, A., AND V. HAMACHER. 1986. Analysis of a star local area network with collision avoidance. In *Proceedings of IEEE INFOCOM'86*, 546–555.

KAMAL, A., J. WONG, AND H. HASSANEIN. 1992. An algorithm for slot reuse in DQDB networks. In *Proceedings of IEEE MAN Workshop* (Taormina, Italy, May).

KAMAT, S., G. AGRAWAL, AND W. ZHAO. 1994. Available bandwidth in FDDI-based reconfigurable networks. In *Proceedings of IEEE INFOCOM'94* (Toronto, June), 1390–1397.

KAROL, M., AND R. GITLIN. 1990. High-performance optical local and metropolitan area networks: enhancements of FDDI and IEEE 802.6 DQDB. *IEEE Journal on Selected Areas in Communications 8*, 8 (October), 1439–1448.

KARVELAS, D., M. PAPAMICHAIL, AND G. POLYZOS. 1991. The rotating slot generator dual bus. Cis-91-26, New Jersey Institute of Technology.

———. 1992. Performance analysis of the rotating slot generator scheme. In *Proceedings of IEEE INFOCOM'92* (Florence, Italy, May), 794–803.

KESSLER, G., AND D. TRAIN. 1991. *Metropolitan Area Networks*. McGraw-Hill.

KIESEL, W., AND P. KÜHN. 1983. A new CSMA/CD protocol for local area networks with dynamic priorities and low collision probability. *IEEE Journal on Selected Areas in Communications 1*, 5, 869–876.

KLEIJNEN, J. 1974-75. *Statistical Techniques in Simulation*. Parts I and II. Marcel Dekker.

KLEINROCK, L., AND H. LEVY. 1987. On the behavior of a very fast bidirectional bus network. In *Proceedings of the 1987 IEEE International Communications Conference* (Seattle, June), 1419–1426.

KNUTH, D. 1973. *The Art of Computer Programming, Volume 3: Sorting and Searching*. Addison-Wesley.

KOBAYASHI, H. 1978. *Modeling and Analysis: An Introduction to System Performance Evaluation Methodology.* Addison-Wesley.

KOCHAN, S., AND P. WOOD. 1989. *UNIX Networking.* Hayden Books.

KUMAR, L., AND A. BOVOPOULOS. 1992. An access protection solution for heavy load unfairness in DQDB. In *Proceedings of IEEE INFOCOM'92* (Florence, Italy, May), 190–199.

LAW, A. 1983. Statistical analysis of simulation output data. *Journal of the Operational Research Society 31*, 983–1029.

LAW, A., AND W. KELTON. 1982. Confidence intervals for steady-state simulation: a survey of sequential procedures. *Management Science 28*, 550–562.

———. 1984. Confidence intervals for steady-state simulation: a survey of fixed sample size procedures. *Journal of the Operational Research Society 32*, 1221–1239.

———. 1991. *Simulation Modeling and Analysis.* 2d ed. McGraw-Hill.

LAW, A. M., AND M. G. McCOMAS. 1994. Simulation software for communication networks: the state of the art. *IEEE Communications Magazine 32*, 3 (March), 44–51.

LEE, B., M. KANG, AND J. LEE. 1993. *Broadband Telecommunications Technology.* Artech House.

LEE, E., AND P. BOULTON. 1983. The principles and performance of Hubnet. *IEEE Journal on Selected Areas in Communications 1*, 5, 711–720.

LEE, E., P. BOULTON, AND B. THOMSON. 1988. Hubnet performance measurements. *IEEE Journal on Selected Areas in Communications 6*, 6, 1025–1032.

LEFFLER, S., M. McKUSICK, M. KARELS, AND J. QUARTERMAN. 1989. *The Design and Implementation of the 4.3BSD UNIX Operating System.* Addison-Wesley.

LELAND, W., M. TAQQU, W. WILLINGER, AND D. WILSON. 1994. On the self-similar nature of Ethernet traffic. *IEEE Transactions on Networking 2*, 1 (February), 1–15.

LIMB, J., AND C. FLORES. 1982. Description of Fasnet, a unidirectional local area communications network. *Bell Systems Technical Journal* (September).

LIPPMAN, S. 1991. *C++ Primer.* Addison-Wesley.

LITZKOW, M., M. LIVNY, AND M. MUTKA. 1988. Condor—a hunter of idle workstations. In *Proceedings of the 8th International Conference on Distributed Computing Systems* (San Jose, CA, June), 104–111.

LITZKOW, M., AND M. SOLOMON. 1992. Supporting checkpointing and process migration outside the UNIX kernel. In *Proceedings of Usenix Winter Conference* (San Francisco, January), 283–290.

LOGRIPPO, L., A. OBAID, J. P. BRIAND, AND M. C. FEHRI. 1988. An interpreter for LOTOS, a specification language for distributed systems. *Software Practice and Experience 18*, 4 (April), 365–385.

LYNCH, W. 1968. Reliable full-duplex transmission over half-duplex telephone lines. *Communications of the ACM 11*, 6, 407–410.

MACDOUGALL, M. 1987. *Simulating Computer Systems: Techniques and Tools.* MIT Press.

MACIEJEWSKI, V. 1990. *Evaluating fairness in broadcast bus networks.* Master's thesis, University of Alberta, Edmonton, Canada.

MACIEJEWSKI, V., W. DOBOSIEWICZ, AND P. GBURZYNSKI. 1990. Behavior of unfair protocols under file server traffic. In *Proceedings of SICON'90* (Singapore, November), 1138–1142.

MAITAN, J., L. WALICHIEWICZ, AND B. WEALAND. 1990a. Integrated communication and information fabric for space applications. In *AIAA/NASA Second International Symposium on Space Information Systems* (September), 1175–1184.

———. 1990b. A new low cost communication scheme for military applications. In *Proceedings of Milcom'90* (Monterey, CA).

MARSAGLIA, G. 1968. Random numbers fall mainly in the planes. *Proceedings of the National Academy of Sciences 60*, 25–28.

MARSAN, M. 1982. Fairness in local computer networks. In *IEEE International Conference on Communications '82*, vol. 1, 2F.4/1–6.

MARTIN, J. 1989. *Local Area Networks.* Prentice-Hall.

MATLOFF, N. 1988. *Probability Modeling and Computer Simulation.* PWS-Kent.

MAXEMCHUK, N. 1985. The Manhattan Street Network. In *Proceedings of GLOBECOM'85*, 255–261.

———. 1987. Routing in the Manhattan Street Network. *IEEE Transactions on Communications 35*, 5 (May), 503–512.

———. 1988. Twelve random access strategies for fiber optic networks. *IEEE Transactions on Communications 36*, 8 (August), 942–950.

———. 1989. Comparison of deflection and store-and-forward techniques in Manhattan-street network and shuffle-exchange networks. In *Proceedings of IEEE INFOCOM'89*, 800–809.

———. 1991. Problems arising from deflection routing. In *High Capacity Local and Metropolitan Networks*, ed. Pugolle, 209–233. Springer-Verlag.

MCQUILLAN, J. 1980. The new routing algorithm for the ARPANET. *IEEE Transactions on Communications 28* (May), 711–719.

MCQUILLAN, J. M., G. FALK, AND I. RICHER. 1978. A review of the development and performance of the ARPANET routing algorithm. *IEEE Transactions on Communications 26* (December), 1802–1811.

MENDEHALL, W., AND R. SHEAFFER. 1973. *Mathematical Statistics with Applications*. Duxbury Press.

METCALFE, R., AND D. BOGGS. 1976. Ethernet: distributed packet switching for local computer networks. *Communications of the ACM 19*, 7 (July), 395–404.

MILLER, M., AND S. AHAMED. 1987. *Digital Transmission Systems and Networks*. Computer Science Press.

MOLLOY, M. 1985. Collision resolution on the CSMA/CD bus. *Computer Networks and ISDN Systems 9*, 209–214.

MOLVA, R., M. DIAZ, AND J. AYACHE. 1987. Observer: a run-time checking tool for local area networks. In *Proceedings of the IFIP WG 6.1 6th Workshop on Protocol Specification, Testing, and Verification*, 495–506, North-Holland.

MUKHERJEE, B., AND S. BANERJEE. 1991. Alternative strategies for improving the fairness in and an analytical model of DQDB networks. In *Proceedings of IEEE INFOCOM'91* (Miami, April), 879–888.

MUKHERJEE, B., AND C. BISDIKIAN. 1991. A journey through the DQDB network literature. Rc 17016, IBM Research Division.

MUKHERJEE, B., AND J. MEDITCH. 1988. The p_i-persistent protocols for unidirectional broadcast bus networks. *IEEE Transactions on Communications 36*, 12 (December), 1277–1286.

NIEDERREITER, H. 1992. Random number generation and quasi Monte Carlo methods. In *CBMS-NSF Regional Conference Series in Applied Mathematics* (Philadelphia), Society for Industrial and Applied Mathematics.

PACH, A., S. PALAZZO, AND D. PANNO. 1992. Improving DQDB throughput by a slot preuse technique. In *Proceedings of ICC'92* (Chicago, June).

PATRINOS, A., AND S. HAKIMI. 1972. The distance matrix of a graph and its tree realization. *Quarterly of Applied Mathematics 30* (October), 255–269.

PAXSON, V., AND S. FLOYD. 1994. Wide-area traffic: the failure of Poisson modeling. In *Proceedings of SIGCOM'94* (London, August).

PETITPIERRE, C. 1984. Meshed local computer networks. *IEEE Communications Magazine 22*, 8 (August), 36–40.

ROCHKIND, M. 1985. *Advanced Unix Programming*. Prentice-Hall.

ROSS, F. 1989. An overview of FDDI: The fiber distributed data interface. *IEEE Journal on Selected Areas in Communications 7*, 7 (September), 1043–1051.

ROSS, S. 1989. *Probability Models*. Academic Press.

———. 1990. *A Course in Simulation*. Macmillan.

SAULNIER, E. T., AND B. J. BORTSCHELLER. 1994. Simulation model reusability. *IEEE Communications Magazine 32*, 3 (March), 64–69.

SCHMEISER, B., AND A. BABU. 1980. Beta variate generation via exponential majorizing functions. *Journal of the Operational Research Society 28*, 917–926.

SCHWARTZ, M. 1987. *Telecommunication Networks: Protocols, Modeling and Analysis*. Addison-Wesley.

SHARON, O., AND A. SEGALL. 1994. On the efficiency of slot reuse in the dual bus configuration. In *Proceedings of IEEE INFOCOM'94* (Toronto, June), 758–765.

SHOCH, J., et al. 1982. Evolution of the Ethernet local computer network. *IEEE Computer 15*, 8 (August), 10–26.

SHOCH, J., et al. 1987. Ethernet. In *Advances in Local Area Networks*, ed. K. Kummerle, F. Tobagi, and J. Limb. IEEE Press.

SILBERSCHATZ, A., AND P. GALVIN. 1994. *Operating System Concepts*. Addison-Wesley.

SIMÕES-PEREIRA, J., AND C. ZAMFIRESCU. 1982. Submatrices of non-tree-realizable distance matrices. *Linear Algebra and Its Applications 44*, 1–17.

SPRAGINS, J., J. HAMMOND, AND K. PAWLIKOWSKI. 1991. *Telecommunications Protocols and Design*. Addison-Wesley.

STALLINGS, W. 1987a. *Handbook of Computer Communications Standards*. Macmillan.

———. 1987b. *Local Networks: An Introduction*. Macmillan.

———. 1990. *Local Networks*. Macmillan.

STAMOULIS, G. D., M. E. ANAGNOSTOU, AND A. D. GEORGANTAS. 1994. Traffic source models for ATM networks: a survey. *Computer Communications 17*, 6 (June), 428–438.

STARR, N. 1966. The performance of a sequential procedure for the fixed-width interval estimation of the mean. *Annals of Mathematical Statistics 37*, 36–50.

STEVENS, W. 1992. *Advanced Programming in the UNIX Environment*. Addison-Wesley.

STROUSTRUP, B. 1989. Multiple inheritance in C++. *USENIX Computer Systems 2*, 4.

———. 1991. *The C++ Programming Language*. Addison-Wesley.

STUCK, B., AND E. ARTHURS. 1985. *A Computer and Communications Network Performance Analysis Primer*. Prentice-Hall.

TAKAGI, H., AND L. KLEINROCK. 1985. Throughput analysis for persistent CSMA systems. *IEEE Transactions on Communications 33*, 7 (July), 627–638.

TANENBAUM, A. 1988. *Computer Networks*. 2d ed. Prentice-Hall.

———. 1992. *Modern Operating Systems*. Prentice-Hall.

TASAKA, S. 1986. Dynamic behaviour of a CSMA/CD system with a finite population of buffered users. *IEEE Transactions on Communications 34*, 6 (June), 576–586.

TASSIULAS, L., AND L. GEORGIADIS. 1994. Any work-conserving policy stabilizes the ring with spatial reuse. In *Proceedings of IEEE INFOCOM'94* (Toronto, June), 66–70.

TOBAGI, F., F. BORGONOVO, AND L. FRATTA. 1983. Express-net: a high-performance integrated-services local area network. *IEEE Journal on Selected Areas in Communication 1*, 5 (November), 898–913.

TOBAGI, F., AND M. FINE. 1983. Performance of unidirectional broadcast local area networks: Expressnet and Fasnet. *IEEE Journal on Selected Areas in Communication 1*, 5 (November), 913–926.

TOBAGI, F., AND V. HUNT. 1980. Performance analysis of carrier sense multiple access with collision detection. *Computer Networks 4*, 5 (October), 245–259.

TODD, T. 1994. The token grid network. *IEEE/ACM Transactions on Networking 2*, 3 (June), 279–287.

WALCH, M., A. WOLISZ, AND J. WOLF-GÜNTHER. 1994. Visualization and performance analysis of formally specified communication protocols. In *Proceedings of MASCOTS'94* (Durham, NC, January), 284–291.

WANG, P. 1987. *An Introduction to Berkeley UNIX*. Wadsworth.

WELCH, P. 1983. The statistical analysis of simulation results. In *Computer Performance Modeling Handbook*, ed. S. Lavenberg. Academic Press.

WILLEBEEK-LeMAIR, M., AND P. SHAHABUDDIN. 1994. Approximating dependability measures of FDDI networks. In *Proceedings of IEEE INFOCOM'94* (Toronto, June), 1372–1381.

WONG, J. 1989. Fairness, priority, and predictability of the DQDB MAC protocol under heavy load. Rz 1929 (#68259) 12/29/89, IBM Research Division, Zurich Research Laboratory.

WU, H., Y. OFEK, AND K. SOHRABY. 1992. Integration of synchronous and asynchronous traffic on the metaring architecture and its analysis. IBM technical report RC 17718.

YANG, J., AND C. N. MANIKOPOULOS. 1992a. Investigation of the performance of a controlled router for the CEBus. *IEEE Transactions on Consumer Electronics*, 4 (November), 831–841.

YANG, J., AND C. N. MANIKOPOULOS. 1992b. Router connected physical media in networking the intelligent home. *IEEE Transactions on Consumer Electronics*, 1 (February), 30–35.

YIN, J., AND C. B. SILIO, JR. 1994. Reliability of FDDI's dual homing network architecture. In *Proceedings of IEEE INFOCOM'94* (Toronto, June), 1382–1389.

ZARETSKI, K. 1965. Postroenie dereva po naboru rastoiani mezhdu visiatchimi vershinami. *Uspekhi Matematicheskikh Nauk 20*, 6, 90–92.

ZIPF, G. 1949. *Human Behavior and the Principle of Least Effort: An Introduction to Human Ecology*. Addison-Wesley.

Index†

---

†Boldface numbers indicate the pages on which the subject is introduced, defined, or described.

I
PH\